ZAGAT®

San Francisco Bay Area Restaurants
2012

LOCAL EDITOR
Meesha Halm
STAFF EDITOR
Cynthia Kilian

Published and distributed by
Zagat Survey, LLC
4 Columbus Circle
New York, NY 10019
T: 212.977.6000
E: sanfran@zagat.com
www.zagat.com

ACKNOWLEDGMENTS

We thank Gayle Keck, Bernard Onken, Katie Robbins, Troy Segal, Ian Turner and Sharron Wood, as well as the following members of our staff: Danielle Borovoy (assistant editor), Aynsley Karps (editorial assistant), Brian Albert, Sean Beachell, Maryanne Bertollo, Reni Chin, Larry Cohn, Nicole Diaz, Kelly Dobkin, Alison Flick, Jeff Freier, Matthew Hamm, Justin Hartung, Marc Henson, Natalie Lebert, Mike Liao, Vivian Ma, James Mulcahy, Polina Paley, Emily Rothschild, Chris Walsh, Jacqueline Wasilczyk, Art Yaghci, Sharon Yates, Anna Zappia and Kyle Zolner.

The reviews in this guide are based on public opinion surveys. The ratings reflect the average scores given by the survey participants who voted on each establishment. The text is based on quotes from, or paraphrasings of, the surveyors' comments. Phone numbers, addresses and other factual data were correct to the best of our knowledge when published in this guide.

Contents

Ratings & Symbols

Zagat Top Spot	Name	Symbols		Cuisine	Zagat Ratings			
					FOOD	DECOR	SERVICE	COST

Area, Address & Contact

Z Tim & Nina's ◑ *Seafood* ▽ 23 | 9 | 13 | $15

Embarcadero | 999 Mission St. (The Embarcadero) | 415-555-7233 | www.zagat.com

Review, surveyor comments in quotes

Open "more or less when T and N feel like it", this bit of unembellished Embarcadero ectoplasm excels at seafood with Asian-Argentinean-Albanian accents; while the "surly" staff seems "fresh off the boat" and the view of the garbage barges is "a drag", no one balks at the "beneficent" "bottom-feeder prices."

Ratings   **Food, Decor** & **Service** are rated on a 30-point scale.

0	– 9	poor to fair
10	– 15	fair to good
16	– 19	good to very good
20	– 25	very good to excellent
26	– 30	extraordinary to perfection
	▽	low response | less reliable

Cost   The price of dinner with a drink and tip; lunch is usually 25% less. For unrated **newcomers** or **write-ins,** the price range is as follows:

I	$25 and below	E	$41 to $65
M	$26 to $40	VE	$66 or above

Symbols
- **Z** highest ratings, popularity and importance
- **◑** serves after 11 PM
- **Ⓩ Ⓜ** closed on Sunday or Monday
- **⊄** no credit cards accepted

Maps   Index maps show restaurants with the highest Food ratings in those areas.

About This Survey

Here are the results of our **2012 San Francisco Bay Area Restaurants Survey,** covering 1,448 eateries in the greater San Francisco Bay Area, including the Monterey Peninsula, Silicon Valley, Wine Country and Lake Tahoe. Like all our guides, this one is based on input from avid local consumers – 10,672 all told. Our editors have synopsized this feedback, highlighting representative comments (in quotation marks within each review). To read full surveyor comments – and share your own opinions – visit **ZAGAT.com,** where you will also find the latest restaurant news, special events, deals, reservations, menus, photos and lots more, **all for free.**

ABOUT ZAGAT: In 1979, we started asking friends to rate and review restaurants purely for fun. The term "user-generated content" had not yet been coined. That hobby grew into Zagat Survey; 32 years later, we have over 375,000 surveyors and cover airlines, bars, dining, fast food, entertaining, golf, hotels, movies, music, resorts, shopping, spas, theater and tourist attractions in over 100 countries. Along the way, we evolved from being a print publisher to a digital content provider, e.g. **ZAGAT.com** and **Zagat To Go** mobile apps (for iPad, iPhone, Android, BlackBerry, Windows Phone 7 and Palm webOS). We also produce marketing tools for a wide range of blue-chip corporate clients. And you can find us on Twitter (twitter.com/zagat), Facebook, Foursquare and just about any other social media network.

THREE SIMPLE PREMISES underlie our ratings and reviews. First, we believe that the collective opinions of large numbers of consumers are more accurate than those of any single person. (Consider that our surveyors bring some 1.6 million annual meals' worth of experience to this survey, visiting restaurants year-round, anonymously – and on their own dime.) Second, food quality is only part of the equation when choosing a restaurant, thus we ask our surveyors to separately rate food, decor and service and report on cost. Third, since people need reliable information in an easy-to-digest, curated format, we strive to be concise and we offer our content on every platform – print, online and mobile. Our Top Ratings lists (pages 10–18) and indexes (starting on page 270) are also designed to help you quickly choose the best place for any occasion, be it for business or pleasure.

THANKS: We're grateful to our local editor, Meesha Halm, who is a Bay Area restaurant critic, cookbook author and youth garden-to-table educator. We also sincerely thank the thousands of surveyors who participated – this guide is really "theirs."

JOIN IN: To improve our guides, we solicit your comments – positive or negative; it's vital that we hear your opinions. Just contact us at **nina-tim@zagat.com.** We also invite you to join our surveys at **ZAGAT.com.** Do so and you'll receive a choice of rewards in exchange.

New York, NY
September 22, 2011

Nina and Tim Zagat

25 Years Later

Much has changed since our first SF Survey in 1987. While the Bay Area was ahead of many others in embracing trends that continue to resonate today – casual dining, exotic cuisines, celeb chefs (remember Stars' Jeremiah Tower?) – our first Tops lists still included plenty of old-school, white-tablecloth places serving up steak Diane, veal piccata and boeuf bourguignon. Alice Waters' reverence for local, organic and sustainably raised larder was not yet commonplace. And the pre–Thomas Keller French Laundry was described by surveyors as a "mellow" place with an average cost of $29.

Flash forward 25 years. Today's hottest restaurants tend to feature bare wooden tables, dressed-down diners and cuisines that run the global gamut. The locavore movement is palpable everywhere – even your local pho joint or taqueria is apt to serve hormone-free meat and heirloom tomatoes. And the French Laundry typifies contemporary culinary theater, complete with a big-name chef, impossible reservations and a price tag roughly 10 times that '87 estimate.

Diners have changed too. Thanks to the explosion of interest in all things food-related, their tastes are more sophisticated and cosmopolitan than ever. They're as comfortable grabbing lunch from a falafel truck as they are exploring the wonders of molecular gastronomy, aka Modernist Cuisine. Here's a look at trends and survey stats from then and now.

DINING TRENDS THEN AND NOW

1987	2012
Bartender	Mixologist
Beer on draft	Wine on tap
Roach coach	Food truck
Smoking between courses	Tweeting between courses
Rooftop patios	Rooftop beehives (and gardens)
Bottled water	Hetch Hetchy tap water
Single-vineyard wines	Single-origin coffee beans
Reservationist	Open Table
Sommelier	iPad wine menu
Closed on Mondays	Pop-up restaurant on Mondays

SURVEY STATS THEN AND NOW

	1987	2012
No. of Cuisines	42	84
No. of Restaurants	400	1,448
Most Popular	Campton Place	Gary Danko
Top Food	Masa's	Gary Danko
Top Decor	Auberge du Soleil	Sierra Mar
Top Newcomer	Square One	Michael Mina
Top French	Masa's	Cyrus
Top Italian	Donatello	Acquerello
Top Japanese	Osome	Sushi Ran
Top Seafood	Swan Oyster Depot	Swan Oyster Depot
Most Expensive	Masa's	French Laundry

Vote at ZAGAT.com

What's New

In this economy, less is more, and hot new budget eateries are popping up around the Bay Area in the form of izakayas, pizzerias and food trucks, while bigger-ticket restaurants are debuting more-affordable offshoots. Of course, surveyors still appreciate high-end dining, as evidenced by **Gary Danko** retaining the No. 1 spot for Food, Service and Popularity, and **Sierra Mar** again reigning for Decor. But the average price per meal – $38.88, nearly the same as last year's $38.78 – reflects continuing efforts to hold the line on prices.

STAR LITE: Fine-dining whiz Michael Mina and his namesake restaurant are back, relocated into the former **Aqua** space where the chef got his start and offering a more approachable (but still pricey) menu. Other less-expensive ventures from marquee names include **Delfina**'s osteria spin-off, **Locanda, Commis'** Asian street-fooder, **Hawker Fare,** and **Kitchen Door,** a cafe from the shuttered **Martini House.**

GOING MOBILE: Frugal feeders are also scoring curbside deals, thanks to the explosion of street food at events like Off the Grid, hosting a roundup of popular trucks including **Liba Falafel** and the **Chairman Bao Bun Truck,** and pop-up food stalls such as **Hapa Ramen** at the Ferry Plaza Market. The Survey's No. 1 food truck, **Spencer on the Go!,** is a roving French takeaway from the beloved **Chez Spencer.**

TOKYO A GO-GO: Japanese cuisine is still in vogue, but these days it's less about extravagant sushi and more about bites like yakitori, as izakayas including **Chotto, Ki** and **Nojo** skewer the competition. Even **Cyrus** chef Douglas Keane is getting into the act with **Shimo Modern Steak,** where the premier dish on the Japanese-inspired steakhouse menu is the customizable bowl of ramen.

PIE-EYED: The obsession with zero-zero flour and crackling crusts intensifies as upstart pizzerias are firing up their ovens all over the region, from **Cupola Pizzeria, Ragazza** and **Una Pizza Napoletana** in the city to San Mateo's **Osteria Coppa** and Sausalito's **Bar Bocce.**

CALIFORNICATION: Locavore cuisine remains a Bay Area passion – 80% of surveyors think menus should change seasonally and 68% are willing to pay more for locally sourced, organic or sustainably raised ingredients. And now chefs are looking beyond the **Chez Panisse** Cal-Med model and putting local spins on the likes of Eastern and Central European fare, as on the revamped menus of **Bar Bambino** and **Bar Tartine** as well as at newcomer **Gaumenkitzel.**

SURVEY SAYS: Respondents report eating out 2.8 times per week (same as last year) . . . Bay Area diners tip an average of 18.6% (vs. 19.2% nationally), which ties with Seattle for lowest in our U.S. surveys . . . 79% think restaurants should be required to post a health inspection letter grade as in LA and NYC . . . 65% won't wait longer than 30 minutes at places that don't take reservations.

San Francisco, CA
September 22, 2011

Meesha Halm

KEY NEWCOMERS

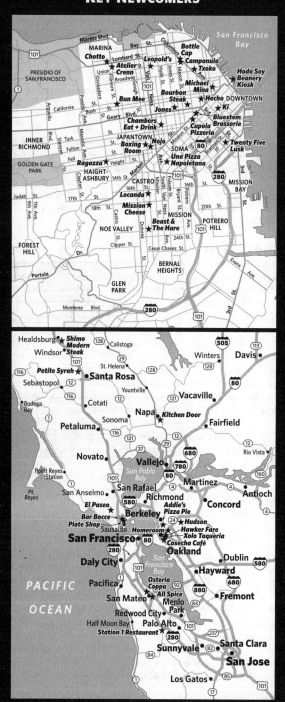

Key Newcomers

Our editors' picks among this year's arrivals. See full list at p. 328.

HOT CHEFS & OPENINGS

Atelier Crenn
Bluestem Brasserie
Bourbon Steak
Boxing Room
El Paseo/N
Hawker Fare/E
Hecho
Kitchen Door/N
Locanda
Michael Mina
Nojo
Plate Shop/N
Shimo Modern Steak/N
Txoko

LOCAL JOINTS

All Spice/S
Beast & The Hare
Bottle Cap
Campanula
Homeroom/E
Hudson/E
Leopold's
Osteria Coppa/S
Petite Syrah/N
Station 1/S

PIZZA

Addie's Pizza Pie/E
Bar Bocce/N
Cupola Pizzeria
Ragazza
Una Pizza Napoletana

SMALL BITES/QUICK

Bun Mee
Cosecha Café/E
Hodo Soy
Mission Cheese
Xolo Taqueria/E

WINE/SPIRITS/BEER

Chambers Eat + Drink
Chotto
Jones
Ki
Twenty Five Lusk

Looking ahead, as if the Mission wasn't already rife with hot dining options, just wait till **Bar Tartine** launches an adjoining sandwich shop, **Amber India** debuts **Amber Dara** and a **Tacolicious** outpost arrives with its adjacent tequila bar, **Mosto**. The delayed **Central Kitchen** and **Salumeria** in the Southern Exposure building from the **Flour + Water** team is scheduled to open in late 2011. Also moving into the Mission, the Marina and Oakland are links of LA's **Umami Burger** chain.

Hub dining is on the horizon too, thanks to mixed-use megaplexes such as the high-profile Proxy project in Hayes Valley, where refurbished shipping containers will serve as temporary homes to a passel of A-list food ventures. Slated to open at any minute are **Biergarten,** a suds-centric outdoor eatery from **Suppenküche; Avedano's Meat Wagon,** a retrofitted ambulance turned sustainable sandwich and meat shop; and a series of pop-up restaurants.

By year's end, jazz and restaurant megacomplex Preservation Hall West is expected in the old New College building at 777 Valencia, bringing several NoLa-inspired eateries including **The Chapel** (a sprawling bistro and bar) and the more informal **Second Line Café.**

But perhaps the biggest thing to happen to the Valencia corridor since the mid-'90s when Charles Phan opened the original **Slanted Door** is the return of Charles Phan with **Wo Hing General Store,** a Southern Chinese street food–inspired restaurant and bar in his long-vacant 584 Valencia space, scheduled for press time.

Most Popular

These restaurants are plotted on the map at the back of this book. Places outside of San Francisco are marked as: E=East of SF; N=North; and S=South. When a restaurant has locations both inside and out of the city limits, we include the notation SF as well.

1. Gary Danko | *American*
2. Boulevard | *American*
3. French Laundry/N | *Amer./Fr.*
4. Slanted Door | *Vietnamese*
5. Chez Panisse/E | *Cal./Med.*
6. Cyrus/N | *French*
7. Kokkari Estiatorio | *Greek*
8. Chez Panisse Café/E | *Cal./Med.*
9. Zuni Café | *Mediterranean*
10. Bouchon/N | *French*
11. Delfina | *Italian*
12. Fleur de Lys | *Californian/French*
13. Acquerello | *Italian*
14. Perbacco | *Italian*
15. Yank Sing | *Chinese*
16. Tadich Grill | *Seafood*
17. A16 | *Italian*
18. Quince | *Italian*
19. Chapeau! | *French*
20. Bottega/N | *Italian*
21. Ad Hoc/N | *American*
22. Bistro Jeanty/N | *French*
23. Auberge du Soleil/N | *Cal./Fr.*
24. Frances | *Californian*
25. Michael Mina | *American*
26. House of Prime Rib | *American*
27. Absinthe | *Fr./Med.*
28. In-N-Out/E/N/S/SF | *Burgers*
29. Redd/N | *Californian*
30. Burma Super/E/SF | *Burmese*
31. Flour + Water | *Italian*
32. Mustards Grill/N | *Amer./Cal.*
33. Evvia/S | *Greek*
34. Aziza | *Moroccan*
35. La Folie | *French*
36. Jardinière | *Californian/French*
37. Amber India/S/SF | *Indian*
38. Greens | *Vegetarian*
39. Scoma's*/N/SF | *Seafood*
40. Nopa | *Californian*
41. Spruce | *American*
42. Tartine Bakery* | *Bakery*
43. Foreign Cinema | *Cal./Med.*
44. Farallon | *Seafood*
45. Buckeye/N | *Amer./BBQ*
46. Barbacco | *Italian*
47. Hog Island/N/SF | *Seafood*
48. Bix | *American/French*
49. À Côté/E | *Fr./Med.*
50. BayWolf/E | *Cal./Med.*

Many of the above restaurants are among the San Francisco area's most expensive, but if popularity were calibrated to price, a number of other restaurants would surely join their ranks. To illustrate this, we have added lists of Best Buys and Prix Fixe Bargains on pages 17–18.

---

* Indicates a tie with restaurant above

Vote at ZAGAT.com

Top Food Overall

29] Gary Danko | American
French Laundry/N | Amer./Fr.

28] Cyrus/N | French
Manresa/S | American
Aubergine/S | Californian
Meadowood Rest./N | Cal.
Acquerello | Italian
Sushi Ran/N | Japanese
Kiss Seafood | Japanese
Chez Panisse/E | Cal./Med.
La Folie | French
Masa's | French

27] Swan Oyster Depot | Seafood
Sierra Mar/S | Cal./Eclectic
Cafe La Haye/N | Amer.
Commis/E | American
Marinus/S | Cal./French
Chez Panisse Café/E | Cal./Med.
Canteen | Californian
Erna's Elderberry/E | Cal./Fr.
Le Papillon/S | French
Kokkari Estiatorio | Greek
Boulevard | American
Kaygetsu/S | Japanese
Terra/N | American

Passionfish/S | Cal./Seafood
Madrona Manor/N | Amer./Fr.
Fleur de Lys | Californian/French
Pizzeria Picco/N | Pizza
Farmhouse Inn/N | Californian
Baumé/S | French
Ad Hoc/N | American
Redd/N | Californian
Cheese Board/E | Bakery/Pizza
Sushi Zone | Japanese
Evvia/S | Greek
Tartine Bakery | Bakery
Bistro des Copains/N | French
Frances | Californian
La Forêt/S | Continental/French
Range | American
Auberge du Soleil/N | Cal./Fr.
Koo | Asian

26] Cafe Gibraltar/S | Med.
Santé/N | Californian/French
Plumed Horse/S | Californian
Chapeau! | French
Quince | Italian
Delfina | Italian
Flea St. Café/S | Cal.

BY CUISINE

AMERICAN (NEW)

29] Gary Danko
French Laundry/N
28] Manresa/S
27] Cafe La Haye/N
Commis/E

AMERICAN (TRAD.)

27] Ad Hoc/N
25] Mama's on Wash.
House of Prime Rib
24] Press/N
Maverick

ASIAN FUSION

27] Koo
26] House
23] Eos
22] Bushi-tei
Namu

BARBECUE

24] Buckeye/N
22] Wexler's

Bo's BBQ/E
21] BarBersQ/N
20] Everett & Jones/E

BURGERS

22] Roam Artisan Burgers
21] In-N-Out/E/N/S/SF
Gott's Roadside/N/SF
20] Trueburger/E
BurgerMeister/E/S/SF

CAJUN/CREOLE/SOUL

24] Brenda's
23] Brown Sugar Kitchen/E
22] Picán/E
21] Chenery Park
1300 on Fillmore

CALIFORNIAN

28] Aubergine/S
Meadowood Rest./N
Chez Panisse/E

Excludes places with low votes

27 Chez Panisse Café/E
Marinus/S

CHINESE

26 Yank Sing
24 R&G Lounge
Great China/E
Koi/E/S
23 Ton Kiang

CONTINENTAL

27 La Forêt/S
23 Anton & Michel/S
Ecco/S
22 Bella Vista/S

DIM SUM

26 Yank Sing
24 Koi /E/S
23 Ton Kiang
Good Luck Dim Sum
22 Tai Pan/S

ECLECTIC

27 Sierra Mar/S
26 Della Fattoria/N
25 Willi's Wine Bar/N
Firefly
24 Va de Vi/E

FRENCH

28 Cyrus/N
La Folie
Masa's
27 Marinus/S
Le Papillon/S

FRENCH (BISTRO)

26 Chapeau!
25 Bistro Jeanty/N
Bouchon/N
Chez Spencer
24 Artisan Bistro/E

INDIAN

25 Ajanta/E
24 Amber India/S/SF
Neela's/N
23 Sakoon/S
Vik's Chaat Corner/E

ITALIAN

28 Acquerello
26 Quince
Delfina
La Ciccia
Cotogna

JAPANESE

28 Sushi Ran/N
Kiss Seafood
27 Kaygetsu/S
Sushi Zone
26 Sebo

MED./GREEK

28 Chez Panisse/E
27 Chez Panisse Café/E
Kokkari Estiatorio
Evvia/S
26 Cafe Gibraltar/S

MEXICAN

25 Taqueria Can Cun
La Taqueria
Tamarindo Antojeria/E
24 C Casa/N
Loló

MIDDLE EASTERN

22 Kabul Afghan/S
Dishdash/S
A La Turca
Helmand Palace
21 Troya

PERUVIAN

25 Mochica
Piqueo's
La Mar Cebicheria
22 Limón
Fresca

PIZZA

27 Pizzeria Picco/N
Cheese Board/E
26 Pizzaiolo/E
Una Pizza Napoletana
25 Tony's Pizza

SANDWICHES

26 Saigon Sandwiches
25 Downtown Bakery/N
Bakesale Betty/E
24 Ike's/S/SF
Sentinel

SEAFOOD

27 Swan Oyster Depot
Passionfish/S
25 Hog Island/N/SF
Pesce
Bar Crudo

SPANISH/BASQUE

25 Piperade
ZuZu/N

24	Contigo			Marnee Thai
	Fringale		23	Lers Ros Thai
	Zarzuela			

VEGETARIAN

25	Millennium
24	Ubuntu/N
	Greens
23	Cha-Ya Vegetarian/E/SF
21	Gracias Madre

STEAK

26	Harris'
	Alexander's Steakhouse/S/SF
25	Cole's Chop House/N
	House of Prime Rib
24	Seasons

VIETNAMESE

26	Tamarine/S
25	Slanted Door
24	Crustacean
	Thanh Long
23	Vanessa's Bistro

THAI

24	Thep Phanom Thai
	Manora's Thai
	Soi4/E

BY SPECIAL FEATURE

BREAKFAST

27	Tartine Bakery
	Mama's on Wash.
25	Boulette's Larder
24	Oliveto Cafe/E
	Chloe's Cafe

25	Station 1 Restaurant/S
24	Osteria Coppa/S
	Ragazza

OPEN LATE

25	Taqueria Can Cun
	Nopa
24	Adesso/E
	Brother's Korean
	Incontro*/E

BRUNCH

27	Canteen
	La Forêt/S
26	Yank Sing
25	Zuni Café
	Navio/S

TRENDY

23	Gitane
22	Beretta
21	Bar Agricole
20	15 Romolo
	Twenty Five Lusk

CHILD-FRIENDLY

25	Tony's Pizza
21	Chenery Park
	Gott's Roadside/N/SF
20	Chow/Park Chow/E/SF
18	Yankee Pier/E/N/S

WINE BARS

24	Barbacco
	A16
23	RN74
	Eos
21	Bounty Hunter /N

FOOD TRUCKS

(see ZAGAT.com for more reviews)

26	Spencer on the Go!
	Mama's Empanadas
25	Fivetenburger*
	RoliRoti
	Chairman Bao Bun Truck

WINNING WINE LISTS

29	Gary Danko
	French Laundry/N
28	Cyrus/N
	Acquerello
26	Quince

HOTEL DINING

28	Aubergine/S (L'Aub. Carmel)
	Meadowood Rest./N
	Masa's (Hotel Vintage Ct.)
27	Sierra Mar/S (Post Ranch Inn)
	Marinus/S (Bernardus Lodge)

WORTH A TRIP

29	French Laundry/N
28	Cyrus/N
	Manresa/S
	Aubergine/S
	Meadowood Rest./N

NEWCOMERS (RATED)

| 26 | Michael Mina |
| | Una Pizza Napoletana |

Top Decor Overall

<u>29</u> Sierra Mar/S
Ahwahnee Din. Rm./E
Auberge du Soleil/N

<u>28</u> Erna's Elderberry/E
Pacific's Edge/S

<u>27</u> Cyrus/N
Garden Court
Twenty Five Lusk
Farallon
Big 4
French Laundry/N
Meadowood Rest./N
Gary Danko
Rotunda
Madrona Manor/N

<u>26</u> Club XIX/S
Sutro's at Cliff Hse.
Bix
Marinus/S
Farm/N

Waterbar
Fleur de Lys
Roy's/S
Navio/S
Spruce
Seasons
Kokkari Estiatorio
Rest. at Ventana/S
John Ash & Co./N
Meritage/Claremont/E
Jardinière
Bar Agricole
Campton Place
La Costanera*/S
Silks*
Plumed Horse/S
Étoile/N
Quince

<u>25</u> Epic Roasthouse
St. Orres/N

OUTDOORS

Angèle/N
Auberge du Soleil/N
Bistro Don Giovanni/N
Étoile/N
Foreign Cinema
La Mar Cebicheria

Murray Circle/N
Nepenthe/S
Rustic/N
Sociale
Tra Vigne/N
Waterbar

ROMANCE

Aziza
Bix
Cafe Jacqueline
Casanova/S
Chez Spencer
Fleur de Lys

Gitane
Jardinière
La Forêt/S
Madrona Manor/N
Marinus/S
Shadowbrook/S

ROOMS

Ahwahnee Din. Rm./E
Boulevard
Farallon
Fleur de Lys
Garden Court
Gitane
Jardinière

Kokkari Estiatorio
Plumed Horse/S
Quince
Redd/N
Spruce
Twenty Five Lusk
Waterbar

VIEWS

Beach Chalet
Bella Vista/S
Greens
Guaymas/N
La Costanera/S
Navio/S

Pacific's Edge/S
Sam's Chowder Hse./S
Sierra Mar/S
Slanted Door
Sutro's at Cliff Hse.
Wolfdale's/E

Vote at ZAGAT.com

Top Service Overall

<u>28</u> Gary Danko
   Cyrus/N
   French Laundry/N
   Seasons

<u>27</u> Acquerello
   Manresa/S
   Meadowood Rest./N
   Masa's
   La Folie
   Erna's Elderberry/E
   Baumé/S
   Benu
   Coi
   La Forêt/S

<u>26</u> Sierra Mar/S
   Le Papillon/S
   Auberge du Soleil/N
   Farmhouse Inn/N
   Commis/E
   Chez Panisse/E

   Madrona Manor/N
   Marinus/S
   Michael Mina
   Terra/N
   Boulevard
   Fleur de Lys
   Aubergine/S
   Kaygetsu/S

<u>25</u> BayWolf/E
   Silks
   Bistro des Copains/N
   Chez Panisse Café/E
   Campton Place
   Harris'
   Jardinière
   La Toque/N
   Quince
   Cafe La Haye/N
   Bistro Moulin/S
   Club XIX/S

Best Buys Overall

Everyone loves a bargain, and the San Francisco area offers plenty of them. For prix fixe menus, call ahead for availability.

BAKERIES

- 27 Cheese Board/E
- Tartine Bakery
- 26 Della Fattoria/N
- Arizmendi/E/N/SF
- 25 Downtown Bakery/N
- Bakesale Betty/E
- 24 Emporio Rulli/N/S/SF
- 23 Gayle's Bakery/S

DINERS

- 26 Dottie's True Blue
- 23 Bette's Oceanview/E
- 22 Red Hut/E
- 21 Gott's Roadside/N/SF
- 20 Rudy's Can't Fail Café/E
- Jimmy Beans/E
- 19 Sears Fine Food
- 18 FatApple's/E

EARLY-BIRD

- 26 Cafe Gibraltar/S ($25)
- Chapeau! ($28)
- 24 Trattoria Corso/E ($29)
- 23 Anton & Michel/S ($28)
- 22 Cetrella/S ($25)
- Mezza Luna/Caffè/S ($10)
- Boca/N ($25)
- Caprice/N ($20)
- Sardine Factory/S ($25)

HOLE-IN-THE-WALL

- 26 Saigon Sandwiches
- 22 Yamo
- A La Turca
- Shalimar/E/S/SF
- 21 Shanghai Dumpling
- Yuet Lee
- House of Nanking
- 18 Tu Lan

NO CORKAGE FEE

- 25 Fig Cafe & Winebar/N
- Anchor Oyster Bar
- 24 Tra Vigne/N
- 23 Rutherford Grill/N
- 22 Cafe Citti/N
- 21 Pizzeria Tra Vigne/N
- 20 Indigo
- 18 Healdsburg B&G/N

NOODLE SHOPS

- 24 O Chamé/E
- 23 San Tung
- 22 Katana-Ya
- Citrus Club
- 21 Osha Thai
- 20 Hotaru/S
- 19 Hotei
- Mifune

PRIX FIXE LUNCH

- 27 Chez Panisse Café/E ($28)
- 25 Ajanta/E ($13)
- Piperade ($26)
- 24 Dry Creek Kitchen/N ($25)
- One Market ($23)
- Bix ($25)
- Chez Papa Resto ($24)
- 23 Chez Papa Bistro ($18)

PRIX FIXE DINNER

- 27 Bistro des Copains/N ($29)
- 26 Isa ($30)
- 25 Esin/E ($28)
- Ajanta/E ($18)
- Eve/E ($25)
- Chantilly/S ($30)
- 24 Harvest Moon Café/N ($28)
- Incontro Ristorante/E ($27)

TAQUERIAS

- 25 Taqueria Can Cun
- La Taqueria
- 23 Tacubaya/E
- Picante Cocina/E
- 22 Nopalito
- La Cumbre Taqueria/S/SF
- Pancho Villa/S/SF
- Tacolicious

TOP CHEF BARGAINS

- 28 Chez Panisse Café/E
- 25 Pizzeria Delfina
- 24 Sentinel
- 23 Bocadillos
- 22 Out the Door
- 21 Bovolo/N
- 19 Burger Bar
- – Hawker Fare

BEST BUYS: CARTS, TRUCKS, SPECIALTY SHOPS

Arinell Pizza/E/SF
Arizmendi/E/N/SF
Bakesale Betty/E
Barney's/E/N/SF
Beautifull
Betty's Fish & Chips/N
Blue Bottle
Boccalone Salumeria
Burger Joint/S/SF
BurgerMeister/E/S/SF
Caspers Hot Dogs/E
Chairman Bao Bun Truck
Cheese Board/E
Cheese Steak Shop/E/N/S
Curry Up Now
Downtown Bakery/N
Dynamo Donut
El Tonayense
Fivetenburger
4505 Meats
Gioia Pizzeria/E
Giorgio's Pizzeria
Golden West
Good Luck Dim Sum

Hapa Ramen
Ike's/S/SF
In-N-Out/E/N/S/SF
Jay's Cheesesteak
Jimtown Store/N
Joe's Cable Car
Lanesplitter/E
Let's Be Frank
Liba Falafel Truck/E/SF
Mama's Empanadas
Model Bakery/N
Patxi's Pizza/E/S/SF
Pica Pica Maize/N/SF
Roam Artisan Burgers
RoliRoti
Rosamunde Sausage
Saigon Sandwiches
Sentinel
Showdogs
Tartine Bakery
Trueburger/E
Underdog
'Wichcraft
Zachary's Pizza/E

BEST BUYS: FULL MENU

A La Turca
Alexis Baking Co./N
American Grilled Cheese
Andalé/E/S/SF
Asqew Grill/E/SF
Avatar's/N
Bette's Oceanview/E
Blue Barn Gourmet
Boogaloos
Brenda's
Brown Sugar Kitchen/E
Cactus Taqueria/E
C Casa/N
Chloe's Cafe
Citrus Club
Dottie's True Blue
El Metate
Emporio Rulli/N/S/SF
Frjtz Fries
Gayle's Bakery/S
Green Chile Kitchen
Joe's Taco/N
Juan's Place/E
Kasa Indian

King of Thai
La Boulange/N/SF
La Corneta/S/SF
La Cumbre Taqueria/S/SF
Little Chihuahua
Mama's on Wash.
Mama's Royal Café/E
Mixt Greens
Muracci's/S/SF
Nick's Crispy Tacos
Pancho Villa/S/SF
Papalote
Picante Cocina/E
Pluto's Fresh Food/S/SF
Pork Store Café
Red Hut/E
Rudy's Can't Fail Café/E
Sol Food/N
St. Francis
Tacubaya/E
Taqueria Can Cun
Vik's Chaat Corner/E
Warming Hut Café
Yamo

DINNER ($40 & UNDER)

Ajanta/E	$19
Alfred's Steak	39
Amber Bistro/E	29
Americano	32
Baker St. Bistro	19
Bellanico/E	26
Bistro des Copains/N	29
Bridges/E	27
Cafe Bastille	30
Casanova/S	29
Chantilly/S	30
Chapeau!	38
Charcuterie/N	20
Chevalier/E	39
Chez Panisse Café/E	30
Cliff House Bistro	25
Cotogna	40
Destino	35
Donato Enoteca/S	35
Esin/E	28
Eve/E	33
Firefly	36
Flora/E	40
Garibaldis	30
Globe	39
Grasing's Coastal/S	33
Great China/E	15
Harvest Moon Café/N	28
Hayes St. Grill	25
Hyde St. Bistro	25
Imperial Tea/E/SF	20
Incontro Ristorante/E	27
Isa	30
Jimmy Beans/E	15
Kyo-Ya	35
Lavanda/S	29
Le Charm Bistro	32
Le P'tit Laurent	22
Luella	33
Mantra/S	29
Metro/E	30
Mezze/E	23
MoMo's	39
Palio d'Asti	31
Plouf	29
Rick & Ann's/E	20
Roy's/S/SF	36
Saha	35
South Park Cafe	39
Tai Pan/S	39
1300 on Fillmore	35
Ton Kiang	38
Town's End	24
Venezia/E	24
Yoshi's/E	29
Zazie	24

LUNCH ($35 & UNDER)

Ajanta/E	$13
Ana Mandara	16
Bellanico/E	18
Bistro Liaison/E	17
Bix	25
Chez Panisse Café	28
Chez Papa Bistro	18
Chez Papa Resto	24
Dry Creek Kitchen/N	25
Espetus Churrascaria/S/SF	24
Fish Story/N	16
Five/E	20
Girl & the Fig/N	34
Hurley's/N	18
Imperial Tea/E/SF	20
Isobune/S	9
Junnoon/S	13
Lark Creek Steak	18
Market Bar	24
One Market	23
Plouf	22
Scala's Bistro	25
Scoma's	25
Sens	20
Tommy Toy's	17
Vik's Chaat Corner/E	6
Waterbar	24
Zibibbo/S	16

CITY OF SAN FRANCISCO

Top Food

29 Gary Danko | *American*

28 Acquerello | *Italian*
Kiss Seafood | *Japanese*
La Folie | *French*
Masa's | *French*

27 Swan Oyster Depot | *Seafood*
Canteen | *Californian*
Kokkari Estiatorio | *Greek*
Boulevard | *American*
Fleur de Lys | *Californian/French*
Sushi Zone | *Japanese*
Tartine Bakery | *Bakery*
Frances | *Californian*
Range | *American*
Koo | *Asian*

26 Chapeau! | *French*
Quince | *French/Italian*
Delfina | *Italian*
Michael Mina | *American*
La Ciccia | *Italian*
Harris' | *Steak*
Cafe Jacqueline | *French*
Cotogna | *Italian*
Saison | *American*
House | *Asian*
Frascati | *Cal./Med.*
Jardinière | *Californian/French*
Benu | *American*
Saigon | *Sandwich/Viet.*
Sebo | *Japanese*

BY CUISINE

AMERICAN (NEW)

29 Gary Danko
27 Boulevard
Range
26 Michael Mina
Saison

AMERICAN (TRAD.)

25 Mama's on Wash.
House of Prime Rib
24 Maverick
Chloe's Cafe
Bix

ASIAN FUSION

27 Koo
26 House
23 Eos
22 Bushi-tei
Namu

BAKERIES

27 Tartine Bakery
26 Arizmendi
24 Emporio Rulli
Dynamo Donut
21 La Boulange

BURGERS

22 Roam Artisan Burgers
21 In-N-Out

Gott's Roadside
20 BurgerMeister
19 Barney's

CALIFORNIAN

27 Canteen
Frances
26 Jardinière
Coi
25 Nopa

CHINESE

26 Yank Sing
24 R&G Lounge
23 Ton Kiang
San Tung
Tommy Toy's

FRENCH

28 La Folie
Masa's
27 Fleur de Lys
26 Cafe Jacqueline
Jardinière

FRENCH (BISTRO)

26 Chapeau!
25 Chez Spencer
24 L'Ardoise
Bistro Central Parc
Gamine

Excludes places with low votes

Vote at ZAGAT.com

INDIAN/PAKISTANI

24 Amber India
22 Indian Oven
   Pakwan
   Shalimar
   Dosa

ITALIAN

28 Acquerello
26 Quince
   Delfina
   La Ciccia
   Cotogna

JAPANESE

28 Kiss Seafood
27 Sushi Zone
   Koo
26 Sebo
   Zushi Puzzle

MED./GREEK

27 Kokkari Estiatorio
26 Frascati
25 Zuni Café
   Campton Place
24 Foreign Cinema

MEXICAN

25 Taqueria Can Cun
   La Taqueria
24 Loló
22 Nopalito
   Mamacita

MIDDLE EASTERN

22 A La Turca
   Helmand Palace
21 Troya
20 La Méditerranée
18 Goood/Chicken

NOODLES

23 San Tung
22 Katana-Ya

   Citrus Club
21 Osha Thai
19 Hotei

PERUVIAN

25 Mochica
   Piqueo's
   La Mar Cebicheria
22 Limón
   Fresca

PIZZA

26 Una Pizza Napoletana
   Arizmendi
25 Tony's Pizza
   Pizzeria Delfina
   Pizzetta 211

SEAFOOD

27 Swan Oyster Depot
25 Hog Island Oyster
   Pesce
   Bar Crudo
   Anchor Oyster Bar

SPANISH/BASQUE

25 Piperade
24 Contigo
   Fringale
   Zarzuela
23 Bocadillos

STEAK

26 Harris'
   Alexander's Steakhouse
25 House of Prime Rib
24 Seasons
   Ruth's Chris

VIETNAMESE

25 Slanted Door
24 Crustacean
   Thanh Long
22 Le Colonial
   Out the Door

BY SPECIAL FEATURE

BREAKFAST

27 Tartine Bakery
25 Mama's on Wash.
   Boulette's Larder
   Campton Place
24 Chloe's Cafe

BRUNCH

27 Canteen
26 Yank Sing

25 Zuni Café
24 Foreign Cinema
   Universal Cafe

CHILD-FRIENDLY

26 Yank Sing
25 Mama's on Wash.
   Tony's Pizza
   Tommaso's
21 Gott's Roadside

GOOD FOR GROUPS

27	Kokkari Estiatorio
26	Aziza
25	Perbacco
24	Foreign Cinema
22	Town Hall

NEWCOMERS (RATED)

26	Michael Mina
	Una Pizza Napoletana
24	Ragazza
	Bourbon
21	Citizen Cake

OPEN LATE

25	Taqueria Can Cun
	Nopa
24	Brother's Korean
23	Lers Ros Thai
	Alembic

OUTDOOR SEATING

25	Chez Spencer
	La Mar Cebicheria
24	Foreign Cinema
23	Sociale
21	Waterbar

PEOPLE-WATCHING

27	Boulevard
26	Jardinière
25	Zuni Café
	Nopa
	La Mar Cebicheria

POWER SCENES

29	Gary Danko
28	Masa's

27	Kokkari Estiatorio
	Boulevard
	Fleur de Lys

ROMANCE

29	Gary Danko
28	Acquerello
	La Folie
	Masa's
27	Boulevard

SMALL PLATES

26	Isa
25	Pesce
	Piqueo's
24	Barbacco
	Terzo

TRENDY

26	Delfina
	Jardinière
	Sebo
25	Slanted Door
	Pizzeria Delfina

VIEWS

25	Slanted Door
	La Mar Cebicheria
24	Greens
21	Epic Roasthouse
18	Cliff House Bistro

WINNING WINE LISTS

29	Gary Danko
28	Acquerello
	La Folie
	Masa's
27	Kokkari Estiatorio

BY LOCATION

CASTRO/NOE VALLEY

27	Sushi Zone
	Frances
26	La Ciccia
25	Incanto
	Firefly

CHINATOWN

24	R&G Lounge
22	Hunan Home/Garden
21	Gold Mountain
	Yuet Lee
	House of Nanking

COW HOLLOW/MARINA

26	Zushi Puzzle
	Isa
25	Capannina
24	Umami
	Greens

DOWNTOWN

28	Masa's
27	Kokkari Estiatorio
	Fleur de Lys
26	Quince
	Michael Mina

EMBARCADERO

27 Boulevard
25 Slanted Door
   Hog Island Oyster
   Boulette's Larder
   La Mar Cebicheria

FISHERMAN'S WHARF

29 Gary Danko
23 Scoma's
21 In-N-Out
   Ana Mandara
20 McCormick/Kuleto

HAIGHT-ASHBURY/
COLE VALLEY

24 Capannina
23 Zazie
   Alembic
   Eos
22 Citrus Club

HAYES VALLEY/
CIVIC CENTER

26 Jardinière
   Sebo
25 Zuni Café
24 Brenda's
23 Bar Jules

LOWER HAIGHT

24 Thep Phanom Thai
22 Indian Oven
   Rosamunde Sausage
   Uva Enoteca
19 Memphis Minnie's

MISSION

27 Tartine Bakery
   Range
26 Delfina
   Saison
   Arizmendi

NOB HILL/
RUSSIAN HILL

28 La Folie
26 Frascati
25 Sons & Daughters
   Pesce
   Rist. Milano

NORTH BEACH

26 Cafe Jacqueline
   House
   Coi
25 Mama's on Wash.
   Tony's Pizza

PACIFIC HEIGHTS/
JAPANTOWN

28 Kiss Seafood
25 Pizzeria Delfina
24 Tataki Sushi & Sake
   SPQR
22 Bushi-tei

RICHMOND

26 Chapeau!
   Aziza
25 Pizzetta 211
   Kabuto
24 Richmond Restaurant

SOMA

26 Benu
   Una Pizza Napoletana
   Yank Sing
   Ame
   Alexander's Steakhouse

SUNSET

27 Koo
24 Thanh Long
   Ebisu
   Marnee Thai
23 San Tung

Top Decor

27 Garden Court
Twenty Five Lusk
Farallon
Big 4
Gary Danko
Rotunda

26 Sutro's at Cliff Hse.
Bix
Waterbar
Fleur de Lys

Spruce
Seasons
Kokkari Estiatorio
Jardinière
Bar Agricole
Campton Place
Silks*
Quince

25 Epic Roasthouse
Boulevard

Top Service

28 Gary Danko
Seasons

27 Acquerello
Masa's
La Folie
Benu
Coi

26 Michael Mina
Boulevard
Fleur de Lys

25 Silks
Campton Place
Harris'
Jardinière
Quince
Big 4
L'Ardoise
Kokkari Estiatorio
Saison
Chapeau!

BEST BUYS: CARTS, TRUCKS, SPECIALTY SHOPS

Arizmendi
Boccalone Salumeria
Chairman Bao Bun Truck
Curry Up Now
El Tonayense
4505 Meats
Hapa Ramen
Ike's

Let's Be Frank
Liba Falafel Truck
RoliRoti
Rosamunde Sausage
Saigon
Sentinel
Showdogs
Tartine Bakery

BEST BUYS: FULL MENUS

A La Turca
American Cupcake
American Grilled Cheese
Arlequin To Go
Brenda's
Chloe's Cafe
Citrus Club
El Metate
Frjtz Fries
Green Chile Kitchen

Kasa Indian
King of Thai
Little Chihuahua
Mama's on Wash.
Mixt Greens
Muracci's
Nick's Crispy Tacos
Papalote
Taqueria Can Cun
Yamo

---

* Indicates a tie with restaurant above

| | FOOD | DECOR | SERVICE | COST |

City of San Francisco

Z Absinthe ● 🅼 *French/Mediterranean* 　22 | 22 | 22 | $47

Hayes Valley | 398 Hayes St. (Gough St.) | 415-551-1590 | www.absinthe.com

"Absinthe makes the heart grow fonder" say supporters of this "hip and happening" Hayes Valley "boîte" where "imaginative" "artisan" cocktails meet "expertly turned" French-Med small and large plates; from the "high-energy", "beautiful" bar to the "more sedate back corners", it's a "sultry", "hot spot pre- and post-ballet, symphony and opera", thanks to "well-honed service" and lots of "pretty people to watch" – "if you can tolerate" the "deafening" din when it's "packed."

Academy Cafe *Eclectic* 　19 | 15 | 14 | $21

Inner Richmond | California Academy of Sciences | 55 Music Concourse Dr. (bet. Fulton St. & Lincoln Way) | 415-876-6121 | www.academycafesf.com

It's "hard to resist" the "fantastic array" of "local, organic and sustainable" "foods from many ethnicities" at this Eclectic eatery run by Charles Phan (the Slanted Door) and located inside the California Academy of Sciences; though "definitely better than your average museum fare", it's "kind of pricey" for a "self-serve cafeteria" and can "get crowded" with "rowdy kids", but the "outdoor patio is a must" when "weather permits"; P.S. admission fee required to enter.

Ace Wasabi's Rock-N-Roll Sushi *Japanese* 　19 | 15 | 18 | $33

Marina | 3339 Steiner St. (bet. Chestnut & Lombard Sts.) | 415-567-4903

The "sake is flowin' and the sushi is rollin'" at this "lively" Marina "pickup scene" where "beautiful people" and "young professionals" meet for "trendy" Japanese rolls at a "great value" (even playing "bingo during happy hour" can knock "a few bucks off your tab"); despite "fun servers", you'll "wait forever" when it's "supercrowded", and "unless you like techno", either "go with earplugs" or opt for takeout.

Acme Burgerhaus ● *Burgers* 　∇ 20 | 11 | 17 | $19

Western Addition | 559 Divisadero St. (Hayes St.) | 415-346-3212

"Tasty" hamburgers are made from "unique meats" (e.g. buffalo or lamb) and topped with a "great selection of add-ons" at this "friendly neighborhood place" in the Western Addition; it's all "very casual" and perfectly "fine" if you're nearby, so add in "cheap beer during happy hour" and fans wonder "what more could you ask?"

Z Acquerello 🅱🅼 *Italian* 　28 | 25 | 27 | $87

Polk Gulch | 1722 Sacramento St. (bet. Polk St. & Van Ness Ave.) | 415-567-5432 | www.acquerello.com

"Like fine wine", this "grande dame" is "getting better with age" proffering "magnificent" "high-end Italian" prix fixes brought by a "well-honed" staff while pouring some of "the best pairings in town" in a "gorgeous" "artful" setting in a "former church" off Polk Street; its "subdued" vibe and "aging clientele" are hardly hip, but judging from "the number of town cars arriving with people dressed to the nines" (jackets are suggested), this "ristorante" "for grown-ups" remains *"paradiso"* for "that special occasion" and "worth every coin."

	FOOD	DECOR	SERVICE	COST

Alamo Square Seafood Grill *French/Seafood* | 18 | 14 | 17 | $33 |

Western Addition | 803 Fillmore St. (Grove St.) | 415-440-2828 |
www.alamosquareseafoodgrill.com

Though this "intimate" French seafooder is "tucked away" in the
Western Addition, fin fans always remember the Alamo for its "simple, fresh fare that won't hurt your wallet" (including a "bargain" prix
fixe option available until 7 PM); there's an option to "customize" fish
dishes with a choice of prep style and sauce, and most consider the
"close-together" tables "cozy", so despite a dip in the Service score, it
remains a "neighborhood find."

A La Turca *Turkish* | 22 | 10 | 18 | $19 |

Tenderloin | 869 Geary St. (Larkin St.) | 415-345-1011 |
www.alaturcasf.com

"What's not to like" about "tasty, tender kebabs", "amazing" bread
and "fantastic appetizer platters" ask enthusiasts of this Tenderloin
Turkish that "packs a lot of flavor for the bucks"; sure, the neighborhood's "a bit sketchy" and the "decor leaves something to be desired",
but the "warm, down-to-earth service" and "huge portions" of "authentic" eats win out, and it's also "a fun place to go with a group."

Albona Ristorante | 25 | 18 | 25 | $46 |
Istriano 🗷🅼 *Italian*

North Beach | 545 Francisco St. (bet. Mason & Taylor Sts.) | 415-441-1040 |
www.albonarestaurant.com

Co-owner Michael Bruno "meets and greets every customer" at the
door, the start of the "delightfully old-world service" at this "intimate"
and "very comfortable" spot "hidden" away "in a residential area of
North Beach"; serving "northern Italian with a twist" (the Istrian menu
is "a perfect amalgamation of Ventian", Croatian and Slovenian), it's a
"place you remember long after you've been there", and the "reasonable prices" add to reasons regulars are "always" "going back."

Alegrias, Food From Spain *Spanish* | 21 | 17 | 22 | $36 |

Marina | 2018 Lombard St. (Webster St.) | 415-929-8888 |
www.alegriassf.com

"Small tastes of Spain await" at this "family-run", "off-the-beaten-path" Marina Iberian dishing up "authentic tapas", paella and other
moderately priced fare; while "not luxurious", the "cozy", "quiet" setting makes you "feel like you're having dinner at their home", an illusion furthered by "attentive" servers; P.S. closed Tuesdays.

Alembic, The ● *Eclectic* | 23 | 19 | 19 | $34 |

Haight-Ashbury | 1725 Haight St. (bet. Cole & Shrader Sts.) | 415-666-0822 |
www.alembicbar.com

"Come for the drinks, stay for the food" at this "energetic" "hipster"
gastropub, a Haight lunch-to-late-night "oasis" dispensing "amazing
cocktails" and "clever", "rich and delish" Eclectic small plates; the tin-ceilinged, "saloon-type" digs get "packed" and servers can seem
"gruff", but overall it's almost "too nice for the neighborhood."

Alexander's Steakhouse *Japanese/Steak* | 26 | 24 | 25 | $84 |
🆕🅴🆆 **SoMa** | 448 Brannan St. (bet. 3rd & 4th Sts.) | 415-495-1111 |
www.alexanderssteakhouse.com
See review in South of San Francisco Directory.

	FOOD	DECOR	SERVICE	COST

Alfred's Steakhouse 🅧Ⓜ *Steak* — 23 | 21 | 22 | $56

Downtown | 659 Merchant St. (bet. Kearny & Montgomery Sts.) |
415-781-7058 | www.alfredssteakhouse.com

"Old-fashioned and proud of it", this "very *Mad Men*" Downtowner
with "comfy intimate booths" is "everything a steakhouse should be",
serving a "reasonably priced", "no-surprise" meat-centric menu and
"massive" martinis that "will put you under the table if you aren't care-
ful"; "professional" waiters "just this side of gruff" serve beef buffs
who fancy "feeling like one of the good old boys", but a minority maintains it's "past its prime"; P.S. serves lunch Thursday only.

Alice's *Chinese* — 19 | 16 | 18 | $23

Noe Valley | 1599 Sanchez St. (29th St.) | 415-282-8999 |
www.alicesrestaurantsf.com

There may be "no surprises" at this outer Noe Valley Chinese but
its "expansive menu", "fresh ingredients" and "pleasing flavors" –
not to mention the "modest cost" – make it a local "staple"; a
"homey" atmosphere, "efficient" staff and fairly easy street parking
seal the deal.

Alioto's *Italian* — 18 | 18 | 19 | $44

Fisherman's Wharf | 8 Fisherman's Wharf (Taylor St.) | 415-673-0183 |
www.aliotos.com

Sure, this "old-school" Fisherman's Wharf Italian "institution" reels in
"tourists galore", but even locals appreciate its "eye-popping" views
of the "fishing boats and Golden Gate"; the Sicilian-accented seafood
is somewhat "pricey" but generally "well prepared" (the crab and
cioppino earn kudos), service is "professional" and it's hard to be un-
happy while "watching the sunset with a couple of cocktails."

🌀 Amber India *Indian* — 24 | 21 | 20 | $38

SoMa | 25 Yerba Buena Ln. (bet. Market & Mission Sts.) | 415-777-0500 |
www.amber-india.com

See review in South of San Francisco Directory.

Ame *American* — 26 | 25 | 25 | $76

SoMa | St. Regis | 689 Mission St. (3rd St.) | 415-284-4040 |
www.amerestaurant.com

"It's really difficult not to have a great meal" at this "high-end" SoMa
"boîte" and sashimi bar in the St. Regis from Terra owners Hiro Sone
and Lissa Doumani, where "haute", "elaborately imaginative" New
American cuisine is infused with "Japanese accents" and "flair"; "entry is steep", but from the moment the "impeccable" staff picks a "fantastic wine" (or "mystery sake"), you'll be in "for an amazing
experience" in the "spa-like" "Zen" setting.

American Cupcake Ⓜ *American/Bakery* — 15 | 16 | 17 | $17

Cow Hollow | 1919 Union St. (Laguna St.) | 415-896-4217 |
www.americancupcake.com

"What's not to like about a place that combines sugar with
alcohol?" ask fans of this Cow Hollow American offering "cupcake/
wine pairings", "candy cocktails" and "savory foods" in "modern"
white digs with color-changing lights; "girlie-girls" simply "love"
it, but critics contend the overall execution leaves "something
to be desired."

American Grilled
Cheese Kitchen *American/Sandwiches*

| 22 | 14 | 17 | $14 |

SoMa | 1 South Park Ave. (2nd St.) | 415-243-0107 | www.theamericansf.com
"Dressed-up" grilled cheese creations "oozing with flavor" draw the "hipster parade" to this "friendly" SoMa sammie shop with an industrial-chic–meets–retro–kitchenette look; there can be "bummer" lines and "seating is mainly outdoors, so pick a sunny day" or "be prepared" to take out; P.S. it also offers soups, salads and more, but no dinner.

Americano *Italian*

| 18 | 20 | 18 | $43 |

Embarcadero | Hotel Vitale | 8 Mission St. (The Embarcadero) | 415-278-3777 | www.americanorestaurant.com
This Embarcadero hotel Italian provides "well-prepared" (if rather "pricey") meals, but it's perhaps better known as an "after-work "hot spot" with an "incredible" patio affording views of the Bay Bridge, Ferry Building and the "young and lovely" "financial types" who hit its "hopping happy hour"; they probably don't notice if "service varies" and the noise can be "through the roof."

Amici's East Coast Pizzeria *Pizza*

| 20 | 14 | 18 | $21 |

AT&T Park | 216 King St. (bet. 3rd & 4th Sts.) | 415-546-6666
Marina | 2200 Lombard St. (Steiner St.) | 415-885-4500
www.amicis.com
Maybe it's "not quite" the real thing, but for a "taste of Noo Yawk" close to home, this "family-friendly" chain's "proper thin-crust", brick-oven pizzas (with "low-carb" and "gluten-free" options) satisfy most; if some cite "Manhattan prices", it's still "cheaper than a flight" back East, and there's "take-and-bake" and "quick delivery" to bypass the at-times "crowded", "loud" conditions and "hit-or-miss" service.

Ana Mandara *Vietnamese*

| 21 | 25 | 21 | $51 |

Fisherman's Wharf | Ghirardelli Sq. | 891 Beach St. (Polk St.) | 415-771-6800 | www.anamandara.com
It's easy to be "swept away" by the "posh", "movie-set Asian village" decor and "interesting", "high-end Vietnamese" fare at this "date-night" spot in Fisherman's Wharf; maybe it's "lost some of its sizzle" over the years and the food and service "don't live up to" its looks, but the upstairs bar is still a "perfect place to cuddle", especially when the "jazz trio" plays (Thursday–Saturday).

Anchor & Hope *Seafood*

| 21 | 20 | 20 | $44 |

SoMa | 83 Minna St. (2nd St.) | 415-501-9100 | www.anchorandhopesf.com
"The interior hearkens" back to "Nantucket", "but the ambiance is all West Coast" at this "cavernous", "nautical-themed" "warehouse" in SoMa where a "friendly", "fresh-faced" staff serves "solid" "fish house" favorites like "a tasty *lobstah* roll that would make a Bostonian proud"; it's "a fun place to indulge in seafood fantasies", but it's "way too loud" lament some landlubbers, who prefer "stopping in for a pint" and "bar bites" during the "standout happy hour."

Anchor Oyster Bar *Seafood*

| 25 | 16 | 21 | $36 |

Castro | 579 Castro St. (bet. 18th & 19th Sts.) | 415-431-3990 | www.anchoroysterbar.com
"Don't let this one get away" wink fans of this "cute little" fish shack in the Castro that keeps "shucking along", serving up "not fussy, just

well-prepared", "super-fresh" "blackboard" specials and "various types of oysters" and pours of cheap "house wines"; service is "efficient" and it's a real "catch", just be prepared to "stand out on the sidewalk" to "snag a seat at the counter" and shell out a few clams.

Andalé *Mexican*   21 | 13 | 15 | $17

Downtown | Westfield San Francisco Ctr. | 865 Market St. (5th St.) | 415-243-8700 | www.andalemexican.com
See review in South of San Francisco Directory.

Andalu *Eclectic*   21 | 19 | 19 | $36

Mission | 3198 16th St. (Guerrero St.) | 415-621-2211 | www.andalusf.com
"Still trendy after all these years", this "reasonably priced" Missionite with "accommodating" servers is "tops for tapas", in this case "creative" Eclectic small plates that take "a little from this culture, a little from that one"; an "excellent date place" (you can "sit in the window" for "people-watching"), the "festive" atmosphere and "sublime sangria" mean it's also "deservedly popular with younger diners", who gather in "large groups" "to see and be seen."

Angkor Borei *Cambodian*   22 | 15 | 22 | $23

Bernal Heights | 3471 Mission St. (Cortland Ave.) | 415-550-8417 | www.cambodiankitchen.com
Stepping inside this "family-run" Bernal Heights "gem" "feels like visiting Cambodia" thanks to "consistently good", "authentic" eats and "exceptionally friendly, hospitable" service; the location and decor may be "humble", but the "warm" vibe and solid "value" keep fans returning.

Anzu *Japanese*   22 | 19 | 21 | $57

Downtown | Hotel Nikko | 222 Mason St. (O'Farrell St.) | 415-394-1100 | www.restaurantanzu.com
"Tucked away on the second floor" of Downtown's Hotel Nikko, this "incredibly civilized" Japanese specializes in "quality" sushi, "outstanding" steak and a "wide selection of sake"; it's "one of the city's best-kept secrets" whisper devotees of the "quiet room", who come for "a quick bite before the theater" or on their way to a concert at the "swank Rrazz Room downstairs", and though some add it would be even "better if the decor were updated", "gracious" service adds to the appeal.

Aperto *Italian*   23 | 17 | 22 | $32

Potrero Hill | 1434 18th St. (bet. Connecticut & Missouri Sts.) | 415-252-1625 | www.apertosf.com
A "warm, homey" "neighborhood charmer", this "reasonably priced" Potrero Hill trattoria "continues to shine" by dishing out "hearty" "Italian comfort food", like "excellent" "homemade pastas" and "well-executed" "blackboard specials" filled with "fresh flavors"; the staff treats you "like family", and since regulars "always run into their neighbors", most don't mind the "tight quarters."

Ariake Japanese ⊠ *Japanese*   23 | 15 | 21 | $36

Outer Richmond | 5041 Geary Blvd. (bet. 14th & 15th Aves.) | 415-221-6210 | www.sfariake.com
"Beautifully prepared" sushi "melts in the mouth" at this "reliable" Outer Richmond Japanese, where surveyors suggest you "sit at the

FOOD DECOR SERVICE COST

bar" and "chitchat with the owner" (and chef), Jin Kim; "order omakase for a transcendent dinner", but the "fun" rolls, "top-grade" fish and "friendly" staff make it a "favorite" no matter which you choose.

Arinell Pizza ⊅ *Pizza* 22 | 5 | 13 | $8
Mission | 509 Valencia St. (16th St.) | 415-255-1303
The "closest thing to a real NY slice" declare fans of the "hot, fresh" pies with "spot-on" crispy crusts at these "cheap" joints in the Mission (a "late-night drinkers" pit stop on weekends) and Berkeley (a student fave); a staff with "Jersey attitude" and "hole-in-the-wall" digs don't faze groupies who say the goods are "best enjoyed while walking."

Arizmendi *Bakery/Pizza* 26 | 12 | 19 | $11
Inner Sunset | 1331 Ninth Ave. (bet. Irving & Judah Sts.) | 415-566-3117 | www.arizmendibakery.org Ⓜ⊅
NEW Mission | 1268 Valencia St. (24th St.) | 415-826-9218 | valencia.arizmendi.coop
"You can taste the love" at this "worker-owned co-op" in the Mission (with separately owned cousins), a "carbohydrate heaven" where "well-informed" staffers dole out "drool-worthy" "sweet and savory" baked goods and a vegetarian "pizza of the day that never disappoints"; though seats are "minimal" and frills "few", you'll "walk away fatter but happier" (and you can always "take out").

Arlequin To Go *Mediterranean* 19 | 15 | 16 | $19
Hayes Valley | 384B Hayes St. (bet. Franklin & Gough Sts.) | 415-626-1211 | www.arlequincafe.com
"Little brother (and neighbor) to upscale Absinthe" and Arlequin Wine Merchant, this "casual" all-day Hayes Valley Med cafe is an "affordable" "winner" for "quick gourmet food" ("tasty" sandwiches, soups, etc.); it's popular "before the ballet or symphony" nearby, with "ample outdoor seating", "friendly" service and free WiFi as bonuses.

AsiaSF Ⓜ *Asian/Californian* 17 | 19 | 22 | $58
SoMa | 201 Ninth St. (Howard St.) | 415-255-2742 | www.asiasf.com
"Gorgeous" "gender illusionists" perform "hourly on the bar catwalks" in-between serving up "fancy" cocktails and "better than you'd expect" Cal-Asian small plates at this "funky" SoMa nightspot; "it may be touristy and a little pricey" but it provides "lots of laughs" for "bachelorette or birthday parties"; P.S. prix fixe–only most nights.

NEW Asiento ☽ *Spanish* – | – | – | I
Mission | 2730 21st St. (Byrant St.) | 415-829-3375 | www.asientosf.com
Befitting its name (it means "seat" in Spanish), this chill Mission haunt feels like a living room – replete with board games and DJs – perfect for gatherings over wine and an affordable menu of tapas ranging from bocadillos to Thai spring rolls; additional draws include $2 Taco Tuesdays, Sunday brunch and an early-bird bonus: the first one in at 5 PM chooses the discounted happy-hour drink.

Ⓩ A16 *Italian* 24 | 20 | 21 | $45
Marina | 2355 Chestnut St. (bet. Divisadero & Scott Sts.) | 415-771-2216 | www.a16sf.com
It's "worth running the gauntlet" through the "buzzing" "younger crowd" at this "total Marina scene" where the "well-executed", "rustic

Italian" menu includes "fresh" pastas, salumi and "phenomenal" "wood-charred" pies; true, the din can be "deafening" and the fare "a bit pricey", but the "harried" staff is a "friendly" guide to the "interesting" wine list, and "sitting at the counter watching the chefs" is "never a miss"; P.S. lunch is served Wednesday–Friday.

Asqew Grill *Californian* | 17 | 12 | 16 | $17 |

Haight-Ashbury | 1607 Haight St. (Clayton St.) | 415-701-9301
Laurel Heights | 3415 California St. (bet. Laurel & Locust Sts.) | 415-386-5608
Marina | 3348 Steiner St. (bet. Chestnut & Lombard Sts.) | 415-931-9200
www.asqewgrill.com

"Almost everything is on a stick" at this Californian "skewer cuisine" mini-chain featuring "tasty", "relatively healthy" "mix-and-match" grilled proteins and veggies plus salads and sides; though "nothing fancy", they're "quick", "cheap" choices "for an easy night out" or "to-go" eats.

NEW Atelier Crenn 🛇Ⓜ *French* | ▽ 26 | 23 | 26 | $105 |

Marina | 3127 Fillmore St. (bet. Filbert & Pixley Sts.) | 415-440-0460 |
www.ateliercrenn.com

Chef Dominique Crenn (ex Luce) has struck out on her own in this new atelier-inspired Marina French where she's turning out "whimsical", "Wonka-like" prix fixe dinners meant to "evoke memories" while bringing "molecular gastronomy" and "artistry" "to a level" fans say is "heretofore unseen in the Bay Area"; add in "spot-on" wine and service, plus a simple, salonlike setting, and though the edible "concepts" might leave some "hungry", most declare it "succeeds in spectacular fashion."

Axum Cafe *Ethiopian* | ▽ 23 | 12 | 20 | $17 |

Lower Haight | 698 Haight St. (Pierce St.) | 415-252-7912 |
www.axumcafe.com

Lower Haight locals frequent this Ethiopian (named after that country's oldest city) for "delicious, filling" fare that's "wonderfully presented" by a "friendly" staff; it may be small and simple, but it's "a real bargain" overseen by "fantastic owners."

🔟 Aziza *Moroccan* | 26 | 22 | 23 | $95 |

Outer Richmond | 5800 Geary Blvd. (22nd Ave.) | 415-752-2222 |
www.aziza-sf.com

"Walk through the entry curtain and you're in the casbah" at this "lushly decorated", "sultry" and "high-end" Outer Richmonder where chef Mourad Lahlou "works some serious magic" in an "exquisite" "modern take" on Moroccan cuisine by way of "Northern California"; "herbalicious cocktails" plus an "amazingly priced prix fixe" and a "pampering staff" all make it "hard to top" for "special occasions"; P.S. it's closed Tuesdays, and plans to serve a more traditional cuisine after a Downtown incarnation opens in early 2012 at 801 Montgomery Street.

Baby Blues BBQ *BBQ/Southern* | 18 | 12 | 17 | $24 |

Mission | 3149 Mission St. (Precita Ave.) | 415-896-4250 |
www.babybluessf.com

"Juicy ribs made Memphis-style", "gut-busting sides" and a "wide selection" of sauces are among the offerings at this "friendly" Mission BBQ joint (by way of Venice, CA); there's "not much" decor and some 'cue connoisseurs deem it "a little pricey" and "nothing special", but it will do the trick "if you need your fix."

Bacco Ristorante   Italian   24 | 21 | 23 | $45

Noe Valley | 737 Diamond St. (bet. Elizabeth & 24th Sts.) | 415-282-4969 | www.baccosf.com

A "delightful" "neighborhood Italian" in true "trattoria tradition", this "cozy" Noe Valley "favorite" serves "nothing fancy", just "excellent housemade pastas", risotto that will "rock your world" and other standbys in "large portions" and at "fair prices"; it's "a nice change of pace from the North Beach usual suspects", with additional props for an "exceptionally warm" staff that "remembers you" and uncorks "fine" all-Boot vinos "without the fine-wine prices."

Baker & Banker Ⓜ American   25 | 23 | 24 | $60

Upper Fillmore | 1701 Octavia St. (Bush St.) | 415-351-2500 | www.bakerandbanker.com

Chef Jeff Banker and pastry whiz Lori Baker are the "talented" couple behind this "cozy" Upper Fillmore storefront where "fantastic" bread from the on-site bakery starts the meal, "heavenly" desserts cap it and there's "outstanding" "farm-to-table" New American "comfort food" in-between; the "upscale tavern-esque" setting gets "crowded and noisy", but a "gracious" staff and "great wine list without the gouge" help make it a "winner"; P.S. dinner only, plus Sunday brunch.

Baker Street Bistro Ⓜ French   19 | 17 | 20 | $38

Marina | 2953 Baker St. (bet. Greenwich & Lombard Sts.) | 415-931-1475 | www.bakerstreetbistro.com

A "bit of Paris hidden in the backstreets of the Marina", this "cozy" bistro earns "repeat customers" because it's "very affordable" and sticks to "the classics" – "nothing fancy, just good French food" and an "ample wine list"; it can feel "a bit crowded" but "doting" service and outdoor seating compensate; P.S. the dinner prix fixe, offered "early-bird" on weekends and till close weeknights, is a "special bargain."

Balboa Cafe   American   19 | 18 | 20 | $37

Cow Hollow | 3199 Fillmore St. (Greenwich St.) | 415-921-3944 | www.balboacafe.com

"Known more for its social scene than anything else" (it's "perpetually busy" with everyone from "ladies who lunch" to "movers and shakers" to "cougars"), this Cow Hollow "classic" (and its "country cousin" in Mill Valley) nonetheless pleases patrons with "traditional" American fare, especially its "legendary" "burgers on a baguette"; some claim it's "firecracker loud" at peak hours, but "generous drinks" and a "solid wine" selection served by a "cheerful" staff mean it's "always fun."

Bar Agricole   Californian   21 | 26 | 20 | $48

SoMa | 355 11th St. (bet. Folsom & Harrison Sts.) | 415-355-9400 | www.baragricole.com

This "hip and hot" contender on "the SoMa scene" "raises the bar" with a Californian menu of "unexpected but delicious" "gastropub" small plates "served family-style" and washed down with "seductive" "handcrafted cocktails" made with "local fresh ingredients"; the "modern, sustainable" (LEED-certified) space feels "funky and rustic" and the staff – including the "knowledgeable bartenders" – is "professional and charming", which all seems "even better" when "somebody else is paying."

Z Barbacco ⓩ *Italian* | 24 | 21 | 22 | $42 |

Downtown | 220 California St. (Front St.) | 415-955-1919 | www.barbaccosf.com

Aka "bargain"-bacco, this "sleek" Downtown 'eno trattoria' – a lower-cost, "lower-key" annex to next-door Perbacco – packs in the power set thanks to "superb" salumi and other regional Italian small plates enhanced by "knowledgeable" service and "eclectic" vinos chosen via "cool" "iPad wine lists"; with a "hip bar" scene (alas, "wine and beer only") and "crowded" communal tables it's "always buzzing" – "who says the FiDi dies after 7 PM?"

Bar Bambino ⓩ *Italian* | 24 | 21 | 21 | $46 |

Mission | 2931 16th St. (Mission St.) | 415-701-8466 | www.barbambino.com

"Terrific" charcuterie, "handcrafted pastas" and "great cheeses" are the holy trinity – and "unique" vinos an extra blessing – at this "chic" Italian cafe/wine bar (with some new Central European accents); "attentive" service and a "lovely" back patio help keep it filled with "trendsetters" who don't mind its "sketch-o" Mission locale or tabs that can mount; P.S. lunch is via to-go boxes only, but upcoming sibling Pronto (3153 17th Street, by the reopened ODC Theater) will serve lunch, light dinner and more.

Bar Crudo Ⓜ *Seafood* | 25 | 18 | 21 | $47 |

Western Addition | 655 Divisadero St. (Grove St.) | 415-409-0679 | www.barcrudo.com

For an "interesting" "change from Japanese sushi", fin fanciers suggest the "Italian version" featuring "amazingly fresh" raw fish "paired with well-balanced ingredients" at this Western Addition spot that also offers hot dishes including "not-to-be-missed" "seafood chowder"; a "top-notch" beer selection is a further draw, while the "industrial-chic" setting is "stark" but "artistic", and though budget-watchers caution that the "small plates can add up", "happy hour is a steal."

Bar Jules Ⓜ *American* | 23 | 17 | 21 | $44 |

Hayes Valley | 609 Hayes St. (Laguna St.) | 415-621-5482 | www.barjules.com

"The new Alice Waters" declare fans of Jessica Boncutter, the "delightful" chef-owner behind this "quirky", "down-home" yet "hip" little Hayes Valley New American where a "limited" but "delicious" "farmer's market-driven" menu is served by "friendly" folks; a few "wish it were cheaper" and not so "noisy" or "impossible to get into" (half the seats are for walk-ins), but overall it's a "neighborhood star"; P.S. no lunch Tuesdays, brunch-only Sundays.

Barney's Gourmet Hamburgers *Burgers* | 19 | 13 | 16 | $17 |

Marina | 3344 Steiner St. (bet. Chestnut & Lombard Sts.) | 415-563-0307
Noe Valley | 4138 24th St. (Castro St.) | 415-282-7770
www.barneyshamburgers.com

"Everybody can get what they like" at this "inexpensive" mini-chain of "almost-gourmet" patty joints, including "large salads", "terrific shakes and malts", "your pick" of fries and an "amazing variety of beef, turkey and veggie burgers with every imaginable topping"; though some find the service "iffy", it helps to take refuge from the often "zoo-like" atmosphere on the "outdoor patio" (at most locations).

Bar Tartine *European* | 24 | 20 | 20 | $41 |

Mission | 561 Valencia St. (bet. 16th & 17th Sts.) | 415-487-1600 | www.bartartine.com

"Revolving chefs have not diminished" the appeal of this "lively" Mission "offshoot" "from the fabulous Tartine folks", a "cozy", "romantic roost" with a "rustic" feel and a "hipster" staff delivering "more than" just "fantastic bread" and "amazing" desserts in a menu that's taken a post-Survey shift toward the food and wines of Eastern and Northern Europe (overseen by ex–Nombe chef Nick Balla); an adjoining sandwich shop is scheduled for a mid-September 2011 opening.

Basil Thai Restaurant & Bar *Thai* | 23 | 19 | 20 | $29 |

SoMa | 1175 Folsom St. (bet. 7th & 8th Sts.) | 415-552-8999

Basil Canteen *Thai*

SoMa | 1489 Folsom St. (11th St.) | 415-552-3963
www.basilthai.com

For a "twist on the traditional South Asian cuisine", SoMa's "hip crowd" turns to the "imaginative, fresh" menu and "Asian-inspired cocktails" served up by "friendly, efficient waiters" in the "modern loft settings" of this Thai twosome; "reasonable prices" (especially for drinks and apps during the Canteen's happy hour) keep the "neighbor-hood gems" "consistently crowded", and if it gets too "hectic" and "noisy", you can always take the "fresh flavors" "home to enjoy."

Beach Chalet Brewery *American* | 15 | 21 | 16 | $32 |

Outer Sunset | 1000 Great Hwy. (bet. Fulton St. & Lincoln Way) | 415-386-8439 | www.beachchalet.com

Thanks to the "million-dollar" vista, this brewpub in "historic" digs at the edge of Golden Gate Park in the Outer Sunset is "always packed" with a "mix of tourists and locals" "throwing back" a "tasty" house-made beer and "reliable" New American eats; "you can't beat the view" of the sun setting "over the Pacific Ocean" (or the "fascinating" "Depression-era" murals on the ground floor), though critics carp about the "unimpressive" menu and "spotty" service.

NEW Beast & | ∇ 20 | 14 | 18 | $39 |
The Hare Ⓜ *American/Californian*

Mission | 1001 Guerrero St. (22nd St.) | 415-821-1001 | www.beastandthehare.com

Inspired by taverns of yore, this tiny Mission newcomer strikes some as the "quintessential SF restaurant", where "dressed-down hipsters" describes the crowd and staff, and the "limited" but "very good" array of Cal-American small and big plates (including oysters and house-cured charcuterie) comes at "reasonable prices"; Sunday is brunch only.

Beautifull *Health Food* | 17 | 13 | 17 | $17 |

Inner Sunset | 816 Irving St. (bet. 9th & 10th Aves.) | 415-664-2033 🅢
Laurel Heights | 3401 California St. (bet. Laurel & Locust Sts.) | 415-728-9080
www.beautifull.com

A "wonderful variety" of "wholesome", "fresh" fare "made from the best ingredients" inspires "busy professionals" to patronize this "quick"

FOOD | DECOR | SERVICE | COST

health-food pair in Laurel Heights and the Inner Sunset; "best for take-out" (though equipped with "minimal" seating indoors and out), they're favorites of those "feeling guilty after having overindulged elsewhere", but penny-pinchers opine the merely "ok" eats are "overpriced."

Bella Trattoria *Italian*
22 | 18 | 22 | $36

Inner Richmond | 3854 Geary Blvd. (3rd Ave.) | 415-221-0305 | www.bellatrattoriasf.com

"Leave the fog of the Richmond" at the door and "indulge in the wonderful fresh pastas" and other "quality, homey" Italian fare at this "comfortable neighborhood" trattoria where regulars are "treated like family" by the "personable staff"; "nothing fancy", it's "not a destination spot" but the "great value" ("free corkage" Monday–Wednesday) "delivers in a pinch."

Benihana *Japanese*
17 | 18 | 20 | $38

Japantown | Japan Ctr. | 1737 Post St. (Webster St.) | 415-563-4844 | www.benihana.com

"Theatric" tableside feats by teppanyaki "performer-chefs" assure this Japanese steakhouse chain "never fails to entertain while filling your belly" with "reliable", "reasonably priced" fare including sushi; while a few gripe that it's "loud", "overcrowded" and "gimmicky", partyers proclaim it "novel fun for office lunches or kids' birthdays" – "children really love it" and you can get "a photo too!"

Benu ⊠ Ⓜ *American*
26 | 23 | 27 | $143

SoMa | 22 Hawthorne St. (bet. Folsom & Howard Sts.) | 415-685-4860 | www.benusf.com

Former French Laundry "wunderkind" Corey Lee "makes a knockout debut" at his "super-duper high-end" SoMa "temple for foodies" where the "sublime" *"nouvelle"* American cuisine, augmented with an "Asian twist" and "innovative wine/beer/sake pairings", is "presented like artwork" on "custom-made" plates by an "incomparable" staff; while the "luxe minimalist decor" and "ridiculously small portions" are "probably too extremely Zen" (considering "you're dropping Benjamins to eat here"), as compensation, consider the "see-through kitchen" that "lets you peek at all the wizardry going on."

Beretta ● *Italian*
22 | 19 | 19 | $39

Mission | 1199 Valencia St. (23rd St.) | 415-695-1199 | www.berettasf.com

Credited with kick-starting the "fancy drink and pizza craze", this "terminally busy" Mission "scene" dispenses "insanely good" thin-crust pies, "creative" Italian small plates and "crafty" cocktails in "hip yet cozy" digs complete with a "bustling bar" staffed by some of SF's "best mixologists"; "if you can deal with the noise", crowds and "long" waits (reserving for six or more only), it "always delivers" for anything from "nocturnal noshing" to "weekend brunch."

Betelnut Pejiu Wu *Asian*
23 | 21 | 20 | $40

Cow Hollow | 2030 Union St. (Buchanan St.) | 415-929-8855 | www.betelnutrestaurant.com

"There is always a great buzz" at this "hip" Cow Hollow "Pan-Asian paradise", where a "stylish crowd" including "lots of date-night couples" feeds on "potent exotic cocktails" and "flavor-packed" fare; the "sumptuous" red-and-gold dining room "can get very noisy", but the "helpful" staff and a check that leaves patrons "pleasantly surprised" mean most maintain it hasn't "lost an ounce of its luster."

B44 *Spanish*
| 21 | 17 | 19 | $39 |

Downtown | 44 Belden Pl. (bet. Bush & Pine Sts.) | 415-986-6287 | www.b44sf.com

It's "great to sit outside" on the "lively patio" and "pretend you're in Spain" at this cafe on Downtown's Belden Place, a "paella heaven" that's also praised for its "flavor-packed tapas" and other "authentic Catalan" chow; some find seating a bit "cramped" and say it can get "noisy", but "sensible prices", a "good wine list" and "helpful" servers compensate.

☑ Big 4 *American*
| 23 | 27 | 25 | $59 |

Nob Hill | Huntington Hotel | 1075 California St. (Taylor St.) | 415-771-1140 | www.big4restaurant.com

"Feel like a Gold Rush fat cat" as you soak in the "old-fashioned country club" decor ("gorgeous" cherry wood paneling, "memorabilia from the railroad barons" era) at this Nob Hill "classy classic" where "almost clairvoyant" servers present "surprisingly good" "traditional American cuisine" "with a creative twist"; it may be an "old-world dining experience with new-world prices", but "the piano player is always a treat", as is "watching the local celebs"; P.S. surveyors "especially love the bar" for its "strong drinks" and "delicious chicken pot pie with sherry."

Bistro Aix *Californian/French*
| 22 | 20 | 21 | $42 |

Marina | 3340 Steiner St. (bet. Chestnut & Lombard Sts.) | 415-202-0100 | www.bistroaix.com

"Old is new again after the remodel" of this "affordable" Marina favorite where "neighborhood families" and "out-of-towners flock" for "French fare with a Californian flair" served by an "attentive staff"; while the new "enclosed patio" with a "beautiful" "olive tree in the center" is much acclaimed, some fret the "food seems to have fallen off a step" ("well prepared but not as creative as before"); still, fans are "so glad it's back."

Bistro Boudin *Californian*
| 20 | 16 | 16 | $28 |

Fisherman's Wharf | 160 Jefferson St. (near Pier 43½) | 415-928-1849 | www.boudinbakery.com

It "may be a cliché", but the "clam chowder bread bowl" and other sourdough specialties are "actually very good" at this Cal veteran with "great views" "on the second story of the Boudin shop"/bakery; it's "overpriced", perhaps – but then, in the "tourist mecca" of Fisherman's Wharf, what isn't?

Bistro Central Parc ⓜ *French*
| 24 | 18 | 23 | $40 |

Western Addition | 560 Central Ave. (Grove St.) | 415-931-7272 | www.bistrocentralparc.com

For "unpretentious", "excellent" "French staples" and a "wonderful wine selection", Francophiles don't mind "going cross-town" to this Western Addition "treasure" where even the "small and intimate" (if "spare") dining room and "warm hosts" (who "used to run Baker Street Bistro") contribute to the "classic Parisian feel"; "word has gotten out quickly" about this "bargain for the quality" "and it's always packed, so make reservations."

	FOOD	DECOR	SERVICE	COST

NEW Bistro SF Grill 🛇Ⓜ *Burgers*

| - | - | - | I |

Pacific Heights | 2119 California St. (Laguna St.) | 415-235-4022 | www.bistrosfgrill.com

Fans of the popular Balkan burger stand at the Sunday Divisadero Farmers' Market (aka SF Grill) can now get their fix daily at this sit-down brick-and-mortar offshoot in Pacific Heights that slings the same cheap eats ranging from tame patties (turkey, chicken, beef) to the exotic (alligator, wild boar, elk), along with fries and salads; the interior is decked out with racy red walls, black booths and colorful art.

❷ Bix *American/French*

| 24 | 26 | 23 | $58 |

Downtown | 56 Gold St. (bet. Montgomery & Sansome Sts.) | 415-433-6300 | www.bixrestaurant.com

Slip on that "little black dress" and "step back in time" at this "swanky", "retro" supper club "hidden in an alley" Downtown, where "waiters in white waistcoats" hoisting cocktail shakers and "all that jazz" ("live" nightly) have patrons thinking "they're the cat's meow"; "you half expect to see Humphrey Bogart" at the "jumpin'" bar, and while it "isn't cheap", it's tops for "a night on the town", a "romantic" dinner of "well-prepared" American-French fare "upstairs" or a "three-olive martini" Friday lunch.

Blowfish Sushi To Die For *Japanese*

| 21 | 19 | 17 | $42 |

Mission | 2170 Bryant St. (20th St.) | 415-285-3848 | www.blowfishsushi.com

"Ready for a party at a moment's notice", with "multiple screens showing anime" and "techno music" reminiscent of "Japanese disco", this "trendy" twosome in the Mission and San Jose is "a fun alternative to traditional sushi bars", serving "innovative rolls and appetizers" in addition to the usual suspects; the "fantastic cocktails" take the edge off the "slow service", but it's "ridiculously loud" say some, who tut it's a "tad overpriced" to boot.

Blue Barn Gourmet *Californian*

| 24 | 17 | 18 | $17 |

Marina | 2105 Chestnut St. (Steiner St.) | 415-441-3232 | www.bluebarngourmet.com

It's "all about the sandwiches" – "simple" but "highly creative" – and the "scrumptious salads" at this "laid-back" "Marina hot spot"; "most people take out" their "pricy" orders of "only-in-California" cuisine, because the "charming but cramped" digs are always "mobbed" with "lululemon-wearing girls"; P.S. a second branch is planned for 2237 Polk Street.

Blue Bottle Café *Californian/Coffeehouse*

| 23 | 14 | 17 | $9 |

Embarcadero | Ferry Bldg. Mktpl. | 1 Ferry Bldg. (The Embarcadero) | 510-653-3394
SoMa | Mint Plaza | 66 Mint St. (Mission St.) | 510-653-3394
Blue Bottle Kiosk 🕏 *Californian/Coffeehouse*
Hayes Valley | 315 Linden St. (Gough St.) | 510-653-3394
Rooftop Garden Blue
Bottle Coffee Bar *Californian/Coffeehouse*
SoMa | SFMOMA | 151 Third St. (bet. Howard & Mission Sts.) | 415-243-0455
www.bluebottlecoffee.net

"Coffee-making is an art form" at this cult chain where "hipster" baristas craft "pricey" drinks using "seriously great beans" and "laboratory-style", "made-to-order" brewing methods; critics deride "the hype" and even fans knock "super-slow" lines and occasional "attitude", but for java "fetishists", the "amazing results" are worth it; P.S. there's "simple" Californian breakfast and lunch fare (pastries only at the Hayes Valley kiosk and SFMOMA rooftop bar).

Blue Plate *American*

24 | 19 | 21 | $40

Mission | 3218 Mission St. (bet. 29th & Valencia Sts.) | 415-282-6777 | www.blueplatesf.com

"The name may conjure up a diner but don't be fooled – this "funky" Missionite run by "friendly" "hipsters" serves "fabulous" and "surprisingly sophisticated" sustainably sourced New American "comfort food" and "killer desserts" while pouring "mainly European" wines, all making it a "foodie favorite" for a midpriced "meal out"; it "can be noisy" "sitting at the bar", but those seeking a "calm vibe" come midweek and opt for the "romantic" "back room" or "lovely outdoor garden."

NEW Bluestem Brasserie *Steakhouse*

- | - | - | E

SoMa | 1 Yerba Buena Ln. (bet. 3rd & 4th Sts.) | 415-547-1111 | www.bluestembrasserie.com

Big, brassy and boasting a rare heated second-floor patio, this SoMa arrival is poised to be the new go-to spot for power lunch, brontosaurus-sized dinners and happy-hour hobnobbing, offering all manner of steakhouse fare (with a choice of classic sauces and sides) along with seafood and rotating plats du jour (e.g. coq au vin Tuesdays); adding to the appeal is a good mix of bottles, plus 12 Californian wines on tap and cleverly named cocktails.

Bocadillos ☒ *Spanish*

23 | 19 | 20 | $33

North Beach | 710 Montgomery St. (Washington St.) | 415-982-2622 | www.bocasf.com

"Creative" "modern Basque tapas" and a "well-priced" "Spanish wine list" "bring a touch of San Sebastián to San Francisco" at this "stylish" spot in North Beach from Piperade's Gerald Hirigoyen; "perfect" "for a quick chic lunch", when diners can "mix and match" the "small sandwiches" for which it's named, it's also popular for "tasty little morsels" at dinner; the "tiny" tables may be "squeezed together" and "the communal tables get a bit tight", but "friendly, personable" servers ensure it feels more "cozy" than cramped.

Boccalone Salumeria *Sandwiches*

26 | 20 | 23 | $12

Embarcadero | Ferry Bldg. Mktpl. | 1 Ferry Bldg. (The Embarcadero) | 415-433-6500 | www.boccalone.com

"Hail to the king of pork products" (Incanto's Chris Cosentino) and "bring on the lardo" cheer the hog-happy fans of this "amazing" deli counter in the Ferry Building known for "stellar" "Italian-style meats", sandwiches and other "salty pig parts"; despite the market's "spectacular setting", this "pricey" porker has only four seats, and "don't let the line scare you away" – "the service is quick" plus you "can't go wrong with a cone of meat"; P.S. closes 6 PM Monday–Saturday, 5 PM Sunday.

Bodega Bistro *Vietnamese*

21 | 13 | 17 | $29

Tenderloin | 607 Larkin St. (Eddy St.) | 415-921-1218 | www.bodegabistro.net

Pho-natics are "hooked" on the "dependable" Vietnamese vittles, from "Hanoi street food" to "indulgent" "French-inspired dishes", at this "friendly" "sleeper in a somewhat seedy section of town" (the Tenderloin); and since the "family-style platters" and "fantastic pho" are just "a fraction of the cost" of Slanted Door delicacies, devotees are too busy "diving into" their meals to mind the simple setting.

Boogaloos *Southwestern*

17 | 13 | 16 | $17

Mission | 3296 22nd St. (Valencia St.) | 415-824-4088 | www.boogaloossf.com

"Go on a weekday or super early on a weekend" to miss the "crazy lines" of "Mission hipsters" who queue at this "no-frills breakfast joint" for "massive quantities" of "creative" AM "staples" with a Southwestern bent (including "lots of vegan options"); however, the "hit-or-miss" service and "schizophrenic" decor draw boos, causing foes to "yawn" it's "not really worth the 45 minute wait."

NEW Bottle Cap 🈂️🅜 *BBQ*

- | - | - | M

North Beach | 1707 Powell St. (Columbus Ave.) | 415-529-2237 | www.bottlecapsf.com

Shepherding in a new era at this historic North Beach gathering place (formerly the Washington Square Bar & Grill) is this American bistro, a breezy, walk-only affair offering a moderately priced, updated retro menu (served all day) and handcrafted classic cocktails in an adjacent lounge; the dark, nostalgia-crammed interior has been replaced by a sunny room outfitted with stenciled blue tables, vintage wallpaper and windows looking out onto nearby Washington Square Park.

Boulette's Larder *American*

25 | 18 | 20 | $35

Embarcadero | Ferry Bldg. Mktpl. | 1 Ferry Bldg. (The Embarcadero) | 415-399-1155 | www.bouletteslarder.com

This "petite" "gastronomic treasure trove" in the Ferry Building sells prepared foods, "exotic spices" and other ingredients "to stock your larder", and also turns out "exceptional" New American breakfast and lunch fare (plus "to die for" beignets at Sunday brunch), offered inside at the "community table" or outside with a "waterfront view"; service gets mixed comments and tabs can be "pricey", but fans find it "irresistible"; P.S. it's retail-only on Saturdays.

🅩 Boulevard *American*

27 | 25 | 26 | $69

Embarcadero | Audiffred Bldg. | 1 Mission St. (Steuart St.) | 415-543-6084 | www.boulevardrestaurant.com

"Power brokers", "celebrities" and "common folk" alike "can always count on" "a phenomenal meal" at Nancy Oakes' "iconic" Embarcadero "showstopper", where a "warm and elegant" belle epoque setting with "lovely Bay views" provides a "marvelous atmosphere" for "heavenly" New American fare and "brilliant" wines "without pretensions"; after nearly "20 years", it "keeps up with the newer, flashier joints" for that "big night out" (whether a "date or on business"), and while it's "a bit noisy", "pricey" and "difficult to get into", "once you are there", you're "treated like royalty" and it "never disappoints."

NEW Bourbon Steak *Steak*

24 | 23 | 24 | $81

Downtown | Westin St. Francis | 355 Powell St. (bet. Geary & Post Sts.) | 415-397-3003 | www.michaelmina.net

Michael Mina "has done it again", having transformed his namesake eatery in Downtown's Westin St. Francis into this first SF link of his luxe chophouse chain; it's "pricey" and the "extensive wine list only adds to your sticker shock", but it "produces the goods", offering "well-prepared" "prime quality beef", "fantastic fixin's and standout apps enhanced by "excellent" service and a "classy but comfortable", dark-hued setting; P.S. yes, those duck-fat fries "are that good."

NEW Boxing Room ● *Cajun/Creole* — | — | — | M

Hayes Valley | 399 Grove St. (Gough St.) | 415-430-6590 | www.boxingroom.com

Kin to nearby Absinthe, this Hayes Valley newcomer finds Louisiana native Justin Simoneaux (ex Moss Room) fusing rare-to-these-parts ingredients (alligator, crawfish) with locally sourced larder for moderately priced Bayou fare, including the requisite gumbo and po' boys; set in a former shirt factory with exposed wood beams and steel bracing, the massive space features stools upholstered with faux alligator skin, and there's a zinc-topped bar stocked with 22 beers and six wines on tap.

Brandy Ho's *Chinese* 19 | 12 | 17 | $24

Castro | 4068 18th St. (bet. Castro & Hartford Sts.) | 415-252-8000
Chinatown | 217 Columbus Ave. (bet. B'way & Pacific Ave.) | 415-788-7527
www.brandyhos.com

"If you ask for 'hot' you better mean it" at this torrid twosome where the "wonderful", "cheap" Hunan fare and "smoked meats" are "a cut above the rest"; surveyors suggest "sitting at the counter to watch the wok masters at work" at the original Chinatown "hole-in-the-wall" (a welcome distraction from the "lackluster ambiance" and "efficient" but "impersonal" service), while the Castro spin-off has a more "mod" look and servers more likely to "smile."

Brazen Head ●⇱ *American* 21 | 20 | 23 | $37

Cow Hollow | 3166 Buchanan St. (Greenwich St.) | 415-921-7600 | www.brazenheadsf.com

"Tucked away" in Cow Hollow, this "charming" "old-school" pub is "perfect for a date" or "meeting your mistress" – "if you can find it"; the "strong drinks" and "earnest" "meat-centric" American menu ("quality steaks and likeminded offerings" that are "worth every dime") contribute to the "clubby vibe", and night owls note the "super-friendly staff" serves you till "late" (1 AM); P.S. "no credit cards."

Brenda's French Soul Food *Creole/Southern* 24 | 14 | 19 | $21

Civic Center | 652 Polk St. (bet. Eddy & Turk Sts.) | 415-345-8100 | www.frenchsoulfood.com

"Leave your weight-watching behind" at this Civic Center "gem" where a "down-to-earth" staff dishes out "scrumptious" Creole-Southern "home cookin'" ("divine" beignets , the "best shrimp and grits") in a "happy, warm" ambiance; known for "amazing" breakfasts and lunches, it now serves dinner too (Wednesday–Saturday) plus beer and wine, and those who've endured "hour-plus waits" will welcome a post-Survey expansion that doubled its size.

NEW Brixton, The *American* 15 | 20 | 15 | $35

Cow Hollow | 2140 Union St. (bet. Fillmore & Webster Sts.) | 415-409-1114 | www.brixtonsf.com

Named after a legendary London rock music venue, this "insanely noisy" Cow Hollow newcomer doles out drinks to "salve the 'thirsty

	FOOD	DECOR	SERVICE	COST

thirties'" who fill its wood-heavy digs adorned with vintage concert posters; however, mixed reviews for its American eats and service suggest it's still "looking for its sea legs" and prompt some to ask "is it a bar or a restaurant?"

Broken Record ●◑⇗ Soul Food   ▽ 24 | 16 | 19 | $18

Excelsior | 1166 Geneva Ave. (Naples St.) | 415-963-1713

"If you're looking for a dive bar with spectacular" comfort and soul food, "follow your nose" to this Excelsior "neighborhood place" where "Mission hipsters" knock back pulled pork sandwiches and mac 'n' goat cheese with "any drink you can imagine", even "whiskey on tap"; cash-only, but it's "unbelievably cheap for the quality."

Brother's Korean Restaurant Korean   24 | 7 | 16 | $28

Inner Richmond | 4014 Geary Blvd. (bet. 4th & 5th Aves.) | 415-668-2028 Ⓜ

Inner Richmond | 4128 Geary Blvd. (bet. 5th & 6th Aves.) | 415-387-7991 ●

"Still the standard-bearer" for "killer" "grill-it-yourself" Korean BBQ, these "no-frills" Inner Richmond joints are "crowded" with DIYers cooking "perfectly marinated" meats over "real charcoal"; you'll "smell like a campfire" afterward and may have a "long" wait before, but prices are "fair", the staff "friendly" and the "multitude" of "tasty" "little side dishes" adds to the "novelty"; P.S. the 4014 Geary branch serves dinner only Friday–Sunday.

B Star Bar Asian   23 | 17 | 19 | $27

Inner Richmond | 127 Clement St. (bet. 2nd & 3rd Aves.) | 415-933-9900 | www.bstarbar.com

"B Star gets an A" from the Inner Richmond "scenester crowd" for "exotic but accessible" takes on Pan-Asian and "Burmese comfort food" – especially during the "excellent weekend brunches" – and "super drinks made with soju"; while some "still prefer the original" ("older sister Burma Superstar") this "less-harried sibling" gets extra credit for a "heated patio" and "best of all, you can make reservations."

Buca di Beppo Italian   15 | 16 | 17 | $28

SoMa | 855 Howard St. (bet. 4th & 5th Sts.) | 415-543-1209 | www.bucadibeppo.com

"Humongous portions" of "simple, red-sauce Italian" dishes make this "loud", "family-style" chain a "go-to place for large parties", especially when there are "kids in tow"; critics call the "kitschy" decor "overdone" and the fare "standard at best", but service is generally "friendly and energetic", so fans sum it up as a "value."

NEW Bun Mee Vietnamese   - | - | - | I

Upper Fillmore | 2015 Fillmore St. (Pine St.) | 415-800-7696 | www.bunmee.co

At this quick-service Vietnamese sandwich shop nestled into the Upper Fillmore, nine different modernized kinds of banh mi come 'served with hot jalapeño pepper, unless you're a sissy', and are accompanied on the menu by rice bowls, salads and housemade beverages including kaffir limeade, lychee aqua fresca and Vietnamese coffee; the small, stylish storefront is decorated with street-food photography, chandeliers made from bicycle wheels and a zinc-topped dining counter.

Burger Bar *Burgers*

19 | 16 | 17 | $29

Downtown | Macy's | 251 Geary St., 6th fl. (bet. Powell & Stockton Sts.) | 415-296-4272 | www.burger-bar.com

"Dare you to think of a burger that they don't have" at this chain link "tucked away in Macy's", which augments the "custom-made" patties with beer floats and alcoholic shakes that "will literally make your head spin"; but despite its pedigree – it's owned by *Top Chef Masters'* Hubert Keller – skeptics snap the offerings "are not that good": "only the bill exceeded our expectations."

Burger Joint *Burgers*

18 | 13 | 17 | $15

AT&T Park | 242 King St. (bet. 3rd & 4th Sts.) | 415-371-1600
Mission | 807 Valencia St. (19th St.) | 415-824-3494
www.burgerjointsf.com

"Solid burgers and fries", "cooked right" with Niman Ranch beef, are the formula behind this "quick, easy, reliable" Bay Area mini-chain; it's a "generic venue, but it beats going to your typical fast-food franchise."

BurgerMeister *Burgers*

20 | 11 | 15 | $16

Castro | 138 Church St. (Duboce Ave.) | 415-437-2874
Cole Valley | 86 Carl St. (Cole St.) | 415-566-1274
North Beach | 759 Columbus Ave. (Greenwich St.) | 415-296-9907
www.burgermeistersf.com

"There's no way you'll leave hungry" after chowing down on "humongous burgers cooked to order" "with all the fixin's" plus "crispy fries, creamy shakes" and "great beers" at this pack of patty joints scattered around the Bay Area; it's a "bit pricey, even if they do use Niman Ranch beef", and while service is "friendly" and "fast", many "grab some grub to go" because you "don't come here for the atmosphere."

☑ Burma Superstar *Burmese*

24 | 14 | 19 | $26

Inner Richmond | 309 Clement St. (4th Ave.) | 415-387-2147 | www.burmasuperstar.com

"Memorable" Myanmar fare that's "a real sensory treat", like the "salty, crunchy, refreshing and surprising" signature tea-leaf salad, makes this "cheap and cheerful" Inner Richmond Burmese a "superstar" swoon groupies willing to endure "cramped" quarters and a "ridiculously long" line (at least they'll "call your cell phone when your table is ready", so you can hit "a nearby bar"); the wait is "not nearly as bad" at the Oakland and Alameda offshoots, and all three share "really helpful servers" who are happy "to explain each dish."

Burmese Kitchen ☒ *Burmese*

▽ 20 | 11 | 22 | $18

Tenderloin | Civic Ctr. | 452 Larkin St. (bet. Golden Gate Ave. & Turk St.) | 415-474-5569 | www.burmesekitchen.com

Despite a "wide selection" of "authentic Burmese dishes", this "unpretentious" place gets "overlooked because of its location in the Tenderloin"; it may not be "haute Asian", but it's "dirt-cheap" and "you won't have to wait in line" for attention from the "warm owner and staff."

Bursa *Mediterranean*

21 | 18 | 21 | $27

West Portal | 60 W. Portal Ave. (bet. Ulloa & Vicente Sts.) | 415-564-4006 | www.bursa415.com

Visiting this "pleasant" "neighborhood kebab house" is like taking "a trip to Turkey" (or maybe a "Persian bazaar") proclaim West Portal pa-

	FOOD	DECOR	SERVICE	COST

trons partial to the "well-prepared" Turkish and Mediterranean menu; the "zesty" salads, "yummy combination platter" and "sumptuous" skewers of meat are a "deal", so "you can afford to visit often", plus friendly servers "make you feel at home."

Bushi-tei *Asian/French* | 22 | 19 | 21 | $49 |

Japantown | 1638 Post St. (bet. Laguna & Webster Sts.) | 415-440-4959 | www.bushi-tei.com

Bushi-tei Bistro *Asian/French*

Japantown | Kinokuniya Bldg. | 1581 Webster St. (Post St.) | 415-409-4959 | www.bushiteibistro.com

"Don't expect sushi and the usual Japanese fare" at this "fantastic find in J-town" proffering "gorgeous" high-end "Asian-fusion" à la carte and "kaiseki meals" as "inventive" as they are "eye candy", "served beautifully" by a "gracious host" in a "modern", "jewel-box" setting outfitted with lots of "old wood"; "dinner's pricey", but Sunday brunch is more affordable, as are the "quick" bites available at its more "casual" bistro "offshoot" near "Sundance Cinema"; P.S. a post-Survey chef change is not reflected in the Food score.

Butler & The Chef Bistro Ⓜ *French* | 22 | 17 | 17 | $27 |

SoMa | 155A South Park Ave. (bet. 2nd & 3rd Sts.) | 415-896-2075 | www.butlerandthechef.com

There's "no fusion, no Californian influences" at this cafe "on quiet, sunny South Park" – just "classic French" breakfast and lunch specialties like a "decadent croque monsieur", "amazing coffee" and quiche that "runs out quickly"; the "campy" interior can be "claustrophobic" and the service "pretentious", but that doesn't stop "hordes of people clamoring for" a bit of "bistro bliss" each day.

Butterfly Ⓜ *Asian/Californian* | 21 | 23 | 21 | $44 |

Embarcadero | Pier 33 (Bay St.) | 415-864-8999 | www.butterflysf.com

With its "glorious setting" "right on the Embarcadero" and "amazing waterside view", it's no wonder that this "warehouse" is "frequented by tourists", but locals agree that the "intensely flavored Cal-Asian" eats can set your "palate aflutter"; "gracious" service and "surprisingly affordable" prices are pluses, but a minority mutters that the menu is "hit-or-miss" and suggests social butterflies simply flit in for the "incredible happy hour", when the focus is on the "stylish libations" and "interesting appetizers."

Cafe Bastille Ⓩ *French* | 20 | 17 | 18 | $35 |

Downtown | 22 Belden Pl. (bet. Bush & Pine Sts.) | 415-986-5673 | www.cafebastille.com

"Lively outdoor seating" and "solid Left Bank cuisine" (e.g. "fantastic moules" and "steak frites") make this "cute" cafe an "authentic" "little slice of Paris in Belden" Place; while the French vibe extends to service with "some attitude", the prix fixe dinner is still "one of the best bargains" around.

Café Claude *French* | 22 | 20 | 21 | $39 |

Downtown | 7 Claude Ln. (bet. Bush & Sutter Sts.) | 415-392-3515 | www.cafeclaude.com

"Tucked away from the hustle and bustle of Union Square", this "hidden gem" offers a "little bit of Paris" to Downtown shoppers and pre-

FOOD | DECOR | SERVICE | COST

theater diners with a "varied menu of tried-and-true French classics" "served up with panache" in a "palpably French" setting "from the zinc bar to the cafe tables" outside; the "cramped booths and boisterous atmosphere" can make it "noisy", but "reasonable prices" and live jazz on weekends dispel any discomfort.

Café de la Presse *French*
18 | 19 | 17 | $33

Downtown | 352 Grant Ave. (bet. Bush & Sutter Sts.) | 415-249-0900 | www.cafedelapresse.com

"Pick up a copy of *Le Monde* and practice your French" at this "*très français*" cafe, which serves up bistro "bites throughout the day" plus "Chimay on tap"; the "snooty staff" and "overpriced" offerings offend some, but that's just part of the "Euro-style" shrug Downtowners who "make this a regular stop on their dining routine."

Café des Amis *French*
19 | 24 | 20 | $52

Cow Hollow | 2000 Union St. (Buchanan St.) | 415-563-7700 | www.cafedesamissf.com

This "posh" "Union Street eatery" with a "stunning interior briskly transports you to Paris" with a "*très authentique* brasserie ambiance" and staff who "move like ninjas"; although the French kitchen still "needs to find its *mer* legs", the place is "flooded with twenty- and thirtysomethings", so if you "prefer to converse, sit on the mezzanine level"; P.S. new chef Mark Sullivan (Spruce) arrived post-Survey.

Cafe Divine *American/Sandwiches*
∇ 18 | 18 | 19 | $27

North Beach | 1600 Stockton St. (Union St.) | 415-986-3414

"Simple, good comfort food" – including sandwiches – served "in a splendid location" adjacent to Washington Square (highly visible through "all the windows") sums up the appeal of this North Beach American cafe; though it can make "conversation difficult", the "rotating musical acts throughout the week" ensure "a large following of regulars", while on weekends, "brunch lives up to their name – divine, indeed."

Café Flore *American*
17 | 16 | 15 | $22

Castro | 2298 Market St. (Noe St.) | 415-621-8579 | www.cafeflore.com

"Snag a table with a view of the locals" at this "playful" "people-watching post", a longtime Castro "community spot for hanging, cruising" and consuming "consistent" American eats; it's "not exactly fine dining" or service ("you order and pay at a cash register, and they bring out your food"), "but the portions are big, the prices are relatively low and on a warm, sunny day, the outdoor patio cannot be beat."

Café Gratitude *Vegan*
17 | 15 | 17 | $25

Mission | 2400 Harrison St. (20th St.) | 415-830-3014 | www.cafegratitude.com

Taking the "hippie-dippy quotient" to "new heights", this trio of "healthy" cafes in the Mission, Berkeley and San Rafael assigns "affirmations" (e.g. "I Am Elated", "I Am Serene") to each of its "gorgeous" plates of "vibrant" vegan (and mostly raw) cuisine; the "nuts and twigs crowd" aver it's "amazing what these folks do" with uncooked ingredients and aren't irked by the "slow" service and "quirky" "California vibe", but cynics sneer "I Am Embarrassed to Order" and ask "who knew quinoa and hemp could be so expensive?"

FOOD | DECOR | SERVICE | COST

Cafe Jacqueline ⓂFrench 26 | 19 | 21 | $54

North Beach | 1454 Grant Ave. (bet. Green & Union Sts.) |
415-981-5565

"Fantastic soufflés of every sort, from savory" to sweet – the "best"
"this side of Paris" and meant for sharing – make this "wonderfully
old-fashioned" French cafe in North Beach a "memorable" "place to
have dinner or dessert"; it's "not for he-men" or the impatient, as
"Madame Jacqueline" still whips up each "ethereal" creation "from
scratch herself", but romantics who "enjoy long candlelit stares into
their loved one's eyes" insist *"c'est bon."*

Café Tiramisu ⓈItalian 22 | 16 | 19 | $43

Downtown | 28 Belden Pl. (bet. Bush & Pine Sts.) | 415-421-7044 |
www.cafetiramisu.com

"Fresh pastas" and "creative interpretations on traditional" Northern
Italian fare "hit the spot" at this "popular Belden Place establishment"
where, on "sunny days" or "beautiful nights", a "mix of regulars and
tourists" disregards the "cramped" quarters to pretend they're dining
alfresco "in Firenzi."

Café Zitouna ⓂMorroccan - | - | - | I

Polk Gulch | 1201 Sutter St. (Polk St.) | 415-673-2622 |
www.sfcafezitouna.com

Fans contend that the "outstanding traditional Tunisian couscous" and
"Moroccan food at its best" offered at this Pork Gulch "local haunt"
make it a "rare" "find in the Bay Area" that's akin to a "quick trip to
North Africa for home cooking"; "don't expect luxury" in the "hole-in-
the-wall" setting and be prepared for sometimes "spotty" service, but
the "awesome plates" at affordable prices are "absolutely worth it."

Cafe Zoetrope Italian ∇ 19 | 18 | 18 | $31

North Beach | 916 Kearny St. (Columbus Ave.) | 415-291-1700 |
www.cafecoppola.com

"A must-do experience for any fan of Francis Ford Coppola", this North
Beach "old-world Italian bistro" attracts groupies for "thin-crust
pizza", pasta cooked "just right" and, of course, a "nice selection"
from the maestro's vineyards; service is a bit "laid-back", but "you
shouldn't be in a rush when dining here" anyway; P.S. don't overlook
its "out-of-the-way" sibling, Mammarella's, at the Napa airport.

Caffe Delle Stelle Italian 17 | 15 | 18 | $34

Hayes Valley | 395 Hayes St. (Gough St.) | 415-252-1110 |
www.dellestelle.com

Popular with "opera/ballet/symphony-goers" grabbing a bite "before
the performance", this "homey" Hayes Valley haunt with "courteous"
servers is a "dependable" "standby" for "lovely pastas" and other "old-
fashioned" Tuscan fare; though it may not be a star – some say the
"simple" menu "lacks a sparkle" – most maintain "it fills the need" for
"Italian comfort food" at a "reasonable price."

Caffè Macaroni ⓈItalian ∇ 19 | 15 | 17 | $29

North Beach | 124 Columbus Ave. (Jackson St.) | 415-956-9737 |
www.caffemacaroni.com

"Old-school food in the North Beach Italian tradition" offers "relief
from the trendier joints up Columbus" at this "family-style" trattoria;

FOOD | DECOR | SERVICE | COST

seatingwise, the "sidewalk is the best" and preferred over the off-putting interior with pasta glued to the ceiling.

Caffè Museo *Italian/Mediterranean* | 18 | 15 | 13 | $23 |

SoMa | SFMOMA | 151 Third St. (bet. Howard & Mission Sts.) | 415-357-4500 | www.caffemuseo.com

"Essentially a high-end cafeteria", this Italian-Med cafe "completes the SFMOMA experience" with "artfully prepared" light bites and pastries that are "pretty good for a museum"; the "crowded", "chilly" space can feel "disorganized", but you can always grab an outside table and "watch the world go by"; P.S. closed Wednesdays.

Cajun Pacific 🅢🅜 *Cajun* | ▽ 19 | 14 | 19 | $43 |

Outer Sunset | 4542 Irving St. (47th Ave.) | 415-504-6652 | www.cajunpacific.com

"Cajun so authentic" is the draw for Big Easy fans who "love" the seafood and "desserts to die for" for "very reasonable prices" at this tiny Outer Sunset joint; the portions are "abundant" but the restaurant isn't, and they're only open Thursday–Saturday, so "make reservations."

🆕 Campanula *American* | - | - | - | M |

North Beach | 701 Union St. (Powell St.) | 415-829-7766 | www.campanulasf.com

One of the new non-touristy restaurants reinvigorating North Beach's dining scene, this arrival (from Frascati power-couple Jon and Rebecca Rader) offers locals a laid-back, cozy setting for enjoying a classic cocktail and noshing on a mélange of New American tapas – think everything from fried sausage–stuffed olives to wild-boar sliders to brioche French toast; P.S. no reservations taken, but guests can call 15 minutes ahead and add their name to the wait list.

Campton Place *Californian/Mediterranean* | 25 | 26 | 25 | $73 |

Downtown | Taj Campton Pl. Hotel | 340 Stockton St. (bet. Post & Sutter Sts.) | 415-781-5555 | www.camptonplacesf.com

Whether you want to "splurge for brunch", join the "ladies who lunch" or enjoy a "romantic" "special night out", this "lovely intimate room" (and its "tiny", "quiet" bar) "hidden" "in a beautiful hotel" "just off Union Square" fits the bill; "bring your banker" ("the tab runs high"), but the "outstanding" "cutting-edge" Cal-Med menu and "gracious" service from the "highly trained" staff add up to an "elegant" experience that's "hard to find" elsewhere; P.S. jacket suggested.

Candybar 🅜 *Dessert* | ▽ 20 | 20 | 20 | $20 |

Western Addition | 1335 Fulton St. (Divisadero St.) | 415-673-7078 | www.candybarsf.com

A "sweet change of pace" from the everyday, this "small" but "sophisticated" Western Addition lounge with a "friendly" staff lures patrons with an "appealing wine list" and "delightful" desserts that please "both the eye and the palate"; it's the "perfect ending to a dinner date" declare lovebirds who "linger" over "bubblies" and "play a board game" from their large collection; just remember the tab "can quickly add up"; P.S. a few savory snacks round out the "limited" menu.

☑ Canteen Ⓜ *Californian* — 27 | 15 | 22 | $50

Tenderloin | Commodore Hotel | 817 Sutter St. (Jones St.) | 415-928-8870 | www.sfcanteen.com

"Despite his expanding empire", Dennis Leary "continues to dazzle diners" at his "teeny-tiny" Tenderloin original producing "damn good" Californian dinners (including a Tuesday night prix fixe and "out-of-this-world" brunch) at a "surprisingly reasonable cost"; even with "well-trained" waiters, it's "not a place to impress a date", but the whole "retro seedy diner atmosphere" "is half the fun", as is having to "fight for a stool" at the counter to watch "the magic happening up close."

Capannina *Italian* — 25 | 19 | 23 | $45

Cow Hollow | 1809 Union St. (Octavia St.) | 415-409-8001 | www.capanninasf.com

The "vivacious" owner "makes everyone feel welcome" (like "one of the family") at this "cozy" Cow Hollow trattoria where the "fresh" "homemade pasta" and "generous portions" of "fabulous" Boot bites "make you feel like you are back in Italy"; if the "intimate" dining room "can get a little tight", the relatively "reasonable prices" (including an "early-bird prix fixe" that's an "excellent deal") and "super-friendly atmosphere" ensure that "a lot of regulars" "love it."

Catch *Seafood* — 18 | 19 | 19 | $36

Castro | 2362 Market St. (bet. Castro & 16th Sts.) | 415-431-5000 | www.catchsf.com

For a "cruise-side" view of the Market Street "pretty people", "power gays" gather on the enclosed "pleasant patio around a circular fireplace" at this "catch in the Castro", which dishes out "varied seafood selections" (and some "non-fish entrees" too) alongside "great cocktails" and piano music on weekend nights; while the "midrange" eats "won't knock your socks off" and service can be "hit-or-miss", it remains a place to "mix and mingle."

Cha Am Thai *Thai* — 19 | 14 | 19 | $23

SoMa | Museum Parc | 701 Folsom St. (3rd St.) | 415-546-9711 | www.chaamthaisf.com

"Tasty Thai treats tempt" at this separately owned Southeast Asian pair; the one "in the heart of North Berkeley's Gourmet Ghetto" has been a "standby" for decades, with decor that "feels like you're in a tree house"; the "more upscale" SoMa sibling is "an easy one-block walk from Moscone Center", making it "good for lunch."

Cha Cha Cha *Caribbean* — 20 | 17 | 16 | $27

Haight-Ashbury | 1801 Haight St. (Shrader St.) | 415-386-5758
Mission | 2327 Mission St. (bet. 19th & 20th Sts.) | 415-648-0504
www.cha3.com

"If you're in a party mood", "bring 10 friends" and start "downing glasses" of "dangerous" "delicioso sangria" at this tapas duo in the Mission and Haight-Ashbury where the "Caribbean-style" meant-for-sharing plates "go great with the bright, tropical atmosphere", complete with "ornate altars on the walls"; since these "noisy" hot spots are "still hoppin' after all these years", there's "usually a wait for a table"; P.S. the new offshoot brings "tasty Cuban delights" to "sleepy Downtown San Mateo."

	FOOD	DECOR	SERVICE	COST

Chairman Bao Bun Truck ⍚ *Chinese* — 25 | 20 | 22 | $10

Location varies; see Twitter | 415-813-8800 | www.twitter.com/chairmantruck

Bao lovers go "bow wow" for this "nicely painted" (with a "commie" motif) Chinese truck found at Off the Grid and "throughout NorCal" "pushing out" its "addictively delicious" "buns galore" ("steamed or baked") in "unusual" combos sporting "the right kick of spice"; the staff's "wit" and "zippy service" are pluses, even if "outrageous" lines send devotees "back to work late from lunch"; just "get out your little red wallet", as it "takes two" of these "wee" snacks "to make a meal."

⚠NEW Chambers Eat + Drink *Californian* — - | - | - | M

Tenderloin | Phoenix Hotel | 601 Eddy St. (Larkin St.) | 415-829-2316 | www.chambers-sf.com

The Phoenix Hotel's days as a legendary Tenderloin rocker hangout inspired its new late-night lair featuring an eclectic midcentury rock 'n' roll look (replete with vintage LPs and lumberjack plaid ottomans), a poolside patio and midpriced Californian cuisine overseen by Trevor Ogden (ex Mission Beach Café); the adjacent marble-topped bar also harks back to earlier times, eschewing today's mixology craze for simple, straightforward spirits (The Tequila Drink, The Whiskey Drink) and serving a bar-bites menu until 1:30 AM.

⚡ Chapeau! *French* — 26 | 20 | 25 | $53

Inner Richmond | 126 Clement St. (bet. 2nd & 3rd Aves.) | 415-750-9787 | www.chapeausf.com

"*Très charmant*", this "unpretentious" bistro "has not missed a beat since moving" to its more "upscale" Inner Richmond digs where diners drink and "eat like a French king" while finding "exceptional value" (particularly when ordering the "early-bird" and "weekday prix fixes"); "*oui, oui*", it's still a "little noisy" and "cramped", but the hardworking "*monsieur le proprietor*" (a real "hoot") and his "terrific" wife "ensure" everyone leaves "happy" with a "firm handshake or a kiss on both cheeks" and "a visit worthy of an exclamation point."

Charanga Ⓜ *Pan-Latin* — ▽ 21 | 16 | 20 | $28

Mission | 2351 Mission St. (bet. 19th & 20th Sts.) | 415-282-1813 | www.charangasf.com

"Creative Pan-Latin" fare "with a hint of island spice" brings "flair" to a Mission night out at this "neighborhood/hip" spot with a "slightly hole-in-the-wall feeling" where locals wash down "large" portions of "innovative" grub with "great red and white sangria"; though "the staff makes an all-out effort to make sure you're having a good time", service can be "slow", but the tabs are relatively "cheap."

Chaya Brasserie *French/Japanese* — 20 | 22 | 20 | $49

Embarcadero | 132 The Embarcadero (Mission St.) | 415-777-8688 | www.thechaya.com

"Sample fantastic views of the Bay Bridge" while munching "creative French-Japanese fare with a twist" at this "romantic", red-accented Embarcadero "winner", a catch for "Asian-inspired seafood dishes", "creative rolls" and a "great cocktail menu" served by an "attentive" staff; since "it's a scene", "it's gonna cost you" – though, "for a less-expensive option", "head to the bar for happy hour", which extends well into the night.

	FOOD	DECOR	SERVICE	COST

Cha-Ya Vegetarian
23 | **13** | **17** | **$22**

Japanese Restaurant ⌁ *Japanese/Vegan*

Mission | 762 Valencia St. (bet. 18th & 19th Sts.) | 415-252-7825

Berkeleyites "stand in line" "for ages" in anticipation of "inventive" vegan fare "that will entice even the most enthusiastic" meat eater at this "tiny, storefront Japanese" while across the bay, Mission denizens are in "paradise" over the "delicate flavors", "fantastic" "vegetarian sushi" and "sweet service" at its sibling; portions may be "small" and decor "lacking", but "the bill is doable" at both locations.

Cheesecake Factory *American*
17 | **18** | **17** | **$29**

Downtown | Macy's | 251 Geary St., 8th fl. (bet. Powell & Stockton Sts.) | 415-391-4444 | www.thecheesecakefactory.com

"How does anyone ever get to the cheesecake?" ask veterans of this midpriced American chain known for its "giant" portions and "ency-clopedic" "menu to please everyone"; the "big", "noisy" setting re-sembles "Vegas in a good way", and any grumbles about variable service and "too much quantity, not enough quality" are drowned out by "ridiculous crowds" dubbing it "perfect for a family outing" – so "be prepared to wait."

Cheese Steak Shop *Cheesesteaks*
20 | **6** | **15** | **$12**

Western Addition | 1716 Divisadero St. (bet. Bush & Sutter Sts.) | 415-346-3712 | www.cheesesteakshop.com

Sure, some Philly "purists may find fault", but the cheesesteaks "grilled in front of you" at this local chain are "as good as it gets on this coast", bringing "tears to the eyes" with their "meaty, cheesy, gooey wonder-fulness" (there's even Cheez "Whiz under the counter"); while the de-cor's "no frills", the service is "efficient", leaving the only drawback the "calorie count."

Chenery Park Ⓜ *American*
21 | **19** | **22** | **$40**

Glen Park | 683 Chenery St. (Diamond St.) | 415-337-8537 | www.chenerypark.com

"The definition of a neighborhood restaurant", this "cozy spot" in Glen Park proffers "scrumptious" portions of "flavorful twists on American classics" with a Southern slant (e.g. "good gumbo"); though the "friendly staff" is "great with kids", non-parents should "beware early Tuesdays" (which is "family night") with a special menu geared to the little ones.

Chez Maman *French*
23 | **13** | **20** | **$29**

Potrero Hill | 1453 18th St. (bet. Connecticut & Missouri Sts.) | 415-824-7166 | www.chezmamansf.com

"Je t'aime, maman!" murmur Francophiles who "love sitting at the counter" to "watch the talented cooks" concoct "classic" "French bis-tro fare" that won't "break the bank"; "seating is very limited" at this "tiny" Potrero Hill haunt, so "be prepared" to "wait", but "no matter how busy" they are, the "suave" staffers are always "a pleasure" – and, *bien sûr*, they have "beautiful accents" to boot.

Chez Papa Bistrot *French*
23 | **18** | **21** | **$42**

Potrero Hill | 1401 18th St. (Missouri St.) | 415-824-8205 | www.chezpapasf.com

"All the elements of an imaginary escape back to Paris" are in evidence at this "cute" "neighborhood *bistrot*" "tucked away on Potrero Hill" –

FOOD | DECOR | SERVICE | COST

"tight quarters", "lively atmosphere", "rich" "classics" like "your French aunt would make" and waiters with whom you can "practice your" *français*; they're skilled "at packing in the guests" and it gets "very noisy", but fans don't mind for a "bit of ooh-la-la" at "fair prices"; P.S. no longer related to Chez Papa Resto.

Chez Papa Resto ☒ *French* — 24 | 22 | 22 | $50

SoMa | 4 Mint Plaza (Stevenson St.) | 415-546-4134 |
www.chezpaparesto.com

"OMG!" tweets the "hip crowd" at this "convivial" SoMa "sleeper" in the "slowly revitalizing Mint Plaza" that serves a "creative" (albeit "pricey") seasonally driven contemporary French menu in a "sexy", "dark" black-and-orange setting befitting a "hot date or dinner with friends" – or "sit outside on a beautiful day" for a "business lunch" or brunch; it gets "very loud", but the "hospitable" staff and "tasty cocktails ease" the pain; P.S. no longer related to Chez Papa Bistrot.

Chez Spencer *French* — 25 | 23 | 23 | $58

Mission | 82 14th St. (bet. Folsom & Harrison Sts.) | 415-864-2191 |
www.chezspencer.net

"Definitely not a formula restaurant", this French "gem" in a "converted warehouse" on a somewhat "sketchy" stretch in the Mission is "hidden" where "you would least expect" to find such a "fabulous" dinner and Sunday brunch spot filled with diners who "actually dress up"; it's a "perfect" "romantic" perch for a "cutting-edge date", and though "pricey", the "über-hip" "party" vibe and "impeccable service" make it "special"; P.S. Spencer on the Go!, its mobile spin-off, parks Wednesday-Saturday at the corner of Folsom and Seventh Streets.

Chile Pies & Ice Cream ⊖ *Dessert* — ∇ 22 | 16 | 18 | $11

Western Addition | 601 Baker St. (Fulton St.) | 415-614-9411 |
www.chilepies.com

"Eat your pie and then go for the ice cream" at this Western Addition stop where the savory options are a setup for "sweet offerings" like "huge and towering" sundaes and 'pie milkshakes'; critics complain about the "small servings" – "especially at those prices!" – but the "nice" staffers and "cool vibe" make it a "good after-dinner (or in lieu of dinner) hangout."

Chloe's Cafe ⊖ *American* — 24 | 12 | 18 | $18

Noe Valley | 1399 Church St. (26th St.) | 415-648-4116

"The price is right" for "breakfast and brunch galore" at this "tiny", "homey" "Noe Valley classic" where "the kitchen has a Master's degree in eggs" and receives honors for American offerings including "exceptional sandwiches", "fluffy pancakes" and "delicious, unique" salads; service is "welcoming", but "get there early", "late or on a weekday" because the queue "starts 15 minutes before they open."

NEW Chotto *Japanese* — ∇ 24 | 20 | 19 | $47

Marina | 3317 Steiner St. (bet. Chestnut & Lombard Sts.) | 415-441-2223 |
www.chottosf.com

It feels "like you're in Tokyo" at this "nice new izakaya in the Marina" filled with handmade lanterns, reclaimed wood planks and barflies who "go early for happy hour with its $1 oysters" and sake cocktails and stay late for "very fresh sushi, good ramen" and "delicate, tasty" small plates and skewers; "the staff hasn't quite worked out the kinks", "however, when the dishes do arrive, they are worth the wait."

Chouchou ⓜ *French* | 21 | 16 | 21 | $42 |

Forest Hills | 400 Dewey Blvd. (Laguna Honda Blvd.) | 415-242-0960 | www.chouchoubistro.com

The "staff oozes Gallic charm at this bistro, which belies its "off location" "tucked away in Forest Hills" with "delicious" French fare that caters to "SF tastes" (don't miss the "perfect fruit tarts"); "the decor is not helping" – "tables too-close-together" make it "noisy" – but it's "nice to have in the neighborhood."

Chow *American* | 20 | 16 | 19 | $26 |

Castro | 215 Church St. (bet. 15th & Market Sts.) | 415-552-2469
Park Chow *American*
Inner Sunset | 1240 Ninth Ave. (bet. Irving St. & Lincoln Way) | 415-665-9912
www.chowfoodbar.com

"It's like eating at mom's house, only better" at this local mini-chain of "American comfort food" joints offering "a little bit of everything", from pizzas to poached lobster, all at an "awesome value"; maybe the "menu could use some updating" – "would a few specials kill you people?" – but they're "always filled with happy, loud families, so not good for those who don't like ambient noise."

Citizen Cake *Californian* | 21 | 17 | 19 | $31 |

Upper Fillmore | 2125 Fillmore St. (bet. California & Sacramento Sts.) | 415-861-2228 | www.citizencake.com

"Desserts rule the roost" at chef-owner Elizabeth Falkner's "pricey" patisserie and American bistro that's "come back to life in a new location on Fillmore Street", but the "excellent cocktails" and Californian-inspired lunch and dinner fare make it an "interesting" "neighborhood spot" anytime; the "spare" Victorian soda-fountain decor and "snooty service" leaves some "cold", but it's still "the best place in SF to do" just "like Marie A once said."

Citizen's Band ⓜ *American* | ▽ 21 | 19 | 20 | $35 |

SoMa | 1198 Folsom St. (8th St.) | 415-556-4901 | www.citizensbandsf.com

You'll need a "six-mile run" after enjoying the "creative" "interpretations of homey classics" at this "funky" American; decorated with "used" furniture, radios and "postcards pinned to the walls", the "quirky diner-esque" digs suffer from "noise, noise, noise" but "affordable prices" and "friendly-for-hipster-SoMa" service have roadies "craving a return trip"; P.S. "don't miss" the "delicious pastries" from Pinkie's Bakery "right next door."

Citrus Club *Asian* | 22 | 12 | 17 | $18 |

Haight-Ashbury | 1790 Haight St. (Shrader St.) | 415-387-6366 | www.citrusclubsf.com

It "looks like nothing from the outside" (or the inside either), but this "loud and busy" Haight-Ashbury Pan-Asian proffers "feel-good soups and delicious noodle plates" that are some of the "best cheap eats" around; "the only problem is the wait" at prime times.

FOOD | DECOR | SERVICE | COST

Cliff House Bistro *Californian*
18 | 24 | 19 | $43

Outer Richmond | 1090 Point Lobos Ave. (Balboa St.) | 415-386-3330 |
www.cliffhouse.com

A "classic for a reason", this Outer Richmond "open, bright" "bistro perched on the side of a cliff overlooking the Pacific Ocean" elicits oohs from "tourists and natives alike" for "a view that can't be beat" ("if the fog permits"); but the verdict on the "pricey" plates is split – friends find the Californian fare "better than average" (especially the "plentiful" popovers), while foes say "it's a wonderful place for sunset libations, but we don't stay for dinner"; P.S. Sunday "brunch is really extraordinary."

Coco500 🅉 *Californian/Mediterranean*
24 | 19 | 21 | $46

SoMa | 500 Brannan St. (4th St.) | 415-543-2222 | www.coco500.com

"Where bankers take SoMa dot-com guys for not-so-casual lunches" and fans "stop before the game", co-chef/owner Loretta Keller's "small", "swanky" Cal-Med "succeeds" by "keeping it simple" with "incredible" farm-"fresh" cocktails that are "always a home run" and "quirky" shared plates ("everyone actually fights over the green beans"); "you absolutely cannot go wrong here", unless you can't handle the "mind-blowing" noise (and occasional "spotty" service) "during peak times" when the "trendy" bar "gets crowded."

Coi 🅉🅜 *Californian/French*
26 | 24 | 27 | $202

North Beach | 373 Broadway (Montgomery St.) | 415-393-9000 |
www.coirestaurant.com

"Gifted" chef-owner Daniel Patterson "leads you on a mind-bending culinary" journey with "sensational", "over-the-top" Cal-French tasting menus that can be matched with "great wine pairings" and are delivered with "sublime" service at his "molecular gastronomy" maverick in North Beach; "chic" "Japanese-inspired" surroundings add to the "soothing" atmosphere, and though prices are "exorbitant" and "not every dish works, overall the experience is a revelation"; P.S. the à la carte lounge menu is no longer served.

Colibrí Mexican Bistro *Mexican*
21 | 18 | 19 | $36

Downtown | 438 Geary St. (bet. Mason & Taylor Sts.) | 415-440-2737 |
www.colibrimexicanbistro.com

"Go for the guac, stay for the mole" duck at this "vibrant Mexican in the thick of the theater district" Downtown, whose dishes "transcend the usual enchilada and fajita choices", as do the "divine" drinks (did you know "margaritas can be both refined and dangerous"?); service can be "confused" and it's "a bit pricey" – but then you "don't go expecting a Mission-area taqueria."

Commonwealth 🅜 *American*
24 | 18 | 23 | $60

Mission | 2224 Mission St. (18th St.) | 415-355-1500 |
www.commonwealthsf.com

"There is nothing common" about this "eccentric" haunt "in the heart of the Mission" that plies the "champagne and caviar set" with the kind of "fantastic" "inventive" New American food, wine list and service they'd expect "at a swank Downtown fine-dining establishment, with none of the pretentiousness"; maybe "edgy" elements like "liquid nitrogen cooled cocktails" "verge on the too-trendy", but the place has got a "good heart", donating "$10 of every tasting menu" to charity; P.S. it's "made even greater" by "free parking."

Comstock Saloon ●⑳ *American*　　16 | 21 | 19 | $34

North Beach | 155 Columbus Ave. (Pacific Ave.) | 415-617-0071 | www.comstocksaloon.com

"Where John Wayne would go for drinks and a bite – if he were a metrosexual cowboy" confide clients of this "beautiful" North Beach "Old Western–style saloon with a piano playing upstairs and nostalgic memorabilia on the walls"; the "throwback" American pub grub is "no match for the top-notch" "libations concocted by the talented bartenders", though, so while "it's fun to do once or twice", it all "ends up feeling kitschy."

Contigo Ⓜ *Spanish*　　24 | 22 | 23 | $45

Noe Valley | 1320 Castro St. (24th St.) | 415-285-0250 | www.contigosf.com

Specializing in artisanal jamón iberico and other "superb tapas" bursting "with strong flavors and eye appeal", this eco-"stylish" "Spanish marvel" "tucked away in Noe Valley" is the place to "re-create those memories" of Barcelona's La Boqueria (the digs "are that close" and "loud"); foodies prefer sitting at the "darling little wine bar" "where the action is", while the back garden is "delightful" for sipping "interesting" Iberian wines the servers "really help with" selecting.

Cosmopolitan, The ⑳ *American*　　18 | 19 | 19 | $50

SoMa | Rincon Ctr. | 121 Spear St. (bet. Howard & Mission Sts.) | 415-543-4001 | www.cosmopolitansf.com

Now in its second decade, this New American remains a "reliable" "generic upscale hangout" "for denizens of the neighborhood offices" around SoMa; but with "unexcitingly" prepared food and servers "going through the motions", it – "like the namesake drink" – "feels a bit played out."

Cotogna ⑳ *Italian*　　26 | 22 | 22 | $50

Downtown | 490 Pacific St. (Montgomery) | 415-775-8508 | www.cotognasf.com

"Hotter than the smoking pizza popping out of their oven", this all-day trattoria, "Quince's sister, has quickly become a go-to" "FiDier's lunch haunt" and celebrity-spotting dinner spot; also offering "silky-smooth pastas" and "worthy spit-fired meats", the "screaming good" daily changing "rustic Italian" menu is further "helped by shockingly fair wine prices" ("all $40 a bottle") and "sensitive service", yet comes "without the formality" of its elder; so despite "close" tables and a "noisy" sound level, the place is always "booked solid"; P.S. Sunday night a family-style prix fixe supper is served.

NEW Criolla Kitchen *Soul Food*　　- | - | - | M

Castro | 2295 Market St. (16th St.) | 415-552-5811 | www.criollakitchen.com

Expect fare from the Islands, the American South, Cuba and anywhere else soul food is found at this moderately priced newcomer in the Castro overseen by New Orleans–born chef Randy Lewis; the corner cafe space – renovated in an airy plantation style – also serves as a backdrop for brunch (think chicken and waffles), lunch and a late-night menu of pan-national street food.

Crustacean *Vietnamese*

| 24 | 19 | 20 | $55 |

Polk Gulch | 1475 Polk St. (California St.) | 415-776-2722 | www.anfamily.com

"Even though you'll look foolish, wear the bib" – all the better to dive right into the buttery "namesake Dungeness crab done to perfection" at this "hidden" "divine Vietnamese" also plying "truly addictive" garlic noodles; its steep tabs, "sporadic service" and Polk Street setting are somewhat "off-putting", but not enough to keep fans from the "decadent" meals.

NEW Cupola Pizzeria *Italian/Pizza*

| - | - | - | M |

Downtown | Westfield San Francisco Ctr. | 845 Market St., 4th fl. (bet. 4th & 5th Sts.) | 415-896-5600 | www.cupolasf.com

Set under the Emporium dome on the fourth floor of the Westfield San Francisco Centre, this midpriced pizzeria serves a variety of thin-crust pizzas, including whole-wheat and vegan options, prepared in a wood-burning oven imported from Naples, along with antipasti such as pulled-to-order mozzarella plus handmade pastas and dolci; designed by Cass Calder Smith, the space has a vibe that's more Milan fashion than rustic Tuscany.

Curry Up Now *Indian*

| 25 | 15 | 21 | $9 |

Location varies; see website | 650-477-3000 | www.curryupnow.com

"Flavorful and filling" "awesome Indian burritos" "with a kick" and "delicious" "deconstructed samosas" are some of the "innovative twists" on classics dispensed from this "always-on-the-move" fleet of San Francisco and Peninsula trucks; given the "horrendously long lines", snarky types suggest the name should be "curry up and wait", plus they're an "effort to track" on Facebook and Twitter, but it's "worth it" for "crave-worthy", if "pricey", "fusion" bites served by "pleasant", "passionate" folks.

Delancey Street Ⓜ *Eclectic*

| 18 | 17 | 22 | $30 |

Embarcadero | 600 The Embarcadero (Brannan St.) | 415-512-5179 | www.delanceystreetfoundation.org

Social-minded surveyors rack up "good karma" at this "reasonably priced" Electic eatery on the Embarcadero, where "ex-cons" and recovering addicts "are remaking their lives" by "learning the restaurant biz"; a minority mutters the menu is "nothing out of the ordinary", but the majority declares it "delivers" with "plentiful and pleasing" plates that represent the "staff's version of comfort food – wherever they may be from", and that the "gorgeous view of the Bay Bridge" (best from the patio seats) "just makes it that much better."

Delarosa ◑ *Italian*

| 22 | 18 | 19 | $32 |

Marina | 2175 Chestnut St. (bet. Pierce & Steiner Sts.) | 415-673-7100 | www.delarosasf.com

The "latest 'it' spot on Chestnut" charms Marina twentysomethings with a "convivial vibe" and a variety of "delicious" "crispy, thin-crust pizza" and "interesting" "Italian tapas", plus a "fantastic beer list" for a "reasonable price"; it can "be too dang busy and hard to get into", and once inside, the "communal seating is a turnoff" for some; but jesters proclaim "a Delarosa by any other name would smell as sweet."

DeLessio Market & Bakery *Bakery*

| 20 | 13 | 15 | $20 |

Hayes Valley | 1695 Market St. (Gough St.) | 415-552-5559
Western Addition | Falletti's Plaza | 302 Broderick St. (Oak St.) |
415-552-8077
www.delessiomarket.com

Help yourself to "a heaping plate of whatever looks good" from the
"treasure trove of treats" at these gourmet buffets, including a "hot
bar with comfort food like your mom never made" and "desserts to
write home about"; the Hayes Valley original sports a patio, but "seating is haphazard" in the Western Addition branch; either way, you
"certainly pay for all this deliciousness" – by the pound, to be precise.

☑ Delfina *Italian*

| 26 | 19 | 23 | $48 |

Mission | 3621 18th St. (bet. Dolores & Guerrero Sts.) | 415-552-4055 |
www.delfinasf.com

Anne and Craig Stoll's "hugely popular" Mission trattoria is the "place
to be" for "casual and delicious" dining, turning out Northern Italian
fare that's "nothing fancy" yet "lusty" while pouring "affordable"
wines in a "vibrant atmosphere" far "away from the tourists"; "in spite
of its hipster rep", "the crowd defines the word diverse" and the "laid-
back" staff is "well versed", so while it's "always packed" and "still impossible to get a reservation", fans attest it's "worth" "everything."

Delica *Japanese*

| 21 | 13 | 15 | $20 |

Embarcadero | Ferry Bldg. Mktpl. | 1 Ferry Bldg. (The Embarcadero) |
415-834-0344 | www.delicasf.com

"Japanese deli by day, sushi bar by night", this Embarcadero eatery
"provides fresh and healthy options to Ferry Building-goers" who love the
"hot and cold" dishes "with a Western twist" (e.g. roast beef sushi),
even if they are a bit "pricey"; however, there's "no seating" so "be prepared to wander around for a long time looking for a place to eat."

Destino *Nuevo Latino*

| 22 | 19 | 20 | $41 |

Castro | 1815 Market St. (bet. Guerrero St. & Octavia Blvd.) |
415-552-4451 | www.destinosf.com

"Trendy tapas" and "divinely refreshing" Latin cocktails are a highlight
of "modern Peruvian comfort fare" at this Nuevo Latino Castro eatery;
surveyors appreciate the "good value" and "warm atmosphere", but bemoan the "cramped" quarters that get "so noisy" you might as well "go
by yourself" – "you won't be able to talk anyway."

Dinosaurs *Vietnamese*

| - | - | - | I |

Castro | 2275 Market St. (16th St.) | 415-503-1421

Hawking "the best banh mi outside the Tenderloin" from a "sunny
storefront with Castro sensibilities" is this new dino-themed, pint-
sized Vietnamese sandwich shop; the "delicious" signature sammies
are stuffed with meats of all stripes, or tofu and taro (a "unique vegetarian option"), by the "super-sweet boys behind the counter."

Domo Sushi *Japanese*

| ▽ 24 | 16 | 20 | $34 |

Hayes Valley | 511 Laguna St. (Linden St.) | 415-861-8887 |
www.domosf.com

"Huge" portions of "inventive rolls" and "high-quality fresh fish" is the
M.O. of this Japanese joint in Hayes Valley; it's a "shoebox-sized place"
and it "doesn't take rezzies", but most find that it's "worth the wait."

	FOOD	DECOR	SERVICE	COST

Dosa *Indian*
22 **22** **19** **$38**

Mission | 995 Valencia St. (21st St.) | 415-642-3672
Upper Fillmore | 1700 Fillmore St. (Post St.) | 415-441-3672
www.dosasf.com

"Spice me up, yogurt me down" holler the heat-hankering fans of this "haute Indian" duo that specializes in "spicy", "not wholly authentic" "namesake dosas" that are "as big as the table", as well as cooling "inventive cocktails"; the "gorgeous" Fillmore locale in an "old bank building" is "more elegant than its Mission sister", but both attract "large tables" of "noisy" "beautiful people", which, along with the "brusque" staff, can make the pair seem "a little too hip for its own chapatis."

Dottie's True Blue Cafe *Diner*
26 **13** **19** **$19**

Tenderloin | 522 Jones St. (bet. Geary & O'Farrell Sts.) | 415-885-2767
Patient patrons "prepared" for "long lines" that "circle the block" (or willing to "get there early" before the 7:30 AM opening) are rewarded with "love on a plate" in the form of "fresh-baked pastries", pancakes to "flip" for and "huge portions" of "fattening to the max" breakfast and lunch fare; the "small" diner may look "like a greasy spoon", but "watching the cook at work" is like observing a maestro "conduct a symphony", and "warm" and "friendly service makes up for" the "inevitable wait" in the "sketchy" Tenderloin; closes at 3 PM; P.S. slated to relocate in fall 2011.

Dragon Well *Chinese*
21 **15** **21** **$25**

Marina | 2142 Chestnut St. (bet. Pierce & Steiner Sts.) | 415-474-6888 | www.dragonwell.com

"Ok, it's Chinese food for Marina residents" (that is, "catered to Western tastes"), but the "California farm-fresh" ingredients make for a "balanced, deliciously healthy" and "well-priced" meal at this "family-friendly" spot; adorned with "high ceilings and contemporary Asian decor", it gets an additional "bravo" for its "attentive" servers.

☒ Dynamo Donut & Coffee Ⓜ *Coffeehouse*
24 **12** **19** **$8**

Mission | 2760 24th St. (bet. Hampshire & York Sts.) | 415-920-1978 | www.dynamodonut.com

"There's always a line" of "Mission hipsters" waiting for the "sublimely conceived works of doughy art" offered in "flavors that get a little crazy" ("bacon in a doughnut!") at this tiny bakery; some "complain about paying $3" a pop, but "the servers are so sweet", there's "perfect coffee" and the occasional focaccia to go with, and a "magical garden" to sit in, making it "worth the splurge now and then"; P.S. closes by 5 PM.

E&O Trading Company *Asian*
20 **21** **19** **$39**

Downtown | 314 Sutter St. (bet. Grant Ave. & Stockton St.) | 415-693-0303 | www.eosanfrancisco.com

Get "transported to the Far East" just steps from Union Square, at this "energetic", Pan-Asian small plates pioneer that trades on its "fabulous kitschy" "tiki interior" and "terrific" "exotic cocktails", especially at the "super happy hour"; cynics sense "a careless attitude" of late, and "in some instances, portions are tiny for the price", but it's still a "delicious" "standby", especially if you "go with several people and really work the menu" ("the corn fritters are a must").

	FOOD	DECOR	SERVICE	COST

E'Angelo Ⓜ *Italian* ▽ 20 | 13 | 17 | $32

Marina | 2234 Chestnut St. (bet. Pierce & Scott Sts.) | 415-567-6164
For a study in "old-school Italian" ristorantes San Francisco–style, this "Marina mainstay" remains "quite crowded" with those seeking "a family-friendly place for the kids"; when ordering, stick to the "good pasta", and expect "easygoing" service and "great prices."

Ebisu *Japanese* 24 | 18 | 19 | $36

Downtown | 336 Kearny St. (bet. Bush & Pine Sts.) | 415-398-2388
Inner Sunset | 1283 Ninth Ave. (Irving St.) | 415-566-1770 Ⓜ
www.ebisusushi.com
"In a neighborhood full of sushi restaurants", the "straight-ahead", "pristine" preparations of a father and son who "know their fish" en-sure this "long-standing Inner Sunset Japanese joint" (with a Downtown lunch counter and quick-service SFO offshoot) keeps its "first-class destination status"; there's usually a "mad crush" at din-ner, but patient patrons can "order a beer and sit on the sidewalk" be-fore bellying up to the bar to "enjoy the banter" of the chefs.

Eiji Ⓜ *Japanese* ▽ 26 | 14 | 19 | $41

Castro | 317 Sanchez St. (bet. 16th & 17th Sts.) | 415-558-8149
"Ethereal tofu made in-house" along with "authentic" dishes almost "never seen elsewhere in San Francisco" are matched by "traditional service" at this "quaint" country Japanese haunt in the Castro; the chef also turns out "very fresh" fish fare, and do "save room for a mo-chi" dessert, but "the place is about the size of postage stamp", so "don't expect to drop in and get a table."

Elite Cafe *American* 19 | 19 | 19 | $42

Pacific Heights | 2049 Fillmore St. (bet. California & Pine Sts.) | 415-673-5483 | www.theelitecafe.com
The "spicy" "Cajun dishes" ("caloric, but worth it") and "lively bar" put you "in a Big Easy kinda mood" at this "old-school" American that's "still going strong" after 30 years; it's a "semisplurge" say some, who wish the "down-home soul food" weren't so "expensive", but "servers who genuinely seem to care" and "old-fashioned" high-backed booths that provide plenty of "privacy" ensure it's "crowded all the time" with Pac Heights patrons.

Eliza's *Chinese* 21 | 16 | 16 | $27

Pacific Heights | 2877 California St. (bet. Broderick & Divisadero Sts.) | 415-621-4819
"Fresh produce" puts this Pac Heights "favorite" "a notch above the rest" for locals who "take out-of-town guests" for its "beautifully pre-sented", uniquely "Californian-influenced" Chinese fare that's "a ma-jor bargain for lunch and a very good value for dinner"; the "eclectic decor of gorgeous blown glass" "isn't for everyone", though, and nei-ther is the often-"sour" service, so many opt to "get it to go."

Ella's *American* 21 | 14 | 18 | $22

Presidio Heights | 500 Presidio Ave. (California St.) | 415-441-5669 | www.ellassanfrancisco.com
"Justifiably famous" for "indulgent" breakfasts and brunches, this "casual" cafe in Presidio Heights "starts your day right" by putting a "twist on traditional favorites", from "amazing baked goods" to

"fantastic" chicken hash; critics decry the "crazy lines on the weekend" and wonder if it's "lost some of its edge", but most maintain there's "plenty to rave about" on the "hearty" American menu; P.S. no dinner.

El Metate *Mexican*

22 | 14 | 17 | $11

Mission | 2406 Bryant St. (22nd St.) | 415-641-7209

Mission-ites maintain you "can't go wrong" with the "always-fresh burritos", tacos and other mainstays at this Mexican joint; the "people are nice", and while it's "nothing fancy", it's "reliable, which is good value right there."

El Porteno ⊘ *Argentinean*

24 | 14 | 19 | $8

Location varies; see website | 415-513-4529 | www.elportenosf.com

"Buttery, flaky" "goodness" is the hallmark of the "authentic Argentinean empanadas" available around the Bay courtesy of this "bright star of the food cart genre" that packs its wallet-friendly wares full of "inventive", "tasty fillings", including "excellent vegetarian options" (the mushroom is the "stuff that dreams are made of"); "swooning" fans "love" the "chatty owner" and "return again and again."

El Tonayense ⊘ *Mexican*

24 | 13 | 21 | $7

Location varies; see website | 415-550-9192
Mission | 3150 24th St. (Shotwell St.) | 415-550-9192
www.eltonayense.com

The "price is right and the portions are large" for the "*muy delicioso*" tacos, "spicy salsa" and "awesome burritos on wheels" served up at this "king of SF taco trucks"; they're so "friendly" and quick" that even with a sister brick-and-mortar Mission outpost, many believe these traveling taquerias are "still the way to go."

El Zocalo ● *Salvadoran*

▽ 19 | 9 | 14 | $18

Bernal Heights | 3230 Mission St. (Valencia St.) | 415-282-2572

"Feel like part of the family" while feasting on "the best pupusas around", plus other Salvadoran seafood ("most served with an abundance of french fries") at this "homey" Bernal Heights hideaway; sure, it's in a "sketchy neighborhood, with the slowest service in town", but for budget-friendly Central American eats, it can't be beat.

Emmy's Spaghetti Shack *Italian*

20 | 14 | 16 | $26

Bernal Heights | 18 Virginia Ave. (Mission St.) | 415-206-2086 | www.emmysspaghettishack.com

Its "name says it all" at this "longtime standout" in the Mission, where the "tattooed staff" serves "super-huge portions" of the eponymous pasta with "delicious sauce" and "flavorful meatballs the size of your fist" (and "rotating specials that never disappoint"); even though it's "loud" and there are "long lines", fans say once you're eating, it's "something magical."

Emporio Rulli *Dessert/Italian*

24 | 21 | 17 | $20

(aka Emporio Rulli Italian Caffe at Union Square)

Downtown | Union Sq. Pavilion | 225 Stockton St. (bet. Geary & Post Sts.) | 415-433-1122 | www.rulli.com

See review in North of San Francisco Directory.

Eos Restaurant & Wine Bar *Asian/Californian*

| 23 | 19 | 20 | $43 |

Cole Valley | 901 Cole St. (Carl St.) | 415-566-3063 | www.eossf.com
"Bring a couple of friends", because this Cole Valley Cal-Asian specializes in "outstanding" "small plates" that are suitable for "sharing"
(witness the "divine" shiitake dumplings that "beckon" boosters to
this sleek industrial eatery); add in "cordial" service and a "good selection of wines" (the "flights are a nice touch") and "it's enough to
make you forget about the lack of parking", but some suggest the
smaller wine salon "next door", which serves the same menu in a
less "noisy" milieu.

Epic Roasthouse *Steak*

| 21 | 25 | 21 | $66 |

Embarcadero | 369 The Embarcadero (bet. Folsom & Harrison Sts.) |
415-369-9955 | www.epicroasthousesf.com
The panorama "at the edge of the Bay Bridge" is "epic" indeed (both
inside and on the "terrific" patio) at this "comfy leather"-furnished
"meat-eater's delight" right on the Embarcadero; while "location,
location, location is what makes this spot of interest", chef Jan
Birnbaum's "big chunks" of steak are certainly "savory" enough,
especially at weekend brunch ("beef and beignets" - "does it get any
better?"); and if it seems all "sooo expensive", you can "soak up the
views for less" in the "bustling bar" upstairs.

Eric's *Chinese*

| 20 | 13 | 16 | $23 |

Noe Valley | 1500 Church St. (27th St.) | 415-282-0919 |
www.ericrestaurant.com
"Dependable, delicious", if "a bit Americanized Chinese food" has
kept this Asian a "standby" for 20 years; but while "you can always
count on the fresh ingredients and tasty sauces", the dishes are
"served carelessly" and the digs are "cramped and crowded", leaving
some to say it "only makes sense if you need to be in the Noe Valley" -
or for "fast takeout."

Esperpento *Spanish*

| 20 | 15 | 16 | $30 |

Mission | 3295 22nd St. (Valencia St.) | 415-282-8867
"Sharing is best" when it comes to enjoying the "wonder-tapas" and
other "authentic" edibles at this "divey Spanish" in the Mission; some
are bothered by "rookie servers", "noisy" sound levels and say that the
"food has gone down" in quality , but it's still "great value" "for a
hearty table of adventurous eaters."

Espetus Churrascaria *Brazilian*

| 22 | 18 | 21 | $65 |

(aka Espetus Churrascaria Brazilian Steakhouse)
Hayes Valley | 1686 Market St. (Gough St.) | 415-552-8792 |
www.espetus.com
It's "a caveman's dream" claim "carnivores" who leave their "vegan
friends" at home when headed to these "friendly" (if fairly "expensive") Brazilian churrascarias in Hayes Valley and San Mateo for "a
good time" partaking of the "endless parade of mouthwatering beef,
pork, chicken and seafood" "piled onto your plate" by "gorgeous"
"waiters in gaucho pants"; a "plentiful" "salad bar buffet" "complements" the "protein deluge", but the "meatatarian" majority prefers
filling up on the "unlimited skewers."

	FOOD	DECOR	SERVICE	COST

Eureka Restaurant & Lounge *American*
| 20 | 20 | 21 | $39 |

Castro | 4063 18th St. (bet. Castro & Hartford Sts.) | 415-431-6000 |
www.eurekarestaurant.com

"Low-key Southernish comfort food", a clientele containing "plenty of
neighborhood eye candy" and a "let's just say, festive" ambiance keep
this Castro New American ("sister restaurant to Chenery Park") a
perpetual discovery; regulars recommend you "sit upstairs" in the
"intimate Victorian" space.

Fang *Chinese*
| 20 | 19 | 17 | $31 |

SoMa | 660 Howard St. (bet. New Montgomery & 3rd Sts.) |
415-777-8568 | www.fangrestaurant.com

A "second outpost from the chef behind the ever-popular House of
Nanking" ("but with a definite step up in decor"), this SoMa "sleeper"
features "fresh, flavorful Chinese fare" that "you can really get your
teeth into" fans say – even as the belligerent bare their fangs at what
they call "Americanized", "average" eats; perhaps the key is to let
owner Peter Fang "order for you, and you won't be disappointed."

☒ Farallon *Seafood*
| 24 | 27 | 24 | $70 |

Downtown | 450 Post St. (bet. Mason & Powell Sts.) | 415-956-6969 |
www.farallonrestaurant.com

The "over-the-top" "deep-sea decor", complete with "jellyfish chandeliers", makes "an impression on out-of-towners and locals alike" at this
"swimmingly good" seafooder Downtown; if a few fret the "meals
don't match" the "whimsically elegant" environs, most maintain the
cuisine can "always be counted on", from chef/co-owner Mark Franz's
"flawlessly fresh" fish to "high-style" desserts, and "stellar" service
takes the sting out of the "whale-size" tab.

Farina *Italian*
| 23 | 21 | 20 | $49 |

Mission | 3560 18th St. (Dearborn St.) | 415-565-0360 |
www.farina-foods.com

"Liguria meets the Mission" at this "lively" location that earns "props"
for its "in-house crafting" of pastas, "fantastic" pesto and "killer focaccia"; though the frugal fuss it's "overpriced for what you get",
Italians are "transported" to their "nonna's hometown" by the "memorable" menu and "well-selected" wine list, even if the "great-looking
space" and "buzzin' atmosphere" are all San Francisco; P.S. offshoot
Antica Pizeria Napoletana is scheduled to open next door.

Farmerbrown *Soul Food*
| 20 | 15 | 18 | $28 |

Tenderloin | 25 Mason St. (bet. Eddy & Turk Sts.) | 415-409-3276 |
www.farmerbrownsf.com

Farmerbrown's Little Skillet ☒⌨ *Soul Food*

SoMa | 360 Ritch St. (bet. Brannan & Townsend Sts.) | 415-777-2777 |
www.littleskilletsf.com

"Soul food as interpreted for SF hipsters" (i.e. made with lots of "local"
and "organic" ingredients) "will knock your socks off" say supporters of
this "funky, spunky" spot that's a "welcome respite" from the "dodgy
Tenderloin"; the "top-notch" "cocktails served in old mason jars" will
"get your night started right", or opt for the "all-you-can-eat Southern
fried fest" for the weekend "buffet brunch"; a "cash-only" "take-out
window" "hidden" on an "alley" serves similar fare to "SoMa workers."

	FOOD	DECOR	SERVICE	COST

15 Romolo ● *Pub Food* | 20 | 18 | 19 | $28 |

North Beach | Basque Hotel | 15 Romolo Pl. (B'way) | 415-398-1359 | www.15romolo.com

"Amazing" "handcrafted" cocktails that "look as good as the bartenders" wash down "interesting takes" on American "bar food" at this "hip", midpriced "old-timey" gastropub in a "dark" North Beach "alleyway"; it's "perfect for happy hour" or a late-night snack, just "be in the mood" for an "often loud" scene of "twenty- and thirtysomethings" plus "plenty of waiting."

Fifth Floor *American/French* | 23 | 23 | 24 | $75 |

SoMa | Hotel Palomar | 12 Fourth St., 5th fl. (Market St.) | 415-348-1555 | www.fifthfloorrestaurant.com

Surveyors suspect the "new chef from Chez Papa Resto" is the cure for what's been a "constantly changing" kitchen at this SoMa "art deco" favorite, swearing that his New American menu with French and Med influences has already "catapulted" it "back to being one of the best"; a "true wine lover's list" and "exquisite service" enhance options including a "multicourse" prix fixe geared to "fat cats" and an à la carte menu, and frugal diners can "stick to the bar" or lounge.

54 Mint ⊠ *Italian* | 21 | 20 | 19 | $46 |

SoMa | 16 Mint Plaza (Jessie St.) | 415-543-5100 | www.54mint.com

Bellissimo cucina cheer champions of the "housemade pasta", "imaginative" small plates and other "well-seasoned" fare at this "authentic but stylish" SoMa Italian "tucked away in Mint Plaza"; while "loud music" and "slow service" are in the mix, most find the setting "cozy" yet "hip", plus "it doesn't cost a mint."

Fior d'Italia *Italian* | 18 | 18 | 19 | $45 |

North Beach | San Remo Hotel | 2237 Mason St. (bet. Chestnut & Francisco Sts.) | 415-986-1886 | www.fior.com

The "oldest Italian restaurant" in town transports you "back to a San Francisco that doesn't exist anymore" aver aficionados of this "authentic", "traditional" trattoria that relocated to North Beach's San Remo Hotel some years back; pickier patrons call the menu "mundane" while others find the "well-prepared" pastas and other "classic" *cucina* "reliably impressive."

Firefly *Eclectic* | 25 | 20 | 23 | $44 |

Noe Valley | 4288 24th St. (Douglass St.) | 415-821-7652 | www.fireflyrestaurant.com

"Nearly two decades after its inception", Brad Levy's "low-key" neighborhood "Noe Valley fixture" still glows, "churning out" an ever-changing slate of "interesting Eclectic food" that's "outlandishly good", whether you go for the shrimp and sea scallop potstickers, an "interesting veggie entree" or fried chicken that's "among the best in the city"; toss in a "homey feeling" and prices that "won't break the bank", and it's clear why the "mismatched chairs" are "always full."

Fish & Farm ⊠ *American/Seafood* | 20 | 16 | 18 | $47 |

Downtown | 339 Taylor St. (bet. Ellis & O'Farrell Sts.) | 415-474-3474 | www.fishandfarmsf.com

"Man-sized portions" of "homestyle" New American dishes "won't leave you hungry" at this "low-key" Downtowner with a focus on sustainability in both cuisine (including seafood) and decor; while the less-enthused say they wouldn't seek out the "locally sourced" fare, given that the location "isn't the best area" and service "varies", others contend it's a "find" "especially for the price."

5A5 Steak Lounge *Steak*
23 | 23 | 21 | $71

Downtown | 244 Jackson St. (bet. Battery & Front Sts.) | 415-989-2539 | www.5a5stk.com

Downtowners desiring "a vacation from the everyday steakhouse" head for this "trendy" "meat-lover's paradise" that offers a "huge variety" of "absolutely outstanding" beef – including the "awesome" A5 Wagyu for which it's named; "dazzling" decor and a notably "non-snooty staff" make most "feel glamorous", and those who balk at paying "big bucks" instead soak up the "cool, futuristic lounge atmosphere" over "after-work drinks and appetizers."

Fivetenburger 🖪Ⓜ *Burgers*
25 | 16 | 22 | $9

Location varies; see website | 510-545-3486 | www.fivetenburger.com

It may be "nothing fancy", but whether made with "organic grass-fed" or natural corn-fed beef, the "really good-and-sloppy burgers" "don't mess around" at this Oakland-based food truck that also serves "delicious" "garlic fries" and sausage sandwiches; P.S. open till 11 PM Thursday–Friday and till 9 PM Saturday.

🗹 Fleur de Lys 🖪Ⓜ *Californian/French*
27 | 26 | 26 | $98

Downtown | 777 Sutter St. (bet. Jones & Taylor Sts.) | 415-673-7779 | www.fleurdelyssf.com

Hubert Keller "shows why he is one of the greatest master chefs" at this "oldie but goodie" Downtown "showstopper" where he and his wife, Chantal, create a dining experience devotees dub "beyond memorable"; the "haute" French-Californian prix fixes "with inspired wine pairings" will "knock your *chaussettes* off", as will the "romantic" "fantasy" "tent" decor (warning: your date may "be the only one in the room not getting a ring"); so forget about "sticker shock" and put this one "on your bucket list."

Florio *French/Italian*
19 | 19 | 20 | $44

Pacific Heights | 1915 Fillmore St. (bet. Bush & Pine Sts.) | 415-775-4300 | www.floriosf.com

Featuring "everything you liked" at that "busy" "little bistro in your arrondissement of Paris", this "charming and cozy" Italian-French eatery with "dark-wood" decor is an "old-school" spot for "simple food done well"; Pac Heights habitués – everyone from "single" women to "couples" to "families" – stick to "roast chicken, steak frites" and "crispy fries", because "classic" "comfort food" is its strong suit, along with drinks doled out by "super-friendly" servers in the "very lively" bar.

🗹 Flour + Water *Italian*
24 | 19 | 21 | $44

Mission | 2401 Harrison St. (20th St.) | 415-826-7000 | www.flourandwater.com

"Reserve weeks ahead" or "you may be eating bread and water" "while you wait" alongside the "terminally hip" at this Mission "'in' spot" "where the "novel" "charred-crust Neapolitan pizza", "ethereal" pastas and "interesting" Italian wines served in quirky "reclaimed-wood" digs "may just live up to" the "hype"; some could do without "the noise"

FOOD DECOR SERVICE COST

and the "attitude at the door" (even for the "community table"), but "the tariff is affordable" and the "bohemian" staffers are "convivial."

Fog City Diner *American* 18 | 19 | 19 | $37

Embarcadero | 1300 Battery St. (The Embarcadero) | 415-982-2000 | www.fogcitydiner.com

Elevating "diner" fare "to another dimension", this "tried-and-true" New American resembling a "gleaming" "old rail car" "still charms after all these years" with its "eclectic" (if slightly "expensive") "comfort food" "and a good bar to boot"; the Embarcadero environs, "not far from Pier 39 and The Wharf", mean it's "a bit touristy", and a few feel it has "lost its old jazz", but most maintain this "stalwart" "still leaves you satisfied."

Fondue Cowboy Ⓜ *Fondue* ▽ 18 | 16 | 19 | $29

SoMa | 1052 Folsom St. (Russ St.) | 415-431-5100 | www.fonduecowboy.com

"Who doesn't like to dip their food and eat?" wonder fondue fans of this "cozy" corner in SoMa, where the sweet and savory sauces "are only eclipsed by the wide variety" of "amazingly fresh seasonal fruits and stunning vegetables" to dunk; having "old silent Westerns playing" is a "cute concept" too, and while "the menu has room to grow", most feel this cowpoke has "great potential."

Forbes Island Ⓜ *American/Seafood* ▽ 15 | 22 | 21 | $57

Fisherman's Wharf | Piers 39 & 41 (The Embarcadero) | 415-951-4900 | www.forbesisland.com

It's a "one-of-a-kind experience" declare deckhands who "take a boat" (sometimes piloted by the "character" "Mr. Forbes" himself) from Fisherman's Wharf to reach this artificial "little island floating off of Pier 39"; landlubbers lament that the "expensive" American and seafood menu is "just ok", but the "dramatic venue" where you can "watch the sunset" from the lighthouse or dine "underwater near a fireplace" make it a "fun place" "to take out-of-town visitors" or celebrate a "special date"; P.S. closed Monday–Tuesday.

Ⓩ Foreign Cinema *Californian/Mediterranean* 24 | 24 | 22 | $48

Mission | 2534 Mission St. (bet. 21st & 22nd Sts.) | 415-648-7600 | www.foreigncinema.com

"After all these years", this Mission "hipster" hideaway that "shows rad foreign films" "on the courtyard wall" still "maintains its delicious reputation"; sure, the setting is "unique" (whether "under the stars" or "fireside" in the "chic" "industrial" interior), but the "amazingly creative" Cal-Med "food lives up to the surroundings" ("order the 'adult' pop tarts" at weekend brunch); the staff is a tad "too cool for school" at times, but overall, it's "one of the best farm-to-table places in the city."

4505 Meats Ⓢ Ⓜ ⏁ *Hot Dogs* 27 | 17 | 21 | $11

Embarcadero | Ferry Bldg. Mktpl. | 1 Ferry Bldg. (The Embarcadero) | 415-255-3094 | www.4505meats.com

From "bacon hot dogs" to "amazing" chicharrones to perhaps the "most succulent burger ever", whatever "rich concoctions of meaty love" "they happen to be slinging" at this "sustainable and local" food stall at the "back of the Ferry Building" "will make your taste buds sing"; "it's not the easiest place to find" and it's often "too crazed" and "crowded", but "when there is no line", they "go out of their way" to be "very accommodating"; P.S. open Thursdays and Saturdays only, until 2 PM.

FOOD | DECOR | SERVICE | COST

⛅ Frances ⓂCalifornian
27 | 19 | 24 | $55

Castro | 3870 17th St. (Pond St.) | 415-621-3870 | www.frances-sf.com

"World-class chef" Melissa Perello and her "genuinely excited" staff prove that "rustic fine dining is no longer an oxymoron" at this "quaint" "neighborhood-y" Castro phenom turning out a changing menu of "seriously wonderful" Californian "comfort food" in a "minuscule storefront"; you "almost need divine intervention to get a table" or a "walk-in" "seat at the bar", and it gets "jammed" and "noisy", but the "ingenious" "pay-for-what-you-drink house wines" policy makes it an "affordable" "treasure for foodies."

Frascati Californian/Mediterranean
26 | 21 | 24 | $52

Russian Hill | 1901 Hyde St. (Green St.) | 415-928-1406 | www.frascatisf.com

"Cable cars" that "clang by" and a "cozy", "comfortable" dining room help make this "intimate" "neighborhood bistro" "one of the most romantic restaurants" in town, with an "excellent" Cal-Med "menu to match the ambiance"; Russian Hill habitués are also "wooed" by the "warm welcome", and since "one can eat without muss, fuss or bankruptcy" (as long as you "make a reservation"), the enraptured are ready to "return" "in a heartbeat."

Fresca Peruvian
22 | 18 | 19 | $36

West Portal | 24 W. Portal Ave. (Ulloa St.) | 415-759-8087
Noe Valley | 3945 24th St. (bet. Noe & Sanchez Sts.) | 415-695-0549
Upper Fillmore | 2114 Fillmore St. (Clay St.) | 415-447-2668
www.frescasf.com

"Who knew there were so many great versions of ceviche?" wonder fans who flock to this "crowd-pleasing", "pleasant Peruvian" trio where the "addictive" lomo saltado is washed down with "innovative" cocktails; the "lively" settings can be "noisy", however, and the "friendly" service "slow", so some "skip dinner and head here for brunch" or lunch instead.

Fringale French/Spanish
24 | 18 | 22 | $52

SoMa | 570 Fourth St. (bet. Brannan & Freelon Sts.) | 415-543-0573 | www.fringalesf.com

"Still going strong" after 20 years, this "delightful" bistro in SoMa "never ceases to amaze" by proffering a "fantastic selection" of "authentic" Gallic goods "with a Basque twist" paired with "perfectly matched wines"; the "cramped quarters" (and tables that are nearly "on top of each other") may discourage "confidential conversations", but the "friendly" staff with a "thick French accent" and "reasonable prices" mean most take away "happy memories."

Frjtz Fries Belgian
17 | 13 | 14 | $17

Hayes Valley | 581 Hayes St. (Laguna St.) | 415-864-7654
Mission | 590 Valencia St. (17th St.) | 415-863-8272
www.frjtzfries.com

"Go to Belgium" or go to this Hayes Valley and Mission "casual counter-service" duo for "fries! fries! fries!" served with "many" "tasty" "dipping sauces" and washed down "with a cold glass of suds"; though there is "other food there", converts concentrate on the "carb snacks", as the rest of the menu is "pricey" in the "Euro-cool", "design-crazy" digs.

	FOOD	DECOR	SERVICE	COST

Front Porch *Caribbean/Southern*
| 20 | 17 | 19 | $29 |

Bernal Heights | 65A 29th St. (bet. Mission St. & San Jose Ave.) | 415-695-7800 | www.thefrontporchsf.com

"You could almost put your feet up, that's how down-home this place is", thanks to the "lip-smacking" "Southern fried comfort" food with Caribbean influences it serves, along with an "awesome beer selection"; it gets "loud and crowded on the weekends" ("plan to wait") and several say "a little light would help" the dark digs, but for most, this Bernal Heights hang is a "charming cave of a restaurant."

Gamine *French*
| 24 | 16 | 24 | $37 |

Cow Hollow | 2223 Union St. (bet. Fillmore & Steiner Sts.) | 415-771-7771 | www.gaminesf.com

The owner "and his whole crew" treat you like a "longtime friend" at this "charming", "little" midpriced Gallic bistro in Cow Hollow; the "casual" confines can be "very crowded" (and there are "no reservations" for groups of fewer than six), but once you snag a seat "at the bar" and "watch them prepare" your fare, or "sit outside" with a glass of wine, it's a "fantastic French experience" that's a "bit of Paris on Union Street."

☑ Garden Court *Californian*
| 19 | 27 | 21 | $59 |

Downtown | Palace Hotel | 2 New Montgomery St. (Market St.) | 415-546-5010 | www.sfpalace.com

"At least once in your life", "step back in time to the belle epoque" by visiting this "beautiful and historical" Palace Hotel "institution", which makes "happy occasions" happier with "opulent" afternoon tea or a "Sunday" or "holiday" "champagne brunch" with a "groaning-board buffet that will leave you full for the next three days"; the service varies and the Cal fare is "expensive" while "not that impressive", but "with a room this beautiful it's doubtful you'll even care."

Garibaldis *Californian/Mediterranean*
| 22 | 21 | 22 | $47 |

Presidio Heights | 347 Presidio Ave. (bet. Clay & Sacramento Sts.) | 415-563-8841 | www.garibaldisrestaurant.com

A "perennial favorite" of Presidio Heights habitués, from "ladies that lunch" to "privileged" patrons fresh from a "portfolio" review, this "elegant" but "understated" "locals' clubhouse" "will surprise and delight" with its "seasonal" Cal-Med menu and "exquisite" wine list; if some sigh it's "lacking" that "special something", fans unfazed by the "close quarters" say servers make you "feel welcome" ensuring a "civilized dinner."

☑ Gary Danko *American*
| 29 | 27 | 28 | $109 |

Fisherman's Wharf | 800 N. Point St. (Hyde St.) | 415-749-2060 | www.garydanko.com

Acolytes could "write a short story" on why Gary Danko's "highly sought-after gastronomic mecca" on the Wharf is again "Numero Uno" for Food, Service and Popularity in the Bay Area Survey; to begin, "like your favorite" "little black dress", it's "perfect for any occasion", proffering "brilliant", customizable New American tasting menus and "stupendous wines" plus an "unequalled" cheese cart in a "gorgeous" room with service that "befits kings and queens" yet has a "refreshing lack of pretension" (you can also "eat at the bar"); in sum, where else can you pay "three- and four-digit prices" and "walk out feeling you more than got your money's worth"?

	FOOD	DECOR	SERVICE	COST

Gaylord India *Indian* — 18 | 16 | 19 | $34

Downtown | 1 Embarcadero Ctr. (Sacramento St.) | 415-397-7775 |
www.gaylords1.com

"Lots of lunchtime workers" depend on the "all-you-can-eat buffet", a
"good value" that "fills you up" with "frequently replaced" "traditional" eats at this Downtown Indian; it gets a nod for "nice service"
and being "so convenient" for nine-to-fivers, who also dine here at dinner, but surlier surveyors say it's "overpriced" and and a dip in the
Decor score suggests "an update is seriously in order."

Georges 🛇 *Californian/Seafood* — ▽ 19 | 18 | 18 | $45

Downtown | Fugazi Bldg. | 415 Sansome St. (Commercial St.) |
415-956-6900 | www.georgessf.com

"Simple but elegant" Californian "sustainable fish" dishes are the hook
for Downtown "seafood lovers" at this "cute little place in FiDi"; still,
some finicky folk refuse to take the bait, citing "sloppy" service and
"food that's not that exciting for the price."

Gialina *Pizza* — 25 | 15 | 19 | $29

Glen Park | 2842 Diamond St. (Kern St.) | 415-239-8500 | www.gialina.com

"Who needs New York?" ask pie-eyed patrons, when you can chow
down on "fantastic" thin-crust versions laced with "imaginative" "seasonally changing" toppings (like nettles or dandelion greens) that "elevate your pizza to gourmet status" at this Glen Park contender; it also
dishes out "outstanding garden-fresh salads" and "one or two roasted
dishes", but the "tiny" "unpretentious" setting gets "cramped and
noisy", so be prepared to line up "at 5 PM when they open."

Giordano Bros. *Sandwiches* — ▽ 23 | 15 | 19 | $15

North Beach | 303 Columbus Ave. (B'way) | 415-397-2767 |
www.giordanobros.com

It's "Primanti Brothers in North Beach" at this sporty sandwich shop,
which serves up a "little slice of Pittsburgh out West" – "cheesesteak
with fries and slaw on the bun"; it "may sound weird to the uninitiated"
but fans suggest "give it a try" and "you won't be disappointed"; adding to the cheer, there's "pretty good music" from live bands Tuesday-
Saturday too; P.S.a branch is slated for 3108 16th Street.

Giorgio's Pizzeria *Pizza* — 20 | 14 | 18 | $21

Inner Richmond | 151 Clement St. (3rd Ave.) | 415-668-1266 |
www.giorgiospizza.com

Even 'za zealots "raised in NYC" return "for years and years" to this
Inner Richmond "traditional pizzeria – just like the kind you remember from childhood" for its "straightforward" pies with "thin
crusts and fresh herby sauce" ("try the calzone too"); with "red-
checkered tablecloths" and "faux vines hanging overhead", the
"dated" decor is "low on pretense, high on feel-good nostalgia", but
they're "very accommodating to families" and prices are "reasonable"; P.S. "now they deliver."

Gitane 🛇Ⓜ *French/Spanish* — 23 | 23 | 21 | $51

Downtown | 6 Claude Ln. (bet. Bush & Sutter Sts.) | 415-788-6686 |
www.gitanerestaurant.com

There's "not a gypsy in sight" at this "mucho sexy", "secretive place"
Downtown named for one, but fans agree your fortune is made if you

choose "to rendezvous with your friends or lover" in the "romantic, darkly lit" setting while dining on an "inspired combination of Spanish, French and Moroccan" dishes and "wonderful nibbles" ("bacon bon bons, oh my"); alas, it's "always booked", so you'll need "good luck" to get a reservation.

Globe ◐ *Californian/Italian* | 18 | 15 | 19 | $45 |

Downtown | 290 Pacific Ave. (bet. Battery & Front Sts.) | 415-391-4132 | www.globerestaurant.com

The "industrial-looking dining room" is "elbow to elbow" at this "noisy" Downtowner with a "wonderful" "urban feel"; the Cal-Italian menu fashioned from "fresh local ingredients" is served till 1 AM" (midnight on Sundays) note night owls, who claim the "crowd is always fun to watch"; but if some say it's "still hitting solidly on all cylinders", a slipping Food score suggests "a bit of the luster has worn off."

Goat Hill Pizza *Pizza* | 18 | 11 | 18 | $20 |

Potrero Hill | 300 Connecticut St. (18th St.) | 415-641-1440
SoMa | 171 Stillman St. (bet. 3rd & 4th Sts.) | 415-974-1303
www.goathill.com

A "sourdough crust is a nice twist" on the pizza presented at this Potrero Hill "neighborhood joint" where "you can't beat all-you-can-eat Mondays", which let you "try lots of different toppings"; however, since the digs are "nothing fancy", many opt for the "fast delivery" (which is the only option at the SoMa sibling).

Godzila Sushi *Japanese* | ▽ 20 | 11 | 17 | $30 |

Pacific Heights | 1800 Divisadero St. (Bush St.) | 415-931-1773

"Go, go, go Godzila!" cheer fans of this "reliable" Pacific Heights sushi "standby" that's plastered with posters and napkin drawings of their namesake monster; the setting is just one "step above a hole-in-the-wall", and the fin fare probably "won't blow you away", but you "can't beat the price" on their "fresh rolls" and other "delectable" dishes that "hit the spot"; P.S. "fast service" suits those in a monster of a hurry.

Golden West ⊠ *Bakery/Sandwiches* | ▽ 24 | 7 | 16 | $13 |

Downtown | 8 Trinity St. (bet. Montgomery & Sutter Sts.) | 415-216-6443

This "great take-out" bakery/sammie shop (actually, more like "a window in the alley") "from the creator of Canteen" beckons Downtowners with the "same good coffee cake and excellent coffee" as its sister act, Sentinel, along with a limited selection of gussied-up American-style breakfast and lunch fare (including a signature short-rib sandwich); it's nothing to look at and only open on weekdays till 2 PM, but owner Dennis Leary's "usual pleasant demeanor" keeps it golden.

Gold Mountain *Chinese* | 21 | 8 | 13 | $24 |

Chinatown | 644 Broadway (bet. Columbus Ave. & Stockton St.) | 415-296-7733

Dim sum devotees suggest "go get sum" along with "all the locals" at this "authentic" Chinatown dumpling destination; there's "no decor" to speak of, and some servers "act like they can't wait for you to leave", but who cares when "the carts just keep rolling" by brimming with "excellent" and "inexpensive" eats; P.S. the kitchen specializes in Hong Kong–style seafood at dinner.

FOOD | DECOR | SERVICE | COST

Good Luck Dim Sum ⊄ *Chinese* 23 | 4 | 10 | $11

Inner Richmond | 736 Clement St. (bet. 8th & 9th Aves.) | 415-386-3388
Why shell out "eight times as much for the fancier places" when you can consume "steaming hot" "fantastic dim sum" like "what you would get in Hong Kong or Taiwan" at this Inner Richmond "hole-in-the-wall" Chinese; there are always "long lines" and the regimented "way of ordering can be intimidating", but a Food score jump attests it's "perfect" for a "grab-and-dash" lunch or early dinner (closes at 6:30 PM).

Goood Frikin' Chicken *Mideastern* 18 | 8 | 15 | $18

Mission | 10 29th St. (Mission St.) | 415-970-2428 | www.gfcsf.com
"Never has a name been more accurate" than the moniker of this Outer Mission Middle Eastern rotisserie joint, which "earns all its 'o's'" for its "moist but heavily herbed" chicken, supported by "really kickin'" hot sauce and hummus for "ridiculously low prices"; "take it home, though" – the "decor is not much to look at."

Gordon Biersch ◑ *Pub Food* 15 | 15 | 16 | $27

Embarcadero | 2 Harrison St. (The Embarcadero) | 415-243-8246 | www.gordonbiersch.com
Whether "for an after-work meal with friends" or to "meet up with the guys and catch the game", this affordable chain fills the bill, offering "lots of beer choices" including a "winning selection of local brews" to wash down "decent" American "brewpub food" including "over-the-top garlic fries"; service is "a bit spotty" and it's "frequently loud and crowded, but you know that going in", so just "pull up a chair" and "enjoy" the "down-to-earth" vibe.

Gott's Roadside *Diner* 21 | 13 | 15 | $19
(fka Taylor's Automatic Refresher)

Embarcadero | Ferry Bldg. Mktpl. | 1 Ferry Bldg. (The Embarcadero) | 866-328-3663 | www.gottsroadside.com
These "nostalgic" "self-serve" "burger joints" are "a perfect antidote to all the fancy-pants dining" offering "delicious all-American" fare and a "diverse" wine list in the "most varied menu of any roadside resto"; the frugal balk at "fast food at restaurant prices" and others skewer the "long lines" and "lackluster service", but most maintain "Gott's has got it right"; P.S. St. Helena has seating at outdoor picnic tables, while the Napa and SF offshoots have indoor tables too.

Gracias Madre *Mexican/Vegan* 21 | 19 | 20 | $26

Mission | 2211 Mission St. (18th St.) | 415-683-1346 | www.gracias-madre.com
"You don't miss the meat or dairy at all" assure fans of this Mission cantina offering "delicious" "stealth" "vegan Mexican" fare with "layered flavors"; some critics "don't like the communal tables", but service is "friendly" and the grateful still say *gracias* to this sister of "Café Gratitude."

Grand Cafe *French* 19 | 25 | 20 | $47

Downtown | Hotel Monaco | 501 Geary St. (Taylor St.) | 415-292-0101 | www.grandcafe-sf.com
The "opulent" art nouveau dining room with a "soaring ceiling" and "regal decor" is "very grand" indeed at this "elegant" bistro and

"charming bar" at Downtown's Hotel Monaco; a "varied menu" of French fare is served from morning till night, but it's especially popular with the "pre-theater" crowd, who can count on the "experienced" servers to get them out "on time"; if a few fuss that the "unimaginative menu" is "not worth the price", most sigh it's "so romantic" to take "a step back in time."

Grandeho's Kamekyo *Japanese* ∇ 25 | 15 | 22 | $40

Fisherman's Wharf | 2721 Hyde St. (bet. Beach & N. Point Sts.) | 415-673-6828

The sushi is "worth every penny" proclaim proponents of this "fantastic" Fisherman's Wharf neighborhood joint "that consistently hits the mark", especially given the "Vietnamese menu that also pairs well with the Japanese side"; the setting is nothing special, but a staff that "remembers the regulars" and "does not rush you out" is also grand.

Grand Pu Bah *Thai* ∇ 19 | 20 | 18 | $34

Potrero Hill | 88 Division St. (Rhode Island St.) | 415-255-8188 | www.grandpubahrestaurant.com

"In the up-and-coming SoMa/Potrero Hill district", this "rare upscale Thai fusion" eatery dishes out "comfort food with an exotic twist" and "great cocktails" at a "reasonable price"; the "relaxed, trendy atmosphere" also makes this grandee a "go-to place."

Great Eastern ● *Chinese* 21 | 10 | 13 | $28

Chinatown | 649 Jackson St. (bet. Grant Ave. & Kearny St.) | 415-986-2500

"Wonderfully fresh seafood", some of it plucked straight "from the fish tank", makes this "brightly lit" location a "solid Chinatown choice"; service is lacking, but that doesn't deter dumpling devotees, who know to go early unless they want to "wait" for the brunch-and-lunch-only dim sum, "fairly priced" fare that you "order from a menu" (meaning "no carts" or "chaos").

NEW Greenburgers *Burgers* - | - | - | I

Lower Haight | 518 Haight St. (Fillmore St.) | 415-829-2491 | www.sfgreenburgers.com

Burgers and other affordable, locally sourced American eats (plus pop made from natural cane sugar and organic, seasonal milkshakes) are the conceit behind this counter-serve arrival in the Lower Haight overseen by a husband-and-wife team; the retro-looking storefront is decked out with family photos, '70s bric-a-brac and a vintage Coca-Cola cooler that doubles as a condiment table.

Green Chile
Kitchen & Market *Southwestern* 23 | 17 | 18 | $19

Western Addition | 1801 McAllister St. (Baker St.) | 415-440-9411 | www.greenchilekitchen.com

"Authentic Southwestern" cuisine "nourishes the soul" at this Western Addition cantina that takes fans "back to New Mexico" thanks to "reasonably priced" "organic and healthy" takes on the likes of "stellar burritos", posole and chile stew (available in red, green or "Xmas-style with both"); since the decor's "no frills" and service is "so-so" in the often "crowded" space, some prefer "takeout."

	FOOD	DECOR	SERVICE	COST

☑ Greens *Vegetarian* — 24 | 23 | 22 | $44

Marina | Fort Mason Ctr., Bldg. A | Marina Blvd. (Buchanan St.) | 415-771-6222 | www.greensrestaurant.com

"Every bite's a Zen dream" at this "white-tablecloth" "vegetarian super-star", which, "like the greens they serve", continues "sprouting up" "surprising and delicious" meals, enhanced by "wonderful" wine pairings, that offer an "epiphany for meat eaters" and vegheads alike; service is "always busy" but "attentive", and for foes who fuss "for a pile of vegetables, the cost is too high", try to "go in daytime", a "more affordable" way to soak up the "spectacular views" of the "killer" Marina setting.

NEW Grub ◗ *American* — ▽ 16 | 16 | 16 | $31

Mission | 758 Valencia St. (19th St.) | 415-431-4782 | www.grubsf.com

"Mission hipsters" hit this "unpretentious foodie happy-land" for "upscale" midpriced American "comfort food" like fancy burgers and an "awesome" "build-your-own mac 'n' cheese option" (regulars recommend "stick to that", as the "fancier" fare can lose some "oomph"); service that varies leaves some reckoning it's "still finding its footing", but "super-cute" "'80s decor" adds to a "fun vibe."

Hakka Restaurant ☒Ⓜ *Chinese* — ▽ 24 | 9 | 18 | $21

Outer Richmond | 4401 Cabrillo (45th Ave.) | 415-876-6898

Once "you convince the skeptical waiter you like real Chinese food", prepare for a "great-tasting variety of flavors" at this Outer Richmond dishing out the likes of "melt-in-your-mouth pork belly" and "delightful" deep-fried pumpkin among the "wide variety of classic and exotic" dishes; yes, it's located "way out" in a simple setting, but cognoscenti contend it's "really worth" the trip, as they "aim to heartily feed and please" at "stunningly low prices."

Hamano Sushi *Japanese* — 20 | 11 | 17 | $36

Noe Valley | 1332 Castro St. (bet. Jersey & 24th Sts.) | 415-826-0825 | www.hamanosushi.com

"Simple, fresh", "honest sushi", "excellent" sashimi and "perfectly made" tempura draw locals to this "dependable" Noe Valley Japanese where neither the prices nor the decor are lavish; true, service can range from "cheerful to indifferent", but the "outstanding fish quality" keeps it a "convenient" "neighborhood favorite."

Hapa Ramen ☒Ⓜ⌗ *Japanese/Noodle Shop* — 20 | 16 | 20 | $11

Location varies; see website | 925-212-3289 | www.haparamensf.com

Chef Richie Nakano (ex Nopa) slow simmers broth that sends fanatics "over the moon" at his ramen stand doling out "filling" bowls of "handmade noodles" and "market veggies" plus "random bits of happiness" like a "sous-vide egg" on top; not everyone's convinced it's "worth the price tag" or "15 minutes in line" when it's open (Tuesdays and Thursdays at the Ferry Building and Fridays at OTG in Fort Mason) but most agree it hits the spot "on cold days."

Hard Knox Cafe *Southern* — 20 | 14 | 18 | $21

Dogpatch | 2526 Third St. (bet. 22nd & 23rd Sts.) | 415-648-3770
Outer Richmond | 2448 Clement St. (bet. 25th & 26th Aves.) | 415-752-3770
www.hardknoxcafe.com

"Just plain good at what it does" – which is "generous portions" of "ribsticking" soul food, like "amazing fried chicken" that's "as tender as a marshmallow during a heat wave" – this "reasonably priced" pair is "a no-brainer" for denizens of Dogpatch and the Outer Richmond; it may be "more hip" "than authentic", but the "friendly staff" and "quirky", "kitschy" setting exude "down-home" "Southern charm."

Harris' *Steak* | 26 | 24 | 25 | $70

Polk Gulch | 2100 Van Ness Ave. (Pacific Ave.) | 415-673-1888 | www.harrisrestaurant.com

"Go hungry, very hungry" to this "classic", "old-school" steakhouse in Polk Gulch that "exceeds expectations" with beef "aged to perfection" and enhanced by "cold martinis" and an "amazing wine list"; sure, you may need your "corporate card" to cover the tab, but the experience provides all the "traditional trappings", from "impeccable service" to "dark wood, plush fabrics" and live "mellow jazz" in the lounge.

Hayes Street Grill *Seafood* | 23 | 17 | 23 | $49

Hayes Valley | 320 Hayes St. (bet. Franklin & Gough Sts.) | 415-863-5545 | www.hayesstreetgrill.com

"Packed to the gunwales before curtain time", this Hayes Valley "stalwart" draws a "pre-performance" crowd, who count on the "professional servers" to get them to their seats "for the first note"; known for its "simply prepared" "super-fresh" sustainable seafood and "fantastic french fries", it's a "reliable" spot for a "sophisticated" evening in an "old-school" setting, and if a handful huffs it's "a little boring", most are thankful it "never changes"; P.S. the post–7:30 PM prix fixe is "a steal."

Heart *Eclectic* | ∇ 19 | 18 | 18 | $29

Mission | 1270 Valencia St. (24th St.) | 415-285-1200 | www.heartsf.com

"Mostly a wine bar"/art gallery, this Mission spot in a "modern, narrow space" serves its "carefully curated" list of sippers in "rustic and charming" "mason jars", befitting the "anti-establishment–type" selection of bottles and glasses; the staff is "knowledgeable", and while the menu of Eclectic small plates is "limited", it's "surprisingly good."

Heaven's Dog ❷ *Chinese* | 20 | 19 | 19 | $40

SoMa | 1148 Mission St. (bet. 7th & 8th Sts.) | 415-863-6008 | www.heavensdog.com

"Bow wow" bark Charles Phan fans who overlook the somewhat "iffy" location of his "SoMa grand" Chinese, focusing instead on the "delightful" small plates and "amazing cocktails" served in this "way-too-cool" "loungey setting" with an adjacent noodle bar; there are a few growls about "pricey" tabs, but it's "open late" and is "easier to get into than its sibling" (the Slanted Door), and a good option before "hitting the clubs or theater."

NEW Hecho 🈺 *Japanese* | – | – | – | M

Downtown | 185 Sutter St. (Kearny St.) | 415-835-6400 | www.hechosf.com

Just the kind of mash-up you'd expect when a tequila-lovin' Italian-American restaurateur opens a sushi restaurant, this Downtown Japanese arrival – masterminded by chef Joseph Manzare (Globe, Tres, Zuppa) – offers authentic Tokyo-style sushi and robata grilled fare alongside an extensive menu of small-batch tequila and seasonal sakes; the 120-seat, bi-level space features a street-level sushi bar and lounge, juxtaposing cultural elements such as Mexican-style Shaker wood tables paired with chairs that resemble Japanese bathing stools.

Heirloom Café ☒ *Californian/Mediterranean* | 23 | 18 | 22 | $47 |

Mission | 2500 Folsom St. (21st St.) | 415-821-2500 | www.heirloom-sf.com
Like its "amazing reserve wine list", this oenocentric yearling run by a "passionate young proprietor"/sommelier is "getting better with age", offering "wonderfully textured" "high-quality Californian"-Med cuisine (including numerous cheeses "of the stinky, strong variety"), served with "fresh, lively energy"; the "deafening sound level detracts from the experience", but overall it "feels like the Mission is a million miles away" at this "sweet" spot.

Helmand Palace *Afghan* | 22 | 15 | 19 | $32 |

Russian Hill | 2424 Van Ness Ave. (bet. Green & Union Sts.) | 415-362-0641 | www.helmandpalace.com
Adventurers eager to "step out of the ordinary rotation" of cuisine choices suggest this Afghan eatery, where the "wonderful pumpkin" and "inexpensive" lamb dishes "redolent of" "spices" might even "stop the war" in the Middle East; the "warm atmosphere" and "attentive service" make it "hard to leave" according to Russian Hill regulars, who "could eat their food forever."

Henry's Hunan *Chinese* | 21 | 8 | 16 | $21 |

Chinatown | 924 Sansome St. (bet. B'way & Vallejo St.) | 415-956-7727
Downtown | 674 Sacramento St. (Spring St.) | 415-788-2234 ☒
Noe Valley | 1708 Church St. (bet. Day & 29th Sts.) | 415-826-9189
SoMa | 1016 Bryant St. (bet. 8th & 9th Sts.) | 415-861-5808 ☒
SoMa | 110 Natoma St. (bet. New Montgomery & 2nd Sts.) | 415-546-4999 ☒
www.henryshunanrestaurant.com
The "smoky, spicy goodness" dished out at this Sino chainlet is "no ordinary Chinese takeout" but rather is served in "mountains" of "tasty authentic Hunan" fare filled with "fresh" ingredients in dishes such as the "famous" "Diana's special meat pie"; service varies and you can "forget atmosphere", but devotees "can't forget the food" and the tab "doesn't hurt" either.

Herbivore *Vegan* | 17 | 13 | 16 | $21 |

Mission | 983 Valencia St. (bet. Liberty & 21st Sts.) | 415-826-5657
Western Addition | 531 Divisadero St. (bet. Fell & Hayes Sts.) | 415-885-7133
www.herbivorerestaurant.com
There's "fake meat so good it makes vegans uncomfortable" at this trio in the Mission, Western Addition and Berkeley offering "much variety" in "flavorful" "veggie choices" such as "tofu scrambles" and other "affordable" "guilt-free" grub; service could be "a bit more attentive" and the utilitarian settings can be "noisy", but on the plus side, there's "outdoor seating."

Hillstone *American* | 22 | 23 | 24 | $41 |

Embarcadero | 1800 Montgomery St. (bet. Bay & Chestnut Sts.) | 415-392-9280 | www.hillstone.com
"Don't be turned off by its chain status" because this Embarcadero link of a national franchise is a "reliable standby" with staffers that "bend over backward to please" while delivering "consistent high-quality" American fare including a "rack of ribs", "absolutely delicious" burgers" and desserts to "save room for"; the "casual" setting is "great-looking", and if the bill's just "a bit pricey", it "comes promptly."

	FOOD	DECOR	SERVICE	COST

NEW Hodo Soy Beanery Kiosk *Vegan*

| | - | - | - | I |

Embarcadero | Ferry Building | 1 Ferry Bldg. (Embarcadero) |
415-983-8030 | www.hodosoy.com

Tofu goes beyond the stir-fry at this take-out kiosk set in San Francisco's
Ferry Building, where it's featured in freshly made vegan breakfast and
lunch items such as smoothies, salads, sandwiches and desserts; the
affordable fare is made with the artisanal, organic goods of the
Oakland-based Hodo Soy Beanery and available to-go only, but noshers can tote their spoils outside and enjoy them on the market hall's
waterfront patio; P.S. closes at market hours.

Hog & Rocks ● *American*

| | 21 | 19 | 21 | $38 |

Mission | 3431 19th St. (San Carlos St.) | 415-550-8627 |
www.hogandrocks.com

"Varied and delicious" "oysters and pig products" are featured at this
"Mission hangout" (from the Maverick and Tres guys), a "sociable
place" to ham it up, sharing "lots of small plates" at communal tables
while watching "the action on the street"; the rest of the American
fare "does not live up to the chef's reputation" – "clearly, their name
indicates what they're best at" – but a "friendly staff" and "hopping
bar scene keep this place packed from brunch to closing"; P.S. a quick-
service BBQ offshoot across the street is slated for winter 2011.

Z Hog Island Oyster Co. & Bar *Seafood*

| | 25 | 17 | 20 | $35 |

Embarcadero | Ferry Bldg. Mktpl. | 1 Ferry Bldg. (The Embarcadero) |
415-391-7117 | www.hogislandoysters.com

"Sure, it's touristy", but "the world really is your oyster" when you're
sitting "on the deck" of this Embarcadero eatery, "slurping down" "tiny
critters" – "shucked with a smile" – and "fabulous and atypical clam
chowder", all "washed down with a local brew"; so while it gets "im-
possibly crowded and noisy", squeeze in for half-price "happy hour
and you'll be happy as a clam"; P.S. there's a Napa offshoot that's
missing only the "fantastic Bay views."

Hong Kong Lounge *Chinese*

| | 20 | 14 | 16 | $29 |

Outer Richmond | 5322 Geary Blvd. (bet. 17th & 18th Aves.) |
415-668-8836

A "favorite" dumpling destination of Outer Richmond residents, who
form "lines out the door" for "excellent made-to-order dim sum", this
"crowded" Cantonese can also be counted on for "delicious" "family-
style" meals; Anglophones advise inviting "a Chinese friend to trans-
late the menu" since service can be "spotty", but boosters say all you
really need to bring is "your appetite", since the "big servings" come
at "bargain" prices.

Hotei *Japanese*

| | 19 | 14 | 17 | $21 |

Inner Sunset | 1290 Ninth Ave. (Lincoln Way) | 415-753-6045 |
www.hoteisf.com

"On a cold, wet winter day" the "soup and slurpy noodles have healing
powers" at this "casual" Japanese shop where "ramen is king" and
"delicious sushi" from sister restaurant Ebisu "across the street" is
also served; the "cramped" room might feel "a little down at the
heels", but service is "fast" and the "bargain" bites "won't hurt your
wallet", so customers leave "warm and contented."

House, The *Asian* | 26 | 15 | 21 | $43 |

North Beach | 1230 Grant Ave. (bet. Columbus Ave. & Vallejo St.) | 415-986-8612 | www.thehse.com

"Superb", "sophisticated" Asian fusion fare, like "divine" miso-marinated cod, "never disappoints" at this North Beach "jewel" with a "skillful" staff; wedging yourself into the "minimalist shoebox" is "like squeezing into somebody's living room" carp claustrophobes, and it's "quite loud" at dinner, but that doesn't "really matter", because "the quality of the food far exceeds" any "inconvenience", and "prices are very reasonable" to boot.

House of Nanking *Chinese* | 21 | 8 | 12 | $23 |

Chinatown | 919 Kearny St. (Columbus Ave.) | 415-421-1429

"Prepare to take orders" (instead of "the other way round") at this Chinatown "dive", where the famously "bossy" staff will "tell you what" to eat; it's all "part of the experience", along with sitting "shoulder to shoulder next to strangers" in this "utilitarian" "hole-in-the-wall", but the "fresh", "flavorful" fare – from "porkalicious" potstickers to other "cheap" "Chinese" chow – is something "special" say supporters, adding that lines that "wrap around the block" "tell the story."

☑ House of Prime Rib *American* | 25 | 20 | 23 | $52 |

Polk Gulch | 1906 Van Ness Ave. (Washington St.) | 415-885-4605 | www.houseofprimerib.net

"If prime rib is your thing", you'll have to be "rolled out" of this Polk Gulch "throwback", where "huge slabs" of the eponymous dish are "served with a flourish" from "stainless-steel" carts (aka the beloved "meat blimps") that "glide around" the "cozy", "dark-wood dining area"; no, it's "not cutting-edge", but "old-school" waiters contribute to the "clubby" vibe, and "perfectly" prepared (and "quite debilitating") martinis help deliver a "big bang for the buck."

HRD Coffee Shop ☑🍴 *Diner/Korean* | ▽ 20 | 5 | 18 | $10 |

SoMa | 521 Third St. (bet. Bayshore Fwy. & Brannan St.) | 415-543-2355 | www.hrdcoffeeshop.com

"The secret is out" about this SoMa "greasy spoon" where "Korean BBQ meets American diner and the result is fantastic" in "cheap, spicy and delicious" "fusion" dishes like a "kimchi burrito and Mongolian cheesesteak"; it also serves "breakfast and lunch", and while the place "looks like a dive from the outside", an "outstanding" staff and "monster portions at ridiculously low prices" make up for that.

Hunan Home's | 22 | 12 | 17 | $26 |
Restaurant *Chinese*

Chinatown | 622 Jackson St. (bet. Grant Ave. & Kearny St.) | 415-982-2844 | www.hunanhomes.com

The "broad" menu ranges from "top-notch" "Chinese-American" chow to "authentic" "hot and hotter" Hunan fare ("peppery enough to make sweat bead on your forehead") at this "reliable" Chinatown-based chainlet with branches in Palo Alto and Los Altos; a "super-efficient staff" and "fair" prices for the "large portions" make it a "staple" for Sinophiles, even if the "minimalist decor" means most "get in, get fed" and "get out."

Hyde Street Bistro   French

21 | 18 | 21 | $43

Russian Hill | 1521 Hyde St. (bet. Jackson St. & Pacific Ave.) | 415-292-4415 | www.hydestreetbistrosf.com

Whether as a "great date spot" or for "casual, local dining", this "cozy neighborhood" Russian Hill bistro "on the Hyde Street cable car" line is a "dependable" choice, proffering "authentic", "basic French" fare including an "outstanding" cassoulet and "fresh seafood" ferried by an "attentive" staff in "cute" (if "tiny") digs; though drivers bemoan "endless circling" "to find parking", budget-watchers dub the tabs "reasonable" "for SF."

NEW Ichi Sushi ⌀ Japanese

∇ 23 | 13 | 21 | $39

Bernal Heights | 3369 Mission St. (Godeus St.) | 415-525-4750 | www.ichisushi.com

Afishionados "kinda don't want to tell outsiders" about this Bernal Heights "tiny neighborhood gem" serving "lovely sushi" and Japanese "sous vide dishes" in an unpretentious, "so not-trendy" atmosphere; a "super-knowledgeable" staff and moderate prices add to the appeal.

Ike's Place   Sandwiches

24 | 7 | 14 | $13

NEW Castro | 3489 16th St. (Sanchez St.) | 415-553-6888 | www.ilikeikesplace.com

"The lines and the sandwiches are both epic" at this "cult" sub shop with a "new location" in the Castro (with takeaway offshoots at Stanford and in Redwood Shores), hawking hot, "heart attack–inducing" "heaven on rolls"; dissenters huff it's "a lot of hullabaloo", wondering why "shell out double digits" "only to end up having to sit on the street just to eat", but those who like Ike argue the "combinations will blow your mind" and "leave you licking your fingers after you're done."

Il Cane Rosso   Italian

23 | 11 | 15 | $22

Embarcadero | Ferry Bldg. Mktpl. | 1 Ferry Bldg. (The Embarcadero) | 415-391-7599 | www.canerossosf.com

For a "lip-smacking meal on the run", "thank your lucky stars" for this "tiny" "walk-up" sandwich shop and rotisserie on the waterfront in the Ferry Building, now solely run by former Delfina chef Lauren Kiino; "there's no decor" or service, and you'll have to "fight for a table", but you get "the quality of fine dining without the price or hassles", plus a "knockout" sight of the Bay – "the cheapest view in SF."

Il Fornaio   Italian

20 | 20 | 20 | $39

Downtown | Levi's Plaza | 1265 Battery St. (bet. Filbert & Greenwich Sts.) | 415-986-0100 | www.ilfornaio.com

"Heavenly" breads and "reliable pastas" typify the "simple, authentic Italian cooking" at this "tried-and-true" chain where "monthly specials roam all over" the country "introducing diners to regional specialties"; a "comfortable", "lively" setting and "efficient" service complete the package, which provides a "pleasant experience" "without breaking the bank."

Imperial Tea Court   Tearoom

19 | 20 | 19 | $23

Embarcadero | Ferry Bldg. Mktpl. | 1 Ferry Bldg. (The Embarcadero) | 415-544-9830 | www.imperialtea.com

Leaf lovers "relax with exotic teas" as they escape the "chaos of the Ferry Building" at this San Francisco tearoom that "makes you feel transported to China", while at the Berkeley branch, they slurp "soothing" "hand-pulled noodles" in quarters "nestled in the upper level of the Epicurious Garden"; partisans praise the "intellectual presentation" and "traditional" pouring offered "with a sweet smile", but caution "because everything is made to order it can be slow."

Incanto *Italian* | 25 | 21 | 23 | $52 |

Noe Valley | 1550 Church St. (Duncan St.) | 415-641-4500 | www.incanto.biz

Chris Cosentino's "edgy", "Dante-themed" "star of Noe Valley" "rocks" the world of "truly adventurous" foodies with a "wild ride" of "exotic offal offerings" spotlighting "animal parts normally thrown away", while keeping the more "faint of heart" "enchanted" with "outstanding pastas", "amazing" charcuterie and other "innovative, high-quality, sophisticated Italian fare"; a "beautiful setting", "intriguing" "regional" wines and "gracious service" complete an experience that's expensive, but leaves most "thoroughly satisfied."

Indian Oven *Indian* | 22 | 17 | 19 | $32 |

Lower Haight | 233 Fillmore St. (bet. Haight & Waller Sts.) | 415-626-1628 | www.indianovensf.com

The "flavorful feast" offered at this midpriced Lower Haight Indian is the "real deal", featuring "consistently good" curries and other "authentic" subcontinental staples; but if you want to grab a seat in the "delightfully casual", "quaint" spot, better "go early", because it "gets crowded fast."

Indigo Ⓜ *American* | 20 | 18 | 20 | $49 |

Civic Center | 687 McAllister St. (Gough St.) | 415-673-9353 | www.indigorestaurant.com

"Ultraconvenient" "before or after" "the ballet or symphony", this "attractive" cobalt-colored Civic Center stop is a "favorite" for "reliable" New American fare with "lots of special touches"; if some sulk it's "solid but a bit boring", the majority appreciates the "professional", "well-paced" service and "reasonable prices", especially for the "outstanding" early-bird prix fixe menu.

◪ In-N-Out Burger ◗ *Burgers* | 21 | 10 | 18 | $9 |

Fisherman's Wharf | 333 Jefferson St. (bet. Jones & Leavenworth Sts.) | 800-786-1000 | www.in-n-out.com

"Double-double, animal-style . . . definitely learn the off-menu terms" to optimize your "fast-food fix" at this "addictive" "iconic California" chain flipping "one of the best burgers around" (and it's "a bargain too"); the "fresh, fresh" patties, "thick shakes" and fries are "presented by the most courteous staff" amid "throwback" decor, but these "cult" "favorites" are "crowded at all hours", so you're "not in and out very fast."

Ironside *Eclectic* | ▽ 17 | 18 | 16 | $29 |

South Beach | Chronicle Books Bldg. | 680 Second St. (bet. Brannan & Townsend Sts.) | 415-896-1127 | www.ironsidesf.com

"Striking a balance between casual and artisanal", this "lively" South Beach Eclectic offers a "funky menu" of "decent" morning fare and "solidly delicious" sandwiches, pizzas and plates the rest of the day in a "rustic", "two-level" space "with cool exposed wood and brick"; some say it's "priced fairly" while others counter "holy schmoly", it's "expensive" for the neighborhood.

Isa *French* 26 | 20 | 22 | $46

Marina | 3324 Steiner St. (bet. Chestnut & Lombard Sts.) | 415-567-9588 | www.isarestaurant.com

There's "flavor bursting from every mouthful" of the "unique" "French-style small plates" at this Marina "favorite" that ups the ante with "wines you don't find elsewhere" all for a "bargain" (the prix fixe is an especially "great deal"); a staff that "makes you feel genuinely welcome" fuels the "festive atmosphere" making it a "delicious experience" for "groups", "a date" or a "special occasion", especially in the "tented back area."

Isobune *Japanese* 19 | 14 | 16 | $30

Japantown | Japan Ctr. | 1737 Post St. (Webster St.) | 415-563-1030 | www.isobunesushi.com

Set sail "early enough to get a seat around the moat" at this Japantown joint and its Burlingame branch, because it's "great fin fun" to watch the countertop "boats go by" and fish off your "favorite sushi"; if a few anglers ask "how long has that piece has been circling?" (and advise you to "ask for something you don't see"), at least it's "not expensive", and the "no-frills service" can't sink the experience, which is "especially pleasant for solo dining" or a meal "with the kids."

Izakaya Sozai Ⓜ *Japanese* 22 | 16 | 18 | $32

Inner Sunset | 1500 Irving St. (16th Ave.) | 415-742-5122 | www.izakayasozai.com

Enterprising eaters eager to "explore Japanese food beyond sushi" enjoy this "amazing" izakaya in the Inner Sunset, which specializes in "to-die-for" egg noodles nestled in a "slowly cooked" broth; bring friends "so you can taste everything" on the "creative" menu of "small plates" and share a bottle from the "tempting" "sake selection", but "come early" or expect to wait, because the "tiny" "wood-themed" space "fills fast" with "local ramen junkies."

Izzy's Steaks & Chops *Steak* 20 | 17 | 19 | $43

Marina | 3345 Steiner St. (bet. Chestnut & Lombard Sts.) | 415-563-0487 | www.izzyssteaks.com

"Carnivores" "won't leave hungry" thanks to the "generous portions" of "well-prepared" "cuts of meat" and "fantastic sides" at this "dependable steakhouse" trio in the Marina and the suburbs; "prices are better than many" with such "old-time" atmosphere, and service is "professional", so while some find it "less-than-stellar", devotees decree it "delivers."

Jackson Fillmore Trattoria Ⓜ *Italian* 21 | 13 | 19 | $39

Upper Fillmore | 2506 Fillmore St. (Jackson St.) | 415-346-5288 | www.jacksonfillmoresf.com

"Large portions" of "garlicky Italian soul food" and a "wide wine selection" are "a great deal" at this "lively neighborhood trattoria" in the Upper Fillmore; it's notably "noisy" and the "decor needs some sprucing up" (critics quip that once "hip", it now "needs a hip replacement"); but most maintain that the "superb pastas" and "jovial atmosphere make up for it."

Jai Yun *Chinese* ▽ 26 | 8 | 16 | $65

Chinatown | 680 Clay St. (Kearny St.) | 415-981-7438

"The one-man wonder that is chef Nei" turns out "exquisite small plates" of "haute Chinese cuisine" "that delight the eyes as well as the taste buds" at this Chinatown "hole-in-the-wall"; true, "he needs to update decor and service", and you'll "need a guide" as "very little English is spoken" and "the rules are impossible to know" (basically, there are "three different" set-priced options at lunch and dinner); but all's forgiven, given the "fantastic" fare.

Jake's Steaks *Cheesesteaks*   ▽ 19 | 10 | 15 | $15

Marina | 3301 Buchanan St. (bet. Lombard & Magnolia Sts.) | 415-922-2211 | www.jakessteaks.net

When "you just gotta have a cheesesteak", the "crowds of Eagles fans spilling out the door" signal that this Marina joint is the "real deal", serving up "awesome" sandwiches on "Amaroso rolls", "waffle fries" and even "Tasty Cakes" flown "in from Philly"; the "menu could be a little bigger" as could the "small" casual digs, but it's "the closest thing" to "Pat's" or "Geno's" around.

NEW Jane *Bakery/Coffeehouse*   - | - | - | I

Upper Fillmore | 2123 Fillmore St. (California St.) | 415-931-5263 | www.janeonfillmore.com

With its snazzy black-and-white interior, lined with tufted black benches and high bar tables for its WiFi-appreciating habitués, this stylish new Upper Fillmore cafe (open until 6 PM daily) could easily be mistaken for one of the luxury housewares shops in the 'hood, but it's actually a next-generation coffeehouse; expect single-origin Four Barrel espressos and organic teas, along with made-from-scratch midday fare including soups, salads, sandwiches and pastries.

❷ Jardinière *Californian/French*   26 | 26 | 25 | $74

Civic Center | 300 Grove St. (Franklin St.) | 415-861-5555 | www.jardiniere.com

"No opera is complete without dinner" "before the curtain" at Traci Des Jardins' "classy" "glitterati" "hangout" located just "a minute" from Civic Center, where "exquisite", "seasonal" "nouvelle" Cal-French fare and a "wow"-inducing "retro-ish" two-tier "supper-club" design combine to "create magic" nightly; "smooth-as-silk" staffers (including "sommeliers who know everything") finesse "the rush", and regulars "love returning" for "bargain" "Monday night prix fixes" or to "sip champagne" at the "beautiful" "round bar."

NEW Jasper's Corner   - | - | - | M
Tap & Kitchen 🅂🅼 *American*

Downtown | Serrano Hotel | 401 Taylor St. (O'Farrell St.) | 415-775-7979 | www.jasperscornertap.com

Poised to be the city's hot new watering hole, this Downtown gastropub adjacent to the Serrano Hotel (in the former Ponzu space) hawks midpriced San Francisco–style tavern fare gussied-up with local ingredients from breakfast through late night; but its raison d'être is its bar program offering beer (on draft and bottles) and handcrafted cocktails by startender Kevin Diedrich (ex Burritt Room), served in the large bi-level dining room and the front bar/lounge filled with TVs.

Jay's Cheesesteak *Cheesesteaks*   17 | 7 | 15 | $11

Mission | 3285 21st St. (bet. Lexington & Valencia Sts.) | 415-285-5200 ⊘

(continued)

Jay's Cheesesteak

Western Addition | 553 Divisadero St. (bet. Fell & Hayes Sts.) | 415-771-5104

www.jayscheesesteak.com

Serving "greasy but ever so tasty" sandwiches that are "as close to a Philly cheesesteak as you can get in SF", these fast-food eateries in the Mission and Western Addition "fill" the "void" when you can't make it back East; lighting that "reminds" some of "elementary school" can be "jarring", but "damn good burgers" provide a "quick" bite, and "vegetarians in search of a junk-food fix" are satisfied by "seitan steak" subs and "fabulous fries."

Joe's Cable Car *Burgers* | 19 | 15 | 15 | $18 |

Excelsior | 4320 Mission St. (bet. Silver Ave. & Tingley St.) | 415-334-6699 | www.joescablecar.com

The "smiling" owner "takes a lot of pride in his work", as evidenced by the fact that the beef that goes into his "juicy" patties is "ground in the front window" of this "quirky" cable car replica in the Excelsior ("you don't see that at McDonald's"); the result is the "best-quality burger you can sink your incisors into", served with "fantastic shakes" and fries, but penny-pinchers are put off by the relatively "exorbitant" tab.

NEW Jones ◐ *Californian/French* | - | - | - | M |

Tenderloin | 620 Jones St. (Geary St.) | 415-496-6858 | www.620-jones.com

Urbanites jonesing for a hot new spot are flocking to this French-Californian in the Tenderloin offering midpriced fare (including $5 happy-hour plates) from Ola Fendert (Oola's); the trendy digs feature three bars – two inside and one on a sprawling heated rooftop patio – which draw late-night diners and drinkers and a Sunday brunch bunch.

Juban *Japanese* | 18 | 13 | 16 | $35 |

Japantown | Kinokuniya Bldg. | 1581 Webster St. (Post St.) | 415-776-5822 | www.jubanrestaurant.com

In-table hibachis allow adults and "children" alike to have "great fun" grilling an "outstanding" selection of "delicious" meats marinated in "tasty" sauces at this Japanese trio in J-town, Burlingame and Menlo Park; where else can you "enjoy a BBQ while sitting cozily inside" other than these "friendly" and "casual" "do-it-yourself" *yakinuki* joints ask enthusiasts; still, a frugal few fuss "it seems like a lot of money to pay to cook your own food."

Just Wonton Ⓜ *Chinese* | ▽ 17 | 5 | 13 | $19 |

Outer Sunset | 1241 Vicente St. (bet. 23rd & 24th Aves.) | 415-681-2999

"Stick to anything with a won ton wrapper and you can't go wrong" at this bargain-basement Outer Sunset Chinese known for its dumplings; "huge plates of rice or noodles" and other "lunch specials" that "go beyond" the titular item are "good too", while the no-frills setting feels distinctly like a "fast-food" joint.

Kabuto Ⓜ *Japanese* | 25 | 12 | 18 | $47 |

Outer Richmond | 5121 Geary Blvd. (bet. 15th & 16th Aves.) | 415-752-5652 | www.kabutosushi.com

"Ridiculously good sushi" made from "fresher-than-fresh fish" takes Japanese fare "to another level" at this "pricey" Outer Richmonder with a "family feel"; sure, the "cramped" setting is "simple" and service can be "slow" ("get here early" to avoid "a long line"), but you can "always count on the chef" for "creative" combos and "imaginative" rolls.

Kappou Gomi M *Japanese*   ▽ 28 | 17 | 25 | $51

Outer Richmond | 5524 Geary Blvd. (20th Ave.) | 415-221-5353

"One of the most authentic Japanese restaurants in the city" (let alone the Outer Richmond), this "quiet" little izakaya is run by "wonderful people"; as the sign in the window announces, it's "not a sushi restaurant" – though "they do serve sashimi" – but rather showcases "real home cooking from Japan" on an "overwhelming" menu with over "200 items to choose from"; divided by ingredient and preparation, the dishes are artistically plated and "simply delicious."

Kasa Indian Eatery *Indian*   18 | 12 | 18 | $15

Castro | 4001 18th St. (Noe St.) | 415-621-6940 | www.kasaindian.com

"Quick", "simple" and "inexpensive" eats draw Castrolites to this Indian "at all hours" for "filling" "kati rolls" and "full Thali" dinners; downsides are "long lines" and "limited" seating, but a "charming staff" and emphasis on "healthy" local ingredients make it an "alternative to fast food"; P.S. the Marina offshoot has closed but their new Kati Roller truck participates in Off the Grid events – check offthegridsf.com for details.

Katana-Ya ● *Japanese*   22 | 10 | 15 | $18

Downtown | 430 Geary St. (bet. Mason & Taylor Sts.) | 415-771-1280

"Riding the wave of the ramen fad that's spreading around town", this "hole-in-the-wall" Downtown Japanese is "always packed" with tourists, students, after-work and "before theater" types, slurping "warm bowls" of "super-chewy" noodles in a variety of "killer broths" (along with "terrific sushi") that it "could easily charge twice as much" for; while the lines are "ridiculous", it's one of "the best places" to have your *Tampopo* moment, and "open late" to boot.

Kate's Kitchen ⊅ *Southern*   ▽ 21 | 13 | 17 | $21

Lower Haight | 471 Haight St. (bet. Fillmore & Webster Sts.) | 415-626-3984

"The love is transparent in the food" at this "funky" Lower Haight "temple" to "solid" Southern breakfasts and lunches, like "rocket fuel" coffee, "amazing" pancakes and flannel hash that "will power you through your Sunday"; "waiting in line" is de rigueur on weekends, but the "heartwarming" service makes you "feel like you are at your in-laws" for brunch, and most maintain you'll "have a better day for having stopped" here; P.S. cash only.

Katia's Russian Tea Room M *Russian*   ▽ 20 | 16 | 21 | $29

Inner Richmond | 600 Fifth Ave. (Balboa St.) | 415-668-9292 | www.katias.com

Chef-owner Katia "makes everyone into a friend" within "minutes of arriving" at this "charming" roost in the Inner Richmond where the "live accordion player" on Saturday nights is "great fun"; "fantastic Russian specialties", like "borscht, pierogi, beef stroganoff" and more, remind Muscovites of "grandmother's cooking", and "the price is right" too; P.S. you need "advance reservations" for their formal tea service, so plan ahead.

Khan Toke Thai House *Thai*

▽ 21 | 23 | 21 | $33

Outer Richmond | 5937 Geary Blvd. (bet. 23rd & 24th Aves.) | 415-668-6654

"Wear good socks" recommend regulars of this affordable Siamese spot, because you'll "check your shoes at the door" before being seated "on the ground" with your legs dangling in "a sunken area under the table"; the "fun" setup and "lovely interior" make the "excellent", "authentic" Bangkok bites that much better, and the "helpful" "Thai hospitality" explains why it's a "favorite" of Outer Richmond residents.

NEW Ki ⊠ *Japanese*

- | - | - | M

SoMa | 540 Howard St. (bet. 1st & 2nd Sts.) | 415-278-0495 |
www.ki-sushisf.com

The wave of izakayas sweeping the San Francisco dining scene shows no signs of abating as evidenced by the debut of this edgy new Japanese at Temple Nightclub; the brainchild of sustainability guru Casson Trenor (Tataki) and Paul Hemming (Zen Compound), it offers responsibly sourced sushi, yakitori and other small plates in an über-modern setting replete with color-changing LED screens and oversized graffiti art.

Kiji Sushi Bar & Cuisine ⊠ *Japanese*

▽ 25 | 21 | 23 | $40

Mission | 1009 Guerrero St. (22nd St.) | 415-282-0400 |
www.kijirestaurant.com

Arguably the "best-kept sushi secret in the city", this Japanese "tucked away" in the Mission quietly proffers a "terrific", "growing list of wild and sustainable fish", along with a "first-rate sake selection"; factor in a "helpful" staff, and a "great vibe", both at the bar and in the dining room comprised of "intimate" alcoves, and you can see why this "small" storefront is a "go-to" for devotees.

King of Thai *Thai*

19 | 9 | 15 | $16

Downtown | 184 O'Farrell St. (bet. Powell & Stockton Sts.) | 415-677-9991 ☽
Inner Richmond | 346 Clement St. (bet. 4th & 5th Aves.) |
415-831-9953 ☽⇟
Inner Richmond | 639 Clement St. (bet. 7th & 8th Aves.) |
415-752-5198 ☽⇟
North Beach | 1268 Grant Ave. (bet. Fresno & Vallejo Sts.) |
415-391-8219 | www.kingofthainoodlehouse.com ☽
Outer Sunset | 1507 Sloat Blvd. (bet. Everglade & Springfield Drs.) |
415-566-9921 ⇟
Outer Sunset | 1541 Taraval St. (bet. 25th & 26th Aves.) | 415-682-9958 ☽

"Hungry crowds" crown this "convenient" Siamese sextet "king of cheap eats", since the "dependable" Thai fare ("filling", "flavorful noodles" and "stir-fries to fit every palate") is proffered for "terrific" prices; they feature "no frills" to speak of, but the "efficient" staff serves you "in a blink of an eye", and "super-late" hours (until at least 1 AM nightly) satisfy clubbers who crave a "drunken" "midnight dinner"; P.S. the Sloat outpost closes earlier, at 10:30 PM.

☒ Kiss Seafood ⊠Ⓜ *Japanese*

28 | 15 | 25 | $74

Japantown | 1700 Laguna St. (Sutter St.) | 415-474-2866

"You won't find chicken teriyaki" or "Americanized sushi" at this "superstar in Japantown", just "the chef and his wife" proffering "fantastic omakase" dinners comprised of the "freshest fish" and "amazingly

FOOD DECOR SERVICE COST

subtle" "non-sushi items" in a reverent "tea ceremony style"; as it "seats only about a dozen people", calling it "intimate" is an understatement, but the owners are "so 'kawaii' (cute) you just want to hug them" and the "extraordinary" meals are "worth every penny."

Kitchenette SF ☒⼝ *Sandwiches* | 24 | 15 | 21 | $13 |

Dogpatch | American Industrial Ctr. | 958 Illinois St. (bet. 20th & 22nd Sts.) | No phone | www.kitchenettesf.com

For a "fresh" and "delicious" weekday lunch of "tasty sandwiches" and a few other "excellent" American sides at "decent prices", Dogpatch denizens descend on this "loading dock" staffed by "nice" folks; "you don't go for the decor" – it's "definitely a grab-and-go kind of place" – but those who tote their takeout to a "nearby" park for a "quick picnic" are repaid with a "happy belly."

Koh Samui & The Monkey *Thai* | 20 | 20 | 19 | $31 |

SoMa | 415 Brannan St. (bet. Ritch & 3rd Sts.) | 415-369-0007 | www.kohsamuiandthemonkey.com

Another Monkey *Thai*

Mission | 280 Valencia St. (14th St.) | 415-241-0288 | www.anothermonkeythai.com

There are "flashes of delight" at this upscale SoMa Thai and its "attractive" younger Mission sister, which dish out "generous" portions of "colorful and lively" midpriced fare including a "standout" pumpkin curry; sometimes "slow" service is nonetheless "friendly", and "excellent" "happy-hour bargains" and "monkey-themed cocktails" make for a "great date night" or "after-work gathering."

☒ Kokkari Estiatorio *Greek* | 27 | 26 | 25 | $57 |

Downtown | 200 Jackson St. (bet. Battery & Front Sts.) | 415-981-0983 | www.kokkari.com

Fans muse that "if Odysseus" had made "his first stop" this "upscale" Greek estiatorio, "his travels" would surely have ended here among Downtown's "power-lunchers" and "luminaries" with their "limos" all "lined up outside", dining on "phenomenal", "rustic" yet "refined" meze and roasted meats from a "fireplace" spit that lends a "warm ambiance" to the "beautiful" rooms; "servers know their stuff and do their best to please" and the bar's a "lively" scene, proving that "after all these years", it's still "amazing all-around."

☒ Koo Ⓜ *Asian* | 27 | 17 | 20 | $38 |

Inner Sunset | 408 Irving St. (bet. 5th & 6th Aves.) | 415-731-7077 | www.sushikoo.com

"Fantastic", "inventive rolls" and "other wonderful", "refined" Asian fusion creations are "made with care" and "served up cheerfully" at this "peaceful" two-room Inner Sunset storefront "on the N-Judah line"; "to-die-for" dishes like the Spoonful of Happiness (uni, quail egg, tobiko ponzu and ankimo served with a sake shot) rate koo-dos, and the "reasonably priced" fare allows you to "stuff your face during happy hour."

Kuleto's *Italian* | 21 | 20 | 20 | $47 |

Downtown | Villa Florence Hotel | 221 Powell St. (bet. Geary & O'Farrell Sts.) | 415-397-7720 | www.kuletos.com

A peek at the "open kitchen" "whets the appetite" at this "ebullient" eatery where a "terrific wine list" "complements" the "well-prepared"

	FOOD	DECOR	SERVICE	COST

Northern Italian menu ("consistent" "year in and year out"); if a few find it "uninspired", partisans praise the "decent prices", "friendly, knowledgeable waiters" and "lively" Downtown digs "convenient to the theater district" and shops "in the heart of Union Square."

Kyo-Ya ☒ *Japanese* | 23 | 19 | 20 | $56

Downtown | Palace Hotel | 2 New Montgomery St. (Market St.) | 415-546-5090 | www.sfpalace.com

Some of the "freshest sushi" in town and other "innovative Japanese" fare is served with "simple" "elegance" at this Downtowner hidden in the Palace Hotel; the "pricey" tab means some save it for a "power business lunch" or special "night out", though the "happy hour is good too", luring in fish fans with lower prices from 5–7 PM.

La Boulange *Bakery* | 21 | 16 | 16 | $16

Cow Hollow | 1909 Union St. (Laguna St.) | 415-440-4450
Cole Valley | 1000 Cole St. (Parnassus St.) | 415-242-2442
Hayes Valley | 500 Hayes St. (Octavia St.) | 415-863-3376
Noe Valley | 3898 24th St. (bet. Sanchez & Vicksburg Sts.) | 415-821-1050
North Beach | 543 Columbus Ave. (bet. Powell & Stockton Sts.) | 415-399-0714
Pacific Heights | 2043 Fillmore St. (bet. California & Pine Sts.) | 415-928-1300
Pacific Heights | 2325 Pine St. (bet. Fillmore & Steiner Sts.) | 415-440-0356
Russian Hill | 2300 Polk St. (Green St.) | 415-345-1107
SoMa | 685 Market St. (bet. Annie & 3rd Sts.) | 415-512-7610 ☒
www.laboulangebakery.com

"Decadent pastries" and "a giant bowl of latte" are "a winning formula" at this chain of "absolutely darling" "self-serve" bakeries with "first-rate croissants", "lovely sandwiches" and other "butter"-y fare; "you have to be quick to snag a seat" since they're "always full of folks" (and "$800 strollers blocking the aisles"), and some sniff the staff has "perfected" the art of "Parisian indifference", but "Francophiles" say they're "a great way to start the day" or "linger" over a "casual" lunch.

La Ciccia �M *Italian* | 26 | 17 | 24 | $45

Noe Valley | 291 30th St. (Church St.) | 415-550-8114 | www.laciccia.com

"If it weren't for the J Church rumbling outside I would think I am in Italy" (vs. the "hinterlands of Noe Valley") swear locals "living it up" at this "fantastic family-run Sardinian" where the "mama and papa" owners "put their hearts in every dish" and "on the floor", "welcoming" guests and guiding them through the "bold", "beyond the familiar" regional *cucina* and vino; the "crowded" digs "could be more refined" for the price, but regulars return "whenever we can get in."

La Corneta *Mexican* | 21 | 11 | 15 | $12

Glen Park | 2834 Diamond St. (bet. Bosworth & Chenery Sts.) | 415-469-8757 ⵟ
Mission | 2731 Mission St. (bet. 23rd & 24th Sts.) | 415-643-7001 www.lacorneta.com

"Incredible rice", "full-of-flavor" beans and "meat grilled while you wait" all "meld together perfectly in burrito form" at this "casual" quartet in the Mission, Glen Park, Burlingame and San Carlos; the "line is often out the door during dinner hours", but "courteous" servers get you in and out of the "cafeteria-style" space "fast", and the "extensive selection" of "fresh" Mexican meals is "very reasonably priced" "to say the least", especially considering the "bountiful" portions.

La Cumbre Taqueria   *Mexican*   22 | 10 | 17 | $12

Mission | 515 Valencia St. (bet. 16th & 17th Sts.) | 415-863-8205
"Fresh" ingredients "tailored right to your tastes" result in "Mexican fast food as it should be" at this "old-school" south-of-the-border spot; don't expect "some fancy dining experience" – "it's a Mission taqueria, people", with a San Mateo sib – but since the "bargain" "gut-busting burritos" "the size of your forearm" "will feed you for days", most keep "coming back" (available until 3 AM on weekends).

Lafitte   *French*   20 | 21 | 19 | $50

Embarcadero | Pier 5, The Embarcadero (B'way) | 415-839-2134 | www.lafittesf.com
"After years" of orchestrating Sub Culture Dining, former Dissident chef Russell Jackson is cooking in plain sight in his "lively", "pirate"-themed Embarcadero brasserie, dishing out "delicious", "inventive" modern French fare (ordered via "iPad") plus a "Jolly Roger" chef's-whim prix fixe; the new menu "changes" less than the "never-the-same" original, with "inspiring cocktails" and a "spectacular view of the Bay" adding to the "pricey" "show."

⚡ La Folie ⍓ *French*   28 | 25 | 27 | $98

Russian Hill | 2316 Polk St. (bet. Green & Union Sts.) | 415-776-5577 | www.lafolie.com
"One of the last bastions" of haute cuisine, chef-owner Roland Passot's "fouffy French" Russian Hill "grande dame" "has stood the test of time" as he "greets the customers" and presents "superb", almost "too beautiful to eat" tasting menus that are "as up to date" as the "elegant" "plush" setting; "from the amuse bouche" and "fabulous" wine pairings by "his brother George" to the "gracious" service that "recalls a bygone era", it "fits the (hefty) bill" "for that very special occasion"; P.S. the lounge next door serves "great apps" and cocktails.

La Mar Cebicheria Peruana   *Peruvian/Seafood*   25 | 24 | 21 | $50

Embarcadero | Pier 1.5 (Washington St.) | 415-397-8880 | www.lamarcebicheria.com
Star chef Gastón Acurio's "Peruvian seafood cornucopia" "overlooking the Bay on the Embarcadero" dishes out "colorful", "superb" South American eats ("ceviche heaven") that patrons promise will "expand your culinary horizons"; the "modern" interior gets as "loud as the inside of a drum", and, while full of "enthusiasm", "your server may vanish for the length" of your stay, but all is forgotten after sipping "your fill of pisco sours" ("incredible and lethal") on the patio or at the "jammed" bar.

La Méditerranée   *Mediterranean/Mideastern*   20 | 15 | 19 | $25

Castro | 288 Noe St. (bet. Beaver & Market Sts.) | 415-431-7210
Upper Fillmore | 2210 Fillmore St. (bet. Clay & Sacramento Sts.) | 415-921-2956
www.cafelamed.com
"Fabulous" "phyllo-filled goodies", "homemade hummus" and other items on the "reasonably priced" Middle Eastern–Med menu have "been the same for ages" at this "tried-and-true" trio in the Castro,

Upper Fillmore and Berkeley; the "low-key", "cozy" confines mean you're "sure to know" your neighbors "by the end of dinner" (even at the "outdoor tables"), but the "helpful" staff delivers a "fast" "fix" of "tasty" fare.

L'Ardoise 🈂️Ⓜ️ *French* | 24 | 21 | 25 | $47 |

Castro | 151 Noe St. (Henry St.) | 415-437-2600 | www.ardoisesf.com
It's "Paris in San Francisco . . . or as close as you'll get" "without the hassle of going through security" say fans of this "cozy corner cafe" in the Castro proffering a daily chalkboard menu of "all the old French standards" "smothered in buttery goodness" and doled out by "charming" garçons; given that it's "not so secret any more" and only "about the size of a closet", it "gets booked up quick."

Lark Creek Steak *Steak* | 23 | 21 | 21 | $54 |

Downtown | Westfield San Francisco Ctr. | 845 Market St., 4th fl. (bet. 4th & 5th Sts.) | 415-593-4100 | www.larkcreeksteak.com
A "lovely respite from the shopping throngs" in Downtown's Westfield Centre, this "wonderful" steakhouse with a "vibrant bar" far exceeds "expectations for a 'mall restaurant'"; "knowledgeable servers" "guide you through" the "wide selection" of beefy yumminess – like "sinful" burgers and a "properly done" porterhouse – as well as the "excellent wine list"; just "expect to spend a pretty extra penny", because those "à la carte" "sides can add up fast."

La Scene Café & Bar Ⓜ️ *Californian/Mediterranean* | ▽ 19 | 18 | 22 | $48 |

Downtown | Warwick Regis | 490 Geary St. (bet. Mason & Taylor Sts.) | 415-292-6430 | www.warwicksf.com
"Everyone will find something to like" at this "charming" "pre-theater venue" with a "prime location" that's "so handy" to the A.C.T. and other Downtown destinations; though a minority labels the Cal-Med fare merely "ok", most are persuaded by the "bargain" prix fixe menu, "very reasonable" wine prices and "attentive" servers who "get you out before curtain time."

La Taqueria 🚫 *Mexican* | 25 | 9 | 16 | $13 |

Mission | 2889 Mission St. (bet. 24th & 25th Sts.) | 415-285-7117
Troops "in the taqueria wars" testify this Mission maker "rivals all" for "authentic, tasty" Mexican – including "amazing tacos" and "burritos so chock-full of fresh ingredients" (but "no rice") "they're really two meals in one"; it's "not much for ambiance", which matches the "bargain" tabs (though it can get "a bit pricey" "with the add-ons"), and unless it's "off hours", expect "lines eternally long and table space eternally short."

La Terrasse *French* | 17 | 18 | 16 | $39 |

Presidio | 215 Lincoln Blvd. (Graham St.) | 415-922-3463 | www.laterrassepresidio.com
The "Presidio setting" and "sheltered" "patio seating" with bay views are "so wonderful" sigh vista votaries, who take their "traditional" French "bistro fare" with a side of "fog horns" in the distance; the unconvinced cite "forgettable" bites and "indifferent service", but "what is wrong" with "a bottle of rosé" and a "look out at the Golden Gate Bridge?" ask aficionados.

La Trappe ⊠Ⓜ *Belgian*

▽ 16 | 22 | 16 | $32

North Beach | 800 Greenwich St. (Mason St.) | 415-440-8727 | www.latrappecafe.com

You'll "think you are in Belgium" in the "super-cool" "subterranean" "lair" of this "awesome" North Beach gastropub known for its "encyclopedia's worth" of "Belgian beer"; the menu – mostly moules frites (with "the best fries this side of the pond") and other Flemish fare – "isn't shabby either", though most are more interested in the "unrivaled" ale options, served by "knowledgeable" (if sometimes "slow") staffers.

Le Central Bistro ⊠ *French*

21 | 19 | 22 | $46

Downtown | 453 Bush St. (bet. Grant Ave. & Kearny St.) | 415-391-2233 | www.lecentralbistro.com

"As clubby" as it can be – "especially on Friday afternoon", when "everyone who is anyone in San Francisco" stops by – this "*charmante*" "traditional" bistro knows "how to do affordable French food", like their "famous cassoulet" that's been cooking away "for many years"; it's "a little tired" tut critics, who reserve it for "people-watching" or indulging in "nostalgia", but habitués who "have been going here since the '70s" claim this "classic" Downtowner is "always a treat."

Le Charm
French Bistro Ⓜ *French*

23 | 19 | 23 | $43

SoMa | 315 Fifth St. (bet. Folsom & Shipley Sts.) | 415-546-6128 | www.lecharm.com

Prepare to "be charmed" at this "aptly named" Gallic bistro in SoMa where the "doting" staffers "go out of their way to make you feel at home"; the "excellent" "old-school" "menu is small in variety but big on flavor" and relatively "affordable" to boot, especially if you order the "popular" prix fixe, and the "lovely" "enclosed patio" is "oh-so-romantic", especially when there's a "live band performing French jazz" on Thursday nights.

Le Colonial *French/Vietnamese*

22 | 24 | 21 | $54

Downtown | 20 Cosmo Pl. (bet. Jones & Taylor Sts.) | 415-931-3600 | www.lecolonialsf.com

The "superb" "sensual" atmosphere suggests "prewar Saigon" at this "impressive" "high-energy" hideout on a Downtown alley; "the check can quickly escalate", but "it's worth every penny" for the "imaginative" menu of "delectable" French-Vietnamese vittles and "wide-ranging wine list" served in a "stylish" setting, plus tipplers tout the upstairs lounge, where "lovely" cocktails accompany "live music or DJs" almost every night.

ℕ𝔼𝕎 Leopold's *Austrian*

▽ 23 | 23 | 22 | $30

Russian Hill | 2400 Polk St. (Union St.) | 415-474-2000 | www.leopoldssf.com

"This ain't your grandma's hofbrau" declare fans of this new "ridiculously good", affordable Austrian with Italian touches on Russian Hill, where "the Wiener schnitzel is cooked to perfection", "the great selection of German beers" and wines are "soothing on the gullet" and the "attentive", "cute" dirndl-clad waitresses are easy on the eyes; the Alpine setting (pine wood booths, antlers on the wall) is "properly kitschy" – "loud, though."

	FOOD	DECOR	SERVICE	COST

Le P'tit Laurent *French* | 23 | 19 | 23 | $39 |

Glen Park | 699 Chenery St. (Diamond St.) | 415-334-3235 |
www.leptitlaurent.net

Glen Park Francophiles feel "lucky" to "live in the neighborhood"
thanks to this "utterly charming" bistro where the "congenial" host
is the owner, Laurent, himself; the "small" size means you'll "get to
know" those near you "whether you want to or not", but the
"cramped" quarters don't deter devotees, who are "always
pleased" with the "generous portions" of "authentic" French fare,
"lovely wine list" and "bargain" prix fixe menu ("what a deal" when
dining Sunday–Thursday).

Lers Ros Thai ● *Thai* | 23 | 9 | 16 | $23 |

Tenderloin | 730 Larkin St. (O'Sarrell St.) | 415-931-6917 | www.lersros.com

"Delicious" "traditional" Bangkok bites, such as "spicy and flavorful"
curries, join more "exotic" items, including an "interesting selection of
game meats", on the "ambitious" menu at this "authentic" Tenderloin
Thai; sure, "the interior needs some love", and a few of the "unusual
offerings" are "not for the squeamish", but the "unique" fare "warms
the soul" say supporters, and "brings a smile" to those "lucky enough"
to eat it; P.S. a second branch is planned for 307 Hayes Street.

Le Soleil *Vietnamese* | ▽ 22 | 17 | 20 | $32 |

Inner Richmond | 133 Clement St. (bet. 2nd & 3rd Aves.) | 415-668-4848 |
www.lesoleilusa.com

With service that's "above par" for such a "small local place", this
Inner Richmond Vietnamese is a "great neighborhood joint" for a
"quiet" meal of lemongrass chicken or whole roasted crabs with garlic
noodles; moderate prices and "lunchtime specials" suit scrimping surveyors, and groupies gush they are "never disappointed" by their
"favorite" "hidden gem."

Let's Be Frank Ⓜ *Hot Dogs* | 20 | 12 | 20 | $8 |

Marina | 3318 Steiner St. (bet. Chestnut & Lombard Sts.) | 415-674-6755
Presidio | Warming Hut Café & Bookstore | Crissy Field (Marine Dr.) |
No phone ⊟
www.letsbefrankdogs.com

Fans fawn over these "great little" franks made from "organic" ingredients and "ethically raised meat" and served with a variety of "extras"
(including "curry and onions") to "gild the lily"; whether noshers hit
the original cart at Crissy Field or get it "to go", or stay while sipping a
beer at the Marina brick-and-mortar "hole-in-the-wall", they're "in
doggie heaven" and just wish the eats weren't so "darn expensive."

Liba Falafel Truck Ⓩ *Mideastern* | 25 | 19 | 24 | $9 |

Location varies; see website | 415-806-5422 | www.libafalafel.com

"I would follow that truck anywhere" swear falafel freaks, who travel
between SF and the East Bay for "amazingly delicious" chickpea patties that are "customizable" with a "distinctive array" of "vibrant"
"housemade" condiments that "make the meal"; some say it's "a bit
expensive" considering the "small" portions (you might "have to add"
the "addicting" sweet potato fries to your order), but since it's all
served "with smiles", most maintain it's a "friendly, feel-good offering" for a Middle Eastern meal.

Liberty Cafe ⓂAmerican | 23 | 18 | 21 | $33 |

Bernal Heights | 410 Cortland Ave. (bet. Andover & Bennington Sts.) | 415-695-8777 | www.thelibertycafe.com

The "cozy", "unpretentious" setting staffed with "sweet" servers "makes you feel like you've been invited to a chef friend's place" for dinner attest admirers of this "real-deal" American "comfort-food" cafe in Bernal Heights with a bakery in the "little cottage in the back" (it's a wine bar at night); boosters extol the "amazing pot pie" and also suggest you "save room for dessert" – easier said than done thanks to the "hearty portions" of "seasonal locavore fare."

Limón Peruvian | 22 | 17 | 20 | $34 |

Mission | 524 Valencia St. (bet. 16th & 17th Sts.) | 415-252-0918 | www.limon-sf.com

Limón Peruvian Rotisserie Peruvian

Mission | 1001 S. Van Ness Ave. (21st St.) | 415-821-2134 | www.limonrotisserie.com

"*Viva la Limón*" cheer champions of this "trendy" Nuevo Peruvian serving "awesome" "puckery-fresh ceviche" and "solid" tapas that are a "nice variation on the usual Latin fare"; it "can get a bit loud", since it's often "crowded" with "young", "hip" Missionites swilling "top-notch sangria", and "small portions" lead some to say it's "a bit overpriced", but the "festive" rotisserie offshoot's "succulent" chicken, "delicious dipping sauces" and "super sides" are more "affordable"; P.S. another rotisserie outpost is planned for 5800 Third Street.

Little Chihuahua Mexican | 21 | 13 | 15 | $14 |

Noe Valley | 4123 24th St. (Castro St.) | 415-648-4157
Western Addition | 292 Divisadero St. (bet. Haight & Page Sts.) | 415-255-8225
www.thelittlechihuahua.com

When "hipsters" want to get "stuffed silly without breaking the bank", they vamoose to this "upscale" taqueria twosome – the "packed" Western Addition original and its "calmer" Noe Valley sib; critics may chafe at the "counter service", since sometimes there's "nowhere to sit", but fans are focused on the "fast", "friendly service" and "fresh", "natural ingredients" filling the "unusual burritos", as well as the "amazing salsa bar" worth a bounty of "bonus points."

Little Nepal Ⓜ Nepalese | ▽ 19 | 17 | 21 | $29 |

Bernal Heights | 925 Cortland Ave. (bet. Folsom & Gates Sts.) | 415-643-3881 | www.littlenepalsf.com

For "wonderful" Nepalese nibbles that you "normally don't get in the city", Kathmandu connoisseurs scale "beautiful" Bernal Heights to this "neighborhood gem" with a "super-nice staff"; the "interesting" menu includes "vegetarian options" and some "spicy" stuff as well, and since the tab is anything but Everest sized, it's a "favorite" of the frugal.

Little Star Pizza Pizza | 24 | 15 | 17 | $23 |

Mission | 400 Valencia St. (15th St.) | 415-551-7827
Western Addition | 846 Divisadero St. (bet. Fulton & McAllister Sts.) | 415-441-1118 Ⓜ
www.littlestarpizza.com

"Delicious deep-dish options" "as Chicago" "as the Cubbies" are the draw at this pizza trio serving up pies with a "flaky-light cornmeal crust" ("crispy", "thin-crust pizzas are fantastic" too); though some say the quarters have "just the right amount of hip" others find them "too dark and noisy" and "long" waits during "crush times" prompt impatient types to "call ahead."

Local Kitchen & Wine Merchant *Californian/Italian*

| 18 | 16 | 17 | $36 |

SoMa | 330 First St. (bet. Folsom & Harrison Sts.) | 415-777-4200 | www.sf-local.com

In an "off-the-beaten-path" part of SoMa, this "sleek" (some say "stark") "urban" Cal-Italian is "worth a detour" for "artisanal" "wood-oven pizzas", "fresh pastas" and an "awesome wine list that isn't marked up very much"; the Sunday supper of all-you-can eat slices "is a must" affirm the famished, who join other "families" for "one of the best deals in SF", delivered with service that's "attentive."

Local Mission Eatery Ⓜ *Californian*

| 23 | 19 | 19 | $37 |

Mission | 3111 24th St. (bet. Folsom & Shotwell Sts.) | 415-655-3422 | www.localmissioneatery.com

Locals wanting to see the mantra of "farm-to-table truly in practice" make it their mission to visit this modest Californian on 24th Street – popular for lunch – where there's "not always a lot on the menu", but what there is, is constantly "creative" and "fresh" – as indicated by the "great bakery in back"; P.S. occasional winemaker and cooking seminars provide food for thought.

NEW Locanda ❶ *Italian*

| - | - | - | M |

Mission | 557 Valencia St. (bet. 16th & 17th Sts.) | 415-863-6800 | www.locandasf.com

Delfina's long-awaited osteria spin-off in the Mission features a daily changing, Roman-inspired menu that leans heavily on meats, including charcoal grill/rotisserie entrees, house-cured salumi and a section devoted to offal; the long, handsome dining room features dark-wood tables with white Escher-like tiles, and there's a bar pouring wines (from anywhere the Roman Empire touched) plus classic cocktails with an Italian twist.

NEW Locavore Ⓜ *Californian*

| ▽ 20 | 17 | 18 | $34 |

Bernal Heights | 3215 Mission St. (Valencia St.) | 415-821-1918 | www.locavoreca.com

"Portlandia" types love the "story behind" the "creative" dishes at this new midpriced Californian in Bernal Heights, where chef-owner Jason Moniz (ex Flora) sources everything (including beer and wine) within a 100-mile radius for menus that "change weekly"; locally made communal tables and art lend a "homey atmosphere", but the staff can also be a bit "green", resulting in "slow service."

Loló 🅂 *Mexican*

| 24 | 19 | 21 | $39 |

Mission | 3230 22nd St. (bet. Mission & Valencia Sts.) | 415-643-5656 | www.lolosf.com

"For a piece of real SF", "take your out-of-towners" or "a big group" of your wildest friends to this "quirky" "Mission favorite" where the "marvelous" midpriced Med-"Mexican mash-up" of mostly "small bites" actually "works" (and is served until midnight on weekends); some are left "dizzy" by the decor, "a massive collection of brightly colored oddities affixed to every square inch of the wall", but the "veteran staff is ever-charming and the short wine list is full of great-tasting values."

L'Osteria del Forno ⌨ *Italian*   24 13 19 $32
North Beach | 519 Columbus Ave. (bet. Green & Union Sts.) | 415-982-1124 | www.losteriadelforno.com
"Locals love to love" this "always busy" "authentic osteria" "on an otherwise touristy main drag in North Beach", whose "superb" "homestyle" Northern Italian food is produced "without a stove-top" ("only what can be made in an oven") in "crammed" "real hole-in-the-wall" digs; it's "not for folks in a rush or those wanting big presentation", and "the servers can sometimes be a little standoffish", but the joint "has a lot of heart and soul" and tabs are "reasonable" to boot.

Lovejoy's Tea Room Ⓜ *Tearoom*   20 22 22 $26
Noe Valley | 1351 Church St. (Clipper St.) | 415-648-5895 | www.lovejoystearoom.com
"Get together with the girls" in this Noe Valley "English living room" setting where "elaborate sofas" and "doilies and lace" are a fitting backdrop for "traditional tea served with flair" plus midpriced treats such as "lemon curd and crumpets" and "delicious scones and clotted cream"; "charming" "mismatched china" and a "knowledgeable, friendly and flexible staff" make it a "favorite" for "Anglophiles", "book clubs, baby showers and birthdays."

Luce *Californian/Italian*   21 20 19 $65
SoMa | InterContinental Hotel | 888 Howard St. (bet. 4th & 5th Sts.) | 415-616-6566 | www.lucewinerestaurant.com
The "perfect" perch for an expense-account "business lunch or dinner" "if you're at a conference at the Moscone Center", this "sleek" SoMa restaurant with a minimalist decor and a popular "grappa bar" proffers ingredient-driven Cal-Ital fare that fans find "superb for a hotel" plus a wine list filled with "some interested choices"; "too many people with name tags" and the "hotel-lobby atmosphere" "diminish the pleasure" for some, particularly since its "star chef" "moved on"; P.S. the post-Survey appointment of a new chef is not reflected in the Food score.

Luella *Californian/Mediterranean*   21 19 20 $43
Russian Hill | 1896 Hyde St. (Green St.) | 415-674-4343 | www.luellasf.com
"Right on the Hyde Street cable car line", this "cozy" bistro with a "friendly" staff serves "fresh and wonderful" Cal-Med fare "prepared with great ingredients"; if a few fret it should "change the menu more frequently" to really "spread its wings", most maintain this "wonderful neighborhood" nook "rocks" their "Russian Hill socks" with a "fantastic" prix-fixe option (Monday–Thursday) and "kid-friendly" Little Luella Menu (Sunday only).

Luna Park *American/French*   19 16 18 $35
Mission | 694 Valencia St. (18th St.) | 415-553-8584 | www.lunaparksf.com
"Urban hipsters" hop to this "solid choice" in the Mission for a "night on the town" that offers "great values" on "fine" French-New American fare – including "fun" "warm goat cheese fondue" and

FOOD | DECOR | SERVICE | COST

"make your own s'mores dessert" – plus an "awesome array of unique drinks" and a "friendly" staff; though a few contend that the "loud and dark" interior could use "some upgrades", it's "always packed", so be sure to make a "reservation."

Lupa Trattoria *Italian*   ∇ 21 | 16 | 21 | $37

Noe Valley | 4109 24th St. (bet. Castro & Diamond Sts.) | 415-282-5872 | www.lupatrattoria.com

Diners think they're "in Italy" at this "cozy", midpriced Noe Valley trattoria where the "housemade pasta", "delicious homemade bread" and other "fabulous, authentic" Roman-style dishes come courtesy of a "passionate" chef-owner; the "welcoming" staff and somewhat "scruffy" decor add to the "kid-friendly", "family-style ambiance", but better "call for reservations" as "seating is limited."

NEW **Ma*Velous** Ⓩ *Coffeehouse*   ∇ 17 | 18 | 19 | $21

Civic Center | 1408 Market St. (Fell St.) | 415-626-8884 | www.maveloussf.com

Sporting an edgy interior (think lizard-green beauty-shop chairs), this Civic Center coffeehouse and wine bar takes its beans "very seriously", brewing "the best" (including cult Norwegian roaster Wendelboe) using methods including Japanese cold slow-drip and siphon; "unfortunately, there isn't a lot more" offered, save some Sandbox Bakery sweets, locally procured cheese and charcuterie and sustainable vino, though the baristas are, naturally, "excellent."

Magnolia Gastropub &   20 | 18 | 17 | $28
Brewery ☻ *Southern*

Haight-Ashbury | 1398 Haight St. (Masonic Ave.) | 415-864-7468 | www.magnoliapub.com

Putting "inventive twists" on your usual bar bites, this "boisterous" boîte in the Upper Haight pairs its "solid" American gastropub grub with "terrific", "creamy" "cult beers" "brewed downstairs"; a few might miss the "simpler, cheaper" menu of years gone by, but "passionate fans" still "pack" in "every night" for the "spirited atmosphere" and locally sourced "Southern-tinged" fare.

Mamacita *Mexican*   22 | 19 | 18 | $34

Marina | 2317 Chestnut St. (Scott St.) | 415-346-8494 | www.mamacitasf.com

The "ingredients are always fresh and sassy" and so are the "pretty Marina girls" who flock to this "raucous", "funky über-hip" haunt for "outstanding" (if "pricey") "creative Mexican" "small plates" with "twists"; diners "over a certain age" might find the "crowds and noise" "a bit much", but "prompt and friendly service" and "awesome" "house margaritas" make up for it.

NEW **Mama's Empanadas** Ⓩ *Italian/Pan-Latin*   26 | 17 | 24 | $8

Location varies; see Twitter | 650-281-6431 | www.twitter.com/mamaempanadassf

Mama's boys and girls "can't stop thinking about" the "super tasty" Pan-Latin empanadas doled out "piping hot and crispy with amazing fillings" from this roving kitchen that also serves some Italian dishes; sure, "service can be slow" and the cost may be relatively "high" but that's only "because you really do want to try everything."

	FOOD	DECOR	SERVICE	COST

Mama's on Washington Square ☒⇗ American

25 | **15** | **18** | **$22**

North Beach | 1701 Stockton St. (Filbert St.) | 415-362-6421 | www.mamas-sf.com

The "rib-sticking" "American-style" eats and "fresh baked goods" – including "inspired waffles", "creative" omelets, and pancakes that are "as light as a feather" – are "close to perfect" at this "cheery" North Beach breakfast and lunch location "with a charming kitchen-table vibe"; "quick" service adds to the "pleasure", but remember that the "long lines" are as "legendary as the food", so steel yourself to join the "crowd of locals" in the queue.

Mandalay Burmese

23 | **14** | **19** | **$26**

Inner Richmond | 4348 California St. (bet. 5th & 6th Aves.) | 415-386-3895 | www.mandalaysf.com

A "warm" staff offers novices "advice on what to order" e.g. the "marvelous tea leaf salad", a "unique combination of ingredients" "mixed at the table" that typifies the "bold", "complex" Burmese cuisine at this "inexpensive" Inner Richmond roost; though not as well known as its Clement Street competitors, "those in the know" note it's "just as good," serving similar "lovely dishes without the crowd and hype."

Manora's Thai Cuisine Thai

24 | **15** | **22** | **$26**

SoMa | 1600 Folsom St. (12th St.) | 415-861-6224 | www.manorathai.com

"Fragrant", "flavorful" Thai cuisine "hits the spot" at this SoMa "sleeper", offering "generous portions" of an "excellent variety of soups", seafood dishes and "great combo plates" that "may be the best lunch deal in town"; sure, "it's been around forever" with the decor to prove it, but the "welcoming" service helps keep it a "neighborhood" favorite.

Mario's Bohemian Cigar Store Cafe Italian/Sandwiches

17 | **16** | **14** | **$18**

North Beach | 566 Columbus Ave. (bet. Green & Union Sts.) | 415-362-0536

"Loved by the locals" for both its "wonderful" focaccia sandwiches and "vintage North Beach vibe", this "mellow" Northern Italian "neighborhood hangout" "next to Washington Square" is a "cheap" "choice for a snack and a glass of vino"; no, it's "not fine dining", but it's all "about the scene" and the "people-watching across the way at the park", which hasn't "changed a bit" "since the 1970s."

MarketBar Mediterranean

16 | **17** | **17** | **$39**

Embarcadero | Ferry Bldg. Mktpl. | 1 Ferry Bldg. (The Embarcadero) | 415-434-1100 | www.marketbar.com

"Sit outside and watch the parade" at this "nonfussy" Embarcadero brasserie "in the Ferry Building", a "convenient" locale to "wine down" and "while away the hours" over "decent" if "unremarkable" Med fare "after a morning of farmer's market shopping"; dissenters decry "hit-or-miss" service and tabs that run "expensive for what you get", but "stick to the simple stuff" and it's "pleasant enough" "on a sunny day."

Marlowe ☒ American/Californian

23 | **17** | **21** | **$40**

SoMa | 330 Townsend St. (4th St.) | 415-974-5599 | www.marlowesf.com

"A great reinvention of the old South space", this "meat-centric" market-driven Californian lunch and late-night bistro near the Caltrain station has quickly become a "SoMa favorite" for fans of "the king of hamburgers" and equally "unbelievable roast chicken"; seating at the communal tables is "tight", and the noise level "horrific", but "personable service" makes up for that.

Marnee Thai *Thai*
24 | 14 | 18 | $25

Inner Sunset | 1243 Ninth Ave. (bet. Irving St. & Lincoln Way) | 415-731-9999 | www.marneethaisf.com
Outer Sunset | 2225 Irving St. (bet. 23rd & 24th Aves.) | 415-665-9500
"The line out the door says it all" at this "super-legit" Sunset duo that's "popular" for its "delicious" "superior Thai" dishes like "sticky and spicy" wings, "awesome" corn cakes and "possibly the best pad Thai" around; the "bustling" quarters can be "cramped" and "crowded", and depending on the customer, service is either "helpful" or "pushy", but the check's indisputably affordable.

⚡ Masa's ⊠Ⓜ *French*
28 | 24 | 27 | $107

Downtown | Hotel Vintage Ct. | 648 Bush St. (bet. Powell & Stockton Sts.) | 415-989-7154 | www.masasrestaurant.com
Acolytes "don't have a vocabulary with enough superlatives to describe the dining experience" at this venerable Downtown "destination"; if "not trendy", it's "stood the test of time" offering a "trifecta" of "incredible" "modern French" tasting menus that display "artistry" (with "top-notch" wine pairings), "complemented by perfect service" and an "elegant and quiet" "setting well suited for adults" (jackets are required); but unless you're "independently wealthy", the high tabs limit it as "a place for celebration."

Matterhorn Swiss Restaurant Ⓜ *Swiss*
22 | 19 | 21 | $41

Russian Hill | 2323 Van Ness Ave. (bet. Green & Vallejo Sts.) | 415-885-6116 | www.thematterhornrestaurant.com
Emmenthal enthusiasts are "very fondue this place" at the foot of Russian Hill, where they "indulge" in "cheesy goodness" and other "wonderful" Alpine fare as well as a wine list with "reasonable" prices; the "Swiss chalet interior" may strike some as "schmaltzy", but nevertheless it's the "real deal" and a "charming", "family-friendly" destination.

Maverick *American*
24 | 17 | 22 | $42

Mission | 3316 17th St. (bet. Mission & Valencia Sts.) | 415-863-3061 | www.sfmaverick.com
Even a "fried chicken special can be extraordinary" at this "hidden" Missionite serving "fabulous" American eats filled with "so much flavor" that the "cozy", "casually upscale" setting "needs to be three times bigger" to accommodate its following; "aside from the impossibility of conversation", it makes for "special evenings", given the "killer wines" suggested by "servers who know the list" – just be sure to "get a reservation."

Max's at the Opera *Deli*
17 | 15 | 17 | $27

Civic Center | Opera Plaza | 601 Van Ness Ave. (Golden Gate Ave.) | 415-771-7301
Max's Market ⊠ *Deli*
Downtown | 555 California St., concourse level (Montgomery St.) | 415-788-6297

(continued)

(continued)

Max's on the Square *Deli*
Downtown | Hotel Frank | 398 Geary St. (Mason St.) | 415-646-8600
www.maxsworld.com

"East Coast meets West" at this Bay Area chain of "lively" "New York-style" delis that "satisfies" a "craving" for "Jewish comfort food" with an "enormous menu" of "straightforward American favorites"; the "ginormous" servings deliver a "good bang for the buck", and the "opera-singing waiters" who "serenade" you at some locations are a "nice touch", but skeptics sneer at the "utilitarian" setting and say they'd "prefer less quantity and more quality."

Maya *Mexican*
20 | 21 | 19 | $39

SoMa | 303 Second St. (bet. Folsom & Harrison Sts.) | 415-543-2928 | www.mayasf.com

"A great reminder that Mexican cuisine is more than just tacos", this "fancy" SoMa spot serves "creative", "flavorful" fare like super ceviche, one of the "things that makes it extra-special"; some find it relatively "expensive", but "young office workers" ensure they do "a brisk business around lunch" as well as during the "amazing happy hour", when "great margaritas" and "some nice tequilas" are sometimes served with "complimentary appetizers."

Mayflower *Chinese*
20 | 13 | 14 | $31

Outer Richmond | 6255 Geary Blvd. (bet. 26th & 27th Aves.) | 415-387-8338 | www.mayflower-seafood.com

"Crazy popular on the weekends", this "palace of Cantonese cuisine" in the Outer Richmond (with suburban sibs in Millbrae and Milpitas) is "worth the wait" for "very reasonably priced" and "delicious dim sum"; "impersonal" service and a setting "that can be as chaotic as traffic in Downtown Beijing" mean it's "not for the timid", but it's often "quieter" in the evening, when "banquet-style dinners" and "fresh" (if occasionally "expensive") Hong Kong–style seafood dishes "surprise with their distinctive flavors."

Maykadeh *Persian*
∇ 23 | 18 | 21 | $34

North Beach | 470 Green St. (Grant Ave.) | 415-362-8286 | www.maykadehrestaurant.com

"A boon to lamb lovers" and connoisseurs of "tasty" kebabs, this "outstanding" North Beach Persian attracts "adventurous" eaters with its "wonderfully aromatic" plates that are "a joy to the senses"; despite the "linen tablecloths" and "restrained" "old-school" vibe, the service is "great" and it's "very reasonably priced."

McCormick & Kuleto's *Seafood*
20 | 23 | 20 | $47

Fisherman's Wharf | Ghirardelli Sq. | 900 N. Point St. (Larkin St.) | 415-929-1730 | www.mccormickandkuletos.com

"Knockout" "views of the bay and Alcatraz" (that are especially beautiful when "bathed in early evening sunlight") accompany a "varied menu" of "fresh, well-prepared fish" at this "touristy but tasty" seafooder located at Fisherman's Wharf; a few penny-pinchers flinch at the "pricey" tab, but most surveyors agree the "attentive" servers who "treat every diner like a real VIP" make it a "winner" "with locals and visitors alike."

	FOOD	DECOR	SERVICE	COST

Mel's Drive-In ☽ *Diner* — 13 | 14 | 15 | $19

Civic Center | 1050 Van Ness Ave. (bet. Geary & Myrtle Sts.) | 415-292-6358
Inner Richmond | 3355 Geary Blvd. (bet. Beaumont & Parker Aves.) | 415-387-2255
Marina | 2165 Lombard St. (bet. Fillmore & Steiner Sts.) | 415-921-2867
SoMa | 801 Mission St. (4th St.) | 415-227-0793
www.melsdrive-in.com

"For late-night munchies", burgers or "hearty breakfasts" served "all day and night", "diner" fans descend upon this "retro" chain in a "'50s throwback on steroids" setting (you almost expect "to see Fonzi"); ok, it's a bit of a "tourist trap" and the "old-time" "comfort food" is merely "cheap, fast" and "average" but at "2 AM" you're "not going for service or great food, just a hot meal and a cup of coffee."

Memphis Minnie's BBQ Joint *BBQ* — 19 | 11 | 15 | $20

Lower Haight | 576 Haight St. (bet. Fillmore & Steiner Sts.) | 415-864-7675 | www.memphisminnies.com

"One of the best" in town for a "Southern-style" "BBQ experience", this counter-service pit stop in the Lower Haight "will satisfy" smokehouse cravings with a "fix" of pulled pork, brisket or other "regional tastes" bolstered by "homemade sauces" and sides; a frill-free "'joint' it is" and Dixie purists insist the grub "has a long way to go", but for 'cue hounds hereabouts "there isn't much competition."

Mescolanza *Italian* — 23 | 17 | 22 | $36

Outer Richmond | 2221 Clement St. (bet. 23rd & 24th Aves.) | 415-668-2221 | www.mescolanza.net

The "classic" Northern Italian *cucina* – "simply prepared with the freshest ingredients" – "hits all the right notes" at this "charming" trattoria that's a "favorite" of Outer Richmond "locals and worth a trip for everyone else"; "definitely get the specials" suggest some, but the "thin-crust" pizzettas and "perfect-textured pasta" (all at "moderate" prices) are also popular, and "helpful" waiters add to the "quaint and cozy" vibe.

Mexico DF *Mexican* — 20 | 17 | 18 | $33

Embarcadero | 139 Steuart St. (bet. Howard & Mission Sts.) | 415-808-1048

"Not your typical Tex-Mex", this "upscale" Embarcadero cantina puts "interesting twists" on "authentic Mexico City food", "the real thing" transported "from the DF to SF"; the service needs an "upgrade", though the setting's "quite nice", and the "wonderfully creative menu", "lip-smacking array" of margaritas and "lots of kinds of tequila" "bring smiles" to the "Downtown crowd."

ⓩ NEW Michael Mina *American* — 26 | 25 | 26 | $103

Downtown | 252 California St. (Battery St.) | 415-397-9222 | www.michaelmina.net

"Michael Mina magic" is behind this "brilliant rebirth" of the "old Aqua space" where the chef got his start, which is now home to his relocated namesake eatery; out are the signature "trios" (plays on one ingredient) in favor of a "superb" "downscaled" – yet still "expensive" – Japanese-inflected New American menu (plus "classics" like "lobster pot pie" and a tasting menu) accompanied by "spectacular wines"; the room is a "less-formal" but "still gorgeous" setting for the "modern gourmand"

and the "power-lunch" crowd, sans "tablecloths" and with an "impeccable" "staff that overlooks jeans without a jacket."

Mifune *Japanese*   19 | 12 | 15 | $21

Japantown | Japan Ctr. | 1737 Post St. (Webster St.) | 415-922-0337 | www.mifune.com

"Still running" after more than three decades, this "basic" Japantown "noodle joint" is a "reliable workhorse" slinging "scrumptious" "homemade" soba, udon and other "slurpy" "comfort food" at a "low cost"; a few are miffed by "iffy" service and a setup that's "not much to look at", but for a "fast" bowl "in a pinch" you "can't go wrong."

Mijita *Mexican*   19 | 12 | 13 | $17

South Beach | AT&T Park | 24 Willie Mays Plaza (3rd St.) | 415-644-0240 M
Embarcadero | Ferry Bldg. Mktpl. | 1 Ferry Bldg. (The Embarcadero) | 415-399-0814
www.mijitasf.com

Traci des Jardins (Jardinière) "makes her *abuelita* proud" at this "small", "self-serve" Mexican at the Ferry Building and larger, "sit-down" sibling "near AT&T Park", where shoppers can grab "outstanding carnitas" or "superb" fish tacos (with "super-fresh salsas" on a "handmade tortilla") and wash it down with a "freshly squeezed juice" or a "lunchtime margarita" while watching "the ferries come in and out"; despite "picnic table" seating, it's a "notch above a taqueria", with "correspondingly higher prices."

Millennium *Vegan*   25 | 22 | 23 | $48

Downtown | Hotel California | 580 Geary St. (Jones St.) | 415-345-3900 | www.millenniumrestaurant.com

Giving vegetarian vittles "a good name", this "sophisticated" "vegan nirvana" in Downtown's Hotel California "elevates" meat-free meals "to lofty heights"; even "confirmed" "carnivores" are "converted" by its "extremely creative" entrees and "creamy desserts untouched by dairy", as well as an "organic wine list" that's "tops"; and if it's a bit "expensive" for everyday, the "attentive" servers and "beautiful atmosphere" make it suitable for a "wonderfully special" occasion.

Miller's East Coast   20 | 8 | 15 | $18
West Delicatessen *Deli/Jewish*

Polk Gulch | 1725 Polk St. (Clay St.) | 415-563-3542 | www.millersdelisf.com
Matzo ball soup, "awesome Reubens" and "huge pastrami and corned beef sandwiches" "with all the trimmings" (including "real" "half-sour pickles") deliver your "Jewish deli fix" at this Polk Gulch eatery; though it's "not a stylish palace", it's still a "haven" for homesick New Yorkers, though a few say it's "not bad" for a "West Coast" copy, but "sigh" it's "not like the real East Coast thing."

Mission Beach Café *Californian*   22 | 16 | 19 | $35

Mission | 198 Guerrero St. (14th St.) | 415-861-0198 | www.missionbeachcafe.com

"Fabulous 'meat candy' bacon" and bucket-size mimosas are among the reasons "hordes" of early birds descend upon this modern cafe with "friendly" service in an "unassuming" Mission locale; "brunch is a zoo" with "terrible waits" but locals "leave happy", especially after chowing down on the "delicious" value-oriented Californian dinners or

	FOOD	DECOR	SERVICE	COST

"better yet", the "fantastic selection of pies"; P.S. past chef Thomas Martinez returned post-Survey.

NEW Mission Cheese Ⓜ *American* — | — | — | M

Mission | 736 Valencia St. (18th St.) | 415-553-8667 | www.missioncheese.net

Turophiles melt for this midpriced Mission newcomer devoted to all-American artisanal fromages culled from across the land by owner and dairy whiz Sarah Dvorak; a chalkboard menu lists regional cheese plates, pressed sandwiches, raclettes and gourmet mac 'n' you-know-what, all served in spare industrial digs featuring a yellow-brick bar and cases chock-full of wedges and wheels; P.S. shoppers with deep pockets can also purchase the goods by the pound.

Mission Chinese Food *Chinese* 21 | 5 | 14 | $23
(fka Misson Street Food)

Mission | Lung Shan Restaurant | 2234 Mission St. (18th St.) | 415-863-2800 | www.missionchinesefood.com

"Chinese with spice and heart" best describes the "classic dishes taken to a new level" that are "hurried" out by a "funky and fun" staff at this "hyped" Mission "hipster" located inside (and sharing a kitchen with) old-school restaurant Lung Shan; though the decor consists of "typical" "plastic covered tables", it's "cheap enough" to eventually try "the entire Sichuan peppercorn–laden menu", plus 75 cents per entree is donated to the SF Food Bank; P.S. closed Wednesday.

Mixt Greens Ⓩ *Health Food/Sandwiches* 20 | 13 | 16 | $14

Downtown | Adam Grant Bldg. | 120 Sansome St. (bet. Bush & Pine Sts.) | 415-433-6498
Downtown | 475 Sansome St. (Commercial St.) | 415-296-9292
Downtown | JP Morgan Chase | 560 Mission St. (bet.1st & 2nd Sts.) | 415-543-2505
www.mixtgreens.com

"Super-fresh" salads – both "already packaged" and "made to order" by "friendly" "tossers" – are packed with a "large selection" of "tasty", "top-notch ingredients" at this "feel-good" health-food trio that earns the "'green' of its name" by using lots of "local" and "organic" ingredients; the frugal flinch at the relatively "steep" tab, even so it's "insanely popular" with Downtown desk jockeys, who declare "your planet and body will thank you" once you endure the "crazy-long" line.

Mochica *Peruvian* 25 | 18 | 22 | $38

SoMa | 937 Harrison St. (bet. 5th & 6th Sts.) | 415-278-0480 | www.mochicasf.com

A "fabulous variety" of "innovative" and "astoundingly good" Peruvian "small plates" are a "big surprise" to some at this "unknown treasure" in an out-of-the-way stretch of SoMa; the "authentic" ceviche "does not disappoint", nor does the "very reasonable wine list", and since "the ambiance is an unexpected delight" (like an "upscale home dining room"), Lima lovers deem it a "favorite" for a "quiet" "dinner date."

Moishe's Pippic Ⓩ⟟ *Deli/Jewish* ∇ 17 | 11 | 18 | $18

Hayes Valley | 425A Hayes St. (Gough St.) | 415-431-2440

"The owner knows from deli" at this "low-key" Hayes Valley haven of Jewish "comfort food", serving up "huge" pastrami and corned beef

FOOD | DECOR | SERVICE | COST

sandwiches, Chicago-style hot dogs and other heart-stopping staples in "kitschy" quarters bedecked with walls full of "sports posters and junk"; but while the eating's "ok" for the Left Coast, choosier noshers caution "it ain't New York"; P.S. closes at 4 PM.

Moki's Sushi & Pacific Grill *Japanese* ▽ 26 | 18 | 20 | $35

Bernal Heights | 615 Cortland Ave. (bet. Anderson & Moultrie Sts.) | 415-970-9336 | www.mokisushi.com

Granted, it's "not your typical Japanese", but this Bernal Heightser is a "neighborhood" standout thanks to the "inventive" flair of its "fresh and terrific" sushi ("try the ecstasy roll") and "fantastic" "grilled items"; a "casual" venue "with a Hawaii/Pacific vibe", it "can get packed with families" who create a "loud and harried atmosphere", but maki mavens still urge "go now, thank me later."

MoMo's *American* 18 | 18 | 18 | $40

South Beach | 760 Second St. (King St.) | 415-227-8660 | www.sfmomos.com

"Packed to the gills before and after" the Giants play, this South Beach spot "right near the ballpark" achieves "ignition and liftoff every game day", when fans fill the "rocking bar" and outdoor patio; "quieter and much more relaxing" at other times, it's a "civilized" spot for a "varied" menu of "solid" New American fare in a dining room decked out in "dark wood"; still, opponents say it's "not a great value" and service is "unpredictable."

Monk's Kettle ◐ *Californian* 20 | 17 | 18 | $28

Mission | 3141 16th St. (Albion St.) | 415-865-9523 | www.monkskettle.com

"More beer options than you can count" bolstered by "reliably appetizing bar bites" make this Mission gastropub with a "seasonal" Californian bent a "neighborhood favorite" for "drinks and a late-night meal"; the "drawback is so many people like it" that there's often a "long wait" for a table in the "loud", "tight quarters", but the "well-educated staff" eases the pain, guiding "you to some terrific" brews.

Morph *Thai* - | - | - | M

Outer Richmond | 5344 Geary Blvd. (bet. 17th & 18th Aves.) | 415-742-5093 | www.morphlife.com

The moniker could allude to the "ever-changing menu" at this Outer Richmond yearling, where Pan-Asian meets traditional Thai for an affordable tour of fusion territory eased along by chic soju cocktails; the space flaunts a futuristic design with mod white chairs, tiles protruding from the wall and morphing LED lights that steep the space in shifting hues.

Morton's The Steakhouse *Steak* 23 | 21 | 23 | $72

Downtown | 400 Post St. (bet. Mason & Powell Sts.) | 415-986-5830 | www.mortons.com

"If it's beef you want", look no further than this "classic go-to steakhouse" chain (with Downtown and San Jose outposts) offering "well-prepared" fare in "copious" portions delivered with service that's "caring and attentive" "without hovering"; "elegant", "clubby" quarters complete the "old-school" "power-play" scene where there are "no surprises, no mistakes" but there is "a steep price tag."

FOOD | DECOR | SERVICE | COST

Moss Room *Californian* 22 | 25 | 22 | $50

Inner Richmond | California Academy of Sciences | 55 Music Concourse Dr. (bet. Fulton St. & Lincoln Way) | 415-876-6121 | www.themossroom.com
"A quiet" lunch "oasis" that's a departure "from the manic scene upstairs", this "sophisticated" gourmet "grotto" is an "excellent (if pricey) way to finish a day" at the Academy of Sciences; the "unique setting" overlooks "a wall of ferns" and a "gorgeous fish tank", while the Californian menu also offers sustainable dinners (Thursday–Sunday) complemented by "attentive" service, "fantastic" desserts and "well-crafted cocktails" via the Coco500 crew.

Mr. Pollo ◐⇄ *Colombian* ▽ 24 | 6 | 19 | $21

Mission | 2823 Mission St. (bet. 24th & 25th Sts.) | 415-374-5546
Surveyors "almost don't want to" share this cash-only South American "masquerading behind a tacky yellow sign" in the Mission where "amazing" "haute Colombian" fare comes at taqueria prices; the signature "arepas stand out" and the "four-course" market-driven "tasting menus for $15" are "spectacular", plus while it's "BYOB" and there's "not much atmosphere" or seating, the "two guys" running it make diners "feel totally at home."

Muracci's Japanese 21 | 8 | 15 | $16
Curry & Grill 🖾 *Japanese*

Downtown | 307 Kearny St. (Bush St.) | 415-773-1101 | www.muraccis.com
"Save a plane ticket to Tokyo" at this Downtown "lunch find" (open weekdays only), a carry-out cubbyhole specializing in "scrumptious" "homestyle" Japanese curry that's "freshly made" "from scratch" and "can't be beat" when ladled over the "tasty" katsu; while both locations are apt to be "jammed" at midday, the full-service Los Altos offshoot offers an expanded menu of the same "real-deal" eats and stays open nights and Saturdays.

My Father's Kitchen 🖾 *Vietnamese* ▽ 18 | 14 | 21 | $17
Pacific Heights | 1655 Divisadero St. (Sutter St.) | 415-829-2610 | www.myfatherskitchensf.com
"Step in for lunch" and slurp down a "steaming bowl" of "fine pho" at this Pacific Heights storefront, which plies a "small menu" of Vietnamese staples in a modest but "friendly setting"; doubters deem the eats "rather average", but the nabe's cost-conscious types still "hope they open for dinner soon"; P.S. closes at 7 PM.

My Tofu House *Korean* 21 | 8 | 14 | $19
Inner Richmond | 4627 Geary Blvd. (bet. 10th & 11th Aves.) | 415-750-1818
A "bubbling" bowl of "fantastic" "spicy tofu soup" is "all you need on a foggy SF day" claim Korean connoisseurs, who "get cravings" for this Inner Richmond roost despite the "no-frills" setting and "hit-or-miss" service; "copious portions" of "good BBQ meats" will also make you a "happy soul" for a song; no wonder it's "usually crowded" with a "mixed" group of "families and couples" singing "ba-da-bing, ba-da-bibimbop."

Naan 'n Curry *Indian/Pakistani* 17 | 6 | 10 | $15
Downtown | 336 O'Farrell St. (bet. Mason & Taylor Sts.) | 415-346-1443 ◐
Inner Sunset | 642 Irving St. (bet. 7th & 8th Aves.) | 415-664-7225
(continued)

(continued)

Naan 'n Curry

North Beach | 533 Jackson St. (Columbus Ave.) | 415-693-0499 ●
www.naancurry.com

"There's nothing 'haute' about the cuisine here", but "curry in a hurry" and other "basic" Indian-Pakistani fare attract fans to this SF and Berkeley chain despite "zero customer service" – "order at the counter" from the "uninterested staff" before you "get your own water and silverware" – and quarters that resemble an "ugly college cafeteria"; "at least it's cheap", though critics warn "you get what you pay for."

Naked Lunch 🖼️Ⓜ️⌂ *Sandwiches* ▽ 19 | 7 | 15 | $15

North Beach | 504 Broadway (Kearny St.) | 415-577-4951 |
www.nakedlunchsf.com

Noontime picks up "panache" via this lunch-only North Beach nook run by a pair of Cafe Majestic vets, a bare-bones over-the-counter outfit with a "daily changing menu" of "gourmet take-out sandwiches" featuring the "well-executed" likes of "signature foie gras" or the Tuesday fried chicken; despite a somewhat costly and "very limited" selection, it's always "worth a look", especially since the "humble digs" expand to patio seating at its new next-door sib, Txoko.

Namu *Californian/Korean* 22 | 17 | 18 | $34

Embarcadero | Ferry Bldg. Mktpl. | 1 Ferry Bldg. (The Embarcadero) |
415-386-8332 Ⓜ️⌂
Inner Richmond | 439 Balboa St. (6th Ave.) | 415-386-8332
www.namusf.com

SF's answer to NYC's "Momofuku", this "trendy" Inner Richmonder "pushes the envelope" with reasonably priced, "innovative" Californian and "Japanese-influenced Korean" small plates (plus "praised" "handmade ramen" and weekend brunch) "in an edgy, black-painted" storefront; fans weary of "circling" for parking and "slow" service opt for the "fusion" tacos at their Ferry Building tent on Thursday and Sunday; P.S. Namu Gaji, an izakaya offshoot, is slated to open in the Mission (499 Dolores Street) in late 2011.

Nettie's Crab Shack *Seafood* 18 | 16 | 18 | $38

Cow Hollow | 2032 Union St. (bet. Buchanan & Webster Sts.) |
415-409-0300 | www.nettiescrabshack.com

"Wonderful", "well-prepared" seafood dishes – the lobster roll's "worth the trip" alone – "transport" diners "to New England" at this "casual" Cow Hollow fish shack; with a "spare" "Cape Cod feeling" inside and a "spectacular" patio out, it's an "inviting space" with "friendly service" (the owner "Nettie herself is a kick"), but "bring your wallet" warn some who say it's "pricey" considering the "small portions" and "uneven quality."

Nick's Crispy Tacos ⌂ *Mexican* 22 | 12 | 13 | $14

Russian Hill | 1500 Broadway (Polk St.) | 415-409-8226

"Those crispy tacos" "are the bomb" at this Russian Hill Mexican "favorite", where compadres "way cooler than you" "chow down" on the namesake ("'Nick's way' is the only way to go") amid "gaudy" "red velvet and crystal chandeliers" in a space that transforms into the club Rouge later at night; "cheap eats" enthusiasts "cannot get enough", especially on $2 Taco Tuesdays when "pure mayhem" prevails.

	FOOD	DECOR	SERVICE	COST

Nihon 🔣Ⓜ *Japanese*

▽ 19 | 20 | 16 | $45

Mission | 1779 Folsom St. (14th St.) | 415-552-4400 |
www.nihon-sf.com

A "well-presented" lineup of Japanese "small plates" rounded out with "imaginative rolls" qualifies this split-level Mission izakaya as "a winner", but for those with an eye to imbibe "the focus" is an "unparalleled" 500-label "whiskey list" that puts the spotlight on single-malts and creative cocktails; the "modern" space houses "intimate dining upstairs" and an "impressive" late-night bar below, and though it's "not cheap", the often "lively" "scene" is "worth every penny."

Nob Hill Café *Italian*

20 | 14 | 20 | $35

Nob Hill | 1152 Taylor St. (bet. Clay & Pleasant Sts.) | 415-776-6500 |
www.nobhillcafe.com

"Excellent" "homemade" pasta – "fresh" and "full of flavor" – and "wonderful" pizzas are some of the Northern Italian eats at this "sweet little trattoria" with "very reasonable" prices atop Nob Hill; no reservations means "the wait can be long" for a seat "packed" amid the other "elbow-touching patrons", but "nothing can equal sitting outside" on a "sunny day" sipping wine from the "simple" list, plus the "lovely staff" ensures a "warm and inclusive feel."

NEW Nojo *American/Japanese*

- | - | - | M

Hayes Valley | 231 Franklin St. (Hayes St.) | 415-896-4587 |
www.nojosf.com

Bringing some Eastern mojo to Hayes Valley, this newcomer from an ex-Ame chef stresses local and seasonal ingredients on a concise New American–Japanese menu highlighting yakitori skewers (traditional chicken or creative variants) backed up by intriguing izakaya-style nibbles and don't-miss desserts; anchored by an open kitchen, the streamlined setup fills with a hip clientele sipping sake and microbrews; P.S. reservations only for parties of six or more.

Nombe *Japanese*

21 | 12 | 19 | $39

Mission | 2491 Mission St. (21st St.) | 415-681-7150 |
www.nombesf.com

Slaking the city's thirst for Japanese "street food", this "casual" Mission izakaya turns out a "terrific assortment" of "late-night bites", weekend brunch and specials, washed down with a "huge" selection of sake and shochu drinks; the "funky" layout and "slow" service can be "off-putting", and serial chef changes have resulted in "hit-or-miss" fare, though some expect it will "only get better" – e.g. there are new build-your-own ramen dishes and kaiseki dinners.

⚡ Nopa ● *Californian*

25 | 21 | 22 | $47

Western Addition | 560 Divisadero St. (Hayes St.) | 415-864-8643 |
www.nopasf.com

The "crown jewel" of the Western Addition, this "late-night" locavore and "hipster refueling station" (now also serving brunch that's "off the hook") "truly stands by" its "philosophy", delivering "simple" yet "brilliantly sourced", "gently" priced Cal meals and "creative cocktails" that change "with the seasons" courtesy of a "smooth" staff; "parking is a bitch" and it's "as hard to get into" as a "Giants-Dodgers game", but "it has it all" – including a "big communal table" for walk-ins.

	FOOD	DECOR	SERVICE	COST

Nopalito *Mexican*
22 | **16** | **21** | **$29**

Western Addition | Falletti's Plaza | 306 Broderick St. (Oak St.) | 415-437-0303 | www.nopalitosf.com

Nopa's little sister "hidden" in a Western Addition shopping mall lures the "smart set" with "inventive", "sustainable, organic" – "and did I mention delicious?" – *cocina* plus "perfectly potent" margaritas and "tasty *paletas*" (ice pops); it's "somewhat expensive" given the "spartan" digs (mostly "communal tables" and an "enclosed patio"), but "knowledgeable" service, a "call-in wait list" and a "free parking" lot add to the "value"; P.S. an Inner Sunset branch is planned for fall 2011 at 1224 Ninth Avenue.

North Beach Pizza *Pizza*
19 | **11** | **15** | **$20**

Excelsior | 4787 Mission St. (bet. Persia & Russia Aves.) | 415-586-1400
Haight-Ashbury | 800 Stanyan St. (Haight St.) | 415-751-2300
North Beach | 1462 Grant Ave. (Union St.) | 415-433-2444
Outer Sunset | 3054 Taraval St. (41st Ave.) | 415-242-9100
www.northbeachpizza.net

"Good gooey pizza" – a "thick", "chewy" crust topped with "tons of cheese" and "interesting topping mixtures" – is "all you could ask for" at this "kid-friendly" "institution" with "several locations" across the Bay Area; pickier patrons lament "it has lost much of its luster" and now it's "just another chain" offering "average" pies, but "reliable" delivery and, at some locations, the option to "run in and pick up a slice" explain why they're "still kicking after all these years."

North Beach Restaurant ☺ *Italian*
22 | **20** | **22** | **$50**

North Beach | 1512 Stockton St. (bet. Green & Union Sts.) | 415-392-1700 | www.northbeachrestaurant.com

Dining at this "classic North Beach" "fixture" is like taking "a step back in time", thanks to the "very traditional" Tuscan fare and "professional" "waiters in tuxedos"; "it still wins new converts" with its "memorable" if "pricey" "Italian dishes that always please" and "great" "house-made prosciutto" ("check out" the "curing room downstairs"), as well as "interesting wine choices", but all this "old-style elegance" "can be a little too retro for some."

O Izakaya Lounge *Japanese*
▽ **18** | **19** | **17** | **$41**

Japantown | Hotel Kabuki | 1625 Post St. (Laguna St.) | 415-614-5431 | www.jdvhotels.com

J-baseball memorabilia and numerous flat-screens lend sporty style to this modern izakaya in Japantown, which caters to the "after-work drinks" crowd with sake and soju cocktails supplemented by share-worthy small plates ("don't miss the pork belly"); but given "over-stretched" service and some merely "passable" picks on the menu, holdouts say it "tries to be novel" but "misses being special."

Old Jerusalem *Mediterannean/Mideastern*
▽ **19** | **8** | **15** | **$19**

Mission | 2976 Mission St. (bet. 25th & 26th Sts.) | 415-642-5958 | www.oldjerusalemsf.com

"Flavors of the Middle East" keep "falafel" fans and "baba ghanoush" groupies "coming back" for the "outstanding" renditions and Med eats on hand at this "bare-bones" Missionite; sure the "fare is simple" but with "lots for your money" it's "enough" "to satisfy"; P.S. no alcohol.

	FOOD	DECOR	SERVICE	COST

One Market ☒ *American*   24 | 22 | 22 | $61

Embarcadero | 1 Market St. (bet. Spear & Steuart Sts.) | 415-777-5577 | www.onemarket.com

A "popular" stop for "expense-account" "business lunches", this "big" and "bustling" multitasker features "quite a fun bar scene for the after-work crowd" and "qualifies" as a "lovely" "upscale" "special-occasion" spot thanks to its "memorable" menu of "sophisticated" New American cuisine; though a few find it "too large and cold", most warm to the "sweeping" "view of the Embarcadero out the window" adding "stellar" service is another reason it's a "knock-your-socks-off favorite."

Oola Restaurant & Bar ◑ *Californian*   19 | 18 | 17 | $41

SoMa | 860 Folsom St. (bet. 4th & 5th Sts.) | 415-995-2061 | www.oola-sf.com

SoMa scene-seekers looking for "cool late-night dining" (till midnight or 1 AM nightly) join the other "interesting patrons" at this "dark" and "mysterious" loftlike space offering "consistent" Californian cuisine that "always hits the spot"; though naysayers mention "questionable" service and suggest it's "underwhelming" for the price, most "have never been disappointed" by chef-owner Ola Fendert's menu and a wine list that's "full of winners."

Oriental Pearl *Chinese*   21 | 13 | 19 | $29

Chinatown | 778 Clay St. (Grant Ave.) | 415-433-1817 | www.orientalpearlsf.com

The "excellent" "dim sum is yum yum" (and at "great" prices too) at this "under-the-radar" Chinatown dumpling destination where "profes-sional" waiters "politely" serve a full menu of "wonderful", "authentic" Chinese chow as well; it "avoids" "the pitfalls" of its competitors ("crowds, noise, lines"), so groupies gush it's a "good place to bring out-of-town guests" with a hankering for Hong Kong fare.

Orson ☒ *Californian*   18 | 20 | 17 | $50

SoMa | 508 Fourth St. (Bryant St.) | 415-777-1508 | www.orsonsf.com

With its "lounge-y" "modern/industrial decor" and "experimental" eats (think a "Caesar salad that explodes" or a sourdough ice cream sundae), co-chef/owner Elizabeth Falkner's SoMa Californian is "hip for the hip" – but "not for the non-adventurous"; maybe that explains the sharp split in surveyor sentiment over this "over-priced" place, though even those who call it "hit-or-miss" admit "the highs can be high."

Osha Thai *Thai*   21 | 19 | 17 | $28

Cow Hollow | 2033 Union St. (bet. Buchanan & Webster Sts.) | 415-567-6742 ◑
Downtown | Embarcadero Ctr. | 4 Embarcadero Ctr., street level (Drumm St.) | 415-788-6742
Glen Park | 2922 Diamond St. (Bosworth St.) | 415-586-6742
Mission | 819 Valencia St. (bet. 19th & 20th Sts.) | 415-826-7738 ◑
SoMa | 149 Second St. (bet. Howard & Mission Sts.) | 415-278-9991
SoMa | 311 Third St. (Folsom St.) | 415-896-6742
Tenderloin | 696 Geary St. (Leavenworth St.) | 415-673-2368 ◑
www.oshathai.com

"There's a reason" this "reasonably priced" Thai chainlet is often "crowded", what with "imaginative", "surprisingly tasty" fare ranging from "well-prepared menu stalwarts" to "signature dishes" like "out-of-this-world" pumpkin curry and "delicious" "volcanic beef"; "great cocktails" and "efficient" service are other pluses, and though a few are less enthusiastic about "shouting" over the "too-noisy" "clublike atmosphere", the "modern-Zen" digs are "inviting."

Ottimista Enoteca-Café ⓜ *Italian/Mediterranean*

▽ 19 | 19 | 18 | $31

Cow Hollow | 1838 Union St. (Octavia St.) | 415-674-8400 | www.ottimistasf.com

The "friendly", "knowledgeable staff will make sure your thin-crust pizza is paired with the perfect glass of vino" at this "cute and charming" Cow Hollow *enoteca* suitable for anything from a "light bite" with one of their "hard-to-find wines" or a "hearty meal" from their Italian-Med menu; "delicious" flights and a varied menu with "plenty to offer" "different-sized appetites" make it a "primo" place say supporters, especially if you "grab a table" on the patio, which is "lovely on a warm day."

Outerlands ⓜ *American*

23 | 17 | 18 | $24

Outer Sunset | 4001 Judah St. (45th Ave.) | 415-661-6140 | www.outerlandssf.com

Located "as far out as you can get before hitting the ocean", this "funky" Outer Sunset cafe – "the kind of place where you pay first at the counter" – "gets packed" with "hipsters and surfers on the weekends" jonesing for "amazing" "open-faced sandwiches" on "big hunking" pieces of "freshly baked bread" and other "hearty" affordable American eats; "seating is very limited" and there's "no reservations", just "plenty of interesting people to share the wait with" – and of late, sit-down dinners and a full bar.

Out the Door *Vietnamese*

22 | 15 | 17 | $27

Downtown | Westfield San Francisco Ctr. | 845 Market St., concourse level (bet. 4th & 5th Sts.) | 415-541-9913

Embarcadero | Ferry Bldg. Mktpl. | 1 Ferry Bldg. (The Embarcadero) | 415-321-3740

Upper Fillmore | 2232 Bush St. (Fillmore St.) | 415-923-9575 www.outthedoors.com

"For a taste of Charles Phan's exquisite" California-meets-Vietnam cooking "without the eardrum-shattering noise", "cost" or "interminable" wait at mother ship the Slanted Door, Downtown "working" folks, "tired shoppers" and swells "gladly accept" this "fabulous" "downscale" sit-down trio that also includes a "take-out" "counter" at the Ferry Building and an Upper Fillmore offshoot; the options are "more limited" and the "beef may not be all the way to shaking, but it is shivering", and "affordable wines on tap" boost the appeal.

Oyaji ⓜ *Japanese*

▽ 24 | 14 | 16 | $40

Outer Richmond | 3123 Clement St. (bet. 32nd & 33rd Aves.) | 415-379-3604

The chef-owner "unveils his sushi magic" at this midpriced "gem" "hidden" in the Outer Richmond "near Lincoln Park" where the "excellent" "fresh" fish is "supplemented" with "authentic" "umami"-infused izakaya items, like pork belly that's "cooked to perfection"; regulars say "don't miss the chance to buy" the *oyaji* ("old man") "a drink" and "let the show begin" as he whips up a "truly memorable meal."

	FOOD	DECOR	SERVICE	COST

Ozumo *Japanese*

| | 23 | 24 | 20 | $54 |

Embarcadero | 161 Steuart St. (bet. Howard & Mission Sts.) |
415-882-1333 | www.ozumo.com

A "young" "see-and-be-seen" set sips "fine" sakes in the "hopping" bar at this "upscale" eatery along the Embarcadero and its equally "elegant" Oakland offshoot; in the "pretty" and comparatively "peaceful" dining room, a "well-mannered" staff serves "pristine" sashimi, "expertly grilled skewers" seared "on the robata grill", and other "phenomenal" Japanese fare; "the sushi is to die for, and so is the price", but it's "worth it" when you're set on "impressing a business partner from Manhattan."

Pacific Café *Seafood*

| | 23 | 17 | 22 | $38 |

Outer Richmond | 7000 Geary Blvd. (34th Ave.) | 415-387-7091

"Exquisitely fresh" fish, "simply and superbly prepared", attracts a "devoted clientele" to the Outer Richmond, where this "untrendy" seafooder appeals to both "the pocket and palate"; the "homey" decor might be "unchanged since it opened" in 1974, but the same could be said of the "very friendly" staff, who render the "interminable wait for a table" "very pleasant" (even "festive"); P.S. "no reservations."

Pacific Catch *Seafood*

| | 19 | 16 | 18 | $26 |

Inner Sunset | 1200 Ninth Ave. (Lincoln Way) | 415-504-6905
Marina | 2027 Chestnut St. (bet. Fillmore & Steiner Sts.) | 415-440-1950
www.pacificcatch.com

Fin fanciers "take the poor man's Hawaiian vacation" at this "attractively priced" trio offering "fresh seafood with a Pan-Pacific touch" plus "don't-miss" "sweet potato fries" and "inventive bar drinks"; the "friendly" staff is "terrific with kids", but while the Sunset and Marin outposts boast plenty of room in the sea, "seating is tight" in the Marina, so "get your food to go and skip the lines."

Pagan Ⓜ *Burmese*

| | ▽ 18 | 12 | 16 | $21 |

Outer Richmond | 3199 Clement St. (33rd Ave.) | 415-751-2598 |
www.pagansf.com

"Refreshing and fresh" "renditions of hard to get Burmese food" like "addictive tea-leaf salad" join the Thai options served in "comfortable", "relaxing" surroundings by a "kind" and "helpful" staff at this Richmonder that's a "good alternative" "without the wait" of the other eateries in the 'hood; it's "friendly to your wallet" too.

Pagolac Ⓜ🍽 *Vietnamese*

| | ▽ 23 | 12 | 19 | $26 |

Tenderloin | 655 Larkin St. (bet. Ellis & Willow Sts.) | 415-776-3234

A "divine experience" of the "famous" "seven courses of beef" is "the way to go" at this "hidden treasure" in the Tenderloin, which is also "highly recommended" for its other Vietnamese fare, from pho to "fresh" rolls; the decor may be "simple", but the "friendly", "family-run" vibe makes it a "great choice" when you're in the 'hood.

Pakwan *Pakistani*

| | 22 | 5 | 9 | $17 |

Mission | 3180-3182 16th St. (bet. Guerrero & Valencia Sts.) |
415-255-2440 🍽
Tenderloin | 501 O'Farrell St. (Jones St.) | 415-776-0160
www.pakwanrestaurant.com

The "biryanis are the best" and the "naan is just right" at this "authentic, fast and easy" Pakistani pack, which "attracts" admirers with a "variety" of "flavorful dishes" at "rock-bottom prices" and another "plus – BYO"; there's "minimal service and no decor" at the "order-at-the-counter", "hole-in-the-wall" spots, leading many to find it "perfect for takeout."

Palio d'Asti ⚠ *Italian*

| 20 | 20 | 20 | $46 |

Downtown | 640 Sacramento St. (bet. Kearny & Montgomery Sts.) | 415-395-9800 | www.paliodasti.com

"Financial District suits" seeking a "better-than-usual" "business lunch" hoof it to this "long-lived" "Italian standby", where a "versatile menu" of "solid" cuisine is served amid "theatrical" equine decor by "accommodating" vets who "really know how to pair wines"; while "not adventurous", it's "priced right" (especially the "$1 pizza happy hour") and the "truffle season" meals are "spectacular."

Pancho Villa Taqueria ◑ *Mexican*

| 22 | 8 | 14 | $13 |

Mission | 3071 16th St. (bet. Mission & Valencia Sts.) | 415-864-8840 | www.panchovillasf.com

"Gut-busting" burritos and "fantastic, fresh salsas" that'll "make your eyes and mouth water" are among the *"muy bueno"* "Mexican fast food" at this "reasonably priced" taqueria twosome in the Mission and San Mateo; "friendly", "fast-acting" servers minimize the wait in "long" "cafeteria-style" lines, and the "uncomfortable" stools "are no deterrent to the faithful", though a few prefer "takeout" to dining in the "fluorescent"-lit interior.

Pane e Vino *Italian*

| 22 | 17 | 22 | $40 |

Cow Hollow | 1715 Union St. (Gough St.) | 415-346-2111 | www.paneevinotrattoria.com

The "consistent" kitchen "never lets you down" at this Cow Hollow "comfy" "neighborhood gem", where the "crispy" "thin-crust pizza", "delicious pastas" and other "tasty" fare is "moderately priced"; if a picky few proclaim the "basic Italian repertoire" "not worth a detour", others who adore the "irresistible charm" of the "enthusiastic" servers dub it "always a winner."

Papalote Mexican Grill *Mexican*

| 22 | 11 | 13 | $14 |

Mission | 3409 24th St. (Valencia St.) | 415-970-8815
Western Addition | 1777 Fulton St. (Masonic Ave.) | 415-776-0106
www.papalote-sf.com

"Furiously good" "taqueria feasts" lure legions to this Mission and Western Addition "hole-in-the-wall" duo, where the "awesome", "never greasy" Mexican staples embrace "vegetarian options" "for health nuts" and the "famous" "tangy salsa" "leaves every mouth smiling"; they "aren't strictly authentic" and "it's a pretty penny for a burrito", but the "limited seating" is "always crowded."

Papito *Mexican*

| ▽ 25 | 15 | 22 | $20 |

Potrero Hill | 317 Connecticut St. (bet. 18th & 19th Sts.) | 415-695-0147 | www.papitosf.com

The owners of Chez Papa jettison berets for sombreros "with delicious results" at this Potrero Hill newcomer where "aim-to-please" servers ferry out "sublime" "organic Mexican" small and larger plates ("the duck confit tacos are a must") along with sangria and bottles of Negra Modelo; at night, it's best to "come early" as the handful of sidewalk tables and interior seats at the copper-topped bar fill up fast.

Parada 22 Ⓜ *Puerto Rican*

▽ 21 | 19 | 19 | $15

Haight-Ashbury | 1805 Haight St. (Shrader St.) | 415-750-1111 | www.parada22.com

Between the cordial "casualness" and generous plates of "authentic Puerto Rican", this Haight-Ashbury yearling truly "reminds you of Old San Juan"; *pernil asado* (roast pork), Cuban sandwiches and other "excellent" island classics are served in suitably tropical digs lined with old-time photos, and the low-dough tabs have addicts "coming back for more."

Park Chalet Garden Restaurant *Californian*

15 | 20 | 15 | $29

Outer Sunset | 1000 Great Hwy. (bet. Fulton St. & Lincoln Way) | 415-386-8439 | www.parkchalet.com

Locals laud the "beautiful setting" of this brewpub at the edge of Golden Gate Park, especially "when it's warm" and they "sit outside" in Adirondack chairs; "the beer and wine selection" gets a nod but the "overpriced" New American–Californian fare sometimes "leaves a lot to be desired", as does the "slow service"; it's still "really" "worth it" though, thanks to the "lovely ambiance."

NEW Pasión *Nuevo Latino/Peruvian*

▽ 22 | 24 | 21 | $45

Inner Sunset | 737 Irving St. (bet. 8th & 9th Aves.) | 415-742-5727 | www.pasionsf.com

This new "offspring of Fresca" is "a great addition to the Inner Sunset and to the Peruvian food scene" proclaim patrons with pasión aplenty for the "wondrous" ceviche and other Nuevo Latino offerings; with crystalline lights, a colorful mural and purple suede booths, the dining room provides "great ambiance", and if service is "friendly but uncoordinated", "the bartenders are so handsome it's worth ordering an extra drink."

Pasta Pomodoro *Italian*

16 | 13 | 17 | $23

Laurel Heights | 3611 California St. (Spruce St.) | 415-831-0900
Noe Valley | 4000 24th St. (Noe St.) | 415-920-9904
www.pastapomodoro.com

"Fast food meets Italian" at this "dependable" chain where "large portions" of "solid if unspectacular" eats come with "a small price tag"; "tasty pastas please adults and kids alike" and "efficient" servers who "can handle anything" add to a "family-friendly" vibe that's "loud" during the "early" dinner hour; while some sniff at the "sterile atmosphere" and "minimal" decor, there's also "pleasant" patio or sidewalk seating at every location.

Patxi's Chicago Pizza *Pizza*

22 | 14 | 17 | $21

Cow Hollow | 3318 Fillmore St. (Lombard St.) | 415-345-3995
Hayes Valley | 511 Hayes St. (bet. Laguna & Octavia Sts.) | 415-558-9991
NEW Noe Valley | 4042 24th St. (bet. Castro & Noe Sts.)
www.patxispizza.com

For a taste of "Chicago without the extreme weather", this burgeoning Bay Area pizzeria chainlet serves up "fantastic deep-dish and stuffed pies" and also dishes out "thin-crust" and "vegan options"; "long" waits are "offset by interesting beers on tap", "big screens" for "watching the game" and a "super-nice" staff (some insiders "call ahead" for fully or half-baked orders and "waltz past the line"); whatever the plan, "you definitely get your money's worth."

	FOOD	DECOR	SERVICE	COST

Pauline's Pizza 🅂🅼 *Pizza*   23 | 14 | 19 | $27

Mission | 260 Valencia St. (bet. Duboce Ave. & 14th St.) | 415-552-2050

Pauline's Wines 🅂🅼 *Pizza*

Mission | 260 Valencia St. (bet. Duboce Ave. & 14th St.) | 415-552-2050
www.paulinespizza.com

Pizzaphiles are "delighted every time" by the "artistry" at this "popular" Mission "hangout", a longtime fixture for "divine" designer pies (the signature pesto variety "is a must") and "fantastic salads", both featuring "fresh organic ingredients" "home-grown" on its own farm; "very drinkable" house-label vinos help make the "bare-bones" dining room and backyard wine bar "a fun place for sure", even if "parking's not so fun."

Paul K 🅼 *Mediterranean*   22 | 18 | 22 | $44

Hayes Valley | 199 Gough St. (Oak St.) | 415-552-7132 |
www.paulkrestaurant.com

A "favorite" for "dinner before the opera or symphony", this "buzzy" Hayes Valley Mediterranean dependably "delivers" "memorable" cuisine in a "cozy", "contemporary setting" staffed by "accommodating" servers who "can work a busy room"; the "small", "crowded space" can be "a challenge", but it's "convenient to all the concert halls" and with "bottomless mimosas and Bloody Marys", "they've perfected the boozy brunch."

🆕 Pause Wine Bar ◑🅂🅼 *American*   - | - | - | E

Hayes Valley | 1666 Market St. (bet. Franklin & Gough Sts.) |
415-241-9463 | www.pausesf.com

Now settled into Cav's onetime digs, this new Hayes Valley enoteca goes typical finger fare one better with small American plates flaunting fresh seafood and locally sourced veggies, which complement a vino list featuring organic and Californian options; given the cozy layout with a zinc bar, flattering lights and wooden banquettes lining a wall paneled with corks, a pause could easily turn into an extended stay.

Pazzia 🅂 *Italian*   23 | 15 | 20 | $35

SoMa | 337 Third St. (bet. Folsom & Harrison Sts.) | 415-512-1693

"Authentically Italian in every way", this "unpretentious" SoMa trattoria is a "neighborhood" "find" for "awesome thin-crust" pizza, "melt-in-your-mouth pastas" and other Boot-alicious specialties "done right" at "fair prices"; arrivals are "warmly greeted" by the "charming owner" and "competent staff", which "more than makes up for" a "small", "crowded" setting that's "kind of in the middle of nowhere."

🗹 Perbacco 🅂 *Italian*   25 | 22 | 23 | $57

Downtown | 230 California St. (bet. Battery & Front Sts.) | 415-955-0663 |
www.perbaccosf.com

Still the "'it' place" for a FiDi "power" lunch or "hot date", this "more formal sister to Barbacco" "packs" in a "high-profile bustling crowd where business deals are made or broken" over "heavenly" "house-made pastas", salumi and other "Piemontese specialties"; the "slick decor", "exceptional" staff and "exciting, off-the-beaten-path wines" complete the package, but "it's noisy as all get out", so "to avoid" the "after-work singles crowd at the bar", "sit upstairs."

	FOOD	DECOR	SERVICE	COST

Pesce *Italian/Seafood* — 25 | 16 | 21 | $39

Russian Hill | 2227 Polk St. (bet. Green & Vallejo Sts.) | 415-928-8025 |
www.pescebarsf.com

"A real sleeper", this "totally unassuming" Italian seafooder in Russian
Hill reels in fans with chef/co-owner Ruggero Gadaldi's "splendid"
Venetian fish dishes and "amazing" pastas "served tapas-style" and
paired with a "well-priced wine list"; it's a "local" "standby" with tight,
"minimalist" quarters and a bar that "rocks", so while the "premium"
cooking "doesn't disappoint", seating's "oftentimes hard to snag."

Pi Bar ● *Pizza* — ▽ 18 | 14 | 18 | $21

Mission | 1432 Valencia St. (25th St.) | 415-970-9670 |
www.pibarsf.com

"Decent" pizza plus "a wide range" of suds sums up this "barlike"
Mission joint, which plies "innovative" "thin-crust" pies (and cleverly
priced $3.14 slices) washed down with "California microbrews" on tap
and a "deep bottle" selection that's "heavy on Belgians"; some say the
"average" eating and "irrational" cost don't compute, but it attracts a
"cool" clientele and stays "open late too" – "'nuff said."

Pica Pica Maize Kitchen *Venezuelan* — 21 | 12 | 16 | $17

Mission | 401 Valencia St. (15th St.) | 415-400-5453 |
www.picapicakitchen.com

See review in North of San Francisco Directory.

Piccino Ⓜ *Italian* — ▽ 23 | - | 21 | $33

Dogpatch | 1001 Minnesota St. (22nd St.) | 415-824-4224 |
www.piccinocafe.com

There's even more to "love" at this "sweet" Cal-Italian cafe "out in the
'patch" that's relocated to "bigger digs down the block", where new
chef Rachel Silcocks (ex Nopa) dishes out "amazing" thin-crust pizzas,
salads and sandwiches featuring "the best of what's growing locally";
communal seating at reclaimed wood tables and the kitchen-view
counter suit an "impromptu lunch or dinner", with the adjacent all-day
coffee bar offering "Blue Bottle" brews and baked goods.

Piperade Ⓩ *Spanish* — 25 | 21 | 23 | $54

Downtown | 1015 Battery St. (bet. Green & Union Sts.) | 415-391-2555 |
www.piperade.com

"For an adventure in dining", devotees "let owner" Gerald
Hirigoyen order for them at this "pip of a restaurant" tucked away
Downtown showcasing "delicious" "high-level" "Franco-Basque"
bistro classics along with "well-priced" Spanish and "hard-to-find
wines" from that region; it's all "served up in an appropriately rustic
room" with an "upbeat" vibe by a staff so "friendly" "you might leave
spontaneously speaking Euskara."

Piqueo's *Peruvian* — 25 | 18 | 21 | $39

Bernal Heights | 830 Cortland Ave. (Gates St.) | 415-282-8812 |
www.piqueos.com

Be "transported" "back to Lima" courtesy of the "excellent small
plates" of "fantastically flavored Peruvian" fare served up at this "favorite" "little neighborhood gem" "off the beaten path" in Bernal
Heights; be warned, "prices can get steep" and service ranges from
"very attentive" to "spotty" in the "crowded but atmospheric" "nook."

Pizza Nostra *Pizza* ▽ 19 | 14 | 18 | $30

Potrero Hill | 300 De Haro St. (16th St.) | 415-558-9493 |
www.pizzanostrasf.com

Offering "more than just pizza", this "consistent" Potrero Hill haunt
serves "excellent" pastas and other Italian entrees along with its
"tasty", "freshly made" pies (the Margherita is "a fave"); though decor
is nothing special, patrons assert the "attentive" staff will reward you
"with a special meal", especially on "warm" days, when the "fantastic"
patio is the place to be.

Pizzeria Delfina *Pizza* 25 | 15 | 18 | $28

Mission | 3611 18th St. (Guerrero St.) | 415-437-6800
Pacific Heights | 2406 California St. (bet. Fillmore & Steiner Sts.) |
415-440-1189
www.pizzeriadelfina.com

"Perfect" "thin-crust" "Cali" meets Naples pie graced with "innovative" toppings "forever makes normal pizza seem tacky" insist fans
"privileged to get a seat" at this "upscale" "pizzeria haven" duo in the
Mission and Pac Heights; expect "crazy-long waits", but the "staff
hustles", the antipasti "have the magic of Delfina's" (their big sister)
and there are "great Italian varietals by the glass", while those eager
to skip the fracas and "blasting" "'80s music" can get 'em "to go."

Pizzetta 211 ⌓ *Pizza* 25 | 12 | 16 | $27

Outer Richmond | 211 23rd Ave. (California St.) | 415-379-9880 |
www.pizzetta211.com

The "crisp" pizzas – "razor-thin crusts" loaded with "impeccable" "artisanal locavore toppings" – are "done to perfection" at this "postage
stamp"-size "hole-in-the-wall" in the Outer Richmond; a few fuss
about the staffers' "too-cool attitude", and even aficionados agree you
should "go early" because the "waiting time is a drag", but it's "totally
worth it" for the "quality" pies.

Plant Cafe Organic *Health Food* 21 | 18 | 17 | $25

Downtown | 101 California St. (Front St.) | 415-693-9730 | ⊠
Embarcadero | Pier 3 (bet. B'way & Washington St.) | 415-984-1973
Marina | 3352 Steiner St. (bet. Chestnut & Lombard Sts.) | 415-931-2777
www.theplantcafe.com

"Plant me here" quip fans of this "casual" health-food trio turning out
"fresh, organic" dishes including a "to-die-for" signature burger,
"great salads" and other "inventive" (if "pricey") fare; service can be
"blissed-out and forgetful" and the Marina locale has "zero ambiance"
while Downtown is "crowded" with "workers", but the Embarcadero
outpost offers "views of the Bay" in a "great waterfront location"
(including an "outside patio").

Plouf ⊠ *French* 21 | 16 | 18 | $41

Downtown | 40 Belden Pl. (bet. Bush & Pine Sts.) | 415-986-6491 |
www.ploufsf.com

Bivalve buffs "slurp up" "superior" mussels prepared in "so many
delicious ways", then "soak up" the sauce "to the very last drop" at this
"lively" Gallic seafooder; the tables may be "very close", but there's
"nothing better" than eating outside on "charming" Belden Place, as
"friendly", "very French waiters" in "striped mariner shirts" help
"transport" you from SF's "Downtown bustle" to the "Rive Gauche."

NEW Plow *Californian*

▽ 25 | 19 | 23 | $23

Potrero Hill | 1299 18th St. (Texas St.) | 415-821-7569 | www.eatatplow.com

"Sublime eggs" and other "innovative" Californian fare made from "fantastic ingredients" has "the see-and-be-seen set" "lined up" "early and often" at this "welcome newcomer" to Potrero Hill; contrary to its folksy decor (salvaged wood floors, tables made from oak barrels), it's a "little "pricey for breakfast"/lunch, but the "bustling but relaxed" vibe and "friendly" staff are "worth the trek" for brunch even "for those who do not live in the vicinity."

Pluto's Fresh Food for a Hungry Universe *American*

21 | 12 | 16 | $14

Inner Sunset | 627 Irving St. (bet. 7th & 8th Aves.) | 415-753-8867
Marina | 3258 Scott St. (bet. Chestnut & Lombard Sts.) | 415-775-8867
www.plutosfreshfood.com

A "huge following" lands at this "simple" and "inexpensive" SF and South Bay mini-chain for a "quick lunch" or to "pick up" dinner when "heading home from the gym" from a menu that includes "create-your-own salads", "hot sandwiches" and turkey and fixin's for "Thanksgiving any day of the week"; despite "fast and efficient" service, the "confusing ordering system" reminds some of "a high school cafeteria", though the "healthy, fresh" grub's "way better."

Poesia *Italian*

21 | 18 | 22 | $45

Castro | 4072 18th St. (bet. Castro & Hartford Sts.) | 415-252-9325 | www.poesiasf.com

"Buon appetito!" say fans of this "charming little" Southern Italian, "one of the better" Castro choices thanks to an "exciting" menu spotlighting Calabresi cuisine, a genial expat staff to "provide knowledgeable advice" and a "vibrant" upstairs setting with Cinecittà flicks "showing silently on the wall"; the tabs leave some "wondering if *poesia* means 'expensive'", but most maintain "the quality justifies the price."

Pomelo *Eclectic*

21 | 13 | 19 | $25

Inner Sunset | 92 Judah St. (bet. 5th & 6th Aves.) | 415-731-6175
Noe Valley | 1793 Church St. (30th St.) | 415-285-2257
www.pomelosf.com

It's "cuisine sans category" at this Eclectic pair, with a "revolving menu" of "healthy", "delicious fusion" dishes "from around the world" served in "huge portions" at a "super value"; service is "spotty" but "friendly", and while the Noe Valley outpost is slightly "bigger and noisier", fans of the "tiny and terrific" Inner Sunset spot love to "sit at the bar and chat with the chef."

Pork Store Café *American*

19 | 11 | 16 | $17

Haight-Ashbury | 1451 Haight St. (bet. Ashbury St. & Masonic Ave.) | 415-864-6981
Mission | 3122 16th St. (bet. Guerrero & Valencia Sts.) | 415-626-5523
www.porkstorecafe.com

The "big, traditional" "greasy-spoon breakfast" at these "no-frills" "true classic" diners will "keep you full for the day" with "out-of-control" portions of "cheap" AM "sustenance" that's "worth the wait"; though the Mission spin-off is "larger and can more easily accommodate" crowds, those seeking a "hash-house feel" say you "must go to

Haight Street"; P.S. the 16th Street branch is also open Thursday 7 PM-3 AM, and Friday–Saturday all day till 3 AM.

Postrio *American*   23 | 22 | 23 | $64

Downtown | Prescott Hotel | 545 Post St. (bet. Mason & Taylor Sts.) | 415-776-7825 | www.postrio.com

Although this Downtowner is "not what it once was" "when Wolfgang roamed the premises", its "front bar"/cafe is still a "great location" for "casual" "pre-theater dining" or an "after-shopping treat" over "wood-fired pizzas" and New American fare; these days, one only descends the "grand staircase" into the "stunning" dining room for breakfast and private parties, but you can still count on "great service" and "a local celeb or two."

Presidio Social Club *American*   19 | 20 | 21 | $39

Presidio | 563 Ruger St. (Lombard St.) | 415-885-1888 | www.presidiosocialclub.com

In a "converted" "enlisted men's barracks" "in the middle of the Presidio", this "unique" New American with a "midcentury officers' club motif" takes diners "back in time" with its "interesting twists" on "classic" "comfort food"; it's a "stunning location", and most recruits "would love to just hang out here all evening", thanks in part to bartenders who do a "masterful" job shaking "classic cocktails" with "a modern sensibility."

Prime Rib Shabu Ⓜ *Japanese*   ▽ 20 | 14 | 17 | $33

Inner Richmond | 308 Fifth Ave. (Geary Blvd.) | 415-379-4678

"If you like shabu, it's hard to beat" all you can eat at this Inner Richmond hot-pot hideout from area impresario Luke Sung, where $26 brings on unlimited servings of "thinly" "hand-cut prime rib", "pristine veggies" and "fresh" seafood for DIY "simmering" in "flavored broth" over table-top burners; maybe the service and surroundings are "nothing to write home about", but given the quality and cost, it "can be addicting."

Prospect *American*   24 | 24 | 23 | $66

SoMa | Infiniti Towers | 300 Spear St. (Folsom St.) | 415-247-7770 | www.prospectsf.com

Once "beyond the din" of the "after-work watering-hole" "scene" awash in "fancy cocktails" up "front" in this "more casual" SoMa "sister" of Boulevard, "fans of Nancy Oakes" are ensconced in a "glamorous", "sleek" dining room with plush "booths" where "innovative" New American dinners and "Sunday brunch" join "great wines" and service that's "just right"; but bring your wallet, as the "prospect" is that it's "more opulent" and "pricey" than you'd expect.

Public House *Pub Food*   16 | 19 | 15 | $29

South Beach | AT&T Park | 24 Willie Mays Plaza (3rd St.) | 415-644-0240 | www.publichousesf.com

Situated in the former "Acme Chophouse" at AT&T Park, this jumbo pub "adds to the ballpark experience" with "dozens of large flat-screens" beaming "sporting events", taps dispensing "a lot of craft beers" and culinary all-star Traci Des Jardins' creative bar bites to "soak up all that alcohol"; but "beware" "on game day" when it's "wall to wall" with "fun-loving" "Giants fans" and so "noisy" "you may experience hearing loss."

	FOOD	DECOR	SERVICE	COST

Q Restaurant & Wine Bar *American* | 20 | 17 | 19 | $27 |

Inner Richmond | 225 Clement St. (bet. 3rd & 4th Aves.) | 415-752-2298 | www.qrestaurant.com

"Cheer yourself up after a long day" with "homestyle cookin'" at this "casual" Inner Richmond American, where the "comforting" fare (BBQ, burgers, "mac 'n' cheese to kill for") is prepared a "bit better than what you'd normally expect" at a "reasonable price"; resembling a "diner" bedecked "with artwork" from "Mars", the "high-energy, high-decibel" milieu is "enjoyable" "for kids and adults" alike.

🅉 Quince *Italian* | 26 | 26 | 25 | $87 |

Downtown | 470 Pacific Ave. (bet. Montgomery St. & Osgood Pl.) | 415-775-8500 | www.quincerestaurant.com

Michael and Lindsay Tusk's "locavore-licious", "oh-so-high-end Italian" is "all grown-up" and wears its "very fancy" "adult" identity "well", from its "quiet" "*très chic*" "new quarters" Downtown "to the suits" on the "formal" staff delivering tasting menus featuring "dreamy pastas" and other "fabulous" fare that's "like art"; wines are "superb" (albeit "outrageously" priced), adding to the "total fine-dining experience" when "you have something to celebrate", and if some miss the original's "intimacy", they're outnumbered by those urging "indulge yourself."

NEW Radish Ⓜ *American* | - | - | - | M |

Mission | 3465 19th St. (Lexington St.) | 415-834-5441 | www.radishsf.com

A new sprout in the Mission, this rad American supplies three squares a day with old-fashioned breakfasts, sandwiches at lunch and small plates by night, all notable for random Southern accents and the freshness of locally sourced fixings and house-baked breads (except the gluten-free versions); a colorfully casual space with paintings lining the crimson walls appeals to cool customers, as do the craft beers and soju cocktails.

Radius Ⓜ *Californian* | ▽ 23 | 18 | 21 | $47 |

SoMa | 1123 Folsom St. (Langton St.) | 415-525-3676 | www.radiussf.com

SoMa locals have quickly taken to this "feel-good" Californian serving "simple", "all-organic" cuisine "sourced from within a 100-mile radius" ("even the wine") in "a stunning, industrial-chic setting" outfitted with "mostly recycled materials"; while reservations are accepted for the sit-down dinner quarters, it's walk-in only at the casual all-day "cafe next door" with its artisanal larder and "cute courtyard"; P.S. a post-Survey chef change is not reflected in the Food score.

NEW Ragazza *Pizza* | 24 | 20 | 21 | $36 |

Western Addition | 311 Divisadero St. (bet. Oak & Page Sts.) | 415-255-1133 | www.ragazzasf.com

Gialina's "super-delicious" spin-off is "a welcome addition to the Divisadero Corridor", firing up "amazing" Neapolitan pies "that go way beyond the typical pepperoni and sausage", along with other "delicious" Italian eats; the vintage black-and-white photos of the *ragazze* (girls) in the chef-owner's family "are a hoot", but the "small" storefront "fills up fast" (no reservations) so "get there early."

R & G Lounge *Chinese*   24 | 13 | 15 | $34

Chinatown | 631 Kearny St. (bet. Clay & Sacramento Sts.) |
415-982-7877 | www.rnglounge.com

The "signature" salt-and-pepper crab is "insanely addictive", but "you can't go wrong with anything" on the "extensive" menu of "real-deal" Cantonese chow at this "buzzy" and "brightly lit" seafooder in Chinatown; servers "can be a little harried" in their attempt to "turn tables", and no, it's "not cheap", but it's "worth fighting the crowds", whether you "rub elbows with the locals" in the "basic" basement or choose the "more elegant" upstairs.

☑ Range *American*   27 | 20 | 23 | $53

Mission | 842 Valencia St. (bet. 19th & 20th Sts.) | 415-282-8283 |
www.rangesf.com

"Sophisticated and funky, just like the Mission" itself, this Valencia Corridor "standby" is "as good as it gets" in the 'hood (certainly "for the money"), doling out "deceptively" "simple" yet "extraordinary" New American fare and seasonal ingredient–driven "fancy cocktails" that "never fail to impress"; the deco digs get "noisy and the tables are too close together", but the bartenders and "gracious" staffers are "some of the best", so folks "love to be home on this range."

Red's Java House *Burgers*   15 | 12 | 12 | $13

Embarcadero | Pier 30 (Bryant St.) | 415-777-5626

"The price is right and so is the view" at this "funky" "bayside shack" that's "been there forever" on the Embarcadero; the food may only be "so-so", but both "blue jeans and Savile Row" types can be found with a "cheap", "greasy burger" and a "cold beer" sitting "outside on the dock" and "studying the underside of the Bay Bridge"; P.S. on game days, when it stays open past 5 PM, Giants fans can enjoy "pregame lubrication."

Regalito Rosticeria *Mexican*   ▽ 23 | 16 | 19 | $30

Mission | 3481 18th St. (bet. Lexington & Valencia Sts.) | 415-503-0650 |
www.regalitosf.com

"For something more sophisticated than your average" Mexican spread, this affordable "find" "truly is a 'little gift' to the Mission" specializing in "remarkably good" rotisserie fare and a "*delicioso*" weekend brunch; a lucky few forgo the "tiny, crowded" interior for "people-watching" from a pair of sidewalk tables.

Restaurant LuLu *French/Mediterranean*   19 | 18 | 18 | $45

SoMa | 816 Folsom St. (bet. 4th & 5th Sts.) | 415-495-5775 |
www.restaurantlulu.com

Despite the "cathedral ceilings", this brasserie is "cozy", thanks to an "open kitchen" with a "warm and inviting" "wood-burning oven" that "turns out numerous winners" on the French-Med menu; it suits a "big, boisterous meal" with "family-style" dining and an "impressive wine list", but some suggest the staff needs to get its "groove back."

Richmond Restaurant & Wine Bar ☑ *Californian*   24 | 19 | 24 | $46

Inner Richmond | 615 Balboa St. (bet. 7th & 8th Aves.) | 415-379-8988 |
www.therichmondsf.com

"If you can find parking" you'll "want to linger all night" at this "cozy little Inner Richmond jewel" where the "menu attracts and the chef delivers" "beautifully plated" Californian cuisine (and the "most delicious cheeseburger and fries") with a "well-priced wine list" to match; tabs are "reasonable", particularly the "excellent-value" prix fixe, and "service is "welcoming and crisp."

Ristobar *Italian*   21 | 21 | 19 | $42

Marina | 2300 Chestnut St. (Scott St.) | 415-923-6464 |
www.ristobarsf.com

An "attractive" successor to the Marina's Emporio Rulli, this "fashionable" Italian's marble bar and "high ceiling" limned with hand-painted frescoes set the scene for a "solid" array of rustic small plates, "wonderful thin-crust" pizzas and "hard-to-pass-up" desserts courtesy of owner and "master baker" Gary Rulli; notwithstanding the "noise level" and sometimes "impersonal service", it's "usually crowded" with "suits" seeking "fine" dining and sipping from a "lovely selection of wines" "without spending a fortune."

Ristorante Ideale *Italian*   23 | 16 | 21 | $37

North Beach | 1309 Grant Ave. (Vallejo St.) | 415-391-4129 |
www.idealerestaurant.com

The chef's "grandma's cooking style from Rome" informs the kitchen at this "casual" trattoria in North Beach, and the "*autentico*" results earn "high marks" from Southern Italian enthusiasts, who "thoroughly enjoy" the "outstanding" "homemade pastas"; overall it's a "great value", and there's a "wide selection" of "wines at various prices", so idealists itch "to come back again and again" and be "welcomed by the friendly staff."

Ristorante Milano *Italian*   25 | 18 | 23 | $43

Russian Hill | 1448 Pacific Ave. (bet. Hyde & Larkin Sts.) | 415-673-2961 |
www.milanosf.com

Though you'll find "many regulars" here, the "gracious" chef-owner and his "friendly" yet "professional" staff always extend a "warm welcome" to newcomers too at this "unpretentious", "family-run" trattoria atop Russian Hill; "extraordinary" "housemade pasta" is among the "traditional" Northern Italian fare "made with top-quality ingredients", just "make a reservation", since it's a "very small" space.

Ristorante Umbria ⊠ *Italian*   18 | 15 | 18 | $42

SoMa | 198 Second St. (Howard St.) | 415-546-6985 |
www.ristoranteumbria.com

The "welcoming atmosphere" and "effusive" owner "add to the authenticity" at this SoMa "neighborhood" Italian, where staffers serve up "old-style" Umbrian staples like "mama would make"; it's "reliable" "as long as you're not expecting cutting-edge food", and frequently "crowded" with "an appreciative clientele", especially at lunchtime.

Ritz-Carlton Dining Room ⊠Ⓜ *French*   - | - | - | E

Nob Hill | Ritz-Carlton San Francisco | 600 Stockton St. (bet. California & Pine Sts.) | 415-773-6198 | www.ritzcarltondiningroom.com

After 20 years, the fine-dining room at Nob Hill's Ritz-Carlton is closing to make way for a more informal, yet-to-be-named restaurant geared to both locals and hotel guests, with a new street entrance and a prominent bar and lounge offering its own menu; the main dining room will feature a modern design and an ingredient-driven New

American à la carte menu from chef Ron Siegel, plus a deep wine list; it's slated to open in December 2011.

RN74 *French*

23 | 24 | 22 | $63

SoMa | Millennium Tower | 301 Mission St. (Beale St.) | 415-543-7474 | www.rn74.com

Michael Mina's "happening" "upscale" bistro in SoMa has the "look and feel" of a "European train station" replete with "a clever departure board counting down" a "constantly changing wine list", and while the New French fare's "terrific", the vino gets the "superstar" treatment from "casual but professional" "stewards"; expect to mingle with "all the suits" at lunch and during the "raucous", "young" "after-work bar scene", and if it's "noisy" and "wildly pricey", it's also a "ride you won't want to miss.

Roam Artisan Burgers *Burgers*

22 | 14 | 16 | $20

Cow Hollow | 1785 Union St. (bet. Gough & Octavia Sts.) | 415-440-7626 | www.roamburgers.com

Those with a penchant for patties and "a need to be green" "roam into" this Cow Hollow yearling for "natural" burgers including "grass-fed beef" and bison, "free-range turkey" or "a great veggie" version, all "totally customizable" and packed with "a lot of flavor"; the "rustic" digs are also home to "delicious" "organic shakes", microbrews and "wines on tap", and tasters assure the "gourmet" munching's "worth the hefty price."

RoliRoti ⚅Ⓜ🚫 *American*

25 | 18 | 20 | $10

Embarcadero | Ferry Bldg. Mktpl. | 1 Ferry Bldg. (The Embarcadero) | 510-780-0300 | www.roliroti.com

Noshers are "as happy as a pig in mud" biting into the "crunchy, fatty" "amazing porchetta" sandwich from this roaster-on-wheels (a nominee for the "bucket list") but "don't miss" the "rosemary potatoes" or the "fragrant" "roti chicken" either; no one really minds the "long wait" at the "personable" Ferry Building truck that also parks at "other farmer's markets in the area", and while it may be "pricey", this "swine candy on a roll" is "worth it."

Rosamunde Sausage Grill 🚫 *German*

22 | 8 | 14 | $13

Lower Haight | 545 Haight St. (bet. Fillmore & Steiner Sts.) | 415-437-6851

Mission | 2832 Mission St. (bet. 24th & 25th Sts.) | 415-970-9015 www.rosamundesausagegrill.com

Go "beyond your typical hot dog" at this "gritty" Lower Haight sausage vendor, where "the local characters" "cannot get enough of" "soul-satisfying" wursts "grilled to perfection" in more varieties "than you can imagine", from brats to vegan; patrons of the original can "take it next door to Toronado" to "enjoy with a brewski", while the Mission spin-off provides ample seating and "plenty of beers on tap."

Rose Pistola *Italian*

21 | 20 | 20 | $47

North Beach | 532 Columbus Ave. (bet. Green & Union Sts.) | 415-399-0499 | www.rosepistolasf.com

After 15 years, la dolce vita types declare this "busy" Italian with a "lively bar scene" (and weekend jazz) "still" hot as a pistola for a "lingering lunch" or evening snack over a "delightful" wood-fired pizza and a "bottle of wine"; some say the "ho-hum" service and Ligurian fare doesn't match "the cost", but watching "the people out and about on Columbus Avenue" from "one of the sidewalk tables" tends to make patrons "forget about it."

Rose's Cafe *Italian*

21 | 17 | 20 | $33

Cow Hollow | 2298 Union St. (Steiner St.) | 415-775-2200 | www.rosescafesf.com

"Everyone seems to be in a good mood" at this "charming" "corner bistro" where "gracious" servers make the Cow Hollow regulars feel like they're "part of a nice family"; serving "terrific" midpriced Italian eats all day, it's a "perfect spot for a ladies' lunch" "after shopping on Union Street", and "popular" for "interesting" brunch items as well ("the breakfast pizza is to die for"); just remember "waits can be long" "on the weekend", especially if you want to "grab a table outside"; P.S. reservations accepted for dinner only.

Roti Indian Bistro *Indian*

21 | 16 | 18 | $33

West Portal | 53 W. Portal Ave. (bet. Ulloa & Vicente Sts.) | 415-665-7684 | www.rotibistro.com

The "deliciously spicy" classics are done "to a T", but those who try the more "unusual offerings" and the "extraordinary" vegetarian fare "will be rewarded with some new favorites" promise patrons of this "upscale" "modern Indian" duo in West Portal and Burlingame; though penny-pinchers find it "quite pricey", partisans "love" the "generous" portions and the "attentive service."

⧖ Rotunda *American*

22 | 27 | 22 | $44

Downtown | Neiman Marcus | 150 Stockton St. (bet. Geary & O'Farrell Sts.) | 415-362-4777 | www.neimanmarcus.com

"Refuel" during "a tough day of shopping" at this "oasis" in the Downtown Neiman Marcus, where "well-heeled" matrons lunch on lobster clubs and other "upscale" American fare ("can't beat those popovers") "delivered with style" in "lovely" surroundings with a stained-glass dome and a view of "Union Square below"; naturally the cost is "a bit precious", but "a taste of the good life" is "worth the dent in your Amex"; P.S. no dinner served.

Roy's *Hawaiian*

23 | 22 | 22 | $50

SoMa | 575 Mission St. (bet. 1st & 2nd Sts.) | 415-777-0277 | www.roysrestaurant.com

"A bit of aloha spirit" enhances chef Roy Yamaguchi's Hawaiian fusion cuisine at this SoMa chain link that gets a special shout-out for its "consistently fresh" fish "prepared perfectly" and "accompanied by varied and delicious sauces"; the "classy" tropical decor and "warm" service make it a "favorite place to celebrate", leaving fans saying yes, "it's a 'formula' restaurant, but the formula is a good one"; P.S. the prix fixe dinners are a bargain.

Ruth's Chris Steak House *Steak*

24 | 21 | 23 | $63

Polk Gulch | 1601 Van Ness Ave. (California St.) | 415-673-0557 | www.ruthschris.com

"Superb" steaks arrive "sizzling in butter", "tender, moist and big" at these chophouse chain links in Polk Gulch and Walnut Creek that also dish out "delicious", "gigantic sides"; the "outstanding" "old-school

FOOD | DECOR | SERVICE | COST

service" matches the traditional woody decor, and although it's "expensive", "they do know how to deliver great cocktails", adding to the value as a "great business meeting place or an impressive date spot."

Ryoko's ● *Japanese* ▽ 24 | 15 | 19 | $38

Downtown | 619 Taylor St. (bet. Post & Sutter Sts.) | 415-775-1028

There's "nowhere else like it in San Francisco" profess fin-atics, who say "yes, please" to "late-night sushi" (served until 1:30 AM) at this "eclectic" Japanese in a dark basement space Downtown; from Thursday to Saturday "the DJ keeps the tunes and vibe flowing" for the "interesting crowd" enjoying "fresh" fish and "inventive" izakaya plates presented by chefs who "know a thing or two"; and if it's "always packed" and notably "noisy", it's nonethess "worth the wait" when you want to "drink, eat and be merry" for a "decent" price.

Saha Arabic Fusion 🗷 Ⓜ *Mideastern* ▽ 26 | 21 | 25 | $41

Tenderloin | Carlton Hotel | 1075 Sutter St. (bet. Hyde & Larkin Sts.) | 415-345-9547 | www.sahasf.com

The "innovative" chef is "a master of Arab cooking" at this "hidden treasure" in the Tenderloin's Carlton Hotel, where the "creative" Middle Eastern menu – full of "fresh fusion flavors" – works "for everyone", "omnivores, veggies" and "vegans" alike and the "prix fixe is a great deal"; adding to the appeal is a "gracious" staff in the "beautiful", "quiet spot."

Saigon Sandwiches ⊄ *Sandwiches/Vietnamese* 26 | 3 | 12 | $7

Tenderloin | 560 Larkin St. (bet. Eddy & Turk Sts.) | 415-474-5698

"Banh mi – oh my!" cry fans of the "amazing Vietnamese sandwiches" sold for "practically nothing" at this Tenderloin "hole-in-the-wall" where the waits get "ridiculously long" as "the ladies crank them out"; there's nowhere to eat except "on the street", but the reward is "the perfect $3.25 meal" – a "crispy baguette" topped "with tender, sweet roast meat and crunchy pickled vegetables"; P.S. closes at 6 PM.

Saison 🗷 Ⓜ *American* 26 | 22 | 25 | $192

Mission | 2124 Folsom St. (17th St.) | 415-828-7990 | www.saisonsf.com

Hidden "off the street" in a "cool", restored stable in the "deep Mission" is this "pop"-up turned "cutting-edge" prix fixe New American from "ambitious chef" Joshua Skene, whose seasonal set menus (predominantly cooked outdoors in a "wood oven") score "high marks" for their "derring-do and originality" while being "paired perfectly with off-the-beaten-path wines"; it's "not for picky eaters" and there are occasional "missteps", but service is "spot-on" and gastronauts dining "at the chef's table" or in the "courtyard" deem it an "adventure" "worth every penny."

Salt House *American* 21 | 19 | 20 | $49

SoMa | 545 Mission St. (bet. 2nd St. & Shaw Alley) | 415-543-8900 | www.salthousesf.com

"Hip and casual", this SoMa New American "favorite" is "always crowded" with a "sleek" crowd nibbling "pricey", "sophisticated riffs on conventional dishes" in a converted 1930s warehouse setting; the "knowledgeable" staff has "no attitude", and like at its siblings Town Hall and Anchor & Hope, there's a "bustling bar scene", heavy on the "din."

Samovar Tea Lounge *Tearoom* | 18 | 21 | 19 | $23 |

Castro | 498 Sanchez St. (18th St.) | 415-626-4700
Hayes Valley | 297 Page St. (Laguna St.) | 415-861-0303
SoMa | 730 Howard St. (bet. 3rd & 4th Sts.) | 415-227-9400
www.samovarlife.com

A "wonderful respite from the cacophony of the city", this "exotic" tearoom trio is the "perfect place to kick back" and "lose a few hours" over an "excellent selection" of "aromatic" "teas galore" paired with a "light meal" from the Asian-inflected eclectic menu; though the "knowledgeable" servers can "keep you waiting", and some find the prices "hard to swallow", no one's at odds with the "chic" "Zen" atmosphere – and in SoMa, a "lovely" patio "looking over the splendid Yerba Buena gardens."

Sam's Grill & Seafood | 22 | 19 | 21 | $44 |
Restaurant ⧅ *Seafood*

Downtown | 374 Bush St. (bet. Kearny & Montgomery Sts.) | 415-421-0594
The menu is "so traditional it still features celery Victor" at this "iconic" Downtowner that's been "going strong since the 1860s"; in fact, "everything about the place is old, except the seafood", which is "impeccably fresh" and always "grilled to perfection"; popular with FiDi "business types" who do deals in the "very private" "curtained booths" over lunch, it "never goes out of style" note nostalgics, who claim the "crusty" "tuxedoed waiters" are merely "part of the charm."

Sam Wo's ◑⇄ *Chinese* | 18 | 8 | 11 | $17 |

Chinatown | 813 Washington St. (Grant Ave.) | 415-982-0596
Venturesome chowhounds who are "hankering for great chow fun" "walk through the kitchen", past the cooks who "yell over the din", then climb the "rickety stairs" "to the upstairs seating" at this "funky" Chinatown "dive" with "eccentric" and "sometimes downright rude" servers; the ambiance may remind you of a "B film noir", but the "tasty, hot, fresh and cheap" Chinese fare – especially the "huge" plates of "great" noodles – provides a "happy Hollywood ending" until 3 AM (except Sunday nights).

Sandbox Bakery *Bakery* | ▽ 20 | 12 | 14 | $10 |

Bernal Heights | 833 Cortland Ave. (Gates St.) | 415-642-8580 |
www.sandboxbakerysf.com
This Japanese-inflected Bernal Heights bakery "has taken the neighborhood by storm" with its "not-too-sugary" baked "goodies" augmented with limited-run bento boxes (weekdays only) and "unique" rice sandwiches; the "tiny" portions are "quite expensive" given that it's "just a counter take-out place", but "service is usually very good", despite "lines out the door on the weekends"; P.S. closes at 3 PM.

Sanraku *Japanese* | 22 | 13 | 18 | $33 |
SoMa | Metreon | 101 Fourth St. (Mission St.) | 415-369-6166
Sanraku Four Seasons *Japanese*
Downtown | 704 Sutter St. (Taylor St.) | 415-771-0803
www.sanraku.com
"Consistent quality" "over the years" racks up "lots of repeat customers" for this "unpretentious Japanese" duo located Downtown and in SoMa's Metreon, where "fresh sushi" and "traditional dishes" are

"done well" and supplemented with an "interesting sake menu"; they're "simple", "non-atmospheric" setups, but "efficient" service and "reasonable value" help make them "a regular stop."

San Tung   *Chinese/Korean* | 23 | 8 | 13 | $21 |

Inner Sunset | 1031 Irving St. (bet. 11th & 12th Aves.) | 415-242-0828 | www.santungrestaurant.com

The "legendary" dry fried chicken wings – "sweet yet savory" and "slightly spicy" – inspire a "feeding frenzy" at "just about every table" of this "lively" Inner Sunset spot, but save room for "price-worthy" portions of other Korean and Chinese chow, from "fantastic dumplings" to "tasty" "hand-pulled noodles"; there's "no decor" to speak of, and wing nuts must "brave the lines" to get their "fix", but at least "efficient" servers "keep things moving" – and you can always get it "to go."

Sauce ⬤   *American* | 17 | 14 | 18 | $43 |

Hayes Valley | 131 Gough St. (Oak St.) | 415-252-1369 | www.saucesf.com

Making the "symphony and opera" set "so happy", this Hayes Valley American offers an "interesting wine list" and cocktails from a "small, excellent bar" to complement "large" portions of "gourmet comfort food" plus an "innovative, changing menu of small plates"; service is "friendly", and though the experience strikes some as "pedestrian", others find it a "warm and inviting" "great place to hang" till the wee hours.

Savor   *Mediterranean* | 18 | 15 | 20 | $22 |

Noe Valley | 3913 24th St. (bet. Noe & Sanchez Sts.) | 415-282-0344

"Portions are huge and there's something for everyone" at this Noe Valley "staple", which "continues to please" with "tasty crêpes", omelets and "homey" Med-inspired bites in a "neighborhood" setting with a "sheltered" patio; go-getters gripe it's "not very exciting", but it's a "best choice" for breakfast or brunch and "if you have kids" it's a life-savor.

Scala's Bistro   *Italian* | 21 | 21 | 20 | $47 |

Downtown | Sir Francis Drake Hotel | 432 Powell St. (bet. Post & Sutter Sts.) | 415-395-8555 | www.scalasbistro.com

Downtown diners in search of "easy eats after a hard day of shopping" or a "convenient pre- or post-theater" meal are "delightfully surprised" at this "elegant" but unstuffy eatery "in the Sir Francis Drake", where "experienced", "accommodating" waiters serve "wonderful rustic Italian fare" along with wines from the "exquisite list"; supporters say "I could eat here every day", but detractors ding the "deafening noise" and note you should "bring your megaphone" or plan to "people-watch" while supping "solo at the bar."

Schmidt's   *German* | 21 | 17 | 19 | $26 |

Mission | 2400 Folsom St. (20th St.) | 415-401-0200 | www.schmidts-sf.com

"The Mission meets Munich" at this German deli-grocery from the "same owners as Walzwerk", which stays "true to the flavors" of the old country with numerous sausages, schnitzel and other Teutonic staples served in "austere" but "conversation-friendly" quarters with a sometimes "boisterous" "communal table"; add "excellent" imported brews and you could do wurst "for a low-cost outing."

	FOOD	DECOR	SERVICE	COST

☑ Scoma's *Seafood* — 23 | 19 | 21 | $47

Fisherman's Wharf | Pier 47 | 1 Al Scoma Way (Jefferson St.) | 415-771-4383 | www.scomas.com

"So what if it's touristy?" ask afishionados of this "classic" seafooder, because you "can't go wrong" with the "top-quality" fin fare that's "worth every penny"; there's "almost too much to choose from", but the "warm and professional" servers can explain the "huge menu" and "excellent" wine list, and both the "old-fashioned" Fisherman's Wharf original and Sausalito sibling sport a "fantastic" "waterfront" location and a "killer view."

Sears Fine Food *Diner* — 19 | 12 | 18 | $22

Downtown | 439 Powell St. (bet. Post & Sutter Sts.) | 415-986-0700 | www.searsfinefood.com

"It's all about" the "great" Swedish "silver dollar pancakes" – "legendary little disks" that are "a blast from the past" – enthuse flapjack fans, who "line up early" in a queue that can "stretch around the block" at this "beloved" Downtown institution; "cheerful waitresses", "vintage decor" and "filling" American diner lunches and dinners, which you can order "without a fear of sticker shock", also "evoke the '50s", though the "unimpressed" opine the eats are "kind of plain."

☑ Seasons *Seafood/Steak* — 24 | 26 | 28 | $70

Downtown | Four Seasons Hotel | 757 Market St., 5th fl. (bet. 3rd & 4th Sts.) | 415-633-3838 | www.fourseasons.com

This "gorgeous" "sleeper" with "large windows" "overlooking Market Street" from the fifth floor of Downtown's Four Seasons "rises above" the "competition" with its "flawless" service and "wonderfully relaxed environment" suitable for "quiet" conversation; the "tasty and tasteful" fare, including "really good cuts of steak" and "excellent" seafood, also "impresses", though the "steep" tab means some save it for a "special occasion"; P.S. opens at 6:30 AM for breakfast.

Sebo Ⓜ *Japanese* — 26 | 19 | 20 | $71

Hayes Valley | 517 Hayes St. (bet. Laguna & Octavia Sts.) | 415-864-2122 | www.sebosf.com

"Bring a full wallet advise fans hooked on this spot in Hayes Valley proffering "sushi done right" and "amazing fresh seafood you'd never heard of before", accompanied by selections from the True Sake store across the street; diehards like to "sit at the bar where you can watch the chefs" in the "Zen-like" room; P.S. the Sunday izakaya-only dinners have proved so popular that several cooked items have been added to the regular menu.

Sens Restaurant Ⓩ *Mediterranean/Turkish* — 17 | 20 | 17 | $42

Downtown | Embarcadero Ctr. | 4 Embarcadero Ctr., promenade level (Drumm St.) | 415-362-0645 | www.sens-sf.com

"Great for group lunches", "meeting after work", "happy-hour specials" or a "business dinner", this "convenient" Downtown destination in the Embarcadero Center "does the job" with "tasty" Turkish-influenced eats that put a "twist" on the typical Med menu; nitpickers find it no better than "serviceable" and say service is "ok", but sens-ational windows provide a "fantastic" "front row seat" of the Ferry Building and Bay Bridge while you're nursing a "nice drink"; P.S. closed weekends.

	FOOD	DECOR	SERVICE	COST

Sentinel, The ⊠ Sandwiches
24 | 8 | 18 | $13

SoMa | 37 New Montgomery St. (bet. Market & Mission Sts.) |
415-284-9960 | www.thesentinelsf.com

A "great Downtown lunch spot", this "hole-in-the-wall" "takeout-only" SoMa sandwich shop run by chef Dennis Leary (Canteen, Golden West) garners "long lines" and much "hoopla" for its "remarkable combinations" built on "freshly made" bread; they're "on the pricey side" and "sell out fast", but weekday workers confess the "great" pastries are the primary "reason to go to work in the morning"; P.S. closes at 2:30 PM.

Serpentine American
22 | 19 | 20 | $38

Dogpatch | 2495 Third St. (22nd St.) | 415-252-2000 | www.serpentinesf.com
Despite the "warehouse" setting "in the middle of nowhere" in Dogpatch, this midpriced "modern" "hipster" haunt still "feels warm and inviting", thanks to "welcoming" servers who "make you feel like regulars right away"; an uptick in the Food score attests to the "delicious" menu of "inventive" New American "comfort food", from sandwiches at lunch to "fresh and bright" entrees at dinner, and the "fancy cocktails" are also "worth the trip."

NEW Seven Hills ⓜ Italian
▽ 24 | 18 | 22 | $43

Nob Hill | 1550 Hyde St. (Pacific Ave.) | 415-775-1550 | www.sevenhillssf.com
Perched atop one of the city's seven hills (hence the name), this "quaint little spot" is a "terrific addition to Russian Hill", showcasing "heavenly" "homemade pastas" and other "creative" Italian staples along with a small international wine list (put together by the young chef-owner's master sommelier papa); it's shaping up to be a "great neighborhood place", thanks to an "earnest" staff and "charming" digs outfitted with reclaimed furnishings, that is right on the cable car route.

Shabu-Sen Japanese
▽ 21 | 13 | 17 | $33

Japantown | 1726 Buchanan St. (bet. Post & Sutter Sts.) | 415-440-0466
"If you love shabu-shabu" or simply crave "an easy sukiyaki meal" (including an all-you-can-eat option Monday–Thursday), this DIY Japanese spot in J-town "is your spot", serving up cauldrons of bubbling broth with "lots of veggies" and a choice of fixin's in a "simple" setting with a horseshoe counter; some say "service could be better", but then again it's "hard to judge since it is a cook-it-yourself" operation.

Shalimar ⊅ Indian/Pakistani
22 | 3 | 11 | $16

Polk Gulch | 1409 Polk St. (Pine St.) | 415-776-4642
Tenderloin | 532 Jones St. (Geary St.) | 415-928-0333 ◗
www.shalimarsf.com

"Perpetually packed" with "cabdrivers" and others who are willing to "brave" the "grouchy guys at the counter", this "hole-in-the-wall" curry quartet serves "mind-meltingly good" Indian-Pakistani plates that most pair with "plenty" of "fabulous" "fresh naan" to "mop up" the "spicy" sauces; sure, they may have a "terrible atmosphere", but at least it's "cheap" – and you can always "get it to go."

Shanghai Dumpling King Chinese
21 | 5 | 13 | $17

Outer Richmond | 3319 Balboa St. (34th Ave.) | 415-387-2088
"It's no exaggeration, they really are the king" claim loyal subjects who journey to this Outer Richmond "linoleum Chinese" hawking "perfect

FOOD | DECOR | SERVICE | COST

xiao long bao" (bits of "juicy exploding goodness") that "live up to their name" and a "host of other wonderful" "Shanghai-style" specialties; service is "indifferent" and the "crowded" room is a "total dump", but "huge portions" and low prices "will keep your belly full" – and "your wallet" too.

Showdogs *Hot Dogs*

18 | 10 | 14 | $13

Downtown | 1020 Market St. (6th St.) | 415-558-9560 |
www.showdogssf.com

This "classed-up" "hot dog stand" with real seating serves a selection of "unusually good" wieners and worthy sides plus a "swell beer selection" to go with them in a Downtown area that's "a bit rough", but even critics "fight through" to get to the "pricey" pups, which are served on "only one kind of bun"; still, it's a great "on-the-go" meal "before or after a show", thanks to its location "near the theater district."

Silks *Californian*

23 | 26 | 25 | $76

Downtown | Mandarin Oriental Hotel | 222 Sansome St., 2nd fl.
(bet. California & Pine Sts.) | 415-986-2020 | www.mandarinoriental.com

"Exceptional" Asian-inflected Californian cuisine creates "lasting memories" at this "gracious" "sleeper" in Downtown's Mandarin Oriental, where "silky-smooth service" and "well-spaced tables" in the "gorgeous" and "quiet" dining room lend the "right ambiance" for a "romantic" occasion or a "business lunch or dinner"; but "bring lots of money", because all this "elegance" requires an "expense account."

Skool *Seafood*

22 | 21 | 22 | $43

Potrero Hill | 1725 Alameda St. (De Haro St.) | 415-255-8800 |
www.skoolsf.com

Fin fanciers give "good grades" to this Potrero seafooder for its "unbelievably fresh", "unique" dishes (including "small plates") combining "Japanese reverence for fine fish" with Californian "culinary flair" at prices that are "quite reasonable"; the staff is "friendly" and "beautiful wood tables" and "floor-to-ceiling windows" lend the space a "Zen sensibility", while the "patio is ideal" for sunny days; P.S. don't miss "Detention Hall Happy Hour."

⚡ Slanted Door *Vietnamese*

25 | 22 | 21 | $52

Embarcadero | Ferry Bldg. Mktpl. | 1 Ferry Bldg. (The Embarcadero) |
415-861-8032 | www.slanteddoor.com

Although fans "still pine" for the old location "with the actual slanted door", Charles Phan's "high-energy", "high-end" Vietnamese "palace" on the Embarcadero "waterfront" remains "the king" for "irresistible" "Saigon-meets-SF" small plates and "perfect pairings" of "obscure wines" delivered by a "fast-moving" staff; the "minimalist" "gleaming glass" digs "aren't cozy", but the "spectacular" "views" and chews "wow", so while it's "noisy", swarming with Ferry "market tourists" and "impossible to get a rez", determined diners continue to "battle for a spot at the bar."

Slow Club *American*

22 | 17 | 18 | $36

Mission | 2501 Mariposa St. (Hampshire St.) | 415-241-9390 |
www.slowclub.com

"Thoughtfully" assembled "seasonal ingredients" result in "satisfying" New American "comfort food" for a "fair" price at this "friendly"

FOOD | DECOR | SERVICE | COST

"boîte" in an "out-of-the-way" stretch of the Mission; a bar that's a "blast" and "fabulous cocktails" contribute to the "so cool" scene with the "local crowd" of "hipsters", but the "dim" "industrial" digs "can be very noisy."

Sociale ⓈItalian
23 | 21 | 23 | $52

Presidio Heights | 3665 Sacramento St. (bet. Locust & Spruce Sts.) | 415-921-3200 | www.caffesociale.com

A "pleasant surprise" "tucked away at the end of an alley" in Presidio Heights, this "charming" "little escape" is "just right for an intimate evening", especially if you score a "romantic" table on the "lovely" "heated patio"; inside, seating is "tight" in the "tiny" room, but in either location expect "well-prepared" and "imaginative" Northern Italian eats and an "impressive" selection of wines served by a "gracious" staff.

Social Kitchen & Brewery American
▽ 15 | 16 | 18 | $28

Inner Sunset | 1326 Ninth Ave. (bet. Irving & Judah Sts.) | 415-681-0330 | www.socialbrewsf.com

"It's all about" the suds at this "friendly" Inner Sunset brewpub, a "local spot" with an "open" bi-level layout where "interesting beers are crafted on-site" to wash down the burgers and New American chow; sober sorts suggest it "needs some honing", but if you're feeling social it's a "decent place to drink a few" and "anything will taste good."

Sons & Daughters American
25 | 20 | 21 | $60

Nob Hill | 708 Bush St. (bet. Mason & Powell Sts.) | 415-391-8311 | www.sonsanddaughterssf.com

This "trendy" "postage stamp–sized" Nob Hill haunt run by "young urban hipsters" is "redefining fine dining", presenting "surprisingly high-end" "molecular gastronomy-esque" New American tasting menus with "inspired wine pairings" for $54 in a "casual setting" (there are à la carte options too); gluttons grumble it's "more of a feast for the eyes than the stomach" ("portions are appallingly small"), but when you factor in "gracious" service "and the theater" of it all, it's "a steal."

NEW Source Pizza/Vegetarian
– | – | – | I

Potrero Hill | 11 Division St. (De Haro St.) | 415-864-9000 | www.source-sf.com

All five senses are engaged at this feel-good vegetarian cafe near SoMa's Design District run by two East Coast restaurant-veteran brothers, who are topping signature pizzas with freshly made mozzarella and baking them in a gas-fired brick oven (with a facade that resembles a fire-breathing dragon); other highlights on the all-day, international comfort-food menu include salads, dosas, faux meat sandwiches (on house-baked bread) and gluten-free desserts, accompanied by elixirs and smoothies.

South Park Cafe Ⓢ French
22 | 18 | 21 | $39

SoMa | 108 South Park St. (bet. 2nd & 3rd Sts.) | 415-495-7275 | www.southparkcafesf.com

"You'll think you're in Europe" at this longtime SoMa "charmer", an "authentic" "little find" that's "still at it" providing "terrific" Cal-French fare and "professional" service in a "bistro setting" that transports

"Paris" to South Park; despite "the tight quarters", the "dependable" cooking and "reasonable" prices (including a dinner prix fixe) mean it's "a great place to be a regular."

Spencer on the Go! 🗷 Ⓜ 🍴 *French*

26 | 17 | 21 | $16

SoMa | Folsom & Seventh Sts. | No phone | www.spenceronthego.com

"It's amazing what comes out of" the SF survey's No. 1 truck, parked Wednesdays–Saturdays in SoMa and dishing out "lobster corn dogs", "escargot lollipops" and other "imaginative French" street fare from "the excellent folks" at Chez Spencer; "you needn't eat on the curb" either, thanks to the Terroir wine bar "across the street", which "welcomes food truckers"; the "price is steep" for the genre, but service is "great" and for such "value", "it's worth paying a little extra."

Spice Kit 🗷 *Asian*

∇ 20 | 11 | 16 | $14

SoMa | 405 Howard St. (bet. 1st & Fremont Sts.) | 415-882-4581 | www.spicekit.com

Like "Momofuku in NYC", this "fusion" "fast-casual" spot run by pedigreed French-trained chefs elevates Pan-Asian street food and banh mi with its "loving care" and "organic ingredients"; "it's a great lunch spot for a quick bite" and one of the few that stays "open late" by SoMa standards – that is, after 6 PM; P.S. daytime only on Saturday.

Spork *American*

20 | 16 | 19 | $37

Mission | 1058 Valencia St. (bet. 21st & 22nd Sts.) | 415-643-5000 | www.sporksf.com

"Housed in an old KFC" gone "kitsch", this Mission New American draws a "diverse crowd" with a "small menu" showcasing the "very satisfying" likes of the signature inside-out burger and "luscious mussels with pork (who knew?)", not to mention sundry "international beers"; "hip service" suits the informally "edgy setting", though it seems "a little overpriced" to those still "looking for that 'wow' factor."

SPQR *Italian*

24 | 18 | 21 | $48

Pacific Heights | 1911 Fillmore St. (bet. Bush & Pine Sts.) | 415-771-7779 | www.spqrsf.com

"Noisy" and "bustling", this "awesome sidekick of A16" is an upscale Pacific Heights "hot" spot for a "dinner or brunch" of "ingenious" modern Pan-Italian–inspired fare and "unusual" by-the-glass selections; the staff gives "good advice" on the offerings, and if you "sit at the bar" you can watch the kitchen "sideshow", but best of all, they "finally take reservations."

🗷 Spruce *American*

25 | 26 | 25 | $71

Presidio Heights | 3640 Sacramento St. (bet. Locust & Spruce Sts.) | 415-931-5100 | www.sprucesf.com

Reminiscent of *"Mad Men"*, this "tony" Presidio Heights "scene" with a "solicitous" staff proffers "luxe", farm-fresh New American "comfort food" and "big markup" wines in "highly styled", "dimly lit" quarters dotted with "ladies who lunch" and scions enjoying a "fancy night out with the parents"; it's "very expensive", but the "riffraff" finds it's "more affordable and just as enjoyable" at the "buzzy bar" with a "classic cocktail" and "unbeatable hamburger."

Stable Café *Coffeehouse* ∇ 20 | 21 | 17 | $14

Mission | 2128 Folsom St. (17th St.) | 415-552-1199 | www.stablecafe.com
Although this "cool Bauhaus"-looking Mission coffeehouse set in a converted carriage house is better known for its stablemates (including back-tenant Saison and an incubator kitchen), habitués come 'round early and often for its "amazingly good, simple" breakfast and lunch fare and French-pressed coffee; it's also a "great place to study" and linger, both in the bi-level interior and on the adjacent courtyard patio.

Stacks *American* 18 | 13 | 18 | $20

Hayes Valley | 501 Hayes St. (Octavia St.) | 415-241-9011 | www.stacksrestaurant.com
"Breakfast junkies" "go hungry" gearing up for "huge portions" of the likes of "eggs and perfect pancakes", and there's also a lunch menu "with something for everyone" at this "laid-back" trio in Hayes Valley, Burlingame and Menlo Park; "be prepared to wait on weekends" when there's "always a long line", though "pleasant service" and "affordable" help keep the experience "satisfying."

Starbelly *Californian* 21 | 19 | 19 | $37

Castro | 3583 16th St. (Market St.) | 415-252-7500 | www.starbellysf.com
"What did we do before it arrived to win over the Castro?" wonder surveyors star-struck by this Californian's "marvelous pizzas", small plates and "creative beer and wine cocktails" plus an "upbeat vibe"; the "fantastic back patio" is "irresistible" for lunch or brunch, but "the no-res thing is a problem", as are the "painfully noisy" digs and the "I'm-too-sexy-for-you servers"; still, the "nice mixed crowd" always "leaves happy" with "money still in their pockets."

St. Francis Fountain *Diner* 17 | 17 | 14 | $16

Mission | 2801 24th St. (York St.) | 415-826-4200 | www.stfrancisfountainsf.com
An "old-school" soda fountain repurposed into "hipster central", this Mission fixture slings "solidly tasty and substantial" diner fare (with the occasional "update" like Guinness shakes and "vegan-friendly versions of many dishes") in surroundings replete with Formica, "spinning stools" and a "retro candy" counter; the servers may still be "learning the ropes", but that doesn't deter the "crowds of hungover" locals who show up for brunch.

Stinking Rose *Italian* 18 | 18 | 19 | $35

North Beach | 325 Columbus Ave. (bet. B'way & Vallejo Sts.) | 415-781-7673 | www.thestinkingrose.com
"Not for the vampire crowd", "you can smell" this "kitschy" Cal-Italian "in the heart of North Beach" "from blocks away" since every dish "has garlic – even the ice cream"; though the "40-clove chicken" and "crusty bread" appetizer win raves and service is "helpful" enough, critics who dub the grub "overpriced" and "all odor no flavor" contend it's "fun for tourists, but once is enough."

Straits Restaurant *Singaporean* 20 | 19 | 17 | $40

Downtown | Westfield San Francisco Ctr. | 845 Market St., 4th fl. (bet. 4th & 5th Sts.) | 415-668-1783 | www.straitsrestaurants.com
Pan-Asian partisans with "adventuresome palates" are partial to this "trendy" Downtowner and its siblings to the south, where the "seri-

ously delicious Singapore-style" fare is served in a "dark and clublike" setting; "go with a group" "so you can share" the "exotic" small plates and "unique" "specialty" cocktails suggest sociable sorts, who aren't daunted by "thumping" soundtrack and sometimes "slow" service.

🆕 Straw *Californian/Sandwiches*   - | - | - | M

Hayes Valley | 203 Octavia St. (Page St.) | 415-431-3663 | www.strawsf.com
For "festival food without the barkers", surveyors step right up to this "interesting new" joint in Hayes Valley hawking a "tasty" selection of midpriced California-ized carnie salads, sandwiches and snacks, along with weekend brunch (Jenga French toast, anyone?) and cheeky cocktails (e.g. a scorpion bowl filled with Swedish fish); adopters give a thumbs-up to the service and "love the vibe" of the colorful "carnival-themed decor", which includes a vintage Tilt-A-Whirl seat.

🆕 Summit 🌣 *Californian*   - | - | - | M

Mission | 780 Valencia St. (19th St.) | 415-861-5330 |
www.thesummit-sf.com
This "cool" "new" Mission mash-up of coffeehouse, art gallery/ workspace and restaurant ("your basic 2012 business incubator") is already "always packed with people on their laptops" downing Blue Bottle coffee and morning pastries or having a "solo working dinner" of affordable artisanal Californian cooking; the loftlike space is comprised mainly of communal seating, but foodies commandeer the eight barstools on Sunday nights when chef Eddie Lau offers Dux, a duck-focused prix fixe.

Sunflower Restaurant *Vietnamese*   21 | 9 | 16 | $20

Mission | 3111 16th St. (bet. Albion & Valencia Sts.) | 415-626-5022
Potrero Hill | 288 Connecticut St. (18th St.) | 415-861-2336
"Bring a friend to help you eat" the "huge portions" of pho and other "delicious" options from the "good-sized menu" of "solid" fare at this Vietnamese duo; followers suggest the Mission original "hole-in-the-wall" is best for takeout or a "quick cheap eat", while the Potrero Hill outpost has a bit more of a "cool neighborhood vibe."

Super Duper *Burgers*   ∇ 21 | 12 | 18 | $12

Castro | 2304 Market St. (bet. Noe & 16th Sts.) | 415-558-8123
🆕 Downtown | 721 Market St. (bet. 3rd & 4th Sts.) | 415-538-3437
www.superdupersf.com
It's only a burger joint, but this "nostalgic"-looking spot in a "killer" Castro location (plus a new FiDi outpost) is "a super-duper alternative" to the big chains, albeit at a "higher price"; the "forward-looking flourishes" ("organic" ingredients, "homemade pickles" and rubbish composts on premises) mean disciples "don't feel guilty" when they indulge, and though the "stark" storefront is "ambiance-free", the counter staff is "quick" and "eager"; P.S. branches are in the works for 2001 Chestnut Street and in the Mill Valley.

Suppenküche *German*   22 | 17 | 19 | $32

Hayes Valley | 601 Hayes St. (Laguna St.) | 415-252-9289 |
www.suppenkuche.com
"Homesick" Germans and a "boisterous" "under-30 set" get their "schnitzel fix" at this "rollicking" Hayes Valley hofbräuhaus where "helpful" servers tend to the "bustlingly Bavarian" "communal tables";

the "amazing beer list" is "where they shine", and "no glutton will be left unsatisfied" with the "incredibly generous" portions of "traditional" Teutonic eats "at reasonable prices", but steel yourself for a "long and loud wait" along with the rest of the crowd.

Suriya Thai *Thai* ▽ 25 | 15 | 20 | $27

SoMa | 1532 Howard St. (bet. 11th & 12th Sts.) | 415-355-9999
"Definitely not the run-of-the-mill" Thai, this SoMa sleeper from chef-owner Suriya Srithong is hailed for its "nice-sized portions" of "wonderful", "authentic" Siamese specialties (just "don't fill up before the pumpkin curry arrives"); it remains a lesser-known destination, but to sample "delicious dishes" that go beyond "mainstream", word is it's "worth going out of your way."

Sushi Groove *Japanese* 21 | 15 | 15 | $39

Russian Hill | 1916 Hyde St. (bet. Green & Union Sts.) | 415-440-1905
SoMa | 1516 Folsom St. (bet. 11th & 12th Sts.) | 415-503-1950 ⊠
www.sushigroove.com
Roll in and "chill out" at this "cool little" Japanese duo, where twenty- and thirtysomethings "have a great time" grooving on the "awesome" sushi, sake cocktails and unpretentious but "funky surroundings"; "reasonable prices" add incentive, but be prepared for "cramped, loud quarters" with "DJ music" upping the volume at the SoMa site.

NEW Sushirrito ⊠ *Japanese* - | - | - | I

SoMa | 59 New Montgomery St. (Market St.) | 415-495-7655 | www.sushirrito.com
At this "hot new" take-out lunch joint in SoMa, a former executive chef from Roy's is crafting "giant" sushi rolls that are "uncut", like a burrito (hence the name); "filled with sustainably sourced" seafood, organic rice and both Latin and Japanese flavors, these bundles of "cultural collision" rack up "outrageous" lines, partly from popularity, partly because each is "made-to-order", but "it's worth it."

Z Sushi Zone ⊠⋣ *Japanese* 27 | 10 | 17 | $35

Castro | 1815 Market St. (bet. Guerrero St. & Octavia Blvd.) | 415-621-1114
"Fabulous sushi for the patient patron" awaits at this "humble" Castro Japanese, a 16-seat "hole-in-the-wall" where the "master" chef sets an "insanely slow" pace slicing "delectable bites" with "taste and texture sensations" that'll "satisfy the most adventurous" at "a very fair price"; just "get there early (preferably before they open)" to join the "long line of eager" fans who promise it's "worth the wait."

Z Sutro's at the Cliff House *Californian* 22 | 26 | 21 | $53

Outer Richmond | 1090 Point Lobos Ave. (Balboa St.) | 415-386-3330 | www.cliffhouse.com
Sure, the "priceless" "ocean view" "is the main attraction" at this glass-encased Outer Richmond overlook perched above Ocean Beach's "rocky shoreline", but both the "well-prepared", seafood-centric Californian cuisine and "attentive service" are "better than expected"; maybe the cost runs "high for what you get", but "what's supposed to be the ultimate tourist trap" proves "worthy" "once in a while even if you live here."

	FOOD	DECOR	SERVICE	COST

🔀 Swan Oyster Depot 🗷⇔ *Seafood* — 27 | 13 | 23 | $32

Polk Gulch | 1517 Polk St. (bet. California & Sacramento Sts.) |
415-673-1101

"Fabulous" seafood "so fresh" that "you expect it to talk back" is the
lure of this "no-frills oyster bar" and "humble fish market" in Polk
Gulch that's been a "family-owned" "fixture" "for decades"; "scoring"
one of the "rickety" stools at the "cramped" "marble counter" "has its
price" – a "long line" "out the door" – but those who pay their dues and
are "prepared to drop some serious coin" (cash only) will be made to
"feel at home" by the "hilarious" "guys in fish-stained aprons" behind
the bar; P.S. closes at 5:30 PM.

NEW Tacko *Mexican* — - | - | - | I

Cow Hollow | 3115 Fillmore St. (Filbert St.) | 415-796-3534 | www.tacko.co
Vintage yachting paraphernalia and nautical elements abound at this
Nantucket-inspired taqueria (yes, you read that right) dropping anchor in Cow Hollow, but aside from a lobster roll, the menu is more
Mexico than Massachusetts; it's the brainchild of Nick Fasanella so
look for carnitas tacos 'Nick's way' (grilled crispy), beer-battered fish
burritos and sundry quesadillas, doused with a dizzying array of hot
sauces and washed down by beer, sangria and cocktails, including one
served scorpion bowl–style in a sand pail.

TacoBar *Mexican* — ∇ 17 | 12 | 15 | $15

Pacific Heights | 2401 California St. (Fillmore St.) | 415-674-7745 |
www.415tacobar.com

Expect "choices you don't normally see" at this Pac Heights Mexican
counter from Jack Schwartz (ex Nick's Crispy Tacos), which uses
"local-sourced ingredients" to craft "cool", "creative" tacos and other
"fresh and quick" *comida* chased with sangria and agave wine margs;
it's "a little pricey" and "unimpressed" purists pout "the preparation's
not authentic", but hey, "it stays busy."

Tacolicious *Mexican* — 22 | 16 | 16 | $27

Embarcadero | Ferry Bldg. Mktpl. | 1 Ferry Bldg. (The Embarcadero) |
No phone 🗷Ⓜ⇔

Marina | 2031 Chestnut St. (Fillmore St.) | 415-346-1966
www.tacolicioussf.com

"Inventive" tacos made with "top-notch ingredients" "that more than
live up to the name" are "perfectly paired" with "homemade salsas"
and "even better" "killer" "margies" and "chupitos" ("mini mixed
drinks"), drawing "ridiculous lines" to this "hip, upscale Mexican" sit-
down sibling to the original Thursday Ferry Plaza stand; it's definitely
a "Marina scene" ("day and night"), and while the noise and service
suffers "during peak" hours, regulars insist "it's a blast"; P.S. a Mission
branch with an adjacent tequila bar, Mosto, is slated to open at 741
Valencia Street in fall 2011.

🔀 Tadich Grill 🗷 *Seafood* — 23 | 21 | 22 | $45

Downtown | 240 California St. (bet. Battery & Front Sts.) | 415-391-1849
This "nostalgic" "throwback to the Barbary Coast" "in the heart of
Downtown" (in business since 1849) has "all the atmosphere of a Sam
Spade novel", with its "old-fashioned" "private wooden booths" and
"crusty" "ancient" "waiters in black tie and aprons"; it "hasn't changed

since forever", down to the "huge" portions of "solidly prepared" "sparkling fresh" fish dishes and "classic" martinis, which is why a "mix" of "businessmen, tourists and serious seafood lovers" brave the "ever-present lines" and "crushing crowds" to "sit at the counter" and "schmooze" with the "entertaining" servers.

Tajine ☒ Moroccan   - | - | - | I

Polk Gulch | 1653 Polk St. (Clay St.) | 415-440-1718 | www.tajinerestaurant.com

After a series of moves, genial chef-owner Mohammed Ghaleb has settled into new Polk Street digs, where he's again catering to frugal types with his signature tajines, kebabs, b'steeya and other authentic Moroccan home cooking, plus traditional mint tea; the 40-seat dining room complete with low-slung seating is open for lunch and dinner, and though no alcohol is served, BYO is welcome.

Takara Japanese   ▽ 23 | 13 | 18 | $34

Japantown | 22 Peace Plaza (bet. Laguna & Webster Sts.) | 415-921-2000 | www.takararestaurant.com

"Hidden away" at the edge of the Japantown mall, this "authentic" Japanese nook, which can "get crowded in the evening" with "families", serves up "fresh" sushi as well as "good combination plates"; the "small" dining room may have seen "better days", but devotees "definitely recommend" the bento boxes and "love" the "lunch specials", which are a "great deal."

Taqueria Can Cun ●☒ Mexican   25 | 9 | 15 | $11

Downtown | 1003 Market St. (6th St.) | 415-864-6773
Mission | 2288 Mission St. (19th St.) | 415-252-9560
Mission | 3211 Mission St. (Valencia St.) | 415-550-1414

"Don't go expecting decor" at this taqueria trio that devotees declare nonetheless "worth a cross-country flight" for its "cheap and delicious" Mexican fare including "huge burritos made right before your eyes from fresh ingredients" and some of "the best tacos" around; with the Downtown option, there's really "no need to go to the Mission" for your fix, though those two outposts are open even later, providing a "hipster" hangout for "a perfect late-night snack."

Taqueria El Buen Sabor ☒☒ Mexican   - | - | - | I

Mission | 697 Valencia St. (18th St.) | 415-552-8816

Compadres count on good flavor and "good prices" at this tiny hideaway in the Mission, where the "fast counter" dispenses "perfectly adequate" takes on the Mexican standards; "less snappy decor" makes it less than a destination, but it's a handy "go-to if you're within three blocks."

�Z Tartine Bakery Bakery   27 | 13 | 15 | $17

Mission | 600 Guerrero St. (18th St.) | 415-487-2600 | www.tartinebakery.com

"Just the smells" "will make you euphoric" at this "ridiculously good" Mission bakery swoon "pastry lovers" and "hipsters" who put up with "almost no seating" and "rude service" for the "sublime pastries", "hot pressed sandwiches" and a shot of nabbing "their iconic loaves" fresh from the oven at 5 PM; the line's "wrapped around the building" "rain or shine" ("despite not having a sign") and prices can be "wince"-inducing, but "carb slaves" confess they can't stay away.

Tataki South *Japanese*

NEW Noe Valley | 1740 Church St. (Day St.) | 415-282-1889

24 | 19 | 21 | $38

Tataki Sushi & Sake Bar *Japanese*

Pacific Heights | 2815 California St. (Divisadero St.) | 415-931-1182 | www.tatakisushibar.com

"If you like your sushi deep-fried, endangered and covered in mayo", you're out of luck at this "tiny" "admirable" Pacific Heights Japanese eatery/sake bar with a larger Noe Valley spawn – because the emphasis here is on "innovative rolls (even for vegetarians)", "sustainable" sashimi and ocean-"friendly" substitutions ("faux nagi"), all of it "without the mercury or eco-guilt" – and "utterly delicious"; a "no-reservations" policy means nightly waits, but the "personable" chefs and "feel-good factor" go a long way to compensate.

Ten-Ichi *Japanese*

23 | 16 | 20 | $33

Upper Fillmore | 2235 Fillmore St. (bet. Clay & Sacramento Sts.) | 415-346-3477 | www.tenichisf.com

An "old-time favorite that hasn't lost a beat", this "comfortable neighborhood" "classic" serves up "traditional Japanese dishes and new innovations" plus "reliable sushi" that's as "fresh as if the fish swam up Fillmore"; the "reasonably priced" fare and "friendly", unhurried service has been bringing "regulars" "back" "for years."

Terzo *Mediterranean*

24 | 21 | 23 | $48

Cow Hollow | 3011 Steiner St. (Union St.) | 415-441-3200 | www.terzosf.com

"Delicious" "seasonal" small plates and "enormously creative" entrees "make you want to order one of everything on the menu" at this "modern" yet "cozy" Cow Hollow Mediterranean that's always a "treat"; though the frugal fuss it's "a bit pricey" to be nominated "the perfect neighborhood dining spot", "half-price wines" from the "large" and "deep" list enthrall the thrifty from Sunday through Wednesday, and "super-friendly" servers ensure you always "feel at home."

Thai House Express *Thai*

21 | 12 | 16 | $20

Castro | 599 Castro St. (19th St.) | 415-864-5000
Tenderloin | 901 Larkin St. (Geary St.) | 415-441-2248 ◐
www.thaiexpresssf.com

Wallet-watchers express their appreciation for this "cheap" Thai twosome, home to a "large menu" of "reliably tasty" if "typical" dishes served up "lickety split"; the location "off the beaten Castro path" is somewhat easier on the eyes while the Tenderloin "joint" is a long-running "go-to" with night-owl hours.

Thanh Long Ⓜ *Vietnamese*

24 | 14 | 18 | $51

Outer Sunset | 4101 Judah St. (46th Ave.) | 415-665-1146 | www.anfamily.com

"The original of the An family restaurants" (including Crustacean), this Vietnamese is "still fabulous" for roasted Dungeness dishes "by which all other crabs should be judged" and garlic noodles cloaked in a "famously" secret sauce; yes, it's "messy" ("wear the bib") and "rather expensive for frozen crab", plus the decor's "age is showing", but most say this "hidden gem" in Outer Sunset is everything it's cracked up to be.

	FOOD	DECOR	SERVICE	COST

Thep Phanom Thai Cuisine *Thai*

24 | 17 | 21 | $29

Lower Haight | 400 Waller St. (Fillmore St.) | 415-431-2526 | www.thepphanom.com

Long favored for "the best spices and freshest flavors", this Lower Haight "neighborhood" phanom-enon still "can't be beat" for an "incredible variety" of "wonderful", real-deal Siamese fare that "satisfies" "time after time"; the "small", colorful confines "get crowded early" with "mostly locals", making it a "treat" that may be even more enjoyable "on a weeknight."

Thermidor Ⓩ *American*

20 | 22 | 18 | $53

SoMa | 8 Mint Plaza (bet. Market & Mission Sts.) | 415-896-6500 | www.thermidorsf.com

"If you're feeling a little *Mad Men*", "old school" meets "today's palate" at this split-level SoMa American "from the Spork guys", a "classy" "throwback" that brings "early-'60s" style to the Mint Plaza; the original menu of "retro dishes" with "modern twists" has been scaled down post-Survey to mostly inexpensive snacks with a spotlight on the "fancy cocktails", though a few entrees (such as the "eponymous" lobster) remain, as does a "super-cool design" mingling chandeliers with knotty pine.

1300 on Fillmore *Soul Food/Southern*

21 | 24 | 21 | $46

Western Addition | 1300 Fillmore St. (Eddy St.) | 415-771-7100 | www.1300fillmore.com

"Black-and-white photos of jazz greats" "pay homage" to the "historic" Western Addition's tuneful past at this "sleek", "swanky" spot serving "down-home cookin' with an uptown vibe"; "Southern classics" with a "sophisticated" New American twist "make you jump and jive" (especially during Sunday's "killer" gospel brunch and Friday's "live music" in the "cozy" lounge), and while service can vary from "extremely professional" to a little "off", most maintain it "makes for a real special night out, y'all!"

Tipsy Pig *American*

18 | 16 | 16 | $31

Marina | 2231 Chestnut St. (bet. Pierce & Scott Sts.) | 415-292-2300 | www.thetipsypigsf.com

A "favorite" "in Biff and Muffy land", this "lively" Marina tavern caters to "the young set" with generous tipples and "stick-to-your-gut" American grub dished out in pubby environs that can get "loud" unless you "hibernate in the library" or head for the patio; but be ready for "lacking" service and a "bar scene" "shoulder to shoulder" with so many "overgrown frat boys" that "anyone over 40 is downright invisible."

Tokyo Go Go *Japanese*

20 | 16 | 18 | $37

Mission | 3174 16th St. (bet. Guerrero & Valencia Sts.) | 415-864-2288 | www.tokyogogo.com

The "trendy" "loungelike" setting and "loud music" on the sound system are what set apart this somewhat "pricey" Japanese joint in the middle of the Mission's 16th Street bars; club kids are crazy about the "great cocktails" that accompany the sushi, rolls and "cooked entrees" like tempura the way it "should be", but pickier patrons maintain the fin fare is merely "mediocre."

	FOOD	DECOR	SERVICE	COST

Tommaso's Ⓜ *Italian*   `25` `16` `21` `$31`

North Beach | 1042 Kearny St. (bet. B'way & Pacific Ave.) | 415-398-9696 | www.tommasosnorthbeach.com

"Even with the explosion of new pizza parlors" in town, North Beach mozzarella mavens "can't stay away" from this "traditional" "red-sauce Italian" whose "crisp" pie is "done just right in their wood-fired oven"; "a relief from the trendy", it also serves "old-school" "home-style" Neapolitan fare at "reasonable prices"; just "be prepared to wait" before the "warm" and "wonderful" servers seat you in the "cozy" (some say "crowded") "basement dining room."

Tommy's Mexican Restaurant *Mexican*   `15` `12` `18` `$27`

Outer Richmond | 5929 Geary Blvd. (bet. 23rd & 24th Aves.) | 415-387-4747 | www.tommystequila.com

"Magnificent margaritas" and an "outstanding" "slew of tequila choices" selected by agave guru Julio Bermejo ("no one knows more on the subject") is the *numero uno* reason this "family-run" Mexican is "worth a trip" to the Outer Richmond; the "decor might not be the fanciest", and a flagging Food score suggests the menu's "pedestrian at best", but tipplers who appreciate the "amazing" staff insist "you'll be glad you had the combo platter" after just "one pitcher."

Tommy Toy's Cuisine Chinoise *Chinese*   `23` `24` `25` `$63`

Downtown | 655 Montgomery St. (bet. Clay & Washington Sts.) | 415-397-4888 | www.tommytoys.com

"Completely different" "from anything in neighboring Chinatown", this "ritzy" Downtowner is an "elegant" destination for "memorable Chinese cuisine" "with a French flair"; you'll need to "bring a wad of cash" or "an expense account", but aficionados agree it's "worth every penny" for the "beautifully presented" plates and especially the "prix fixe and signature menus" that "shine"; and, since the "outstanding" servers are "as good as any in the city", the "quiet" dining room is the "perfect" place to "impress that fabulous date."

Tonga Room Ⓜ *Asian/Pacific Rim*   `13` `25` `16` `$47`

Nob Hill | Fairmont San Francisco | 950 Mason St. (bet. California & Sacramento Sts.) | 415-772-5278 | www.tongaroom.com

"Come on, live a little" at this "much-loved" Nob Hill "blast from the past", a "tiki-hut-tastic" "icon" of "crazy Polynesian" "excess" with "totally camp" attractions like a boat-borne band and "indoor tropical storms"; the Pan-Asian–Pacific Rim chow is "forgettable" ("especially for the price"), but between the happy-hour buffet, "potent" "tropical drinks" and "entertainment value" "you've got to do it once" "before it disappears."

Ton Kiang *Chinese*   `23` `12` `16` `$29`

Outer Richmond | 5821 Geary Blvd. (bet. 22nd & 23rd Aves.) | 415-387-8273 | www.tonkiang.net

"Go early" and "pace yourself" because "the carts just keep coming and coming" at this bi-level Outer Richmond "dim sum palace" far "away from the crowds in Chinatown" that racks up "weekend lines" "longer than for Lady Gaga" with its "fantastic" array of "high-quality" dumplings "served all the time" (along with Hakka-style dinners); critics carp this "longtime favorite" has become "run-down" of late, and service gets "harried", but it's still a "Chinese foodie's paradise" that's "worth every penny."

Tony's Coal-Fired Pizza & Slice House Ⓜ *Pizza*

| 24 | 12 | 15 | $21 |

North Beach | 1556 Stockon St. (Union St.) | 415-835-9888 | www.tonyspizzanapoletana.com

Fans say "the only way to make Tony's pizza better is to take away the wait time", which is possible at "maestro" Gemignani's new walk-up adjacent to his North Beach mother ship; in addition to slinging single slices of his "excellent" pies, including a new coal-fired version, it offers "out-of-this world" meatball subs and Italian ices – but "no atmosphere" or seating, so most "get it to go and have a picnic" in Washington Square Park.

Tony's Pizza Napoletana Ⓜ *Italian*

| 25 | 15 | 20 | $30 |

North Beach | 1570 Stockton St. (Union St.) | 415-835-9888 | www.tonyspizzanapoletana.com

"Whether you like your pizza à la NYC or Napoli", this North Beach "instant classic" "is the place to go", particularly when "celebrity" chef-owner Tony Gemignani is in the house and "you get to watch him make" his "award-winning" "phenomenal" pies cooked in "four different ovens"; a few gripe it's "overpriced" and "overhyped", but a "full bar" helps with the "frustrating long waits" and the staff's "friendly and warm."

Town Hall *American*

| 22 | 20 | 20 | $52 |

SoMa | 342 Howard St. (Fremont St.) | 415-908-3900 | www.townhallsf.com

Wriggle "past the yuppie bar scene" at this "see-and-be-seen" SoMa "tavern" and your "patience" is rewarded with "spot-on" New American "comfort food with a Southern bent" (including "magnificent desserts") as "delicious" as a "trip to New Orleans" and graciously served in a "lively" (i.e. "noisy") "exposed-brick" room; it's a veritable "town hall" for everything from a "business lunch", "date night" or "after-work" beer, but drop-ins can join the party at the "community table."

Town's End Restaurant & Bakery Ⓜ *American/Bakery*

| 21 | 16 | 19 | $29 |

Embarcadero | South Beach Marina Apts. | 2 Townsend St. (The Embarcadero) | 415-512-0749 | www.townsendrb.com

"After rolling out of bed", "locals" head to this "surprising find along the Embarcadero", where the highlight of breakfast or brunch is the "basket of fresh baked treats", while later risers deem the New American "evening meals even better" and the prix fixe "three-course deal" "an excellent value"; service "can be a touch slow" and "when there's a game" "parking is nearly impossible", but the "comfortable", "bright atmosphere" keeps it "popular."

Trattoria Contadina *Italian*

| 21 | 16 | 21 | $38 |

North Beach | 1800 Mason St. (Union St.) | 415-982-5728 | www.trattoriacontadina.com

"A little off the main drag" (and thus "away from the hordes of tourists on Columbus Avenue"), this "lively" trattoria in North Beach is known for its "hearty" servings of "traditional" Italian fare including "excep-

| | FOOD | DECOR | SERVICE | COST |

tional" pastas that are prepared "perfectly al dente"; the "cozy" confines can be "crowded" say some of the "neighborhood locals", but the "warm", "welcoming" servers and "inexpensive" tab mean it "never misses the target."

Tres *Mexican* | 17 | 18 | 16 | $34 |
(fka Tres Agaves)
South Beach | 130 Townsend St. (bet. 2nd & 3rd Sts.) | 415-227-0500 | www.tressf.com

It's "hard not to have fun" at this "loud" and "trendy" South Beach boîte, where a "zillion tequilas" and an "outrageous selection" of "stellar" margaritas accompany the "inventive" takes on Mexican fare; near AT&T Park, it's a "favorite starting point" before the Giants play, when the "lively" "vibe gets you in the mood for the game", but critics contend that beyond the "outstanding guacamole" and other "good apps" the menu doesn't merit the "pricey" tab.

Tropisueño *Mexican* | 18 | 17 | 16 | $27 |
SoMa | 75 Yerba Buena Ln. (bet. Market & Mission Sts.) | 415-243-0299 | www.tropisueno.com

"Museumgoers, convention attendees" and clued-in locals are drawn to the "lively", "warm *ambiente*" at this "reasonably priced" SoMa Mexican, which offers a "taqueria-style" "counter for lunch" and full service for dinner; "pretty respectable" "down-home" dishes and "margaritas to die for" ("especially the next day") keep it "bustling" in an area where similar options are "limited."

Troya *Turkish* | 21 | 17 | 21 | $29 |
Inner Richmond | 349 Clement St. (5th Ave.) | 415-379-6000 | www.troyasf.com

"Generous portions" of "delicious" Turkish fare come "with style" at this "cozy neighborhood place" in the Inner Richmond where the "excellent, fresh, well-prepared" "large plates" "offer a wide range of flavors and spices" and nibblers who "love every single meze" can choose all "appetizers for dinner"; "service is almost always fantastic" and "regulars hit up happy hour" for "deals" on bites and wine.

Truly Mediterranean *Mediterranean* | ▽ 22 | 6 | 17 | $12 |
Mission | 3109 16th St. (bet. Guerrero & Valencia Sts.) | 415-252-7482 | www.trulymedsf.com

True believers head to this Mission niche for "awesome, excellently priced" Med–Middle Eastern favorites (notably "terrific shawarma" and falafel on "delicious lavash bread") fixed up "fresh" and "quick"; but the bare-bones sliver of a space is "really not a place to stop and eat", so prepare "to grab and go."

Tsunami Sushi & Sake Bar ●🅩 *Japanese* | 21 | 22 | 20 | $41 |
South Beach | 301 King St. (4th St.) | 415-284-0111
Western Addition | 1306 Fulton St. (Divisadero St.) | 415-567-7664
www.nihon-sf.com

A "super sake selection" and a "great happy hour" make this piscatory pair in the Western Addition and South Beach "excellent" "for a big group" looking for a "hip and happening" scene, but the "inventive" menu of sushi (some of it "on the spicy side") also satisfies afishionados; those "on a budget" say it's "a bit overpriced for what you are getting", but most are still lured in by the "delicious fish" and "good" crowd.

Tu Lan ☒⊅ *Vietnamese* | 18 | 2 | 11 | $12

SoMa | 8 Sixth St. (Market St.) | 415-626-0927

It's "worth braving the Tenderloin" to "eat yourself silly" at this SoMa "greasy-spoon Vietnamese", a "run-down" '70s survivor "famous" for turning out "giant portions" of "super-cheap", "reliably good" grub that "Julia Child raved about"; it's also a "hot", "stuffy" "dump" in a "seedy 'hood" (i.e. "the other wine country"), so you "wouldn't want to take mom."

☒**NEW** Twenty Five Lusk *American* | 20 | 27 | 21 | $59

SoMa | 25 Lusk St. (bet. 3rd & 4th Sts., off Townsend) | 415-495-5875 | www.twentyfivelusk.com

"Wear your Louboutins" to this "architecturally beautiful" *Sex and the City* send-up in SoMa, the new "after-work" haunt of "young techies" to "meet some friends" (and a "celebrity or two") over "delicious cocktails" and bites; despite its "club atmosphere" and "moody lighting", the "sleek Scandinavian" brick-and-wood dining room is the setting for "inventive" if "expensive" New American meals with "attentive" service; partyers prefer to chill in the "shwanky" basement lounge "warmed" with '60s-"retro" "hanging fireplaces."

2223 Restaurant *Californian* | 22 | 19 | 21 | $40

Castro | 2223 Market St. (bet. Noe & Sanchez Sts.) | 415-431-0692 | www.2223restaurant.com

Castro crowds "dress to be seen" at this "delightfully quirky" "down-home" Cal–New American where the "fresh" (if "rich") "comfort food" "doesn't break the bank" and includes "Tuesday night specials" that are an especially "great deal"; the modern quarters "can get a bit noisy" during the "incredibly busy" weekend brunch, but service is "attentive and sweet", all adding up to a "tried-and-true" "favorite."

NEW Txoko ☒Ⓜ *Spanish* | – | – | – | E

North Beach | 504 Broadway (Kearny St.) | 415-500-2744 | www.txokosf.com

Channeling the spirit of San Sebastian in the heart of San Francisco's North Beach, this late-night Basque boîte set in the historic former space of Beat haunt Enrico's is the long-anticipated full-scale sibling to Ian Begg and Ryan Maxey's adjacent Naked Lunch; it serves a mash-up of locally sourced pintxos, as well as small and large plates, complemented by wines and cocktails from the Iberian Peninsula, in a rough-hewn tavernlike setting (with a cartoony "Last Supper"-esque mural) that includes a dining room, a stand-up bar and a heated patio.

Udupi Palace ⊅ *Indian/Vegetarian* | 21 | 8 | 15 | $18

Mission | 1007 Valencia St. (21st St.) | 415-970-8000 | www.udupipalaceca.com

"Spicy curries, crispy dosas" and "light pooris" plus "humongous" portions make this chainlet the place for "vegetarian South Indian food"; decor is "bare-bones", but the staff is "cheerful" and can "steer you to some amazing dishes", including a few that will "clear your sinuses", all at "incredibly low prices" to "satisfy both the wallet and belly"; P.S. there are also "many options for gluten-free" diners.

FOOD | DECOR | SERVICE | COST

Umami ☒ *Japanese* | 24 | 21 | 21 | $40

Cow Hollow | 2909 Webster St. (Union St.) | 415-346-3431 |
www.umamisf.com

The "inventive" and "tasty" izakaya dishes and "to-die-for tempura"
"are equal" to the "terrific sushi" that seems like it "swims fresh from
the sea into your mouth" at this "high-end" "Los Angeles–like"
Japanese joint that attracts a "good-looking" Cow Holllow crowd; it's
"not a cheap place", but the "great deals" and "wicked cocktails" during the "excellent" "sumo hour" (nightly 5:30–7 PM) "can't be beat",
making this "hip" haunt "easy to like."

NEW Una Pizza Napoletana ☒☒ *Pizza* | 26 | 15 | 17 | $31

SoMa | 210 11th St. (Howard St.) | 415-861-3444 | www.unapizza.com

"NYC transplant" Anthony Mangieri brings his "pizza auteur" – or is it
"pizza nazi"? – act to SoMa with this "sparse"-looking newcomer;
"there's a lot of attitude", "no reservations", only five varieties (all
meatless) and "yes, it's $20 a pie", but if you "follow the rules" and
"don't ask for appetizers" or sides, the "ethereal" Neapolitan
"masterpieces" – "all made personally" in a "huge" center-stage blue-
tiled oven – are "worth" the hour-long waits "to get in" and get served.

Underdog ⊄ *Hot Dogs* | 22 | 12 | 19 | $13

Inner Sunset | 1634 Irving St. (bet. 17th & 18th Aves.) | 415-665-8881 |
www.underdogorganic.com

Green-leaners "will be in hog heaven" at this "no-frills" Inner Sunset
tubesteak stop, where a "tasty" array of "organic meat", veggie and
vegan hot dogs are served "with a friendly smile" along with tater tots
and other all-natural sides; "the vibe is unapologetically counter-
cultural", but unless you're feeling communal, cramped conditions
mean it's "not a place to dine in."

Unicorn Pan Asian Cuisine ☒ *Asian* | ▽ 22 | 18 | 21 | $40

Downtown | 191 Pine St. (Battery St.) | 415-982-9828 |
www.unicorndining.com

For a "happy-hour get together" or a "sit-down lunch in the thick of the
Financial District", Downtown types turn to this midpriced Pan-Asian
spot, which offers an "innovative menu" and a "bargain wine list" (now
cocktails too) served by a "gracious, welcoming staff"; as for atmosphere, while some say there's "not much", others find it "just right."

Universal Cafe ☒ *American* | 24 | 17 | 21 | $36

Mission | 2814 19th St. (bet. Bryant & Florida Sts.) | 415-821-4608 |
www.universalcafe.net

The "essence of local farm-to-table" is served up at this "sophisticated" Mission "faithful standby" for midpriced New American dinners, "lunch on the sidewalk" and "out-of-this-universe" brunches
("OMG fresh hot doughnuts"); despite service that's "a joy" and a "relaxed vibe", it can get "noisy" inside, however, "sitting outside" when
it's warm can be "priceless"; P.S. Tuesdays are dinner only.

Urban Tavern *American* | 16 | 15 | 16 | $41

Downtown | Hilton San Francisco Union Sq. | 333 O'Farrell St.
(bet. Mason & Taylor Sts.) | 415-923-4400 | www.urbantavernsf.com

A "good pre-theater choice" since the "attentive" servers "get you out
in time", this "beautifully designed" all-day New American gastropub

FOOD DECOR SERVICE COST

in the Hilton also delivers for Downtown "business meetings" and "a nightcap" for those staying at the hotel; groupies gush about the "great tavern feel" and "perfectly cooked" steaks, but just as many mutter about the "noisy" setting and "inconsistent" quality, commenting "there are better options."

Uva Enoteca *Italian*
22 | 21 | 21 | $37

Lower Haight | 568 Haight St. (bet. Fillmore & Steiner Sts.) | 415-829-2024 | www.uvaenoteca.com

Gracing the "proudly grungy Lower Haight" with a "happy marriage of wine and food", this "appealing" enoteca is "great for grazing" on "must-try" "salumeria antipasti" and "creative pizzas" complemented by an affordable, "Italian-focused" vino lineup; the stylishly "small" quarters "can get crowded", but with a "well-versed" staff to "provide excellent pairing suggestions", it's a "solid" choice "every time."

Venticello *Italian*
23 | 22 | 22 | $47

Nob Hill | 1257 Taylor St. (Washington St.) | 415-922-2545 | www.venticello.com

"It may not be splashy", but this "rustic" trattoria atop Nob Hill just "says San Francisco", thanks to the "city views" "from some tables" and sound of the "rattling" "cable cars going by"; the "mouthwatering" Northern Italian menu ("order anything" from the "wood-burning oven") and "divine" desserts are a "good deal", and the service is "warm and friendly", which is why it's "deservedly popular" for a "really romantic" "neighborhood rendezvous."

Vitrine *American*
▽ 24 | 23 | 23 | $55

SoMa | St. Regis | 125 Third St., 4th fl. (Mission St.) | 415-284-4049 | www.stregis.com

A "serene" "oasis in SoMa" – a "secret" hidden away "on the fourth floor" of the St. Regis Hotel – this "very upscale" New American will "impress most palates" with its "carefully prepared" fare featuring "local ingredients"; it's no surprise that the "elegant" experience can be "pricey", but the "sunny" dining room is the "perfect place for a quiet business lunch" or "excellent" brunch; P.S. closes at 2 PM.

Walzwerk *German*
21 | 17 | 20 | $30

Mission | 381 S. Van Ness Ave. (bet. 14th & 15th Sts.) | 415-551-7181 | www.walzwerk.com

For anyone nostalgic for the Cold War, this "retro East German" in the Mission werks up "hearty" servings of "authentic" schnitzel, bratwurst and other regional fare in a setting that mirrors Berlin "back before the wall came down"; the "stark" "decor is an acquired taste", but the "welcoming" expat staff and Teutonic "beer selection" have fans waltzing "back regularly."

Warming Hut Café & Bookstore *Sandwiches*
14 | 17 | 15 | $14

Presidio | Presidio Bldg., Crissy Field | 983 Marine Dr. (Long Ave.) | 415-561-3040 | www.parksconservancy.org

"At the end of a stroll" through Crissy Field and the "infamous fog", ramblers can "pop in" to this Presidio cafe/bookstore for a breather over a "piping cup of hot joe" and "simple", "wholesome" sandwiches, salads and sweets while taking in "a million-dollar view" of the Golden

Gate Bridge; have-nots huff it's "overpriced", but for those who warm to the "scenic" locale "it hits the spot."

Waterbar *Seafood*   21 | 26 | 21 | $58

Embarcadero | 399 The Embarcadero (Folsom St.) | 415-284-9922 | www.waterbarsf.com

A "sure winner for out-of-town guests", this Embarcadero fish house with a "remarkably romantic location just under the Bay Bridge" and "attentive" service lures the "young" "elites" with "sustainable sea-food" and "zowie decor" anchored by "giant" aquarium towers; critics carp it's "overpriced", but the "outdoor patio is divine" and the "bar is a blast", particularly during the day when oysters are $1.

Waterfront Restaurant *Californian/Seafood*   20 | 22 | 20 | $49

Embarcadero | Pier 7 (B'way) | 415-391-2696 | www.waterfrontsf.com

The "spectacular" vista of "the Bay Bridge and the beautiful SF bay" "from every table" is "the ticket" at this "versatile" "Embarcadero landmark" with seating both indoors and out on an enclosed patio; the "superb happy hour" and "well-priced lunch" satisfy frugal fish fans, who deem dinner a "bit expensive", but surveyors are split on the Californian seafood, with some saying the "fresh, local" fare satisfies "real foodies" and the rest wishing the "food matched the view."

Wayfare Tavern *American*   22 | 23 | 21 | $53

Downtown | 558 Sacramento St. (bet. Montgomery & Sansome Sts.) | 415-772-9060 | www.wayfaretavern.com

"Crowds flock" to Tyler Florence's "formidable" FiDi "expense-account lunch" spot and "after-work" "watering hole" where "generous por-tions" of "devilishly good", "elevated" Traditional American "comfort food" and "great" old-timey drinks are "served by pros" in a "fantastic" "Barbary Coast" "hunting lodge" setting that's "a nod to simpler times"; upstairs is "an acoustic nightmare", prompting some to joke "you pay by the decibel", but fans who snag "a seat at the kitchen counter" and catch the "star chef" "hard" at work find it "impressive."

Weird Fish ⊅ *Seafood*   - | - | - | M

Mission | 2193 Mission St. (18th St.) | 415-863-4744 | www.weirdfishsf.com

After bumpy waters that saw this eclectic Mission cafe close and reopen in a four-month span, the home of the "suspicious fish" dish (revealed only "when it is actually served") is back under a new chef serving much of the same "worthy", "reasonably priced" fin fare along with plenty of veggie and "vegan options" from "local, sustainable ingredi-ents", plus the famed "fried pickles"; quarters are "tight", but the "down-to-earth" staff and "hip" "nautical thrift-shop" vibe (including a new DJ booth) make it a "precious find."

Wexler's ⌧ *BBQ*   22 | 18 | 21 | $41

Downtown | 568 Sacramento St. (Montgomery St.) | 415-983-0101 | www.wexlerssf.com

Explore the "nuance of smoke" via "a different take on Southern" cookin' at this "adventurous" Downtown American, which "attempts to redefine BBQ" with "terrific" "upscale" renderings of "classic" pit dishes plus "unbelievable Scotch eggs" and "sophisticated" cocktails; lodged in a "cool little space" with a "massive wooden wave" as decor, it's al-ways "interesting" even if traditionalists still "long for the basic rub."

FOOD | DECOR | SERVICE | COST

'Wichcraft *Sandwiches*

18 | **13** | **15** | **$16**

Downtown | Westfield San Francisco Ctr. | 868 Mission St., ground fl. (bet. 4th & 5th Sts.) | 415-593-3895 | www.wichcraftnyc.com

"Sensational" "gourmet" sandwiches make a "tasty" and "convenient" "shopping day lunch" at this "sunny" and "pleasant" spot in Downtown's Westfield Centre, "an outpost of Tom Colicchio's NYC" chain; "quick and friendly" servers assemble "fresh ingredients" into "excellent" salads, "delicious vegetarian 'wiches" and other "quality" combos, but wallet-watchers find it "hard to justify" the prices; P.S. closes at 6 PM.

NEW Wise Sons Deli 🗷Ⓜ🍴 *Deli*

23 | **15** | **20** | **$11**

Location varies; see website | 415 787-3354 | www.wisesonsdeli.com

"Heavenly brisket" and "can't-be-beat pastrami and corned beef" are among the "excellent" sandwiches turned out at this pop-up that's arguably "as good as it gets for SF deli"; though the "guys are awesome", the hungry hordes suggest they "need to step up serving techniques" and those with frequent cravings wish the sons would just get a "storefront already"; P.S. currently serving Saturday brunch at Beast & The Hare.

Woodhouse Fish Company *Seafood*

21 | **15** | **19** | **$31**

Castro | 2073 Market St. (14th St.) | 415-437-2722
Pacific Heights | 1914 Fillmore St. (bet. Bush & Pine Sts.) | 415-437-2722
www.woodhousefish.com

Even "East Coasters" concede they "really nail" the "New England style" at this "casual" Castro and Pac Heights pair, which "fill a niche" with "tantalizing" takes on "no-nonsense" seafood staples hooked up with "well-selected wines" and "served with a smile"; despite debate over the cost ("fair" vs. "inflated"), the "spare" "nautical" settings overflow with fin fans who know they "get the job done."

Woodward's Garden 🗷Ⓜ *Californian*

24 | **16** | **24** | **$51**

Mission | 1700 Mission St. (Duboce Ave.) | 415-621-7122 | www.woodwardsgarden.com

While the Mission location "near the freeway" is "not the greatest", this "surprise find" more than atones with "ethereal" Cal cooking and "attentive" service that have "stood the test of time" for "a loyal clientele"; while slightly "pricey" given the "intimate" (and gardenless) setting's "quaint" "shabbiness", for a "quiet" interlude it's still "worth looking for."

Yamo 🗷🍴 *Burmese*

22 | **6** | **13** | **$12**

Mission | 3406 18th St. (Mission St.) | 415-553-8911

"Be prepared" to "squeeze in at the counter" of this "tiny" Mission "true hole-in-the-wall" with "no service, no ambiance" but plenty of "noodles, noodles, noodles" and other "incredible Burmese" bites; "lines usually run out the door" but the initiated assure that "once you get seated" it's "quick" and "seriously budget-friendly."

🆉 Yank Sing *Chinese*

26 | **18** | **19** | **$39**

SoMa | Rincon Ctr. | 101 Spear St. (bet. Howard & Mission Sts.) | 415-957-9300
SoMa | 49 Stevenson St. (bet. 1st & 2nd Sts.) | 415-541-4949
www.yanksing.com

"The Taj Mahal of dim sum joints", this duo of "white-tablecloth" Cantonese "banquet" halls in SoMa featuring an "endless parade of carts" bearing dumplings and other bites whose "originality, diversity and quality are unexcelled" gets "crazy busy at lunch" and "week-end brunch" with "first-timers", "extended Chinese families and tourists"; "it's a bit Westernized" and probably "twice the price" of Chinatown, but the "slick setting" and "helpful" staff, plus "free parking on week-ends" at Rincon, are "well worth it."

Yoshi's San Francisco *Japanese*   21 | 23 | 19 | $48

Western Addition | Fillmore Heritage Ctr. | 1330 Fillmore St. (Eddy St.) | 415-655-5600 | www.yoshis.com

"High notes" abound at this "fab" eatery and "music venue", a "stylish" Western Addition satellite of the "Oakland mother ship" that hosts "world-class jazz" nightly while providing "inspired Japanese cuisine" and "superb sakes" in a "contemporary" milieu; the servers "aren't real quick" and it "isn't cheap", but hepcats hankering for "memorable" "eating and entertainment together" still ask "what could be better?"

Yuet Lee ● *Chinese*   21 | 6 | 10 | $24

Chinatown | 1300 Stockton St. (B'way) | 415-982-6020

Yes, it's "bare-bones" with "harsh fluorescent lights" and "horrible" "green colors", but "get past the appearance" and this Chinatown vet is about "as authentic as it gets" for "inexpensive" Cantonese seafood, "especially if you're willing to be adventurous"; it's also known as a "late-night institution" that accommodates marinated munchers till 3 AM on weekends.

Yumma's *Mideastern*   ∇ 21 | 13 | 20 | $11

Inner Sunset | 721 Irving St. (bet. 8th & 9th Aves.) | 415-682-0762

A "quick" fix for Middle Eastern prepared "the way it should be", this Inner Sunset spot plies "fresh and delicious" shawarma, "homemade hummus", falafel and other grub at a price that's "tough to beat"; the setup's decidedly "casual" (and alcohol-free), but it's "reliable" when you're ready to "chow down."

Zadin ⓜ *Vietnamese*   ∇ 23 | 19 | 22 | $30

Castro | 4039 18th St. (Hartford St.) | 415-626-2260 | www.zadinsf.com

"Distinct flavors" and a vaguely "upscale" feel "right here in the neighborhood" entice Castrolites to this "inventive" Vietnamese and its menu of "rich" phos and other "excellent" specialties, delivered by "friendly" staffers "with a knack for explaining" the nuances; with many gluten-free items to "also set it apart", it's "not exactly the real thing" but always "such a comfortable place to be."

Z & Y *Chinese*   ∇ 24 | 10 | 14 | $21

Chinatown | 655 Jackson St. (bet. Grant Ave. & Kearny St.) | 415-981-8988 | www.zandyrestaurant.com

"Kick up your senses and venture outside of the generic" Chinatown haunts at this wallet-friendly "authentic" Sino where the expat chef's "skilled use of spices and aromatics" and "chiles galore" results in "really good" Sichuan fare that's "the real thing"; "don't expect to be wowed by the ambiance" (it's "the usual" lanterns-and-screens decor) or service, but those who like it hot are "overjoyed" by cuisine that "more than tickles the taste buds"; P.S. it validates two-hour parking at the Portsmouth Square Garage.

	FOOD	DECOR	SERVICE	COST

Zante Pizza & Indian Cuisine *Indian/Pizza* ▽ 20 | 7 | 15 | $19

Bernal Heights | 3489 Mission St. (Cortland Ave.) | 415-821-3949 |
www.zantespizza.com

"When you can't decide" between "pizza or curry", "get both in one" at
this Bernal Heights stalwart, which "rocks" with "fantastic Indian" pies
topped with anything from lamb to tandoori chicken; also a "super
place for vegetarians", it's "a unique" hybrid that's "pretty tasty too", just
don't plan on eating in, as it's no frills; P.S. delivery is free citywide.

Zaré at Fly Trap ⊠ *Californian/Mediterranean* 22 | 21 | 22 | $47

SoMa | 606 Folsom St. (2nd St.) | 415-243-0580 | www.zareflytrap.com
"Gregarious" "chef-owner Hoss Zaré epitomizes the perfect host" as
he "amazes the palate" at this "convivial" SoMa "hot spot", where
"spectacular", "Persian-inspired" Cal-Med "creations" and "superior
drinks" are "served with style" in a "classy" "landmark" setting that's
faithful to "the history of the Fly Trap"; "for something a little different",
it's a haven of "warmth" and "flair" "that doesn't cost an arm and a leg."

Zarzuela ⊠M *Spanish* 24 | 17 | 22 | $38

Russian Hill | 2000 Hyde St. (Union St.) | 415-346-0800
It "definitely feels like the real deal" at this Russian Hill Spaniard,
which "dependably" turns out "superb tapas" and "authentic" paella
served by a "gracious", "cordial staff" in a "casual" but "charming"
space "right on the cable car line"; even with "parking hassles" and a
"no-reservations" policy, it's an "affordable" "standby for a date" and
"fun for a group."

Zazie *French* 23 | 18 | 20 | $28

Cole Valley | 941 Cole St. (bet. Carl St. & Parnassus Ave.) |
415-564-5332 | www.zaziesf.com

"Tops" for "French-style brunch", this "neighborhoody" Cole Valley
"haunt" is a weekend "winner" serving the "super-delicious" likes of
gingerbread pancakes and reenvisioned eggs Benny ("it's very hard to
choose") provided you "have patience with" the "daunting" "crowds"
and "big wait"; otherwise it's a source of "solid bistro fare" at a "reasonable" cost, but regardless of "cute" quarters with "a wonderful garden", "they need to expand."

Zeitgeist ●⊄ *Burgers* 14 | 15 | 11 | $15

Mission | 199 Valencia St. (Duboce Ave.) | 415-255-7505 |
www.zeitgeistsf.com

"Show your tats" and "do not overdress" at this Mission "hangout",
"a dive in the best sense" favored for the "sunny" backyard where
"juicy" burgers "from the grill" are "excellent for soaking up" the
"craft brews" and "stiff Bloodies" that help "wipe away any memories of the gruff service"; since it's "no longer" a "locals' secret",
"the picnic tables fill up" quickly; P.S. "if you're lucky", "you'll cross
paths with the Tamale Lady."

Zero Zero *Italian/Pizza* 24 | 20 | 20 | $37

SoMa | 826 Folsom St. (4th St.) | 415-348-8800 |
www.zerozerosf.com

While you can get "fancy pizza" (at lower prices) at "one-zero-zero
other places", the upper crust deduce Bruce Hill's "hip" SoMa entrant
"stands out" with its "edgy", "blistery" wood-fired "Neapolitan-style"

pies "named after SF neighborhoods", along with "excellent" pastas; factor in a "lively bar scene", "wines on tap" and "super-friendly service" and it's "definitely a 10 (not a zero)"; P.S. "kids (and adults) love the DIY soft-serve ice cream" sundaes.

☑ Zuni Café Ⓜ *Mediterranean*   25 | 20 | 22 | $52

Hayes Valley | 1658 Market St. (bet. Franklin & Gough Sts.) | 415-552-2522 | www.zunicafe.com

Surveyors "always count on" Judy Rodgers' "perennially awesome" Hayes Valley "golden oldie" for "dependably delicious", market-driven Med meals, a "buzzing crowd" and a "zinc bar worth coming early for" to swig "classic cocktails" and slurp "fantastically fresh oysters"; it attracts "a real slice of San Francisco" from "lunch" till "late night", so even if the staff can dish out some "attitude", the "signature" "roast chicken and Caesar salad" (plus "burgers" at lunch and after 10 PM) are the stuff of many a "last meal request."

Zuppa *Italian*   19 | 16 | 18 | $39

SoMa | 564 Fourth St. (bet. Brannan & Bryant Sts.) | 415-777-5900 | www.zuppa-sf.com

While "nothing fancy", this SoMa Southern Italian wins zupport in a "hip neighborhood" serving "consistently decent" "thin-crust pizza" and pastas in a lofty, concrete-walled setting that channels "Rust Belt chic"; the tabs run "a little higher than one might expect", but it's "customer-friendly" enough to be "worth a stop" "every once in a while."

Zushi Puzzle Ⓢ *Japanese*   26 | 11 | 17 | $44

Marina | 1910 Lombard St. (Buchanan St.) | 415-931-9319 | www.zushipuzzle.com

"Don't let the Lombard Street location fool you"– this Japanese "hole-in-the-wall" slices up the "most creative, exotic sushi/sashimi in town"; "you can order from the menu in the dining room if you're on a budget", but the "loyal band of early birds" knows to "reserve a seat at the small sushi bar" and let "ringmaster"/chef-owner Roger Chong "decide what you eat."

EAST OF SAN FRANCISCO

Top Food

28 Chez Panisse | *Cal./Med.*	Chevalier | *French*
27 Commis | *American*	Tratt. La Siciliana | *Italian*
Chez Panisse Café | *Cal./Med.*	Kirala | *Japanese*
Erna's Elderberry | *Cal./Fr.*	Oliveto Restaurant | *Italian*
Cheese Board | *Bakery/Pizza*	Lalime's | *Cal./Med.*
26 Pizzaiolo | *Italian/Pizza*	Ajanta | *Indian*
Rivoli | *Cal./Med.*	Eve | *American*
BayWolf | *Cal./Med.*	Gioia Pizzeria* | *Pizza*
Wood Tavern | *Californian*	Tamarindo Antojeria* | *Mex.*
25 Esin | *Amer./Med.*	Dopo | *Italian*

BY CUISINE

AMERICAN

- **27** Commis
- **25** Esin
- Eve
- **22** Lark Creek
- **21** Flora

CALIFORNIAN

- **28** Chez Panisse
- **27** Chez Panisse Café
- Erna's Elderberry
- **24** Wente Vineyards
- Wolfdale's

CHINESE

- **24** Great China
- Koi Garden
- **22** Shen Hua
- **21** Rest. Peony
- **19** Imperial Tea Court

FRENCH

- **25** Chevalier
- **24** Artisan Bistro
- À Côté
- **23** Café Fanny
- **22** Bistro Liaison

INDIAN

- **25** Ajanta
- **23** Vik's Chaat Corner
- **22** Pakwan
- Shalimar
- **21** Udupi Palace

ITALIAN

- **26** Pizzaiolo
- **25** Tratt. La Siciliana
- Oliveto Restaurant
- Dopo
- **24** Prima

JAPANESE

- **25** Kirala
- **24** O Chamé
- Uzen
- **23** Ozumo
- Cha-Ya Vegetarian

MEDITERRANEAN

- **28** Chez Panisse
- **27** Chez Panisse Café
- **26** Rivoli
- BayWolf
- **25** Esin

MEXICAN/PAN-LATIN

- **25** Tamarindo Antojeria
- **23** Tacubaya
- Fonda Solana
- Picante Cocina
- **22** César

PIZZA

- **27** Cheese Board
- **26** Pizzaiolo
- **25** Gioia Pizzeria
- **24** Little Star Pizza
- Zachary's Chicago Pizza

SOUTHEAST ASIAN

- **24** Soi4
- Burma Superstar
- **23** Vanessa's Bistro
- Pho 84
- **22** Xyclo

Excludes places with low votes; *indicates a tie with restaurant above

Vote at ZAGAT.com

BY SPECIAL FEATURE

BREAKFAST/BRUNCH

24 Wente Vineyards
Oliveto Cafe
23 Venus
Bette's Oceanview
Café Fanny

CHILD-FRIENDLY

24 Zachary's Chicago Pizza
Great China
23 Bellanico
Picante Cocina
22 Lo Coco's

MEET FOR A DRINK

24 Adesso
22 Sidebar
21 Flora
20 Luka's Taproom
Revival Bar*

OPEN LATE

24 Adesso
23 Fonda Solana
22 César
20 Caspers Hot Dogs
17 Lanesplitter

OUTDOOR SEATING

25 Dopo
24 Wente Vineyards
À Côté
Oliveto Cafe
22 La Note

PEOPLE-WATCHING

27 Chez Panisse Café
24 À Côté

Va de Vi
Oliveto Cafe
23 Ozumo

ROMANCE

28 Chez Panisse
27 Erna's Elderberry
25 Lalime's
24 Wente Vineyards
Wolfdale's

SMALL PLATES

24 À Côté
Adesso
Va de Vi*
22 César
21 Barlata

TRENDY

27 Commis
24 À Côté
Adesso
21 Flora
20 Revival Bar

VIEWS

27 Erna's Elderberry
26 Rivoli
25 Meritage/Claremont
24 Wente Vineyards
18 Ahwahnee Din. Rm.

WINNING WINE LISTS

28 Chez Panisse
27 Chez Panisse Café
Erna's Elderberry
24 Adesso
22 César

BY LOCATION

BERKELEY

28 Chez Panisse
27 Chez Panisse Café
Cheese Board
26 Rivoli
25 Tratt. La Siciliana

LAKE TAHOE AREA

24 Wolfdale's
23 PlumpJack Cafe

22 Red Hut Café
Dragonfly
18 Jake's on the Lake

OAKLAND

27 Commis
26 Pizzaiolo
BayWolf
Wood Tavern
25 Oliveto Restaurant

Top Decor

29	Ahwahnee Din. Rm.	23	Postino
28	Erna's Elderberry		Picán
26	Meritage/Claremont		Bridges
25	Wente Vineyards		Adagia
	Lake Chalet		Ippuku
			Jake's on the Lake
24	Wolfdale's		Chez Panisse Café
	Sasa	22	O Chamé
	Chez Panisse		Esin
	Ozumo		Gar Woods Grill
	Bocanova		

Top Service

27	Erna's Elderberry		Meritage/Claremont
26	Commis		Ruth's Chris
	Chez Panisse		Incontro Ristorante
25	BayWolf		PlumpJack Cafe
	Chez Panisse Café		Bridges
24	Rivoli		Wood Tavern
	Lalime's		Oliveto Restaurant
	Esin		Chevalier
	Wente Vineyards	22	Ajanta
23	Wolfdale's		Artisan Bistro

BEST BUYS: SPECIALTY SHOPS

Arinell Pizza	Cheese Steak Shop
Arizmendi	Gioia Pizzeria
Bakesale Betty	Grégoire
Barney's	Imperial Tea Court
BurgerMeister	In-N-Out
Caspers Hot Dogs	Lanesplitter
Cheese Board	Zachary's Chicago Pizza

BEST BUYS: FULL MENUS

Asqew Grill	LCX/Le Cheval
Bette's Oceanview	Mama's Royal Cafe
Bo's BBQ	Picante Cocina
Breads of India	Red Hut Café
Brown Sugar Kitchen	Rick & Ann's
Burma Superstar	Rudy's Can't Fail Café
Cactus Taqueria	Shen Hua
Chow	Tacubaya
Fentons Creamery	Venus
Juan's Place	Vik's Chaat Corner

Vote at ZAGAT.com

East of San Francisco

	FOOD	DECOR	SERVICE	COST

Z À Côté *French/Mediterranean* | 24 | 20 | 22 | $41

Oakland | 5478 College Ave. (Taft Ave.) | 510-655-6469 |
www.acoterestaurant.com

"Every neighborhood deserves a place like this" "intimate"
Mediterranean in Oakland's Rockridge area that "out-Frenches the
French" with small plates to "tickle your palate and warm your heart";
whether it's "girls' night out" or "a romantic dinner", the "culinary
mini-masterpieces", "helpful staff" and "eclectic wine list" are "worth
the parking hassles" and "pricey" tabs – plus the "backyard patio is
a hidden gem."

Adagia Restaurant ☒ *Californian* | 20 | 23 | 20 | $39

Berkeley | Westminster Hse. | 2700 Bancroft Way (College Ave.) |
510-647-2300 | www.adagiarestaurant.com

The "baronial dining room" complete with a fireplace recalls "a Harry
Potter movie" at this "elegant academic" hangout immediately
"across the street" from UC Berkeley that makes a "gracious setting"
for an "imaginative", "organic" Cal-Med menu; though the "fabulous"
decor sometimes "outshines the food" and "well-meaning" service
can be "spotty", it's super "convenient" "before a concert on campus",
and the "sunny patio" is also "great for lunch."

NEW Addie's Pizza Pie ☒ *Pizza* | ∇ 21 | 15 | 19 | $24

Berkeley | 3290 Adeline St. (Alcatraz Ave.) | 510-547-1100 |
www.addiespizzapie.com

Set in a "restored historic building", this "family-friendly" South
Berkeley pizzeria from pastry whiz Jennifer Millar and Flora chef Tom
Schnetz delivers "solid East Coast–style" eats including "delicious",
"slightly upscale" thin-crust pies, salads and housemade desserts
such as frozen custard; add in the "friendliness of the highly competent staff" plus "interesting beers and wines", and pie-sanos feel
they've "struck gold."

Adesso ●☒ *Italian* | 24 | 18 | 21 | $34

Oakland | 4395 Piedmont Ave. (Pleasant Valley Ave.) | 510-601-0305 |
www.dopoadesso.com

This "bustling", "modern" Oakland enoteca (Dopo's "younger sister")
is "a salumi-lover's dream" with a "friendly" staff ferrying "superb"
"house-cured delights", "pâtés galore" and other "excellent" Italian
small plates, plus "exceptional, reasonably priced" vino and cocktails;
regulars say that the twice-nightly aperitivo hours can get "extremely
crowded and noisy" as "after-work" and late-night throngs "descend
upon" the "generous" free apps "like it's the last supper", but otherwise, "what's not to like?"

Z Ahwahnee Dining Room *Californian* | 18 | 29 | 21 | $62

Yosemite | Ahwahnee Hotel | 1 Ahwahnee Way (Tecoya Rd.) |
Yosemite National Park | 209-372-1489 | www.yosemitepark.com

After "racing down from the top of Nevada Fall", national park visitors
"revel in the historic parkitecture" of this "stately" hotel dining hall
with "magnificent high wood ceilings" and "huge picture windows" that
overlook "the granite wall of Yosemite"; while "the setting is priceless",

FOOD | DECOR | SERVICE | COST

the Cal-American food and service are "definitely not the stars of the show", though "the all-you-can-eat" Sunday brunch, annual events such as "Bracebridge" and the chef and vintner dinners "do shine."

Ajanta *Indian*
25 | 20 | 22 | $30

Berkeley | 1888 Solano Ave. (bet. Fresno Ave. & The Alameda) | 510-526-4373 | www.ajantarestaurant.com

Devotees declare "all Indian restaurants should outsource their kitchens" to this "den of heavenly tastes" in Berkeley, where an "ever-changing", "mostly organic" menu with "awesome spice combinations" assures diners "never get bored"; "you can have a quiet conversation" in the "upscale" room that's "fancy enough for a birthday", while the "unfailingly solicitous" staff serves with "style and grace", all resulting in a "quality-for-dollar ratio" that "can't be beat."

Amber Bistro Ⓢ *Californian*
21 | 19 | 22 | $41

Danville | 500 Hartz Ave. (Church St.) | 925-552-5238 | www.amberbistro.com

"Consistent and well-priced" Californian fare is served up by a "hospitable" staff at this "intimate" "little bistro" in Danville that "always hits the spot", particularly with its "value" "fixed-price dinner"; a "good selection of wines", "unique cocktails" and "excellent happy hour" complete the package.

Amici's East Coast Pizzeria *Pizza*
20 | 14 | 18 | $21

Danville | Rose Garden Ctr. | 720 Camino Ramon (Sycamore Valley Rd.) | 925-837-9800
Dublin | 4640 Tassajara Rd. (bet. Central Pkwy. & Dublin Blvd.) | 925-875-1600
www.amicis.com
See review in City of San Francisco Directory.

Andalé *Mexican*
21 | 13 | 15 | $17

Oakland | Oakland Int'l Airport | Terminal 2 (Ron Cowan Pkwy.) | 510-638-6000 | www.andalemexican.com
See review in South of San Francisco Directory.

Arinell Pizza ⊄ *Pizza*
22 | 5 | 13 | $8

Berkeley | 2119 Shattuck Ave. (Addison St.) | 510-841-4035
See review in City of San Francisco Directory.

Arizmendi *Bakery/Pizza*
26 | 12 | 19 | $11

Emeryville | 4301 San Pablo Ave. (43rd St.) | 510-547-0550 | www.arizmendi-bakery.org
Oakland | 3265 Lakeshore Ave. (MacArthur Fwy.) | 510-268-8849 | lakeshore.arizmendi.coop
See review in City of San Francisco Directory.

Artisan Bistro Ⓜ *Californian/French*
24 | 17 | 22 | $49

Lafayette | 1005 Brown Ave. (Mt. Diablo Blvd.) | 925-962-0882 | www.artisanlafayette.com

Fans feel this "darling little restaurant in a vintage restored house" might "finally put Lafayette on the culinary map" with "amazing, inventive, fresh" Cal-French cuisine that's "well executed" and served by an "attentive" staff; some caution that "the noise level inside is ridiculous", but fortunately there's always the "lovely" patio area.

	FOOD	DECOR	SERVICE	COST

Asqew Grill *Californian*   17 | 12 | 16 | $17

Emeryville | Bay Street Mall | 5614 Bay St., 3rd fl. (Shellmound St.) | 510-595-7471 | www.asqewgrill.com
See review in City of San Francisco Directory.

Bakesale Betty 🅂🅼 *Bakery*   25 | 10 | 21 | $13

Oakland | 2228 Broadway (W. Grand Ave.) | 510-251-2100
Oakland | 5098 Telegraph Ave. (51st St.) | 510-985-1213
www.bakesalebetty.com

"Phenomenal baked goods", savory pot pies and "massive" "awesome fried chicken sandwiches" draw "a line around the block" at these "iconic" "kitschy" bakery and take-out counters in Oakland; it's "fun" "sitting at an ironing board" (at Telegraph Avenue only), and "blue-haired babe" Betty and her "friendly" crew keep the crowds "happy" and moving "quickly" with their cheerful attitude, "cheap eats" and "occasional free cookie"; P.S. breakfast and lunch only.

Barlata *Spanish*   21 | 17 | 18 | $34

Oakland | 4901 Telegraph Ave. (49th St.) | 510-450-0678 | www.barlata.com
Surveyors who "love Spain" suggest "save your airfare" and head for this "authentic" Temescal District spot serving "some of the best tapas this side of Barcelona", e.g. housemade *latas* that are "fun to eat out of a tin can"; happy hour offers the "best bang for your buck", but service can be "a bit awkward" and "the small dining room gets crowded quickly", so expect "jet-engine volume at times"; P.S. lunch served Wednesday–Sunday.

Barney's Gourmet Hamburgers *Burgers*   19 | 13 | 16 | $17

Berkeley | 1591 Solano Ave. (Ordway St.) | 510-526-8185
Berkeley | 1600 Shattuck Ave. (Cedar St.) | 510-849-2827
Oakland | 4162 Piedmont Ave. (Linda Ave.) | 510-655-7180
Oakland | 5819 College Ave. (Chabot Rd.) | 510-601-0444
www.barneyshamburgers.com
See review in City of San Francisco Directory.

🇿 BayWolf *Californian/Mediterranean*   26 | 21 | 25 | $50

Oakland | 3853 Piedmont Ave. (Rio Vista Ave.) | 510-655-6004 | www.baywolf.com

"After all these years" (since 1975), Michael Wild's "howling good" "East Bay stalwart" still keeps it "fresh" and local with "outstanding" "seasonal" Cal-Med dishes ("especially the duck"), "stellar wines" and new experimental Monday dinners; it might lack "the excitement" of Oakland's new-wave eateries and "prices are on the high side", but the "gracious service" and "quiet" "Craftsman" setting with a "delight-ful" patio make it "enchanting" for "special occasions and casual din-ing both"; P.S. lunch is no longer served.

Bellanico *Italian*   23 | 18 | 22 | $40

Oakland | 4238 Park Blvd. (Wellington St.) | 510-336-1180 | www.bellanico.net

It's "worth jamming into" this Glenview "neighborhood jewel" (sibling of SF's Aperto) for the "fun vibe" and "imaginative", "delicious, un-fussy" Italian offerings including a "high-end tasting menu at reality-based prices"; wine flights are "a great deal", and adding to the enjoy-ment, staffers "take care of you, even with antsy kids."

	FOOD	DECOR	SERVICE	COST

Bette's Oceanview Diner *Diner*

23 | 16 | 20 | $19

Berkeley | 1807 Fourth St. (bet. Hearst Ave. & Virginia St.) | 510-644-3230 | www.bettesdiner.com

"You'll want to lick your plate" at this daytime-only "Berkeley legend" with a "'50s diner vibe" say fans who don't mind that there's "no ocean view" as they "just give in" to "giant plates" of breakfast "carbs" and "coffee that will grow hair on your chest"; the staff is "calmly professional", and though weekend waits get "tediously long", you can "browse the trendy stores on Fourth Street" or stock up on pancake mix from their take-out shop next door.

Bistro Liaison *French*

22 | 20 | 22 | $41

Berkeley | 1849 Shattuck Ave. (bet. Delaware St. & Hearst Ave.) | 510-849-2155 | www.liaisonbistro.com

"*Mais oui!*" exclaim proponents of the "French bistro fare" at this "little piece of Paris" in Berkeley, with "belle epoque" ambiance, "friendly" service and "quite reasonable" prices; it's a "fine choice" before the "Berkeley Rep or Aurora Theater", and you might even leave feeling "like you've had a vacation in France."

Blackberry Bistro *Southern*

21 | 14 | 17 | $20

Oakland | 4240 Park Blvd. (Wellington St.) | 510-336-1088 | www.theblackberrybistro.com

Dishing up "great" breakfasts, "imaginative lunches" and brunch that's "a cut above", this Southern bistro in the Oakland hills earned an improved Food rating while offering a "wide choice, from hearty to sensible", with "reasonable prices"; just "be prepared to wait" for your "gargantuan-sized waffle" – service is "very cordial but sometimes slow"; P.S. no dinner.

Blackhawk Grille *Californian*

20 | 22 | 21 | $44

Danville | Blackhawk Plaza | 3540 Blackhawk Plaza Circle (Camino Tassajara) | 925-736-4295 | www.blackhawkgrille.com

"Ask to sit outside alongside the water" for a "lovely" dining perch at this Danville Californian in Blackhawk Plaza offering a "value-based menu" of "interesting" fare delivered with "courteous" service; it's "child-friendly" too, all making for a "nice suburban spot for lunch or dinner."

Blue Bottle Roastery & Coffee Bar *Californian/Coffeehouse*

23 | 14 | 17 | $9

Oakland | 300 Webster St. (3rd St.) | 510-653-3394 | www.bluebottlecoffee.net

See review in City of San Francisco Directory.

Bocanova *Pan-Latin*

21 | 24 | 20 | $41

Oakland | Jack London Sq. | 55 Webster St. (Embarcadero W.) | 510-444-1233 | www.bocanova.com

The dining "renaissance in Oakland continues" at this "lively" Pan-Latin in Jack London Square where "each bite is an adventure" of "innovative south-of-the-border cuisine" – though the "cost depends" on whether you fill up on "tasty small plates" or entree-size portions; service is "engaging" (if sometimes "slow"), and the atmosphere is "vibrant" with "beautiful decor" inside and an "outside terrace" overlooking the marina that's "just magical on a sunny day."

FOOD | DECOR | SERVICE | COST

Boot & Shoe Service ⓂItalian/Pizza   24 | 18 | 20 | $32

Oakland | 3308 Grand Ave. (Elmwood Ave.) | 510-763-2668 |
www.bootandshoeservice.com

The "monumental wait times" are "worth it" at this "mobbed" spin-off
from the Pizzaiolo "mother ship" featuring "unbelievably great thin-
crust pizza", "clever appetizers" and cocktails that "rock" amid "arty
but spare decor"; fans "dream" about the "superb creations" and service is "accommodating", and while some gripe it's "way too loud"
others counter that's "expected in this type of place"; P.S. an adjacent
cafe has opened for coffee, baked goods and lunch.

Bo's Barbecue Ⓜ BBQ   22 | 12 | 16 | $24

Lafayette | 3422 Mt. Diablo Blvd. (Brown Ave.) | 925-283-7133

"Bo's knows BBQ" bellow believers in the "huge portions" of "smokin'
eats" at this Lafayette "order-at-the-counter" "roadside find", which
complements the "huge portions" with an "extensive beer selection"
and, interestingly, "nice wines"; some sniff the smoked stuff's strictly
for "gentrified suburbanites", but it can be "a fun place on the weekend" when "local jazz bands play."

Breads of India & Gourmet Curries Indian   19 | 13 | 17 | $24

Berkeley | 2448 Sacramento St. (Dwight Way) | 510-848-7684
Oakland | 948 Clay St. (bet. 9th & 10th Sts.) | 510-834-7684 🗷
Walnut Creek | 1358 N. Main St. (bet. Cypress & Duncan Sts.) |
925-256-7684 Ⓜ
www.breadsofindia.com

Indian aficionados "tired of ho-hum tikka this and tikka that" perk
up when "reading the menu" at this "unpretentious" East Bay trio
with a "revolving" selection of "really interesting" and oft-organic
options "from across the subcontinent"; the "generous portions"
are "good for the dough" maintain most, and the selection of "incredible" breads is undoubtedly "impressive", but heat-seeking
patrons who deem the dishes "a tad bland" are naan-plussed
by their popularity.

Bridges Restaurant Asian/Californian   23 | 23 | 23 | $47

Danville | 44 Church St. (Hartz Ave.) | 925-820-7200 |
www.bridgesdanville.com

"Once sort of an exclusive spot" "made famous" by *Mrs. Doubtfire,* this
Danville "favorite" now appeals to a "more casual diner", offering a
"new-style" Cal-Asian menu and "bargain" prix fixe (Sunday–
Wednesday), served "without snooty airs" in "beautiful" environs; if
doubters suggest it's "still trying to find its identity", fans insist it has
its "groove back"; P.S. an "excellent" nightly happy-hour menu and
"wonderful" patio make for a "great date night."

Bridgetender Tavern Pub Food   ▽ 18 | 20 | 17 | $19

Tahoe City | 65 W. Lake Blvd. (Rte. 89) | 530-583-3342

Munching a burger while "sitting outside, next to the river, is as good
as it gets" sigh fans of this "rustic" Tahoe City site; "everything else is
secondary" to the "ambiance in summer", though the "comforting"
pub grub and "down-home" atmosphere makes this a "great après-ski
refueling destination" as well.

Brown Sugar Kitchen Ⓜ *Soul Food*

23 | 17 | 19 | $22

Oakland | 2534 Mandela Pkwy. (26th St.) | 510-839-7685 |
www.brownsugarkitchen.com

"Soul food meets French culinary technique" at this "hip" West
Oakland breakfast and lunch spot serving up "amazing" chicken with
"crispy" cornmeal waffles "so light they take your breath away"; admirers overlook "uninspired decor" begging "please open for dinner",
because it's "jammed" on weekends, though a "coffee bar" and
"delicious beignets" ease "atrocious" waits; P.S. a San Francisco
branch is in the works.

Bucci's Ⓩ *Californian/Italian*

21 | 20 | 21 | $35

Emeryville | 6121 Hollis St. (bet. 59th & 61st Sts.) | 510-547-4725 |
www.buccis.com

At lunchtime, "Emeryville artists, movers and shakers" invade this
"neighborhood haunt" that offers "enough room between tables" for
discreet conversations, while in the evening it "feels like going over to
friends' for dinner", with "reliable" Cal-Italian "home cooking" tallying
in at "reasonable prices"; "Bucci herself" "patrols the dining room"
amid "interesting local art" and flanked by a "friendly, helpful staff."

BurgerMeister *Burgers*

20 | 11 | 15 | $16

Alameda | 2319 Central Ave. (bet. Oak & Park Sts.) | 510-865-3032
Berkeley | 2237 Shattuck Ave. (Kittredge St.) | 510-649-1700
www.burgermeistersf.com
See review in City of San Francisco Directory.

Ⓩ Burma Superstar *Burmese*

24 | 14 | 19 | $26

Alameda | 1345 Park St. (Central Ave.) | 510-522-6200 Ⓜ
Oakland | 4721 Telegraph Ave. (bet. 47th & 48th Sts.) | 510-652-2900
www.burmasuperstar.com
See review in City of San Francisco Directory.

Cactus Taqueria *Mexican*

20 | 11 | 15 | $13

Berkeley | 1881 Solano Ave. (bet. Fresno Ave. & The Alameda) |
510-528-1881
Oakland | 5642 College Ave. (Keith Ave.) | 510-658-6180
www.cactustaqueria.com

"Fresh, fresh, fresh", "carefully sourced" Mexican fare ("don't miss the
crispy chicken tacos" and "interesting salsa bar") brings "large numbers of families" to this "loud and cheap", "cafeteria-style" duo in
Berkeley and Oakland; "if you don't want to deal with the chaos and
noise", avoid "the moms with their infant assault vehicles" and "get it
to go", just be sure to "double-check your order before walking away."

Café Fanny *French*

23 | 12 | 17 | $20

Berkeley | 1603 San Pablo Ave. (Cedar St.) | 510-524-5451 |
www.cafefanny.com

"Only in Berkeley" would people "pay $8 to drink coffee like a French
truck driver" and consider it a "gem of the local food movement" snarl
cynics of Alice Waters' "informal" "stand-up" "breakfast/lunch
counter" "tucked away" in a parking lot; but given that the Gallic menu
offers "the perfect egg, the perfect sandwich, the perfect pastry" – all
"made with highest quality of ingredients" – "the discomfort and the
wait" are forgiven by fans who feel "Fanny is the manny!"

	FOOD	DECOR	SERVICE	COST

Café Fiore *Italian*

∇ **24** | **21** | **25** | **$47**

South Lake Tahoe | 1169 Ski Run Blvd. (Tamarack Ave.) | 530-541-2908 |
www.cafefiore.com

For a "romantic après-ski" evening, canoodlers "call ahead" for a table
"by the window" at this "very intimate" Northern Italian in South Lake
Tahoe; the "exceptional" pastas and "light", "fresh" sauces are "always
outstanding" (it would "even do well in SF", say some), but "don't go
there if you have a large party", because there are only seven tables,
plus a few more on the patio in summer.

Café Gratitude *Vegan*

17 | **15** | **17** | **$25**

Berkeley | 1730 Shattuck Ave. (bet. Francisco & Virginia Sts.) |
510-578-4928 | www.cafegratitude.com
See review in City of San Francisco Directory.

Café Rouge *Californian/Mediterranean*

22 | **19** | **20** | **$41**

Berkeley | Market Plaza | 1782 Fourth St. (bet. Hearst Ave. & Virginia St.) |
510-525-1440 | www.caferouge.net

"Meat is king" at this Berkeley Cal-Med bistro with an "on-site
butcher" shop and "charcuterie" – but there's also a "super oyster
bar", including daily $1 oyster "happy hours" that are "a killer deal";
carnivores roar about the "awesome burger" and "rotisserie chicken"
and tables on the "patio" to allow diners to "partake of the scene" on
"trendy Fourth Street."

Camino *Californian/Mediterranean*

22 | **20** | **20** | **$47**

Oakland | 3917 Grand Ave. (Sunny Slope Ave.) | 510-547-5035 |
www.caminorestaurant.com

"Chez Panisse alum" Russell Moore is literally "blazing his own trail"
with this "deceptively simple" Oakland Cal-Med offering a "very limited", "based on what's fresh that day" array of "open-fire cooked
food" in a "raw-chic room" "made cozy" by the "wood-burning hearth"
and "all-communal seating"; fans find it all "inventive and interesting",
but malcontents mutter about a "minimal menu to match the minimal
setting" – and "choppy" service to boot.

Casa Orinda *Italian/Steak*

18 | **19** | **20** | **$37**

Orinda | 20 Bryant Way (bet. Davis Rd. & Moraga Way) | 925-254-2981 |
www.casaorinda.net

It's "like time never moved" when you step into the "Old West atmosphere" of this Orinda Italian steakhouse "institution", where even the
"lively bar" looks "out of a movie set"; though a few grouse about "out-
dated preparations", "regulars" come for the "famous" fried chicken
and "heavenly biscuits that float off the plate" plus other "no-nonsense"
fare at "no-nonsense prices" delivered with "warm service."

Caspers Hot Dogs ⊘ *Hot Dogs*

20 | **7** | **15** | **$9**

Albany | 545 San Pablo Ave. (bet. Brighton Ave. & Garfield St.) |
510-527-6611
Dublin | 6998 Village Pkwy. (bet. Amador Valley & Dublin Blvds.) |
925-828-2224
Hayward | 21670 Foothill Blvd. (Grove Way) | 510-581-9064 ●
Hayward | 951 C St. (bet. Main St. & Mission Blvd.) | 510-537-7300
Oakland | 5440 Telegraph Ave. (55th St.) | 510-652-1668

(continued)

(continued)

Caspers Hot Dogs

Pleasant Hill | 6 Vivian Dr. (Contra Costa Blvd.) | 925-687-6030 ◐
Richmond | 2530 MacDonald Ave. (Civic Ctr. St.) | 510-235-6492
Walnut Creek | 1280 Newell Hill Pl. (bet. Newell Ave. & San Miguel Dr.) |
925-930-9154
www.caspershotdogs.com

Frank-ophiles "keep coming back" to these "old-fashioned" East Bay "joints" where "counter 'girls'", who've "been here since the place opened" in 1934, dish up the "best dogs outside of *Lassie*", "steamed" and "with all the trimmings"; they "snap in your mouth when you take a bite" and "explode with flavor" – just "be prepared for the juices that follow the pop."

César España ◐ *Spanish*

22 | 20 | 19 | $36

Berkeley | 1515 Shattuck Ave. (bet. Cedar & Vine Sts.) | 510-883-0222

César Latino ◐ *Pan-Latin*

Oakland | 4039 Piedmont Ave. (bet. 40th & 41st Sts.) | 510-985-1200
www.barcesar.com

It's "Barcelona in Berkeley", for fans of this "bold, loud" midpriced Spanish cafe turning out "delightful little-bitty plates of huge flavors and textures" to wash down with a "great selection of Iberian reds"; the "lively" Oakland outpost is a "place to see and be seen, cocktail in hand" – though the revamped Pan-Latin menu has some sniffling that they "miss the old César" and urging "bring back the tapas."

Cha Am Thai *Thai*

19 | 14 | 19 | $23

Berkeley | 1543 Shattuck Ave. (Cedar St.) | 510-848-9664
See review in City of San Francisco Directory.

Cha-Ya Vegetarian
Japanese Restaurant ⊘ *Japanese/Vegan*

23 | 13 | 17 | $22

Berkeley | 1686 Shattuck Ave. (bet. Lincoln & Virginia Sts.) | 510-981-1213
See review in City of San Francisco Directory.

◪ Cheese Board
Collective ⊠Ⓜ⊘ *Bakery/Pizza*

27 | 13 | 19 | $13

Berkeley | 1512 Shattuck Ave. (bet. Cedar & Vine Sts.) | 510-549-3183 |
www.cheeseboardcollective.coop

"They only make one" "unique pizza per day" (find the week's "incredible" always-vegetarian combinations online) at this "icon" that's a "quintessential Berkeley experience" whether you sit on the "grassy" "road median", eat in the cafe listening to "live music" or take home "half-baked pies"; each "gargantuan" slice is a "little piece of heaven" for a "pittance", and "don't despair", the "jaw-dropping" line "moves pretty fast"; P.S. the adjacent shop features "out-of-this-world" bread and pastries, plus an "amazing variety of cheeses."

Cheesecake Factory *American*

17 | 18 | 17 | $29

Pleasanton | Stoneridge Shopping Ctr. | 1350 Stoneridge Mall Rd.
(Foothill Rd.) | 925-463-1311 | www.thecheesecakefactory.com

"How does anyone ever get to the cheesecake?" ask veterans of this midpriced American chain known for its "giant" portions and "encyclopedic" "menu to please everyone"; the "big", "noisy" setting resembles "Vegas in a good way", and any grumbles about variable service and "too much quantity, not enough quality" are drowned out by "ridiculous crowds" dubbing it "perfect for a family outing" – so "be prepared to wait."

Cheese Steak Shop *Cheesesteaks*

20 | 6 | 15 | $12

Alameda | Blanding Shopping Ctr. | 2671 Blanding Ave. (Tilden Way) | 510-522-5555
Berkeley | 1054 University Ave. (bet. San Pablo Ave. & 10th St.) | 510-845-8689
Concord | 3478 Clayton Rd. (Roslyn Dr.) | 925-687-6116
Lafayette | 3455 Mt. Diablo Blvd. (2nd St.) | 925-283-1234
Oakland | 3308 Lakeshore Ave. (bet. Lake Park Ave. & Mandana Blvd.) | 510-832-6717
Pleasanton | Gateway Square Shopping Ctr. | 4825 Hopyard Rd. (Stoneridge Dr.) | 925-734-0293
San Ramon | Crow Canyon Crest Shopping Ctr. | 3110 Crow Canyon Pl. (Crow Canyon Rd.) | 925-242-1112
Walnut Creek | 1626 Cypress St. (bet. California Blvd. & Locust St.) | 925-934-7017
www.cheesesteakshop.com
See review in City of San Francisco Directory.

Ⓩ Chevalier Ⓜ *French*

25 | 19 | 23 | $52

Lafayette | 960 Moraga Rd. (Moraga Blvd.) | 925-385-0793 | www.chevalierrestaurant.com
"In out-of-the-way Lafayette", "chef-owner Philippe Chevalier welcomes you" into his "cozy" lair, preparing big-"city quality", "classic Provençal" fare at this "suburban charmer"; "it isn't cheap" and the staff, though "warm", "could use one more" body, but the "lovely garden terrace" more than makes up for the "nondescript mini-strip mall" surroundings.

Ⓩ Chez Panisse Ⓢ *Californian/Mediterranean*

28 | 24 | 26 | $84

Berkeley | 1517 Shattuck Ave. (bet. Cedar & Vine Sts.) | 510-548-5525 | www.chezpanisse.com
Alice Waters' "legendary" Berkeley prix fixe "temple" remains the "ne plus ultra" of "fresh, local, organic" Cal-Med meals served with "no flash", just "gorgeous ingredients" "exquisitely handled", and continues to elicit "audible sighs" "night after night" in the "wondrous Craftsman wood" dining room with a "view of the open kitchen" "where it all started" (pilgrims can "request a tour"); the "superb" staff can seem "self-important", but the "integrity, vision and talent" behind this "gastronomic experience" is worth the effort and "investment."

Ⓩ Chez Panisse Café Ⓢ *Californian/Mediterranean*

27 | 23 | 25 | $52

Berkeley | 1517 Shattuck Ave. (bet. Cedar & Vine Sts.) | 510-548-5049 | www.chezpanisse.com
To experience the "same care, creativity and commitment" to the "field-to-plate ethos" as at "the mother ship" downstairs "sans the sanctimonious airs" and "full expense", "it's worth the climb" – "on your hands, backward even" for a "relaxing lunch" or dinner at Alice Waters' à la carte cafe turning out "perfect pizza" and other "simple" Cal-Med "deliciousness" in a "lovely Craftsman setting" tended by a "well-trained" staff; best of all, you can still "take a tour of the kitchen."

	FOOD	DECOR	SERVICE	COST

Chop Bar *Californian* — 22 | 20 | 21 | $27

Oakland | 247 Fourth St. (Alice St.) | 510-834-2467 |
www.oaklandchopbar.com

"Comfort food with flair" is turned out by a "sublimely inventive kitchen"
and delivered by a "friendly staff" at this "funky, hip" and "reasonably
priced" Californian that's a "great addition to the loft scene" near
Oakland's Jack London Square; "owners dedicated to local foods and
brews" offer changing "on-tap wines", plus monthly "Sunday pig
roasts" in the summertime, when they roll up the "garage-door front."

Chow *American* — 20 | 16 | 19 | $26

Danville | 445 Railroad Ave. (Hartz Ave.) | 925-838-4510
Lafayette | La Fiesta Sq. | 53 Lafayette Circle (Mt. Diablo Blvd.) |
925-962-2469
www.chowfoodbar.com
See review in City of San Francisco Directory.

Christy Hill *Californian/Mediterranean* — ▽ 22 | 24 | 19 | $59

Tahoe City | 115 Grove St. (Rte. 28) | 530-583-8551 | www.christyhill.com
After coming aboard in 2010, the current "owners have cranked up the
menu to match the stupendous view" (almost) at this Tahoe City
Cal-Med focusing on "creative" small plates that manage to be "surprisingly fresh and delicious" "in sleet and snow and summer heat"; the elements permitting, eating on the "appealing deck" is "recommended."

⚡ Commis Ⓜ *American* — 27 | 21 | 26 | $109

Oakland | 3859 Piedmont Ave. (Rio Vista Ave.) | 510-653-3902 |
www.commisrestaurant.com

"Isn't Oakland lucky?" fawn "intense foodies" who relish "sitting at the
counter" of this "unmarked" New American "hipster-haute" "jewel box"
watching "gifted chef"-owner James Syhabout and crew "work like
precision engineers" crafting "thought-provoking" molecular gastronomic prix fixes; the "subdued minimalist setting" is "not for everyone"
and it's "tough to get a reservation", but "you definitely get your money's
worth", from the "exotic" amuse bouche to the "spot-on service."

NEW Cosecha Café Ⓢ *Mexican* — - | - | - | M

Oakland | Swan's Mkt. | 907 Washington St. (bet. 9th & 10th Sts.) |
510-452-5900 | www.cosechacafe.com

At this new quick-service, Californian-inspired Mexican in Oakland's
Swan's Market, Dominca Rice (a former Chez Panisse line cook) offers
midpriced, traditional *comida* made from scratch – think tamales,
tacos, posole – to be enjoyed at a communal table, the counter or to
go; it's primarily a daytime affair, offering fresh baked goods in the
morning followed by lunch fare and a happy hour until 6 PM, plus
weekend brunch items; P.S. a family-style pop-up dinner series
is planned too.

Cottonwood *Eclectic* — ▽ 26 | 24 | 25 | $49

Truckee | 10142 Rue Hilltop (Brockway Rd.) | 530-587-5711 |
www.cottonwoodrestaurant.com

Perched "on a hillside" with a "commanding view of Downtown
Truckee", this upscale Eclectic combines a "menu that rivals anything
you can find in San Francisco" (all hail the "incredible Caesar salad for
two") with a "fun and funky bar where locals and tourists mingle with

ease"; a "neat place to hang after skiing" or to "sit on the deck in the summer", it's "one of the best near the lake."

NEW Disco Volante ◑ *Californian*   - | - | - | M

Oakland | 347 14th St. (Webster St.) | 510-663-0271 | www.discovolanteoakland.com

Funky beats and affordable Californian eats are the come-on at this Oakland newcomer, a restaurant-cum-nightclub that draws Downtown workers and night owls alike; the refurbished art deco venue, featuring high ceilings and reclaimed stained-glass panes, hosts daily happy hours and DJs, plus live music some nights after 10 PM; P.S. it's also open for lunch on weekdays.

Doña Tomás ⊠Ⓜ *Mexican*   22 | 18 | 19 | $35

Oakland | 5004 Telegraph Ave. (bet. 49th & 51st Sts.) | 510-450-0522 | www.donatomas.com

It's "a real restaurant, not a taco joint" – so "don't expect the usual Mexican" bites at this "hot spot" in Oakland's Temescal where instead you'll find midpriced meals such as "off-the-hook" carnitas and chiles rellenos "foodied-up" "with the best ingredients, gourmet technique and brilliant presentation"; "some are just in it for the fabulous margaritas", as a "noisy bar" scene suggests, and as long as you don't require swift service, it's "very pleasant on the back patio."

Dopo ⊠ *Italian*   25 | 17 | 22 | $37

Oakland | 4293 Piedmont Ave. (Echo Ave.) | 510-652-3676 | www.dopoadesso.com

Recently "expanded quarters mean less waiting for a table" at this "cozy" Oakland trattoria run by "ex Oliveto dudes" that "continues to astound" with its "brilliant" "ultra-thin-crust pizza", "superb salumi" and crudos that rival those "in Italy", expertly matched with "reasonably priced" vinos; whether you lunch "at the bar" or dine on the "coveted patio", don't be a dope – "just go"; P.S. Saturday is dinner only.

Dragonfly *Asian/Californian*   22 | 18 | 20 | $39

Truckee | Porter Simon Bldg. | 10118 Donner Pass Rd., 2nd fl. (Spring St.) | 530-587-0557 | www.dragonflycuisine.com

"Maybe the most solid place to dine in Truckee" is this "Californian-Asian fusion plus sushi bar" that "goes beyond the traditional" offerings with "inventive dishes" and "superb wine"; service is "attentive", and while the place is "well decorated", regulars recommend "eat outside if you can – the trains heading to and from Donner Summit are fun to watch."

Duck Club *American*   20 | 22 | 21 | $50

Lafayette | Lafayette Park Hotel & Spa | 3287 Mt. Diablo Blvd. (Pleasant Hill Rd.) | 925-283-7108 | www.lafayetteparkhotel.com
See review in South of San Francisco Directory.

Élevé Ⓜ *Vietnamese*   ∇ 21 | 22 | 21 | $37

Walnut Creek | 1677 N. Main St. (Civic Dr.) | 925-979-1677 | www.eleverestaurant.com

"Vietnam with a Californian twist" epitomizes the experience at this "nice addition to Walnut Creek", where "imaginative eats", augmented by a "well-aligned wine list" and a "great selection of vintage cocktails", are served in a "fancy", "two-story glass enclosed showcase" by a "friendly" staff; but big eaters beware – several find it somewhat "*élevé*" pricewise, given the "skimpy" portions.

Emilia's Pizzeria 🗷Ⓜ⇗ *Pizza* ▽ 27 | 10 | 20 | $19

Berkeley | 2995 Shattuck Ave. (Ashby Ave.) | 510-704-1794 | www.emiliaspizzeria.com

This "tiny closet" of a pizzeria "deserves all the accolades", Berkeleyites gush, for New York–style pies that leave them "floating on a dreamy cloud of pizza tranquility"; be forewarned, you'll have to "jump through hoops" to score the goods, so "call right when they open" to order your 'za, and "don't plan on eating in" without a reservation, since the room only seats eight.

Encuentro Cafe & Wine Bar 🗷 *Vegetarian* ▽ 23 | 21 | 23 | $29

Oakland | 200 Second St. (Jackson St.) | 510-832-9463 | www.encuentrooakland.com

"People in the know" venture "off the beaten path" ("just a block or two") to this midpriced "neighborhood joint" near Oakland's Jack London Square, where they warn "meat eaters beware", "this place could change your tune" with "vegetarian fare prepared as a meal, not a sacrament"; the quarters are "small" but the staff is "great", and organic, sustainable or biodynamic wines help keep the vibe "pleasant."

𝗡𝗘𝗪 Enoteca Molinari 🗷Ⓜ *Italian* - | - | - | M

Oakland | 5474 College Ave. (Taft Ave.) | 510-428-4078 | www.enoteca-molinari.com

You might need "an advanced degree in Italian wine" to navigate the list at this "new seat on the block" in Oakland, but this enoteca's early adopters insist its "fantastic" small plates, handmade pastas and "friendly" staff are "easy to appreciate"; it's not very big and "it can be hard to get in", particularly at happy hour when crowds belly up to the curved wood bar for $5 snacks and vinos; however, it offers limited reservations online.

𝗭 Erna's Elderberry House *Californian/French* 27 | 28 | 27 | $99

Oakhurst | Château du Sureau | 48688 Victoria Ln. (Hwy. 41) | 559-683-6800 | www.elderberryhouse.com

"If you're going to Yosemite", "you must stop" at this "astounding" hotel eatery in Oakhurst, where "quintessential hostess" Erna "attends to every last detail" in an "elegant" dining room, proffering "spectacular" "multicourse gourmet" New French–Californian dinners; while "certainly pricey", it's "the height of perfection" (not to mention the "only option for a high-end meal" for miles); P.S. "if you really want to impress your lady-love", "stay overnight and indulge the rest of you at the super-pampering spa."

𝗭 Esin Restaurant & 25 | 22 | 24 | $45
Bar *American/Mediterranean*

Danville | Rose Garden Ctr. | 750 Camino Ramon (Sycamore Valley Rd.) | 925-314-0974 | www.esinrestaurant.com

"Why go to SF?" Danvillians ask, when there's this "fresh, friendly, focused" and "fabulous" New American–Med situated in a local "shopping center", serving "creative and inventive" cuisine and "excellent housemade desserts" for a "not-so-hefty price"; a "smart" staff is overseen by the married chef-owners, who manage to "whip up

Bay Area sophistication" in both the setting and menu, keeping repeat customers "impressed."

Evan's American Gourmet Cafe *American* ▽ 27 | 23 | 27 | $61

South Lake Tahoe | 536 Emerald Bay Rd. (15th St.) | 530-542-1990 | www.evanstahoe.com

Evan-gelists attest this New American is a Tahoe "must-go", thanks to "unique", "flavorful" "food that you expect to find in the heart of SF", and they're "sure glad" to add that the tabs are much less than those in the city; there are "no pretensions" in this converted cabin, just "gracious service" that makes it "the kind of place" fans "go back to year after year."

Eve Ⓢ Ⓜ *American* 25 | 17 | 22 | $50

Berkeley | 1960 University Ave. (bet. Bonita Ave. & Milvia St.) | 510-868-0735 | www.eve-berkeley.com

A "talented" "husband-and-wife cook in the open kitchen" of this New American nook in Berkeley, turning out "exquisitely prepared" fare from an "innovative, although small, menu"; if pessimists find it "a little precious", protesting "tiny portions" and "service that tends to disappear if the place is crowded", smitten surveyors see this "diamond in the rough" as offering "the East Bay's version of gastronomique cuisine."

Everett & Jones Barbeque *BBQ* 20 | 11 | 14 | $22

Berkeley | 1955 San Pablo Ave. (University Ave.) | 510-548-8261 ⊟
Hayward | 296 A St. (Fuller Ave.) | 510-581-3222
Oakland | Jack London Sq. | 126 Broadway (bet. Embarcadero W. & 2nd St.) | 510-663-2350
www.eandjbbq.com

For "juicy", "fall-off-the-bone" ribs "dripping with sauce", "large portions" and "cheap" prices, BBQ fans are willing to accept the "no-frills" decor and service with "attitude" at this East Bay threesome; Hayward and Berkeley are counter-service spots, while Jack London Square is a sit-down location with live music Fridays.

FatApple's *Diner* 18 | 14 | 17 | $20

Berkeley | 1346 Martin Luther King Jr. Way (bet. Berryman & Rose Sts.) | 510-526-2260
El Cerrito | 7525 Fairmount Ave. (bet. Carmel & Ramona Aves.) | 510-528-3433

There may be "no frills" at these "informal", "family-friendly" diners in Berkeley and El Cerrito, but "who needs 'em" when you can order "dependable" "all-American fare" from the "exceptionally nice servers"; the "juicy" burgers, "meal-sized salads" and "delicious" breakfasts are a "good value", just remember to "save room for a slice of pie."

Fentons Creamery *Ice Cream* 20 | 14 | 17 | $16

Oakland | 4226 Piedmont Ave. (bet. Entrada & Glenwood Aves.) | 510-658-7000
Oakland | Oakland Int'l Airport | Terminal 2 (Ron Cowan Pkwy.) | No phone
www.fentonscreamery.com

"A throwback to another era", this "cheerful" "old-fashioned soda fountain" is an "Oakland institution" where you can "gorge yourself" on "amazing" "super-huge" sundaes and other "oozy ice cream goodies"; the savory selections are "solid" if "nothing special" (save the "great crab sandwich"), and the impatient are irked by "long" lines, but it's a "family-friendly" spot to "celebrate a child's birthday" – or just "feel like a kid again" yourself; P.S. the outpost at the Oakland airport "almost makes waiting for a plane palatable."

Five *American/Californian* | 20 | 22 | 20 | $44 |

Berkeley | Hotel Shattuck Plaza | 2086 Allston Way (Oxford St.) | 510-225-6055 | www.five-berkeley.com

The "stylish decor" at this "beautifully" refurbished Cal-American in Berkeley's Hotel Shattuck Plaza is "reminiscent of an earlier era", while a "small, carefully selected menu" offers "innovative" dishes, "well executed with local ingredients"; noting the name evokes "all five senses", some wish they'd "dial down the noise" and go instead for "four", but on the plus side, prices are "reasonable" and the "staff tries to please."

Flora 🅂 Ⓜ *American* | 21 | 20 | 20 | $45 |

Oakland | 1900 Telegraph Ave. (19th St.) | 510-286-0100 | www.floraoakland.com

Located in a "revamped art deco–style flower mart", this "pricey" Uptown Oakland New American sibling of Doña Tomás "serves a bouquet of delicious dishes" and "amazing", "artfully crafted" cocktails amid "cool '30s New York decor"; it's "great before Paramount Theatre events", just "get there early if you can't take the noise" – and psst – "don't tell the SF crowd about this jewel."

Fonda Solana ❶ *Pan-Latin* | 23 | 20 | 20 | $36 |

Albany | 1501 Solano Ave. (Curtis St.) | 510-559-9006 | www.fondasolana.com

Head for the border – "between Albany and Berkeley", that is – to find this "hopping, late-night hipster" spot serving "upscale", "vibrantly fresh" Pan-Latin small plates (including tacos in "terrific" duck and "divine" fish versions) plus "handcrafted" drinks; the brick-walled space lends a "warm atmosphere", and though "teensy portions" mean it's hard "to fill up without emptying your savings", budget-watchers praise the "bargains after 9 PM."

Forbes Mill Steakhouse *Steak* | 22 | 20 | 22 | $59 |

Danville | Livery Mercantile | 200 Sycamore Valley Rd. W. (San Ramon Valley Blvd.) | 925-552-0505 | www.forbesmillsteakhouse.com

See review in South of San Francisco Directory.

Gar Woods Grill & Pier *American/Mediterranean* | 17 | 22 | 19 | $38 |

Carnelian Bay | 5000 N. Lake Blvd. (Center St.) | 530-546-3366 | www.garwoods.com

If you seek a "beautiful location on the lake", this "casual" Carnelian Bay standby (always "hopping" with those who "went to Bzerkeley") may well float your boat; for "pitchers of Wet Woodies" "and munchies" "on a summer evening out on the deck", it "can't be beat", and if the "overpriced" Mediterranean–New American fare is "inconsequential", well, "everything tastes better with a view."

Gather *Californian* | 23 | 20 | 21 | $39 |

Berkeley | David Brower Ctr. | 2200 Oxford St. (Allston Way) | 510-809-0400 | www.gatherrestaurant.com

Offering "a little bit of *Portlandia*" "near the UC campus", this indoor/outdoor "darling of the Berkeley dining scene" gathers "super-yoga mamas", "food snobs" and "meat and potatoes" guys who all "find something to drool about" from the "unique" Californian "locally grazed, raised and grown delights" (especially the "vaunted" vegan charcuterie); if a few find it "too precious", most "feel healthier just reading the menu."

NEW Gaumenkitzel M German
- | **-** | **-** | **M**

Berkeley | 2121 San Pablo Ave. (Addison St.) | 510-647-5016 | www.gaumenkitzel.net

Fueling the current zeitgeist for all things German, this Berkeley newcomer finds a husband-and-wife duo from Hamburg presenting breakfast, lunch, tea-time and early supper fare from the Northern regions – everything from muesli and linzertorte to soups and beef with braised cabbage; open Tuesday–Sunday till 6:30 PM (with full dinner hours coming soon), the laid-back digs feature a vaulted wood ceiling, a communal table and sidewalk seating.

Gioia Pizzeria Pizza
25 | **9** | **17** | **$12**

Berkeley | 1586 Hopkins St. (bet. McGee & Monterey Aves.) | 510-528-4692 | www.gioiapizzeria.com

"Ex-New Yorkers" praise the pie at this family "favorite" as "an ideal blending of Brooklyn and Berkeley", since the "thin" and "blistered" East Coast–style crust comes with "fresh" "locally sourced toppings"; it's "not much more than a take-out counter", so "don't expect a seat" (there are only six stools), but the "creative combo slices" "never fail to please", much like the "friendly" service.

Great China Chinese
24 | **10** | **14** | **$26**

Berkeley | 2115 Kittredge St. (bet. Fulton St. & Shattuck Ave.) | 510-843-7996 | www.greatchinaberkeley.com

"Don't go for decor or service, just go for" the "tasty" "unique" fare including "incomparable Peking duck" and "amazing" "double-skin salad" at this "authentic" East Bay favorite turning out the "best Chinese food in Berkeley" while offering a wine list that "will blow your mind"; the signature dish "bumps up the average price", but tabs are generally "very reasonable", just aim to "go early or late" because the "chaotic" spot gets "crowded" and "noisy."

Grégoire French
21 | **8** | **14** | **$21**

Berkeley | 2109 Cedar St. (bet. Shattuck Ave. & Walnut St.) | 510-883-1893
Oakland | 4001B Piedmont Ave. (40th St.) | 510-547-3444
www.gregoirerestaurant.com

"How can such a small space deliver such a huge taste?" ask admirers of the "affordable", "elegant takeout" from these "authentic" French Berkeley and Oakland twins offering "interesting twists to old cafe/bistro standbys" on a menu that changes monthly; you "can inhale a truckload" of the signature potato puffs, just don't plan on sitting down, as there are scant seats.

NEW Hawker Fare ⑤ SE Asian
- | **-** | **-** | **I**

Oakland | 2300 Webster St. (23rd St.) | 510-832-8896 | www.hawkerfare.com

Oakland native James Syhabout (Commis) ditches his fine-dine pyrotechnics to crank out reinterpreted Southeast Asian street food at this Uptown arrival situated in the very Thai restaurant his mom used to run when he was growing up; the tiny storefront – filled with Bruce Lee posters, graffiti art and thumping old-school funk and hip-hop – sets the stage for rice bowls topped with various meats and the requisite fried egg (all priced under $10), chased by Straus soft-serve flavored with condensed milk.

Herbivore *Vegan*
17 | 13 | 16 | $21

Berkeley | 2451 Shattuck Ave. (Haste St.) | 510-665-1675 | www.herbivorerestaurant.com
See review in City of San Francisco Directory.

Hibiscus Ⓜ *Caribbean*
20 | 19 | 18 | $39

Oakland | 1745 San Pablo Ave. (18th St.) | 510-444-2626 | www.hibiscusoakland.com
"In a blossoming Uptown" Oakland neighborhood, chef Sarah Kirnon (ex Front Porch) is serving up a "tasty" "take on nouveau Caribbean"-Creole fare, say surveyors, who are particularly partial to her "smashing fried chicken" ("pour on the housemade habanero hot sauce"); though some find the experience "uneven", others applaud the "great lunch scene", "accommodating" staff and upbeat "after-work" vibe; P.S. closed Monday and Tuesday.

Home of Chicken & Waffles ◑ *Southern*
∇ 16 | 11 | 16 | $19

Oakland | 444 Embarcadero W. (B'way) | 510-836-4446 | www.homeofchickenandwaffles.com/
NEW Walnut Creek | 1653 Mt. Diablo Blvd. (S. California Blvd.) | 925-280-1653 | www.homeofchickenandwaffles.com
A "dive" in a "good" sense, this Oakland soul fooder turns out "delicious Southern cooking" that hits a high note with its "combo" of "great fried chicken" and "flat, round old-fashioned waffles"; true, it's "not exactly healthy" but the vibe's "friendly" and it won't dent your wallet, so most say it's a "treat" "you have to experience"; P.S. there's a new branch in Walnut Creek.

NEW Homeroom Ⓜ *American*
- | - | - | I

Oakland | 400 40th St. (Shafter Ave.) | 510-597-0400 | www.homeroom510.com
Many mac 'n' cheese iterations (including vegan and gluten-free versions) made with local-sustainable fromage, accompanied by beer, wine and house-brewed root beer, are on offer at this newcomer in Oakland's Temescal neighborhood; the school theme is carried through to the decor with reclaimed bleachers, an old card catalog (to hold punch cards for a customer loyalty program) and a chalkboard map marking the kitchen's sources.

NEW Hudson *American*
∇ 20 | 19 | 20 | $46

Oakland | 5356 College Ave. (Manila Ave.) | 510-595-4000 | www.hudsonoakland.com
Opened by the same "wonderful owners" in the "former Garibaldi's/Marzano space", this "latest incarnation has gotten it right" report Oaklanders, who cite the "sleek" digs and "imaginative comfort food to match"; a blend of New American and Italian fare, including wood-fired pizzas, the menu offers "something for everyone", and there's an expanded "lively bar" scene too.

	FOOD	DECOR	SERVICE	COST

Il Fornaio *Italian* | 20 | 20 | 20 | $39 |

Walnut Creek | 1430 Mt. Diablo Blvd. (bet. B'way & Main St.) |
925-296-0100 | www.ilfornaio.com
See review in City of San Francisco Directory.

Imperial Tea Court *Tearoom* | 19 | 20 | 19 | $23 |

Berkeley | Epicurious Gdn. | 1511 Shattuck Ave. (bet. Cedar & Vine Sts.) |
510-540-8888 | www.imperialtea.com
See review in City of San Francisco Directory.

Incontro Ristorante ● *Italian* | 24 | 17 | 23 | $41 |

San Ramon | 2065 San Ramon Valley Blvd. (bet. Hooper Dr. & Purdue Rd.) |
925-820-6969

Surveyors feel they've "arrived in Italy" at this "small restaurant with a big heart" in San Ramon that's "becoming well-known" for its "wonderful, authentic Italian cuisine" (e.g. "feather-light gnocchi") and "lovely" wines by the glass or bottle; sure, the space might need "a face-lift", but "very personal" service led by the "welcoming and gracious" owners helps make it "one of the best values in the East Bay."

☒ In-N-Out Burger ● *Burgers* | 21 | 10 | 18 | $9 |

Oakland | 8300 Oakport St. (bet. Pendleton & Roland Ways) | 800-786-1000 |
www.in-n-out.com
See review in City of San Francisco Directory.

Ippuku *Japanese* | 23 | 23 | 20 | $44 |

Berkeley | 2130 Center St. (Shattuck Ave.) | 510-665-1969 |
www.ippukuberkeley.com

"A lot of the menu is unfamiliar" at this new, "brilliant" Berkeley-based "izakaya/yakitori restaurant" "with an emphasis on chicken" in all its forms, plus "lots of liquor" (over 24 sakes and 50 shochus); yes, it gets "a bit smoky from the grill" cooking "delicious small skewers", but "sit tatami-mat style or in a booth of repurposed elegant wood, and you'll swear you went through the portal to Japan."

Izzy's Steaks & Chops *Steak* | 20 | 17 | 19 | $43 |

San Ramon | 200 Montgomery St. (bet. Alcosta Blvd. & Market Pl.) |
925-830-8620 | www.izzyssteaks.com
See review in City of San Francisco Directory.

Jake's on the Lake *Californian* | 18 | 23 | 19 | $41 |

Tahoe City | Boatworks Mall | 780 N. Lake Blvd. (Jackpine St.) |
530-583-0188 | www.jakestahoe.com

"Plan dinner at around sunset" (or just come for lunch), the better to appreciate the "unsurpassed" view from the "lakeside" deck of this "busy" Tahoe City standby; the "predictable" Californian menu veers from "surprisingly good" to "so-so" (some suggest you "save room" for the "delicious hula pie"), but who cares when you're enjoying an "appetizer and a drink" with all the "beautiful people" "on the patio"; P.S. weekends bring live music to the bar.

Jimmy Beans *Diner* | 20 | 11 | 15 | $19 |

Berkeley | 1290 Sixth St. (Gilman St.) | 510-528-3435 |
www.jimmybeans.com

All-day "breakfast rocks" at this Berkeley "go-to", which "can't be beat" for AM eats like "scrambled egg wraps" and "silver-dollar pancakes" you "can't resist", while also getting kudos for its "three-course $15 deal" for dinner; so look past the "industrial area" and downscale "homey ambiance" and step up to "order at the counter", because fans say this one's a "funky" "find."

Juan's Place *Mexican* | 18 | 10 | 20 | $18 |

Berkeley | 941 Carleton St. (9th St.) | 510-845-6904

"Great Mexican food for cheap" includes "flour tortilla chips" that "are too good for calorie-watchers" to pass up at this "funky", "old-school" Berkeley "hole-in-the-wall"; it's "family-run and you can tell" – the staff "knows what you want even before you order", and it remains "popular" for "large gatherings" (and birthdays) even "after all these years."

Kirala *Japanese* | 25 | 15 | 19 | $36 |

Berkeley | 2100 Ward St. (Shattuck Ave.) | 510-549-3486

Kirala 2 *Japanese*

Berkeley | Epicurious Gdn. | 1511 Shattuck Ave. (bet. Cedar & Vine Sts.) | 510-649-1384
www.kiralaberkeley.com

Although it offers "impeccably fresh" fish "for the serious sushi addict", the "great grill specialties" and "other Japanese dishes (tempura, noodles)" are the true "stars" of this "popular" standby in Berkeley; to "avoid the wait", line up no later than "five minutes after they open" (or at lunchtime), lest you "end up drinking too much sake" biding your time at the bar; P.S. bento boxes and pre-made rolls are available at the takeaway-only Epicurious Garden outpost.

Koi Garden *Chinese* | 24 | 16 | 14 | $36 |

Dublin | Ulferts Ctr. | 4288 Dublin Blvd. (bet. Glynnis Rose Dr. & John Monego Ct.) | 925-833-9090 | www.koipalace.com

See Koi Palace review in South of San Francisco Directory.

Koryo Wooden Charcoal BBQ *Korean* | ∇ 21 | 10 | 17 | $31 |

Oakland | 4390 Telegraph Ave. (bet. 43rd & 44th Sts.) | 510-652-6007

"Delicious", "reasonably priced" Korean fare gets the "seal of approval" from fans of this "authentic" Oakland spot where it's "fun to barbecue at the table"; "you won't be disappointed" with the "dolsot bibimbop" (dolsot is the stone bowl its cooked in), and though the decor is pretty "bare", it does the trick for "late-night eats."

Lake Chalet *Californian* | 14 | 25 | 15 | $38 |

Oakland | Lake Merritt Boathse. | 1520 Lakeside Dr. (bet. 14th & 17th Sts.) | 510-208-5253 | www.thelakechalet.com

This "gorgeously restored boathouse" is a "breathtakingly beautiful spot" with "awesome views" of Lake Merritt that make dining "like being on Lake Como, without the attitude"; while some are "pleasantly surprised by the food", others gripe that the "pricey" seafood and Cal fare is "not up to the beautiful location" and service is "erratic", advising "drinks and apps are the way to go."

Lalime's *Californian/Mediterranean* | 25 | 22 | 24 | $52 |

Berkeley | 1329 Gilman St. (bet. Neilson St. & Peralta Ave.) | 510-527-9838 | www.lalimes.com

"The food takes center stage" at this Cal-Med "secret delight" "hidden in north Berkeley", the K2 restaurant group's "flagship" where an "expert kitchen" has been "presenting what is fresh and in season" for over 25 years; the "romantic", "impeccably civilized" experience is further enhanced by an "intimate" setting and "attentive" service, making it a "great choice for special occasions" – and "worth every penny."

La Méditerranée *Mediterranean/Mideastern*   20 | 15 | 19 | $25

Berkeley | 2936 College Ave. (bet. Ashby Ave. & Russell St.) | 510-540-7773 | www.cafelamed.com
See review in City of San Francisco Directory.

Lanesplitter Pub & Pizza ● *Pizza*   17 | 12 | 16 | $17

Albany | 1051 San Pablo Ave. (Monroe St.) | 510-527-8375
Berkeley | 2033 San Pablo Ave. (bet. Addison St. & University Ave.) | 510-845-1652
Emeryville | 3645 San Pablo Ave. (Adeline St.) | 510-594-9400
Oakland | 4799 Telegraph Ave. (48th St.) | 510-653-5350
Oakland | 536 Lake Park Ave. (Lakeshore Ave.) | 510-893-4001
www.lanesplitterpizza.com
When East Bay eaters hanker for "simple, cheap" pie, this "laid-back" quintet of "thin-crust" "New York-style" pizzerias do the trick; the 'za may be "basic", but the "beer choices are terrific" (and the calzone's "the size of a football"), plus you might even spot "entertaining tattoos" on the staff; P.S. the Albany and Lake Park Avenue locations are takeout or delivery only.

La Note *French*   22 | 20 | 18 | $27

Berkeley | 2377 Shattuck Ave. (bet. Channing Way & Durant Ave.) | 510-843-1535 | www.lanoterestaurant.com
Regulars insist this "charming country French in the heart of Berkeley" is "aptly named", since "their breakfasts make you want to sing" about the likes of "crème fraîche pancakes" at prices that are "moderate"; it's "never empty of spirit or of diners" and "lines to get in" at brunch can be "insane", but the "green and yellow" Provençal decor is "calming and relaxing", plus there's a "wonderful back patio for warmer months"; P.S. dinner is served Thursday–Saturday.

Lark Creek *American*   22 | 21 | 22 | $46

Walnut Creek | 1360 Locust St. (bet. Cypress St. & Mt. Diablo Blvd.) | 925-256-1234 | www.larkcreek.com
Devotees declare some of the "best comfort food in comfortville" (aka Walnut Creek) is dished out at this "solid" American featuring "classic", mostly organic "feel-good eats", plus a few "seasonal surprises" in a "charming" and, yes, "comfortable setting"; true, it can be a little "predictable" and "pricey", but thanks to "pleasant" service and "a kids' menu", it's "great for family get-togethers."

LCX *Vietnamese*   20 | 15 | 17 | $26

Oakland | 1019 Clay St. (10th St.) | 510-763-8495
Le Cheval Ⓜ *Vietnamese*
Walnut Creek | 1375 N. Broadway (bet. Cypress & Duncan Sts.) | 925-938-2288
Le Petit Cheval Ⓜ⇄ *Vietnamese*
Berkeley | YWCA | 2600 Bancroft Way (Bowditch St.) | 510-704-8018
www.lecheval.com
Fans were "worried" when the "gigantic, old" Oakland flagship of this triumvirate closed, but now that it's resurfaced "up the block" at

"about a tenth of the size" with a "much more limited menu" in an "elegant" new space, early samplers deem the "upscale Vietnamese" fare "better than ever"; the Berkeley "little sister" leaves "much to be desired" with its "school cafeteria" atmosphere, though it's good for "quick", "cheap eats next to campus", while Walnut Creek is a classier setting that attracts "families."

Liba Falafel Truck ⊠ M *Mideastern* 25 | 19 | 24 | $9

Emeryville | Location varies; see website | 415-806-5422 | www.libafalafel.com

See review in City of San Francisco Directory.

Little Star Pizza *Pizza* 24 | 15 | 17 | $23

Albany | 1175 Solano Ave. (Cornell Ave.) | 510-526-7827 | www.littlestarpizza.com

See review in City of San Francisco Directory.

Lo Coco's Restaurant & Pizzeria M *Italian* 22 | 14 | 21 | $27

Berkeley | 1400 Shattuck Ave. (Rose St.) | 510-843-3745
Oakland | 4270 Piedmont Ave. (Echo Ave.) | 510-652-6222
www.lococospizzeria.com

"Year in, year out", these "old-fashioned" Oakland and Berkeley trattorias with an "honest neighborhood feel" "never disappoint" with their "homey" Silician specialties like "simple red-sauce pastas" and "amazing" pizzas (the best "value" on the menu); alas, it "can be very crowded and noisy", but the "busy" servers still make you "feel like a welcome regular", and "takeout" is always an option.

Luka's Taproom & Lounge ◐ *Californian/French* 20 | 14 | 16 | $30

Oakland | 2221 Broadway (W. Grand Ave.) | 510-451-4677 | www.lukasoakland.com

A "favorite Oakland hangout" for a "casual business lunch", a "very happy hour" or even dancing "late in the evening" to nightly DJs, this "happening" Cal-French brasserie is "beloved" for its "fantastic burgers", "fabulous Belgian-style fries" and "lots of beers on tap"; "long waits" and "inconsistent" service irk the impatient, who are also exasperated by the "earsplitting noise", so regulars recommend "arrive early", when it's not so "crowded."

Mama's Royal Cafe ⊄ *American* 22 | 13 | 18 | $17

Oakland | 4012 Broadway (40th St.) | 510-547-7600 | www.mamasroyalcafeoakland.com

"Breakfast is the star" at this "very reasonably priced" daytime diner, known for "killer pancakes and waffles", "fluffy omelets" and "just plain good cooking"; "helpful" yet "informal" servers contribute to the "funky", "very Oakland" vibe, and partyers are prepared for "long weekend waits" when they want to nurse a "hangover" with "homey" American "comfort food."

Mangia Mi M *Italian* ∇ 21 | 14 | 21 | $29

Danville | 406 Hartz Ave. (Prospect Ave.) | 925-831-3276 | www.mangia-mi.com

The "outgoing" owner and "attentive" servers make everyone "feel welcome" at this "tiny" Danville destination, deemed a "winner" by fans of the Italian fare fashioned from fresh, all-natural ingredients; diners nettled by the "noise level" "sit outside" on the patio, but "authentic" dishes like lasagna – as well as an extensive list of "nice wines" – take the sting out of the "jet-engine" din.

Manzanita Lake Tahoe *Californian/French*   ▽ 23 | 26 | 24 | $59

Truckee | Ritz-Carlton Lake Tahoe | 13031 Ritz Carlton Highlands Ct. (Hwy. 267) | 530-562-3050 | www.manzanitalaketahoe.com

"High above the Northstar Resort" in Truckee, this "knockout gorgeous" restaurant and bar from celebrity chef Traci Des Jardins (Jardinière) pumps up the Tahoe "food scene" by offering "outstanding" patio views and "tram" access so that you can "ski to lunch"; the "special occasion"–quality Cal-French fare and service, plus the "wonderful" lodgelike setting, make it "worth a trip up the mountain" anytime, though you do "pay the price" of being "at the Ritz."

Marica *Seafood*   ▽ 27 | 19 | 27 | $39

Oakland | 5301 College Ave. (B'way) | 510-985-8388

Hidden "just a few blocks from the many busy bistros of Rockridge", this "ever-pleasing, family-run" seafooder is "a real find" that "locals adore" for its "affordably priced" "wonderful standbys" like twice-cooked lobster served with "spectacular side dishes"; the staff's "generous attitude", plus "terrific" prix fixes, "$6 cocktails and $1 oyster" specials at the "appealing" oak bar mean "satisfied diners return again and again."

Marzano *Italian/Pizza*   23 | 19 | 21 | $36

Oakland | 4214 Park Blvd. (Glenfield Ave.) | 510-531-4500 | www.marzanorestaurant.com

They make "magic with the wood-fired oven" cheer champions of the "innovative and inspired" Neapolitan pies at this "tightly packed" Oakland Italian where "super-friendly servers" also deliver "swoonable" "small plates" and entrees at prices that are "downright reasonable"; the setting's "reminiscent of" a "trattoria", and those who "sit at the bar" can "chat with the pie maker."

Max's Diner and Bar ⊠ *Deli*   17 | 15 | 17 | $27

Oakland | Oakland City Ctr. | 500 12th St. (bet. B'way & Clay St.) | 510-451-6297

Max's Restaurant of San Ramon *Deli*

San Ramon | 2015 Crow Canyon Pl. (Crow Canyon Rd.) | 925-277-9300 | www.maxsworld.com

See review in City of San Francisco Directory.

Meritage at The Claremont *Californian*   25 | 26 | 23 | $65

Berkeley | The Claremont Hotel | 41 Tunnel Rd. (Claremont Ave.) | 510-292-4562 | www.meritageclaremont.com

"Breathtaking views of San Francisco" and the Golden Gate Bridge complement the "refined", "innovative" fare proffered at this Californian set in the historic Claremont Hotel, where "high-end dining in a high-end setting" includes "superb" wines and "friendly, knowledgeable and attentive service"; P.S. fans of the "flexible menu" think it's "nice that they offer" dishes in "a half-portion size" too.

Metro *Californian/French*   21 | 19 | 21 | $40

Lafayette | 3524 Mt. Diablo Blvd. (bet. 1st St. & Moraga Rd.) | 925-284-4422 | www.metrolafayette.com

"There's always something new to try" at this "lively" Lafayette Cal-French that "has a cosmopolitan feel despite its suburban locale"; the "fresh, tasty fare" is "consistently good" and moderately priced, and when the noise level of the "modern" interior gets "deafening", many seek out the "delightful" patio.

Mezze *Californian/Mediterranean*
23 | 20 | 22 | $39

Oakland | 3407 Lakeshore Ave. (bet. Mandana Blvd. & Trestle Glen Rd.) | 510-663-2500 | www.mezze.com

The "friendly" owners and their "wonderful" staff "make everyone feel like regulars" at this "pleasant" and "airy" neighborhood "charmer" in Oakland, "but the kitchen is the shining star", thanks to "innovative Cal-Med dishes" that are "prepared to perfection"; the prix fixe is a real "deal", and with a "nice selection" of wines and a "great cocktail menu", it's a "surefire winner."

Miss Pearl's Jam House *Southern*
18 | 18 | 17 | $35

Oakland | Waterfront Plaza Hotel | 1 Broadway (Embarcadero W.) | 510-444-7171 | www.misspearlsjamhouse.com

Situated in a "great Jack London Square location" "on the water", this former SF spot "reinvented in Oakland" now "seems to have the Southern basics down", dishing out midpriced dishes that are "rich and comfort food–centric" with "friendly" service in eclectic surroundings suggesting a funky mansion; a few who find the fare "so-so" still go for "drinks and happy-hour snacks" or to enjoy the live music on weekends.

Moody's Bistro & Lounge *American*
∇ 25 | 20 | 25 | $46

Truckee | Truckee Hotel | 10007 Bridge St. (Donner Pass Rd.) | 530-587-8688 | www.moodysbistro.com

There's "fine dining" in Downtown Truckee ("who knew?") courtesy of this stylish New American, where "the kitchen does itself proud" with "amazing" dishes full of "lots of contrasts" while "attentive" service ensures "a wonderful meal"; a "warm, cozy" ambiance from "dark woods", moody lighting and live "jazz in the bar" Thursday–Sunday are "such a pleasure" "for after skiing or a special night out."

Naan 'n Curry *Indian/Pakistani*
17 | 6 | 10 | $15

Berkeley | 2366 Telegraph Ave. (bet. Channing Way & Durant Ave.) | 510-841-6226 | www.naancurry.com

See review in City of San Francisco Directory.

Naked Fish *Japanese*
∇ 23 | 17 | 22 | $32

South Lake Tahoe | 3940 Lake Tahoe Blvd. (bet. Hwy. 50 & Pioneer Trail) | 530-541-3474 | www.thenakedfish.com

"First-rate sushi" that would impress "anywhere" it was served elevates this "friendly" Japanese "above the rest" in South Lake Tahoe, with fin fans touting the "reliable" "freshness" of its "classic" rolls and "fun innovations" as well as the in-season "happy-hour specials"; insiders attest the food's "much better than" the stripped-down setting suggests, "which is to your benefit when the check comes"; P.S. the Decor score does not reflect a recent expansion.

Nan Yang Rockridge *Burmese*
22 | 14 | 20 | $26

Oakland | 6048 College Ave. (Claremont Ave.) | 510-655-3298 | www.nanyangrockridge.com

Regulars suggest neophytes "look for the specials" at this "neighborhood" Rockridge Burmese, where the "consistently fresh and tasty" regular menu includes "excellent garlic noodles" with seafood and "ginger salad" that diners "dream of"; decor that's merely "fine" matters little given the "lovely" service and "reasonable" tabs.

North Beach Pizza *Pizza* | 19 | 11 | 15 | $20 |

Berkeley | 1598 University Ave. (California St.) | 510-849-9800 |
www.northbeachpizza.net
See review in City of San Francisco Directory.

O Chamé *Japanese* | 24 | 22 | 22 | $35 |

Berkeley | 1830 Fourth St. (bet. Hearst Ave. & Virginia St.) | 510-841-8783
"Giant bowls of soba" floating in "ethereal broth" "replenish the shopper's soul" at this "sophisticated" "Japanese-esque oasis"; "although most come for the noodles", the "refined" fare also includes "wonderful bento boxes"; it's a "lovely" "lunch or dinner spot" "while running errands on Fourth Street", even if the "steep"-for-what-you-get tabs and the "minimalist" digs are not everyone's cup of green tea.

Oliveto Cafe *Italian* | 24 | 20 | 20 | $35 |

Oakland | 5655 College Ave. (Shafter Ave.) | 510-547-5356 |
www.oliveto.com
"Like a bit of old Europe next to the Rockridge BART", this "popular pizza and vino" outpost at the Market Hall is a "delightful place" for "chic" Oaklanders "to sit back" and "people-watch" while enjoying a "delicious" "breakfast pizza", "special lunch" or "lingering mochacino"; dinner is "equally fabulous" say "bargain-hunters" who prefer the "one-page daily menu" of "rustic Italian cafe cuisine", "informal setting" and "friendly" service over the "more formal" restaurant upstairs.

Oliveto Restaurant *Italian* | 25 | 22 | 23 | $56 |

Oakland | 5655 College Ave. (Shafter Ave.) | 510-547-5356 |
www.oliveto.com
"Although the chef has changed", this "white-tablecloth" Northern Italian "grande dame" "continues to define elegant dining" in Oakland, putting out "brilliantly rustic", "ingredient-driven" pastas and rotisserie meats complemented by "an imaginatively aligned wine list" in a "beautiful, sleek space"; a few sense a "taking ourselves way too seriously vibe", but it remains for many "the place" "for really special occasions"; P.S. "local foodies watch for" "their special themed dinners, such as truffle, whole hog or heirloom tomato."

Ozumo *Japanese* | 23 | 24 | 20 | $54 |

Oakland | 2251 Broadway (W. Grand Ave.) | 510-286-9866 |
www.ozumo.com
See review in City of San Francisco Directory.

Pacific Crest Grill at
Bar of America *Mediterranean* | - | - | - | M |

Truckee | 10042 Donner Pass Rd. (Bridge St.) | 530-587-2626 |
www.barofamerica.net
Adjacent to honky-tonk sibling Bar of America, this upscale white-tablecloth bistro offers "interesting" Cal-Med midpriced fare and a serious international wine list; run by the owners of Pianeta and Christy Hill, it's a "great place to have a nice dinner" "in the cute town of Truckee" after a day on the slopes or at the Lake, while live music at the bar adds extra incentive on the weekends.

Pakwan *Pakistani*
22 | 5 | 9 | $17

Fremont | 41068 Fremont Blvd. (Irvington Ave.) | 510-226-6234 Ⓜ�︎
Hayward | 25168 Mission Blvd. (Central Blvd.) | 510-538-2401
www.pakwanrestaurant.com
See review in City of San Francisco Directory.

Pappo Ⓜ *Californian/Mediterranean*
▽ 24 | 19 | 22 | $42

Alameda | 2320 Central Ave. (bet. Oak & Park Sts.) | 510-337-9100 |
www.papporestaurant.com
"Imaginative" Cal-Med dishes – often "terrific" – make this "cozy" "local treasure" the "go-to" for Alameda inhabitants who don't "want to leave the island" for "fine" dining; the menu might be "limited", but since it's "cozy without being crowded" and the "great staff" "sticks around year after year", a visit is "very enjoyable", and a "value" to boot.

Pasta Pomodoro *Italian*
16 | 13 | 17 | $23

Emeryville | Bay Street Mall | 5614 Shellmound St. (Bay St.) | 510-923-1173
Oakland | 5500 College Ave. (Lawton Ave.) | 510-923-0900
www.pastapomodoro.com
See review in City of San Francisco Directory.

Patxi's Chicago Pizza *Pizza*
22 | 14 | 17 | $21

Lafayette | The Clocktower | 3577 Mt. Diablo Blvd. (Lafayette Circle) |
925-299-0700 | www.patxispizza.com
See review in City of San Francisco Directory.

Peasant & the Pear Ⓜ *Mediterranean*
22 | 20 | 21 | $39

Danville | The Clock Tower | 267 Hartz Ave. (Diablo Rd.) | 925-820-6611 |
www.thepeasantandthepear.com
"The chef treats everyone like family" at this Danville Med proffering "intriguing" "yet honest, well-executed and comforting" fare (including "outstanding" lamb) with frequent "menu changes" to "keep it interesting"; an "experienced" staff and moderate prices add to the overall "pleasant" vibe in a "cute setting" that's complete with "patio seating."

Pho 84 🆂 *Vietnamese*
23 | 12 | 16 | $21

Oakland | 354 17th St. (bet. Franklin & Webster Sts.) | 510-832-1338 |
www.pho84.com
"Popular with the local lunch crowd", who "line up" to get their "pho fix" in "huge steaming bowls" of the "namesake" dish, this Oakland "favorite" is more "relaxed" at dinner and on weekends, when you can order with "less jostling and rubbing elbows"; the "extensive" menu of other Vietnamese vittles, including "awesome" "rice and noodle dishes" with just "the right amount of spice", is "inexpensive" to boot, so no one much minds the "no-frills" decor.

Pianeta *Italian/Mediterranean*
▽ 24 | 21 | 23 | $42

Truckee | 10096 Donner Pass Rd. (Brockway Rd.) | 530-587-4694 |
www.pianetarestaurant.com
"All of this in Downtown Truckee!" marvel admirers of this Italian-Med "go-to", where the "excellent choices" include "lamb cooked just right", a "variety of pastas" and other "sturdy" "traditional" fare for "après-ski carbo-loading"; with "personal" service and a "cozy" duplex space "that feels rustic yet luxurious", it's "everything a restaurant in Tahoe should be" – but it's also "a locals' favorite."

Piatti *Italian*
19 | 19 | 19 | $40

Danville | 100 Sycamore Valley Rd. W. (San Ramon Valley Blvd.) | 925-838-2082 | www.piatti.com

The "affordable" Italian fare, from "solid" pizzas to "enormous portions" of "homemade pastas", "doesn't disappoint" at this "very lively" (some say "noisy") Bay Area chain; though a few are put off by a "predictable" menu that's missing a "spark", supporters are sold on servers who are always "accommodating and then some", as well as "beautiful outdoor seating" that's a "bonus in warm weather"; P.S. the Mill Valley venue benefits from a "pleasant view of Richardson Bay."

Picán *Southern*
22 | 23 | 21 | $44

Oakland | 2295 Broadway (23rd St.) | 510-834-1000 | www.picanrestaurant.com

This "luxurious" Southern spot near the Paramount Theatre is "the epitome of Oakland style", where you're as likely to find "church ladies" in "hats and Sunday best" as you are "young urbanites", all "having the time of their lives" dining on "richly decadent" "upscale soul food"; tabs are a little "pricey", but service is "warm" and "welcoming" in the plantationlike setting, plus there's an "incredible bourbon selection."

Picante Cocina Mexicana *Mexican*
23 | 14 | 19 | $17

Berkeley | 1328 Sixth St. (bet. Camelia & Gilman Sts.) | 510-525-3121 | www.picanteberkeley.com

"Everyone from vegans to carnivores to kids will be pleased" at this "cafeteria-style" East Bay "family fiesta", which serves "great, fresh Mexican food" including burritos and "fabulous" "housemade corn tortillas" with "tons of bang for your buck"; despite "all of Berkeley on line ahead of you" there's "quick turnover of the tables", and though it's "perhaps a little too family-friendly" you "can still have a conversation."

Pizza Antica *Pizza*
20 | 15 | 17 | $28

Lafayette | 3600 Mt. Diablo Blvd. (Dewing Ave.) | 925-299-0500 | www.pizzaantica.com

See review in South of San Francisco Directory.

⧉ Pizzaiolo ⧉ *Italian/Pizza*
26 | 18 | 21 | $36

Oakland | 5008 Telegraph Ave. (bet. 49th & 51st Sts.) | 510-652-4888 | www.pizzaiolooakland.com

Thanks to "outstanding variety and incisive flavors", this Oakland pizzeria turning out "wood-fired, brick-oven" pies "just keeps getting better", and even "excels at much more than just pizza", prompting patrons to "try new things and share" "interesting" Southern Italian dishes; the high-ceilinged space, "cool, relaxed atmosphere" and "casually awesome" service all add up to a "hip, moderately priced heaven", just be sure to reserve "well ahead."

Pizza Rustica *Pizza*
20 | 11 | 17 | $21

Oakland | 5422 College Ave. (bet. Kales & Manila Aves.) | 510-654-1601
Oakland | 6106 La Salle Ave. (Mountain Blvd.) | 510-339-7878
www.caferustica.com

"You can't go wrong" with the "freshly made" "specialty pizzas", "wonderful" rotisserie chicken and "equally good salads" say fans of this Oakland pie pair; "cramped seating" is "part of the charm" at the "low-key" College Avenue location (with "bonus of a tiki bar upstairs")

and La Salle Avenue is no-frills, but both are "go-to" spots for "takeout and delivery."

Plum *Californian* | 24 | 20 | 21 | $49 |

Oakland | 2214 Broadway (W. Grand Ave.) | 510-444-7586
Daniel Patterson (of SF's Coi) "raises the bar for East Bay restaurants" with this Californian where he crafts "brilliant" (if sometimes "downright strange") small plates; despite "backless" "hard-wood" seats and "communal tables" that "detract" from experience and "molecule-sized portions" that are "not the greatest value around", it gets plumb full of smitten fans who love to watch the chef and his crew of "perfectionists" "perform miracles"; P.S. lunch prices are "more acceptable."

PlumpJack Cafe *Californian/Mediterranean* | 23 | 21 | 23 | $59 |

Olympic Valley | PlumpJack Squaw Valley Inn | 1920 Squaw Valley Rd. (Hwy. 89) | 530-583-1576 | www.plumpjackcafe.com
"After taking off your ski boots for the day", this "resort" retreat sited "on the mountain" in North Tahoe's Olympic Valley is "a pleasant surprise", matching "fantastic" Cal-Med cuisine and "wines from Napa" with "top-notch" service in a rustic, fireplace-equipped space that's stylish but "nothing stuffy"; "satisfied" slopers say it's "expensive" but "well worth a try, and more than once", if your wallet's plump.

Postino *Italian* | 22 | 23 | 22 | $50 |

Lafayette | 3565 Mt. Diablo Blvd. (Lafayette Circle) | 925-299-8700 | www.postinorestaurant.com
"Romantic", "warm and comfortable", this "upscale Italian" situated in a former Lafayette post office makes for a "special night out", evoking "old-world style" with "beautiful" interiors and a "gorgeous outdoor garden"; though some say the fare "isn't all that innovative", it is "wonderfully fresh" and delivered by a "caring staff."

NEW Prickly Pear Cantina *Mexican* | - | - | - | I |

Danville | Blackhawk Plaza | 3421 Blackhawk Plaza Circle (Camino Tassajara) | 925-984-2363 | www.thepricklypearcantina.com
A fresh entry from Peasant & the Pear chef-owner Rodney Worth, this contempo cantina moves into Coa's former quarters in a Danville shopping complex with casual Mexican chow like the house-special carnitas burrito or an "interesting taco combo" uniting five varieties; there's nothing prickly about the "good prices" and "terrific margaritas" from a staggering tequila selection.

Prima *Italian* | 24 | 22 | 22 | $57 |

Walnut Creek | 1522 N. Main St. (bet. Bonanza St. & Lincoln Ave.) | 925-935-7780 | www.primawine.com
Walnut Creek locals praise the "wonderful, authentic seasonal Italian dishes", "knowledgeable staff" and "remarkable" wine list (which "includes many bottles" from the "wine shop next door") at this Main Street mainstay helmed by "wonderful" chef-owner Peter Chastain; the "ambiance" can range from "romantic" to "noisy", and though "it ain't cheap", it's certainly "cheaper than flying to Italy."

Red Hut Café *Diner* | 22 | 12 | 19 | $16 |

South Lake Tahoe | 2749 Lake Tahoe Blvd. (Al Tahoe Blvd.) | 530-541-9024

(continued)
Red Hut Café
South Lake Tahoe | Ski Run Ctr. | 3660 Lake Tahoe Blvd. (Hwy. 50) |
530-544-1595
www.redhutcafe.com

"A must-visit greasy spoon tradition" for ski bunnies and other visitors to South Lake Tahoe, this diner duo is "terrific" for "healthy portions" of "inexpensive" breakfasts, as well as "never-miss" lunchtime burgers and other American fare (be sure to check out the "tasty daily specials listed on the blackboard"); though "they close before dinner" at 2 PM, early-risers are treated to "wonderful" servers who deliver the goods "with a smile"; P.S. a third hut is across the border in Stateline, Nevada.

Restaurant Peony *Chinese*
21 | 13 | 11 | $25

Oakland | Pacific Renaissance Plaza | 388 Ninth St. (bet. Franklin & Webster Sts.) | 510-286-8866 | www.restaurantpeony.com

The "expansive" menu of "yum yum dim sum", "Peking Duck as good as in China" and other "delicious Chinese standards" keeps this "super-big Hong Kong–style" Oakland joint "very crowded", especially "on weekends"; expect "unhelpful" "non-service" and a "long wait at times", with the usual affordable prices.

Revival Bar & Kitchen Ⓜ *Californian*
20 | 21 | 21 | $45

Berkeley | 2102 Shattuck Ave. (Addison St.) | 510-549-9950 |
www.revivalbarandkitchen.com

Chef Amy Murray (Venus) "has done it again" at this Californian in the Berkeley "theater district" offering a "delicious root-to-shoot, head-to-hoof, locavore-focused menu" that "works for meat eaters and vegetarians" alike; an "attentive" staff also serves "well-crafted cocktails" in the "funky interior" of the 1901-era building.

Rick & Ann's *American*
21 | 14 | 18 | $24

Berkeley | 2922 Domingo Ave. (bet. Ashby & Claremont Aves.) |
510-649-8538 | www.rickandanns.com

It's like "mom's cooking without having to do the dishes" at this Berkeley family favorite dishing out "down-home" American "comfort food" including "challah French toast" and "great mac 'n' cheese"; "the place is jumping on the weekends" despite decor that's "nothing to write home about" and "slow" service, and there's "always a wait" for breakfast – but fans agree it's "worth it."

ⓩ Rivoli *Californian/Mediterranean*
26 | 21 | 24 | $53

Berkeley | 1539 Solano Ave. (bet. Neilson St. & Peralta Ave.) |
510-526-2542 | www.rivolirestaurant.com

The husband-and-wife duo behind this "crown jewel of Solano" "just knows how to run a restaurant" attest admirers of the "superlative" "locavore-based" Cal-Med meals and "deep" wine list that's "right up there with the best of them", all ferried by a "caring" staff; it "can't be beat" for celebrations, "but don't wait for a special occasion", as the setting that "looks out on a lovely garden" is a "perfect alternative to all the trendy" spots around.

Rudy's Can't Fail Café ❶ *Diner*
20 | 18 | 18 | $20

Emeryville | 4081 Hollis St. (Park Ave.) | 510-594-1221

(continued)

(continued)

Rudy's Can't Fail Café

NEW Oakland | 1805 Telegraph Ave. (bet 18th & 19th Sts.) |
510-251-9400
www.iamrudy.com

"A regular haunt" with a "rocker vibe", this "hip" Emeryville diner with
a new Uptown Oakland outpost is a "beloved" "go-to" for "big servings" of "solid" "homestyle" eats in "quirky" digs with "altered
Barbies" on display; it's in "high demand" whether for "breakfast all
day", a "late-night snack" or an "affordable brunch", and those who
can "tolerate" the "loud" soundtrack and "lackadaisical" service from
the staff say it "never fails."

Ruth's Chris Steak House *Steak*   24 | 21 | 23 | $63

Walnut Creek | 1553 Olympic Blvd. (bet. Locust & Main Sts.) |
925-977-3477 | www.ruthschris.com
See review in City of San Francisco Directory.

Sasa *Japanese*   23 | 24 | 21 | $46

Walnut Creek | 1432 N. Main St. (Lincoln Ave.) | 925-210-0188 |
www.sasawc.com

"Pretty hip for Walnut Creek", this "terrific izakaya" offers "lots of innovative" "Japanese tapas" highlighting "delicious and unusual fusion" influences plus sushi and clever cocktails in a century-old
building freshened by a "beautiful" makeover that extends to the lush
patio and "active bar"; while "noisy" and slightly "pricey", for something "far beyond the typical", it's a "very nice surprise."

Saul's Restaurant & Delicatessen *Deli*   19 | 13 | 17 | $22

Berkeley | 1475 Shattuck Ave. (bet. Rose & Vine Sts.) |
510-848-3354 | www.saulsdeli.com

Berkeley noshers declare the "next-best thing to being in New York" is
this deli with "a great buzz", "efficient service" and "typical" atmosphere that "continues to deliver" with affordable bites including
"house-roasted turkey", "house-cured pastrami" and "Acme rye
bread"; while some shrug it off as "the best we can do in the East Bay",
those who "have a yen" ask "vat's not to like, dahlink?"

Scott's Seafood *Seafood*   20 | 20 | 21 | $42

Oakland | 2 Broadway (Embarcadero W.) | 510-444-3456 |
www.scottseastbay.com
Walnut Creek | 1333 N. California Blvd. (bet. Bonanza St. & Mt. Diablo Blvd.) |
925-934-1300 | www.scottswc.com

"As chains go, this is one of the better" for "solid seafood standards" plus
a "good selection of wine by the glass", "great cocktails" – and an "excellent", "famous" brunch in Walnut Creek; service varies and critics call
the bites "bland" and prices "a little high", but the settings are "classy"
and "comfortable" (some have "patio seating" or "live music") with a
"waterfront" "view" in Oakland and "overlooking the city" in San Jose.

Sea Salt *Seafood*   21 | 17 | 19 | $40

Berkeley | 2512 San Pablo Ave. (Dwight Way) | 510-883-1720 |
www.seasaltrestaurant.com

This "quirky" Berkeley storefront "by the people behind Lalime's"
serves "sparkling fresh" seafood with a sustainable focus on a "cre-

ative menu" that always offers "something new to try"; "the lobster roll rocks" and fish 'n' chips rival those "even in London", but perhaps best of all are the "dollar oysters" at the "fantastic happy hour" (from 3 to 9 PM Mondays) – a bonus to the usual "reasonable pricing" and "knowledgeable" service.

Shalimar ⊄ *Indian/Pakistani*

| 22 | 3 | 11 | $16 |

Fremont | 3325 Walnut Ave. (bet. Liberty St. & Paseo Padre Pkwy.) | 510-494-1919 | www.shalimarsf.com

See review in City of San Francisco Directory.

Shen Hua *Chinese*

| 22 | 15 | 19 | $25 |

Berkeley | 2914 College Ave. (bet. Ashby Ave. & Russell St.) | 510-883-1777

"Reliable", "fresh" Sino fare places this affordable Berkeley bastion "a cut above your typical neighborhood joint" for its "killer" hot-and-sour soup and menu boasting "every traditional Chinese dish you can think of" in "huge portions"; even though the staff is "friendly", at dinner it's "one noisy restaurant", so you may want to "take out to avoid the cacophony of Berkeley families."

Sidebar ⊠ *Californian/Mediterranean*

| 22 | 19 | 22 | $35 |

Oakland | 542 Grand Ave. (bet. Euclid Ave. & MacArthur Blvd.) | 510-452-9500 | www.sidebar-oakland.com

"Everything tastes, looks" and "feels homemade, down to the fries" at this Oakland gastropub that's hit its "groove" with "high-quality" small and large Californian plates and cocktails "fit for mixology geeks"; the moderately priced menu is a bit limited, but specials like "Monday mussel madness" "add variety", and "stylish" digs filled with "lively conversation" plus service they "love" make it "heaven" for locals.

Soi4 *Thai*

| 24 | 17 | 20 | $33 |

Oakland | 5421 College Ave. (bet. Kales & Manila Aves.) | 510-655-0889 | www.soifour.com

The Bangkok bites look "almost too pretty to eat" at this "trendy", "atypical" Oakland Thai in an "upscale" modern setting that "always delivers" with a "wonderfully fresh and interesting menu"; "servers are very helpful with recommendations" on dishes that are "modestly priced", all adding up to a real "College Avenue jewel."

Soule Domain *American*

| ▽ 24 | 24 | 26 | $48 |

Kings Beach | 9983 Cove Ave. (Stateline Rd.) | 530-546-7529 | www.souledomain.com

"Around for years", this woodsy Kings Beach New American "still turns out wonderful dining" for the Tahoe set founded on "lovely food" and an "interesting" log-cabin locale that's "rustic" from the rough-hewn rafters to the stone hearth; loyalists insist it's "as good as it gets at the lake" and "definitely worth one visit."

NEW Southie *American*

| - | - | - | I |

Oakland | 6311 College Ave. (bet. Alcatraz Ave. & 63rd St.) | 510-654-0100 | www.southieoakland.com

It's a hands-on experience at this new Rockridge nook from the owners of neighboring hot spot Wood Tavern, an East Coast–inspired outfit specializing in inventive sandwiches (pulled pork, Dungeness crab roll, Niman Ranch meatballs) supplemented with salads, desserts and dinnertime small plates; the snug, diner-esque space finds room for counter seating and a bar tapping craft beers and wine.

Stomp *Eclectic* ∇ | 16 | 17 | 15 | $32

Danville | Blackhawk Plaza | 3451 Blackhawk Plaza Circle (Camino Tassajara) | 925-309-4417 | www.stompsf.com

This workaday wine bar puts its stamp on Danville's Blackhawk Plaza with "tasty", globally influenced small plates and charcuterie and a flight-driven vino lineup to match; it's "satisfying" for a shopping break or "a casual evening" (with live music on Thursdays), and those who deem the decor "a bit cold and stark" can "opt for patio seating."

Sunnyside Resort *Seafood/Steak* ∇ | 18 | 24 | 19 | $42

Tahoe City | 1850 W. Lake Blvd. (bet. Pineland Dr. & Sequoia Ave.) | 530-583-7200 | www.sunnysideresort.com

"Don't miss the patio on a summer afternoon" or winter nights by the fire at this veteran Tahoe City surf 'n' turfer, where the "spectacular lakeside setting" "is a dream come true"; even if "the food and service fall short", sunny surveyors out to "enjoy a drink and appetizers" say you "can't beat it" as a place to "linger."

NEW Table 24 *American* 18 | 16 | 19 | $27

Orinda | 2 Theater Sq. (Brookwood Rd.) | 925-254-0124 | www.table24orinda.com

It's "nothing fancy", but "families" stuck "in the 'burbs" "welcome" this "Orinda arrival" as an "accommodating" stop for New American "comfort food plus" (think Niman Ranch burgers and lamb chop lollipops) served "almost any time of day" in a "smallish" setting that's already "bustling" and "noisy"; despite "a few kinks to work out", most agree the nabe "needs a place like this."

Tacubaya *Mexican* 23 | 14 | 15 | $17

Berkeley | 1788 Fourth St. (bet. Hearst Ave. & Virginia St.) | 510-525-5160 | www.tacubaya.net

"When you need a break from shopping on Fourth street" this "hopping little" Berkeley "gourmet Mexican" sibling of Doña Tomás is "not your rice-and-bean Tex-Mex joint", instead serving "innovative, seasonal" fare with "top-quality ingredients" from a menu that "changes frequently"; "you order first and they bring the food to you", and fans quip about getting the "best *lengua* taco" without "lip from the employees."

Tamarindo Antojeria Mexicana Ⓢ *Mexican* 25 | 17 | 20 | $36

Oakland | 468 Eighth St. (bet. B'way & Washington St.) | 510-444-1944 | www.tamarindoantojeria.com

Putting a fresh spin on small plates, this "adventurous", "new-style Mexican" in Oakland offers "intriguing little dishes" that are "zesty and different", thanks to "high-quality ingredients" and attention "to the details"; the dining room is "charming" and "cozy", and while some note the tab can be "a bit pricey", they're quick to add "it's worth it."

Thai Buddhist Temple Mongkolratanaram Ⓜ⇄ *Thai* ∇ | 21 | 7 | 12 | $12

Berkeley | Wat Mongkolratanaram Buddhist Temple | 1911 Russell St. (bet. Martin Luther King Jr. Way & Otis St.) | 510-849-3419

What a scene, chant surveyors enchanted by the "once-a-week" makeshift backyard buffet brunches held Sundays at this Berkeley Buddhist temple, "one of the most amazing" and unusual spots to "cheaply" consume "wonderful Thai food" (if "toned down a bit for Western tastes"); to partake, "come early and stand in line", then "find a spot to sit" and "eat outside community-style"; in addition, you're "supporting the temple . . . all positives."

Townhouse Bar & Grill 🖂 Californian
21 | 17 | 20 | $38

Emeryville | 5862 Doyle St. (bet. 59th & Powell Sts.) | 510-652-6151 | www.townhousebarandgrill.com

This Emeryville "hidden gem" might look "like a dive on the outside", but it's "the epitome of a neighborhood find", dishing out "well-prepared", midpriced Californian "comfort food with an upscale twist" in surroundings reminiscent of "an old-time saloon"; the staff's "been there a long time", the wine list is "diverse" and fans joke they'd "gladly offer sex for the Brussels sprouts", so just add in an "alfresco terrace" plus "valet parking" and "life is good."

Trader Vic's Polynesian
17 | 22 | 19 | $46

Emeryville | 9 Anchor Dr. (Powell St.) | 510-653-3400 | www.tradervicsemeryville.com

The "fantasy" menu of "throwback tiki drinks" is "as great and goofy as ever" at this somewhat "pricey" "Polynesian time warp" chain with "ticky-tacky" South Seas decor; critics carp you shouldn't "count on the food", but there are a "lot of happy people" who "stick to the pupu platter" and mai tais that "need no introduction" delivered by "energetic" servers; P.S. the "newly redone" Emeryville "original" sports a "spectacular view" of "bobbing boats" in the harbor, while the Palo Alto offshoot has a "wonderful" "outdoor patio."

Trattoria Corso Italian
24 | 18 | 21 | $40

Berkeley | 1788 Shattuck Ave. (Delaware St.) | 510-704-8004 | www.trattoriacorso.com

Co-chef/owner "Wendy Brucker of Rivoli brings her magic" to this "casual", "little" Tuscan trattoria near Berkeley Rep that does its "gourmet ghetto" setting "proud", turning out "simple but excellently prepared", "affordable" *cucina* and "lots of Italian wines you've never heard of before"; it gets "very loud", but the staff takes "good care of you" and "adds to the charm."

🗷 Trattoria La Siciliana 🗭 Italian
25 | 16 | 18 | $36

Berkeley | 2993 College Ave. (bet. Ashby Ave. & Webster St.) | 510-704-1474 | www.trattorialasiciliana.com

If you can't be in Sicily, surveyors suggest "just send your mouth to Italy" via this "authentic" Berkeley "bastion of phenomenal, rustic Southern Italian" fare that's "bursting" at its "narrow" "seams with atmosphere and presence"; sure, "the wait can be long" even "with a reservation", and it's "cash-only", but the "amazingly good" pastas, "great breads with dipping oil" and "friendly staff" are all "worth it."

T Rex Barbecue BBQ
18 | 17 | 17 | $31

Berkeley | 1300 10th St. (Gilman St.) | 510-527-0099 | www.t-rex-bbq.com

"Meat eaters" go for the *"Flintstone-sized"* portions of "big, honkin'", "messy" ribs and "Cali-interpretations of comfort food" that "hits your cozy spot" at this "upscale airplane hangar" of a Berkeley barbecue place from the K2 group; naysayers quip that it "'rex' your wallet" because "sides are all extra", but fans counter with the "great happy hour", particularly the Bloody Mary with a "beef-jerky swizzle stick."

Trueburger ☒ *Burgers*

| 20 | 12 | 17 | $15 |

Oakland | 146 Grand Ave. (bet. Harrison & Valdez Sts.) | 510-208-5678 | www.trueburgeroakland.com

Fans flip for this "burger nirvana" near Lake Merritt serving "tried-and-true" "comfort food to the max", citing the "delectable, high-quality meat" on "amazing" buns, "killer fries" and "thick and decadent" milk-shakes; "everything is from scratch", the staff is "super-friendly" and there's "cool art of Oakland" on the walls – but "why don't they stay open later on the weekends?"; P.S. dinner Wednesday–Saturday only.

Udupi Palace ⊉ *Indian/Vegetarian*

| 21 | 8 | 15 | $18 |

Berkeley | 1901-1903 University Ave. (Martin Luther King Jr. Way) | 510-843-6600
Newark | 5988 Newpark Mall Rd. (bet. Cedar Blvd. & Mowry Ave.) | 510-794-8400
www.udupipalaceca.com

See review in City of San Francisco Directory.

Uzen ☒ *Japanese*

| 24 | 15 | 18 | $32 |

Oakland | 5415 College Ave. (bet. Kales & Manila Aves.) | 510-654-7753

"Masters" of the knife are to be found at this "hidden bargain sushi joint" in Oakland, starting with the owner, Kazu, who provides "an aesthetic experience" of "impeccable" and "interesting sushi"; cooked fare including "light-as-air tempura" is also on offer in a "minimalist" setting of "Zen simplicity" that fans feel "matches the cuisine."

Va de Vi *Eclectic*

| 24 | 21 | 21 | $47 |

Walnut Creek | 1511 Mt. Diablo Blvd. (Main St.) | 925-979-0100 | www.vadevibistro.com

"Va-va-voom" Eclectic small plates that look like "works of art" and "beg to be shared" are the draw at this "chic" Walnut Creek tapas spot with "a lively bar scene"; "big appetites" could require you to "spend a small fortune", so "pace it" with help from the "savvy" staff – and if weather permits, "sit outside under the tree" on the "romantic" back patio.

Vanessa's Bistro *French/Vietnamese*

| 23 | 18 | 22 | $35 |

Berkeley | 1715 Solano Ave. (Ensenada Ave.) | 510-525-8300
Vanessa's Bistro 2 *French/Vietnamese*
Walnut Creek | 1329 N. Main St. (Duncan St.) | 925-891-4790
www.vanessasbistro2.com

"Vanessa's family makes you feel at home" while she's "in back cooking" "superb French-Vietnamese small-plate dishes" at this "classy" North Berkeley "bistro" (with a new Walnut Creek sibling) that's "a great sleeper"; expect "interesting combinations of flavors and textures" that are "fresh", "unique" and "wonderfully presented" – though some wish they'd "find a larger venue", since the "cramped space detracts from the ambiance"; P.S. closed Tuesday.

Venezia *Italian*

| 18 | 21 | 21 | $35 |

Berkeley | 1799 University Ave. (Grant St.) | 510-849-4681 | www.caffevenezia.com

"Nothing changes" at this Berkeley "institution", and "that's good" say loyal locals, contending it "has something for everybody on the menu,

	FOOD	DECOR	SERVICE	COST

even the kids", who especially "love the laundry hanging on the line" overhead in the "kitschy, cute Italian streetscape interior"; the "comforting pastas" are a "great value", making it also popular for "big parties."

Venus ⓜ *Californian* 23 | 16 | 20 | $29

Berkeley | 2327 Shattuck Ave. (bet. Bancroft Way & Durant Ave.) | 510-540-5950 | www.venusrestaurant.net

For "fresh", "seasonal" "organic cooking" – including "out-of-this-world" desserts – Berkeley locals suggest setting your trajectory for this Downtown Californian that will "delight" "vegetarians and meat eaters alike"; it's "the kind of food you think you could make at home if you tried, but you can't", at "fair prices" and served by a "gracious" and "alert" staff.

Vic Stewart's ⓜ *Steak* 22 | 22 | 21 | $58

Walnut Creek | 850 S. Broadway (bet. Mt. Diablo Blvd. & Newell Ave.) | 925-943-5666 | www.vicstewarts.com

"Come hungry" and "leave sated" at this steakhouse in a vintage Walnut Creek train depot, where "even poultry and seafood are also well prepared"; the "knowledgeable staff", "clubby atmosphere" and option of dining in an old Pullman "railroad car" make it "a place for special occasions" – especially since the "pricey" tab might make you wish "somebody else paid for the meal."

Vik's Chaat Corner ⓜ *Indian* 23 | 11 | 13 | $15

Berkeley | 2390 Fourth St. (Channing Way) | 510-644-4432 | www.vikschaatcorner.com

You may be tempted to try "one of everything" on the mind-boggling menu at this Berkeley "street-food" "nirvana" where "Indian mamas" cook up "the best" subcontinental "dishes you've never had" at "bargain prices"; the atmosphere resembles a "hip college cafeteria", complete with "eco-friendly compostable plates" and, yes, it's a "madhouse", but you get to rub elbows with "all of humanity", plus there's also a "well-stocked market"; P.S. closes at 6 PM Tuesday–Thursday, 8 PM Friday–Sunday.

Wente Vineyards, The Restaurant at *Californian/Mediterranean* 24 | 25 | 24 | $58

Livermore | 5050 Arroyo Rd. (Wetmore Rd.) | 925-456-2450 | www.wentevineyards.com

This "great escape" in the Livermore Wine Country "consistently delivers" with wine-friendly Cal-Med cuisine – including produce from its own organic garden – served in "a beautiful setting near the vineyards"; after visiting the tasting room, guests can enjoy "a terrific lunch on the patio", while the "elegant", "romantic" dining area and "attentive-but-not-intrusive service" also make it "a great place for special celebrations"; P.S. dinner packages include the summer music series.

Wild Goose *American* ∇ 23 | 25 | 23 | $40

Tahoe Vista | 7320 N. Lake Blvd. (Pino Grande Ave.) | 530-546-3640 | www.wildgoosetahoe.com

"The goose is on the loose" honk Sierra surveyors now able to partake of the "great views", "great service" and local and seasonally driven New American menu at this once-private Tahoe Vista supper club perched right on the North Shore that's now "open to the public" for

	FOOD	DECOR	SERVICE	COST

its second season; decor resembles the interior of a wooden ship, while the bar opens at 2 PM on weekends and the deck is HQ for sunset happy hours; open mid-May till mid-October.

Wolfdale's *Californian* — 24 | 24 | 23 | $60

Tahoe City | 640 N. Lake Blvd. (Grove St.) | 530-583-5700 | www.wolfdales.com

"They've still got it" bay "totally impressed" boosters of this Tahoe City "classic", celebrated as "consistently" "the most interesting" option on the North Shore thanks to an "exquisite" Californian menu showcasing Asian-inflected seafood to "savor"; add "fantastic" service and smart surroundings with a "bonus" lakeside deck and bocce court, and "it's a definite wow" that's "expensive but worth it" for "a special night out."

✖ Wood Tavern *Californian* — 26 | 20 | 23 | $44

Oakland | 6317 College Ave. (bet. Alcatraz Ave. & 63rd St.) | 510-654-6607 | www.woodtavern.net

Smitten surveyors swoon over this Rockridge gastropub's "superb", "upscale, updated" Californian "comfort food"; yes, there's a "wall-to-wall cram" at dinner, causing an "appalling" noise level that can leave your "ears ringing", but still, "you can feel the presence of the owners and the commitment" of the "exceptional, really caring" staff.

NEW Xolo Taqueria ✖ *Mexican* — - | - | - | I

Oakland | 1916 Telegraph Ave. (19th St.) | 510-986-0151 | www.xolotaqueria.com

Billed as the little brother of Doña Tomás, this quick-service Uptown Oakland taqueria hawks upscale tacos, (rice-free) burritos and other Mexican *especiales* such as 'Danger Dogs' (bacon-wrapped hot dogs), birria (goat stew, served Fridays and Saturdays) and churritos (tortilla fritters); the kitsch-filled, colorful bi-level storefront is perfect for grabbing a quick bite before a show at the Fox Theater or a michelada and late-night snack on the tiny patio.

Xyclo *Vietnamese* — 22 | 17 | 19 | $28

Oakland | 4218 Piedmont Ave. (bet. Entrada & Ridgeway Aves.) | 510-654-2681 | www.xyclorestaurant.com

Locals laud the "inventive", "deliciously vibrant" fare at this neighborhood Oakland spot as "not just your average Vietnamese" by virtue of its "fresh ingredients" and "beautiful" presentation; the room is modern with wood accents, and though some complain service can be somewhat "distant", tipplers toast it "for cocktails", with "zippy" and "strong" mojitos in flavors like "lychee" and "mango."

Yankee Pier *New England/Seafood* — 18 | 15 | 19 | $36

Lafayette | Lafayette Mercantile Bldg. | 3593 Mt. Diablo Blvd. (bet. Dewing Ave. & Lafayette Circle) | 925-283-4100 | www.yankeepier.com

See review in North of San Francisco Directory.

Yoshi's at Jack London Square *Japanese* — 20 | 20 | 18 | $42

Oakland | Jack London Sq. | 510 Embarcadero W. (bet. Clay & Washington Sts.) | 510-238-9200 | www.yoshis.com

Surveyors are tuned into this Oakland Japanese attached to a "world-class" jazz club that offers riffs on "surprisingly creative and pristine"

	FOOD	DECOR	SERVICE	COST

"fusion" fare, including "excellent sushi" and "daring" rolls with "unique flavors"; some find it a tad "costly", while others groove on the "comfortable" room, "professional" service and "priority on club seating" given to diners.

Zachary's Chicago Pizza *Pizza*

| 24 | 12 | 17 | $21 |

Berkeley | 1853 Solano Ave. (The Alameda) | 510-525-5950
Oakland | 5801 College Ave. (bet. Claremont Ave. & Grove Shafter Fwy.) | 510-655-6385
San Ramon | Crow Canyon Crest Shopping Ctr. | 3110 Crow Canyon Pl. (Crow Canyon Rd.) | 925-244-1222
www.zacharys.com

Some "dream about" this East Bay pizza trio's "deep-dish wonders", saying the "killer, fresh-from-the garden tomato sauce" and "unashamedly buttery crust" are akin to "cheesy crack"; alas, it's "a tad pricey", and when you have a "Zach-attack", the wait is as "legendary" as the pies in the "minimal" digs (despite the "efficient" staff) – so consider carryout or "the half-baked option" – just "be prepared for a pizza coma."

Zatar 🗷Ⓜ🍽 *Mediterranean*

| ▽ 23 | 19 | 22 | $39 |

Berkeley | 1981 Shattuck Ave. (University Ave.) | 510-841-1981 | www.zatarrestaurant.com

Local "seasonal restaurant fruits and vegetables" – many of which are "homegrown" in the owners' organic garden – go into the "splendid, creative" fare at this midpriced Berkeley Med; though some bemoan "slow" service, others say the "cozy" "decor and atmosphere" are mostly a "real treat"; P.S. open Wednesday–Saturday.

NEW Zut! *American/Mediterranean*

| 20 | 19 | 21 | $41 |

Berkeley | 1820 Fourth St. (bet. Hearst Ave. & Virginia St.) | 510-644-0444 | www.zutonfourth.com

"Off to a nice start", this "upbeat" Berkeley newcomer ("a reinvention of Eccolo") "gets it right" for "shoppers, stroller moms" and the rest of "the Fourth Street crowd" with an "inviting" lineup of "generous" Med-New American plates; add "courteous" service and a "comfortable", muraled space with a "great bar", and most already "look forward to a return visit."

NORTH OF SAN FRANCISCO

Top Food

29 French Laundry | *Amer./Fr.*
28 Cyrus | *French*
Meadowood Rest. | *Californian*
Sushi Ran | *Japanese*
27 Cafe La Haye | *American/Cal.*
Terra | *American*
Madrona Manor | *Amer./Fr.*
Pizzeria Picco | *Pizza*
Farmhouse Inn | *Californian*
Ad Hoc | *American*

Redd | *Californian*
Bistro des Copains | *French*
Auberge du Soleil | *Cal./Fr.*
26 Santé | *Californian/French*
La Toque | *French*
Scopa | *Italian*
Solbar | *Californian*
Morimoto Napa | *Japanese*
Della Fattoria | *Bakery/Eclectic*
Cook St. Helena | *Italian*

BY CUISINE

AMERICAN

29 French Laundry
27 Cafe La Haye
Terra
Madrona Manor
Ad Hoc

CALIFORNIAN

28 Meadowood Rest.
27 Farmhouse Inn
Redd
Auberge du Soleil
26 Solbar

ECLECTIC

26 Della Fattoria
25 Willi's Wine Bar
23 Willow Wood Mkt.
Celadon
Ravenous Cafe

FRENCH

28 Cyrus
27 Bistro des Copains
26 Santé
La Toque
Bistro Jeanty

ITALIAN

26 Scopa
Cook St. Helena

25 Oenotri
Cucina Paradiso
Bottega

JAPANESE/SUSHI

28 Sushi Ran
26 Morimoto Napa
25 Hana Japanese
24 Osake∇
22 Tsukiji Sushi∇

MEDITERRANEAN

24 Harvest Moon Café
Insalata's
23 Willow Wood Mkt.
Brix
Underwood Bar

PIZZA

27 Pizzeria Picco
25 Rosso Pizzeria
Diavola Pizzeria
23 Azzurro Pizzeria
21 Pizzeria Tra Vigne

SEAFOOD/STEAK

25 Hog Island Oyster Co.
Cole's Chop House
24 Press
Fish
Willi's Seafood

Excludes places with low votes, unless otherwise indicated

Vote at ZAGAT.com

BY SPECIAL FEATURE

BREAKFAST/BRUNCH

- 25 Downtown Bakery
- 23 Girl & the Fig
- Willow Wood Mkt.
- 22 Alexis Baking Co.
- 20 Tavern at Lark Creek
- 18 Dipsea Cafe

CHILD-FRIENDLY

- 25 Rosso Pizzeria
- 24 Fish
- 21 Pizzeria Tra Vigne
- Gott's Roadside
- 20 Pizza Antica

OUTDOOR SEATING

- 27 Madrona Manor
- Auberge du Soleil
- 24 Tra Vigne
- Angèle
- Bistro Don Giovanni

PEOPLE-WATCHING

- 27 Redd
- 26 Solbar
- Morimoto Napa
- 25 Bouchon
- 24 Bistro Don Giovanni

ROMANCE

- 29 French Laundry
- 28 Cyrus
- 27 Terra
- Madrona Manor
- Farmhouse Inn

SMALL PLATES

- 25 Picco
- Willi's Wine Bar
- 24 Willi's Seafood
- 23 Underwood Bar
- 20 Monti's Rotisserie

TASTING MENUS

- 29 French Laundry
- 28 Cyrus
- Meadowood Rest.
- 27 Terra
- Redd
- 26 La Toque

VIEWS

- 27 Auberge du Soleil
- 24 Murray Circle
- 23 Brix
- Albion River Inn
- 22 Caprice

WINE BARS

- 28 Sushi Ran
- 25 Étoile
- Willi's Wine Bar
- Fig Cafe & Winebar
- 21 Bounty Hunter

WINNING WINE LISTS

- 29 French Laundry
- 28 Cyrus
- Meadowood Rest.
- 27 Terra
- 26 La Toque

BY LOCATION

MARIN COUNTY

- 28 Sushi Ran
- 27 Pizzeria Picco
- 25 Marché aux Fleurs
- Picco
- 24 Fish

MENDOCINO COUNTY

- 25 955 Ukiah
- Cafe Beaujolais
- 24 MacCallum House
- 23 St. Orres
- Mendo Bistro

NAPA COUNTY

- 29 French Laundry
- 28 Meadowood Rest.
- 27 Terra
- Ad Hoc
- Redd

SONOMA COUNTY

- 28 Cyrus
- 27 Cafe La Haye
- Madrona Manor
- Farmhouse Inn
- Bistro des Copains

Top Decor

28 Auberge du Soleil	Murray Circle
27 Cyrus	Bottega
French Laundry	Albion River Inn
Meadowood Rest.	24 Tra Vigne
Madrona Manor	Morimoto Napa
26 Farm	Bardessono
John Ash & Co.	Dry Creek Kitchen
Étoile	Farmhouse Inn
25 St. Orres	Press
Caprice	MacCallum House

Top Service

28 Cyrus	Étoile
French Laundry	Solbar
27 Meadowood Rest.	Ad Hoc
26 Auberge du Soleil	Marché aux Fleurs
Farmhouse Inn	24 John Ash & Co.
Madrona Manor	Il Davide
Terra	Redd
25 Bistro des Copains	Santé
La Toque	Bottega
Cafe La Haye	Kenwood

BEST BUYS: SPECIALTY SHOPS

Arizmendi	Downtown Bakery
Avatar's	In-N-Out
Barney's	Jimtown Store
Betty's Fish & Chips	Model Bakery
Bovolo	Napa General Store
Cafe Citti	Pica Pica Maize
Cheese Steak Shop	Pizzeria Picco

BEST BUYS: FULL MENUS

Alexis Baking Co.	La Boulange
Azzurro Pizzeria	Neela's
Boon Fly Café	Norman Rose Tavern
C Casa	Pacific Catch
Diavola Pizzeria	Pizza Antica
Emporio Rulli	Pizzeria Tra Vigne
Fig Cafe & Winebar	Rosso Pizzeria
Hog Island Oyster Co.	Royal Thai
Hopmonk Tavern	Sol Food
Joe's Taco	Willow Wood Mkt.

Vote at ZAGAT.com

North of San Francisco

	FOOD	DECOR	SERVICE	COST

Z Ad Hoc *American*   27 | 21 | 25 | $68
Yountville | 6476 Washington St. (bet. Mission St. & Oak Circle) |
707-944-2487
NEW Addendum 🅢🅜 *American*
Yountville | 6476 Washington St. (bet. Mission St. & Oak Circle) |
707-944-1565
www.adhocrestaurant.com

"'Ad' me to the list of fans" declare devotees of this now "permanent
fixture in Yountville" where "riffs" on "down-home" American "family-
style prix fixe suppers" (and Sunday brunch) come "with the same
incredible attention" diners expect from Thomas Keller and his "enthusiastic staff"; quibblers who find it "a bit pricey" for "everyday"
meals (albeit "swoon-worthy" fried chicken "on alternating Mondays")
and wine served in "water glasses" can always "sit at the bar" and "order
à la carte" or pick up lunch to-go (Thursday–Saturday) at the just-
opened takeout, Addendum; P.S. closed Tuesdays and Wednesdays.

Albion River Inn *Californian*   23 | 25 | 24 | $51
Albion | 3790 N. Hwy. 1 (Spring Grove Rd.) | 707-937-1919 |
www.albionriverinn.com
It's "worth the trip" up the "north coast" to Albion and this
"special-occasion" spot proffering "marvelous", "creative" takes on
seasonal Californian cuisine along with an "exceptional" wine list and
"all those single malts" (130 kinds); even with "professional and un-
obtrusive" service and "live piano music", it's the "spectacular view"
of the "Pacific as far as the eye can see" that sets the scene for a "wonderfully intimate romantic" dinner.

Alexis Baking Company *Bakery*   22 | 12 | 16 | $18
(aka ABC)
Napa | 1517 Third St. (bet. Church & School Sts.) | 707-258-1827 |
www.alexisbakingcompany.com
A "big locals' hangout", this colorful Napa bakery/coffee shop is "the
go-to breakfast place" for many ("huevos rancheros keep me coming
back", "pancake heaven") and also makes a "great" burger and other
lunch fare; just know that "service isn't always stellar", and the "small
space and high demand" mean "go early" or risk a "long" line.

All Seasons Bistro 🅜 *Californian*   ▽ 23 | 19 | 19 | $37
Calistoga | 1400 Lincoln Ave. (Washington St.) | 707-942-9111 |
www.allseasonsnapavalley.net
The "local" Cal cuisine at this "lovely little" bistro "right on the main
street" in Calistoga "may not be glitzy enough for the tourists", but
neighbors are crazy about the "delicious creations" and the "casual"
"country" interior with "fresh flowers on every table"; "a hidden gem of a
retail wine shop in the rear" attracts oenophiles, who know they can
"buy any bottle", pay $15 corkage and "enjoy" it with dinner.

Amici's East Coast Pizzeria *Pizza*   20 | 14 | 18 | $21
San Rafael | 1242 Fourth St. (bet. B & C Sts.) | 415-455-9777 |
www.amicis.com
See review in City of San Francisco Directory.

	FOOD	DECOR	SERVICE	COST

Angèle *French*

24 | 22 | 23 | $50

Napa | Hatt/Napa Mill Bldg. | 540 Main St. (5th St.) | 707-252-8115 |
www.angelerestaurant.com

The setting is "delightful" – an old boathouse with a "lovely", "rustic"
interior and "airy" patio overlooking the river – and the "excellent"
"French comfort food" from an "updated", "much improved" menu
more than holds its own at this "welcoming" Napa standby; "polished
service", "fair" prices, an "enviable wine list" and "vibrant bar scene"
also help make it a "locals' favorite."

Applewood

25 | 21 | 23 | $54

Inn & Restaurant 🗷Ⓜ *Californian*

Guerneville | 13555 Hwy. 116 (River Rd.) | 707-869-9093 |
www.applewoodinn.com

"Tucked among the redwoods" in a "charming European-style inn" near
"funky Guerneville", this "Russian River gem" proffers Californian à la
carte and prix fixe dinners created with "care and artistry" and centered
around "local vegetables" and regional wines in a "romantic", fire-lit
setting; "the fact that it's away from the self-important puffery of
Napa" and staffed by an "attentive but unpretentious" crew "only adds
to its allure"; P.S. closed Sunday–Monday.

Arizmendi *Bakery/Pizza*

26 | 12 | 19 | $11

San Rafael | 1002 Fourth St. (A St.) | 415-456-4093 |
fourthstreet.arizmendi.coop

See review in City of San Francisco Directory.

🄯 Auberge du Soleil *Californian/French*

27 | 28 | 26 | $85

Rutherford | Auberge du Soleil | 180 Rutherford Hill Rd. (Silverado Trail) |
707-967-3111 | www.aubergedusoleil.com

The "unparalleled" view "of the Napa Valley vineyards" "alone is worth
the trip", but this "(very) special-occasion spot" in Rutherford delivers
the "total package", including "marvelous" Cal-French cuisine, a "fabulous wine list" and "knowledgeable" servers who "pamper you
shamelessly"; "make sure to bring the platinum AmEx" because you'll
"pay dearly" for the experience, but you can't put a price on
"perfection" – or the "unforgettable experience" of "watching the sunset" on the "spectacular terrace", where a more affordable bar
menu is served.

Avatar's 🗷 *Indian*

22 | 11 | 20 | $20

Sausalito | 2656 Bridgeway (Coloma St.) | 415-332-8083
Avatar's Punjabi Burrito *Indian*
Mill Valley | 15 Madrona St. (bet. Lovell & Throckmorton Aves.) |
415-381-8293 🗷
Petaluma | 131 Kentucky St. (bet. Washington St. & Western Ave.) |
707-765-9775
www.enjoyavatars.com

Fans "can't get enough of the punjabi enchiladas" and other Indian
"gourmet fusion" fare at this affordable North Bay trio, with special
praise for the "unique burritos" (e.g. "curried lamb and pumpkin") at
the Petaluma and small Mill Valley locales; Sausalito is also appreci-
ated for the "ebullient" owner, who will "direct you through" this
"cross-cultural" "change of pace."

Azzurro Pizzeria & Enoteca *Pizza* | 23 | 17 | 18 | $28 |

Napa | 1260 Main St. (Clinton St.) | 707-255-5552 | www.azzurropizzeria.com

"Hip and delicious coexist" at this "sleek", "lively" Napa pie place known for "designer pizza with real flavor" plus "excellent salads" and "reasonably priced" wine; a "locals' spot", it can get "noisy", but with a "friendly, knowledgeable staff", it's still "a keeper."

Baci Cafe & Wine Bar *Italian/Mediterranean* | ∇ 22 | 19 | 20 | $40 |

Healdsburg | 336 Healdsburg Ave. (North St.) | 707-433-8111 | www.bacicafeandwinebar.com

A Healdsburg "hangout", this "family-run" Italian-Med cafe/wine bar offers an "easy, tasty" menu featuring "flavorful pastas" and wood-oven pizza, delivered by a "friendly" crew in pleasant environs; "good-value" pricing that extends to the "excellent local wine list" also earns kisses.

Balboa Cafe *American* | 19 | 18 | 20 | $37 |

Mill Valley | 38 Miller Ave. (Presidio Ave.) | 415-381-7321 | www.balboacafe.com

See review in City of San Francisco Directory.

BarBersQ *BBQ* | 21 | 16 | 18 | $31 |

Napa | Bel Aire Plaza | 3900 Bel Aire Plaza (Redwood Rd.) | 707-224-6600 | www.barbersq.com

"Soak up a Napa wine-tasting tour" at this "Q shack gone upscale" with "lick-your-lips ribs", pulled pork, "housemade BBQ sauces" and "authentic sides" that all come at "reasonable" prices; while the "strip-mall" setting "isn't the most romantic of locales" and service can be "spotty", "a fabulous wine list" helps to soften any negatives.

NEW Bar Bocce *Pizza* | - | - | - | M |

Sausalito | 1250 Bridgeway (bet. Pine & Turney Sts.) | 415-331-0555 | www.barbocce.com

Despite the Italianate name, this Sausalito waterfront hangout (from the folks behind Buckeye Roadhouse and Bungalow 44) is pure California – hawking an ingredient-driven, midpriced menu of wood-fired sourdough pizzas, garden-fresh salads and a 21-and-over 'winesicle'; Marin swells can kick back by the fire pit and bocce court on the back patio, knocking back cask vinos, brews and wine-based cocktails.

Bardessono *American* | 21 | 24 | 22 | $65 |

Yountville | Bardessono Hotel & Spa | 6526 Yount St. (bet. Finnell Rd. & Washington St.) | 707-204-6030 | www.bardessono.com

"If you like green" and "you've got green", this "opulent", "Zen-like" American at a "cutting-edge eco" "Yountville resort" makes a "stunning" setting for diners to "relax" while enjoying an "ambitious", "creative" "farm-to-table" menu; a staff that's "eager to please" adds to the appeal, and though the fare is somewhat less "impressive" than the surroundings, it's altogether "a great escape"; the Food score does not reflect a chef change.

Barndiva Ⓜ *American* | 23 | 23 | 20 | $49 |

Healdsburg | 231 Center St. (Matheson St.) | 707-431-0100 | www.barndiva.com

"Inventive and exciting" "farm-fresh" "twists with old concepts" make a "mouthwatering impression" on patrons of this upscale Healdsburg

FOOD DECOR SERVICE COST

American "charmer" boasting a "romantic" "backyard with lights in the trees" and an "innovative" "barnlike" interior; service is "attentive without hovering", though it "needs improvement" to complete a "great experience" say surveyors who either "love or hate" the "ultracool atmosphere."

Barney's Gourmet Hamburgers Burgers | 19 | 13 | 16 | $17 |

San Rafael | 1020 Court St. (4th St.) | 415-454-4594 |
www.barneyshamburgers.com
See review in City of San Francisco Directory.

Betty's Fish & Chips British/Seafood | 21 | 10 | 17 | $19 |

Santa Rosa | 4046 Sonoma Hwy. (bet. Bush Creek Rd. & Mission Blvd.) |
707-539-0899
The "only thing missing is the London cabs in front" of this "unpretentious" seafooder specializing in "consistently delicious fish 'n' chips"; set "in an out-of-the-way Santa Rosa mini–strip mall", the nautical-themed digs are rather "casual", but the "greasy" grub is "wonderful for the price" and "nothing beats the pie that these folks make fresh every day."

☑ Bistro des Copains French | 27 | 21 | 25 | $43 |

Occidental | 3782 Bohemian Hwy. (bet. Coleman Valley & Graton Rds.) |
707-874-2436 | www.bistrodescopains.com
A "find in the boondocks", this "quaint", "cozy" Occidental bistro delivering "all the joy of buttery French food without the pretension" is an "outstanding value" and "worth the drive" for its "off the charts good" Provençal classics "updated" with "California ingredients"; add in "warm service", "well-priced" wines and "reduced corkage" for Sonoma wines (waived Thursdays) and it's the place you "wish was just down the street."

Bistro Don Giovanni Italian | 24 | 22 | 21 | $47 |

Napa | 4110 Howard Ln. (bet. Oak Knoll & Salvador Aves.) |
707-224-3300 | www.bistrodongiovanni.com
"Is there a more pleasant dining experience in Napa?" ponder patrons of this Italian "favorite" offering "excellent" *cucina* (with French accents) and "fairly priced" wines in a "dreamy" "indoor/outdoor setting" amid the vineyards; "warm" service extends to the "endless hospitality" of "charming Giovanni himself", so no wonder it gets "busy and noisy" with fans who deem it a "great value" for the area.

☑ Bistro Jeanty French | 25 | 21 | 23 | $51 |

Yountville | 6510 Washington St. (Mulberry St.) | 707-944-0103 |
www.bistrojeanty.com
Philippe Jeanty's "bustling" Yountville bistro "looks and tastes like Paris", with a "jaunty" staff serving *"magnifique"*, "country-style" French "comfort food" with "no pretensions" at "sensible prices"; some say the "quaint" rooms and "rarely changed menu" could use a "refresher", but it's still a "best bet for lunch between winery visits" (especially on the patio) or a "relaxed" dinner when you "aren't counting calories."

Bistro Ralph Californian/French | 24 | 19 | 23 | $47 |

Healdsburg | 109 Plaza St. (bet. Center St. & Healdsburg Ave.) |
707-433-1380 | www.bistroralph.com
"An old standby among all the new and upscale places" hitting Healdsburg, this bistro lets tourists "eat with the locals and eat very

well" from a "simple, straightforward selection" of French-Cal cuisine, including "fantastic" frites and "beautiful fish dishes" paired with a "great list of Sonoma wines" and "old-school" martinis served by "knowledgeable" waiters; if the menu is "rarely changing", it "rarely disappoints", and while the place is "tiny", it's "right on the square."

Boca *Argentinean/Steak*
| 22 | 21 | 21 | $42 |

Novato | 340 Ignacio Blvd. (Rte. 101) | 415-883-0901 | www.bocasteak.com

"When you want meat, this is your spot" in Novato say aficionados of this "Argentine steakhouse", which also offers "excellent empanadas" and "amazing" "complimentary pickles" along with its "grass-fed steak" – all served in a "dark and inviting" atmosphere (or on the "super outside patio", weather permitting); "if you are on a budget, try their happy hour when everything in the bar menu is half-off."

Boon Fly Café *Californian*
| 21 | 18 | 20 | $33 |

Napa | Carneros Inn | 4048 Sonoma Hwy. (Old Sonoma Rd.) | 707-299-4900 | www.thecarnerosinn.com

A "cute" and "casual" Californian in "a comfortable red barn", this "upscale diner" in Napa's Carneros Inn is a midpriced option from breakfast through dinner; "there's usually a line" for the "super Sunday brunch", when the housemade "doughnuts are to-die-for", but a "friendly" staff "that cares" means it's "well worth a stop" on the "way to or from the Wine Country."

☑ Bottega *Italian*
| 25 | 25 | 24 | $58 |

Yountville | V Mktpl. | 6525 Washington St. (Yount St.) | 707-945-1050 | www.botteganapavalley.com

It's "the quintessential Napa Valley" hot spot – complete with a celeb chef "making the rounds" – yet Michael Chiarello's "chic" Yountville "showcase" also boasts "outstanding", "rustic" Italian food that's both "full of flavor" and a "good value", backed by wines at "reasonable" prices, "warm" service and a "gorgeous" "farmhouse" setting including "roaring fireplaces" outside; it's a hit with "tourists and locals", thus reservations are "a must"; P.S. it's dinner-only on Monday.

☑ Bouchon *French*
| 25 | 23 | 24 | $59 |

Yountville | 6534 Washington St. (Yount St.) | 707-944-8037 | www.bouchonbistro.com

"The master's handiwork shines" at Thomas Keller's "true Parisian bistro" in Yountville (a more "affordable" "backup" to his "place up the street"), proffering "rock-solid", "classic French fare" and "skillful" yet "casual" service; its "dead-on" "authenticity" – down to the "noisy", "tight quarters" and "champagne and oyster" bar – keeps the place "hopping" from lunch "straight through late night"; P.S. don't miss the "terrific bakery next door" selling "lovely desserts", breads, sandwiches and other boulangerie fare from 7 AM–7 PM daily.

Bounty Hunter Wine Bar & Smokin' BBQ *BBQ*
| 21 | 19 | 21 | $35 |

Napa | 975 First St. (Main St.) | 707-226-3976 | www.bountyhunterwinebar.com

"Try a new wine (or two or three)" at this "casual", "inviting Downtown Napa" pit stop "right near the river", which has a "huge by-the-glass list" (including a house label) to accompany its "smokin' hot" "ribs, BBQ and,

| | FOOD | DECOR | SERVICE | COST |

of course, the beer-can chicken", all served up by a "knowledgeable" staff; "go on off-hours", otherwise "good luck finding a place to sit" – and hearing yourself think (the Western-themed digs get "so loud").

Bovolo *Italian*   21 | 9 | 14 | $25

Healdsburg | Copperfield's Bookstore | 106 Matheson St. (Healdsburg Ave.) | 707-431-2962 | www.bovolorestaurant.com

"It's all about the pig" at this "unpretentious" "little" Healdsburg Italian where pork is "lovingly incorporated" into "creative" sandwiches, "artisan pizza" and breakfasts that are a "bacon lover's dream" (there's "imaginative" gelato too); run by the Zazu folks, it's a "no-ambiance" counter-service joint in "back of a bookstore", but it's "budget-friendly" and the back patio is a "quiet" "escape" from Wine Country crowds; P.S. closes at 4 PM weekdays, later on weekends.

NEW Branches Wood   – | – | – | M
Fired Chophouse *American*

Ukiah | 1180 Airport Park Blvd. (Talmage Rd.) | 707-468-5400 | www.branchesrestaurant.com

Encompassing an American restaurant, butcher shop, bakery and sports bar, this "cavernous" newcomer in Ukiah aims to be a destination for Mendocino County foodies; the chophouse allows one to "indulge in huge steaks", naturally, but also pulls a "wide-ranging menu" from its fires, "including many vegetarian options", within a rustic atmosphere.

Brannan's Grill *American/French*   18 | 20 | 19 | $41

Calistoga | 1374 Lincoln Ave. (Washington St.) | 707-942-2233 | www.brannansgrill.com

Locals "keep going back" for the "well-prepared" American-French "meat and potatoes" at this Calistoga "standby" "that's been around for years"; if a few fret that it "never truly wows", most maintain the "pretty" decor and "large windows" where you can watch "the locals passing by" make for a "memorable experience", and "live jazz" on weekends "is a nice touch."

Brick & Bottle *Californian*   19 | 16 | 19 | $39

Corte Madera | 55 Tamal Vista Blvd. (Sandpiper Circle) | 415-924-3366 | www.brickandbottle.com

"Comfort food, done comfortably in everyone's comfort zone" is the consensus on this Corte Madera Californian, though surveyors split on whether that's "delightful" or "disappointing"; while chef "Scott Howard can surely cook", the fare here seems a bit "ordinary" – as does the staff and the "noisy" digs, but at least you "can't beat that $5 corkage."

Brix *Californian/Mediterranean*   23 | 23 | 22 | $53

Napa | 7377 St. Helena Hwy. (Yount Mill Rd.) | 707-944-2749 | www.brix.com

This "Napa landmark" exudes a "laid-back, yet inviting" vibe, thanks to its "scenic" outdoor seating area with views of the "sunset over the vineyard and the mountains" – and the "beautiful garden" whose bounty shines in an "intriguing" Cal-Med "seasonal menu of fresh ingredients"; some say there's "a corporate feel" (perhaps due to the gift shop), but those "lavish wine choices" make this "a real Valley outing"; P.S. scores don't reflect the replacement of chef Anne Gingrass-Paik by Chris Jones (ex The Girl & The Fig and Estate).

	FOOD	DECOR	SERVICE	COST

Z Buckeye Roadhouse *American/BBQ*　24 | 24 | 23 | $47

Mill Valley | 15 Shoreline Hwy. (Hwy. 101) | 415-331-2600 |
www.buckeyeroadhouse.com

This "festive" "high-end roadhouse" in Mill Valley with a "fantastic
hunting lodge atmosphere" gets "crowded as all get out" with "hiker/
biker/kayaker" types refueling, "families celebrating birthdays" and
the "old guard of Marin" hobnobbing over "tasty" New American
"comfort food" that "entirely satisfies" (particularly "anything from
the smoker"); the "fortysomething"- singles bar is a total "scene", but
with "generous libations", a "roaring fire" and "professionally personable" staff, "heck, what else do you want?"

Bungalow 44 *American*　21 | 19 | 20 | $44

Mill Valley | 44 E. Blithedale Ave. (Sunnyside Ave.) | 415-381-2500 |
www.bungalow44.com

"You really can't go wrong" at this "always abuzz" Mill Valley New
American that's "run by the same outfit as the Buckeye"; "it can be a
bit of a singles scene" (and "cougar central at the bar"), but "for a
more mellow experience" you can sit "in the back near the fireplace"
or on the "covered patio" to enjoy the "responsive service" and "innovative twists" that make the "comfort food" "seem special."

Cafe Beaujolais *Californian/French*　25 | 20 | 23 | $54

Mendocino | 961 Ukiah St. (bet. Evergreen & School Sts.) | 707-937-5614 |
www.cafebeaujolais.com

"After all these years", this "charming" "white-tablecloth" "country
bistro" is still "one of the reasons to return" to "picturesque
Mendocino", proffering "lovingly prepared", organically oriented Cal-
French fare along with "local Anderson Valley wines" in a "traditional
Victorian" farmhouse; even without its original owners, it "hasn't lost
its special appeal", most say, be it for "dinner with your significant
other during your romantic weekend getaway" or lunch in the "delightful" garden (Wednesday–Sunday); P.S. "the cafe's bakery window
sells breads and pastries to go."

Cafe Citti *Italian*　22 | 12 | 19 | $27

Kenwood | 9049 Sonoma Hwy./Hwy. 12 (Shaw Ave.) |
707-833-2690 | www.cafecitti.com

"The almost-cafeteria setup", not to mention the "minimal decor",
"belies the fine food" served by "this roadhouse on Sonoma Highway
in Kenwood" – "melt-in-your-mouth pizza", "fresh pastas" and other
"great garlicky Italian casual" fare, including a "Caesar salad that will
keep the vampires away"; it's a "no-frills" experience, but a
"great-value" "stop for a bit while wine-tasting", plus there's no corkage.

Café Gratitude *Vegan*　17 | 15 | 17 | $25

San Rafael | 2200 Fourth St. (W. Crescent Dr.) | 415-578-4928 |
www.cafegratitude.com

See review in City of San Francisco Directory.

Z Cafe La Haye 🅂🅜 *American/Californian*　27 | 19 | 25 | $52

Sonoma | 140 E. Napa St. (bet. 1st & 2nd Sts.) | 707-935-5994 |
www.cafelahaye.com

"Everything works" at this "charming, tiny place off the Sonoma
Square", from the "thoughtful menu" of "perfectly prepared" New

American–"Californian comfort food" to the sips from the "winning wine list"; "top-notch" service and "great prices" make it highly "popular with locals", so "book ahead" because scoring a table is the "envy of Wine Country."

Caprice, The ⓜ American
| 22 | 25 | 22 | $56 |

Tiburon | 2000 Paradise Dr. (Mar W. St.) | 415-435-3400 | www.thecaprice.com

With a "spectacular view of the bay and the GG bridge", "your date will just melt" in the "pleasant but understated interior" of this Tiburon "special-occasion" New American; the "improved" menu of "Californian-style" "standbys" "now stands well on its own", but even with "better food" and "excellent" service, "nothing could top" that panorama "worth pretty much a million dollars."

Carneros Bistro &
Wine Bar Californian
| ▽ 24 | 19 | 23 | $49 |

Sonoma | The Lodge at Sonoma | 1325 Broadway (bet. Clay St. & Leveroni Rd.) | 707-931-2042 | www.thelodgeatsonoma.com

This "undiscovered gem of Sonoma" "hidden" in a "chain hotel" lures "hotel guests" and "locals" with its "wonderful" "local" Cal fare served breakfast through dinner, enhanced by "ingredients grown on the property", "great wine pairings" and "warm service"; even after "toooo many wineries", the recently refreshed dining room and bar (plus the fire pit seating) are "worth checking out", especially on Thursdays for 'Celebrity Wine-tender' tastings; P.S. a post-Survey chef change is not reflected in the Food score.

C Casa Mexican
| 24 | 14 | 18 | $18 |

Napa | Oxbow Public Mkt. | 610 First St. (bet. Silverado Trail & Soscol Ave.) | 707-226-7700 | www.myccasa.com

"Where have you been all my life?" surveyors ask this "casual" cantina "inside Oxbow Public Market", which dishes up "made-to-order Mexican small plates" and "dreamy" tortillas stuffed with "super-fresh", "unusual" ingredients like buffalo, lamb or mahi mahi; since it's situated in "the social hub for locals", these "fancy" "little" tacos are "pricier than they should be" (those with "hearty appetites and thin wallets will leave hungry"), but it's nevertheless a "nice change of pace for Napa."

Celadon American/Eclectic
| 23 | 21 | 24 | $51 |

Napa | The Historic Napa Mill | 500 Main St. (5th St.) | 707-254-9690 | www.celadonnapa.com

Combining "comfort food with flavors that will send you to the moon", "a wonderful" "historic setting" "right near the riverfront" and "a dedicated staff", this American-Eclectic makes co-chef/owner Greg Cole something of "a local hero" to his Napa neighbors; though the "tables near the outdoor fireplace are best", "eating at the bar" is also "great."

Central Market Californian/Mediterranean
| 22 | 20 | 22 | $45 |

Petaluma | 42 Petaluma Blvd. (Western Ave.) | 707-778-9900 | www.centralmarketpetaluma.com

Gregarious chef-owner "Tony Najiola puts his heart" into transforming "fresh, local and the seasonal best" of ingredients into "creative" Cal-Med dishes "with New Orleans touches" at this "cavernous", "noisy" space in Downtown Petaluma; some grumble it's "slipping" a bit and the staff, while "attentive", "could use a shot of caffeine", but "locals and out-of-towners alike" still have "a lot of fun" here.

Chapter & Moon Ⓜ American
▽ 21 | 15 | 18 | $33

Fort Bragg | 32150 N. Harbor Dr. (S. Main St.) | 707-962-1643
"Honest-to-goodness fresh seafood from Noyo Harbor boats" and "scrumptious salads served in large wooden bowls" comprise the "simple, but solid" American eats at this "funky find" hidden "off the beaten path" in Fort Bragg; the digs and servers are "homey, maybe to a fault", but the "beautiful location" "down near the water" makes it "worth a stop."

Charcuterie French
21 | 18 | 21 | $37

Healdsburg | Healdsburg Plaza | 335 Healdsburg Ave. (Plaza St.) | 707-431-7213 | www.charcuteriehealdsburg.com
"Meat eaters delight" in "returning time and time again" to this "consistent", "casual" spot "in a convenient location off Healdsburg square", offering not only the namesake "wonderful pork dishes", but "flavorful French" classics as well; the "pig-heavy decor" has been "toned down to a more manageable level" in the "warm and friendly atmosphere", but it's still "cramped quarters", so "keep your elbows in at all times."

Cheesecake Factory American
17 | 18 | 17 | $29

Corte Madera | The Village at Corte Madera | 1736 Redwood Hwy. (Hwy. 101) | 415-945-0777 | www.thecheesecakefactory.com
See review in City of San Francisco Directory.

Cheese Steak Shop Cheesesteaks
20 | 6 | 15 | $12

Santa Rosa | 750 Stony Point Rd. (Sebastopol Rd.) | 707-527-9877 | www.cheesesteakshop.com
See review in City of San Francisco Directory.

Cindy's Backstreet Kitchen Californian
24 | 20 | 23 | $45

St. Helena | 1327 Railroad Ave. (bet. Adams St. & Hunt Ave.) | 707-963-1200 | www.cindysbackstreetkitchen.com
Maybe "it's not Mustard's", but "famous chef"-owner Cindy Pawlcyn's "cozier", "quaint" St. Helena venue offers a "nice departure from the overdone Napa Valley" dining circuit, pairing "fabulous" "high-end" Californian ("with a south-of-the-border influence") comfort food with "great local wines" and "casual, warm" service; the "full bar" is "an added draw", and if you end up "scoring a patio table", you have an experience that's "backstreet in name only."

Cole's Chop House Steak
25 | 22 | 22 | $64

Napa | 1122 Main St. (bet. 1st & Pearl Sts.) | 707-224-6328 | www.coleschophouse.com
"Meat Central for the Valley", this Napa "staple" ("probably one of the best steakhouses north of SF") is at the "top of its game" for "high-quality, dry-aged beef, expertly prepared and presented", plus "first-rate" sides, a "well-selected" (if "expensive") wine list and "birdbath-sized martinis", all courtesy of "comfort-food king Greg Cole" and his "attentive" staff; just "stake out your table early" because there's often a "wait (even with reservations)."

Cook St. Helena *Italian*

26 | 16 | 22 | $42

St. Helena | 1310 Main St. (Hunt Ave.) | 707-963-7088 |
www.cooksthelena.com

"You have to fight the locals to get in" to this cafe in "cute Downtown St. Helena", which wins raves for "Italian food done to perfection", including "innovative pasta dishes" "lovingly prepared" with "wonderfully fresh ingredients", an enhanced, "affordable wine list" and "cheerful staff"; the "teensy- tiny" space gets "loud", but "dinner is worth the din."

Cucina Paradiso Ⓢ *Italian*

25 | 21 | 23 | $41

Petaluma | 114 Petaluma Blvd. N. (bet. Washington St. & Western Ave.) |
707-782-1130 | www.cucinaparadisopetaluma.com

This "unpretentious" Petaluma trattoria "knows how to marry pasta with sauce to perfection", in addition to assembling "amazing veal" and other "authentic Italian" dishes; "superb" vino "by the glass, a full bar and a charming staff round out the experience"; but the "room can get horribly noisy as voices rise with wine consumption."

Cucina Restaurant & Wine Bar Ⓜ *Italian*

22 | 15 | 20 | $38

San Anselmo | 510 San Anselmo Ave. (Tunstead Ave.) | 415-454-2942 |
www.cucinarestaurantandwinebar.com

"For reliable Italian comfort food" and pizza (every night except Friday and Saturday), this "low-key" "homestyle" trattoria in San Anselmo is "a wonderful neighborhood tradition", thanks to "ample servings" and a "nice selection" of wines; though it "can get crowded and noisy", an "agreeable staff" helps keep this "cozy" spot a "winner."

Cuvée ⦿ *American* (aka Cuvée Napa)

∇ 22 | 20 | 23 | $49

Napa | 1650 Soscol Ave. (Vallejo St.) | 707-224-2330 |
www.cuveenapa.com

Even Napa natives sometimes "forget about" this "underappreciated" American that some deem a "local treasure" for its "outdoor seating" in a spacious courtyard plus "unusual mixed drinks" featuring local fruits, vegetables and spirits that put it "ahead of the cocktail curve"; dissenters dub it only "average", but most agree the "new chef has made a big difference" for "the better", plus it "won't put too big a dent in your wallet", especially on Wednesdays, when the prix fixe menu is a "great deal."

⊠ Cyrus *French*

28 | 27 | 28 | $138

Healdsburg | Les Mars Hotel | 29 North St. (Foss St.) | 707-433-3311 |
www.cyrusrestaurant.com

"The caviar and champagne cart" alone "is enough to convince" "starry-eyed" tourists and other "froufrou" fanciers that this New French Healdsburg "destination" is the place for a "blow-out fine-dining" dinner or Saturday lunch in otherwise "casual" Sonoma; you can "save yourself a ton of money" dining "à la carte in the bar", but chef Douglas Keane's "magnificent" prix fixes with "wine pairings" and "all the extras" proffered in a "gorgeous setting" with a near "1:1" "staff-to-guest ratio" are what gives other temples of "haute cuisine" "a run for their money."

	FOOD	DECOR	SERVICE	COST

Della Fattoria
Downtown Café *Bakery/Eclectic*

| 26 | 17 | 19 | $25 |

Petaluma | 141 Petaluma Blvd. N. (bet. Washington St. & Western Ave.) | 707-763-0161 | www.dellafattoria.com

"I'd drive a hundred miles for their bread" declare members of the "huge cult following" inspired by this "great bakery/bistro", a "real foodie's paradise" in Petaluma serving "habit-forming", if "high"-priced, Eclectic eats for breakfast, lunch and late on Friday ("wish they were open for dinner more"); the scene is fairly "no frills", but staffed by "nice, nice people."

Della Santina's *Italian*

| 22 | 20 | 20 | $38 |

Sonoma | 133 E. Napa St. (1st St. W.) | 707-935-0576 | www.dellasantinas.com

Enoteca Della Santina Ⓜ *Italian*

Sonoma | 127 E. Napa St. (bet. 1st & 2nd Sts.) | 707-938-4200 | www.enotecadellasantina.com

It's "the real Italian deal" at this "delicious hideaway" "off the Sonoma Square", which is "popular with locals" for its Lucca-inspired "home cooking" and "good wines at fair prices"; "although you may have trouble flagging down your server, the food is well worth the wait", and "springtime" in the "garden is beautiful"; P.S. the small enoteca offers the same menu.

Diavola Pizzeria & Salumeria *Italian*

| 25 | 18 | 21 | $33 |

Geyserville | 21021 Geyserville Ave. (Hwy. 128) | 707-814-0111 | www.diavolapizzeria.com

"More than a pizzeria", this "adorable" old-timey-looking Italian with a "neighborly vibe" in the "small quaint town of Geyserville" is a "foodie's dream", turning out "home-cured salumi" and masterful dinner "plates full of brains and sweetbreads" alongside "sublime" wood-fired thin-crust pies, all to be washed down with local beer and wines; it's a devil of a "drive in the country" to reach it, but that mitigates the waiting hordes ("it doesn't take reservations" for groups under eight).

Dipsea Cafe *American*

| 18 | 15 | 18 | $21 |

Mill Valley | 200 Shoreline Hwy./Hwy. 1 (Hwy. 101) | 415-381-0298 | www.dipseacafe.com

On weekends, you'll need to "go early and get your name on the list" to enjoy the "good old comfort food" like "fluffy pancakes", omelets and "homemade Southern-style biscuits" at this "Mill Valley brunch tradition"; some dub the American grub "overpriced for the quality" – you're "paying for the location, access to the beach and Mount Tam" – but at least "they dish out steaming hot coffee while you are waiting in line."

Downtown Bakery & Creamery ⊅ *Bakery*

| 25 | 11 | 19 | $16 |

Healdsburg | 308A Center St. (bet. Matheson & Plaza Sts.) | 707-431-2719 | www.downtownbakery.net

This "long-established bakery" off the Healdsburg Plaza is as much a "community gathering spot" as a "gotta-stop-here" "favorite" for a "cup of coffee" or to "stock up" on a "fantastic array" of "sinful" morning pastries, "artisanal breads" and, of course, "excellent ice cream", along with "filling" breakfast and lunch fare; P.S. there's now a European-style cafe open Friday–Mondays.

Drake's Beach Café *Californian*

▽ 21 | 15 | 21 | $37

Inverness | Point Reyes Nat'l Seashore | 1 Drake's Beach Rd.
(Sir Francis Drake Blvd.) | 415-669-1297 | www.drakescafe.com

During or "after a day hiking in Point Reyes", this weather-beaten beach shack near the Visitor Center makes "a perfect place" to refuel on its namesake oysters, "burgers and fries" and other simple Cal fare "made from wonderfully fresh ingredients"; P.S. mainly a summer option, it operates Friday–Monday off-season and is not open for dinner.

Dry Creek Kitchen *Californian*

24 | 24 | 23 | $65

Healdsburg | Hotel Healdsburg | 317 Healdsburg Ave. (Matheson St.) | 707-431-0330 | www.charliepalmer.com

This "celebrity-chef hangout" from chef-restaurateur Charlie Palmer is "yet another reason Healdsburg is becoming a mecca for foodies", presenting "killer" Cal fare (seemingly "better when he is there") in an "open, airy" space that creates a "convivial", "relaxed atmosphere"; "it's not inexpensive", but the "amazingly friendly service", "no corkage fee for Sonoma County wines" and "sophisticated platings" make it an idyllic spot, especially if you can sit "outside under the vines."

Duck Club *American*

20 | 22 | 21 | $50

Bodega Bay | Bodega Bay Lodge & Spa | 103 S. Hwy. 1 (Doran Park Rd.) | 707-875-3525 | www.bodegabaylodge.com

See review in South of San Francisco Directory.

El Dorado Kitchen *Californian/Mediterranean*

22 | 23 | 20 | $52

Sonoma | El Dorado Hotel | 405 First St. W. (Spain St.) | 707-996-3030 | www.eldoradosonoma.com

A "sophisticated" yet "soul-satisfying" Cal-Med menu and "refreshing cocktails" are as good as gold at this "modern, minimalist" space in Sonoma's El Dorado Hotel; the "urban" setup is a welcome change from the "typical" Wine Country setting, and "from spring to autumn" the "lovely" poolside patio is perfect for a "romantic" dinner, all "topped off with beyond-the-call service."

NEW El Paseo *Steak*

- | - | - | E

Mill Valley | 17 Throckmorton Ave. (E. Blithedale Ave.) | 415-388-0741 | www.elpaseomillvalley.com

Having conquered San Francisco (Wayfare Tavern) and Napa Valley (Rotisserie & Wine), Tyler Florence turns his attention to Mill Valley, where he and business partner Sammy Hagar have finally opened their long-awaited rustic American chophouse; the pricey menu features gussied-up, locally sourced standards, while the warren of rooms and patios in its historic brick-building setting have been outfitted with a multitude of curios, gas lanterns and fireplaces.

Emporio Rulli *Dessert/Italian*

24 | 21 | 17 | $20

Larkspur | 464 Magnolia Ave. (bet. Cane & Ward Sts.) | 415-924-7478 | www.rulli.com

This Larkspur "local legend" has pastry *paesani* purring over "heavenly" baked goods, gelato and the "best lattes" in the "gorgeous" "mid-20th-century setting" that provides a "charming" spot to "relax and watch the world go by"; the Union Square sister in SF offers a "great picker-upper" for "power-shoppers", and while the staff's somewhat "disorganized", it's still "faster than flying back home to

Italy"; P.S. it now also offers its patented "little piece of Italy" in three spots at the airport.

Estate *Californian/Italian* | 21 | 23 | 24 | $45 |

Sonoma | 400 W. Spain St. (4th St.) | 707-933-3663 | www.estate-sonoma.com

"General Vallejo's daughter's home" sets a "lovely, historic" scene for "delightful in-season bounty from Sonoma" prepared with a Cal-Italian "twist" and "relaxed but efficient" service at owner Sondra Bernstein's "Wine Country hot spot"; if some protest the "price is a bit more than the food deserves", the four-course, family-style prix fixe is a "helluva delicious deal"; P.S. "eat on the deck in summertime."

Étoile *Californian* | 25 | 26 | 25 | $76 |

Yountville | Domaine Chandon Winery | 1 California Dr. (St. Helena Hwy./ Rte. 29) | 707-944-2892 | www.chandon.com

"One of the stars" of Yountville, this "elegant" eatery "at the Domaine Chandon Winery" is "everything you would expect of a Wine Country experience" – "bubbles abound" and the Californian fare "rivals the finest New York restaurants" in an atmosphere of "Napa casual sophistication"; "lunch on the terrace" overlooking the "idyllic" gardens is "a perfect way to split up a day of winery visits" and also "dodge the high prices"; P.S. closed Tuesday and Wednesday.

Farm *American* | 24 | 26 | 23 | $61 |

Napa | Carneros Inn | 4048 Sonoma Hwy. (Old Sonoma Rd.) | 707-299-4882 | www.thecarnerosinn.com

Not your everyday farm, this one's a "beautifully designed", "wonderful culinary stop" with "terrific preparations of locally sourced everything" on its New American menu; the staff is "friendly", and it boasts "the best patio in Napa", "with beautiful fire pits" and views of the bocce courts, which has most agreeing it's "expensive but well worth it."

☑ Farmhouse Inn & Restaurant Ⓜ *Californian* | 27 | 24 | 26 | $90 |

Forestville | Farmhouse Inn | 7871 River Rd. (Wohler Rd.) | 707-887-3300 | www.farmhouseinn.com

Set in a "real farmhouse", this "charming" "countryside extravaganza" "in the middle of nowhere" (Forestville, actually) "is very much worth seeking out" "if you are visiting Russian River Wine Country" advise fans of the "rabbit three ways" and other "elegant" source-centric Californian prix fixe dinners delivered with "spot-on" service; "outstanding" "sommelier"-selected "local" and "old-world" wine pairings gild the lily, but expect "wealthy tourists'" pricing; P.S. dinner served Thursday–Monday only.

Farmstead *Californian* | 20 | 22 | 19 | $44 |

St. Helena | Long Meadow Ranch | 738 Main St. (Charter Oak St.) | 707-963-9181 | www.farmsteadnapa.com

"The food could only be fresher if they moved the tables into the garden" gush advocates of this "rustic" Cal-New American with upscale prices in St. Helena, whose "large and barnish" environs "feel like you've been invited into the farmhouse" to dine "with the family"; however, "the acoustics are tough" and the service "occasionally" drifts "off-track" but it's "full of good intentions."

FOOD | DECOR | SERVICE | COST

Fig Cafe & Winebar *French*
25 | 20 | 24 | $35

Glen Ellen | 13690 Arnold Dr. (O'Donnell Ln.) | 707-938-2130 |
www.thefigcafe.com

Fans "almost hate" to hail this "hidden gem in Glen Ellen", because it'll
make the "wait for a table" even longer; but *c'est la vie* when you have
"top-notch" French bistro food combined with "no corkage – a big plus
in Wine Country" and "served with smiles and knowledge"
amid "quaint" decor.

Fish ⊘ *Seafood*
24 | 14 | 15 | $32

Sausalito | 350 Harbor Dr. (Gates 5 Rd.) | 415-331-3474 |
www.331fish.com

"Everyone and their dog" "queues up" at this Sausalito seafood shack,
waiting to "chow down" "with a clear conscience" on "locally sourced"
"sustainably caught fish" "so fresh it's like you're eating it straight
from the ocean"; some say the prices will "fillet your wallet" considering the "waterfront-dive atmosphere" but supporters swear it's "fresh,
fresh, fresh" and "fantastic."

Fish Story *Seafood*
18 | 21 | 19 | $45

Napa | Napa Riverfront | 790 Main St. (3rd St.) | 707-251-5600 |
www.fishstorynapa.com

Overlooking "the riverfront in Downtown Napa", this year-old all-day
seafooder hooks in a "mix of locals and tourists" who shell out big
clams for "straightforward", "sustainable" fish and "wines on tap" in
the "modern, attractive" setting replete with an "indoor aquarium";
"the concept is fine", "but something is missing" – "surprising, given
that it's a Lark Creek Group restaurant"; P.S. a post-Survey chef change
is not reflected in the Food score.

Flavor *Californian/Eclectic*
20 | 18 | 20 | $31

Santa Rosa | 96 Old Courthouse Sq. (bet. 3rd & 4th Sts.) |
707-573-9600 | www.flavorbistro.com

"Locals meet" at this "low-key" bistro with "great buzz" "on Santa
Rosa's Courthouse Square", drawn by the "varied" Cal-Eclectic edibles
and the beers, all at a "reasonable price"; but while "widely accommodating", the menu contains "nothing exciting" and the service is often
"distracted", leaving skeptics to say the "flavor is" "lacking" here.

Fort Bragg Bakery ⊠Ⓜ⊘ *Bakery/Eclectic*
▽ 22 | 14 | 18 | $17

Fort Bragg | 360 N. Franklin St. (Laurel St.) | 707-964-9647 |
www.fortbraggbakery.com

"In working-class Fort Bragg", this "wonderful bakery" run by
Christopher Kump (ex Cafe Beaujolais) is a "cool" place for breakfast
or lunch, offering "decadent" pastries, "really good crusty bread" and
organic, "outstanding pizza" from the "wood-fired oven"; get "the
goods to go" or washed down with local beer and apple juice on the
tiny, "casual" premises.

NEW Frank and Ernie's *Steak*
- | - | - | M

Healdsburg | 9 Mitchell Ln. (Healdsburg Ave.) | 707-433-2147
"Finally, a reasonably priced restaurant in Healdsburg" say supporters of
this newcomer where "the locals are flooding in" for "good simple steaks,
burgers and great fries" – and "a real bar", to boot; if cynics sniff it's
"nothing exciting", friends of Frank retort it's fair fare "for the rest of us."

Frantoio   *Italian*

20 | 20 | 21 | $42

Mill Valley | 152 Shoreline Hwy. (Hwy. 101) | 415-289-5777 | www.frantoio.com

"Home away from home" for regulars, this "comfortable" trattoria, set in a "peaked-ceiling room with a modern operating olive oil press", brings "true Italian flavors" to Mill Valley; perhaps it's "a bit inconsistent" – the "kitchen goes from solid to inspired" and the service "declines when they get too busy" – but for a dinner that "doesn't kill the wallet", it's "superior" (now, "if only they'd change" the location "next to a motel").

Fremont Diner   *Diner*

▽ 21 | 15 | 16 | $21

Sonoma | 2698 Fremont Dr. (S. Central Ave.) | 707-938-7370

"Take a break from the pretentious Wine Country" when you step into this "funky with a capital 'F'" roadside diner (it's literally "almost in the road") "just outside Sonoma"; "if you are craving Southern cookin'", you'll enjoy the "hearty breakfasts", pulled pork sandwiches and "soda served in mason jars", despite the "so-so service" and "extremely limited" seating; P.S. it's currently open through lunch, but rumor has it "they are soon to add dinner."

☑ French Laundry   *American/French*

29 | 27 | 28 | $297

Yountville | 6640 Washington St. (Creek St.) | 707-944-2380 | www.frenchlaundry.com

Like a "natural wonder", Thomas Keller's "rarified" stone "temple of gastronomy" in Yountville bedazzles surveyors with tasting menus of New American–French fare that "defies description" delivered with "service that borders on clairvoyant", creating an "absolutely amazing" "four-hour dream" evening or afternoon (Friday–Sunday) "of culinary theater" by a "master"; "it takes an act of God to snare a slot" and the "incredible" wine list looks to have "500% markup", but like a "Chanel suit", "if you have to ask" if it's "worth the money", you're "not worthy."

NEW Fresh by

▽ 24 | 18 | 18 | $28

Lisa Hemenway   *Californian/French*

Santa Rosa | 5755 Mountain Hawk Way (Hwy. 12) | 707-595-1048 | www.freshbylisahemenway.com

Whether it's "a market, a restaurant" or "a cafe", this hybrid, "tucked inside a high-end grocery store", is a "great addition to the local foodie scene" in Santa Rosa offering Californian-French "comfort food at amazing prices" (be sure to "snag one of the pot pies"); the staff's still a bit "wet behind the ears", but chef-owner Lisa Hemenway's "expertise in creating a dining experience for everyone shines through."

Fumé Bistro & Bar   *American*

19 | 16 | 21 | $42

Napa | 4050 Byway E. (Avalon Ct.) | 707-257-1999 | www.fumebistro.com

Fans say "Napa Valley's number one sleeper" is this New American offering a "familiar menu" that's "attractive to a broad range of tastes"; the "crazy paintings on the walls" are "a major detractor", but the "comfortable atmosphere" created by the staff makes it a favorite "for locals that don't have tourist money."

Gary Chu's ☒ *Chinese*   22 | 17 | 20 | $34

Santa Rosa | 611 Fifth St. (bet. D St. & Mendocino Ave.) |
707-526-5840 | www.garychus.com

"Good Chinese is scarce in the Wine Country", but "masterfully pre-pared" Mandarin and Sichuan dishes made with "ultrafresh ingredients" make this Santa Rosa eatery "best of the breed"; if connoisseurs quibble it's a "far cry from the quality served in SF", the "understated service" and "reasonable price" "continue to draw them in."

Girl & the Fig *French*   23 | 21 | 22 | $45

Sonoma | Sonoma Hotel | 110 W. Spain St. (1st St.) | 707-938-3634 |
www.thegirlandthefig.com

From the burgers "done so right" to an "amazing cheese plate" and the "interesting twists" on French standards, "wonderful food abounds" at this "down-to-earth" "corner of Provence on the corner" of the square; the "cozy setting encourages flirtation", as does the "remarkable" Cal-Rhône selection and "vibrant" staff; so, while it "can be crowded" (and "overrun with tourists"), it remains "the place to go in Sonoma."

Gott's Roadside *Diner*   21 | 13 | 15 | $19
(fka Taylor's Automatic Refresher)

Napa | Oxbow Public Mkt. | 644 First St. (bet. Silverado Trail & Soscol Ave.) |
707-224-6900

St. Helena | 933 Main St. (Pope St.) | 707-963-3486
www.gottsroadside.com

"Super on a sunny day", since you "sit outside" at "picnic tables", these "nostalgic" "self-serve" "burger joints" are "a perfect antidote to all the fancy-pants dining" in the Wine Country offering "delicious all-American" fare and a "diverse" wine list in the "most varied menu of any roadside resto"; the frugal balk at "fast food at restaurant prices" and others skewer the "long lines" and "lackluster service", but most maintain "Gott's has got it right"; P.S. the Napa and SF offshoots have indoor tables too.

Guaymas *Mexican*   17 | 21 | 16 | $36

Tiburon | 5 Main St. (Tiburon Blvd.) | 415-435-6300 |
www.guaymasrestaurant.com

The "dynamite view" "of the bay and San Francisco skyline" "is the biggest selling point" at this "festive" Mexican seafooder with a "prime location" on Tiburon's waterfront; the "upscale" menu meanders from "mediocre to delicious" (and it's "no bargain" to boot), but that's all "incidental" insist vista-ficionados, who "pick a seat on the deck" and sip "strong" margaritas ("the best item" on offer), obliterating the memory of the "marginal service."

Hana Japanese Restaurant *Japanese*   25 | 16 | 23 | $46

Rohnert Park | 101 Golf Course Dr. (Roberts Lake Rd.) |
707-586-0270 | www.hanajapanese.com

"Omakase, OMG" gush groupies of this "admirable Japanese", a "surprise find in Rohnert Park" where chef-owner "Ken-san keeps a tight watch over the kitchen and sushi bar" while turning out "outstanding" cooked entrees and a "wide selection of fish, including less common choices"; a "huge selection of sakes" and "pleasant, prompt service" add to the appeal, so "who cares if it's in a weird strip-mall zone?"

Harmony Restaurant *Chinese*
20 | 20 | 19 | $31

Mill Valley | Strawberry Vill. | 800 Redwood Hwy. (Belvedere Dr.) |
415-381-5300 | www.harmonyrestaurantgroup.com

"Creative chefs" who "love vegetables" put a "Marin-style" spin on
Chinese chow by putting in "fresh" (and often "organic") "local ingredients" while leaving out the MSG at this midpriced Mill Valley spot;
just "don't be fooled" by the "shopping-center" setting, because the
dim sum (available for both lunch and dinner) is "loaded with flavor"
and "dumpling fans will be in heaven."

Harvest Moon Café *Californian/Mediterranean*
24 | 18 | 23 | $45

Sonoma | 487 First St. W. (Napa St.) | 707-933-8160 |
www.harvestmooncafesonoma.com

Locals "pass up the big names" for this "wonderful" "mellow" "little
gem on Sonoma square", where a "friendly" husband-and-wife team
creates "delightful memories nightly"; the "fantastic" Cal-Med "menu
changes with whatever is the freshest fare of the day", but always
comes at "extremely fair prices", and since the Provençal-inspired dining room overlooking the "tiny kitchen" is "somewhat cramped", the
"outdoor garden" "is the place to be", particularly "on Wednesdays
when they screen movies."

Healdsburg Bar & Grill *American*
18 | 15 | 16 | $32

Healdsburg | 245 Healdsburg Ave. (bet. Matheson & Mill Sts.) |
707-433-3333 | www.healdsburgbarandgrill.com

"Just what a bar and grill should be", this "casual" "burger joint" in
Healdsburg "from the Cyrus team" serves "incredibly tasty" American
"basics" with the usual distractions ("esoteric brews" and "sports on
the tubes") and no corkage to boot; it's "often too loud", and "spotty"
service mars "the hype", but the "beautiful" "patio" is the "perfect lunch
or dinner spot" when wearing "your biker gear or vineyard jeans."

☒ Hog Island Oyster Co. & Bar *Seafood*
25 | 17 | 20 | $35

Napa | Oxbow Public Mkt. | 610 First St. (bet. Silverado Trail &
Soscol Ave.) | 707-251-8113 | www.hogislandoysters.com
See review in City of San Francisco Directory.

Hopmonk Tavern *Eclectic*
18 | 19 | 18 | $30

Sebastopol | 230 Petaluma Ave. (bet. Abbott Ave. & Burnett St.) |
707-829-7300
NEW **Sonoma** | 691 Broadway (Andrieux St.) | 707-935-9100
www.hopmonk.com

"It's all about the beers" at this "hoppin' place in Sebastopol" (from
Dean Biersch of Gordon Biersch) where a "stunning" list of brews
complements a "solid" menu of midpriced Eclectic "modern pub"
grub; the "outstanding" patio and "beer garden" plus "friendly staff"
make for a "perfect afternoon", while most nights have "live music",
keeping the vibe "loud and fun"; P.S. "the new sister restaurant in
Sonoma" "is really catching on with locals."

Hot Box Grill ☒ *Californian*
▽ 23 | 11 | 21 | $49

Sonoma | 18350 Hwy. 12 (Calle Del Monte) | 707-939-8383 |
www.hotboxgrill.com

"Don't let the unusual location turn you off" – this new, "small"
Highway 12 roadside spot is run by a "former chef at Cafe La Haye",

and he's offering "explosions of tasty, naughty" Californian food like duck fat fries with béarnaise sauce and locally sourced wines served in carafes; the "uptown prices for downscale decor" are not so hot, but early supporters say this is a "super-addition to the Sonoma area."

Hurley's Restaurant & Bar *Californian/Mediterranean*

21 | 19 | 22 | $45

Yountville | 6518 Washington St. (Yount St.) | 707-944-2345 | www.hurleysrestaurant.com

At this "humble gem in Yountville", "chef Bob Hurley continues to make magic" with "hearty" Cal-Med fare and "wild-game dishes", offering "refreshingly unpretentious" fare and service "in the land of the celebrity chef"; while "there are better places (and more expensive)" in town, "no corkage" and "killer" "vintner lunch" specials keep it a "reliable standby", whether in the "comfortable" dining room or out on the patio with a "view of the mountains and vineyards."

Il Davide ⓜ *Italian*

24 | 19 | 24 | $40

San Rafael | 901 A St. (bet. 3rd & 4th Sts.) | 415-454-8080 | www.ildavide.net

This "warm" San Rafael "neighborhood Italian" is "an enduring favorite" – with imporved Food and Service scores to show it – where "beautifully prepared" Tuscan fare, including "excellent" "homemade" pastas, is a "solid value"; the "caring" staff "makes you feel at home", and even chef /co-owner David himself "pays personal attention to every table"; just remember there are "lots of regulars", which is why some "recommend reservations."

Il Fornaio *Italian*

20 | 20 | 20 | $39

Corte Madera | Town Ctr. Corte Madera | 223 Corte Madera Town Ctr. (Madera Blvd.) | 415-927-4400 | www.ilfornaio.com

See review in City of San Francisco Directory.

Ⓩ In-N-Out Burger ◑ *Burgers*

21 | 10 | 18 | $9

Mill Valley | 798 Redwood Hwy. (Belvedere Dr.)
Napa | 820 Imola Ave./Hwy. 121 (Napa Vallejo Hwy.)
800-786-1000 | www.in-n-out.com

See review in City of San Francisco Directory.

Insalata's *Mediterranean*

24 | 22 | 22 | $46

San Anselmo | 120 Sir Francis Drake Blvd. (Barber Ave.) | 415-457-7700 | www.insalatas.com

An "open and airy" dining room is a "charming setting" for chef-owner Heidi Krahling's "imaginative" Mediterranean fare built with "locally sourced" and "sustainable" ingredients; San Anselmans are "never disappointed" with the "wonderfully seasoned" offerings including "meat-free entrees" and the "professional" service that make it "impressive in a quiet, consistent way"; P.S. a "take-out counter" caters to those on the run.

Jimtown Store *Deli*

21 | 16 | 15 | $19

Healdsburg | 6706 Hwy. 128 (Alexander Valley Rd.) | 707-433-1212 | www.jimtown.com

"Go for a sandwich or salad, stay for the vintage candy and gifts" at this "funky", "high-quality deli"/general store "in the heart of Anderson Valley"; yes, it's "a little pricey", but it's a "great place to break up the

FOOD | DECOR | SERVICE | COST

day" when hitting Healdsburg's wineries, "and the shopping might make you laugh"; P.S. closes at 5 PM, and earlier in off-season.

Joe's Taco Lounge & Salsaria *Mexican* | 20 | 17 | 18 | $18 |

Mill Valley | 382 Miller Ave. (bet. Evergreen & Montford Aves.) | 415-383-8164

"Hike Mount Tam" and then "take your grubby self here for sustenance" suggest supporters of this "cheerful" Mill Valley Mexican with "endless bottles of hot sauce lined up on the walls"; the "fish tacos rock", and all the "fresh" fare is "very inexpensive", but even the "efficient" and "super-friendly" servers can't keep up with the "young families" at times, so "go late" if you want to arrive "after the kids" or avoid the "crazy" "crowds."

John Ash & Co. *Californian* | 24 | 26 | 24 | $61 |

Santa Rosa | 4330 Barnes Rd. (River Rd.) | 707-527-7687 | www.vintnersinn.com

"Though John Ash is long gone from the premises", this Santa Rosa standby, "blessed with lovely decor" in a "beautiful vineyard setting", is "still one of the best choices" "after a long afternoon of wine tasting" or a "special night out", "particularly if you can grab a table outside" overlooking "Pinot Noir land"; under "chef Tom Schmidt", the Cal menu's "on the rebound", augmented by local varietals "carefully chosen to please", but the bar also makes "a great stop to wet the whistle" and consume snacks.

Jole *American* | ▽ 27 | 18 | 23 | $47 |

Calistoga | Mount View Hotel | 1457 Lincoln Ave. (bet. Fair Way & Washington St.) | 707-942-5938 | www.jolerestaurant.com

"Fabulous" "tasting" menus and small plates of New American fare are "ingeniously prepared with farm-fresh ingredients" at this stylish Calistoga "treasure" that also offers a "super selection of interesting small-production wines" "available by the glass, half bottle or full bottle"; "service is slow but friendly" while nibblers enjoy "matching the various tastes and dishes."

K&L Bistro ⓼ *French* | 24 | 17 | 22 | $46 |

Sebastopol | 119 S. Main St. (bet. Bodega Ave. & Burnett St.) | 707-823-6614

"Simply spectacular" "Gallic comfort food" – "several notches above" the "standard" – makes this "likable" French "bistro in Sebastopol" a "hometown favorite"; it can get "awfully cramped" and "crowded", but the "good-value" vittles nevertheless "exceed expectations", and the "folksy" setting is "just plain comfortable" thanks to "delightful chef-owners" who lead the "warm" staff; P.S. an expansion is in the works.

Kenwood Ⓜ *American/French* | 23 | 23 | 24 | $48 |

Kenwood | 9900 Sonoma Hwy./Hwy. 12 (Libby Ave.) | 707-833-6326 | www.kenwoodrestaurant.com

In a "beautiful setting" "surrounded by" "rolling vineyards", this "reliable" roadhouse "off the beaten path" in Kenwood does a "fantastic job" with its "fairly extensive menu" of New American–French fare and "outstanding" service; "it may be a bit old school", but most maintain there's "nothing quite like" "a good glass of Pinot" on the patio, which "looks like a Renoir painting" "in the summer."

NEW Kitchen Door *Eclectic* — | — | — | I

Napa | Oxbow Public Mkt. | 644 First St. (bet. Silverado Trail & Soscal Ave.) | 707-226-1560 | www.kitchendoornapa.com

Fans of St. Helena's shuttered Martini House can again enjoy chef Todd Humphries' creations at this new quick-service Eclectic cafe in Napa's Oxbow Market, where inexpensive local, seasonal, handmade multiculti comfort food is meant for sharing; the space has a grange hall–chic vibe with no tablecloths, no waiters and no reservations (except for groups), though the open kitchen boasts a wood-fired rotisserie and the patio overlooks the Napa River.

La Boulange *Bakery* 21 | 16 | 16 | $16

Mill Valley | Strawberry Vill. | 800 Redwood Hwy. (Belvedere Dr.) | 415-381-1260

Novato | Hamilton Mktpl. | 5800 Nave Dr. (bet. N. Hamilton Pkwy. & Roblar Dr.) | 415-382-8594
www.laboulangebakery.com

See review in City of San Francisco Directory.

La Gare ⓂⓂ *French* ▽ 21 | 16 | 22 | $38

Santa Rosa | 208 Wilson St. (3rd St.) | 707-528-4355 | www.lagarerestaurant.com

The "superbly prepared" "beef Wellington and Châteaubriand" may not be "cutting-edge", but these and other "excellent menu choices" have kept this "traditional", "family-owned" French "a Santa Rosa fixture for some 30 years" (since 1979); though a minority dings it as "dated", most maintain it's a "real treat", since "everyone feels like family."

La Ginestra Ⓜ *Italian* 19 | 13 | 20 | $32

Mill Valley | 127 Throckmorton Ave. (bet. Madrona St. & Miller Ave.) | 415-388-0224

"Wonderful" "homestyle" fare, including "fabulous housemade ravioli", "fine pizzas" and "perfectly" cooked "fresh fish", is served by a "friendly" staff at this "popular" Mill Valley Southern Italian; the "plain setting" may be nothing to write home about, but loyalists who "eat more meals here" than elsewhere "love" the "moderate prices" and "unpretentious" "down-home setting"; P.S. no reservations.

LaSalette *Portuguese* 24 | 19 | 24 | $43

Sonoma | Mercado Ctr. | 452 First St. E. (bet. Napa & Spain Sts.) | 707-938-1927 | www.lasalette-restaurant.com

Chef-owner "Manny Azevedo is a master" at blending "his native dishes with Californian sensibilities" at this "charming" Portuguese "off the square" in Sonoma, where the "lusty" "homestyle" fare from the "wood-fire oven" boasts "beguiling" flavors; "cozy" "during cooler months", it also has a patio that's "welcome" on "warm evenings", and "friendly service" makes it "truly a treat" for a "reasonably priced" meal.

Las Camelias *Mexican* 20 | 14 | 19 | $28

San Rafael | 912 Lincoln Ave. (bet. 3rd & 4th Sts.) | 415-453-5850 | www.lascameliasrestaurant.com

"Excellent" "south-of-the-border" bites – "*muy auténtica*" and "always a good value" – make this "enduring Mexican classic" "worth a trip" to Downtown San Rafael; though tipplers tut that "they don't use real tequila in their margaritas" (they serve a less-alcoholic agave version), "the owner's artwork adds a quirky flair" to the "cozy" dining room.

La Toque *French*   26 | 23 | 25 | $107

Napa | Westin Verasa | 1314 McKinstry St. (Soscol Ave.) | 707-257-5157 | www.latoque.com

"From the original in Los Angeles to this latest iteration in Napa", "toque of the town" Ken Frank shows that he "knows his craft and practices it with imagination and dedication"; the "relatively modern dining room in the Westin Verasa" may lack curb appeal, but the "outstanding" "mix-and-match" New French prix fixes (don't miss the "seasonal truffle menu"), delivered with "a lot of fanfare" and paired with "perfect, nuanced wines", make it a "great occasion restaurant."

Ledford House Ⓜ *California/Mediterranean*   ▽ 23 | 22 | 23 | $52

Albion | 3000 N. Hwy. 1 (Spring Grove Rd.) | 707-937-0282 | www.ledfordhouse.com

"Warm and inviting" owners ensure "everything runs smoothly" at this "unpretentious" Albion eatery where you can "watch the sun sink into the Pacific" along "the Mendocino coast"; the "spectacular view" is matched by the "marvelous" Cal-Med menu and "wonderful wine list", making it suitable for a "special occasion" or just to "sip a local gerwurtz" while listening to the nightly live jazz; P.S. closed Monday and Tuesday.

Left Bank *French*   19 | 20 | 19 | $41

Larkspur | Blue Rock Inn | 507 Magnolia Ave. (Ward St.) | 415-927-3331 | www.leftbank.com

"Simple" Gallic fare "expertly prepared" (if "not so sparklingly original") is the hallmark of these "buzzy" brasseries with "reasonably priced" outposts in Larkspur, Menlo Park and San Jose; service, though oft "friendly", "can be so-so", and critics cry it's "too noisy" for conversation, but partisans who like to "watch the world go by from an outdoor table" declare "there is none better" when you need a "French fix."

Little River Inn *California/Seafood*   22 | 21 | 24 | $45

Little River | Little River Inn | 7901 N. Hwy. 1 (Little River Airport Rd.) | 707-937-5942 | www.littleriverinn.com

Choose between the "beautiful" dining room with an "unexpected" "garden view" or "bliss at the bar", which boasts a "perfect" vista of the "Pacific coastline" at this "welcoming" "destination" near Mendocino; in addition to "delicious, expensive" Cal seafood and a "superb wine list", "buttery" "Swedish pancakes" seduce the brunch bunch who "spend the weekend" here for a "romantic" "getaway" (it's a "historic inn" as well).

Lotus Cuisine of India *Indian*   22 | 17 | 20 | $27

San Rafael | 704 Fourth St. (Tamalpais Ave.) | 415-456-5808 | www.lotusrestaurant.com

Anokha Cuisine of India *Indian*

Novato | 811 Grant Ave. (Reichert Ave.) | 415-892-3440 | www.anokharestaurant.com

Café Lotus *Indian*

Fairfax | 1912 Sir Francis Drake Blvd. (bet. Claus & Taylor Drs.) | 415-457-7836 | www.cafelotusfairfax.com

For "a reasonably priced visit to Delhi" North Bayers head to this trio where a "sweet staff" serves "Indian food done right", with a health-conscious bent and made "spicy if you ask"; the San Rafael original is "warm and inviting", especially "when they open the sliding roof", Novato's "hopping" and both offer "bargain" lunch buffets, while the cafe dishes out more casual, mostly organic bites.

MacCallum House *Californian*   24 | 24 | 23 | $53

Mendocino | MacCallum House Inn | 45020 Albion St. (bet. Hesser & Kasten Sts.) | 707-937-5763 | www.maccallumhouse.com

"Start your night in the Grey Whale Bar" sipping "spectacular artisanal cocktails made with fresh organic ingredients" before moving on to the "cozy", "warm" and "charming" Victorian dining room proffering "consistently excellent, creative" Californian fare at this Mendocino B&B; the wine list and service add to the "lovely experience" that's "worth the price" for a "romantic dinner" or other "special occasions"; P.S. there's a separate bar menu.

☒ Madrona Manor Ⓜ *American/French*   27 | 27 | 26 | $90

Healdsburg | Madrona Manor | 1001 Westside Rd. (W. Dry Creek Rd.) | 707-433-4231 | www.madronamanor.com

You'll surely "impress your date" "as soon as you drive onto the property" of this "elegant" "old Victorian with wonderful gardens" in Healdsburg, where "exquisite", "beautifully plated" French–New American à la carte meals and a "wonderful" chef's menu are offered with "wine pairings that are well conceived and generous"; "impeccable" service and "dimly lit" quarters add to the allure, though most save it for a "bank-breaking" "treat"; P.S. closed Monday and Tuesday.

NEW Mamma Pig's Ⓜ *American*   - | - | - | I
(fka Mirepoix)

Windsor | 275 Windsor River Rd. (Honsa Ave.) | 707-838-7447 | www.restaurantmirepoix.com

Hawking America's fab four – barbecue, burgers, bacon and beer – this down-home, counter-serve arrival in the former Mirepoix space (it's from the same owners) offers tri-tip, pulled pork, Texas-style brisket and an array of pig specialties – including pig on a stick (seared pork belly), bacon mac 'n' cheese and bacon waffles, accompanied by Moonlight Brewery beers and a few wines; rounding out the menu are sides such as baked beans and collards, along with housemade ice cream and pies.

Mammarella's Ⓢ *Italian*   ∇ 19 | 18 | 18 | $31

Napa | Napa Airport | 630 Airpark Rd. (Airport Blvd.) | 707-256-3441 | www.cafecoppola.com

See Cafe Zoetrope review in City of San Francisco Directory.

Marché aux Fleurs ⓈⓂ *French*   25 | 21 | 25 | $52

Ross | 23 Ross Common (Lagunitas Rd.) | 415-925-9200 | www.marcheauxfleursrestaurant.com

The "delightful couple" that owns this "intimate" bistro in Ross "make it seem like you are friends visiting their home", but it's unlikely your pals can prepare such "excellent" New French fare from fresh seasonal ingredients, or own such an "inspired" selection of "boutique" wines that "you won't find anywhere else"; all in all it's "so romantic", especially on a "warm night", when the "wonderful patio" resembles "Provence."

	FOOD	DECOR	SERVICE	COST

Marinitas *Mexican/Pan-Latin*

| | 20 | 21 | 18 | $34 |

San Anselmo | 218 Sir Francis Drake Blvd. (Bank St.) | 415-454-8900 | www.marinitas.net

"Always packed", this "inviting" San Anselmo "offshoot of Insalata's" is a "favorite" among "Marin-ites" enjoying a "limited" but "well-executed" lineup of "flavorful" Mexican and Pan-Latin bites in "kind of upscale" cantina quarters; the "terrific margaritas" fuel a "bustling" "bar scene", and Sunday brunch features an "interesting" Bloody Mary buffet.

Market *American*

| | 23 | 21 | 23 | $44 |

St. Helena | 1347 Main St. (bet. Adams St. & Hunt Ave.) | 707-963-3799 | www.marketsthelena.com

This "unhidden gem" in St. Helena stays "in high demand" with day-trippers and natives in the market for "affordable" "American comfort food" prepared with "pizzazz" and amiably served "along with excellent local wines" in a "rustic", fieldstone-lined space; "consistent" "quality and value" from a menu that "hits the spot" secures "a loyal clientele."

Max's Cafe of Corte Madera *Deli*

| | 17 | 15 | 17 | $27 |

Corte Madera | 60 Madera Blvd. (Hwy. 101) | 415-924-6297 | www.maxsworld.com

See review in City of San Francisco Directory.

Meadowood, The Grill *Californian*
(aka The Grill at Meadowood)

| | 22 | 22 | 24 | $49 |

St. Helena | Meadowood Napa Valley | 900 Meadowood Ln. (Silverado Trail) | 707-968-3144 | www.meadowood.com

"Locals" and visitors agree "it doesn't get much better" than the "magical setting" of this "casual" Californian "hidden" in St. Helena at the Meadowood resort, where you can dine "outside on the deck with a view down the fairways of the golf course" while being tended to by an "excellent" staff; the "standard grill fare" (served breakfast through dinner) is a "night-and-day difference" from its tonier "big brother upstairs", but it's "one of the most reliable" and "calming" places in the Napa Valley "that won't break the bank."

☑ Meadowood, The Restaurant ☒ *Californian*
(aka The Restaurant at Meadowood)

| | 28 | 27 | 27 | $163 |

St. Helena | Meadowood Napa Valley | 900 Meadowood Ln. (Silverado Trail) | 707-967-1205 | www.meadowood.com

Tucked away past the "guarded entrance" of St. Helena's Meadowood resort, this "special-occasion" hillside hideaway "surrounded by trees" and croquet lawns is an "absolutely gorgeous setting" for dining on "exquisite" Californian tasting menus by chef Christopher Kostow at "the top of his game", matched by a "deep wine list" and delivered by a staff that anticipates "every need"; "an open and expansive" room and details such as "Riedel crystal" place it "a world away from the routine dining-out experience", though it's one "you'll pay dearly for."

Melting Pot *Fondue*

| | 16 | 18 | 18 | $50 |

Larkspur | 125 E. Sir Francis Drake Blvd. (Larkspur Landing Circle) | 415-461-6358 | www.meltingpot.com

"When only fondue will do", surveyors head for these chain links where "eating hot cheese from a communal pot with a glass of wine in hand" makes for "a fun night out whether with the girls, a date or family"; Larkspur's "interesting" setting is "inside an old brick kiln" while San Mateo is in the train station, and if budget-watchers brand it "expensive for what it is" – i.e. "cooking for yourself" – "you gotta do it once."

Mendo Bistro   *American*   23 | 18 | 23 | $41

Fort Bragg | The Company Store | 301 N. Main St., 2nd fl. (Redwood Ave.) | 707-964-4974 | www.mendobistro.com

"If you're up this way", it's "worth the extra drive" to "pay homage" to chef Nicholas Petti at this "remarkable" Fort Bragg New American, which "reflects local sourcing" with a "something-for-everyone" menu "fit for foodies" ("the crab cakes are a must" in-season) paired with "well-priced" wines from area vintners; with a staff that's "hospitable to all" and "a second-floor view" of Downtown from the Arts and Crafts-inspired former Company Store, it's "a real treat" "every time."

Mendocino Café   *Eclectic*   20 | 16 | 19 | $33

Mendocino | 10451 Lansing St. (Albion St.) | 707-937-6141 | www.mendocinocafe.com

"A distinct bohemian feel" sets this "little" fixture apart from "the more touristy places in Mendo", as does a "healthy" and "tasty" selection of globe-trotting "Eclectic plates" à la the "house specialty" Thai burrito; the "relaxed" pace means service may "take a while", but the "humble setting" is heightened by a leafy deck with an "excellent view" and it continues "to pack 'em in."

Mendocino Hotel   *Californian*   18 | 21 | 19 | $42

Mendocino | Mendocino Hotel | 45080 Main St. (bet. Kasten & Lansing Sts.) | 707-937-0511 | www.mendocinohotel.com

"Well worth a visit" to admire the "beautiful setting", this "lovely old hotel" sports refurbished Victorian decor that's like a "charming" "step into the past" whether you fancy bistro bites under a stained-glass dome in the "genteel" Lobby Lounge or upmarket Californian cuisine matched with local vinos in the "quiet", antiques-adorned dining room; either way it aims to "please the palate", though it's the backdrop that'll make you "want to stay overnight."

Meritage Martini   ∇ 22 | 19 | 21 | $44
Oyster Bar & Grille   *Italian*

Sonoma | 165 W. Napa St. (bet. 1st & 2nd Sts.) | 707-938-9430 | www.sonomameritage.com

"Start off with oysters" and a "good" martini "at the bar with all the lo-cals" before moving on to "something from the grill" or the other "excellently prepared" fare of this "inventive" Northern Italian in Sonoma under "maestro chef"-owner Carlo Cavallo; "team service" helps make it a "great place to grab lunch" on a "sunny" weekend (or dinner any night of the week) and leaves its champions "champing at the bit to go back."

Model Bakery   *Bakery*   22 | 11 | 17 | $15

Napa | Oxbow Public Mkt. | 644 First St. (bet. Silverado Trail & Soscol Ave.) | 707-963-8192

St. Helena | 1357 Main St. (bet. Adams St. & Hunt Ave.) | 707-963-8192 www.themodelbakery.com

"Casual" "breakfast and lunch spots" from a mom-and-daughter team, this "reasonably priced" St. Helena bakery/cafe and its Napa "take-out" adjunct "really deliver" with "homemade" specialties "for every desire", including brick-oven pizza, sandwiches prepared with "fantastic" artisanal breads, "legendary English muffins" and "decadent pastries"; whether for picnic supplies or a "quick snack", they're a model of "old-fashioned goodness."

Monti's Rotisserie & Bar *American/Mediterranean*
20 | 19 | 21 | $37

Santa Rosa | Montgomery Vill. Shopping Ctr. | 714 Village Ct. (Farmers Ln.) | 707-568-4404 | www.starkrestaurants.com

"The aromas of the rotisserie lure you in" to this "comfortable" "family favorite" ("the place to meet and greet in Santa Rosa"), where "very good daily specials" join raw-bar bites and "heartier meat entrees" on the New American–Med menu; the location "in a shopping center" may be "a bit odd", but admirers agree it's still "charming", perhaps because "the price is right" and "service is always spot on."

Moosse Café *Californian*
22 | 18 | 22 | $44

Mendocino | The Blue Heron Inn | 390 Kasten St. (Albion St.) | 707-937-4323 | www.themoosse.com

"A wonderful surprise" "in the heart of Mendocino", this "gem" anchoring the quaint Blue Heron Inn is a "top local spot" "for lunch or a light dinner" with a "seasonal menu" of "delightful" Californian fare set down by "lovely" servers who "remember you year after year"; a "gorgeous garden" with ocean views offsets the interior's "tight quarters", and most sojourners say they'd "go back in a heartbeat."

Morimoto Napa *Japanese*
26 | 24 | 22 | $77

Napa | 610 Main St. (5th St.) | 707-252-1600 | www.morimotonapa.com

Morimoto's Downtown Napa "kitchen stadium" with a "beautiful view" of the river is "flashy" and "splashy", just like the "television star" himself, but the "artistic", "innovative" Japanese "creations" and "fanatically fresh" sushi ably served in a "strikingly modern" setting are a welcome "relief" from the typical "Wine Country" stops – even with a bar that's "six deep"; *Iron Chef* fans don't mind the steep tabs and "cacophony" insisting just the chance to "have your tofu freshly made by the big man himself" is worth all the "hype."

Murray Circle *Californian*
24 | 25 | 23 | $68

Sausalito | Cavallo Point Resort in Fort Baker | 602 Murray Circle (Sausalito Lateral Rd.) | 415-339-4750 | www.murraycircle.com

Don your "fedora and bring your gal" to this "classy" Sausalito spot just "past the GG Bridge" offering "super-delicious", "creative" Californian meals in an "old army fort" that feels like a "different world" with its "serene postcard setting" and "service to match"; whether for "executive lunch", Sunday brunch "on the porch" or appetizers "by the fireplace" bar, it's "all-around terrific"; P.S. a post-Survey chef change may outdate the Food score.

⊠ Mustards Grill *American/Californian*
25 | 19 | 22 | $49

Yountville | 7399 St. Helena Hwy./Hwy. 29 (bet. Oakville Grade Rd. & Washington St.) | 707-944-2424 | www.mustardsgrill.com

Blink and "you might drive by" chef Cindy Pawlcyn's "casual yet refined" "gourmet truck stop" deep in Yountville that's "still packing them in" "after all these years" with its "wonderful roadhouse ambi-

FOOD DECOR SERVICE COST

ance", "friendly" service and "plentiful", "down-home" Cal–New American meals "straight from the garden out back"; despite "more upscale" tabs and being "noisy and rushed", it's always "welcoming", even "at the bar" that's filled with "locals", "wine geeks" and other "happy" "tourists" "slumming it" without reservations.

Napa General Store *Californian/Eclectic*   18 | 15 | 18 | $26

Napa | Hatt/Napa Mill Bldg. | 540 Main St. (5th St.) | 707-259-0762 | www.napageneralstore.com

"Fun for breakfast" or "a leisurely lunch", this rustic culinary emporium's cafe provides "a varied menu" of "dependable" Cal-Eclectic eats in a converted feed mill with patio seating "overlooking the Napa River"; it's also "convenient" for provisioning "your picnic in the vineyards", and the new wine-tasting bar offers a chance to sample select vintages from small local producers; P.S. closes at 5 PM.

Napa Valley Wine Train *Californian*   18 | 22 | 21 | $75

Napa | 1275 McKinstry St. (bet.1st St. & Soscol Ave.) | 707-253-2111 | www.winetrain.com

Taking one of the "beautiful" "period dining cars" on "a slow ride through Napa Valley" while "attentive" servers deliver a "rolling gourmet meal" of "excellent" Californian cuisine is a "leisurely" "way to eat, drink and sightsee" all at the same time; the experience "gets a lot of flack" for catering to "tourists", and it's "pricey" as well, but most maintain even locals should "do it once" so they can pretend to "be a railroad baron for a day."

Neela's ⓜ *Indian*   24 | 19 | 22 | $36

Napa | 975 Clinton St. (Main St.) | 707-226-9988 | www.neelasnapa.com

"Run, don't walk to this bastion of fine Indian cooking" urge Napa fans of Neela Paniz (ex LA's Bombay Cafe) who promise you'll be "well-fed" with "outstanding" perfectly spiced pan-regional dinners and prix fixe Thali lunches; prices are relatively "high" and service can be "very slow", but the setting is "attractive", plus "vegetarian evenings" and Bollywood videos in the bar help "keep things interesting."

Nick's Cove *Californian*   19 | 21 | 19 | $44

Marshall | Nick's Cove & Cottages | 23240 Hwy. 1 (4 mi. north of Marshall-Petaluma Rd.) | 415-723-1071 | www.nickscove.com

"It doesn't get much better than a plate of oysters harvested from right outside" wax surveyors who "laze away" the day at this "restored roadhouse" overlooking "wind-swept" Tomales Bay in Marshall; it's a "must" for "fresh" (if "pricey") Californian seafood when "you're cruising along" "the coast", if "just to get a drink and walk to the end of the pier" to enjoy "the view at sunset"; P.S. ownership changed post-Survey.

955 Ukiah ⓜ *American/French*   25 | 19 | 24 | $44

Mendocino | 955 Ukiah St. (School St.) | 707-937-1955 | www.955restaurant.com

"Charming" and "always welcoming", this "upscale" Mendocino New American–French lures "a lot of locals" for its "excellent" cuisine made with "fresh" ingredients and delivered by "knowledgeable servers"; "homey", "comfortable" decor adds to the "intimate dining" experience, and acolytes assure "you can't go wrong" here.

Norman Rose Tavern *American*

FOOD	DECOR	SERVICE	COST
20	19	19	$32

Napa | 1401 First St. (Franklin St.) | 707-258-1516 |
www.normanrosenapa.com

"Popular day and night", this "casual", "convivial" Downtown Napa hangout from the Azzurro crew purveys "good ol' American" "saloon food" (notably the "superb" burgers) chased with "brewpub beers" and "wines by the glass"; while "barhoppers" and "sports" on the tube contribute to "the expected high noise level", the "collegial" vibe and "reasonable" cost are well liked by the "locals, and no wonder."

North Coast Brewing Company *American*

FOOD	DECOR	SERVICE	COST
18	17	20	$28

Fort Bragg | 455 N. Main St. (Pine St.) | 707-964-3400 |
www.northcoastbrewing.com

Located across the street from the Fort Bragg microbrewery crafting what quaffers call "some of the best brews" around, this rustic, "kid-friendly" American tavern is a natural "spot for a pub nosh" and some "fresh" "suds"; the midpriced fare's "decent" enough and the service has improved, but the main draw's the "beer selection."

Oco Time Ⓢ *Japanese*

FOOD	DECOR	SERVICE	COST
-	-	-	M

Ukiah | 111 W. Church St. (School St.) | 707-462-2422 |
www.ocotime.com

"Authentic Japanese village food is translated for California lifestyles" (e.g. a "strong emphasis on vegetarian" options and "organic and sustainable ingredients") at this cafe in Ukiah in a "down-home" setting; though it's relatively unknown to outsiders, "the lines form early" for its signature okonomiyaki (a multilayered savory pancake) as well as sushi, which is also available at its adjacent take-out annex, It's Time.

Oenotri *Italian*

FOOD	DECOR	SERVICE	COST
25	20	21	$47

Napa | Napa Sq. | 1425 First St. (bet. Franklin & School Sts.) |
707-252-1022 | www.oenotri.com

Opened in spring 2010 by two Oliveto alums, this Southern Italian is "not so new anymore, but they work as hard as if it were", turning out a "creative" rotating slate of "wonderful homemade pastas", "fantastic salumi" and "superb" Neapolitan-style pizzas, complemented by "extensive" Boot bottlings and "accommodating" servers; sadly, "it's not a secret" anymore, and "pricey" for the "undersize" portions, but it's emerged as one of the "new stars of Napa."

Olema Inn *Californian*

FOOD	DECOR	SERVICE	COST
18	21	18	$46

Olema | Olema Inn | 10000 Sir Francis Drake Blvd. (Hwy. 101) |
415-663-9559 | www.theolemainn.com

"If you're out that way (and it is out there)", this picturesque Olema inn is an "agreeable" stop-off where the Californian "comfort food" is enhanced by locally produced vinos and the "rustic elegance" of the "calming", whitewashed interior and back garden; however, it's "changed hands a number of times" and critics contend the cooking's only "fair" for the upmarket cost.

Osake Ⓢ *Californian/Japanese*

FOOD	DECOR	SERVICE	COST
▽ 24	19	21	$35

Santa Rosa | 2446 Patio Ct. (Farmers Ln.) | 707-542-8282 |
www.garychus.com

Chef-owner Gary Chu is "the man!" cheer finatics, who "sit at the sushi bar" and "let him pick rolls to make" while enjoying "his warmth and humor"; the other "creative" Cal-Japanese eats (including martini prawns that some are "still dreaming of") are "amazing" too, which is why it's a "neighborhood favorite", "even though" it's in a Santa Rosa "strip mall."

Osteria Stellina *Italian* | 23 | 17 | 21 | $44 |

Point Reyes Station | 11285 Hwy. 1 (bet. 2nd & 3rd Sts.) | 415-663-9988 | www.osteriastellina.com

A "delicious find in out-of-the-way Point Reyes Station", this Italian turns out "fabulous locavore food", like an "amazing goat" shoulder and "perfectly done" pizza with oysters; despite the "minimal rustic decor", it's "worth the drive" to "while away the afternoon" or enjoy a "romantic night out" enlivened with "local wines" and "friendly" service.

Oxbow Wine | ∇ 18 | 17 | 19 | $45 |
Merchant *Californian/Mediterranean*

Napa | Oxbow Public Mkt. | 610 First St. (bet. Silverado Trail & Soscol Ave.) | 707-257-5200 | www.oxbowwinemerchant.com

Newly relocated to the main hall among the Oxbow Public Market's "cool little shops", this Cal-Med retailer/eatery is like "the best food court you could ask for", with a vino bar decanting vintages from the stock on display and a "delicious variety" of charcuterie and artisanal fromage from the on-site cheese counter; it's a rare chance to "taste before buying", and the outdoor seating fronting the Napa River is a plus.

Pacific Catch *Seafood* | 19 | 16 | 18 | $26 |

Corte Madera | Town Ctr. Corte Madera | 133 Corte Madera Town Ctr. (off Hwy. 101) | 415-927-3474 | www.pacificcatch.com
See review in City of San Francisco Directory.

Pasta Pomodoro *Italian* | 16 | 13 | 17 | $23 |

Mill Valley | Strawberry Vill. | 800 Redwood Hwy. (Belvedere Dr.) | 415-388-1692 | www.pastapomodoro.com
See review in City of San Francisco Directory.

Patrona Restaurant & | - | - | - | E |
Lounge 🅂🅼 *Californian*

Ukiah | 130 W. Standley St. (School St.) | 707-462-9181 | www.patronarestaurant.com

This locavore Californian near Downtown's County Courthouse Square brings "fine dining" to Ukiah, proffering an "eclectic" menu (served all day) featuring "fresh", regionally sourced ingredients along with lots of "local" "wines-by-the-glass"; the old brick storefront with "modern, loungelike decor" makes for a "great vibe", and a well-stocked bar befits its calling as "the cornerstone" of the town's "nightlife."

Pearl 🅂🅼 *Californian* | ∇ 24 | 19 | 23 | $36 |

Napa | 1339 Pearl St. (bet. Franklin & Polk Sts.) | 707-224-9161 | www.therestaurantpearl.com

"Popular with locals" who consider it "the real pearl inside" "the ever more upscale oyster of the Downtown Napa restaurant" scene, this "long-standing" "hard-to-find" family-run bistro is worth seeking out for "fresh, fresh" bivalves along with "simple but well-prepared" Californian fare that "holds its own in the land of foodies"; it's all

	FOOD	DECOR	SERVICE	COST

served up by "professional" staffers for prices that provide "more bang for the buck than the tourist spots a few blocks south."

Peter Lowell's *Italian*

∇ 23	18	21	$35

Sebastopol | 7385 Healdsburg Ave. (Florence Ave.) | 707-829-1077 | www.peterlowells.com

This "tiny" "politically correct" LEED certified organic Italian cafe in Sebastopol turns out a "small" but "remarkably good" selection of "healthy" breakfasts, thin-crust pizza and a few token sustainably sourced fish and meat dishes, washed down with biodynamic wines; it's a "great" "casual" stop "on the way to the Sonoma coast", but the "limited" seating "requires sharing tables with strangers" (both inside and on the patio), and the "friendly" staff seems a tad green.

NEW Petite Syrah *Californian*
(fka Syrah)

-	-	-	M

Santa Rosa | 205 Fifth St. (Davis St.) | 707-568-4002 | www.petitesyrah.com

Changing with the times, chef-owner Josh Silvers has reinvented his 12-year-old bistro, Syrah, in Santa Rosa's Railroad Square into this more casual and affordable small-plates Californian, showcasing seasonal ingredients in cutting-edge creations served nonstop from lunch through dinner; while still offering seats overlooking the exhibition kitchen and in the atrium, the renovated space has added salvaged wood tables and bar-height tables ideal for sampling over two dozen wines by the three- or 5.5-ounce glass.

Piaci Pub & Pizzeria *Pizza*

∇ 25	18	22	$28

Fort Bragg | 120 W. Redwood Ave. (Hwy. 1) | 707-961-1133 | www.piacipizza.com

"The local Fort Braggarts" boast this "hole-in-the-wall" pub's "inventive" roster of "first-class" pizza is "very satisfying", "and if you like beer" it aims to oblige "with tons of microbrews on tap"; yes, it's "always crowded" and "noisy" and you might "have to search for the waiter", but it's also "one of the funnest" destinations "on the Mendocino coast."

Piatti *Italian*

19	19	19	$40

Mill Valley | 625 Redwood Hwy. (Hwy. 101) | 415-380-2525 | www.piatti.com
See review in East of San Francisco Directory.

Piazza D'Angelo *Italian*

20	19	21	$39

Mill Valley | 22 Miller Ave. (bet. Sunnyside & Throckmorton Aves.) | 415-380-2000 | www.piazzadangelo.com

This "stunningly popular" "place to be seen" "right on the square" in Mill Valley "never fails to please" fans of its "tasty" Italian eats, "attentive" staff and owners who are "always there"; attached to a "dynamic bar" filled with a "lively local crowd", it's a "reasonably priced" option for a "fun" night out, but "sit in back by the fireplace" if you left your "noise reduction headphones" home.

Pica Pica Maize Kitchen *Venezuelan*

21	12	16	$17

Napa | Oxbow Public Mkt. | 610 First St. (bet. Silverado Trail & Soscol Ave.) | 707-251-3757 | www.picapicakitchen.com

Get a "hard-to-come-by" taste of "Venezuelan fast food" at this Oxbow Market outlet (with an adjacent ceviche bar) and its Mission spin-off, which "fill a hungry void" with "fresh", "authentic" arepas and other "corn-based", "gluten-free" specialties dressed with "savory stuffings" and "tangy" salsas; both "flavorful" "and very affordable", they're "a must-try" "for something a little different."

Picco *Italian*   25 | 20 | 23 | $48

Larkspur | 320 Magnolia Ave. (King St.) | 415-924-0300 | www.restaurantpicco.com

Even diners who "hate sharing plates" happily "share the bounty" at this "wildly popular" Larkspur Cal-Italian (a more serious "sidekick to the popular Pizzeria Pico next door") turning out "vividly delicious" "familiar and innovative" dishes that are a "joy to look at, smell and eat"; the "precious" pricing and "deafening" sound level in the "rustic brick and redwood digs" detract slightly", but locals like the "capable" service, sophisticated bar scene and "imaginative" cooking.

Pine Cone Diner ⊅ *Diner*   ▽ 23 | 15 | 18 | $20

Point Reyes Station | 60 Fourth St. (B St.) | 415-663-1536 | www.pineconediner.com

"Don't judge this book by its cover" recommend regulars of this "blast from the past" in Point Reyes Station, because although it's "not fancy", the "excellent" New American fare "satisfies"; they "only serve breakfast and lunch", but those "on the way home from an early hike" can join "locals" for an "ample plateful" of "quality", largely "organic" eats "in a diner setting" – as long as they don't mind "a lot of attitude" served alongside.

Pizza Antica *Pizza*   20 | 15 | 17 | $28

Mill Valley | Strawberry Vill. | 800 Redwood Hwy. (Belvedere Dr.) | 415-383-0600 | www.pizzaantica.com

See review in South of San Francisco Directory.

⊉ Pizzeria Picco *Pizza*   27 | 16 | 19 | $29

Larkspur | 316 Magnolia Ave. (King St.) | 415-945-8900 | www.pizzeriapicco.com

Larkspur locals "have waited many a summer evening" to "snag an outside table" or seat at the wine bar of co-chef/owner Bruce Hill's *piccolo* Southern Italian pizzeria, which slings "sensational" "Neapolitan thin, blistered-crust pie" "fresh out of the wood-burning oven"; "creative" salads, "great" vino and "to-die-for soft serve" ice cream (topped with "EVOO & salt if you dare") round out the casual meals here that, some advocates argue, "beats the restaurant"-sibling next door "hands down"; P.S. the pizzas can be "bought frozen to take home."

Pizzeria Tra Vigne *Pizza*   21 | 16 | 18 | $27

St. Helena | Inn at Southbridge | 1016 Main St. (bet. Charter Oak Ave. & Pope St.) | 707-967-9999 | www.pizzeriatravigne.com

"Wood-fired", "crispy pies" assure "it's all about the pizza" at this "quick, family-friendly" St. Helena "favorite" where other dishes like salads, "pasta and sandwiches" are also "pretty solid" and "no corkage" adds to the appeal; despite "lots of room" and a "courtyard", it's "crowded at peak hours", and if some dub the slices "nothing special", it's still a "lower-key option in the high-end Napa Valley restaurant scene" that's a "good deal" to boot.

	FOOD	DECOR	SERVICE	COST

NEW Plate Shop M *Californian* ▽ - | 20 | 19 | $49

Sausalito | 39 Caledonia St. (Johnson St.) | 415-887-9047 |
www.plateshop.net

With a name and "simple, attractive" decor paying homage to the
area's pre-WWII ship-building days, this newcomer is a "great addition to the budding Sausalito foodie scene"; despite an early chef
change, it's staying the course with seasonal, ingredient-driven Cal-
Med fare sourced from local farmers and ranchers as well as from its
own on-site herb garden, overseen by chef Peter Erickson (of the shuttered 1550 Hyde); the beverage program also incorporates backyard
clippings into über-fresh cocktails.

Poggio *Italian* 23 | 24 | 23 | $48

Sausalito | Casa Madrona | 777 Bridgeway (Bay St.) | 415-332-7771 |
www.poggiotrattoria.com

A "treat for any occasion", this "convivial" ristorante smack "in the
middle" of Sausalito's "tourist Mecca" ("equally known for its bar
scene" and "dependable" Tuscan eats) draws "both locals and visitors" to its "lovely", "dark-wood booths" and "sidewalk patio" for
watching "pedestrians strolling by" and "boats bobbing in the water
nearby"; it's "honestly priced", the waiters "allow you to eat at your
own pace" and "seasonal specials" "raise it up a notch", so all consid-
ered, "what's not to like?"

Press M *American/Steak* 24 | 24 | 23 | $75

St. Helena | 587 St. Helena Hwy. (White Ln.) | 707-967-0550 |
www.pressthelena.com

"You will leave amazed" promise impressed partisans of this "top-
drawer" St. Helena American, where "great grilling" yields an all-local
lineup of "fantastic" prime beef and sides that "excel", paired with a
"deep wine list" showcasing Napa reds; "exceptional" servers oversee
a "beautiful", "spacious" room that's akin to a "formal" farmhouse,
and while it's ultra-"pricey", the performance is "on par with any" and
there's a reduced menu in the "surprisingly fun bar."

Ravenous Cafe M *Californian/Eclectic* 23 | 17 | 20 | $40

Healdsburg | 420 Center St. (bet. North & Piper Sts.) | 707-431-1302

"After a day of wine tasting", revive over "creative and filling fare" at
this "cute" Healdsburg "favorite" in a converted Craftsman bungalow,
whose "handwritten menus" of "delectable" Cal-Eclectic dishes from
"local, seasonal ingredients" deliver "solid value for the money"; just
know that the "snug" space gets "crowded" with a "loyal following"
and some ravenous regulars find the "friendly staff" "a little slow
during the rush."

Ravens' Restaurant *Vegan* ▽ 26 | 23 | 25 | $41

Mendocino | Stanford Inn & Spa | 44850 Comptche Ukiah Rd. (Hwy. 1) |
707-937-5615 | www.ravensrestaurant.com

A "unique experience" of "the highest quality" wins raves for this
"wonderful" "retreat" in a coastal Mendocino inn, where "inventive"
vegetarian and vegan dishes featuring "the freshest" harvest from the
on-site organic farm burst "with flavor" whether for dinner or a "fabulous" breakfast; "warm" servers who "truly care" and "windows with
breathtaking views" mean it's "not to be missed" even by "meat eaters."

	FOOD	DECOR	SERVICE	COST

⊠ Redd Restaurant *Californian*   27 | 23 | 24 | $70

Yountville | 6480 Washington St. (bet. Mission St. & Oak Circle) | 707-944-2222 | www.reddnapavalley.com

Surveyors say Richard Reddington's "modern" "Yountville trendsetter" offering "exquisite presentations" of "inventive" Californian fare exhibiting a touch of "fusion" flair (the pork buns are "beyond belief") and delivered by a "West Coast–relaxed" staff is "as good as anywhere" in Napa but "without the pretension" and "over-the-top prices"; the "chic decor" "is either modern or cold depending" on who's talking, but "outdoor seating", brunch and a bar that "comes alive at night" provide additional reasons "the young and wealthies" are "Redd-y to come back."

Restaurant, The *American/Eclectic*   ▽ 25 | 22 | 21 | $37

Fort Bragg | 418 N. Main St. (Laurel St.) | 707-964-9800 | www.therestaurantfortbragg.com

"If you were to stop by Fort Bragg for any reason", this mom-and-pop joint is "a must" that's been cranking out the "freshest seafood" and other dependably "good" midpriced Eclectic–New American dinners for "30-plus years and counting"; it's virtually unknown to outsiders, but the "funky" storefront – filled with an extensive folk doll collection and oils from the local painter Olaf Palm – offers a "relaxing atmosphere" in which to enjoy a low-key meal.

Restaurant at Stevenswood *American*   ▽ 21 | 24 | 22 | $62

Little River | Stevenswood Lodge | 8211 Shoreline Hwy./N. Hwy. 1 (1 mi. south of Mendocino) | 707-937-2810 | www.stevenswood.com

A "dining experience" "to seek out on the Mendocino coast", this New American hideaway in a woodsy Little River resort furnishes a "limited" but "superb" menu in "comfortably art-influenced" environs warmed by "a fireplace" and "excellent" service; the "quiet and intimate" setting where twosomes "can carry on a conversation" is "not bad at all" "for a romantic" rendezvous; P.S. dinner is not served Wednesdays.

Risibisi *Italian*   ▽ 20 | 19 | 22 | $39

Petaluma | 154 Petaluma Blvd. N. (Washington St.) | 707-766-7600 | www.risibisirestaurant.com

Surveyors who have "stumbled upon" this "surprise find" "in the middle of Downtown Petaluma" "hope to return again" thanks to the "darling" decor, "wine list" and especially the "divine" (and "good value") Venetian cuisine like "fresh" pasta topped with "great sauces"; the owner pays "special attention" to diners and leads a staff that's "all heart", leading Italophiles to insist it's a "pleasure to eat" at this "delightful" "jewel."

Robata Grill & Sushi *Japanese*   ▽ 21 | 17 | 20 | $37

Mill Valley | 591 Redwood Hwy. (Seminary Dr.) | 415-381-8400 | www.robatagrill.com

"After all these years", this Mill Valley "neighborhood Japanese" remains "a Marin fave" for a "wide variety" of edibles encompassing "consistently tasty sushi" as well as "grilled stuff" hot off the robata; with its "predictable" performance and "accommodating" service, it's a "top choice" in these parts for everyday dining.

FOOD | DECOR | SERVICE | COST

Rocker Oysterfellers ⓜ American

▽ 21 | 17 | 21 | $39

Valley Ford | Valley Ford Hotel | 14415 Hwy. 1 (School St.) | 707-876-1983 | www.rockeroysterfellers.com

Dishing out "honest", "Southern-style" American chow that's surprisingly "delicious" for a "small-town restaurant", this "funky, laid-back" Valley Ford saloon with a "cute name" and "lots of locals" is a fine gathering spot "on the way to Bodega Bay"; it offers $1 Tomales Bays on Thursdays, live music on Sunday and "great hospitality" all the time; P.S. now serving Saturday lunch.

Rosso Pizzeria & Wine Bar Italian/Pizza

25 | 17 | 23 | $32

Santa Rosa | Creekside Ctr. | 53 Montgomery Dr. (3rd St.) | 707-544-3221 | www.rossopizzeria.com

While outwardly "unassuming", this Santa Rosa pie maestro "impresses" with "fabulous" "wafer-thin" pizza, flatbreads piled with "farm-fresh" salad fixings, "sublime homemade burrata" and "not-to-be-missed" daily specials ("roasted pig, yum!"); the site in a "shopping mall" is "nothing fancy", but between the "welcoming staff", "wonderful" wines and "lively" vibe with an "emphasis on soccer", it's "a delightful surprise"; there are plans to expand to Petluma and Sebastopol.

Rotisserie & Wine American

22 | 21 | 21 | $57

(fka Tyler Florence Rotisserie & Wine)

Napa | Napa Riverfront | 720 Main St. (3rd St.) | 707-254-8500 | www.rotisserieandwine.com

Getting in on the resurgence of Downtown Napa's riverfront, this Wine Country American with an adjacent kitchen store from "celeb" chef Tyler Florence (Wayfare Tavern, El Paseo) cranks out "interesting and creative" (if "expensive") "comfort-type" fare served "family-style" by a "friendly" staff; housemade pies and (unsurprisingly) "rotisserie items are the winners" in the "cool" (albeit "noisy") vino-themed indoor/outdoor setting where lunch is also served Wednesday–Sunday.

Royal Thai Thai

23 | 16 | 18 | $28

San Rafael | 610 Third St. (Irwin St.) | 415-485-1074 | www.royalthaisanrafael.com

Serving "fantastic", "full-of-flavor" Thai food, this "reliable" roost in San Rafael is a "bargain" according to royal subjects who praise the "bright" salads, "delicate" "lacy crêpe" and "especially good pad Thai"; a crowd-pleaser "for a quick lunch" or takeout "for decades", it's also "one of the best" options in town for a "value"-priced dinner, thanks to the "quaint" setting in a converted house.

Rustic, Francis's Favorites Italian

19 | 22 | 20 | $39

Geyserville | Francis Ford Coppola Winery | 300 Via Archimedes (Fredson Rd.) | 707-857-1400 | www.franciscoppolawinery.com

"Splendid views of the vineyards" and an "ambiance you can only find in the Wine Country" make Francis Ford Coppola's new winery venture "worth the very long drive" to Geyserville for pizza and other "home-style" Italian favorites proffered in a "giant" room boasting an Argentinean-style *parrilla* grill; critics sneer it's "more of a theme park than a restaurant", overrun with "kids swimming" and "movie memorabilia", but it's "pleasant enough" and a "professional staff and accessible prices" are the "frosting" on the cake.

	FOOD	DECOR	SERVICE	COST

Rutherford Grill *American*

| 23 | 20 | 22 | $42 |

Rutherford | 1180 Rutherford Rd. (Hwy. 29) | 707-963-1792 |
www.hillstone.com

The "updated" "American comfort food", like the signature "finger-licking ribs" from the "wood-burning oven", makes this "casual" Rutherford link in the Hillstone chain a "satisfying" "sunny day stop" for a "lunch break while wine tasting"; "no reservations" before 5 PM means "long waits", "especially during weekends", but the "accommodating" staff and "great" "no-corkage policy" make it a "fun" place to join the "Napa vintners" on the "pleasant" patio.

☑ Santé *Californian/French*

| 26 | 23 | 24 | $70 |

Sonoma | Fairmont Sonoma Mission Inn & Spa | 100 Boyes Blvd. (Sonoma Hwy.) | 707-939-2415 | www.fairmont.com

"This is a class act" affirm admirers of this Sonoma stalwart, which ups the ante with "amazing" but "nonfussy" Cal-French cuisine "prepared with real dedication" and paired with some 600 "excellent" vinos ("try the tasting menu for the full range of flavors"); "polite" service suits the "exclusive atmosphere", and though "you may need an extra glass of wine when you get the check", it's "definitely" an occasion to "splurge and enjoy."

NEW Sazon *Peruvian*

| - | - | - | M |

Santa Rosa | 1129 Sebastopol Rd. (McMinn Ave.) | 707-523-4346 | www.sazonsr.com

So "exciting to have Peruvian in Santa Rosa" say suburbanites who "love the ceviche" and other "excellent" midpriced fare that doesn't hold back on the sazon ('seasoning' in Spanish) at this "not-to-be missed" family-run newcomer, which also offers beer, wine and Inca Kola imported from the Andes; it's tiny, with just 30 seats, including six at the bar and a walk-up window hawking South American–flavored ice creams.

Schat's Courthouse Bakery ⊠ *Bakery*

| - | - | - | I |

Ukiah | 113 W. Perkins St. (bet. School & State Sts.) | 707-462-1670 | www.schats.com

A "good choice for lunch" or breakfast in "the heart of Downtown Ukiah", this "wonderful bakery" and counter-service cafe is a locals' "go-to place" for "tasty soups", "large salads" and "delicious" sandwiches built on "homemade bread", "followed by a sweet treat" and cup of Peet's Coffee; it closes at 6 PM, but "you can take home a loaf" "for enjoying later on."

☑ Scoma's *Seafood*

| 23 | 19 | 21 | $47 |

Sausalito | 588 Bridgeway (Princess St.) | 415-332-9551 | www.scomassausalito.com

See review in City of San Francisco Directory.

☑ Scopa Ⓜ *Italian*

| 26 | 18 | 22 | $45 |

Healdsburg | 109A Plaza St. (bet. Center St. & Healdsburg Ave.) | 707-433-5282 | www.scopahealdsburg.com

"Rustic Italian food" that "brings a tear to the eye – it's that good", a wine list containing "top-quality Chianti" plus regional vinos and staffers "wanting to please" add up to a "lively" evening at this sidewalk osteria "right off the square in Healdsburg"; true, seating's "tight" ("you get to know your neighbors") and it's "loud enough to cost you your hearing", but it's "justifiably popular"; P.S. "go for the Wednesday wine dinners, when local winemakers" "market their latest vintages."

NEW Shimo Modern Steak Ⓜ *Japanese/Steak* ∇ - | 23 | 28 | M

Healdsburg | 241 Healdsburg Ave. (bet. Matheson & Mill Sts.) | 707-433-6006 | www.shimomodernsteak.com

Less than a year after opening, this Healdsburg newcomer from Cyrus chef-owner Douglas Keane has downscaled from a "very elegant" Japanese-inspired modern steakhouse into a more casual, small-plates izakaya; you can still expect "nonpareil" service and a few "spectacularly flavorful and buttery-smooth" steaks, but now there's a customizable noodle bar (ramen or soba) plus other small plates offered at lunch and dinner, in both the bar area and modern-looking main dining room; P.S. the bar pours only sake, beer and cocktails, but wine lovers can BYO for no corkage.

Solbar *Californian* 26 | 23 | 25 | $56

Calistoga | Solage Resort | 755 Silverado Trail (bet. Brannan St. & Pickett Rd.) | 707-226-0850 | www.solbarnv.com

"Dueling" Californian menus (some "good-for-you", some "hedonistic"), "brilliantly prepared" by an ex-French Laundry chef and served adroitly by a staff "devoid of pretensions", "make for a refreshing combination" at this Calistoga spot "on the Silverado Trail"; its "quintessential" Wine Country setting, with a "modern but warm" interior and "terrific outdoor patio" with a "view of the pool" and fire pits, is ideal for an "elegant lunch between wineries" or a "heavenly dinner – and at "reasonable prices (for the Napa Valley)."

Sol Food *Puerto Rican* 23 | 15 | 16 | $19

San Rafael | 732 Fourth St. (Lincoln Ave.) | 415-451-4765
San Rafael | 901 Lincoln Ave. (3rd St.) | 415-451-4765
www.solfoodrestaurant.com

"Perfecto" for a "taste of the islands", these "addictive" San Rafaelites are a "solid" source of "filling" Puerto Rican "home cooking" doused in "spicy sauce" and priced at an "awesome value"; whether at the full-service Lincoln Avenue eatery with its "funky" "Borinqueño backdrop" or the nearby "to-go stand", they're "favorites of locals" albeit "not a place to linger or bring a first date."

Spoonbar *Mediterranean* 18 | 21 | 18 | $42

Healdsburg | H2hotel | 219 Healdsburg Ave. (bet. Mill & W. Matheson Sts.) | 707-433-7222 | www.spoonbar.com

Offering a "great respite from wine tasting" and the usual "high-priced spreads" in Healdsburg, this "ultramodern" "see-and-be-seen" Cal-Med eatery/late-night lounge attached to the H2hotel offers primo people-watching from its "lively" open-air bar and dining room filled with locals and tourists; the seasonal small plates are "good" enough, but revelers insist startender Scott Beattie's "artisanal" ingredient-driven classic cocktail program "tops everything", including the "rookie" service.

Stark's Steakhouse *Steak* - | - | - | E

Santa Rosa | 521 Adams St. (7th St.) | 707-546-5100 | www.starkssteakhouse.com

"A winner" in the Railroad Square section of Santa Rosa, this big-city meatery (sib to Monti's Rotisserie, Willi's Seafood and Willi's Wine

Bar) cossets carnivores with "damn good steak", "all the sides" and a well-rounded roster of local wines; the brick-lined setting adopts a vintage '40s feel – think chocolate-brown booths and firelight – that fits seamlessly with the retro bill of fare.

Starlight Wine Bar & Restaurant M *American*

▽ 22 | 24 | 21 | $41

Sebastopol | 6167 Sebastapol Ave. (bet. Morris St. & Petaluma Ave.) | 707-823-1943 | www.starlightwinebar.com

Installed in a converted Pullman coach sporting well-preserved "train decor" and deco accents, this Sebastopol vino junction engineers a "delicious" New American–Creole menu of "old standbys" matched with vintages from select small producers; akin to a wining and "dining car" run by "knowledgeable" folks who "love their job", most aboard consider it "an absolute treat."

Station House Cafe *Californian*

18 | 17 | 19 | $38

Point Reyes Station | 11180 State Rte. 1 (2nd St.) | 415-663-1515 | www.stationhousecafe.com

"The perfect place to go after a day on the trails" in West Marin, this "refuge" in "postcard-cute" Point Reyes Station "keeps locals happy and day-trippers satisfied" with its "enjoyable" "homestyle" Californian cuisine full of "local ingredients"; if some say the menu is the "same old, same old", outdoor enthusiasts always emerge with a "glow" thanks to "friendly" service and the "fragrant gardens"; P.S. closed Wednesday.

St. Orres *Californian*

23 | 25 | 23 | $61

Gualala | St. Orres Hotel | 36601 S. Hwy. 1 (Seaside School Rd.) | 707-884-3335 | www.saintorres.com

A "longtime favorite" "on the North Coast", this "special-occasion" Gualala getaway "overlooking the ocean" lures pilgrims with "interesting game dishes" and locally foraged all-inclusive Californian dinners; sure, the "blast-from-the-past fern-bar decor" and "quirky" menu ("red hots or popcorn in your salad?") "hasn't changed in 25 years" and service can be stiff, but devotees insist it's worth navigating the "windy" roads just to "sit in the spectacular dining room" set in an "onion-domed tower."

☒ Sushi Ran *Japanese*

28 | 21 | 23 | $59

Sausalito | 107 Caledonia St. (bet. Pine & Turney Sts.) | 415-332-3620 | www.sushiran.com

The "cult following" drives "over the bridge" and spends "a week's wages" for "Japan-like sushi" that "tastes as though plucked from the sea seconds before hitting your chopsticks" and "gorgeous", "cooked" "kaiseki dishes" served by the "gracious hosts" at this Sausalito stalwart; "parking is a pain" and they "pack you in like on a Tokyo subway", but lunch is a "bargain" and the easier to get into "cute wine bar" with "outside seating" delivers a real "sake-to-me experience."

Table Café ☒M *Californian*

▽ 22 | 13 | 19 | $24

Larkspur | 1167 Magnolia Ave. (Estelle Ave.) | 415-461-6787 | www.table-cafe.com

This "friendly" "local find" in Larkspur lends an "interesting and delicious" Californian spin to its signature dosas and other "healthy" daylight bites made with sustainable ingredients from the local farmer's market; although a "casual" setup with "not much sitting" space, it's "terrific for lunch" and an "affordable" stop-off for "home-made" desserts or "dinner to go" for your own table.

Table 128 *Californian*

- | - | - | E

Boonville | Boonville Hotel | 14050 Hwy. 128 (Lambert Ln.) | 707-895-2210 | www.boonvillehotel.com

Diners en route to Mendocino "always stop" at this Californian country kitchen in the Boonville Hotel presenting simple "but oh-so-good" "real food" served family-style; considering it's in the boondocks, the set dinners "can get pricey", and the "limited" options and hours (Thursday–Sunday in high season, Friday–Sunday only in winter) are somewhat inconvenient; still, come summer, the rustic Shaker-style venue offers "the best outdoor dining around."

Tavern at Lark Creek *American*

20 | 23 | 21 | $42

Larkspur | 234 Magnolia Ave. (Madrone Ave.) | 415-924-7766 | www.tavernatlarkcreek.com

A "lovely wooded setting" in a Victorian dwelling marks this "comfy" Larkspur New American, where the "high-quality" "homestyle" menu "offers something for everyone" in "tastefully" tavernesque surroundings with a skylight and patio "oasis"; sticklers still say it's "not as exciting" "since it went a little more casual", but the "continuing warm ambiance" and "reasonable prices" are "a winner" for most.

⚡ Terra *American*

27 | 24 | 26 | $73

St. Helena | 1345 Railroad Ave. (bet. Adams St. & Hunt Ave.) | 707-963-8931 | www.terrarestaurant.com

Just like at their San Francisco restaurant, Ame, Hiro Sone and Lissa Doumani's "classy", older St. Helena stalwart "continues to evoke the spirit of Japanese food" with "creative" New American prix fixes and "superlative desserts"; the "formal" dining room boasts "stone walls" and a "quiet", "romantic atmosphere" and "hits all the high notes" with "top-notch service"; alas, prices are steep, but at the "new", "more casual" adjacent Bar Terra, drop-ins can enjoy a "full bar and great small plates" for far "less."

Terrapin Creek 🅜 *Californian*

∇ 25 | 21 | 24 | $46

Bodega Bay | 1580 Eastshore Rd. (Hwy. 1) | 707-875-2700 | www.terrapincreekcafe.com

"Hidden away" in the "home of the chowderhouses", this Bodega Bay "gem" delivers "wonderful dining" courtesy of a "gracious" chef-owner couple whose "top-notch" Californian fare is "expertly prepared" and served with a "very personal touch" in "warm and inviting" cottage quarters; those in the know salute an "outstanding job" done "with verve" saying it's "certainly worth the drive"; P.S. open Thursday–Sunday.

Toast *American*

19 | 15 | 18 | $24

Mill Valley | 31 Sunnyside Ave. (bet. Blithedale & Miller Aves.) | 415-388-2500 | www.toastmillvalley.com
Novato | Hamilton Mktpl. | 5800 Nave Dr. (bet. N. Hamilton Pkwy. & Roblar Dr.) | 415-382-1144 | www.toastnovato.com

"An easy choice" when you're "out with the family", this "very casual" couple offers "ample" helpings of "decent" American "comfort food" "at fair prices" whether at the Mill Valley grill or the outsized Novato offshoot with an ultramodern design that reminds some "of a dorm cafeteria"; consensus calls them "solid performers for breakfast and lunch" though some sniff they're "too run-of-the-mill for dinner."

Tra Vigne *Italian*   24 | 24 | 22 | $57

St. Helena | 1050 Charter Oak Ave. (Main St.) | 707-963-4444 | www.travignerestaurant.com

"Despite its age", "there isn't a more pleasant place" to "sit among the vines" and dine than at this St. Helena "destination trattoria" that turns out handcrafted "Northern Italian" *cucina* in a "beautiful" villa setting with a "charming" Tuscan-inspired "courtyard"; "it's open all day" for whenever "your wine tour schedule dictates", and "there's no corkage charge" (making it a "real bargain") with service that's "not stuffy at all."

Tsukiji Sushi Ⓜ *Japanese*   ▽ 22 | 16 | 18 | $47

Mill Valley | 24 Sunnyside Ave. (Parkwood St.) | 415-383-1382 | www.tsukijisushimv.com

Named after the renowned "fish market in Tokyo", this easygoing Mill Valley Japanese imports seafood to craft a strong lineup of "very fresh" and "authentic sushi" via the blade of ex–Sushi Ran chef Haruo Komatsu; the traditional cooked dishes, "interesting sake choices" and "relaxing" atmospherics are also "a welcome addition to Downtown", though a few tougher customers shrug "nice try."

Ubuntu *Californian/Vegan*   24 | 21 | 23 | $51

Napa | 1140 Main St. (Pearl St.) | 707-251-5656 | www.ubuntunapa.com

Who knew "roots and tubers could be so good"? marvel omnivores who eat their way through a veritable "garden constructed with tweezers" at this "phenomenal", ultra-"Zen" Californian in Napa ("there's a yoga studio upstairs, after all") that continues to take vegan and "vegetarian cooking to a whole new level"; the wine list is "great" and the staff will "guide you" through the "weird stuff", so while "skimpy portions and high prices" leave some wondering "what all the fuss is about", most predict "uwantu go back, again and again."

Ukiah Brewing Company & Restaurant *Pub Food*   - | - | - | M

Ukiah | 102 S. State St. (Perkins St.) | 707-468-5898 | www.ukiahbrewingco.com

Crunchy sorts "on a trip north" can sip and scarf at this eco-friendly Ukiah microbrewery's adjoining eatery, where the menu of burgers and other "organic pub grub" abounds with vegan and vegetarian picks; slackers who can abide the "bar atmosphere" "really enjoy this place", though many actually "go for" the house-brand suds and nightly bands.

Underwood Bar & Bistro Ⓜ *Mediterranean*   23 | 20 | 21 | $42

Graton | 9113 Graton Rd. (Edison St.) | 707-823-7023 | www.underwoodgraton.com

"Quite a surprise" in the "tiny town of Graton", this "upbeat" "rural gem" is a "favorite watering hole" for a "who's who" of "West County winemakers" where the "delicious" Med tapas and entrees, "killer" vino list and "mixologist" cocktails deliver "quality while avoiding any pretension"; tended by a "professional staff", it's "always bustling" and the "noise level's very high", so "bring a pad and pencil to communicate."

Uva Trattoria & Bar Ⓜ *Italian* ▽ 21 | 17 | 21 | $45

Napa | 1040 Clinton St. (bet. Brown & Main Sts.) | 707-255-6646 | www.uvatrattoria.com

For "down-home Italian, reasonably priced", this "local" "hangout" in Downtown Napa offers a "wide menu of well-prepared dishes" and an "extensive wine list"; free corkage on your first BYO bottle and no-cover "cool jazz" some nights make for a "satisfying evening" and "a great alternative to the pricey tourist eateries."

Vin Antico Ⓜ *Italian* 23 | 23 | 22 | $41

San Rafael | 881 Fourth St. (bet. Cijos St. & Lootens Pl.) | 415-454-4492 | www.vinantico.com

"The buzz is big" at this "dark" and "cozy" little trattoria in San Rafael, a "great date restaurant" where chef Ed Vigil puts out "fantastic" Cal-Italian fare that "shines"; "space is limited" and the tables "close", but enthusiasts enjoy the "intimacy" and "warm", "attentive service", and since the "imaginative eats are a "bargain" compared to big-"city prices", fans affirm its "a real find."

Volpi's Ristorante & Bar Ⓜ *Italian* ▽ 19 | 18 | 21 | $36

Petaluma | 124 Washington St. (bet. Keller St. & Telephone Alley) | 707-762-2371

Go "back in time" in a setting with "red-checked tablecloths" and "Chianti bottles with a candle stuck in them" as a backdrop for "old-fashioned" Italian dishes served up "family-style" at this Petaluma stalwart; there's even "an old speakeasy bar" in the back of the historic building, and on lucky days, someone from the family breaks out an accordion.

Water Street Bistro *French* ▽ 22 | 15 | 18 | $26

Petaluma | 100 Petaluma Blvd. N. (Western Ave.) | 707-763-9563 | www.waterstreetbistro.net

Like "a little bit of France on the Petaluma River", this "sweet little bistro" is run by a "passionate" chef-owner who "lovingly" prepares "exquisite", Gallic-accented breakfast and lunch fare and "hard-to-resist" desserts priced "at a fraction of what it would cost elsewhere"; unsurprisingly, the "tiny, cramped interior" tends to be "crowded", so it's "best to" "sit outside" on the waterfront patio; P.S. monthly special dinners are by reservation only.

Willi's Seafood & Raw Bar *Seafood* 24 | 19 | 20 | $44

Healdsburg | 403 Healdsburg Ave. (North St.) | 707-433-9191 | www.willisseafood.net

Healdsburg habitués suggest you go with "a group" so you can "mix and match" the "amazing" seafood tapas (little "bites of heaven") and "awesome" raw-bar items, then "wash it all down" with one of their "specialty cocktails" or "always interesting wines" from "a lot of the local vineyards"; the "small portions" can "add up" "to big bucks", but "unpretentious" yet "professional" servers help make it a "delightful" destination, especially if you score "outdoor seating" "in the summer"; P.S. a post-Survey expansion is not reflected in the Decor score.

Willi's Wine Bar *Eclectic*

25 | 19 | 22 | $44

Santa Rosa | 4404 Old Redwood Hwy. (Ursuline Rd.) | 707-526-3096 | www.williswinebar.net

A "memorable" "sharing experience", this Santa Rosa "favorite" is an Eclectic "adventure" "even to well-traveled eaters" "nibbling away" on an "innovative" "array" of "perfectly executed small plates" while "sipping" flights and "various sized pours" of "wines from the area"; the "comfortable" room expands with a "back porch", and while the "grazing" can "add up" willy-nilly, "heaven in your mouth" is "worth the price tag."

Willow Wood
Market Cafe *Eclectic/Mediterranean*

23 | 17 | 18 | $30

Graton | 9020 Graton Rd. (Edison St.) | 707-823-0233 | www.willowwoodgraton.com

"*The* place for breakfast and lunch" "in rural Graton", this "friendly" cafe-cum-country store (sib to local nexus Underwood) "consistently" supplies "delicious" Eclectic-Med "home cooking" the natives proudly hail as "the best food you'll get at this price"; the "offbeat" digs and patio are "busy all the time", often with "out-of-towners" in need of a "pre- or post-winery" "sponge."

Wine Spectator Greystone *Californian*

21 | 22 | 21 | $55

St. Helena | Culinary Institute of America | 2555 Main St. (bet. Deer Park Rd. & Pratt Ave.) | 707-967-1010 | www.ciachef.edu

As part of the CIA's Left Coast campus, this St. Helena "ex-winery" sports a "show kitchen" where "student chefs" work alongside seasoned pros to turn out "quite good" Cal-Eclectic fare matched with an all-California, flight-intensive vino list; set in an "impressive" 19th-century "manor" with a terrace affording "a perfect view of Napa Valley", it's not cheap, but it's "a real treat" to be "treated so well."

Yankee Pier *New England/Seafood*

18 | 15 | 19 | $36

Larkspur | 286 Magnolia Ave. (bet. King St. & William Ave.) | 415-924-7676 | www.yankeepier.com

"Better than you might expect" for seafood "in suburbia", this "local chain" is a "family favorite" that's "pretty dependable" for "rockin'" "chowdah", lobster rolls and other "straightforward" New England faves in "casual" "clam shack" quarters that can get "busy" and "noisy"; still, mutineers maintain service "fluctuates" and the food's "just so-so" "for the price."

Zazu Ⓜ *American/Italian*

25 | 18 | 22 | $50

Santa Rosa | 3535 Guerneville Rd. (Willowside Rd.) | 707-523-4814 | www.zazurestaurant.com

You can "taste the provenance and the love" at this back-country Santa Rosa "roadhouse" "abuzz with locals and people who have come from afar" for married chef-owners Duskie Estes and John Stewart's "inventive" New American–Northern Italian "cuisine du terroir" featuring "produce from just outside the kitchen door" and "porktacular", home-cured black pig bacon; the "barnyard atmosphere" and "personable staff" add to the laid-back vibe, and while it's "rather pricey", the thrice-weekly "Pizza and Pinot Nights" provide some relief to the wallet."

Zin *American*

23 | 19 | 22 | $43

Healdsburg | 344 Center St. (North St.) | 707-473-0946 |
www.zinrestaurant.com

There's Zinfandel and "so much more" at this "comfy" Healdsburg
New American specializing in "Southern spins on local ingredients"
where "just about everything is housemade" with "fresh veggies right
out of their garden"; the "blue-plate specials" offer "bang for your
buck" in a "casual" setting with a "friendly staff", and while it's
certainly "not highbrow dining", fans say it's "not very far from it."

Zinsvalley ◐ *American*

∇ 17 | 16 | 18 | $43

Napa | 1106 First St. (Main St.) | 707-224-0695 | www.zinsvalley.com

"Full of energy and good-looking people", this New American in
Downtown Napa "has earned lots of local business over the years"
serving "comfort food with an extra flair" at "fair prices"; regulars say
the newer location is "not like the old place", though the "patio" has its
supporters, as does the "comfy bar" for a "liquid diet."

ZuZu *Spanish*

25 | 18 | 22 | $39

Napa | 829 Main St. (bet. 2nd & 3rd Sts.) | 707-224-8555 |
www.zuzunapa.com

Established on Napa's Riverfront long before it was 'revitalized', this
"busy" Spaniard is a "local" lunch and dinner favorite furnishing "excellent tapas" (both "classic and unusual ones") and "hard-to-find"
Iberian wines by the glass, ably paired by the staff to "truly enhance
the experience"; just remember – while it's "so much fun to try the little plates", the tabs "add up quickly"; P.S. it's "best" to "sit upstairs if
you want to have quiet conversation."

SOUTH OF SAN FRANCISCO

Top Food

<u>28</u> Manresa | *American* Aubergine | *Californian*	<u>26</u> Cafe Gibraltar | *Mediterranean* Plumed Horse | *Californian*
<u>27</u> Sierra Mar | *Cal./Eclectic* Marinus | *French* Le Papillon | *French* Kaygetsu | *Japanese* Passionfish | *Cal./Seafood* Baumé | *French* Evvia | *Greek* La Forêt | *Continental/French*	Flea St. Café | *Californian* Tamarine | *Vietnamese* Nick's on Main | *American* Dio Deka | *Greek* Alexander's | *Japanese/Steak* Village Pub | *American*
	<u>25</u> John Bentley's | *Californian* Navio | *American*

BY CUISINE

AMERICAN

<u>28</u> Manresa
<u>26</u> Nick's on Main
Village Pub
<u>25</u> Navio
Station 1 Restaurant*

ASIAN

<u>26</u> Tamarine
<u>24</u> Flying Fish (Carmel)
<u>21</u> Xanh
<u>20</u> Straits
<u>19</u> Three Seasons

CALIFORNIAN

<u>28</u> Aubergine
<u>27</u> Sierra Mar
<u>26</u> Plumed Horse
Flea St. Café
John Bentley's

CHINESE

<u>24</u> Koi Palace
<u>22</u> Tai Pan
Hunan Home/Garden
<u>20</u> Mayflower/HK Flower
Chef Chu's

CONTINENTAL

<u>27</u> La Forêt
<u>23</u> Anton & Michel
Ecco
<u>22</u> Bella Vista

FRENCH

<u>27</u> Marinus
Le Papillon
Baumé

<u>25</u> Bistro Moulin
Chantilly

INDIAN

<u>24</u> Amber India
<u>23</u> Sakoon
<u>22</u> Shalimar
Junnoon
<u>21</u> Mantra

ITALIAN

<u>24</u> Osteria Coppa
Pasta Moon
<u>23</u> Casanova
Osteria
<u>22</u> Donato Enoteca

JAPANESE

<u>27</u> Kaygetsu
<u>26</u> Alexander's
<u>25</u> Gochi
<u>24</u> Ebisu
<u>23</u> Fuki Sushi

MED./GREEK

<u>27</u> Evvia
<u>26</u> Cafe Gibraltar
Dio Deka
<u>23</u> Fandango
<u>22</u> Cetrella

SEAFOOD

<u>27</u> Passionfish
<u>24</u> Flying Fish (Carmel)
Koi Palace
<u>22</u> Flying Fish (Half Moon Bay)
<u>21</u> Old Port Lobster

Excludes places with low votes, unless otherwise indicated; * indicates a
tie with restaurant above

Vote at ZAGAT.com

BY SPECIAL FEATURE

BREAKFAST/BRUNCH

- 27 La Forêt
- 25 Navio
- 24 Koi Palace
- 23 Gayle's Bakery
- 22 Madera

OUTDOOR SEATING

- 27 Sierra Mar
- 24 Roy's
- 23 Anton & Michel
- 20 Sam's Chowder Hse.
- 16 Nepenthe

PEOPLE-WATCHING

- 26 Tamarine
- Dio Deka
- Village Pub
- 22 Madera
- 21 Lion & Compass

ROMANCE

- 28 Aubergine
- 27 Sierra Mar
- Marinus
- La Forêt
- 23 Casanova

SINGLES SCENES

- 22 Junnoon
- 21 Joya
- Xanh

- 19 Sino
- 18 Hula's

SMALL PLATES

- 26 Tamarine
- 23 Chez Shea
- 22 Junnoon
- 21 Joya
- Cascal

TASTING MENUS

- 28 Manresa
- Aubergine
- 27 Marinus
- Kaygetsu
- Baumé

VIEWS

- 27 Sierra Mar
- 25 Navio
- 24 Roy's
- Pacific's Edge
- 21 La Costanera
- 16 Nepenthe

WINNING WINE LISTS

- 27 Sierra Mar
- Marinus
- Passionfish
- 26 Plumed Horse
- Village Pub

BY LOCATION

CARMEL/MONTEREY

- 28 Aubergine
- 27 Marinus
- 25 Bistro Moulin
- 24 Café Rustica
- Pacific's Edge

HALF MOON BAY/COAST

- 26 Cafe Gibraltar
- 25 Navio
- 24 Pasta Moon
- 23 Chez Shea
- 22 Cetrella

PALO ALTO/MENLO PARK

- 27 Kaygetsu
- Baumé
- Evvia
- 26 Flea St. Café
- Tamarine

PENINSULA

- 26 Village Pub
- John Bentley's
- 25 Station 1 Restaurant
- Chantilly
- 22 Donato Enoteca

SANTA CRUZ/CAPITOLA

- 26 Cellar Door Café∇
- La Posta∇
- 23 Gayle's Bakery
- 18 Hula's
- Shadowbrook

SILICON VALLEY

- 28 Manresa
- 27 Le Papillon
- La Forêt
- 26 Nick's on Main
- Dio Deka

Top Decor

29	Sierra Mar
28	Pacific's Edge
26	Club XIX
	Marinus
	Roy's
	Navio
	Rest. at Ventana
	La Costanera
	Plumed Horse
25	Chantilly

	Casanova
	Nepenthe
	Manresa
	Le Papillon
24	Madera
	Anton & Michel
	Shadowbrook
	Village Pub
	Aubergine
	La Forêt

Top Service

27	Manresa
	Baumé
	La Forêt
26	Sierra Mar
	Le Papillon
	Marinus
	Aubergine
	Kaygetsu
25	Bistro Moulin
	Club XIX

	Chantilly
	Plumed Horse
	Passionfish
	Navio
	Alexander's
24	Pacific's Edge
	Cafe Gibraltar
	Anton & Michel
	John Bentley's
	Flea St. Café

BEST BUYS: SPECIALTY SHOPS

Applewood Pizza	Ebisu
Burger Joint	Gayle's Bakery
BurgerMeister	Ike's
Calafia	In-N-Out
Cheese Steak Shop	Patxi's Chicago Pizza
Chez Shea	Pizza Antica
Cool Café	Pluto's Fresh Food

BEST BUYS: FULL MENUS

Amber India	Half Moon Bay Brewing Co.
Andalé	Hunan Home/Garden
Barbara's Fish Trap	Kabul
Cafe Gibraltar	Krung Thai
Cascal	La Corneta
Cha Cha Cha	La Cumbre Taqueria
Chef Chu's	Mezza Luna
Dishdash	Muracci's
Duarte's Tavern	Pancho Villa
Emporio Rulli	Roti Indian

South of San Francisco

Acqua Pazza *Italian*
21 | 19 | 22 | $38

San Mateo | 201 E. Third Ave. (bet. B St. & San Mateo Dr.) |
650-375-0903 | www.acqua-pazza.com

"Real Italian hospitality" assures "you feel like one of the family" at this "midrange" San Mateo ristorante that's "improving like a good bottle of Barolo", serving up "very good" pastas, pizzas and even some "wow" entrees; though the simple two-story corner setting is "attractive" and "bustling", a few warn that it can get "somewhat noisy", especially when there's "live music."

Alexander's Steakhouse *Japanese/Steak*
26 | 24 | 25 | $84

Cupertino | Cupertino Sq. | 10330 N. Wolfe Rd. (bet. Rte. 280 & Stevens Creek Blvd.) | 408-446-2222 | www.alexanderssteakhouse.com

"Marvelous" meat and "expertly prepared East-meets-West cuisine" corral carnivores at this "extravagant" "Japanese-influenced steakhouse" in Cupertino and its younger sis in SoMa; "tender" beef that's "bigger than your head" is served by your "own herd" of "spectacular" servers who "attend to your every need", but the "crazy expensive" menu is "priced for VCs and bankers" "with very deep pockets" sigh some, who have to save it for a "special occasion."

NEW All Spice Ⓜ *Indian*
▽ 24 | 22 | 25 | $43

San Mateo | 1602 S. El Camino Real (Borel Ave.) | 650-627-4303 | www.allspicerestaurant.com

"Blink" and "you'll pass" this "brilliant" newcomer "tucked away" in a converted Victorian house in San Mateo where chef Sachin Chopra (Sakoon) and his "welcoming" wife proffer "upscale" "eclectic" Indian food with a Californian touch that often "knocks it out of the park"; as the name suggests, spices abound in everything from the unusual house-made ice creams to the color choices of the vibrantly painted walls.

☒ Amber India *Indian*
24 | 21 | 20 | $38

Mountain View | Olive Tree Shopping Ctr. | 2290 W. El Camino Real (bet. Ortega & S. Rengstorff Aves.) | 650-968-7511
San Jose | Santana Row | 377 Santana Row (Olin Ave.) | 408-248-5400

☒ Amber Café *Indian*

Mountain View | 600 W. El Camino Real (View St.) | 650-968-1751
www.amber-india.com

The Indian eats "range from comfortably mild" (the "fantastic" butter chicken) to "incendiary" at this fab foursome that "stands out" among the competition; outposts range from the "supremely casual" cafe to the "beautifully decorated" San Jose and SoMa spots with their "glamorous" bars and "proficient" servers; and though it's a pity that "prices are a little steep", the lunch buffet ("full of delectable surprises", though not available on El Camino Real) is "an incredible bargain."

Amici's East Coast Pizzeria *Pizza*
20 | 14 | 18 | $21

Cupertino | 10310 S. De Anza Blvd. (Rodrigues Ave.) | 408-252-3333
Mountain View | 790 Castro St. (Yosemite Ave.) | 650-961-6666
Redwood Shores | 226 Redwood Shores Pkwy. (Twin Dolphin Dr.) | 650-654-3333

(continued)

(continued)

Amici's East Coast Pizzeria

San Jose | 225 W. Santa Clara St. (N. Almaden Ave.) | 408-289-9000
San Mateo | 69 Third Ave. (San Mateo Dr.) | 650-342-9392
www.amicis.com
See review in City of San Francisco Directory.

Andalé *Mexican*

21 | 13 | 15 | $17

Los Gatos | 21 N. Santa Cruz Ave. (W. Main St.) | 408-395-8997
Los Gatos | 6 N. Santa Cruz Ave. (W. Main St.) | 408-395-4244
South San Francisco | San Francisco Int'l Airport | Int'l Terminal, G Concourse (Hwy. 101) | 650-821-8201
NEW **South San Francisco** | San Francisco Int'l Airport |
United Domestic Departure Terminal 2 (Hwy. 101) | 650-821-9306
www.andalemexican.com

They're "nothing fancy", but for a "reasonable", "reliable quick bite", it's tough to beat the "fresh" and "tasty" eats at these "old faithful" Los Gatos Mexicans (with airport and SF Westfield Centre outposts); the smaller original (6 North Santa Cruz) is "great for takeout" while the larger sib across the street has a "pretty backyard patio."

Anton & Michel Restaurant *Continental*

23 | 24 | 24 | $59

Carmel | Mission St. (bet. Ocean & 7th Aves.) | 831-624-2406 |
www.antonandmichel.com

"Old school at its best" sums up this "special-occasion" Carmel Continental where an "excellent" menu including "Caesar salad made tableside" is smartly served in an "elegant", "romantic" setting with fireplaces and a fountain-filled courtyard; though a few find it a "bit stuffy" and say it "could use a makeover", others insist you simply "need to be old enough to appreciate" this "quiet winner."

Applewood Pizza *Pizza*

21 | 10 | 14 | $20

Menlo Park | 1001 El Camino Real (Ravenswood Ave.) |
650-324-3486 | www.applewoodpizza.com

"Reliably good pizza" with a "scarily addictive buttery crust" and some "unique" toppings win fans for this "casual", "family-friendly" Menlo Park joint; there's "nothing fancy" about the setting or service, but modest prices (the lunch special is a "steal") and "fantastic" beer choices make it easy to "close your eyes" and enjoy.

Aquarius *American*

▽ 21 | 21 | 17 | $40

Santa Cruz | Santa Cruz Dream Inn | 175 W. Cliff Dr. (Bay St.) |
831-460-5012 | www.aquariussantacruz.com

It's "upscale" for Santa Cruz, so "put down the surfboard and slip on some shoes" to enjoy "fresh fish" and other New American fare at this breakfast-through-dinner option in the Dream Inn; some find the menu "unremarkable" and say service can be "disorganized" (though "pleasant"), but a "wow setting" with "dynamite" Pacific views works in its favor.

Arcadia *American*

▽ 20 | 19 | 18 | $58

San Jose | San Jose Marriott | 100 W. San Carlos St. (Market St.) |
408-278-4555 | www.michaelmina.net

"Well-prepared" steakhouse fare gets a New American twist thanks to owner Michael Mina (he of the "legendary" "lobster corn dogs") at this "quiet", "relaxing" roost in the San Jose Marriott; suitable for a "special date or a power business dinner", it "always hits a home run" say some, though critics sniff "the ambiance is a little sterile" and the service "unpolished."

Attic Ⓢ Ⓜ *Asian* ▽ 18 | 17 | 17 | $32

San Mateo | 234 S. B St. (2nd Ave.) | 650-342-4506 | www.atticrestaurant.com

"Tasty" Filipino and Pan-Asian shared plates washed down with "exotic" tropical cocktails in an airy second-floor setting make this moderately priced and "hip"-as-can-be newcomer a "great addition to the dining scene" in Downtown San Mateo; the dining room is tricked out with wooden lanterns and low-slung gong-topped tables, while the downstairs bar, Under the Attic, hosts a "solid happy hour" with more "Americanized" bar bites.

Z Aubergine *Californian* 28 | 24 | 26 | $116

Carmel | L'Auberge Carmel | Monte Verde St. (7th Ave.) | 831-624-8578 | www.laubergecarmel.com

It's the "crème of Carmel" and "special in every way" gush groupies of this "charming", "intimate" Relais & Châteaux Californian turning out "absolutely exquisite" prix fixe meals "with wine pairings that will leave you talking for days" ferried by service "so good it raises the bar"; true, it also "pushes the envelope on price" and can be "a bit pretentious", but if you "don't come underdressed" (jackets suggested) and "bring several credit cards", "you'll be richly rewarded"; P.S. the arrival of a new chef might not be fully reflected in the Food score.

Barbara's Fish Trap ⊄ *Seafood* 21 | 14 | 17 | $25

Princeton by the Sea | 281 Capistrano Rd. (Hwy. 1) | 650-728-7049

"Loyal customers" are hooked on this affordable Princeton by the Sea "shack" that dishes out "generous portions" of "fantastically fresh" seafood including "tasty fish 'n' chips" and "white chowder"; though there's a "great view of the harbor", those opting out on the "brusque service" and "noisy", "tight quarters" instead "line up" at the "take-out stand" and "eat perched over the water."

Basin, The *American* ▽ 20 | 19 | 20 | $46

Saratoga | 14572 Big Basin Way (5th St.) | 408-867-1906 | www.thebasin.com

"Organic, fresh foods", "great cocktails" and an "excellent wine list" make this "warm and inviting" American a "popular" "Saratoga hang-out", particularly if you snag a table on the "romantic outdoor dining patio"; service is "gracious", and if some call the menu "solid but nothing to text home about", others find it "pretty special."

Basque Cultural Center Ⓜ *French* 19 | 12 | 18 | $32

South San Francisco | Basque Cultural Ctr. | 599 Railroad Ave. (bet. Orange & Spruce Aves.) | 650-583-8091 | www.basqueculturalcenter.com

"True to the Basque tradition", this "old-school" French "find" in South City features "big portions" of "authentic", "hearty" dishes (like "pork chops and peppers") that you won't "find just anywhere"; the "clubby", "relaxed" atmosphere can feel a bit "dreary" and "service can be quite slow", but the "family-style dinners" are a "real value", making it "great for big groups" who "come hungry, leave happy."

FOOD | DECOR | SERVICE | COST

✦ Baumé 🅜 *French* — 27 | 23 | 27 | $153

Palo Alto | 201 S. California Ave. (Park Ave.) | 650-328-8899 |
www.baumerestaurant.com

"A spritz here, a foam there" – "master of his craft" Bruno Chemel
leaves admirers "blown away" at this Palo Alto New French, where "innovative" tasting menus that mix classical techniques with "cutting-
edge molecular gastronomy" turn meals into "ethereal" "entertainment"; a "stellar" staff works the "small", "Zen"-like space, and if a
few demur ("Ferrari prices", "self-conscious"), the bottom line is
"there's nothing like it in the South Bay"; P.S. closed Monday–Tuesday.

Bella Vista 🅂🅜 *Continental* — 22 | 23 | 23 | $56

Woodside | 13451 Skyline Blvd. (5 mi. south of Rte. 92) | 650-851-1229 |
www.bvrestaurant.com

It's "worth the drive up a curvy road" to "breathe the romance" at this
"charming" Woodside "special-occasion" "hideaway" proffering "pan-
oramic" views of the Bay and "traditional" but "delicious" Continental
cuisine and an extensive wine list served by "old-fashioned" professionals; critics complain it's "overpriced", given that some dishes "can
be a little disappointing", but c'mon – "where can one get steak Diane
prepared tableside anymore?"

Benihana *Japanese* — 17 | 18 | 20 | $38

Burlingame | 1496 Old Bayshore Hwy. (Mahler Rd.) | 650-342-5202
Cupertino | Cupertino Sq. | 2074 Vallco Fashion Park (Vallco Pkwy.) |
408-253-1221
www.benihana.com
See review in City of San Francisco Directory.

Big Sur Bakery & Restaurant *American/Bakery* — 22 | 17 | 19 | $37

Big Sur | Hwy. 1 (½ mi. south of Pfeiffer State Park) | 831-667-0520 |
www.bigsurbakery.com

"Beloved by locals", this "rustic" roadhouse "along Highway 1" is a "must
visit" for its "memorable" breads and pastries, wood-fired pizza and
other "creative", affordable American fare; dining alfresco is especially "relaxing" – just "do not go in a coat and tie" or expect "speedy
service" since "this is real Big Sur"; P.S. only the bakery is open Mondays.

Bistro Moulin *French* — 25 | 20 | 25 | $49

Monterey | 867 Wave St. (bet. David & Irving Aves.) | 831-333-1200 |
www.bistromoulin.com

"In a sea of tacky tourist fish joints", this Monterey "favorite" is "clearly
where the locals go" for "fabulous" "French country and bistro classics" "prepared with love" and served by the "friendly but discreet"
owners and their staff; a "terrific value", the "warm, cozy" "petit
place" is "always busy", so "reservations are a must."

Blowfish Sushi To Die For *Japanese* — 21 | 19 | 17 | $42

San Jose | Santana Row | 335 Santana Row (Alyssum Ln.) | 408-345-3848 |
www.blowfishsushi.com
See review in City of San Francisco Directory.

Buca di Beppo *Italian* — 15 | 16 | 17 | $28

Campbell | Pruneyard Shopping Ctr. | 1875 S. Bascom Ave. (Campbell Ave.) |
408-377-7722
Palo Alto | 643 Emerson St. (bet. Forest & Hamilton Aves.) | 650-329-0665

(continued)

Buca di Beppo

San Jose | Oakridge Mall | 925 Blossom Hill Rd. (bet. Santa Teresa & Winfield Blvds.) | 408-226-1444
www.bucadibeppo.com
See review in City of San Francisco Directory.

Burger Joint *Burgers*

| 18 | 13 | 17 | $15 |

Burlingame | 1401 Burlingame Ave. (Primrose Rd.) | 650-558-9232
South San Francisco | San Francisco Int'l Airport |
Int'l Terminal, Boarding Area A (Hwy. 101) | 650-821-0582
www.burgerjointsf.com
See review in City of San Francisco Directory.

BurgerMeister *Burgers*

| 20 | 11 | 15 | $16 |

Daly City | 507 Westlake Ctr. (John Daly Blvd.) | 650-755-1941 |
www.burgermeistersf.com
See review in City of San Francisco Directory.

Café Brioche *Californian/French*

| 21 | 16 | 18 | $33 |

Palo Alto | 445 S. California Ave. (bet. Ash St. & El Camino Real) |
650-326-8640 | www.cafebrioche-paloalto.com
Well-known to Palo Altans, this "charming" Cal-French cafe is a "go-to" for "excellent brunch" or a "perfect romantic" evening, thanks to its "consistent", "down-to-earth" fare and highly "reasonable prices"; while "friendly", the service "is pretty slow", so "be prepared for a wait."

☒ Cafe Gibraltar Ⓜ *Mediterranean*

| 26 | 22 | 24 | $44 |

El Granada | 425 Ave. Alhambra (Palma St.) | 650-560-9039 |
www.cafegibraltar.com
Chef/co-owner Luis Ugalde "makes magic with local, sustainable ingredients while taking diners on a journey through the Mediterranean" at his "fantastico" cafe endowed with "dreamy" casbah atmosphere – "you can even sit on pillows" while enjoying "exotic" meze and mains; add in the well-matched wines and "impeccable service", and you have a "knock your socks off", yet "affordable", experience; if only "it weren't in out-of-the-way El Granada."

Café Rustica Ⓜ *Californian*

| 24 | 18 | 21 | $39 |

Carmel Valley | 10 Del Fino Pl. (bet. Carmel Valley & Pilot Rds.) |
831-659-4444 | www.caferusticacarmel.com
"Beautiful Carmel Valley views" make this "pleasant" "neighborhood spot" a "family favorite" for "high-quality" "homestyle" Californian cuisine, including "wonderful pizzas" and "fresh" salads at a "great value"; "inside can be noisy", so request "the lovely patio" and remember "reservations are a must", as the locals "dine here regularly."

NEW Café Tradition Ⓢ *French/Moroccan*

| - | - | - | M |

San Mateo | 123 W. 25th Ave. (Hacienda St.) | 650-345-2233
Husband-and-wife team Jean-Roger and Drissia Rafael, who hail from Marseilles and Fes, respectively, are behind this San Mateo arrival, a simple white-tablecloth storefront bistro offering moderately priced French and Moroccan cuisine; expect the likes of escargot in puff pastry and lamb tagine, accompanied by a wine list that spans from France and North Africa to California.

Calafia *Californian* | 17 | 17 | 17 | $29 |

Palo Alto | Town & Country Vill. | 855 El Camino Real (Embarcadero Rd.) | 650-322-9200 | www.calafiapaloalto.com

"Former Google chef" Charlie Ayers "has the perfect algorithm for pleasing the palate" say "Silicon Valley types" who tout this "crowded" Palo Alto cafe with a "creative" "seasonal" Cal menu; if some say service is "slow" and it's "a bit pricey" for "people not pulling down" "tech company salaries", most maintain that the dishes (including "lots" of vegan and "unique" veggie choices) "trump the noise and the wait."

Cannery Row Brewing Company *American* | ▽ 17 | 18 | 18 | $33 |

Monterey | 95 Prescott Ave. (Wave St.) | 831-643-2722 | www.canneryrowbrewingcompany.com

An "off-the-charts" beer selection (74 on tap alone) makes this yearling a "super addition to Cannery Row" for hopsheads who revel in the elements of a "typical brewery-type evening" (augmented by a "meat market" scene on weekends); the American pub grub "is ok" – "the burger is their best item", with 10 types to choose from – and there are outdoor fire pits to warm you if the staff seems cold.

Cantinetta Luca *Italian* | 21 | 21 | 19 | $45 |

Carmel | Dolores St. (bet. Ocean & 7th Aves.) | 831-625-6500 | www.cantinettaluca.com

Fans say the "passion for food and wines" runs hot at this "happening spot", which, despite its rich-toned, "style-forward" digs, remains "true to its Italian roots" with "crispy wood-fired pizzas" and "outstanding" housemade salumi; the "customer service could use some spiffing" and the digs get "loud and crowded, but the food will make you forget the chaos"; P.S. it's "pricey, but so is all of Carmel."

Casanova *French/Italian* | 23 | 25 | 21 | $56 |

Carmel | Fifth Ave. (bet. Mission & San Carlos Sts.) | 831-625-0501 | www.casanovarestaurant.com

The "place to be with the true love of your life", this Carmel "nook" "exudes romance", divided into several rooms with different "rustic" themes and serving a "creative menu" of "delicious" French-Italian "country cuisine" that's supported by a "wonderful wine cellar"; it's "expensive" for dinner, but also remains a "charming place to lunch", especially on the patio that "allows furry friends."

Cascal *Pan-Latin* | 21 | 21 | 19 | $36 |

Mountain View | 400 Castro St. (California St.) | 650-940-9500 | www.cascalrestaurant.com

"Buzzing" with a "convivial" Mountain View crowd, this Pan-Latin lounge with "brightly colored walls" serves "inventive" tapas (small plates with "huge flavors") and "full entrees" along with "creative" cocktails; fans say it's "great for groups", who can "share" the fare at a "fair price" and listen to "live music" on weekends, but the "noise level" necessitates "lip reading", and some suggest you "sit outside" "when the weather is nice."

Cellar Door Café Ⓜ *Californian* | ▽ 26 | 24 | 24 | $44 |

Santa Cruz | Bonny Doon Vineyard | 328 Ingalls St. (bet. Fair Ave. & Swift St.) | 831-425-6771 | www.bonnydoonvineyard.com

Though the original "chef moved onward", this "hip as it gets" Santa Cruz Californian is "still a very enjoyable" spot for sharing "OMG wonderful, inventive" farm-to-table prix fixes nightly (plus à la carte offerings and weekend lunch) with "great pairings" of "Bonny Doon wines" – the place ("a creatively designed warehouse") is part of the vineyard's tasting room; tabs get "a bit pricey", but there are also cheaper "small bites", craft beers and non-proprietary wines in the new lounge.

Cetrella Ⓜ *Mediterranean*   22 | 24 | 22 | $51

Half Moon Bay | 845 Main St. (Monte Vista Ln.) | 650-726-4090 | www.cetrella.com

"With a ceiling-high fireplace dominating the main dining room" and "live music on weekends" in the lounge, "ambiance is part of the dining experience" at this "big, attractive Half Moon Bay" establishment whose "timely, knowledgeable" staff has earned a Service score boost; fans also feel the pricey Mediterranean fare with "decidedly French inspiration" "has never been better."

NEW Cha Cha Cha Cuba *Caribbean/Cuban*   20 | 17 | 16 | $27

San Mateo | 112 S. B St. (First Ave.) | 650-347-2900

See review in City of San Francisco Directory.

Chantilly Ⓢ *French/Italian*   25 | 25 | 25 | $64

Redwood City | 3001 El Camino Real (Selby Ln.) | 650-321-4080 | www.chantillyrestaurant.com

"For special occasions, it's elegant and romantic" to visit this Redwood City "war horse", offering "a stable of favorites" from the realm of "quintessential French"–Northern Italian haute cuisine, "beautifully plated" and served with "stellar" wines by "knowledgeable waiters"; some sniff the "formal Continental atmosphere" is "old world for older folks", but admirers enjoy the sense of a "restaurant of yesteryear."

Cheesecake Factory *American*   17 | 18 | 17 | $29

Palo Alto | 375 University Ave. (bet. Florence & Waverly St.) | 650-473-9622

San Jose | 925 Blossom Hill Rd. (bet. Santa Teresa & Winfield Blvds.) | 408-225-6948

Santa Clara | Westfield Shoppingtown Valley Fair | 3041 Stevens Creek Blvd. (Santana Row) | 408-246-0092

www.thecheesecakefactory.com

See review in City of San Francisco Directory.

Cheese Steak Shop *Cheesesteaks*   20 | 6 | 15 | $12

San Jose | Monterey Plaza | 5524 Monterey Rd. (Blossom Hill Rd.) | 408-972-0271

Sunnyvale | 832 W. El Camino Real (Hollenbeck Ave.) | 408-530-8159 ⊞

www.cheesesteakshop.com

See review in City of San Francisco Directory.

Chef Chu's *Chinese*   20 | 14 | 19 | $29

Los Altos | 1067 N. San Antonio Rd. (El Camino Real) | 650-948-2696 | www.chefchu.com

"Exuberant" celebrity chef Lawrence Chu and his "manager son, Larry, really know how to run a restaurant", using "high-quality ingredients" to produce an "extensive menu" of "delicious" (if oft "Americanized") Mandarin fare at "moderate" prices; it's a "mainstay" in Los Altos, decorated with "lots of pictures" of "celebrities who have been there", but pickier patrons prefer to "phone in for takeout", saying that "everything shines except the dreary surroundings."

	FOOD	DECOR	SERVICE	COST

Chez Shea *Eclectic* — 23 | 14 | 15 | $24

Half Moon Bay | 408 Main St. (Mill St.) | 650-560-9234 |
www.chez-shea.com

"Come as you are" to the "casual" "offshoot of Cafe Gibraltar" in Half Moon Bay, where "Eclectic, creative" plates and tapas running from "South African to south-of-the-border" are made with "locally focused" "superlative ingredients"; the space is "narrow" and service is "questionable", but there's a "nice patio out back" and it's a "great value."

Chez TJ 🈂️Ⓜ️ *French* — 24 | 20 | 24 | $111

Mountain View | 938 Villa St. (bet. Bryant & Franklin Sts.) | 650-964-7466 |
www.cheztj.com

This Mountain View vet proffers "beautifully presented", "inspired *nouveau*" French prix fixes and "fine" wine in a "comfortable, if not fancy" (a bit "down-at-heel", in fact) Victorian bungalow; critics call out the small portions ("come hungry and leave the same way") and the kitchen's "chef merry-go-round" (including a departure during this Survey); still, it remains a destination to "take your honey when you've cashed in a few stock options" and want to "feel totally catered to."

Ⓩ Club XIX 🈂️Ⓜ️ *Californian/French* — 23 | 26 | 25 | $71

Pebble Beach | The Lodge at Pebble Beach | 1700 17 Mile Dr. (Cypress Dr.) |
831-625-8519 | www.pebblebeach.com

"You might have to elbow out Arnold Palmer for the best table" at this "posh" eatery in that duffers' delight, The Lodge at Pebble Beach; while "the view of Stillwater Cove is the real star", followed by "outstanding" service, the Cal-French fare is "cooked superbly" and the tab "matches" the experience, but it's "heaven if you're a golfer."

Cool Café *Californian* — 20 | 14 | 15 | $22

Menlo Park | Menlo Business Park | 1525 O'Brien Dr. (University Ave.) |
650-325-3665 🈂️

Stanford | Stanford Univ. Cantor Arts Ctr. | 328 Lomita Dr. (Museum Way) |
650-725-4758 Ⓜ️
www.cooleatz.com

It's "artistic all around" at this quick-service cafe that's ideal for "alfresco lunches" (and Thursday dinners) "when visiting the Cantor Museum or other afternoon events at Stanford"; true, the "tasty and healthy" Cal fare from Jesse Cool (Flea St. Café), served on compostable tableware, is "a bit pricey", but you "can't beat the view of the Rodin sculpture garden"; P.S. the Menlo Park outpost is open only on weekdays.

Crouching Tiger *Chinese* — ▽ 19 | 16 | 15 | $24

Redwood City | 2644 Broadway St. (El Camino Real) | 650-298-8881 |
www.crouchingtigerrestaurant.com

Fans contend "some of the best Chinese" in the area is at this Redwood City "favorite go-to" for "all the standards", "Sichuan-style" – "authentic oily, spicy", "flavorful food" – at "reasonable prices"; you can "eat in or take out, both work."

Dasaprakash *Indian* — ▽ 22 | 13 | 21 | $21

Santa Clara | 2636 Homestead Rd. (bet. Kiely Blvd. & Layton St.) |
408-246-8292 | www.dasaprakash.com

The "great" grub – "vegetarian" South Indian eats, and much of it "good for vegans too" – does "a Kathakali dance in your mouth" at this "quiet" "family-owned" location that "stands out" in Santa Clara; if you want to "try something different", don't let the "strip-mall location deter you", because it's an "outstanding value", and everyone receives a "warm welcome."

Davenport Roadhouse Restaurant & Inn 🅼 *Californian/Coffeehouse*

▽ 16 | 14 | 16 | $25

Davenport | 1 Davenport Ave. (Hwy. 1/Cabrillo Hwy.) | 831-426-8801 | www.davenportroadhouse.com

"Between Santa Cruz and San Francisco on Highway 1", this "locals' place" in the "tiny town of Davenport" is good for a pit stop and some "funky" affordable Californian fare in a "casual", woody setting complete with "laid-back vibe" and live music (with no cover) some nights.

Deetjen's Big Sur Restaurant *Californian*

23 | 23 | 22 | $50

Big Sur | Deetjen's Big Sur Inn | 48865 Hwy. 1 (30 mi. south of Carmel) | 831-667-2378 | www.deetjens.com

"For a real Big Sur experience", this "ramshackle" yet "romantic" redwoods-sheltered 1937 inn serving "cozy breakfast with the fire going" and "unpretentious" candlelit Californian dinners is "where the locals eat" (despite the "big guns up on the hill"); maybe "grandpa Deetjen's ghost" "wouldn't recognize the prices" nowadays, "but if you're going to spend the day hiking or mousing up and down Highway 1", it's a "truly enchanting" start or finish.

Dio Deka *Greek*

26 | 23 | 23 | $61

Los Gatos | Hotel Los Gatos | 210 E. Main St. (High School Ct.) | 408-354-7700 | www.diodeka.com

"The height of Greek civilization"– or at least Hellenic dining in Los Gatos – this big fat "festive" estiatorio is filled with a "loud", happy crowd noshing on "gosh-darn expensive" but "fantastic" "nouveau" meals; a "new chef" is on the scene, but steady scores indicate this "modern" "Mondrian atmosphere" remains the "'it' place" to "dress up" and "bring family, friends or those to impress."

Dishdash 🅶 *Mideastern*

22 | 15 | 18 | $29

Sunnyvale | 190 S. Murphy Ave. (Washington Ave.) | 408-774-1889 | www.dishdash.com

🆕 Dish n Dash 🅶 *Mideastern*

Sunnyvale | 736 N. Mathilda Ave. (San Anselmo) | 408-530-9200 | www.dishndashrestaurant.com

It's "worth a detour" to Downtown Sunnyvale for the "melt-in-your-mouth Middle Eastern" meals dished by this "lively" spot; it gets "busy, busy, busy at lunch", but the "staff manages to keep up" and "their outdoor seating is restored", which should ease the squeeze; P.S. the newly opened sister on North Mathilda Avenue offers a fast-food alternative.

Donato Enoteca *Italian*

22 | 20 | 21 | $45

Redwood City | 1041 Middlefield Rd. (bet. Jefferson Ave. & Main St.) | 650-701-1000 | www.donatoenoteca.com

"Bellissimo" bellow Peninsula patrons who feel "lucky to have" "hit-the-spot" Northern "Italian fare to scratch that Tuscan itch", matched with a "wide array of carefully selected" vinos, in Downtown Redwood City; service ranges from "customer-friendly" to "inattentive when

FOOD | DECOR | SERVICE | COST

they get busy", but with seats "at the bar", on the outdoor patio or in the "elegant white-tablecloth back room", this "reasonably priced" "continuing favorite" works for "date night" or "family get-togethers" alike.

Don Pico's Original Mexican Bistro ⧄Ⓜ Mexican

17 | 14 | 17 | $26

San Bruno | 461 El Camino Real (Jenevein Ave.) | 650-589-1163 | www.donpicosbistro.com

It's "always a packed house" at this San Bruno Mexican cantina, which offers "modern takes as well as traditional dishes" with "good margaritas" and a "grab-bag of live musical entertainment" in "colorful, worn" surroundings; purists pout that "better food can be found elsewhere" for fewer pesos, but they plan "to expand into the space next door", which may outdate the Decor score.

Duarte's Tavern American

20 | 12 | 19 | $29

Pescadero | 202 Stage Rd. (Pescadero Creek Rd.) | 650-879-0464 | www.duartestavern.com

A "destination restaurant for generations", this "funky mainstay" with "authentic roadhouse decor" and "friendly" service off the "scenic coast" of Pescadero inspires internal debates in those who "can't choose between the green chili and the cream of artichoke soups" – so they "ask for the half and half", making sure to "leave room for warm olallieberry pie"; "seafood specialties" also stand out on the American menu.

Duck Club Grill American

20 | 22 | 21 | $50

Monterey | Monterey Plaza Hotel & Spa | 400 Cannery Row (Wave St.) | 831-646-1700 | www.woodsidehotels.com

"Wonderfully prepared" New American fare "with some nice twists" brings out-of-towners, "ladies who lunch" and "deal-making" business diners to this flock of "quiet" "upscale" hotel restaurants; the Monterey and Bodega Bay branches boast a "beautiful setting" with "drop-dead" "views of the water", and the Lafayette branch is "very comfortable" and "serene" too, but the adventuresome "duck this" trio, citing a "staid" atmosphere and "lackluster" service.

Ebisu ❶Ⓜ Japanese

24 | 18 | 19 | $36

South San Francisco | San Francisco Int'l Airport | Int'l Terminal, Main Hall, N. Food Court (Hwy. 101) | 650-588-2549 | www.ebisusushi.com

See review in City of San Francisco Directory.

Ecco Restaurant ⧄ Californian/Continental

23 | 22 | 24 | $49

Burlingame | 322 Lorton Ave. (bet. Burlingame & Donnelly Aves.) | 650-342-7355 | www.eccorestaurant.com

"Sort of a throwback" to an earlier era, this Burlingame "gem" "delivers big time" with "reliable" Continental-Cal cuisine "cooked to perfection" (in addition to rack of lamb, "specials are a highlight"); add in "friendly", "professional" servers and "fair" prices and the result is a "comfortable" spot for an "unrushed" "business dinner" or a "quiet" tête-à-tête.

Emporio Rulli Dessert/Italian

24 | 21 | 17 | $20

South San Francisco | San Francisco Int'l Airport | Domestic Terminal 3
South San Francisco | San Francisco Int'l Airport | Lower Int'l Loop
South San Francisco | San Francisco Int'l Airport | Upper Int'l Loop ◗
888-887-8554 | www.rulli.com

See review in North of San Francisco Directory.

	FOOD	DECOR	SERVICE	COST

Espetus Churrascaria *Brazilian*

| | 22 | 18 | 21 | $65 |

(aka Espetus Churrascaria Brazilian Steakhouse)

San Mateo | 710 S. B St. (bet. 7th & 8th Aves.) | 650-342-8700 | www.espetus.com

See review in City of San Francisco Directory.

☑ Evvia *Greek*

| | 27 | 23 | 23 | $53 |

Palo Alto | 420 Emerson St. (bet. Lytton & University Aves.) | 650-326-0983 | www.evvia.net

Not your "typical" "taverna" but instead an "elegant" "Hellenic" hot spot, this "convivial" Palo Altan "artfully" captures "the spirit of Greek cuisine", with "palate pleasers galore", like "beautifully cooked lamb" prepared "every which way you can think of" and "amazing" fish; it may be "almost as hard to get into as Stanford", but that's because the "fantastic" staff and "warm" atmosphere "make an unbeatable combination"; the "only drawback" to this "little sister" of SF's Kokkari is the "noisy ambiance", which "can either be exciting or exhausting depending on your mood."

Fandango *Mediterranean*

| | 23 | 22 | 23 | $48 |

Pacific Grove | 223 17th St. (bet. Laurel & Lighthouse Aves.) | 831-372-3456 | www.fandangorestaurant.com

"Nothing is missed at this Pacific Grove institution", a "large" place both physically and figuratively – from the "extensive" menu offering "all the classics" of "superb Mediterranean fare" to the "wine list that reads like a novel"; everything's "graciously served" throughout the "converted old house", though "if you want romance, ask for one of the small front rooms"; "otherwise, the main salon is a fun, boisterous party."

Fishwife at Asilomar Beach *Californian/Seafood*

| | 20 | 14 | 19 | $32 |

Pacific Grove | 1996½ Sunset Dr. (Asilomar Ave.) | 831-375-7107 | www.fishwife.com

"After seeing a spectacular sunset" at Asilomar Beach, surveyors partake of the "Caribbean fish preparations" at this "casual" Californian; the "simple" fare is "not for the fussy gourmet", and it's "not a beautiful place", but "generous portions" and "knowledgeable" service make it "one of the better values in the Monterey Peninsula."

Flea St. Café Ⓜ *Californian*

| | 26 | 22 | 24 | $53 |

Menlo Park | 3607 Alameda de las Pulgas (Avy Ave.) | 650-854-1226 | www.cooleatz.com

"One of the original Californian cuisine" champions, Jesse Ziff Cool still "visits the tables" and "does her magic" at her "flagship" "locavore" "icon" in Menlo Park proffering "organic and delicious", "creative" American dinners in a refreshingly "quiet", "charming" and "intimate" eco-chic setting; "for the price" it "better be good . . . and it is", fans attest, down to the "biodynamic wines" and "unique cocktails" (don't expect "the usual diet drinks" here), making it "a very special place on the Peninsula."

Flying Fish Grill *Californian/Seafood*

| | 24 | 20 | 22 | $47 |

Carmel | Carmel Plaza | Mission St. (bet. Ocean & 7th Aves.) | 831-625-1962

"Tucked away in the lower level of a shopping center", this Carmel Californian seafooder offers "heaven in a basement", in the form of "fresh, inventive" fish "prepared with an Asian twist"; the staff is "knowledgeable", and on special nights, "chef/co-owner Kenny Fukumoto will welcome you with a warm pithy comment or his guitar", making this "small" but "serene" site a "winner."

Flying Fish Grill *Californian/Seafood* 22 | 12 | 17 | $22

Half Moon Bay | 211 San Mateo Rd. (Main St.) | 650-712-1125 | www.flyingfishgrill.net

"Fresh fish to the max" makes this Californian seafooder a real catch in Half Moon Bay for chowder, ceviche and "to-die-for" fish tacos; the quarters are a little "cramped" and the service can be a tad "slow", but the "good value" makes it "worth a stopover" nonetheless.

Forbes Mill Steakhouse *Steak* 22 | 20 | 22 | $59

Los Gatos | 206 N. Santa Cruz Ave. (Royce St.) | 408-395-6434 | www.forbesmillsteakhouse.com

When hankering for a "hunk of prime rib" or other "tender and tasty" beef "cooked to perfection", Los Gatos and Danville diners "know they can count on" this "elegant" twosome of "traditional" steakhouses; the "high prices" hinder some, who save it for sealing a "business deal" over meat and "martinis", but "superior" service, from the "front door to the check", helps make it "worth it."

Fuki Sushi *Japanese* 23 | 18 | 19 | $46

Palo Alto | 4119 El Camino Real (bet. Arastradero & Page Mill Rds.) | 650-494-9383 | www.fukisushi.com

Silicon Valley sushi lovers say this Palo Alto "institution" is a "favorite" for "wonderful quality fish" (even if "you pay for it like you're visiting Japan") or cooked Japanese fare; the "authentic atmosphere" includes "quiet and tranquil" tatami rooms and "slow" but "professional" servers.

Gabriella Café *Californian/Italian* ▽ 22 | 17 | 18 | $46

Santa Cruz | 910 Cedar St. (bet. Church & Locust Sts.) | 831-457-1677 | www.gabriellacafe.com

"Warmth and simplicity" rule at this "tiny, romantic cafe in Santa Cruz", which dishes up "wonderfully fresh and tasty", if "expensive for SC", Cal-Italian seasonal plates; while "tables too close together" mean you may be "playing footsie with a stranger", at least you get to check out "others' plates as well as your own."

Gayle's Bakery & Rosticceria *Bakery* 23 | 15 | 18 | $19

Capitola | Upper Capitola Shopping Ctr. | 504 Bay Ave. (Capitola Ave.) | 831-462-1200 | www.gaylesbakery.com

There's "always a treat waiting" at this Capitola "institution" beloved for "divine" "bakery goods" along with "wonderful" rotisserie meats and "great sandwiches"; eat them in the "enclosed patio" or pick up "picnicking provisions" – the preferred option for curmudgeons, who confide "this is really" a "fancy deli with fancy prices."

Gochi Japanese Fusion Tapas Ⓢ *Japanese* 25 | 16 | 18 | $39

Cupertino | 19980 Homestead Rd. (bet. Blarney & Heron Aves.) | 408-725-0542 | www.gochifusiontapas.com

"Japanese tapas are all the rage these days", but for several years this Cupertino spot has been "one of the better modern izakaya-type" places around – where you can "blow your whole paycheck and feel good about it" on the "superb" fare; while the "random strip-mall decor" "could use updating" and the service is just "ok", "the food is worth it" – as those enduring the "wait" will attest.

Gordon Biersch *Pub Food* `15` `15` `16` `$27`

Palo Alto | 640 Emerson St. (bet. Forest & Hamilton Aves.) | 650-323-7723
San Jose | 33 E. San Fernando St. (bet. S. 1st & 2nd Sts.) | 408-294-6785
www.gordonbiersch.com
See review in City of San Francisco Directory.

Grasing's Coastal Cuisine *Californian* `23` `21` `22` `$56`

Carmel | Jordan Ctr. | Sixth Ave. (Mission St.) | 831-624-6562 | www.grasings.com

This "classic Carmel" Californian from chef/co-owner Kurt Grasing offers up "delicious, seasonally fresh foods, prepared with care" and served in a "subdued, refined atmosphere" or out on the "dog-friendly" "heated patio"; a "special-occasion" spot, its prices can strain "pocketbooks", but the "prix fixe menu is an excellent bargain" and a recently "added bar" has made it even "more welcoming."

Hachi Ju Hachi Ⓜ *Japanese* ▽ `23` `15` `22` `$52`

Saratoga | 14480 Big Basin Way (3rd St.) | 408-647-2258 | www.hachijuhachi88.com

A "small surprise tucked in Saratoga", this "authentic Japanese" goes "beyond the usual" thanks to the "high standards" of "amusing and charming host Mr. Suzuki", who delivers "memorable" "izakaya-style" eats from "housemade tofu" to small plates and sushi; the space might have "very few tables", but you can always grab a seat at the "huge bar" and watch the action.

Half Moon Bay `16` `17` `17` `$29`
Brewing Company *Pub Food/Seafood*

Half Moon Bay | 390 Capistrano Rd. (bet. Cabrillo Hwy. & Prospect Way) | 650-728-2739 | www.hmbbrewingco.com

"Bring on the bay" cheer fans of this "casual" Half Moon Bay pub with "standard bar" fare plus "fresh" "seafood options" including "thick", "rich" clam chowder; patrons "stick to the basics" on the midpriced Californian menu while quaffing "locally brewed beer" on the "dog-friendly" patio with a "spectacular" view or sitting "outside by the fire pit and heaters on a foggy, coast-side day."

Happy Cafe Restaurant Ⓜ⇄ *Chinese* ▽ `21` `6` `13` `$14`

San Mateo | 250 S. B St. (bet. 2nd & 3rd Aves.) | 650-340-7138 | www.happycaferestaurant.blogspot.com

"No frills, great dumplings" might just be the motto for this San Mateo "hole-in-the-wall" dispensing "fresh and well-made" dim sum and other "delicious", "unusual" Shanghainese fare; the "cheap" eats coupled with "sweet and caring" service keeps many "going back", so on weekends better "get there early or you will have to wait"; P.S. closed Mondays and Tuesdays.

Hotaru *Japanese* `20` `11` `16` `$24`

San Mateo | 33 E. Third Ave. (bet. El Camino Real & San Mateo Dr.) | 650-343-1152 | www.hotarurestaurant.com

San Mateans who "crave Japanese" but "don't want to break the bank" head to this "friendly", "no-frills" Nippon nook that satisfies with "high-quality" "homestyle fare" – everything from "fresh sushi" "to teriyaki" to "tons of bento boxes for a very decent price"; there's "no atmosphere to speak of", and "limited seating" means there's likely a "line out the door", but the antsy can always order takeaway or eat "early or late."

Hula's *Hawaiian* | 18 | 18 | 19 | $32 |

Monterey | 622 Lighthouse Ave. (Hoffman Ave.) | 831-655-4852
Santa Cruz | 221 Cathcart St. (bet. Cedar St. & Pacific Ave.) | 831-426-4852
www.hulastiki.com

"Hula your way over" for the "fine island nostalgia" at this "laid-back tiki hut" duo in Santa Cruz and Monterey, where a midpriced "Hawaiian menu" with global influences combines with "tropical drinks" that warrant "a second mai tai"; "lively", "kitschy" digs with "looping surf footage" and "so-friendly" service plus "one of the best happy hours" around all add to the "funky" "fun", and part of 'Mahalo Monday' sales go to charity.

Hunan Home's Restaurant *Chinese* | 22 | 12 | 17 | $26 |

Los Altos | 4880 El Camino Real (Jordan Ave.) | 650-965-8888 |
www.hunanhomes.com

Hunan Garden *Chinese*

Palo Alto | 3345 El Camino Real (bet. Fernando & Lambert Aves.) |
650-565-8868 | www.chineserestauranthunangarden.com
See review in City of San Francisco Directory.

Iberia *Spanish* | 22 | 21 | 16 | $51 |

Menlo Park | 1026 Alma St. (Ravenswood Ave.) | 650-325-8981 |
www.iberiarestaurant.com

"Tucked away" in Menlo Park, this "romantic" Iberian does double duty, serving an "impressive selection of tapas" "by the fire" in the "intimate" bar and "classic Spanish cuisine" like "super" paella in the more "formal" dining room and on the "enchanting" patio; a "pitcher" of the "wonderful" "sangria spells comfort" aver advocates, who "just relax and enjoy" the "Euro-speed" (i.e. slow) experience, though others are irked by the "mandatory tip" considering the "inconsistent" service.

Ike's Lair 🛃 *Sandwiches* | 24 | 7 | 14 | $13 |

NEW **Redwood City** | 2655 Broadway (El Camino Real) | 650-365-2200 Ⓜ
Redwood Shores | 555 Twin Dolphin Dr., Ste. 115 (Redwood Shores Pkwy.) |
650-637-8903
www.ikeslair.com

Ike's Place *Sandwiches*

NEW **Stanford** | Stanford Univ. Huang Engineering Ctr. | 475 Via Ortega Dr.
(Campus Dr.) | 650-322-1766 | www.ilikeikesplace.com
See review in City of San Francisco Directory.

Il Fornaio *Italian* | 20 | 20 | 20 | $39 |

Burlingame | 327 Lorton Ave. (Donnelly Ave.) | 650-375-8000
Carmel | The Pine Inn | Ocean Ave. (Monte Verde St.) | 831-622-5100
Palo Alto | Garden Ct. Hotel | 520 Cowper St. (bet. Hamilton &
University Aves.) | 650-853-3888
San Jose | Sainte Claire Hotel | 302 S. Market St. (San Carlos St.) |
408-271-3366
www.ilfornaio.com
See review in City of San Francisco Directory.

Il Postale *Italian*

21 | 18 | 22 | $37

Sunnyvale | 127 W. Washington Ave. (bet. Frances St. & Murphy Ave.) | 408-733-9600 | www.ilpostale.com

"Authentic, delicious" and "just right" "homemade Italian" fare makes for a "pleasant lunch or dinner" at this Sunnyvale "favorite" that draws the "Silicon Valley" bunch with "large portions" of pasta, "savory sauces" and "varying specials" at a "decent price"; though it can get "a bit crowded" and "noisy", "quick" service "with a smile" and a "small", "intimate" setting provide "storybook ambiance."

☑ In-N-Out Burger ● *Burgers*

21 | 10 | 18 | $9

Millbrae | 11 Rollins Rd. (bet. Adrian Rd. & E. Millbrae Ave.)
Mountain View | 1159 N. Rengstorff Ave. (Amphitheatre Pkwy.)
Mountain View | 53 W. El Camino Real (bet. Bay St. & Grant Rd.)
San Jose | 550 Newhall St. (Chestnut St.)
San Jose | 5611 Santa Teresa Blvd. (Blossom Hill Rd.)
Daly City | 260 Washington St. (Sullivan Ave.)
800-786-1000 | www.in-n-out.com
See review in City of San Francisco Directory.

Isobune *Japanese*

19 | 14 | 16 | $30

Burlingame | 1451 Burlingame Ave. (bet. El Camino Real & Primrose Rd.) | 650-344-8433
See review in City of San Francisco Directory.

Izzy's Steaks & Chops *Steak*

20 | 17 | 19 | $43

San Carlos | 525 Skyway Rd. (Hwy. 101) | 650-654-2822 | www.izzyssteaks.com
See review in City of San Francisco Directory.

Jin Sho ☒ *Japanese*

▽ 23 | 16 | 17 | $53

Palo Alto | 454 S. California Ave. (bet. Ash St. & El Camino Real) | 650-321-3454 | www.jinshorestaurant.com

The "talented" chefs, alums of NYC's Nobu, make this a "favorite" of Palo Altans "willing to pay for" "high-quality" sushi "with a fusion twist"; the setting is "nothing pretentious", and service is "sometimes slow", but those who order omakase or "lots of small plates" along with a "sake sampler" contend it's "head and shoulders above" the competition.

John Bentley's ☒ *Californian*

26 | 21 | 24 | $59

Redwood City | 2915 El Camino Real (Selby Ln.) | 650-365-7777 | www.johnbentleys.com

A "quiet", "refined" dining room – neither "too formal" nor "too casual" – is just right for "appreciating" the "well-thought-out" menu of "elegantly prepared" Californian cuisine and "creative cocktails" at this "upscale getaway" in Redwood City; although old-timers "miss the ambiance" of the now "defunct" digs in Woodside, it's "consistently one of the best on the Peninsula", with "reasonable" prices considering the "quality", and since the "superb" servers "know how to take care of you", it's suitable for "special occasions."

Joya Restaurant *Nuevo Latino*

21 | 24 | 20 | $44

Palo Alto | 339 University Ave. (Florence St.) | 650-853-9800 | www.joyarestaurant.com

"Dark" and "sexy surroundings" make you feel like "part of the 'in' crowd" at this "lively" Nuevo Latino, perhaps "the hippest place in Palo

FOOD DECOR SERVICE COST

Alto"; "the prices on those little dishes sure add up" though, leading some to suggest "drinks at the bar" ("the main draw") "before moving on", but between the "accommodating" service, "superb sangria" and "tantalizing tapas", the "beautiful people" keep "going back."

Juban *Japanese*
18 | 13 | 16 | $35

Burlingame | 1204 Broadway (Laguna Ave.) | 650-347-2300
Menlo Park | 712 Santa Cruz Ave. (bet. Chestnut & Curtis Sts.) | 650-473-6458
www.jubanrestaurant.com
See review in City of San Francisco Directory.

Junnoon *Indian*
22 | 22 | 21 | $46

Palo Alto | 150 University Ave. (High St.) | 650-329-9644 | www.junnoon.com

"If you want the usual Indian", then "go elsewhere", but for "beautifully presented" small and large plates that "pique one's interest", this "lovely" Palo Altan is "worth a special trip"; putting an "upscale", "artistic" spin on the usual subcontinental "classics", it's "never boring", and "friendly" service adds to the "wonderful atmosphere", but penny-pinchers peg it as "overpriced" and "too fancy by half."

Kabul Afghan Cuisine *Afghan*
22 | 16 | 20 | $31

Burlingame | 1101 Burlingame Ave. (California Dr.) | 650-343-2075
San Carlos | San Carlos Plaza | 135 El Camino Real (bet. Hull Dr. & Spring St.) | 650-594-2840
www.kabulcuisine.com

Despite the "pretty plain" decor and "unlikely" locations (in Burlingame and "hidden" "in a strip mall" in San Carlos), visiting this "dignified" duo is like taking "an exotic trip to a faraway place" where you receive "a warm welcome as an honored guest"; the "authentic" Afghan fare "smells divine and tastes just as good", from the "large variety of lamb dishes" to "perfectly cooked" kebabs, and considering they come in "ample portions", the "prices are outstanding" too.

Kanpai ⓢ *Japanese*
▽ 22 | 17 | 21 | $38

Palo Alto | 330 Lytton Ave. (bet. Bryant & Florence Sts.) | 650-325-2696

"The key here is to trust the sushi chef" (and "let him select the sake for you too"), because the "creative omakase" (as "good as it is in Japan") is tops at Palo Alto's "friendly" "sister restaurant" to Menlo Park's Naomi; if some say this "star" "has lost its shine", most maintain the "menu standards" and "specials handwritten on a small white board" are a "wonderful surprise."

ⓩ Kaygetsu Ⓜ *Japanese*
27 | 19 | 26 | $89

Menlo Park | Sharon Heights Shopping Ctr. | 325 Sharon Park Dr. (Sand Hill Rd.) | 650-234-1084 | www.kaygetsu.com

"Brilliant sushi and sashimi" ("served like little jewels" "and priced accordingly") and a "meticulously orchestrated" kaiseki menu that "changes every month" (order "in advance") are examples of the "delicate" "Japanese food done to ultimate perfection" at this "popular" Menlo Park place; add a "sake sampler" and the tab can really "mount", but "solicitous" service and a "sedate" "minimalist" setting that belies the "suburban strip-mall" location make it a "favorite splurge" of fin-atics.

	FOOD	DECOR	SERVICE	COST

Kitchen, The ● *Chinese*   ▽ 19 | 12 | 12 | $31

Millbrae | 279 El Camino Real (La Cruz Ave.) | 650-692-9688

"Super-crowded on weekends", when "lots of families with kids" line up for the "substantial" selection of "tasty" dim sum (available at lunchtime only), this "noisy" Millbrae dumpling destination also serves a full menu of "excellent Cantonese cuisine"; critics concur the competition has "better decor" and service is only "ok", but the "consistently" "fresh" fare "makes up for it" say admirers, who insist it's "enjoyable for all."

Koi Palace *Chinese*   24 | 16 | 14 | $36

Daly City | Serramonte Plaza | 365 Gellert Blvd. (bet. Hickey & Serramonte Blvds.) | 650-992-9000 | www.koipalace.com

The South Bay's standby to "get your dumpling fix", this "upper-scale" Chinese in Daly City (with a Dublin bro) is still "rockin' the dim sum", along with the "freshest seafood" and "Cantonese-style" banquet dinners in a setting that "actually looks like a palace on the inside", complete with koi pond and "more fish tanks than the local aquarium"; "horribly long lines and curt staff" mean it "is not for the faint of heart, but it is an experience to remember."

Krung Thai *Thai*   19 | 12 | 15 | $23

Mountain View | San Antonio Shopping Ctr. | 590 Showers Dr. (bet. California & Latham Sts.) | 650-559-0366

San Jose | 642 S. Winchester Blvd. (bet. Moorpark Ave. & Riddle Rd.) | 408-260-8224 | www.newkrungthai.com

"Tasty curries" are among the "interesting flavors" that keep these "solid" Thai twins in San Jose and Mountain View "packed and noisy" with fans of their "amazing pad Thai" and other affordable "noodle dishes"; though the atmosphere is "relaxed and pleasant", the decor is "nothing fancy" and service can be so "quick" it's "rushed", but there's always the option for "takeout."

La Corneta *Mexican*   21 | 11 | 15 | $12

Burlingame | 1123 Burlingame Ave. (bet. Hatch Ln. & Lorton Ave.) | 650-340-1300

San Carlos | 1147 San Carlos Ave. (El Camino Real) | 650-551-1400 www.lacorneta.com

See review in City of San Francisco Directory.

La Costanera Ⓜ *Peruvian*   21 | 26 | 18 | $46

Montara | 8150 Cabrillo Hwy. (bet. 1st & 2nd Sts.) | 650-728-1600 | www.lacostanerarestaurant.com

"Go before sunset" if you want to "enjoy" the "stunning" "view of the Pacific" at this "dazzling" "destination spot" in Montara; supporters suggest sipping one of their "creatively concocted cocktails" ("start with any pisco-based" drink) "at the fire pit" "on the deck overlooking the ocean" before indulging in "a delicious parade" of "pricey" Peruvian plates; service that "needs polish" "doesn't mesh" with the "spectacular setting", but most maintain it's "another winner" from the chef behind SF's Piqueo's and Mochica.

La Cumbre Taqueria *Mexican*   22 | 10 | 17 | $12

San Mateo | 28 N. B St. (bet. Baldwin & Tilton Aves.) | 650-344-8989

See review in City of San Francisco Directory.

FOOD | DECOR | SERVICE | COST

🔟 La Forêt Ⓜ *Continental/French* — 27 | 24 | 27 | $77

San Jose | 21747 Bertram Rd. (Almaden Rd.) | 408-997-3458 |
www.laforetrestaurant.com

"Bring your sweetheart", because the "gorgeous", "woodsy" "creekside setting" makes this "serene" "throwback" "hidden away" "at the end of Almaden Valley" (on the outskirts of San Jose) "a romantic retreat"; the kitchen "delivers" "wonderful" "old-fashioned" Continental-French cuisine, "premium wine" and "impeccable" "service to match", so the "expensive" tab doesn't deter devotees, who claim "you cannot go wrong" here when celebrating a "special occasion."

La Posta Ⓜ *Italian* — ▽ 26 | 19 | 23 | $36

Santa Cruz | 538 Seabright Ave. (Watson St.) | 831-457-2782 |
www.lapostarestaurant.com

The "excellent changing menu" of Italian eats focuses on "fresh" "seasonal ingredients" (which "makes all the difference") at this "very pleasant" "hideaway" housed in a former post office in Santa Cruz; a Boot-focused wine list complements the "colorful" salads and pizzas featuring "great combinations of toppings, textures" and "flavors", and the prices are "well below" what you "would expect given the loving care" lavished on "each dish."

La Strada *Italian* — 19 | 17 | 18 | $39

Palo Alto | 335 University Ave. (bet. Bryant & Florence Sts.) |
650-324-8300 | www.lastradapaloalto.com

An "interesting variety" of "well-prepared" fare, from "wonderful" antipasti to "incredible" specials, is served by an "accommodating staff" at this "welcoming" Italian; some call it "solid, not spectacular" and best for "casual" "weeknight" meals, but seats along Palo Alto's main *strada* are a "great" place "to watch the Stanford students" say locals who "sit at the bar and share" the "reasonably priced" plates.

Lavanda *Mediterranean* — 20 | 18 | 20 | $48

Palo Alto | 185 University Ave. (Emerson St.) | 650-321-3514 |
www.lavandarestaurant.com

"Unique takes on Mediterranean cuisine" – in small and large plates – are paired with a "beautifully chosen wine list" (including bottles "from less-well-known places") at this "swanky spot" in Palo Alto; if a frugal few fret it "ought to be better" in light of the "high" prices, the prix fixe "Sunday suppers" are a "deal", and most maintain the "inventive" eats and "refined" "romantic" ambiance are "hard to beat."

LB Steak *Steak* — 20 | 21 | 20 | $53

San Jose | Santana Row | 334 Santana Row (Alyssum Ln.) |
408-244-1180 | www.lbsteak.com

Surveyors say "bring your inner T. rex", because chef Roland Passot does beef "right" at this French-inflected steakhouse in San Jose's Santana Row; it's "not cheap", but the eats are "high-quality", from the "dry-aged" rib-eye to "great sides", and since the setup is "fancy without being overly formal", and "super" staffers treat you "like a queen", it's deemed a "reliable" destination for "dates, business meals or groups."

	FOOD	DECOR	SERVICE	COST

Left Bank *French*
19 | 20 | 19 | $41

Menlo Park | 635 Santa Cruz Ave. (Doyle St.) | 650-473-6543
San Jose | Santana Row | 377 Santana Row (Olsen Dr.) | 408-984-3500
www.leftbank.com

See review in North of San Francisco Directory.

⚡ Le Papillon *French*
27 | 25 | 26 | $85

San Jose | 410 Saratoga Ave. (Kiely Blvd.) | 408-296-3730 |
www.lepapillon.com

"Masterfully prepared" New French fare is "pretty as a picture" and tastes just as "irresistible" at this "elegant" eatery that's "worth the splurge" for an "upscale" experience; never mind the "weird" location next to a San Jose strip mall, because the "cozy", "intimate" dining room is really "romantic", and "very fine" service enhances your "quiet tête-à-tête."

Lion & Compass ⓢ *American*
21 | 17 | 21 | $44

Sunnyvale | 1023 N. Fair Oaks Ave. (Weddell Dr.) | 408-745-1260 |
www.lionandcompass.com

"The place to see and be seen in Silicon Valley", this stalwart in Sunnyvale with a "tropical" "greenhouse" setting "still delivers" "fine" New American fare with "old-school service"; a few ding the "dated" decor, declaring it "detracts from the experience", but nevertheless it's "very busy at lunchtime", when filled with the "business-lunch" crowd wielding "the corporate credit card."

NEW Locanda Positano Ⓜ *Pizza*
– | – | – | M

San Carlos | 617 Laurel St. (San Carlos Ave.) | 650-591-5700 |
www.locanda-positano.com

Fueling the ever-popular Neapolitan pizza craze, this casual all-day San Carlos newcomer is run by the AcquaPazza guys and headed up by an award-wining Naples-born pizzaiolo, who specializes in thin-crust pies baked in an 800-degree gas-fired oven, along with other midpriced Southern Italian specialties (including a killer weekend brunch); the sleek digs, centered around a large bar and exhibition kitchen, channels la dolce vita of coastal Italy with oversized photos of Positano and lemon trees flanking the entrance.

MacArthur Park *American*
17 | 20 | 19 | $41

Palo Alto | 27 University Ave. (El Camino Real) | 650-321-9990 |
www.macarthurparkpaloalto.com

An "open, airy" dining room in a "historic" "building designed by Julia Morgan" is a "beautiful" setting for the "tried-and-true" menu of Traditional American fare at this Palo Altan in "close proximity to the Stanford campus"; "it's all about the ribs" aver aficionados, who call it a "comfortable" spot for "quiet" conversation, but snarky surveyors quip "someone left the cake out in the rain."

Madera *American*
22 | 24 | 23 | $74

Menlo Park | Rosewood Sand Hill | 2825 Sand Hill Rd. (Hwy. 280) |
650-561-1540 | www.maderasandhill.com

"Beautiful views", "beautiful food" and "beautiful people" converge at this Peninsula New American inside the Rosewood Hotel that's a "hot spot with a young vibe" and "upscale all the way" including the "classy setting", "terrific" food and "outstanding" service; the "break-the-bank prices" prompt some to say it could be in "Paris, London or Manhattan, not Menlo Park", but on the plus side, the "outside patio is terrific in the summer."

Ma Maison ⓜ *French*

▽ 24 | 22 | 22 | $55

Aptos | 9051 Soquel Dr. (Rio Del Mar Blvd.) | 831-688-5566 | www.mamaisonrestaurant.com

A "secret no longer", this "lovely place tucked away off Highway 1 in Aptos" has a chef-owner who "prepares luscious French-inspired entrees with the freshest of ingredients" and offers them with a "nice wine list"' and "very friendly" service; it's "great" "to have lunch" on the patio or a "romantic" "special dinner" inside the "cozy" "country-style bistro", and there's also an "early-bird prix fixe dinner."

Mandaloun *Californian/Mediterranean*

▽ 20 | 20 | 20 | $37

Redwood City | 2021 Broadway St. (bet. Jefferson Ave. & Main St.) | 650-367-7974 | www.mandaloun.biz

Whether you're seated near the "romantic fireplace" or on the "delightful outdoor patio", you "can always rely" on a "relaxed" meal at this "fun" and "friendly" Redwood City slicker that's a "perfect pre-movie meeting spot"; if a few fuss the fare is "a bit hit"-or-"miss", most gush about the "eclectic" menu, which ranges from "yummy" small plates to pizza to "generous" Cal-Med entrees.

☒ Manresa ⓜ *American*

28 | 25 | 27 | $150

Los Gatos | 320 Village Ln. (bet. N. Santa Cruz & University Aves.) | 408-354-4330 | www.manresarestaurant.com

"Four-hour" meals filled with "inventions of which Edison would be proud" are turned out by "magician" chef-owner David Kinch at this "elegant", "experimental", "special-occasion" New American in Los Gatos that takes diners on "an unforgettable journey" via "Japanese-influenced" tasting menus featuring his own biodynamic produce; a "synchronized dance" of servers and sommeliers "bring it together" and "it may set you back" some serious coin, but it makes "true foodies' hearts skip a beat"; P.S. there's a new cocktail bar and lounge.

Mantra *Californian/Indian*

21 | 21 | 22 | $41

Palo Alto | 632 Emerson St. (bet. Forest & Hamilton Aves.) | 650-322-3500 | www.mantrapaloalto.com

Bringing your usual Bombay bites "up a few notches", this "upscale" Palo Altan puts a lot of "pizzazz" into its Californian-Indian "fusion" fare, as well as the "great drinks" mixed at the "elegant bar"; those who deemed it "a little overpriced" will appreciate a shift to a more casual, "lower-priced" small-plates menu (with a new "lunch buffet") and a more relaxed design "makeover" (not fully reflected in the scores), while the "half-price" happy-hour specials and "accommodating" service remain.

☒ Marinus ⓜ *Californian/French*

27 | 26 | 26 | $95

Carmel Valley | Bernardus Lodge | 415 Carmel Valley Rd. (Laureles Grade Rd.) | 831-658-3595 | www.bernardus.com

It's "a bit of a drive if you're not staying at the lodge", but "worth every mile" for some of the "best food on the Monterey Peninsula" swoon foodies who trek to this "elegant" "classic in Carmel Valley" to "be coddled" and "bask in the glow" of its "cheery fireplace"-lit "old-world

| | FOOD | DECOR | SERVICE | COST |

ambiance"; chef Cal Stamenov's "exquisite" "*nouveau* French"–Californian tasting menu "is the star here", and for "special occasions when price does not matter", "let the sommelier guide you to wines perfectly paired to your dinner"; P.S. closed Monday and Tuesday.

Martins West ☒ *Scottish* — 22 | 19 | 18 | $36

Redwood City | 831 Main St. (bet. B'way & Middlefield Rd.) | 650-366-4366 | www.martinswestgp.com

"Who knew Scottish food could be this good?" marvel newcomers to this Redwood City "true gastropub" that's a "secret location" for "delicious fare" including "fish 'n'chips that are among the best", "not-to-be-missed" Scotch eggs and "the best haggis-on-a-stick west of Edinburgh" plus a "great beer and whiskey selection"; there's a "convivial", "cool vibe" underscored by "reclaimed decor", though service varies and penny-pinchers lament "alas, prices are, well pricey."

Max's Cafe of Redwood City *Deli* — 17 | 15 | 17 | $27

Redwood City | Sequoia Station | 1001 El Camino Real (James Ave.) | 650-365-6297

Max's Opera Cafe of Palo Alto *Deli*

Palo Alto | Stanford Shopping Ctr. | 711 Stanford Shopping Ctr. (Sand Hill Rd.) | 650-323-6297

Max's Restaurant and Bar *Deli*

Burlingame | 1250 Old Bayshore Hwy. (B'way) | 650-342-6297
www.maxsworld.com

See review in City of San Francisco Directory.

Mayfield Bakery & Café *Bakery/Californian* — 20 | 18 | 18 | $37

Palo Alto | Town & Country Vill. | 855 El Camino Real (Embarcadero Rd.) | 650-853-9200 | www.mayfieldbakery.com

"Large and always bustling", this Californian sibling of Village Pub and Spruce situated in Palo Alto's Town & Country "strip mall" serves "wholesome" fare all day that includes produce "straight from a local farm" plus desserts and "excellent bread from its own bakery next door"; while service needs "polish", backers say it's a "great place" to "celebrity-watch" for noteworthy "VCs."

Mayflower *Chinese* — 20 | 13 | 14 | $31

Milpitas | 428 Barber Ln. (Bellew Dr.) | 408-922-2700

Hong Kong Flower Lounge *Chinese*

Millbrae | 51 Millbrae Ave. (bet. B'way & El Camino Real) | 650-692-6666
www.mayflower-seafood.com

See review in City of San Francisco Directory.

McCormick & Schmick's *Seafood* — 21 | 20 | 20 | $45

San Jose | Fairmont San Jose | 170 S. Market St. (San Carlos St.) | 408-283-7200 | www.mccormickandschmicks.com

"Classic seafood" and "great views" combine at this "upscale" chain link situated just inside the Fairmont San Jose, whose menu "changes daily and always has many tantalizing options"; "lots of wood and brass" contribute to a "festive environment" where "you're treated very well", and if some find it all "predictable" and "overpriced", those who "come for happy hour instead" "love" the "values."

	FOOD	DECOR	SERVICE	COST

Melting Pot *Fondue* | 16 | 18 | 18 | $50 |

San Mateo | 2 N. B St. (Baldwin Ave.) | 650-342-6358 |
www.meltingpot.com

See review in North of San Francisco Directory.

Mezza Luna *Italian* | 22 | 19 | 22 | $37 |

Princeton by the Sea | 459 Prospect Way (Capistrano Rd.) |
650-728-8108 | www.mezzalunabythesea.com

Caffè Mezza Luna *Italian*

Half Moon Bay | Oceana Hotel & Harbor Vill. | 240 Capistrano Rd.
(Hwy. 1) | 650-560-0137

"Lovely Italian classics", including fish prepared "correctly",
served by a "charming" staff in a "simply beautiful location adjacent to the marina" make this Princeton by the Sea trattoria an "informal go-to"; the cafe "offshoot" in Half Moon Bay "doesn't quite
meet expectations", but you "can't go wrong with any of the sandwiches and salad choices", especially if you snag "a window seat
for the view."

Mistral *French/Italian* | 20 | 19 | 20 | $42 |

Redwood Shores | 370-6 Bridge Pkwy. (Marine Pkwy.) |
650-802-9222 | www.mistraldining.com

Popular for both "business and pleasure", this "lovely" bistro "off
the beaten path" in Redwood Shores is a "solid value" for "fresh"
French-Italian fare that's both "consistent" with a varied wine list
that "should keep you interested" if you're an oenophile; the "attentive" servers and "stunning patio" "overlooking the water" contribute to the "lovely ambiance."

Montrio Bistro *Californian* | 23 | 22 | 23 | $51 |

Monterey | 414 Calle Principal (Franklin St.) | 831-648-8880 |
www.montrio.com

"The mood is friendly and casual, just like Downtown Monterey itself"
at this "lively" "winner", where the "consistently" "excellent"
Californian fare (with Southwestern and Italian accents) is crafted
from "fresh local ingredients" and served with "great wines" by staffers who "genuinely care"; set in a "pretty" revamped firehouse, it's
"where the locals go – for a reason" – and favored by visitors who
"would be regulars" if they "lived closer."

Morton's The Steakhouse *Steak* | 23 | 21 | 23 | $72 |

San Jose | 177 Park Ave. (bet. Almaden Blvd. & Market St.) |
408-947-7000 | www.mortons.com

See review in City of San Francisco Directory.

Mundaka *Spanish* | ∇ 24 | 15 | 20 | $39 |

Carmel | San Carlos St. (bet. Ocean & 7th Aves.) | 831-624-7400 |
www.mundakacarmel.com

There's "never a dull moment" at this "engaging" Spaniard in
Downtown Carmel, an "inspired take on the traditional tapas bar"
where chef Brandon Miller's selection of "inventive, flavorful" small
plates "changes nightly" and an "informed staff cheerfully guides you
through"; DJs regularly enliven a "funky", earthy space constructed
from reclaimed materials, and with "reasonable" wine prices and
housemade sangria flowing freely, it's "just a blast."

	FOOD	DECOR	SERVICE	COST

Muracci's Japanese Curri & Grill 🅱 *Japanese*

21 | 8 | 15 | $16

Los Altos | 244 State St. (bet. 2nd & 3rd Sts.) | 650-917-1101 | www.muraccis.com

See review in City of San Francisco Directory.

Naomi Sushi 🅼 *Japanese*

▽ 20 | 12 | 20 | $34

Menlo Park | 1328 El Camino Real (bet. Glenwood & Oak Grove Aves.) | 650-321-6902 | www.naomisushi.com

"Sit at the bar", "say 'omakase' and wait for the very fresh and inventive food to come" at this Menlo Park Japanese "go-to"; the setting may be "simple", but the chef "will do you right" with his "beautiful" sushi, and a "great selection of sake" complements the cuisine.

Navio *American*

25 | 26 | 25 | $73

Half Moon Bay | Ritz-Carlton Half Moon Bay | 1 Miramontes Point Rd. (Hwy. 1) | 650-712-7000 | www.ritzcarlton.com

A "stunning ocean view" and "ship-shaped" dining room set the stage for this "jewel on the Coast", where "excellent" New American cuisine delivered with the "spot-on" service "expected from Ritz" make it "the place to be in Half Moon Bay" for a "special experience"; granted, tabs are "steep" but "worth it" for the "limitless Sunday brunch" (especially "if you like caviar") or a "romantic sunset dinner."

Nepenthe *American*

16 | 25 | 17 | $35

Big Sur | 48510 Hwy. 1 (¼ mi. south of Ventana Inn & Spa) | 831-667-2345 | www.nepenthebigsur.com

"It's worth a drive down the coast" for "the views (simply breathtaking)" and "the vibe (Big Sur bohemian)" at this "mythic", "Frank Lloyd Wright-esque" "hippie" haunt "perched on a cliff"; "yes, it's a tourist stop" with "epic waits" and "pokey" service, and "you'll pay out the nose" for basic "burgers" and bottles, but "when it's not fogged in", the patio vista will "blow your mind, man."

Nick's on Main 🅱🅼 *American*

26 | 20 | 24 | $53

Los Gatos | 35 E. Main St. (College Ave.) | 408-399-6457 | www.nicksonmainst.com

Besides being a "great host", "personable" chef-owner Nick Difu is "an artist in the kitchen" who'll "dazzle" with his "inspiring" "creations" at this "real find" in Los Gatos, a "teensy" "gem" that "entices" with "simply" "wonderful" New American fare "cooked to perfection" and served by an "excellent" team; diners are "crammed together" in "noisy" quarters ("a nice neighbor is imperative"), but it's "all so worth" any "seating issues" – in fact, the "one problem" is "it's impossible to get a table."

North Beach Pizza *Pizza*

19 | 11 | 15 | $20

San Mateo | 240 E. Third Ave. (B St.) | 650-344-5000 | www.northbeachpizza.net

See review in City of San Francisco Directory.

Old Port Lobster Shack *Seafood*

21 | 11 | 16 | $31

Redwood City | 851 Veteran's Blvd. (bet. Jefferson Ave. & Middlefield Rd.) | 650-366-2400 | www.oplobster.com

"If you can't get to Bar Harbor", this "New England–style" "seafood shack" with "an unlikely location" in a Redwood strip mall is "the next best thing" for "fantastic fresh" lobster rolls (try 'em "naked with just drawn butter") partnered with "Allagash ale" and "a cup of chowdah"; "tacky" quarters with "picnic tables and benches" mean the "comfort level is low" while "prices are high", but for Yankee "refugees" "longing for Maine" it's "authentic as heck" and "cheaper than flying."

O'mei Ⓜ Chinese ▽ 20 | 13 | 14 | $31

Santa Cruz | 2316 Mission St. (Fair Ave.) | 831-425-8458 | www.omeichow.com

The "excellent" Chinese chow – "everything tastes fresh" and each dish has a "distinct" flavor – is the "best" in Santa Cruz aver aficionados of the "addicting" green beans and other "creatively prepared" fare; "o'mei, oh my", the "surly" "service leaves a lot to be desired", as does the "run-down" location "in a nondescript strip mall", but most maintain that's worth enduring for some of the "most innovative" Sichuan around.

Original Joe's ❶ American/Italian 22 | 16 | 21 | $33
(aka Joe's, OJ's)

San Jose | 301 S. First St. (San Carlos St.) | 408-292-7030 | www.originaljoes.com

"A throwback to the past", this "seriously old-school" "Downtown San Jose institution" delivers "huge portions" of "traditional" Italian-American fare, like "meat and fish done simply but well" ("anything off the grill" is "best"); if some surveyors say it's "solid but not spectacular", nostalgists counter that "the experience is the draw", from the "top-of-the-line professional servers" to "watching the chefs" from a perch at the counter.

Osteria Ⓢ Italian 23 | 15 | 18 | $36

Palo Alto | 247 Hamilton Ave. (Ramona St.) | 650-328-5700

"Fantastic" "fresh" pasta – "served piping hot" in "large portions" – "more than offsets" the "utilitarian" decor at this perpetually "packed" trattoria in Palo Alto; "tight" seating and "over-the-top noise" rankle some, as do servers who swerve from "efficient" to "brusque", but "you won't care" claim patrons, since the Italian fare is "absolutely delicious" and "you won't have to pay an arm and a leg for it" either.

NEW Osteria Coppa Italian/Pizza 24 | 18 | 21 | $42

San Mateo | 139 S. B St. (bet. 1st & 2nd Aves.) | 650-579-6021 | www.osteriacoppa.com

"City-quality" artisanal pizzas and "darn good" "homemade pastas" are the double bill at this new suburban Italian ("think Tuscany in San Mateo") where an "alum of Quince" turns out "carefully prepared", seasonally "soulful" cucina (albeit in "very small portions"), accompanied by quartinos of Boot vinos; aside from the "rock-band" level of noise from the "'too-cool-for school' bar scene" and "struggling" service during "peak hours", "it's a delightful find" on the Peninsula, particularly if you perch "on the patio."

Oswald Restaurant Ⓜ American ▽ 25 | 21 | 23 | $41

Santa Cruz | 121 Soquel Ave. (Front St.) | 831-423-7427 | www.oswaldrestaurant.com

"Every dish is a winner" at this "urban" enclave in Santa Cruz, where "sterling" New American fare is "expertly prepared" by chef Damani

Thomas from "incredibly fresh" local ingredients and matched with "delightful specialty drinks", a "robust wine list" and "outstanding" service; "concrete floors, stainless-steel finishes" and a "view into the kitchen" make for a "metro feel", and while "loud" "at peak times", some feel it's the "best" pick Downtown; P.S. the $29 "Wednesday prix fixe dinner" "is a steal."

☑ Pacific's Edge American/French
24 | 28 | 24 | $81

Carmel | Hyatt Highlands Inn | 120 Highlands Dr. (Hwy. 1) | 831-622-5445 | www.pacificsedge.com

"Usually places with great views have lousy food", but this spot "set on a cliff by the Pacific" "breaks the mold" – not only does it serve up "stunning views of the surf" ("take the earliest reservation you can get so you don't miss" the sight), it offers "outstanding" New American-French tasting menus, "impeccable service" and a "wine list that literally looks like an encyclopedia"; while it "doesn't come cheap", well-heeled types maintain there is "no better place" in Carmel to "watch the sunset", be it at a window table in the "swank" "formal dining room" or, more affordably, over "drinks in the bar."

Pampas Brazilian
22 | 23 | 23 | $56

Palo Alto | 529 Alma St. (bet. Hamilton & University Aves.) | 650-327-1323 | www.pampaspaloalto.com

"Cholesterol be damned" declare "hungry" "carnivores", who "go crazy" "gorging" themselves at this "huge" Palo Alto Brazilian churrascaria offering "endless servings" of an "impressive" selection of "delicious" grilled meats that servers "bring to the table"; it's "simply heaven for meat lovers", but there's an "incredible salad selection" as well, and a "live jazz band" on weekends makes the "elegant" environs even more "energetic" and "fun."

Pancho Villa Taqueria Mexican
22 | 8 | 14 | $13

San Mateo | 365 S. B St. (bet. 3rd & 4th Aves.) | 650-343-4123 | www.smpanchovilla.com

See review in City of San Francisco Directory.

Parcel 104 Californian
23 | 20 | 21 | $65

Santa Clara | Santa Clara Marriott | 2700 Mission College Blvd. (bet. Freedom Circle & Great America Pkwy.) | 408-970-6104 | www.parcel104.com

An "oasis" for "Silicon Valley types" who require a "quiet atmosphere" for a "perfect" "power lunch", this "beautifully decorated" Californian in the Santa Clara Marriott also receives kudos for its "inventive" menu and "very good wine list"; "you'll forget you're eating in a hotel" thanks to the "excellent" fare "with a focus on fresh local produce" and the "professional service", though the "pricey" tab leaves some saying "I love going here when someone else is paying."

☑ Passionfish Californian/Seafood
27 | 20 | 25 | $47

Pacific Grove | 701 Lighthouse Ave. (Congress Ave.) | 831-655-3311 | www.passionfish.net

"Creatively prepared", "nicely plated", "eco-friendly" fish dishes plus "phenomenal" "alternatives" for carnivores, served by a "sincere and efficient" staff, ensure "lines out the door" at this "neighborhood" Californian in Pacific Grove; everyone "loves the sustainable ethos", but oenophiles are especially "passionate" about the "killer" wine list "priced just a few dollars over retail" – all of which "offsets the crowded" digs.

Pasta Moon *Italian*

| 24 | 21 | 22 | $40 |

Half Moon Bay | 315 Main St. (Kelly St.) | 650-726-5125 | www.pastamoon.com

"Just as the name" suggests, "some of the tastiest pastas around" "lead the parade" of "creative" cuisine fashioned from "local produce" at this "welcoming" "favorite" in "beautiful" Half Moon Bay; it "may not have a view", but still it's "worth the trip over the hill", since the "the prices are not outrageous" and the "welcoming atmosphere" (courtesy of the chef-owner and his staff) "makes you want to linger over a luscious Barolo" on the "adventurous" "all-Italian wine list."

Pasta Pomodoro *Italian*

| 16 | 13 | 17 | $23 |

Redwood City | 490 El Camino Real (Whipple Ave.) | 650-474-2400
San Bruno | Bayhill Ctr. | 811A Cherry Ave. (San Bruno Ave.) | 650-583-6622
San Jose | Evergreen Mkt. | 4898 San Felipe Rd. (Yerba Buena Blvd.) | 408-532-0271
San Mateo | Bay Meadows | 1060 Park Pl. (Saratoga Dr.) | 650-574-2600
www.pastapomodoro.com
See review in City of San Francisco Directory.

Patxi's Chicago Pizza *Pizza*

| 22 | 14 | 17 | $21 |

Palo Alto | 441 Emerson St. (bet. Lytton & University Aves.) | 650-473-9999 | www.patxispizza.com
See review in City of San Francisco Directory.

Piatti *Italian*

| 19 | 19 | 19 | $40 |

Santa Clara | 3905 Rivermark Plaza (Montague Expwy.) | 408-330-9212 | www.piatti.com
See review in East of San Francisco Directory.

Pizza Antica *Pizza*

| 20 | 15 | 17 | $28 |

San Jose | Santana Row | 334 Santana Row (Alyssum Ln.) | 408-557-8373 | www.pizzaantica.com

"Happy families" "in the 'burbs" "couldn't live without" this "very popular" in-state chain, "a safe choice" for "casual" Italian bites led by "tasty" "flatbread-style pizza" that merges a "crispy crust" with "interesting toppings"; but while the eating's "surprisingly good" "for the price point", "service varies" and "kid-friendly" antics create an "earsplitting" "din" "during peak periods", so aim to "snag a table outside."

🅩 Plumed Horse 🅈 *Californian*

| 26 | 26 | 25 | $90 |

Saratoga | 14555 Big Basin Way (4th St.) | 408-867-4711 | www.plumedhorse.com

"Recently morphed into a very upscale" establishment, this South Bay "staple" might feel "more at home in Manhattan than sleepy Saratoga", trotting out "fantastic" Californian fare in an über-modern" dining room that "exudes refinement"; "prices are ridiculously high" and the "attentive staff" can be "a bit snobbish", but it's definitely designed "for a special occasion" or to "bring your wine-loving friends for theatrics involving one-of-a-kind glassware", an "à la carte champagne cart" and a "cellar like no other."

	FOOD	DECOR	SERVICE	COST

Pluto's Fresh Food for a Hungry Universe *American* | 21 | 12 | 16 | $14 |

Palo Alto | 482 University Ave. (Cowper St.) | 650-853-1556
San Jose | Santana Row | 3055 Olin Ave. (S. Winchester Blvd.) |
408-247-9120
www.plutosfreshfood.com
See review in City of San Francisco Directory.

Quattro Restaurant & Bar *Italian* | 22 | 22 | 23 | $57 |

East Palo Alto | Four Seasons Hotel | 2050 University Ave. (Woodland Ave.) |
650-470-2889 | www.fourseasons.com
The "ultramodern" dining room with "high ceilings" is a "handsome"
setting for the "imaginative" menu at this "elegant" "hidden gem" in
East Palo Alto that delivers "Four Seasons quality" from the kitchen in
the form of a "fresh" take on "classic" Italian fare delivered with "superior service" worthy of the "wonderful hotel" in which it's located;
undoubtedly "expensive", it's still "worth it" insist expense-
accounters, who come to conduct "quiet" "business discussions."

Restaurant at Ventana *Californian* | 21 | 26 | 23 | $59 |

Big Sur | Ventana Inn & Spa | 48123 Hwy. 1 (Coast Ridge Rd.) |
831-667-2331 | www.ventanainn.com
"Unforgettable" "on a nice day", this "classy" Californian boasts a rustic interior "to match the inn" and an "expansive terrace" that's a
"stunning" daytime aerie with "spectacular views" overlooking "the
beautiful coast" of Big Sur; while the spendy seasonal fare is "very
good" and service is "gracious", it's the "one-of-a-kind" setting that'll
make you want to "stay forever."

Rio Grill *Californian* | 21 | 19 | 22 | $42 |

Carmel | Crossroads Shopping Ctr. | 101 Crossroads Blvd. (Rio Rd.) |
831-625-5436 | www.riogrill.com
You "can always count on a fun time" at this "casual" Carmel "roadhouse", where the "great bar" and "nice choice of wines" stoke a "festive" vibe; "don't be turned off by the strange location" "in a shopping
center", say supporters, because the "well-trained" staff brings "generous portions" of "wonderful" Californian cuisine "with a slant to the
Southwest", and since "prices are reasonable for the area", it attracts
a "loyal" "local" clientele "year after year."

Ristorante Avanti *Californian/Italian*   ▽ | 24 | 16 | 21 | $37 |

Santa Cruz | Palm Shopping Ctr. | 1711 Mission St. (Bay St.) |
831-427-0135 | www.ristoranteavanti.com
"One of Santa Cruz's finest" since 1987, this Cal-Italian "treasure"
"tucked inconspicuously in a shopping strip" "always stuns" with "superlative fare" "prepared with a light touch" from "incredibly fresh",
"very local" and "mostly organic" ingredients and paired with an "innovative wine list"; with its "outgoing, professional staff" and "super-
inviting" ambiance, it's "deservedly popular" with natives who advise
"don't pass by."

Ristorante Capellini *Italian* | 20 | 20 | 19 | $40 |

San Mateo | 310 Baldwin Ave. (B St.) | 650-348-2296 | www.capellinis.com
Perhaps it's the wood-burning oven, but the aromas at this "old
standby" in San Mateo "make the mouth water"; "outstanding for

groups", the Pat Kuleto–designed interior has four different dining areas, including a "kitchen bar" where you can "watch the guys cook" while sipping a "great" martini; and though service can vary, aficionados agree that the midpriced Italian menu – which includes many "wonderful" meat dishes – is "consistently good."

Roti Indian Bistro Indian   21 | 16 | 18 | $33
Burlingame | 209 Park Rd. (bet. Burlingame & Howard Aves.) | 650-340-7684 | www.rotibistro.com
See review in City of San Francisco Directory.

Roy's at Pebble Beach Hawaiian   24 | 26 | 23 | $58
Pebble Beach | The Inn at Spanish Bay | 2700 17 Mile Dr. (Congress Rd.) | 831-647-7423 | www.roysrestaurant.com
Arguably "the best Roy's on the mainland", this "reliably Yamaguchi" venue in Pebble Beach turns out the same "delicious" "faithfully" "Asian fusion"–Hawaiian fare proffered at all the branches – only here it's augmented by a "gorgeous location overlooking the golf course and ocean at Spanish Bay"; yes, you're surrounded by "argyle-sweater" clad "snobbies", but service is above par, as are "drinks on the terrace by a fire pit" replete with a "sunset view" and "bagpiper coming through the dunes."

Sakae Sushi Noboru Japanese   ∇ 26 | 18 | 21 | $62
Burlingame | 243 California Dr. (bet. Burlingame & Howard Aves.) | 650-348-4064 | www.sakaesushi.com
"If you like raw fish, you'll love" the "fantastic sushi" at this "incredible" Burlingame Japanese, where "elegant" presentations of "the freshest" catch "flown in from Tsukiji Market in Tokyo" (and "creative" "cooked offerings") distract from the nondescript decor; with primo sakes to "top it off" "the tab will run up quickly", but finthusiasts who "have yet to be disappointed" deem it "a treat" "on par with the best."

Sakoon Indian   23 | 22 | 19 | $36
Mountain View | 357 Castro St. (bet. California & Dana Sts.) | 650-965-2000 | www.sakoonrestaurant.com
There's plenty of "eye candy" at this "cooler-than-cool" Mountain View "modern Indian", where the "crazy" decor is "like eating in a Bollywood movie" – but no slum dogs, please, since it's far more "upscale" than the "typical strip-mall" affair and the "innovative" "fusion" menu "overflows with robust" flavors; there's a "personable" staff, or serve yourself at the "great lunch buffet with all the stars of the menu."

Sam's Chowder House Seafood   20 | 19 | 18 | $36
Half Moon Bay | 4210 N. Cabrillo Hwy. (Capistrano Rd.) | 650-712-0245 | www.samschowderhouse.com
"Awesome views" entice "tourists" and natives alike to this "casual" surfside seafooder on Half Moon Bay to relish "traditional" "Eastern chowder" and "signature lobster rolls" as they "soak in" the "glorious" "sunset over the ocean"; spoilers say it's "spendy" for "quite average" food, but "it's got location going for it" so "huge crowds" turn up "no matter what the weather"; P.S. Sam's Chowdermobile roves the Bay (www.samschowdermobile.com).

	FOOD	DECOR	SERVICE	COST

Sardine Factory *American/Seafood* | 21 | 22 | 22 | $57 |

Monterey | 701 Wave St. (Prescott Ave.) | 831-373-3775 |
www.sardinefactory.com

A "veteran" that's "kept its standards", this Cannery Row "institution" remains a "fave" among out-of-towners for "consistent" American seafood served in "comfortable" confines with an "old-style" dining room and "awesome" glassed-in conservatory; critics claim it's "overpriced" ("especially the wine menu") and "a little long in the tooth", but it "still delivers" for the faithful.

Scott's of Palo Alto *Seafood* | 20 | 20 | 21 | $42 |

Palo Alto | Town & Country Vill. | 855 El Camino Real (Embarcadero Rd.) |
650-323-1555 | www.scottsseafoodpa.com

Scott's of San Jose *Seafood*

San Jose | 185 Park Ave. (bet. Almaden Blvd. & Market St.) |
408-971-1700 | www.scottsseafoodsj.com
See review in East of San Francisco Directory.

Sent Sovi Ⓜ *Californian* | 23 | 19 | 23 | $77 |

Saratoga | 14583 Big Basin Way (5th St.) | 408-867-3110 |
www.sentsovi.com

It's a "superb way to celebrate" at this "charming" Saratoga standout that "really caters to your every desire" with "delicious", "thoughtfully prepared" Californian fare and an "exceptionally edited wine list" delivered by "attentive" but "unpretentious" staffers in a "very intimate" country-cottage setting that's "perfect for a romantic evening"; the prix fixe specials and theme dinners "showcase" the chef's "creativity", but if you've got "deep pockets", "go for the tasting menu."

71 Saint Peter Ⓧ *Californian/Mediterranean* | 20 | 17 | 18 | $41 |

San Jose | San Pedro Sq. | 71 N. San Pedro St. (bet. W. Santa Clara &
W. St. John Sts.) | 408-971-8523 | www.71saintpeter.com

Devout diners "watch the world go by" at this "funky", brick-walled bistro situated in San Jose's San Pedro Square that serves a "creative" Cal-Med menu, including a "great-value seasonal prix fixe"; though some confess "service could be better", most find it an "interesting" (even "romantic") choice for the area, and there's an outdoor patio too.

Shadowbrook *Californian* | 18 | 24 | 20 | $50 |

Capitola | 1750 Wharf Rd. (Capitola Rd.) | 831-475-1511 |
www.shadowbrook-capitola.com

The "sublime" setting, with "views of a babbling brook" in Capitola, makes this "romantic" destination a "tourist favorite", but even locals like to "take the tram" through the "luscious" garden to celebrate a "special night out" in this "lovely fantasy world"; the "well-prepared" Cal menu strikes some as merely "satisfactory", and the frugal are fond of the "festive" bar, for a "better deal" and a "more casual" experience.

Shalimar ⊅ *Indian/Pakistani* | 22 | 3 | 11 | $16 |

Sunnyvale | 1146 W. El Camino Real (bet. Bernardo & Grape Aves.) |
408-530-0300 | www.shalimarsv.com
See review in City of San Francisco Directory.

Shokolaat 🔲Ⓜ️ *Californian* ▽ 17 | 16 | 17 | $41

Palo Alto | 516 University Ave. (Cowper St.) | 650-289-0719 |
www.shokolaat.com

"Creative" Californian cuisine joins "outlandishly lovely chocolates"
and other desserts at this Palo Alto multitasker where the "nice
owner" has combined a restaurant and patisserie in one; some say it's
a "solid" "sleeper", but the less-impressed indicate the "itty-bitty
dishes" are "not really worth the prices", and quip it's "great if you're
on a diet and an expense account."

🆉 Sierra Mar *Californian/Eclectic* 27 | 29 | 26 | $93

Big Sur | Post Ranch Inn | Hwy. 1 (30 mi. south of Carmel) |
831-667-2200 | www.postranchinn.com

"Stellar views" of the Pacific "elevate the experience" at this "truly exceptional" "clifftop" "destination" – voted the Bay Area's No. 1 for
Decor – in Big Sur's Post Ranch Inn, an "elegant" overlook with "walls
of windows" that's "equally spectacular" for its "sophisticated"
Cal-Eclectic cuisine, an "enormous" wine list and "personalized" service; "prices are also in the stratosphere", but "pampered" epicures
consider it "well worth the splurge" (and lunch "on the terrace"
is "memorable" too).

Sino *Chinese* 19 | 21 | 16 | $36

San Jose | Santana Row | 377 Santana Row (Olsen Dr.) |
408-247-8880 | www.sinorestaurant.com

For "dim sum yum" and other "tasty" "Chinese-influenced" chow, San
Jose's "young professional" crowd congregates at this "trendy" spot
on Santana Row; it's a "little pricey" but "very enjoyable" maintain
most, who join the "happy" throngs in the "thumping" lounge, but critics carp about "high" prices and "hit-or-miss service", as well as how
"noisy" it is "as the night wears on."

Soif Wine Bar *Californian* ▽ 25 | 21 | 23 | $46

Santa Cruz | 105 Walnut Ave. (Pacific Ave.) | 831-423-2020 |
www.soifwine.com

With its "perfect nibbles" and "plethora of wines", this "laid-back"
Santa Cruz vino bar "will surely please the palate" as the "knowledgeable staff" supplies "superb small plates" (or "full entrees") paired
with "fantastic" vinos poured "by the glass or in a flight" from bottles
available at the adjoining retailer; but bring a "well-prepared wallet"
as the tab "adds up quickly" "when you indulge."

Stacks *American* 18 | 13 | 18 | $20

Burlingame | 361 California Dr. (Lorton Ave.) | 650-579-1384
Menlo Park | 600 Santa Cruz Ave. (El Camino Real) | 650-838-0066
www.stacksrestaurant.com

See review in City of San Francisco Directory.

🆕 Station 1 Restaurant Ⓜ️ *Californian* 25 | 19 | 22 | $63

Woodside | 2991 Woodside Rd. (Mountain Home Rd.) |
650-851-4988 | www.station1restaurant.com

Set in a "cozy" historic firehouse, this Californian "start-up on the
'main drag' of Woodside" is already "firing on all engines", proffering
an "innovative", three-course prix fixe dinner dictated by "fresh, local
ingredients" and accompanied by "interesting" wines (by the glass or

pour) and pre-Prohibition cocktails; it's a "great cost-to-value proposition" and the staff is "incredibly warm", plus there's an à la carte Sunday Supper too.

St. Michael's Alley ⓈⓂ *Californian*   22 | 22 | 22 | $45

Palo Alto | 140 Homer Ave. (High St.) | 650-326-2530 | www.stmikes.com
"Imaginative" fare "emphasizing local seasonal ingredients" is matched with "wonderful" wines at this "popular" Palo Altan that moved to a "more comfortable" "light-filled space" in 2009; though a few find the Californian menu "a little too predictable", most maintain the prices are "reasonable" and the "smiling" service ensures "a warmth permeates the atmosphere"; P.S. brunch is served at the original location "a few blocks away" (806 Emerson Street) and it's "worth the wait."

Straits Restaurant *Singaporean*   20 | 19 | 17 | $40

Burlingame | 1100 Burlingame Ave. (California Dr.) |
650-373-7883
San Jose | Santana Row | 333 Santana Row (Alyssum Ln.) | 408-246-6320
www.straitsrestaurants.com

Straits Cafe *Singaporean*

Palo Alto | 3295 El Camino Real (Lambert Ave.) | 650-494-7168 |
www.straitscafepaloalto.com
See review in City of San Francisco Directory.

Sumika Ⓜ *Japanese*   ▽ 22 | 16 | 20 | $42

Los Altos | 236 Central Plaza (bet. 2nd & 3rd Sts.) | 650-917-1822 |
www.sumikagrill.com
"Dig into stick after stick of yakitori" at this "surprising" Japanese "find" in a "hide-and-seek" Los Altos locale, which reaches "Tokyo's level" according to kushiyaki connoisseurs craving "delicious" "grilled-on-a-skewer" specialties ("come with an open mind") and "outstanding donburi for lunch"; it may seem "expensive" given the spare setting, but the "amazing attention to detail and fresh ingredients make all the difference."

Tai Pan *Chinese*   22 | 21 | 20 | $39

Palo Alto | 560 Waverley St. (bet. Hamilton & University Aves.) |
650-329-9168 | www.taipanpaloalto.com
Accolytes attest you can "taste the quality" of the "authentic", "winning" "Hong Kong-style" eats, including a "variety" of "elegant dim sum" ("from a menu, not a cart") at this Palo Alto "old standard" near Stanford; "your parents will approve" of the "attentive service" and "beautiful" "white-tablecloth" decor, and while it may be "pricey for Chinese", "it's worth it."

Tamarine *Vietnamese*   26 | 23 | 23 | $55

Palo Alto | 546 University Ave. (bet. Cowper & Webster Sts.) |
650-325-8500 | www.tamarinerestaurant.com
"Hot" and "hip", this Palo Alto Vietnamese delivers "seductive" flavors, luring a "trendy" crowd "back again and again" for "creative", "delicious and beautifully prepared" (if "pricey") "small plates" and "fancy", "fabulous cocktails"; service is "refined" in the "lovely" modern setting, but it can get "crowded and noisy", so be sure to "make a reservation", or come at lunch when the "set menu is a bargain."

Taqueria Tlaquepaque *Mexican* ▽ 20 | 9 | 12 | $19

San Jose | 2222 Lincoln Ave. (bet. Curtner & Franquette Aves.) | 408-978-3665

San Jose | 699 Curtner Ave. (Canoas Garden Ave.) | 408-448-1230 ⬧

San Jose | 721 Willow St. (Delmas Ave.) | 408-287-9777

"Homegrown San Jose folk" swear by the "cheap" eats at this trio of Mexican cubbyholes, which depend on their specialty chile verde and other traditional faves to distract from eyesore decor and nonchalant service; critics counter the food's "not as great" as its champions claim, though all applaud the 'Super Chavela' blend of "beer and tequila."

Tarpy's Roadhouse *American* 20 | 21 | 21 | $42

Monterey | 2999 Monterey-Salinas Hwy. (Canyon Del Rey Blvd.) | 831-647-1444 | www.tarpys.com

They "give roadhouses a very good name" at this "unpretentious" outpost situated "away from everything" in Monterey, long a "dependable" stop for "well-prepared" "Americana", "local wines" and Sunday brunch; whether in the "warm, comfortable" interior of the old stone homestead or on the "leisurely" "patio", "generally everyone leaves happy."

Thea Mediterranean Cuisine *Greek/Mediterranean* 19 | 21 | 19 | $37

San Jose | Santana Row | 3090 Olsen Dr. (S. Winchester Blvd.) | 408-260-1444 | www.thearestaurant.com

The "beautiful" "open" dining room as well as the "outside seats" where you can watch Santana Row "shoppers stroll by" are a "favorite" San Jose setting for a "fun social night out" say diners who "go with a group" to share items on the midpriced Med menu; though the "crowd can be stifling" "on weekends" and some suggest "there are better Greek restaurants" around, devotees declare "they do a more than adequate job", and there's "even a belly dancer" on Friday and Saturday nights.

Three Seasons *Vietnamese* 19 | 18 | 18 | $40

Palo Alto | 518 Bryant St. (University Ave.) | 650-838-0353 | www.threeseasonsrestaurant.com

"Tucked into a Downtown alley", this "hip" Palo Alto Vietnamese offers a "wonderful combination of seasonings and flavors" in "tasty tidbits" that come at moderate tabs; service is helpful and friendly in the room with a tropical look, though some stick to the outside terrace for lunch or for "people-watching and drinks" on "a summer evening."

Trader Vic's *Polynesian* 17 | 22 | 19 | $46

Palo Alto | Dina's Garden Hotel | 4269 El Camino Real (bet. Charleston & San Antonio Rds.) | 650-849-9800 | www.tradervicspaloalto.com
See review in East of San Francisco Directory.

Twist Café Ⓜ *American/French* 18 | 15 | 17 | $37

Campbell | 247 E. Campbell Ave. (bet. 1st & 2nd Sts.) | 408-374-8982 | www.twist-cafe.com

Furnishing "European flair in Campbell" with a "homemade" twist, this local hang adds "authentic French" accents to "well-prepared" New American fare served in a daytime-only cafe with "outside" seating; it's widely liked for "casual meals", though a "full house" can hamper "kitchen efficiency" and "cause service delays."

231 Ellsworth ⬧ *American*

23 | 21 | 23 | $62

San Mateo | 231 S. Ellsworth Ave. (bet. 2nd & 3rd Aves.) | 650-347-7231 | www.231ellsworth.com

A "perennial favorite" for a "romantic date" or sealing a "lucrative business deal", this "quiet", intimate San Mateo "institution" proffers "imaginative", "elegantly prepared" New American fare and a "wide, well-selected wine selection"; the tasting menu, while "pretty pricey", is "done to perfection", and though a few find the decor a "bit stuffy", the "stellar" staff can be counted on "to meet your needs."

Udupi Palace *Indian/Vegetarian*

21 | 8 | 15 | $18

Sunnyvale | 976 E. El Camino Real (Poplar Ave.) | 408-830-9600 | www.udupipalaceca.com

See review in City of San Francisco Directory.

Village Pub, The *American*

26 | 24 | 24 | $67

Woodside | 2967 Woodside Rd. (Whiskey Hill Rd.) | 650-851-9888 | www.thevillagepub.net

"As welcoming as the name implies", this Woodside "classic" buzzes with "Silicon Valley celebrities", "titans of tech and the venture capitalists who fund them", who settle into its "comfy booths" for everything from "super lunches" to "special occasions" featuring "sophisticated" New American "comfort food" and "premier cru wines", "leisurely" enjoyed by the fireplace; "pampering" waiters seal the deal, but if you're not among the "well-heeled", not to worry: the "more reasonably priced" bar is the "place to come if you are in boots."

Viognier *Californian/French*

23 | 20 | 22 | $61

San Mateo | Draeger's Mktpl. | 222 E. Fourth Ave. (bet. B St. & Ellsworth Ave.) | 650-685-3727 | www.viognierrestaurant.com

The "surprisingly" "excellent seasonal tasting menus" – "fit for foodies" and made from the "freshest ingredients" – overcome the "odd location" "atop" an "upscale supermarket" at this "elegant and understated" San Mateo "special-event" spot; the Cal-French menu is "costly", say some, but it's "worth the price" proclaim partisans, who are partial to the "incredible wine list" and "engaging" staff.

Wakuriya ⓜ *Japanese*

▽ 27 | 22 | 27 | $98

(aka Japanese Kitchen Wakuriya)

San Mateo | Crystal Springs Vill. Shopping Ctr. | 115 De Anza Blvd. (bet. Parrott Dr. & Polhemus Rd.) | 650-286-0410 | www.wakuriya.com

Despite being "hidden" in a San Mateo strip mall, this "small" "haute Japanese" run by a "husband-and-wife team (both formerly of Kaygetsu)" dazzles diners with "exquisite" "artfully designed" seasonally changing kaiseki dinners that "hit one high note after another"; "impeccable service", along with "exceptional, but also expensive" "well-coordinated flights" of sake up the ante, so while there's only "one menu per night" and you must "book one month in advance", for an "indulgence", it's "as good as it comes."

	FOOD	DECOR	SERVICE	COST

Wicket's Bistro *Californian*

| | - | - | - | E |

Carmel Valley | Bernardus Lodge | 415 Carmel Valley Rd.
(Laureles Grade Rd.) | 831-658-3400 | www.bernardus.com

The "beautiful patio" "is the place to be" at this Carmel Valley Californian, "a more casual" sidekick to the Bernardus Lodge's tony Marinus where the "heavenly" "outdoor setting" with a "view of the lawns" compensates for a "quite bland" interior; serving an abbreviated menu of pricey, "solid" bistro fare, it's a "dependable" retreat "on a warm day" or by the open-air fireplace when the temperature dips.

Will's Fargo Dining House & Saloon *Seafood/Steak*

| | ▽ 21 | 22 | 23 | $48 |

Carmel Valley | Carmel Valley Vill. | 16 W. Carmel Valley Rd.
(bet. Purton Ln. & Village Dr.) | 831-659-2774 | www.bernardus.com

Done up as a ritzy roadhouse, this circa-1959 surf 'n' turf trouper indulges Carmel Valley carnivores with "surprisingly excellent" steaks and "California wines" from its nearby partner, Bernardus Winery; the "warm service" and "charming atmosphere" are especially welcome since for an old-fashioned red meat spree, it's about "the only game in town"; P.S. closed Tuesday and Wednesday.

Xanh *Vietnamese*

| | 21 | 21 | 19 | $39 |

Mountain View | 110 Castro St. (Evelyn Ave.) | 650-964-1888 |
www.xanhrestaurant.com

"Hip young things" throng to this "trendy" Mountain View Vietnamese to "mingle" over "distinctively delicious" "artisanal" dishes and "fabulous cocktails" against a "glam" backdrop with a "wall of water" and "cool blue" color scheme; it's "wildly popular" both for its "outstanding" weekday "lunch buffet deal" and "pulsing", "clublike ambiance" after dark, complete with "off-the-charts" din when there's a weekend DJ.

Yankee Pier *New England/Seafood*

| | 18 | 15 | 19 | $36 |

San Jose | Santana Row | 378 Santana Row (Olsen Dr.) | 408-244-1244
South San Francisco | San Francisco Int'l Airport |
United Domestic Departure Terminal 3 (Hwy. 101) | 650-821-8938
www.yankeepier.com

See review in North of San Francisco Directory.

Yuzu Sushi & Grill *Japanese*

| | ▽ 22 | 14 | 18 | $38 |

San Mateo | 54 37th Ave. (S. El Camino Real) | 650-358-0298

"Despite its suburban location", this San Mateo "gem" (a cut-rate companion to Sakae Sushi Noburu) "delivers" "authentic, high-end sushi" and Japanese "small dishes", including options "not normally seen" in a "neighborhood" "joint"; even with occasionally "slow service" it's "a real find", but "be warned" – the "teeny-tiny" space fills up fast.

Zibibbo ⊠ *Mediterranean*

| | 19 | 18 | 19 | $45 |

Palo Alto | 430 Kipling St. (bet. Lytton & University Aves.) |
650-328-6722 | www.zibibborestaurant.com

"Come hungry and bring friends" to this "relaxed" Palo Alto adjunct of SF's Restaurant Lulu, a "favorite" among "corporate" characters gathered in "groups" for "satisfying" Mediterranean "small plates", "bountiful platters" of rotisserie and "grilled meats" and flights from a "cool wine list"; naysayers knock the "cavernous space" and "uneven" execution, but a "convenient location" keeps the scene "boisterous."

INDEXES

LOCATION MAPS

All places are in San Francisco unless otherwise noted (East of San Francisco=E; North of San Francisco=N; South of San Francisco=S).

Cuisines

Includes names, locations and Food ratings.

AFGHAN

Helmand Palace | **Russian Hill** 22
Kabul Afghan | **multi.** 22

AMERICAN

🆉 Ad Hoc/Addendum | **Yountville/N** 27
🆉 Ahwahnee | **Yosemite/E** 18
Ame | **SoMa** 26
Amer. Cupcake | **Cow Hollow** 15
Amer. Grilled Cheese | **SoMa** 22
Aquarius | **Santa Cruz/S** 21
Arcadia | **San Jose/S** 20
Baker/Banker | **Upper Fillmore** 25
Balboa Cafe | **multi.** 19
Bardessono | **Yountville/N** 21
Bar Jules | **Hayes Valley** 23
Barndiva | **Healdsburg/N** 23
Basin | **Saratoga/S** 20
Beach Chalet | **Outer Sunset** 15
Benu | **SoMa** 26
🆉 Big 4 | **Nob Hill** 23
Big Sur | **Big Sur/S** 22
🆉 Bix | **Downtown** 24
Blue Plate | **Mission** 24
🆕 Bluestem Brass. | **SoMa** –
🆕 Bottle Cap | **N Beach** –
Boulette Larder | **Embarcadero** 25
🆉 Boulevard | **Embarcadero** 27
🆕 Bourbon | **Downtown** 24
🆕 Branches | **Ukiah/N** –
Brannan's Grill | **Calistoga/N** 18
Brazen Head | **Cow Hollow** 21
🆕 Brixton | **Cow Hollow** 15
🆉 Buckeye | **Mill Valley/N** 24
Bungalow 44 | **Mill Valley/N** 21
Café Flore | **Castro** 17
🆉 Cafe La Haye | **Sonoma/N** 27
🆕 Campanula | **N Beach** –
Cannery/Brew | **Monterey/S** 17
Caprice | **Tiburon/N** 22
Celadon | **Napa/N** 23
🆕 Chambers | **Tenderloin** –
Chapter & Moon | **Ft Bragg/N** 21
Cheesecake | **multi.** 17
Chenery Park | **Glen Pk** 21
Chloe's Cafe | **Noe Valley** 24
Chow | **multi.** 20
Citizen's Band | **SoMa** 21
🆉 Commis | **Oakland/E** 27

Commonwealth | **Mission** 24
Comstock | **N Beach** 16
Cosmopolitan | **SoMa** 18
Cuvée | **Napa/N** 22
Dipsea Cafe | **Mill Valley/N** 18
Duarte's | **Pescadero/S** 20
Duck Club | **multi.** 20
Elite Cafe | **Pacific Hts** 19
Ella's | **Presidio Hts** 21
🆉 Esin | **Danville/E** 25
Eureka | **Castro** 20
Evan's | **S Lake Tahoe/E** 27
Eve | **Berkeley/E** 25
Farm | **Napa/N** 24
Farmstead | **St. Helena/N** 20
15 Romolo | **N Beach** 20
Fifth Floor | **SoMa** 23
Fish & Farm | **Downtown** 20
Five | **Berkeley/E** 20
Flea St. Café | **Menlo Pk/S** 26
Flora | **Oakland/E** 21
Fog City Diner | **Embarcadero** 18
Forbes Island | **Fish. Wharf** 15
🆉 French Laundry | **Yountville/N** 29
Fumé Bistro | **Napa/N** 19
Gar Woods | **Carnelian Bay/E** 17
🆉 Gary Danko | **Fish. Wharf** 29
Gordon Biersch | **multi.** 15
Gott's Roadside | **multi.** 21
🆕 Grub | **Mission** 16
Healdsburg B&G | **Healdsburg/N** 18
Hillstone | **Embarcadero** 22
Hog & Rocks | **Mission** 21
🆕 Homeroom | **Oakland/E** –
🆉 House/Prime | **Polk Gulch** 25
🆕 Hudson | **Oakland/E** 20
Indigo | **Civic Ctr** 20
🆉 In-N-Out | **multi.** 21
🆕 Jasper's Corner | **Downtown** –
Jole | **Calistoga/N** 27
Kenwood | **Kenwood/N** 23
Kitchenette SF | **Dogpatch** 24
Lark Creek | **Walnut Creek/E** 22
Liberty Cafe | **Bernal Hts** 23
Lion/Compass | **Sunnyvale/S** 21
Luna Park | **Mission** 19
MacArthur Pk. | **Palo Alto/S** 17

Madera | **Menlo Pk/S**	22
🔼 Madrona | **Healdsburg/N**	27
Magnolia | **Haight-Ashbury**	20
Mama's on Wash. | **N Beach**	25
Mama's Royal | **Oakland/E**	22
NEW Mamma Pig's | **Windsor/N**	-
🔼 Manresa | **Los Gatos/S**	28
Market | **St. Helena/N**	23
Maverick | **Mission**	24
Mendo Bistro | **Ft Bragg/N**	23
NEW Michael Mina | **Downtown**	26
NEW Mission Cheese | **Mission**	-
Mixt Greens | **Downtown**	20
MoMo's | **S Beach**	18
Monti's | **Santa Rosa/N**	20
Moody's Bistro | **Truckee/E**	25
🔼 Mustards | **Yountville/N**	25
Navio | **Half Moon Bay/S**	25
Nepenthe | **Big Sur/S**	16
Nick's on Main | **Los Gatos/S**	26
955 Ukiah | **Mendocino/N**	25
NEW Nojo | **Hayes Valley**	-
Norman Rose | **Napa/N**	20
North Coast Brew | **Ft Bragg/N**	18
One Market | **Embarcadero**	24
Original Joe's | **San Jose/S**	22
Oswald | **Santa Cruz/S**	25
Outerlands | **Outer Sunset**	23
🔼 Pacific's Edge | **Carmel/S**	24
Park Chalet | **Outer Sunset**	15
NEW Pause | **Hayes Valley**	-
Pine Cone Diner | **Pt Reyes/N**	23
Pluto's | **multi.**	21
Pork Store | **multi.**	19
Postrio | **Downtown**	23
Presidio Social | **Presidio**	19
Press | **St. Helena/N**	24
Prospect | **SoMa**	24
Q Rest. | **Inner Rich**	20
NEW Radish | **Mission**	-
🔼 Range | **Mission**	27
Red Hut | **S Lake Tahoe/E**	22
Restaurant | **Ft Bragg/N**	25
Rest./Stevenswood | **Little River/N**	21
Rick & Ann | **Berkeley/E**	21
Rocker Oyster | **Valley Ford/N**	21
RoliRoti | **Embarcadero**	25
Rotisserie & Wine | **Napa/N**	22
🔼 Rotunda | **Downtown**	22
Rudy's | **multi.**	20
Rutherford Grill | **Rutherford/N**	23

Saison | **Mission**	26
Salt House | **SoMa**	21
Sardine Factory | **Monterey/S**	21
Sauce | **Hayes Valley**	17
Scott's | **multi.**	20
Sears | **Downtown**	19
Serpentine | **Dogpatch**	22
Shadowbrook | **Capitola/S**	18
Slow Club | **Mission**	22
Social Kit. | **Inner Sunset**	15
Sons/Daughters | **Nob Hill**	25
Soule Domain | **Kings Bch/E**	24
NEW Southie | **Oakland/E**	-
Spork | **Mission**	20
🔼 Spruce | **Presidio Hts**	25
Stacks | **multi.**	18
Starlight | **Sebastopol/N**	22
NEW Straw | **Hayes Valley**	-
NEW Table 24 | **Orinda/E**	18
Tarpy's | **Monterey/S**	20
Tav./Lark Creek | **Larkspur/N**	20
🔼 Terra | **St. Helena/N**	27
Thermidor | **SoMa**	20
1300/Fillmore | **W Addition**	21
Tipsy Pig | **Marina**	18
Toast | **multi.**	19
Town Hall | **SoMa**	22
Town's End | **Embarcadero**	21
Trueburger | **Oakland/E**	20
🔼**NEW** 25 Lusk | **SoMa**	20
Twist | **Campbell/S**	18
231 Ellsworth | **San Mateo/S**	23
2223 | **Castro**	22
Universal Cafe | **Mission**	24
Urban Tavern | **Downtown**	16
Village Pub | **Woodside/S**	26
Vitrine | **SoMa**	24
Warming Hut | **Presidio**	14
Wayfare Tav. | **Downtown**	22
Wild Goose | **Tahoe Vista/E**	23
Woodward's Gdn. | **Mission**	24
Zazu | **Santa Rosa/N**	25
Zin | **Healdsburg/N**	23
Zinsvalley | **Napa/N**	17
NEW Zut! | **Berkeley/E**	20

ARGENTINEAN

Boca | **Novato/N**	22
El Porteno | **Loc varies**	24

ASIAN

AsiaSF | **SoMa**	17
Betelnut Pejiu | **Cow Hollow**	23
Bridges | **Danville/E**	23

B Star Bar | **Inner Rich**	23
Butterfly | **Embarcadero**	21
Dragonfly | **Truckee/E**	22
E&O Trading | **Downtown**	20
Eos | **Cole Valley**	23
Flying Fish | **Carmel/S**	24
NEW Hawker Fare | **Oakland/E**	–
House | **N Beach**	26
Spice Kit | **SoMa**	20
Tonga Rm. | **Nob Hill**	13
Unicorn | **Downtown**	22

AUSTRIAN

NEW Leopold's | **Russian Hill**	23

BAKERIES

Alexis Baking | **Napa/N**	22
Amer. Cupcake | **Cow Hollow**	15
Arizmendi | **multi.**	26
Bakesale Betty | **Oakland/E**	25
Big Sur | **Big Sur/S**	22
☑ Cheese Board | **Berkeley/E**	27
Citizen Cake | **Upper Fillmore**	21
DeLessio | **multi.**	20
Della Fattoria | **Petaluma/N**	26
Downtown Bakery | **Healdsburg/N**	25
☑ Dynamo Donut | **Mission**	24
Emporio Rulli | **multi.**	24
Fort Bragg | **Ft Bragg/N**	22
Gayle's Bakery | **Capitola/S**	23
Golden West | **Downtown**	24
NEW Jane | **Upper Fillmore**	–
La Boulange | **multi.**	21
Liberty Cafe | **Bernal Hts**	23
Mama's on Wash. | **N Beach**	25
Mayfield | **Palo Alto/S**	20
Model Bakery | **multi.**	22
Sandbox | **Bernal Hts**	20
Schat's/Bakery | **Ukiah/N**	–
☑ Tartine | **Mission**	27
Town's End | **Embarcadero**	21

BARBECUE

Baby Blues BBQ | **Mission**	18
BarBersQ | **Napa/N**	21
Bo's BBQ | **Lafayette/E**	22
Bounty Hunter | **Napa/N**	21
☑ Buckeye | **Mill Valley/N**	24
Everett/Jones | **multi.**	20
Memphis Minnie | **Lower Haight**	19
Q Rest. | **Inner Rich**	20
T Rex BBQ | **Berkeley/E**	18
Wexler's | **Downtown**	22

BELGIAN

Frjtz Fries | **multi.**	17
La Trappe | **N Beach**	16

BRAZILIAN

Espetus | **multi.**	22
Pampas | **Palo Alto/S**	22

BRITISH

Betty's Fish | **Santa Rosa/N**	21
Lovejoy's Tea | **Noe Valley**	20

BURGERS

Acme Burger | **W Addition**	20
Balboa Cafe | **multi.**	19
Barney's | **multi.**	19
NEW Bistro SF Grill | **Pacific Hts**	–
Burger Bar | **Downtown**	19
Burger Joint | **multi.**	18
BurgerMeister | **multi.**	20
Cannery/Brew | **Monterey/S**	17
FatApple's | **multi.**	18
Fivetenburger | **Loc varies**	25
Gott's Roadside | **multi.**	21
NEW Greenburgers | **Lower Haight**	–
Healdsburg B&G | **Healdsburg/N**	18
☑ In-N-Out | **multi.**	21
Joe's Cable Car | **Excelsior**	19
Mel's Drive-In | **multi.**	13
Red's Java | **Embarcadero**	15
Roam | **Cow Hollow**	22
Super Duper | **multi.**	21
Trueburger | **Oakland/E**	20
Zeitgeist | **Mission**	14

BURMESE

☑ Burma Superstar | **multi.**	24
Burmese Kitchen | **Tenderloin**	20
Mandalay | **Inner Rich**	23
Nan Yang | **Oakland/E**	22
Pagan | **Outer Rich**	18
Yamo | **Mission**	22

CAJUN

NEW Boxing Rm. | **Hayes Valley**	–
Cajun Pacific | **Outer Sunset**	19
Chenery Park | **Glen Pk**	21
Elite Cafe | **Pacific Hts**	19

CALIFORNIAN

Adagia | **Berkeley/E**	20
☑ Ahwahnee | **Yosemite/E**	18
Albion River Inn | **Albion/N**	23
All Seasons | **Calistoga/N**	23
Amber Bistro | **Danville/E**	21

Applewood Inn | **Guerneville/N**	25
Artisan Bistro | **Lafayette/E**	24
AsiaSF | **SoMa**	17
Asqew Grill | **multi.**	17
Z Auberge/Soleil | **Rutherford/N**	27
Z Aubergine | **Carmel/S**	28
Bar Agricole | **SoMa**	21
Z BayWolf | **Oakland/E**	26
NEW Beast/Hare | **Mission**	20
Bistro Aix | **Marina**	22
Bistro Boudin | **Fish. Wharf**	20
Bistro Ralph | **Healdsburg/N**	24
Blackhawk Grille | **Danville/E**	20
Blue Barn | **Marina**	24
Blue Bottle | **multi.**	23
Boon Fly | **Napa/N**	21
Brick/Bottle | **Corte Madera/N**	19
Bridges | **Danville/E**	23
Brix | **Napa/N**	23
Bucci's | **Emeryville/E**	21
Butterfly | **Embarcadero**	21
Cafe Beaujolais | **Mendocino/N**	25
Café Brioche | **Palo Alto/S**	21
Café Rouge | **Berkeley/E**	22
Café Rustica | **Carmel Valley/S**	24
Calafia | **Palo Alto/S**	17
Camino | **Oakland/E**	22
Campton Place | **Downtown**	25
Z Canteen | **Tenderloin**	27
Carneros Bistro | **Sonoma/N**	24
Cellar Door Café | **Santa Cruz/S**	26
Central Market | **Petaluma/N**	22
NEW Chambers | **Tenderloin**	-
Z Chez Panisse | **Berkeley/E**	28
Z Chez Panisse Café | **Berkeley/E**	27
Chop Bar | **Oakland/E**	22
Christy Hill | **Tahoe City/E**	22
Cindy's | **St. Helena/N**	24
Citizen Cake | **Upper Fillmore**	21
Cliff House | **Outer Rich**	18
Z Club XIX | **Pebble Bch/S**	23
Coco500 | **SoMa**	24
Coi | **N Beach**	26
Cool Café | **multi.**	20
Davenport | **Davenport/S**	16
Deetjen's Big Sur | **Big Sur/S**	23
NEW Disco Volante | **Oakland/E**	-
Dragonfly | **Truckee/E**	22
Drake's | **Inverness/N**	21
Dry Creek | **Healdsburg/N**	24
Ecco | **Burlingame/S**	23
El Dorado | **Sonoma/N**	22
Eos | **Cole Valley**	23
Erna's | **Oakhurst/E**	27
Estate | **Sonoma/N**	21
Étoile | **Yountville/N**	25
Z Farmhse. Inn | **Forestville/N**	27
Farmstead | **St. Helena/N**	20
Fishwife | **Pacific Grove/S**	20
Five | **Berkeley/E**	20
Flavor | **Santa Rosa/N**	20
Flea St. Café | **Menlo Pk/S**	26
Z Fleur de Lys | **Downtown**	27
Flying Fish | **Carmel/S**	24
Flying Fish | **Half Moon Bay/S**	22
Z Foreign Cinema | **Mission**	24
Z Frances | **Castro**	27
Frascati | **Russian Hill**	26
NEW Fresh/Lisa | **Santa Rosa/N**	24
Gabriella Café | **Santa Cruz/S**	22
Z Garden Ct. | **Downtown**	19
Garibaldis | **Presidio Hts**	22
Gather | **Berkeley/E**	23
Georges | **Downtown**	19
Globe | **Downtown**	18
Grasing's Coastal | **Carmel/S**	23
Half Moon Brew | **Half Moon Bay/S**	16
Harvest Moon | **Sonoma/N**	24
Heirloom | **Mission**	23
Hot Box Grill | **Sonoma/N**	23
Hurley's | **Yountville/N**	21
Jake's/Lake | **Tahoe City/E**	18
Z Jardinière | **Civic Ctr**	26
John Ash | **Santa Rosa/N**	24
John Bentley | **Redwood City/S**	26
NEW Jones | **Tenderloin**	-
Lake Chalet | **Oakland/E**	14
Lalime's | **Berkeley/E**	25
La Scene | **Downtown**	19
Ledford Hse. | **Albion/N**	23
Little River Inn | **Little River/N**	22
Local Kitchen | **SoMa**	18
Local Mission | **Mission**	23
NEW Locavore | **Bernal Hts**	20
Luce | **SoMa**	21
Luella | **Russian Hill**	21
Luka's Taproom | **Oakland/E**	20
MacCallum | **Mendocino/N**	24
Mandaloun | **Redwood City/S**	20
Mantra | **Palo Alto/S**	21
Manzanita | **Truckee/E**	23
Z Marinus | **Carmel Valley/S**	27
Marlowe | **SoMa**	23
Mayfield | **Palo Alto/S**	20
Meadowood Grill | **St. Helena/N**	22
Z Meadowood Rest. | **St. Helena/N**	28

Mendo Hotel | **Mendocino/N**	18
Meritage/Claremont | **Berkeley/E**	25
Metro | **Lafayette/E**	21
Mezze | **Oakland/E**	23
Mission Bch. Café | **Mission**	22
Monk's Kettle | **Mission**	20
Montrio Bistro | **Monterey/S**	23
Moosse Café | **Mendocino/N**	22
Moss Room | **Inner Rich**	22
Murray Circle | **Sausalito/N**	24
Z Mustards | **Yountville/N**	25
Namu | **multi.**	22
Napa General | **Napa/N**	18
Napa Wine Train | **Napa/N**	18
Nick's Cove | **Marshall/N**	19
Z Nopa | **W Addition**	25
Olema Inn | **Olema/N**	18
Oola | **SoMa**	19
Orson | **SoMa**	18
Osake | **Santa Rosa/N**	24
Oxbow Wine | **Napa/N**	18
Pacific Crest | **Truckee/E**	-
Pappo | **Alameda/E**	24
Parcel 104 | **Santa Clara/S**	23
Park Chalet | **Outer Sunset**	15
Z Passionfish | **Pacific Grove/S**	27
Patrona | **Ukiah/N**	-
Pearl | **Napa/N**	24
NEW Petite Syrah | **Santa Rosa/N**	-
Piccino | **Dogpatch**	23
Picco | **Larkspur/N**	25
NEW Plate Shop | **Sausalito/N**	-
NEW Plow | **Potrero Hill**	25
Plum | **Oakland/E**	24
Z Plumed Horse | **Saratoga/S**	26
PlumpJack | **Olympic Valley/E**	23
Radius | **SoMa**	23
Ravenous | **Healdsburg/N**	23
Z Redd | **Yountville/N**	27
Rest./Ventana | **Big Sur/S**	21
Revival Bar | **Berkeley/E**	20
Richmond Rest. | **Inner Rich**	24
Rio Grill | **Carmel/S**	21
Rist. Avanti | **Santa Cruz/S**	24
Z Rivoli | **Berkeley/E**	26
Z Santé | **Sonoma/N**	26
Sent Sovi | **Saratoga/S**	23
71 St. Peter | **San Jose/S**	20
Shadowbrook | **Capitola/S**	18
Shokolaat | **Palo Alto/S**	17
Sidebar | **Oakland/E**	22
Z Sierra Mar | **Big Sur/S**	27
Silks | **Downtown**	23
Soif Wine Bar | **Santa Cruz/S**	25

Solbar | **Calistoga/N**	26
Starbelly | **Castro**	21
Station House | **Pt Reyes/N**	18
NEW Station 1 | **Woodside/S**	25
Stinking Rose | **N Beach**	18
St. Michael's | **Palo Alto/S**	22
St. Orres | **Gualala/N**	23
NEW Summit | **Mission**	-
Z Sutro's | **Outer Rich**	22
Table Café | **Larkspur/N**	22
Table 128 | **Boonville/N**	-
Terrapin Creek | **Bodega Bay/N**	25
Townhouse B&G | **Emeryville/E**	21
2223 | **Castro**	22
Ubuntu | **Napa/N**	24
Venus | **Berkeley/E**	23
Vin Antico | **San Rafael/N**	23
Viognier | **San Mateo/S**	23
Waterfront | **Embarcadero**	20
Wente Vineyards | **Livermore/E**	24
Wicket's | **Carmel Valley/S**	-
Wine Spectator | **St. Helena/N**	21
Wolfdale's | **Tahoe City/E**	24
Z Wood Tavern | **Oakland/E**	26
Woodward's Gdn. | **Mission**	24
Zaré/Fly Trap | **SoMa**	22

CAMBODIAN

Angkor Borei | **Bernal Hts**	22

CARIBBEAN

Cha Cha | **multi.**	20
Fishwife | **Pacific Grove/S**	20
Front Porch | **Bernal Hts**	20
Hibiscus | **Oakland/E**	20

CHEESESTEAKS

Cheese Steak Shop | **multi.**	20
Jake's Steaks | **Marina**	19
Jay's | **multi.**	17

CHICKEN

Goood Frikin' Chicken | **Mission**	18
Green Chile | **W Addition**	23
Home of Chicken | **multi.**	16
Il Cane Rosso | **Embarcadero**	23
RoliRoti | **Embarcadero**	25

CHINESE

(* dim sum specialist)

Alice's | **Noe Valley**	19
Brandy Ho's | **multi.**	19
Chairman Bao Bun* | **Loc varies**	25
Chef Chu's | **Los Altos/S**	20
Crouching Tiger | **Redwood City/S**	19
Dragon Well | **Marina**	21

Eliza's | **Pacific Hts**	21
Eric's | **Noe Valley**	20
Fang | **SoMa**	20
Gary Chu's | **Santa Rosa/N**	22
Gold Mountain* | **Chinatown**	21
Good Luck* | **Inner Rich**	23
Great China | **Berkeley/E**	24
Great Eastern* | **Chinatown**	21
Hakka Restaurant | **Outer Rich**	24
Happy Cafe* | **San Mateo/S**	21
Harmony* | **Mill Valley/N**	20
Heaven's Dog* | **SoMa**	20
Henry's Hunan | **multi.**	21
HK Flower/Mayflower* | **multi.**	20
Hong Kong Lounge* | **Outer Rich**	20
House/Nanking | **Chinatown**	21
Hunan | **multi.**	22
Imperial Tea Ct.* | **multi.**	19
Jai Yun | **Chinatown**	26
Just Wonton | **Outer Sunset**	17
Kitchen* | **Millbrae/S**	19
Koi* | **multi.**	24
Mission Chinese | **Mission**	21
O'mei | **Santa Cruz/S**	20
Oriental Pearl* | **Chinatown**	21
R&G Lounge | **Chinatown**	24
Rest. Peony* | **Oakland/E**	21
Sam Wo's | **Chinatown**	18
San Tung | **Inner Sunset**	23
Shanghai Dumpling | **Outer Rich**	21
Shen Hua | **Berkeley/E**	22
Sino* | **San Jose/S**	19
Tai Pan* | **Palo Alto/S**	22
Tommy Toy | **Downtown**	23
Ton Kiang* | **Outer Rich**	23
Z Yank Sing* | **SoMa**	26
Yuet Lee | **Chinatown**	21
Z & Y | **Chinatown**	24

COFFEEHOUSES

Blue Bottle | **multi.**	23
Davenport | **Davenport/S**	16
Z Dynamo Donut | **Mission**	24
NEW Jane | **Upper Fillmore**	-
NEW Ma*Velous | **Civic Ctr**	17
Stable Café | **Mission**	20
Warming Hut | **Presidio**	14

COFFEE SHOPS/ DINERS

Alexis Baking | **Napa/N**	22
Bette's Oceanview | **Berkeley/E**	23
FatApple's | **multi.**	18
Fog City Diner | **Embarcadero**	18
Fremont Diner | **Sonoma/N**	21
Gott's Roadside | **multi.**	21
HRD Coffee | **SoMa**	20
Jimmy Beans | **Berkeley/E**	20
Joe's Cable Car | **Excelsior**	19
Mel's Drive-In | **multi.**	13
Pine Cone Diner | **Pt Reyes/N**	23
Red Hut | **S Lake Tahoe/E**	22
Rudy's | **multi.**	20
Sears | **Downtown**	19
St. Francis | **Mission**	17

COLOMBIAN

Mr. Pollo | **Mission**	24

CONTINENTAL

Anton/Michel | **Carmel/S**	23
Bella Vista | **Woodside/S**	22
Ecco | **Burlingame/S**	23
Z La Forêt | **San Jose/S**	27

CREOLE

NEW Boxing Rm. | **Hayes Valley**	-
Brenda's | **Civic Ctr**	24
Hibiscus | **Oakland/E**	20
Starlight | **Sebastopol/N**	22

CUBAN

Cha Cha | **San Mateo/S**	20

DELIS

Boccalone | **Embarcadero**	26
Jimtown Store | **Healdsburg/N**	21
Max's | **multi.**	17
Miller's Deli | **Polk Gulch**	20
Moishe's Pippic | **Hayes Valley**	17
Saul's Rest./Deli | **Berkeley/E**	19
Schmidt's | **Mission**	21
NEW Wise Sons | **Loc varies**	23

DESSERT

Amer. Cupcake | **Cow Hollow**	15
Cafe Jacqueline | **N Beach**	26
Candybar | **W Addition**	20
Cheesecake | **multi.**	17
Chile Pies | **W Addition**	22
DeLessio | **multi.**	20
Downtown Bakery | **Healdsburg/N**	25
Emporio Rulli | **multi.**	24
Z Farallon | **Downtown**	24
Gayle's Bakery | **Capitola/S**	23
La Boulange | **multi.**	21
Mayfield | **Palo Alto/S**	20
Model Bakery | **multi.**	22
Orson | **SoMa**	18

CUISINES

Shokolaat | **Palo Alto/S**	17
Z Tartine | Mission	27
Town Hall | **SoMa**	22

ECLECTIC

Academy Cafe | **Inner Rich**	19
Alembic | **Haight-Ashbury**	23
Andalu | **Mission**	21
Celadon | **Napa/N**	23
Chez Shea | **Half Moon Bay/S**	23
Cottonwood | **Truckee/E**	26
Delancey St. | **Embarcadero**	18
Della Fattoria | **Petaluma/N**	26
Firefly | **Noe Valley**	25
Flavor | **Santa Rosa/N**	20
Fort Bragg | **Ft Bragg/N**	22
Heart | **Mission**	19
Hopmonk Tav. | **multi.**	18
Ironside | **S Beach**	17
NEW Kitchen Door | **Napa/N**	–
Mendo Café | **Mendocino/N**	20
Napa General | **Napa/N**	18
Pomelo | **multi.**	21
Ravenous | **Healdsburg/N**	23
Restaurant | **Ft Bragg/N**	25
Z Sierra Mar | Big Sur/S	27
Stomp | **Danville/E**	16
Va de Vi | **Walnut Creek/E**	24
Willi's Wine | **Santa Rosa/N**	25
Willow Wood | **Graton/N**	23

ETHIOPIAN

Axum Cafe | **Lower Haight**	23

FILIPINO

Attic | **San Mateo/S**	18

FONDUE

Fondue Cowboy | **SoMa**	18
Matterhorn Swiss | **Russian Hill**	22
Melting Pot | **multi.**	16

FRENCH

Z À Côté | Oakland/E	24
Angèle | **Napa/N**	24
NEW Atelier Crenn | **Marina**	26
Z Auberge/Soleil | Rutherford/N	27
Basque Cultural | **S San Francisco/S**	19
Z Baumé | Palo Alto/S	27
Bistro Aix | **Marina**	22
Z Bistro/Copains | Occidental/N	27
Bistro Moulin | **Monterey/S**	25
Z Bix | Downtown	24
Brannan's Grill | **Calistoga/N**	18
Bushi-tei | **Japantown**	22
Cafe Beaujolais | **Mendocino/N**	25

Café Fanny | **Berkeley/E**	23
Cafe Jacqueline | **N Beach**	26
NEW Café Tradition | **San Mateo/S**	–
Casanova | **Carmel/S**	23
Chantilly | **Redwood City/S**	25
Chaya | **Embarcadero**	20
Z Chevalier | Lafayette/E	25
Chez TJ | **Mtn View/S**	24
Z Club XIX | Pebble Bch/S	23
Coi | **N Beach**	26
Z Cyrus | Healdsburg/N	28
Z Erna's | Oakhurst/E	27
Fifth Floor | **SoMa**	23
Fig Cafe/Wine | **Glen Ellen/N**	25
Z Fleur de Lys | Downtown	27
Z French Laundry | Yountville/N	29
NEW Fresh/Lisa | **Santa Rosa/N**	24
Gitane | **Downtown**	23
Grégoire | **multi.**	21
Isa | **Marina**	26
Z Jardinière | Civic Ctr	26
NEW Jones | **Tenderloin**	–
Kenwood | **Kenwood/N**	23
La Boulange | **multi.**	21
Lafitte | **Embarcadero**	20
Z La Folie | Russian Hill	28
Z La Forêt | San Jose/S	27
La Gare | **Santa Rosa/N**	21
La Toque | **Napa/N**	26
Le Colonial | **Downtown**	22
Z Le Papillon | San Jose/S	27
Luna Park | **Mission**	19
Z Madrona | Healdsburg/N	27
Ma Maison | **Aptos/S**	24
Manzanita | **Truckee/E**	23
Marché/Fleurs | **Ross/N**	25
Z Marinus | Carmel Valley/S	27
Z Masa's | Downtown	28
Metro | **Lafayette/E**	21
Mistral | **Redwood Shores/S**	20
955 Ukiah | **Mendocino/N**	25
Z Pacific's Edge | Carmel/S	24
Rest. LuLu | **SoMa**	19
Ritz-Carlton | **Nob Hill**	–
RN74 | **SoMa**	23
Z Santé | Sonoma/N	26
Twist | **Campbell/S**	18
Vanessa's Bistro | **multi.**	23
Viognier | **San Mateo/S**	23

FRENCH (BISTRO)

Alamo Sq. | **W Addition**	18
Artisan Bistro | **Lafayette/E**	24

Baker St. Bistro | **Marina** 19
Bistro Central Parc | **W Addition** 24
🔁 Bistro Jeanty | **Yountville/N** 25
Bistro Liaison | **Berkeley/E** 22
Bistro Ralph | **Healdsburg/N** 24
Bodega Bistro | **Tenderloin** 21
🔁 Bouchon | **Yountville/N** 25
Butler & The Chef Bistro | **SoMa** 22
Cafe Bastille | **Downtown** 20
Café Brioche | **Palo Alto/S** 21
Café Claude | **Downtown** 22
Café de la Presse | **Downtown** 18
🔁 Chapeau! | **Inner Rich** 26
Charcuterie | **Healdsburg/N** 21
Spencer/Go | **Potrero Hill** 23
Chez Papa Bistrot | **Potrero Hill** 23
Chez Papa Resto | **SoMa** 24
Chez Spencer | **Mission** 25
Chouchou | **Forest Hills** 21
Florio | **Pacific Hts** 19
Fringale | **SoMa** 24
Gamine | **Cow Hollow** 24
Girl & the Fig | **Sonoma/N** 23
Grand Cafe | **Downtown** 19
Hyde St. Bistro | **Russian Hill** 21
K&L Bistro | **Sebastopol/N** 24
La Note | **Berkeley/E** 22
L'Ardoise | **Castro** 24
La Terrasse | **Presidio** 17
Le Central Bistro | **Downtown** 21
Le Charm Bistro | **SoMa** 23
Le P'tit Laurent | **Glen Pk** 23
Plouf | **Downtown** 21
South Park | **SoMa** 22
Spencer/Go | **SoMa** 26
Water St. Bistro | **Petaluma/N** 22
Zazie | **Cole Valley** 23

FRENCH
(BRASSERIE)

🔁 Absinthe | **Hayes Valley** 22
Café des Amis | **Cow Hollow** 19
Left Bank | **multi.** 19
Luka's Taproom | **Oakland/E** 20

GASTROPUB

Alembic | Eclectic | 23
  Haight-Ashbury
Bar Agricole | Cal. | **SoMa** 21
Comstock | Amer. | **N Beach** 16
15 Romolo | Amer. | **N Beach** 20
Hopmonk Tav. | Eclectic | 18
  Sebastopol/N
La Trappe | Belgian | **N Beach** 16
Magnolia | Amer. | **Haight-Ashbury** 20

Martins West | Scottish | 22
  Redwood City/S
Monk's Kettle | Cal. | **Mission** 20
Norman Rose | Amer. | **Napa/N** 20
Salt House | Amer. | **SoMa** 21
Sidebar | Cal. | **Oakland/E** 22
Social Kit. | Amer. | **Inner Sunset** 15
Tipsy Pig | Amer. | **Marina** 18
Urban Tavern | Amer. | **Downtown** 16

GERMAN

NEW Guamenkitzel | **Berkeley/E** –
Rosamunde | **multi.** 22
Schmidt's | **Mission** 21
Suppenküche | **Hayes Valley** 22
Walzwerk | **Mission** 21

GREEK

Dio Deka | **Los Gatos/S** 26
🔁 Evvia | **Palo Alto/S** 27
🔁 Kokkari | **Downtown** 27
Thea Med. | **San Jose/S** 19

HAWAIIAN

Hula's | **multi.** 18
Roy's | **SoMa** 23
Roy's | **Pebble Bch/S** 24

HEALTH FOOD

(See also Vegetarian)
Beautifull | **multi.** 17
Mixt Greens | **Downtown** 20
Plant Cafe Organic | **multi.** 21

HOT DOGS

Caspers Hot Dogs | **multi.** 20
4505 Meats | **Embarcadero** 27
Let's Be Frank | **multi.** 20
Showdogs | **Downtown** 18
Underdog | **Inner Sunset** 22

ICE CREAM PARLORS

Fentons | **Oakland/E** 20

INDIAN

Ajanta | **Berkeley/E** 25
NEW All Spice | **San Mateo/S** 24
🔁 Amber India | **multi.** 24
Avatar's | **multi.** 22
Breads/India | **multi.** 19
Curry Up Now | **Loc varies** 25
Dasaprakash | **Santa Clara/S** 22
Dosa | **multi.** 22
Gaylord India | **Downtown** 18
Indian Oven | **Lower Haight** 22
Junnoon | **Palo Alto/S** 22

Kasa Indian | **Castro**	18
Anokha/Lotus | **multi.**	22
Mantra | **Palo Alto/S**	21
Naan/Curry | **multi.**	17
Neela's | **Napa/N**	24
Roti Indian | **multi.**	21
Sakoon | **Mtn View/S**	23
Shalimar | **multi.**	22
Udupi Palace | **multi.**	21
Vik's Chaat | **Berkeley/E**	23
Zante | **Bernal Hts**	20

ITALIAN

(N=Northern; S=Southern)

Acqua Pazza | S | **San Mateo/S**	21
Z Acquerello | **Polk Gulch**	28
Adesso | **Oakland/E**	24
Albona Rist. | N | **N Beach**	25
Alioto's | S | **Fish. Wharf**	18
Americano | **Embarcadero**	18
Aperto | **Potrero Hill**	23
Z A16 | S | **Marina**	24
Azzurro Pizzeria | **Napa/N**	23
Bacco | **Noe Valley**	24
Baci Cafe | **Healdsburg/N**	22
Z Barbacco | **Downtown**	24
Bar Bambino | **Mission**	24
Bellanico | **Oakland/E**	23
Bella Trattoria | S | **Inner Rich**	22
Beretta | **Mission**	22
Bistro Don Giovanni | **Napa/N**	24
Boot/Shoe | **Oakland/E**	24
Z Bottega | **Yountville/N**	25
Bovolo | **Healdsburg/N**	21
Buca di Beppo | **multi.**	15
Bucci's | **Emeryville/E**	21
Cafe Citti | N | **Kenwood/N**	22
Café Fiore | N | **S Lake Tahoe/E**	24
Café Tiramisu | N | **Downtown**	22
Cafe Zoetrope/Mammarella's | S | **multi.**	19
Caffe Delle Stelle | N | **Hayes Valley**	17
Caffè Macaroni | S | **N Beach**	19
Caffè Museo | **SoMa**	18
Cantinetta Luca | **Carmel/S**	21
Capannina | **Cow Hollow**	25
Casanova | N | **Carmel/S**	23
Casa Orinda | **Orinda/E**	18
Chantilly | N | **Redwood City/S**	25
Cook St. Helena | N | **St. Helena/N**	26
Cotogna | **Downtown**	26
Cucina Paradiso | S | **Petaluma/N**	25
Cucina Rest. | **San Anselmo/N**	22

NEW Cupola Pizzeria | S | **Downtown**	–
Delarosa | **Marina**	22
Z Delfina | N | **Mission**	26
Della Santina | N | **Sonoma/N**	22
Diavola | **Geyserville/N**	25
Donato | N | **Redwood City/S**	22
Dopo | **Oakland/E**	25
E'Angelo | **Marina**	20
Emmy's Spaghetti | **Bernal Hts**	20
Emporio Rulli | **multi.**	24
NEW Enoteca Molinari | **Oakland/E**	–
Estate | **Sonoma/N**	21
Farina | **Mission**	23
54 Mint | S | **SoMa**	21
Fior d'Italia | N | **N Beach**	18
Florio | **Pacific Hts**	19
Z Flour + Water | **Mission**	24
Frantoio | N | **Mill Valley/N**	20
Gabriella Café | **Santa Cruz/S**	22
Gialina | **Glen Pk**	25
Globe | **Downtown**	18
Il Cane Rosso | **Embarcadero**	23
Il Davide | N | **San Rafael/N**	24
Il Fornaio | **multi.**	20
Il Postale | **Sunnyvale/S**	21
Incanto | N | **Noe Valley**	25
Incontro | **San Ramon/E**	24
Jackson Fillmore | **Upper Fillmore**	21
Kuleto's | N | **Downtown**	21
La Ciccia | **Noe Valley**	26
La Ginestra | S | **Mill Valley/N**	19
La Posta | **Santa Cruz/S**	26
La Strada | **Palo Alto/S**	19
NEW Leopold's | **Russian Hill**	23
Local Kitchen | **SoMa**	18
NEW Locanda | **Mission**	–
Lo Coco | S | **multi.**	22
L'Osteria | N | **N Beach**	24
Luce | **SoMa**	21
Lupa Trattoria | S | **Noe Valley**	21
NEW Mama's Empanadas | **Loc varies**	26
Mangia Mi | **Danville/E**	21
Mario's Bohemian | N | **N Beach**	17
Marzano | S | **Oakland/E**	23
Meritage Martini | N | **Sonoma/N**	22
Mescolanza | N | **Outer Rich**	23
Mezza Luna | S | **multi.**	22
Mistral | **Redwood Shores/S**	20
Nob Hill Café | N | **Nob Hill**	20
North Bch. Rest. | N | **N Beach**	22
Oenotri | S | **Napa/N**	25

Koo* | **Inner Sunset**	27
Kyo-Ya* | **Downtown**	23
Mifune | **Japantown**	19
Moki's Sushi* | **Bernal Hts**	26
Morimoto* | **Napa/N**	26
Muracci's | **multi.**	21
Naked Fish* | **S Lake Tahoe/E**	23
Naomi Sushi* | **Menlo Pk/S**	20
Nihon | **Mission**	19
NEW Nojo | **Hayes Valley**	-
Nombe | **Mission**	21
O Chamé | **Berkeley/E**	24
Oco Time* | **Ukiah/N**	-
O Izakaya | **Japantown**	18
Osake* | **Santa Rosa/N**	24
Oyaji* | **Outer Rich**	24
Ozumo* | **multi.**	23
Prime Rib Shabu | **Inner Rich**	20
Robata Grill* | **Mill Valley/N**	21
Ryoko's* | **Downtown**	24
Sakae Sushi* | **Burlingame/S**	26
Sanraku* | **multi.**	22
Sasa | **Walnut Creek/E**	23
Sebo* | **Hayes Valley**	26
Shabu-Sen | **Japantown**	21
NEW Shimo | **Healdsburg/N**	-
Sumika | **Los Altos/S**	22
Sushi Groove* | **multi.**	21
Z Sushi Ran* | **Sausalito/N**	28
NEW Sushirrito* | **SoMa**	-
Z Sushi Zone* | **Castro**	27
Takara* | **Japantown**	23
Tataki* | **multi.**	24
Ten-Ichi* | **Upper Fillmore**	23
Tokyo Go Go* | **Mission**	20
Tsukiji Sushi* | **Mill Valley/N**	22
Tsunami* | **multi.**	21
Umami* | **Cow Hollow**	24
Uzen* | **Oakland/E**	24
Wakuriya | **San Mateo/S**	27
Yoshi's* | **Oakland/E**	20
Yoshi's SF | **W Addition**	21
Yuzu Sushi | **San Mateo/S**	22
Zushi Puzzle* | **Marina**	26

JEWISH

Miller's Deli | **Polk Gulch**	20
Moishe's Pippic | **Hayes Valley**	17
Saul's Rest./Deli | **Berkeley/E**	19
NEW Wise Sons | **Loc varies**	23

KOREAN

(* barbecue specialist)

Brother's Korean* | **Inner Rich**	24
HRD Coffee | **SoMa**	20
Koryo BBQ* | **Oakland/E**	21
My Tofu* | **Inner Rich**	21
Namu | **multi.**	22
San Tung | **Inner Sunset**	23

MEDITERRANEAN

Z Absinthe | **Hayes Valley**	22
Z À Côté | **Oakland/E**	24
Adagia | **Berkeley/E**	20
Arlequin | **Hayes Valley**	19
Baci Cafe | **Healdsburg/N**	22
Z BayWolf | **Oakland/E**	26
Brix | **Napa/N**	23
Bursa | **W Portal**	21
Z Cafe Gibraltar | **El Granada/S**	26
Café Rouge | **Berkeley/E**	22
Caffè Museo | **SoMa**	18
Camino | **Oakland/E**	22
Campton Place | **Downtown**	25
Central Market | **Petaluma/N**	22
Cetrella | **Half Moon Bay/S**	22
Z Chez Panisse | **Berkeley/E**	28
Z Chez Panisse Café | **Berkeley/E**	27
Christy Hill | **Tahoe City/E**	22
Coco500 | **SoMa**	24
Dio Deka | **Los Gatos/S**	26
El Dorado | **Sonoma/N**	22
Z Esin | **Danville/E**	25
Fandango | **Pacific Grove/S**	23
Z Foreign Cinema | **Mission**	24
Frascati | **Russian Hill**	26
Garibaldis | **Presidio Hts**	22
Gar Woods | **Carnelian Bay/E**	17
Harvest Moon | **Sonoma/N**	24
Heirloom | **Mission**	23
Hurley's | **Yountville/N**	21
Insalata's | **San Anselmo/N**	24
Lalime's | **Berkeley/E**	25
La Méditerranée | **multi.**	20
La Scene | **Downtown**	19
Lavanda | **Palo Alto/S**	20
Ledford Hse. | **Albion/N**	23
Luella | **Russian Hill**	21
Mandaloun | **Redwood City/S**	20
MarketBar | **Embarcadero**	16
Mezze | **Oakland/E**	23
Monti's | **Santa Rosa/N**	20
Old Jerusalem | **Mission**	19
Ottimista | **Cow Hollow**	19
Oxbow Wine | **Napa/N**	18
Pacific Crest | **Truckee/E**	-
Pappo | **Alameda/E**	24
Paul K | **Hayes Valley**	22
Peasant & the Pear | **Danville/E**	22

Pianeta	**Truckee/E**	24
PlumpJack	**Olympic Valley/E**	23
Rest. LuLu	**SoMa**	19
Z Rivoli	**Berkeley/E**	26
Savor	**Noe Valley**	18
Sens	**Downtown**	17
71 St. Peter	**San Jose/S**	20
Sidebar	**Oakland/E**	22
Spoonbar	**Healdsburg/N**	18
Terzo	**Cow Hollow**	24
Thea Med.	**San Jose/S**	19
Truly Med.	**Mission**	22
Underwood Bar	**Graton/N**	23
Wente Vineyards	**Livermore/E**	24
Willow Wood	**Graton/N**	23
Zaré/Fly Trap	**SoMa**	22
Zatar	**Berkeley/E**	23
Zibibbo	**Palo Alto/S**	19
Z Zuni Café	**Hayes Valley**	25
NEW Zut!	**Berkeley/E**	20

MEXICAN

Andalé	**multi.**	21
Cactus Taqueria	**multi.**	20
C Casa	**Napa/N**	24
Colibrí	**Downtown**	21
NEW Cosecha Café	**Oakland/E**	-
Doña Tomás	**Oakland/E**	22
Don Pico	**San Bruno/S**	17
El Metate	**Mission**	22
El Tonayense	**multi.**	24
Gracias	**Mission**	21
Guaymas	**Tiburon/N**	17
NEW Hecho	**Downtown**	-
Joe's Taco	**Mill Valley/N**	20
Juan's	**Berkeley/E**	18
La Corneta	**multi.**	21
La Cumbre	**multi.**	22
Las Camelias	**San Rafael/N**	20
La Taqueria	**Mission**	25
Little Chihuahua	**multi.**	21
Loló	**Mission**	24
Mamacita	**Marina**	22
Marinitas	**San Anselmo/N**	20
Maya	**SoMa**	20
Mexico DF	**Embarcadero**	20
Mijita	**multi.**	19
Nick's Crispy	**Russian Hill**	22
Nopalito	**W Addition**	22
Pancho Villa	**multi.**	22
Papalote	**multi.**	22
Papito	**Potrero Hill**	25
Picante Cocina	**Berkeley/E**	23
NEW Prickly Pear	**Danville/E**	-

Regalito Rosticeria	**Mission**	23
NEW Tacko	**Cow Hollow**	-
TacoBar	**Pacific Hts**	17
Tacolicious	**multi.**	22
Tacubaya	**Berkeley/E**	23
Tamarindo	**Oakland/E**	25
Taqueria Can Cun	**multi.**	25
Taqueria/Sabor	**Mission**	-
Taqueria Tlaquepaque	**San Jose/S**	20
Tommy's Mex.	**Outer Rich**	15
Tres	**S Beach**	17
Tropisueño	**SoMa**	18
NEW Xolo Taqueria	**Oakland/E**	-

MIDDLE EASTERN

Dishdash	**Sunnyvale/S**	22
Goood Frikin' Chicken	**Mission**	18
La Méditerranée	**multi.**	20
Liba Falafel	**multi.**	25
Old Jerusalem	**Mission**	19
Saha	**Tenderloin**	26
Truly Med.	**Mission**	22
Yumma's	**Inner Sunset**	21

MOROCCAN

Z Aziza	**Outer Rich**	26
NEW Café Tradition	**San Mateo/S**	-
Café Zitouna	**Polk Gulch**	-
Tajine	**Polk Gulch**	-

NEPALESE

Little Nepal	**Bernal Hts**	19

NEW ENGLAND

Old Port Lobster	**Redwood City/S**	21
Yankee Pier	**multi.**	18

NOODLE SHOPS

Citrus Club	**Haight-Ashbury**	22
Hapa Ramen	**Loc varies**	20
Hotaru	**San Mateo/S**	20
Hotei	**Inner Sunset**	19
Katana-Ya	**Downtown**	22
King of Thai	**multi.**	19
Mifune	**Japantown**	19
O Chamé	**Berkeley/E**	24
Osha Thai	**multi.**	21
San Tung	**Inner Sunset**	23

NUEVO LATINO

Destino	**Castro**	22
Joya	**Palo Alto/S**	21
Limón	**Mission**	22
NEW Pasión	**Inner Sunset**	22

PACIFIC RIM

Pacific Catch | **multi.**	19
Tonga Rm. | **Nob Hill**	13

PAKISTANI

Naan/Curry | **multi.**	17
Pakwan | **multi.**	22
Shalimar | **multi.**	22

PAN-LATIN

Bocanova | **Oakland/E**	21
Cascal | **Mtn View/S**	21
César | **Oakland/E**	22
Charanga | **Mission**	21
Fonda Solana | **Albany/E**	23
NEW Mama's Empanadas | **Loc varies**	26
Marinitas | **San Anselmo/N**	20

PERSIAN

Maykadeh | **N Beach**	23

PERUVIAN

Fresca | **multi.**	22
La Costanera | **Montara/S**	21
La Mar | **Embarcadero**	25
Limón | **Mission**	22
Mochica | **SoMa**	25
NEW Pasión | **Inner Sunset**	22
Piqueo's | **Bernal Hts**	25
NEW Sazon | **Santa Rosa/N**	-

PIZZA

NEW Addie's | **Berkeley/E**	21
Amici's | **multi.**	20
Applewood Pizza | **Menlo Pk/S**	21
Arinell Pizza | **multi.**	22
Arizmendi | **multi.**	26
Azzurro Pizzeria | **Napa/N**	23
NEW Bar Bocce | **Sausalito/N**	-
Beretta | **Mission**	22
Boot/Shoe | **Oakland/E**	24
Cafe Zoetrope/Mammarella's | **N Beach**	19
Z Cheese Board | **Berkeley/E**	27
NEW Cupola Pizzeria | **Downtown**	-
Delarosa | **Marina**	22
Diavola | **Geyserville/N**	25
Emilia's | **Berkeley/E**	27
Z Flour + Water | **Mission**	24
Gialina | **Glen Pk**	25
Gioia Pizzeria | **Berkeley/E**	25
Giorgio's | **Inner Rich**	20
Goat Hill Pizza | **multi.**	18
La Ginestra | **Mill Valley/N**	19
Lanesplitter | **multi.**	17

Little Star | **multi.**	24
Local Kitchen | **SoMa**	18
NEW Locanda Positano | **San Carlos/S**	-
Lo Coco | **multi.**	22
Marzano | **Oakland/E**	23
North Bch. Pizza | **multi.**	19
Palio d'Asti | **Downtown**	20
Patxi's Pizza | **multi.**	22
Pauline's | **Mission**	23
Piaci | **Ft Bragg/N**	25
Pi Bar | **Mission**	18
Pizza Antica | **multi.**	20
Z Pizzaiolo | **Oakland/E**	26
Pizza Nostra | **Potrero Hill**	19
Pizza Rustica | **Oakland/E**	20
Pizzeria Delfina | **multi.**	25
Z Pizzeria Picco | **Larkspur/N**	27
Pizzeria Tra Vigne | **St. Helena/N**	21
Pizzetta 211 | **Outer Rich**	25
Postrio | **Downtown**	23
NEW Ragazza | **W Addition**	24
Rosso Pizzeria | **Santa Rosa/N**	25
Rustic | **Geyserville/N**	19
NEW Source | **Potrero Hill**	-
Starbelly | **Castro**	21
Tommaso's | **N Beach**	25
Tony's Coal-Fired Pizza | **N Beach**	24
Tony's Pizza | **N Beach**	25
NEW Una Pizza | **SoMa**	26
Zachary's Pizza | **multi.**	24
Zante | **Bernal Hts**	20
Zero Zero | **SoMa**	24

POLYNESIAN

Trader Vic's | **multi.**	17

PORTUGUESE

LaSalette | **Sonoma/N**	24

PUB FOOD

Bridgetender | **Tahoe City/E**	18
Gordon Biersch | **multi.**	15
Half Moon Brew | **Half Moon Bay/S**	16
Public House | **S Beach**	16
Ukiah Brew | **Ukiah/N**	-

PUERTO RICAN

Parada 22 | **Haight-Ashbury**	21
Sol Food | **San Rafael/N**	23

RUSSIAN

Katia's Tea | **Inner Rich**	20

SALVADORAN

El Zocalo | **Bernal Hts**	19

SANDWICHES

Amer. Grilled Cheese | **SoMa**	22
Bakesale Betty | **Oakland/E**	25
Bocadillos | **N Beach**	23
Boccalone | **Embarcadero**	26
Cafe Divine | **N Beach**	18
Cheese Steak Shop | **multi.**	20
Dinosaurs | **Castro**	-
Downtown Bakery | **Healdsburg/N**	25
Fort Bragg | **Ft Bragg/N**	22
4505 Meats | **Embarcadero**	27
Gayle's Bakery | **Capitola/S**	23
Giordano | **N Beach**	23
Golden West | **Downtown**	24
Ike's | **multi.**	24
Il Cane Rosso | **Embarcadero**	23
Jimtown Store | **Healdsburg/N**	21
Kitchenette SF | **Dogpatch**	24
Mario's Bohemian | **N Beach**	17
Max's | **multi.**	17
Mixt Greens | **Downtown**	20
Model Bakery | **multi.**	22
Naked Lunch | **N Beach**	19
Pluto's | **multi.**	21
Saigon Sandwich | **Tenderloin**	26
Sentinel | **SoMa**	24
NEW Southie | **Oakland/E**	-
Spice Kit | **SoMa**	20
NEW Straw | **Hayes Valley**	-
Warming Hut | **Presidio**	14
'Wichcraft | **Downtown**	18

SCOTTISH

Martins West | **Redwood City/S**	22

SEAFOOD

Alamo Sq. | **W Addition**	18
Alioto's | **Fish. Wharf**	18
Anchor & Hope | **SoMa**	21
Anchor Oyster | **Castro**	25
Aquarius | **Santa Cruz/S**	21
Barbara's | **Princeton Sea/S**	21
Bar Crudo | **W Addition**	25
Betty's Fish | **Santa Rosa/N**	21
Cajun Pacific | **Outer Sunset**	19
Catch | **Castro**	18
Chapter & Moon | **Ft Bragg/N**	21
Z Farallon | **Downtown**	24
Fish | **Sausalito/N**	24
Fish & Farm | **Downtown**	20
Fish Story | **Napa/N**	18
Fishwife | **Pacific Grove/S**	20
Flying Fish | **Carmel/S**	24

Flying Fish | **Half Moon Bay/S**	22
Forbes Island | **Fish. Wharf**	15
Georges | **Downtown**	19
Great Eastern | **Chinatown**	21
Guaymas | **Tiburon/N**	17
Half Moon Brew | **Half Moon Bay/S**	16
Hayes St. Grill | **Hayes Valley**	23
Hog & Rocks | **Mission**	21
Z Hog Island | **multi.**	25
HK Flower/Mayflower | **multi.**	20
Koi | **multi.**	24
Lake Chalet | **Oakland/E**	14
La Mar | **Embarcadero**	25
Little River Inn | **Little River/N**	22
Marica | **Oakland/E**	27
McCormick/Kuleto | **Fish. Wharf**	20
McCormick/Schmick | **San Jose/S**	21
Meritage Martini | **Sonoma/N**	22
Nettie's Crab | **Cow Hollow**	18
Old Port Lobster | **Redwood City/S**	21
Pacific Café | **Outer Rich**	23
Pacific Catch | **multi.**	19
Z Passionfish | **Pacific Grove/S**	27
Pesce | **Russian Hill**	25
Plouf | **Downtown**	21
Sam's Chowder | **Half Moon Bay/S**	20
Sam's Grill | **Downtown**	22
Sardine Factory | **Monterey/S**	21
Z Scoma's | **multi.**	23
Scott's | **multi.**	20
Sea Salt | **Berkeley/E**	21
Z Seasons | **Downtown**	24
Skool | **Potrero Hill**	22
Sunnyside | **Tahoe City/E**	18
Z Swan Oyster | **Polk Gulch**	27
Z Tadich Grill | **Downtown**	23
Waterbar | **Embarcadero**	21
Waterfront | **Embarcadero**	20
Weird Fish | **Mission**	-
Willi's Seafood | **Healdsburg/N**	24
Will's Fargo | **Carmel Valley/S**	21
Woodhse. | **multi.**	21
Yankee Pier | **multi.**	18

SINGAPOREAN

Straits | **multi.**	20

SMALL PLATES

(See also Spanish tapas specialist)

Z Absinthe | **French/Med.** | **Hayes Valley**	22
Z À Côté | **French/Med.** | **Oakland/E**	24
Adesso | **Italian** | **Oakland/E**	24

Andalu | Eclectic | **Mission**	21
AsiaSF | Asian/Cal. | **SoMa**	17
☑ Barbacco | Italian | **Downtown**	24
NEW Campanula | Amer. | **N Beach**	-
Cascal | Pan-Latin | **Mtn View/S**	21
César | Pan-Latin | **Oakland/E**	22
Cha Cha | Carib. | **multi.**	20
Chez Shea | Eclectic | **Half Moon Bay/S**	23
E&O Trading | Asian | **Downtown**	20
Eos | Asian/Cal. | **Cole Valley**	23
Heart | Eclectic | **Mission**	19
Isa | French | **Marina**	26
Jole | Amer. | **Calistoga/N**	27
Joya | Nuevo Latino | **Palo Alto/S**	21
Junnoon | Indian | **Palo Alto/S**	22
Lavanda | Med. | **Palo Alto/S**	20
Monti's | Med. | **Santa Rosa/N**	20
Nihon | Japanese | **Mission**	19
Ottimista | Italian/Med. | **Cow Hollow**	19
Oxbow Wine | Cal. | **Napa/N**	18
Park Chalet | Amer. | **Outer Sunset**	15
NEW Pause | Amer. | **Hayes Valley**	-
Pesce | Italian/Seafood | **Russian Hill**	25
NEW Petite Syrah | Cal. | **Santa Rosa/N**	-
Picco | Italian | **Larkspur/N**	25
Piqueo's | Peruvian | **Bernal Hts**	25
Ristobar | Italian | **Marina**	21
Starbelly | Cal. | **Castro**	21
Stomp | Eclectic | **Danville/E**	16
Straits | Singapor. | **multi.**	20
Tamarine | Viet. | **Palo Alto/S**	26
Terzo | Med. | **Cow Hollow**	24
Three Seasons | Viet. | **Palo Alto/S**	19
Underwood Bar | Med. | **Graton/N**	23
Va de Vi | Eclectic | **Walnut Creek/E**	24
Willi's Seafood | Seafood | **Healdsburg/N**	24
Willi's Wine | Eclectic | **Santa Rosa/N**	25
Zibibbo | Med. | **Palo Alto/S**	19

SOUL FOOD

Broken Record | **Excelsior**	24
Brown Sugar | **Oakland/E**	23
NEW Criolla Kitchen | **Castro**	-
Elite Cafe | **Pacific Hts**	19
Farmerbrown | **multi.**	20
Hard Knox | **multi.**	20
Home of Chicken | **multi.**	16

Picán | **Oakland/E**	22
Starlight | **Sebastopol/N**	22
1300/Fillmore | **W Addition**	21

SOUTHERN

Baby Blues BBQ | **Mission**	18
Blackberry Bistro | **Oakland/E**	21
Brenda's | **Civic Ctr**	24
Everett/Jones | **multi.**	20
Front Porch | **Bernal Hts**	20
Hard Knox | **multi.**	20
Home of Chicken | **multi.**	16
Kate's Kitchen | **Lower Haight**	21
Magnolia | **Haight-Ashbury**	20
Miss Pearl's | **Oakland/E**	18
Picán | **Oakland/E**	22
1300/Fillmore | **W Addition**	21

SOUTHWESTERN

Boogaloos | **Mission**	17
Green Chile | **W Addition**	23

SPANISH

(* tapas specialist)

Alegrias* | **Marina**	21
NEW Asiento* | **Mission**	-
Barlata* | **Oakland/E**	21
B44* | **Downtown**	21
Bocadillos* | **N Beach**	23
César* | **Berkeley/E**	22
Contigo* | **Noe Valley**	24
Esperpento* | **Mission**	20
Fonda Solana* | **Albany/E**	23
Gitane | **Downtown**	23
Iberia* | **Menlo Pk/S**	22
Mundaka* | **Carmel/S**	24
Piperade | **Downtown**	25
NEW Txoko | **N Beach**	-
Zarzuela* | **Russian Hill**	24
ZuZu* | **Napa/N**	25

STEAKHOUSES

Alexander's | **multi.**	26
Alfred's Steak | **Downtown**	23
Arcadia | **San Jose/S**	20
NEW Bluestem Brass. | **SoMa**	-
Boca | **Novato/N**	22
NEW Bourbon | **Downtown**	24
Casa Orinda | **Orinda/E**	18
Cole's Chop | **Napa/N**	25
NEW El Paseo | **Mill Valley/N**	-
Epic Roasthse. | **Embarcadero**	21
Espetus | **multi.**	22
5A5 Steak | **Downtown**	23
Forbes Mill | **multi.**	22

NEW Frank/Ernie's | Healdsburg/N	–
Harris' | Polk Gulch	26
Z House/Prime | Polk Gulch	25
Izzy's Steak | multi.	20
Lark Creek Steak | Downtown	23
Morton's | multi.	23
Press | St. Helena/N	24
Ruth's Chris | multi.	24
Z Seasons | Downtown	24
NEW Shimo | Healdsburg/N	–
Stark's | Santa Rosa/N	–
Sunnyside | Tahoe City/E	18
Vic Stewart | Walnut Creek/E	22
Will's Fargo | Carmel Valley/S	21

SWISS

Matterhorn Swiss | Russian Hill	22

TEAROOMS

Imperial Tea Ct. | multi.	19
Lovejoy's Tea | Noe Valley	20
Samovar Tea | multi.	18

THAI

Basil | SoMa	23
Cha Am Thai | multi.	19
Grand Pu Bah | Potrero Hill	19
Khan Toke | Outer Rich	21
King of Thai | multi.	19
Another Monkey/Koh | multi.	20
Krung Thai | multi.	19
Lers Ros Thai | Tenderloin	23
Manora's Thai | SoMa	24
Marnee Thai | multi.	24
Morph | Outer Rich	–
Osha Thai | multi.	21
Royal Thai | San Rafael/N	23
Soi4 | Oakland/E	24
Suriya Thai | SoMa	25
Thai Buddhist | Berkeley/E	21
Thai House | multi.	21
Thep Phanom | Lower Haight	24

TUNISIAN

Café Zitouna | Polk Gulch	–

TURKISH

A La Turca | Tenderloin	22
Bursa | W Portal	21

Sens | Downtown	17
Troya | Inner Rich	21

VEGETARIAN

(* vegan)

Café Gratitude* | multi.	17
Cha-Ya Veg.* | multi.	23
Encuentro | Oakland/E	23
Gracias* | Mission	21
Z Greens | Marina	24
Herbivore* | multi.	17
NEW Hodo Soy* | Embarcadero	–
Millennium* | Downtown	25
Ravens'* | Mendocino/N	26
NEW Source | Potrero Hill	–
Ubuntu* | Napa/N	24
Udupi Palace | multi.	21

VENEZUELAN

Pica Pica Maize | multi.	21

VIETNAMESE

Ana Mandara | Fish. Wharf	21
Bodega Bistro | Tenderloin	21
NEW Bun Mee | Upper Fillmore	–
Crustacean | Polk Gulch	24
Dinosaurs | Castro	–
Élevé | Walnut Creek/E	21
LCX/Le Cheval | multi.	20
Le Colonial | Downtown	22
Le Soleil | Inner Rich	22
My Father's Kit. | Pacific Hts	18
Out the Door | multi.	22
Pagolac | Tenderloin	23
Pho 84 | Oakland/E	23
Saigon Sandwich | Tenderloin	26
Z Slanted Door | Embarcadero	25
Sunflower | multi.	21
Tamarine | Palo Alto/S	26
Thanh Long | Outer Sunset	24
Three Seasons | Palo Alto/S	19
Tu Lan | SoMa	18
Vanessa's Bistro | multi.	23
Xanh | Mtn View/S	21
Xyclo | Oakland/E	22
Zadin | Castro	23

CUISINES

Locations

Includes names, cuisines, Food ratings and, for locations that are mapped, top list with map coordinates.

City of San Francisco

AT&T PARK/ SOUTH BEACH

(See map on page 308)

TOP FOOD

Tsunami	*Japanese*	**G5**	21
Amici's	*Pizza*	**G5**	20
Mijita	*Mex.*	**H5**	19

LISTING

Amici's	*Pizza*	20
Burger Joint	*Burgers*	18
Ironside	*Eclectic*	17
Mijita	*Mex.*	19
MoMo's	*Amer.*	18
Public House	*Pub*	16
Tres	*Mex.*	17
Tsunami	*Japanese*	21

BERNAL HEIGHTS

Angkor Borei	*Cambodian*	22
El Zocalo	*Salvadoran*	19
Emmy's Spaghetti	*Italian*	20
Front Porch	*Carib./Southern*	20
NEW Ichi Sushi	*Japanese*	23
Liberty Cafe	*Amer.*	23
Little Nepal	*Nepalese*	19
NEW Locavore	*Cal.*	20
Moki's Sushi	*Japanese*	26
Piqueo's	*Peruvian*	25
Sandbox	*Bakery*	20
Zante	*Indian/Pizza*	20

CASTRO

(See map on page 306)

TOP FOOD

Sushi Zone	*Japanese*	**A6**	27
Frances	*Cal.*	**D4**	27
Anchor Oyster	*Seafood*	**E3**	25
L'Ardoise	*French*	**C3**	24
Ike's	*Sandwiches*	**C4**	24

LISTING

Anchor Oyster	*Seafood*	25
Brandy Ho's	*Chinese*	19
BurgerMeister	*Burgers*	20
Café Flore	*Amer.*	17
Catch	*Seafood*	18

Chow	*Amer.*	20
NEW Criolla Kitchen	*Soul Food*	–
Destino	*Nuevo Latino*	22
Dinosaurs	*Viet.*	–
Eiji	*Japanese*	26
Eureka	*Amer.*	20
Z Frances	*Cal.*	27
Ike's	*Sandwiches*	24
Kasa Indian	*Indian*	18
La Méditerranée	*Med./Mideast.*	20
L'Ardoise	*French*	24
Poesia	*Italian*	21
Samovar Tea	*Tea*	18
Starbelly	*Cal.*	21
Super Duper	*Burgers*	21
Z Sushi Zone	*Japanese*	27
Thai House	*Thai*	21
2223	*Cal.*	22
Woodhse.	*Seafood*	21
Zadin	*Viet.*	23

CHINA BASIN/ DOGPATCH

Hard Knox	*Southern*	20
Kitchenette SF	*Sandwiches*	24
Piccino	*Italian*	23
Serpentine	*Amer.*	22

CHINATOWN

(See map on page 304)

TOP FOOD

R&G Lounge	*Chinese*	**G7**	24
Hunan	*Chinese*	**F6**	22
Gold Mountain	*Chinese*	**F6**	21

LISTING

Brandy Ho's	*Chinese*	19
Gold Mountain	*Chinese*	21
Great Eastern	*Chinese*	21
Henry's Hunan	*Chinese*	21
House/Nanking	*Chinese*	21
Hunan	*Chinese*	22
Jai Yun	*Chinese*	26
Oriental Pearl	*Chinese*	21
R&G Lounge	*Chinese*	2
Sam Wo's	*Chinese*	1
Yuet Lee	*Chinese*	2
Z & Y	*Chinese*	2

Vote at ZAGAT.co

COW HOLLOW

(See map on page 303)

TOP FOOD

Capannina | *Italian* | **H5**	25
Umami | *Japanese* | **G5**	24
Gamine | *French* | **F5**	24
Terzo | *Med.* | **F5**	24
Betelnut Pejiu | *Asian* | **G5**	23

LISTING

Amer. Cupcake | *Amer./Bakery*	15
Balboa Cafe | *Amer.*	19
Betelnut Pejiu | *Asian*	23
Brazen Head | *Amer.*	21
NEW Brixton | *Amer.*	15
Café des Amis | *French*	19
Capannina | *Italian*	25
Gamine | *French*	24
La Boulange | *Bakery*	21
Nettie's Crab | *Seafood*	18
Osha Thai | *Thai*	21
Ottimista | *Italian/Med.*	19
Pane e Vino | *Italian*	22
Patxi's Pizza | *Pizza*	22
Roam | *Burgers*	22
Rose's Cafe | *Italian*	21
NEW Tacko | *Mex.*	-
Terzo | *Med.*	24
Umami | *Japanese*	24

DOWNTOWN

(See map on page 304)

TOP FOOD

Masa's | *French* | **H5**	28
Kokkari | *Greek* | **F8**	27
Fleur de Lys | *Cal./French* | **I4**	27
Quince | *Italian* | **F7**	26
Michael Mina | *Amer.* | **H8**	26

LISTING

Alfred's Steak | *Steak*	23
Andalé | *Mex.*	21
Anzu | *Japanese*	22
Z Barbacco | *Italian*	24
B44 | *Spanish*	21
Z Bix | *Amer./French*	24
NEW Bourbon | *Steak*	24
Burger Bar | *Burgers*	19
Cafe Bastille | *French*	20
Café Claude | *French*	22
Café de la Presse | *French*	18
Café Tiramisu | *Italian*	22
Campton Place | *Cal./Med.*	25
Cheesecake | *Amer.*	17
Colibrí | *Mex.*	21

Cotogna | *Italian*	26
NEW Cupola Pizzeria | *Italian/Pizza*	-
E&O Trading | *Asian*	20
Ebisu | *Japanese*	24
Emporio Rulli | *Dessert/Italian*	24
Z Farallon | *Seafood*	24
Fish & Farm | *Amer./Seafood*	20
5A5 Steak | *Steak*	23
Z Fleur de Lys | *Cal./French*	27
Z Garden Ct. | *Cal.*	19
Gaylord India | *Indian*	18
Georges | *Cal./Seafood*	19
Gitane | *French/Spanish*	23
Globe | *Cal./Italian*	18
Golden West | *Bakery/Sandwiches*	24
Grand Cafe | *French*	19
NEW Hecho | *Japanese*	-
Henry's Hunan | *Chinese*	21
Il Fornaio | *Italian*	20
NEW Jasper's Corner | *Amer.*	-
Katana-Ya | *Japanese*	22
King of Thai | *Thai*	19
Z Kokkari | *Greek*	27
Kuleto's | *Italian*	21
Kyo-Ya | *Japanese*	23
Lark Creek Steak | *Steak*	23
La Scene | *Cal./Med.*	19
Le Central Bistro | *French*	21
Le Colonial | *French/Viet.*	22
Z Masa's | *French*	28
Max's | *Deli*	17
Z NEW Michael Mina | *Amer.*	26
Millennium | *Vegan*	25
Mixt Greens | *Health/Sandwiches*	20
Morton's | *Steak*	23
Muracci's | *Japanese*	21
Naan/Curry | *Indian/Pakistani*	17
Osha Thai | *Thai*	21
Out the Door | *Viet.*	22
Palio d'Asti | *Italian*	20
Z Perbacco | *Italian*	25
Piperade | *Spanish*	25
Plant Cafe Organic | *Health*	21
Plouf | *French*	21
Postrio | *Amer.*	23
Z Quince | *Italian*	26
Z Rotunda | *Amer.*	22
Ryoko's | *Japanese*	24
Sam's Grill | *Seafood*	22
Sanraku | *Japanese*	22
Scala's Bistro | *Italian*	21

LOCATIONS

Sears	*Diner*	19
🔢 Seasons	*Seafood/Steak*	24
Sens	*Med./Turkish*	17
Showdogs	*Hot Dogs*	18
Silks	*Cal.*	23
Straits	*Singapor.*	20
Super Duper	*Burgers*	21
🔢 Tadich Grill	*Seafood*	23
Taqueria Can Cun	*Mex.*	25
Tommy Toy	*Chinese*	23
Unicorn	*Asian*	22
Urban Tavern	*Amer.*	16
Wayfare Tav.	*Amer.*	22
Wexler's	*BBQ*	22
'Wichcraft	*Sandwiches*	18

EMBARCADERO

Americano	*Italian*	18
Blue Bottle	*Cal./Coffee*	23
Boccalone	*Sandwiches*	26
Boulette Larder	*Amer.*	25
🔢 Boulevard	*Amer.*	27
Butterfly	*Asian/Cal.*	21
Chaya	*French/Japanese*	20
Delancey St.	*Eclectic*	18
Delica	*Japanese*	21
Epic Roasthse.	*Steak*	21
Fog City Diner	*Amer.*	18
4505 Meats	*Hot Dogs*	27
Gordon Biersch	*Pub*	15
Gott's Roadside	*Diner*	21
Hillstone	*Amer.*	22
NEW Hodo Soy	*Vegan*	-
🔢 Hog Island	*Seafood*	25
Il Cane Rosso	*Italian*	23
Imperial Tea Ct.	*Tea*	19
Lafitte	*French*	20
La Mar	*Peruvian/Seafood*	25
MarketBar	*Med.*	16
Mexico DF	*Mex.*	20
Mijita	*Mex.*	19
Namu	*Cal./Korean*	22
One Market	*Amer.*	24
Out the Door	*Viet.*	22
Ozumo	*Japanese*	23
Plant Cafe Organic	*Health*	21
Red's Java	*Burgers*	15
RoliRoti	*Amer.*	25
🔢 Slanted Door	*Viet.*	25
Tacolicious	*Mex.*	22
Town's End	*Amer./Bakery*	21
Waterbar	*Seafood*	21
Waterfront	*Cal./Seafood*	20

EXCELSIOR

Broken Record	*Soul*	24
Joe's Cable Car	*Burgers*	19
North Bch. Pizza	*Pizza*	19

FISHERMAN'S WHARF

(See map on page 304)

TOP FOOD

Gary Danko	*Amer.*	**B2**	29
Scoma's	*Seafood*	**A3**	23
In-N-Out	*Burgers*	**A3**	21
Ana Mandara	*Viet.*	**B1**	21

LISTING

Alioto's	*Italian*	18
Ana Mandara	*Viet.*	21
Bistro Boudin	*Cal.*	20
Forbes Island	*Amer./Seafood*	15
🔢 Gary Danko	*Amer.*	29
Grandeho Kamekyo	*Japanese*	25
🔢 In-N-Out	*Burgers*	21
McCormick/Kuleto	*Seafood*	20
🔢 Scoma's	*Seafood*	23

FOREST HILLS/ WEST PORTAL

Bursa	*Med.*	21
Chouchou	*French*	21
Fresca	*Peruvian*	22
Roti Indian	*Indian*	21

GLEN PARK

Chenery Park	*Amer.*	21
Gialina	*Pizza*	25
La Corneta	*Mex.*	21
Le P'tit Laurent	*French*	23
Osha Thai	*Thai*	21

HAIGHT-ASHBURY/ COLE VALLEY

Alembic	*Eclectic*	23
Asqew Grill	*Cal.*	17
BurgerMeister	*Burgers*	20
Cha Cha	*Carib.*	20
Citrus Club	*Asian*	22
Eos	*Asian/Cal.*	23
La Boulange	*Bakery*	21
Magnolia	*Southern*	20
North Bch. Pizza	*Pizza*	19
Parada 22	*Puerto Rican*	21
Pork Store	*Amer.*	19
Zazie	*French*	23

HAYES VALLEY/
CIVIC CENTER

☑ Absinthe	French/Med.	22
Arlequin	Med.	19
Bar Jules	Amer.	23
Blue Bottle	Cal./Coffee	23
NEW Boxing Rm.	Cajun/Creole	-
Brenda's	Creole/Southern	24
Caffe Delle Stelle	Italian	17
DeLessio	Bakery	20
Domo Sushi	Japanese	24
Espetus	Brazilian	22
Frjtz Fries	Belgian	17
Hayes St. Grill	Seafood	23
Indigo	Amer.	20
☑ Jardinière	Cal./French	26
La Boulange	Bakery	21
NEW Ma*Velous	Coffee	17
Max's	Deli	17
Mel's Drive-In	Diner	13
Moishe's Pippic	Deli/Jewish	17
NEW Nojo	Amer./Japanese	-
Patxi's Pizza	Pizza	22
Paul K	Med.	22
NEW Pause	Amer.	-
Samovar Tea	Tea	18
Sauce	Amer.	17
Sebo	Japanese	26
Stacks	Amer.	18
NEW Straw	Cal./Sandwiches	-
Suppenküche	German	22
☑ Zuni Café	Med.	25

INNER RICHMOND

Academy Cafe	Eclectic	19
Bella Trattoria	Italian	22
Brother's Korean	Korean	24
B Star Bar	Asian	23
☑ Burma Superstar	Burmese	24
☑ Chapeau!	French	26
Giorgio's	Pizza	20
Good Luck	Chinese	23
Katia's Tea	Russian	20
King of Thai	Thai	19
Le Soleil	Viet.	22
Mandalay	Burmese	23
Mel's Drive-In	Diner	13
Moss Room	Cal.	22
My Tofu	Korean	21
Namu	Cal./Korean	22
Prime Rib Shabu	Japanese	20
Q Rest.	Amer.	20
Richmond Rest.	Cal.	24
Troya	Turkish	21

INNER SUNSET

Arizmendi	Bakery/Pizza	26
Beautifull	Health	17
Chow	Amer.	20
Ebisu	Japanese	24
Hotei	Japanese	19
Izakaya Sozai	Japanese	22
☑ Koo	Asian	27
Marnee Thai	Thai	24
Naan/Curry	Indian/Pakistani	17
Pacific Catch	Seafood	19
NEW Pasión	Nuevo Latino/Peruvian	22
Pluto's	Amer.	21
Pomelo	Eclectic	21
San Tung	Chinese/Korean	23
Social Kit.	Amer.	15
Underdog	Hot Dogs	22
Yumma's	Mideast.	21

JAPANTOWN

Benihana	Japanese	17
Bushi-tei	Asian/French	22
Isobune	Japanese	19
Juban	Japanese	18
☑ Kiss Seafood	Japanese	28
Mifune	Japanese	19
O Izakaya	Japanese	18
Shabu-Sen	Japanese	21
Takara	Japanese	23

LAUREL HEIGHTS/
PRESIDIO HEIGHTS

Asqew Grill	Cal.	17
Beautifull	Health	17
Ella's	Amer.	21
Garibaldis	Cal./Med.	22
Pasta Pomodoro	Italian	16
Sociale	Italian	23
☑ Spruce	Amer.	25

LOWER HAIGHT

Axum Cafe	Ethiopian	23
NEW Greenburgers	Burgers	-
Indian Oven	Indian	22
Kate's Kitchen	Southern	21
Memphis Minnie	BBQ	19
Rosamunde	German	22
Thep Phanom	Thai	24
Uva Enoteca	Italian	22

MARINA

(See map on page 303)

TOP FOOD

Zushi Puzzle	Japanese	G4	26
Isa	French	F4	26

Greens | *Veg.* | **G2**	24
Blue Barn | *Cal.* | **F3**	24
A16 | *Italian* | **E3**	24

LISTING

Ace Wasabi's | *Japanese*	19
Alegrias | *Spanish*	21
Amici's | *Pizza*	20
🆉 A16 | *Italian*	24
Asqew Grill | *Cal.*	17
🆕 Atelier Crenn | *French*	26
Baker St. Bistro | *French*	19
Barney's | *Burgers*	19
Bistro Aix | *Cal./French*	22
Blue Barn | *Cal.*	24
🆕 Chotto | *Japanese*	24
Delarosa | *Italian*	22
Dragon Well | *Chinese*	21
E'Angelo | *Italian*	20
🆉 Greens | *Veg.*	24
Isa | *French*	26
Izzy's Steak | *Steak*	20
Jake's Steaks | *Cheesestks.*	19
Let's Be Frank | *Hot Dogs*	20
Mamacita | *Mex.*	22
Mel's Drive-In | *Diner*	13
Pacific Catch | *Seafood*	19
Plant Cafe Organic | *Health*	21
Pluto's | *Amer.*	21
Ristobar | *Italian*	21
Tacolicious | *Mex.*	22
Tipsy Pig | *Amer.*	18
Zushi Puzzle | *Japanese*	26

MISSION

(See map on page 306)

TOP FOOD

Tartine | *Bakery* | **D6**	27
Range | *Amer.* | **E6**	27
Delfina | *Italian* | **D5**	26
Saison | *Amer.* | **D8**	26
Arizmendi | *Bakery/Pizza* | **G6**	26
Taqueria Can Cun | *Mex.* | **E7** | **I7**	25
La Taqueria | *Mex.* | **H7**	25
Pizzeria Delfina | *Pizza* | **D6**	25
Chez Spencer | *French* | **B8**	25

LISTING

Andalu | *Eclectic*	21
Arinell Pizza | *Pizza*	22
Arizmendi | *Bakery/Pizza*	26
🆕 Asiento | *Spanish*	-
Baby Blues BBQ | *BBQ/Southern*	18
Bar Bambino | *Italian*	24
Bar Tartine | *Euro.*	24

🆕 Beast/Hare | *Amer./Cal.*	20
Beretta | *Italian*	22
Blowfish Sushi | *Japanese*	21
Blue Plate | *Amer.*	24
Boogaloos | *SW*	17
Burger Joint | *Burgers*	18
Café Gratitude | *Vegan*	17
Cha Cha | *Carib.*	20
Charanga | *Pan-Latin*	21
Cha-Ya Veg. | *Japanese/Vegan*	23
Chez Spencer | *French*	25
Commonwealth | *Amer.*	24
🆉 Delfina | *Italian*	26
Dosa | *Indian*	22
🆉 Dynamo Donut | *Coffee*	24
El Metate | *Mex.*	22
El Tonayense | *Mex.*	24
Esperpento | *Spanish*	20
Farina | *Italian*	23
🆉 Flour + Water | *Italian*	24
🆉 Foreign Cinema | *Cal./Med.*	24
Frjtz Fries | *Belgian*	17
Goood Frikin' Chicken | *Mideast.*	18
Gracias | *Mex./Vegan*	21
🆕 Grub | *Amer.*	16
Heart | *Eclectic*	19
Heirloom | *Cal./Med.*	23
Herbivore | *Vegan*	17
Hog & Rocks | *Amer.*	21
Jay's | *Cheesestks.*	17
Kiji Sushi Bar | *Japanese*	25
Another Monkey/Koh | *Thai*	20
La Corneta | *Mex.*	21
La Cumbre | *Mex.*	22
La Taqueria | *Mex.*	25
Limón | *Peruvian*	22
Little Star | *Pizza*	24
Local Mission | *Cal.*	23
🆕 Locanda | *Italian*	-
Loló | *Mex.*	24
Luna Park | *Amer./French*	19
Maverick | *Amer.*	24
Mission Bch. Café | *Cal.*	22
🆕 Mission Cheese | *Amer.*	-
Mission Chinese | *Chinese*	21
Monk's Kettle | *Cal.*	20
Mr. Pollo | *Colombian*	24
Nihon | *Japanese*	19
Nombe | *Japanese*	21
Old Jerusalem | *Med./Mideast.*	19
Osha Thai | *Thai*	21
Pakwan | *Pakistani*	22
Pancho Villa | *Mex.*	22
Papalote | *Mex.*	22

    Vote at ZAGAT.com

Pauline's	*Pizza*	23
Pi Bar	*Pizza*	18
Pica Pica Maize	*Venez.*	21
Pizzeria Delfina	*Pizza*	25
Pork Store	*Amer.*	19
NEW Radish	*Amer.*	-
Z Range	*Amer.*	27
Regalito Rosticeria	*Mex.*	23
Rosamunde	*German*	22
Saison	*Amer.*	26
Schmidt's	*German*	21
Slow Club	*Amer.*	22
Spork	*Amer.*	20
Stable Café	*Coffee*	20
St. Francis	*Diner*	17
NEW Summit	*Cal.*	-
Sunflower	*Viet.*	21
Taqueria Can Cun	*Mex.*	25
Taqueria/Sabor	*Mex.*	-
Z Tartine	*Bakery*	27
Tokyo Go Go	*Japanese*	20
Truly Med.	*Med.*	22
Udupi Palace	*Indian/Veg.*	21
Universal Cafe	*Amer.*	24
Walzwerk	*German*	21
Weird Fish	*Seafood*	-
Woodward's Gdn.	*Cal.*	24
Yamo	*Burmese*	22
Zeitgeist	*Burgers*	14

NOB HILL

(See map on page 304)

TOP FOOD

Sons/Daughters	*Amer.*	**H5**	25
Venticello	*Italian*	**G4**	23
Big 4	*Amer.*	**H4**	23

LISTING

Z Big 4	*Amer.*	23
Nob Hill Café	*Italian*	20
Ritz-Carlton	*French*	-
NEW Seven Hills	*Italian*	24
Sons/Daughters	*Amer.*	25
Tonga Rm.	*Asian/Pac. Rim*	13
Venticello	*Italian*	23

NOE VALLEY

(See map on page 306)

TOP FOOD

La Ciccia	*Italian*	**K5**	26
Incanto	*Italian*	**I5**	25
Firefly	*Eclectic*	**H2**	25
Tataki	*Japanese*	**J5**	24
Contigo	*Spanish*	**H3**	24

LISTING

Alice's	*Chinese*	19
Bacco	*Italian*	24
Barney's	*Burgers*	19
Chloe's Cafe	*Amer.*	24
Contigo	*Spanish*	24
Eric's	*Chinese*	20
Firefly	*Eclectic*	25
Fresca	*Peruvian*	22
Hamano Sushi	*Japanese*	20
Henry's Hunan	*Chinese*	21
Incanto	*Italian*	25
La Boulange	*Bakery*	21
La Ciccia	*Italian*	26
Little Chihuahua	*Mex.*	21
Lovejoy's Tea	*Tea*	20
Lupa Trattoria	*Italian*	21
Pasta Pomodoro	*Italian*	16
Patxi's Pizza	*Pizza*	22
Pomelo	*Eclectic*	21
Savor	*Med.*	18
Tataki	*Japanese*	24

NORTH BEACH

(See map on page 304)

TOP FOOD

Cafe Jacqueline	*French*	**E6**	26
House	*Asian*	**E6**	26
Coi	*Cal./French*	**F7**	26
Mama's on Wash.	*Amer.*	**D6**	25
Tony's Pizza	*Italian*	**E6**	25

LISTING

Albona Rist.	*Italian*	25
Bocadillos	*Spanish*	23
NEW Bottle Cap	*American*	-
BurgerMeister	*Burgers*	20
Cafe Divine	*Amer./Sandwiches*	18
Cafe Jacqueline	*French*	26
Cafe Zoetrope/Mammarella's	*Italian*	19
Caffè Macaroni	*Italian*	19
NEW Campanula	*Amer.*	-
Coi	*Cal./French*	26
Comstock	*Amer.*	16
15 Romolo	*Pub*	20
Fior d'Italia	*Italian*	18
Giordano	*Sandwiches*	23
House	*Asian*	26
King of Thai	*Thai*	19
La Boulange	*Bakery*	21
La Trappe	*Belgian*	16
L'Osteria	*Italian*	24
Mama's on Wash.	*Amer.*	25

LOCATIONS

Mario's Bohemian | *Italian/Sandwiches*	17
Maykadeh | *Persian*	23
Naan/Curry | *Indian/Pakistani*	17
Naked Lunch | *Sandwiches*	19
North Bch. Pizza | *Pizza*	19
North Bch. Rest. | *Italian*	22
Rist. Ideale | *Italian*	23
Rose Pistola | *Italian*	21
Stinking Rose | *Italian*	18
Tommaso's | *Italian*	25
Tony's Coal-Fired Pizza | *Pizza*	24
Tony's Pizza | *Italian*	25
Tratt. Contadina | *Italian*	21
NEW Txoko | *Spanish*	-

OUTER RICHMOND

Ariake | *Japanese*	23
Z Aziza | *Moroccan*	26
Cliff House | *Cal.*	18
Hakka Restaurant | *Chinese*	24
Hard Knox | *Southern*	20
Hong Kong Lounge | *Chinese*	20
Kabuto | *Japanese*	25
Kappou Gomi | *Japanese*	28
Khan Toke | *Thai*	21
HK Flower/Mayflower | *Chinese*	20
Mescolanza | *Italian*	23
Morph | *Thai*	-
Oyaji | *Japanese*	24
Pacific Café | *Seafood*	23
Pagan | *Burmese*	18
Pizzetta 211 | *Pizza*	25
Shanghai Dumpling | *Chinese*	21
Z Sutro's | *Cal.*	22
Tommy's Mex. | *Mex.*	15
Ton Kiang | *Chinese*	23

OUTER SUNSET

Beach Chalet | *Amer.*	15
Cajun Pacific | *Cajun*	19
Just Wonton | *Chinese*	17
King of Thai | *Thai*	19
Marnee Thai | *Thai*	24
North Bch. Pizza | *Pizza*	19
Outerlands | *Amer.*	23
Park Chalet | *Cal.*	15
Thanh Long | *Viet.*	24

PACIFIC HEIGHTS

NEW Bistro SF Grill | *Burgers*	-
Elite Cafe | *Amer.*	19
Eliza's | *Chinese*	21
Florio | *French/Italian*	19
Godzila Sushi | *Japanese*	20

La Boulange | *Bakery*	21
My Father's Kit. | *Viet.*	18
Pizzeria Delfina | *Pizza*	25
SPQR | *Italian*	24
TacoBar | *Mex.*	17
Tataki | *Japanese*	24
Woodhse. | *Seafood*	21

POLK GULCH

(See map on page 304)

TOP FOOD

Acquerello | *Italian* | **G1**	28
Swan Oyster | *Seafood* | **H1**	27
Harris' | *Steak* | **F1**	26

LISTING

Z Acquerello | *Italian*	28
Café Zitouna | *Moroccan*	-
Crustacean | *Viet.*	24
Harris' | *Steak*	26
Z House/Prime | *Amer.*	25
Miller's Deli | *Deli/Jewish*	20
Ruth's Chris | *Steak*	24
Shalimar | *Indian/Pakistani*	22
Z Swan Oyster | *Seafood*	27
Tajine | *Moroccan*	-

POTRERO HILL

Aperto | *Italian*	23
Spencer/Go | *French*	23
Chez Papa Bistrot | *French*	23
Goat Hill Pizza | *Pizza*	18
Grand Pu Bah | *Thai*	19
Papito | *Mex.*	25
Pizza Nostra | *Pizza*	19
NEW Plow | *Cal.*	25
Skool | *Seafood*	22
NEW Source | *Pizza/Veg.*	-
Sunflower | *Viet.*	21

PRESIDIO

La Terrasse | *French*	17
Let's Be Frank | *Hot Dogs*	20
Presidio Social | *Amer.*	19
Warming Hut | *Sandwiches*	14

RUSSIAN HILL

(See map on page 304)

TOP FOOD

La Folie | *French* | **E1**	28
Frascati | *Cal./Med.* | **E3**	26
Pesce | *Italian/Seafood* | **E1**	25

LISTING

Frascati | *Cal./Med.*	26
Helmand Palace | *Afghan*	22

Vote at ZAGAT.com

Hyde St. Bistro	*French*	21
La Boulange	*Bakery*	21
Ⓩ La Folie	*French*	28
🆕 Leopold's	*Austrian*	23
Luella	*Cal./Med.*	21
Matterhorn Swiss	*Swiss*	22
Nick's Crispy	*Mex.*	22
Pesce	*Italian/Seafood*	25
Rist. Milano	*Italian*	25
Sushi Groove	*Japanese*	21
Zarzuela	*Spanish*	24

SOMA

(See map on page 308)

TOP FOOD

Benu	*Amer.*	**H3**	26
Una Pizza	*Pizza*	**B2**	26
Yank Sing	*Chinese*	**I1**	**J2**	26
Ame	*Amer.*	**H2**	26
Alexander's	*Japanese/Steak*	**G4**	26

LISTING

Alexander's	*Japanese/Steak*	26
Ⓩ Amber India	*Indian*	24
Ame	*Amer.*	26
Amer. Grilled Cheese	*Amer./Sandwiches*	22
Anchor & Hope	*Seafood*	21
AsiaSF	*Asian/Cal.*	17
Bar Agricole	*Cal.*	21
Basil	*Thai*	23
Benu	*Amer.*	26
Blue Bottle	*Cal./Coffee*	23
🆕 Bluestem Brass.	*Steak*	-
Buca di Beppo	*Italian*	15
Butler & The Chef Bistro	*French*	22
Caffè Museo	*Italian/Med.*	18
Cha Am Thai	*Thai*	19
Chez Papa Resto	*French*	24
Citizen's Band	*Amer.*	21
Coco500	*Cal./Med.*	24
Cosmopolitan	*Amer.*	18
Fang	*Chinese*	20
Farmerbrown	*Soul Food*	20
Fifth Floor	*Amer./French*	23
54 Mint	*Italian*	21
Fondue Cowboy	*Fondue*	18
Fringale	*French/Spanish*	24
Goat Hill Pizza	*Pizza*	18
Heaven's Dog	*Chinese*	20
Henry's Hunan	*Chinese*	21
HRD Coffee	*Diner/Korean*	20
🆕 Ki	*Japanese*	-
Another Monkey/Koh	*Thai*	20
La Boulange	*Bakery*	21

Le Charm Bistro	*French*	23
Local Kitchen	*Cal./Italian*	18
Luce	*Cal./Italian*	21
Manora's Thai	*Thai*	24
Marlowe	*Amer./Cal.*	23
Maya	*Mex.*	20
Mel's Drive-In	*Diner*	13
Mochica	*Peruvian*	25
Oola	*Cal.*	19
Orson	*Cal.*	18
Osha Thai	*Thai*	21
Pazzia	*Italian*	23
Prospect	*Amer.*	24
Radius	*Cal.*	23
Rest. LuLu	*French/Med.*	19
Rist. Umbria	*Italian*	18
RN74	*French*	23
Roy's	*Hawaiian*	23
Salt House	*Amer.*	21
Samovar Tea	*Tea*	18
Sanraku	*Japanese*	22
Sentinel	*Sandwiches*	24
South Park	*French*	22
Spencer/Go	*French*	26
Spice Kit	*Asian*	20
Suriya Thai	*Thai*	25
Sushi Groove	*Japanese*	21
🆕 Sushirrito	*Japanese*	-
Thermidor	*Amer.*	20
Town Hall	*Amer.*	22
Tropisueño	*Mex.*	18
Tu Lan	*Viet.*	18
Ⓩ🆕 25 Lusk	*Amer.*	20
🆕 Una Pizza	*Pizza*	26
Vitrine	*Amer.*	24
Ⓩ Yank Sing	*Chinese*	26
Zaré/Fly Trap	*Cal./Med.*	22
Zero Zero	*Italian/Pizza*	24
Zuppa	*Italian*	19

TENDERLOIN

(See map on page 304)

TOP FOOD

Canteen	*Cal.*	**I4**	27
Saigon Sandwich	*Sandwiches/Viet.*	**K2**	26
Dottie's	*Diner*	**J4**	26

LISTING

A La Turca	*Turkish*	22
Bodega Bistro	*Viet.*	21
Burmese Kitchen	*Burmese*	20
Ⓩ Canteen	*Cal.*	27
🆕 Chambers	*Cal.*	-
Dottie's	*Diner*	26

Farmerbrown	*Soul Food*	20
NEW Jones	*Cal./French*	-
Lers Ros Thai	*Thai*	23
Osha Thai	*Thai*	21
Pagolac	*Viet.*	23
Pakwan	*Pakistani*	22
Saha	*Mideast.*	26
Saigon Sandwich	*Sandwiches/Viet.*	26
Shalimar	*Indian/Pakistani*	22
Thai House	*Thai*	21

UPPER FILLMORE

Baker/Banker	*Amer.*	25
NEW Bun Mee	*Viet.*	-
Citizen Cake	*Cal.*	21
Dosa	*Indian*	22
Fresca	*Peruvian*	22
Jackson Fillmore	*Italian*	21
NEW Jane	*Bakery/Coffee*	-
La Méditerranée	*Med./Mideast.*	20
Out the Door	*Viet.*	22
Ten-Ichi	*Japanese*	23

WESTERN ADDITION

Acme Burger	*Burgers*	20
Alamo Sq.	*French/Seafood*	18
Bar Crudo	*Seafood*	25
Bistro Central Parc	*French*	24
Candybar	*Dessert*	20
Cheese Steak Shop	*Cheesestks.*	20
Chile Pies	*Dessert*	22
DeLessio	*Bakery*	20
Green Chile	*SW*	23
Herbivore	*Vegan*	17
Jay's	*Cheesestks.*	17
Little Chihuahua	*Mex.*	21
Little Star	*Pizza*	24
🗹 Nopa	*Cal.*	25
Nopalito	*Mex.*	22
Papalote	*Mex.*	22
NEW Ragazza	*Pizza*	24
1300/Fillmore	*Soul Food/Southern*	21
Tsunami	*Japanese*	21
Yoshi's SF	*Japanese*	21

East of San Francisco

ALAMEDA

BurgerMeister	*Burgers*	20
🗹 Burma Superstar	*Burmese*	24
Cheese Steak Shop	*Cheesestks.*	20
Pappo	*Cal./Med.*	24

ALBANY

Caspers Hot Dogs	*Hot Dogs*	20
Fonda Solana	*Pan-Latin*	23
Lanesplitter	*Pizza*	17
Little Star	*Pizza*	24

BERKELEY

Adagia	*Cal.*	20
NEW Addie's	*Pizza*	21
Ajanta	*Indian*	25
Arinell Pizza	*Pizza*	22
Barney's	*Burgers*	19
Bette's Oceanview	*Diner*	23
Bistro Liaison	*French*	22
Breads/India	*Indian*	19
BurgerMeister	*Burgers*	20
Cactus Taqueria	*Mex.*	20
Café Fanny	*French*	23
Café Gratitude	*Vegan*	17
Café Rouge	*Cal./Med.*	22
César	*Spanish*	22
Cha Am Thai	*Thai*	19
Cha-Ya Veg.	*Japanese/Vegan*	23
🗹 Cheese Board	*Bakery/Pizza*	27
Cheese Steak Shop	*Cheesestks.*	20
🗹 Chez Panisse	*Cal./Med.*	28
🗹 Chez Panisse Café	*Cal./Med.*	27
Emilia's	*Pizza*	27
Eve	*Amer.*	25
Everett/Jones	*BBQ*	20
FatApple's	*Diner*	18
Five	*Amer./Cal.*	20
Gather	*Cal.*	23
NEW Guamenkitzel	*German*	-
Gioia Pizzeria	*Pizza*	25
Great China	*Chinese*	24
Grégoire	*French*	21
Herbivore	*Vegan*	17
Imperial Tea Ct.	*Tea*	19
Ippuku	*Japanese*	23
Jimmy Beans	*Diner*	20
Juan's	*Mex.*	18
Kirala	*Japanese*	25
Lalime's	*Cal./Med.*	25
La Méditerranée	*Med./Mideast.*	20
Lanesplitter	*Pizza*	17
La Note	*French*	22
LCX/Le Cheval	*Viet.*	20
Lo Coco	*Italian*	22
Meritage/Claremont	*Cal.*	25
Naan/Curry	*Indian/Pakistani*	17
North Bch. Pizza	*Pizza*	19
O Chamé	*Japanese*	24
Picante Cocina	*Mex.*	2.

Revival Bar	*Cal.*	20
Rick & Ann	*Amer.*	21
Ⓩ Rivoli	*Cal./Med.*	26
Saul's Rest./Deli	*Deli*	19
Sea Salt	*Seafood*	21
Shen Hua	*Chinese*	22
Tacubaya	*Mex.*	23
Thai Buddhist	*Thai*	21
Trattoria Corso	*Italian*	24
Ⓩ Tratt. La Sicil.	*Italian*	25
T Rex BBQ	*BBQ*	18
Udupi Palace	*Indian/Veg.*	21
Vanessa's Bistro	*French/Viet.*	23
Venezia	*Italian*	18
Venus	*Cal.*	23
Vik's Chaat	*Indian*	23
Zachary's Pizza	*Pizza*	24
Zatar	*Med.*	23
NEW Zut!	*Amer./Med.*	20

CONCORD

Cheese Steak Shop	*Cheesestks.*	20

DANVILLE

Amber Bistro	*Cal.*	21
Amici's	*Pizza*	20
Blackhawk Grille	*Cal.*	20
Bridges	*Asian/Cal.*	23
Chow	*Amer.*	20
Ⓩ Esin	*Amer./Med.*	25
Forbes Mill	*Steak*	22
Mangia Mi	*Italian*	21
Peasant & the Pear	*Med.*	22
Piatti	*Italian*	19
NEW Prickly Pear	*Mex.*	-
Stomp	*Eclectic*	16

DUBLIN

Amici's	*Pizza*	20
Caspers Hot Dogs	*Hot Dogs*	20
Koi	*Chinese*	24

EL CERRITO

FatApple's	*Diner*	18

EMERYVILLE

Arizmendi	*Bakery/Pizza*	26
Asqew Grill	*Cal.*	17
Bucci's	*Cal./Italian*	21
Lanesplitter	*Pizza*	17
Liba Falafel	*Mideast.*	25
Pasta Pomodoro	*Italian*	16
Rudy's	*Diner*	20
Townhouse B&G	*Cal.*	21
Trader Vic's	*Polynesian*	17

FREMONT/NEWARK

Pakwan	*Pakistani*	22
Shalimar	*Indian/Pakistani*	22
Udupi Palace	*Indian/Veg.*	21

HAYWARD

Caspers Hot Dogs	*Hot Dogs*	20
Everett/Jones	*BBQ*	20
Pakwan	*Pakistani*	22

LAFAYETTE

Artisan Bistro	*Cal./French*	24
Bo's BBQ	*BBQ*	22
Cheese Steak Shop	*Cheesestks.*	20
Ⓩ Chevalier	*French*	25
Chow	*Amer.*	20
Duck Club	*Amer.*	20
Metro	*Cal./French*	21
Patxi's Pizza	*Pizza*	22
Pizza Antica	*Pizza*	20
Postino	*Italian*	22
Yankee Pier	*New Eng./Seafood*	18

LAKE TAHOE

Bridgetender	*Pub*	18
Café Fiore	*Italian*	24
Christy Hill	*Cal./Med.*	22
Cottonwood	*Eclectic*	26
Dragonfly	*Asian/Cal.*	22
Evan's	*Amer.*	27
Gar Woods	*Amer./Med.*	17
Jake's/Lake	*Cal.*	18
Manzanita	*Cal./French*	23
Moody's Bistro	*Amer.*	25
Naked Fish	*Japanese*	23
Pacific Crest	*Med.*	-
Pianeta	*Italian/Med.*	24
PlumpJack	*Cal./Med.*	23
Red Hut	*Diner*	22
Soule Domain	*Amer.*	24
Sunnyside	*Seafood/Steak*	18
Wild Goose	*Amer.*	23
Wolfdale's	*Cal.*	24

LIVERMORE

Wente Vineyards	*Cal./Med.*	24

OAKLAND

Ⓩ À Côté	*French/Med.*	24
Adesso	*Italian*	24
Andalé	*Mex.*	21
Arizmendi	*Bakery/Pizza*	26
Bakesale Betty	*Bakery*	25
Barlata	*Spanish*	21
Barney's	*Burgers*	19

Ƶ BayWolf	Cal./Med.	26
Bellanico	Italian	23
Blackberry Bistro	Southern	21
Blue Bottle	Cal./Coffee	23
Bocanova	Pan-Latin	21
Boot/Shoe	Italian/Pizza	24
Breads/India	Indian	19
Brown Sugar	Soul Food	23
Ƶ Burma Superstar	Burmese	24
Cactus Taqueria	Mex.	20
Camino	Cal./Med.	22
Caspers Hot Dogs	Hot Dogs	20
César	Pan-Latin	22
Cheese Steak Shop	Cheesestks.	20
Chop Bar	Cal.	22
Ƶ Commis	Amer.	27
NEW Cosecha Café	Mex.	-
NEW Disco Volante	Cal.	-
Doña Tomás	Mex.	22
Dopo	Italian	25
Encuentro	Veg.	23
NEW Enoteca Molinari	Italian	-
Everett/Jones	BBQ	20
Fentons	Ice Cream	20
Flora	Amer.	21
Grégoire	French	21
NEW Hawker Fare	SE Asian	-
Hibiscus	Carib.	20
Home of Chicken	Southern	16
NEW Homeroom	Amer.	-
NEW Hudson	Amer.	20
Ƶ In-N-Out	Burgers	21
Koryo BBQ	Korean	21
Lake Chalet	Cal.	14
Lanesplitter	Pizza	17
LCX/Le Cheval	Viet.	20
Lo Coco	Italian	22
Luka's Taproom	Cal./French	20
Mama's Royal	Amer.	22
Marica	Seafood	27
Marzano	Italian/Pizza	23
Max's	Deli	17
Mezze	Cal./Med.	23
Miss Pearl's	Southern	18
Nan Yang	Burmese	22
Oliveto	Italian	24
Oliveto Rest.	Italian	25
Ozumo	Japanese	23
Pasta Pomodoro	Italian	16
Pho 84	Viet.	23
Picán	Southern	22
Ƶ Pizzaiolo	Italian/Pizza	26
Pizza Rustica	Pizza	20
Plum	Cal.	24

Rest. Peony	Chinese	21
Rudy's	Diner	20
Scott's	Seafood	20
Sidebar	Cal.	22
Soi4	Thai	24
NEW Southie	Amer.	-
Tamarindo	Mex.	25
Trueburger	Burgers	20
Uzen	Japanese	24
Ƶ Wood Tavern	Cal.	26
NEW Xolo Taqueria	Mex.	-
Xyclo	Viet.	22
Yoshi's	Japanese	20
Zachary's Pizza	Pizza	24

ORINDA

Casa Orinda	Italian/Steak	18
NEW Table 24	Amer.	18

PLEASANT HILL

Caspers Hot Dogs	Hot Dogs	20

PLEASANTON

Cheesecake	Amer.	17
Cheese Steak Shop	Cheesestks.	20

RICHMOND

Caspers Hot Dogs	Hot Dogs	20

SAN RAMON

Cheese Steak Shop	Cheesestks.	20
Incontro	Italian	24
Izzy's Steak	Steak	20
Max's	Deli	17
Zachary's Pizza	Pizza	24

WALNUT CREEK

Breads/India	Indian	19
Caspers Hot Dogs	Hot Dogs	20
Cheese Steak Shop	Cheesestks.	20
Élevé	Viet.	21
Home of Chicken	Southern	16
Il Fornaio	Italian	20
Lark Creek	Amer.	22
LCX/Le Cheval	Viet.	20
Prima	Italian	24
Ruth's Chris	Steak	24
Sasa	Japanese	23
Scott's	Seafood	20
Va de Vi	Eclectic	24
Vanessa's Bistro	French/Viet.	23
Vic Stewart	Steak	22

YOSEMITE/OAKHURST

Ƶ Ahwahnee	Cal.	18
Ƶ Erna's	Cal./French	27

Vote at ZAGAT.com

North of San Francisco

BODEGA BAY

Duck Club	*Amer.*	20
Terrapin Creek	*Cal.*	25

CALISTOGA

All Seasons	*Cal.*	23
Brannan's Grill	*Amer./French*	18
Jole	*Amer.*	27
Solbar	*Cal.*	26

CORTE MADERA

Brick/Bottle	*Cal.*	19
Cheesecake	*Amer.*	17
Il Fornaio	*Italian*	20
Max's	*Deli*	17
Pacific Catch	*Seafood*	19

FAIRFAX

Anokha/Lotus	*Indian*	22

FORESTVILLE

☑ Farmhse. Inn	*Cal.*	27

GEYSERVILLE

Diavola	*Italian*	25
Rustic	*Italian*	19

GLEN ELLEN/ KENWOOD

Cafe Citti	*Italian*	22
Fig Cafe/Wine	*French*	25
Kenwood	*Amer./French*	23

GUERNEVILLE

Applewood Inn	*Cal.*	25

HEALDSBURG/ WINDSOR

Baci Cafe	*Italian/Med.*	22
Barndiva	*Amer.*	23
Bistro Ralph	*Cal./French*	24
Bovolo	*Italian*	21
Charcuterie	*French*	21
☑ Cyrus	*French*	28
Downtown Bakery	*Bakery*	25
Dry Creek	*Cal.*	24
NEW Frank/Ernie's	*Steak*	-
Healdsburg B&G	*Amer.*	18
Jimtown Store	*Deli*	21
☑ Madrona	*Amer./French*	27
NEW Mamma Pig's	*Amer.*	-
Ravenous	*Cal./Eclectic*	23
Scopa	*Italian*	26
NEW Shimo	*Japanese/Steak*	-
Spoonbar	*Med.*	18

Willi's Seafood	*Seafood*	24
Zin	*Amer.*	23

LARKSPUR

Emporio Rulli	*Dessert/Italian*	24
Left Bank	*French*	19
Melting Pot	*Fondue*	16
Picco	*Italian*	25
☑ Pizzeria Picco	*Pizza*	27
Table Café	*Cal.*	22
Tav./Lark Creek	*Amer.*	20
Yankee Pier	*New Eng./Seafood*	18

MENDOCINO COUNTY

Albion River Inn	*Cal.*	23
NEW Branches	*Amer.*	-
Cafe Beaujolais	*Cal./French*	25
Chapter & Moon	*Amer.*	21
Fort Bragg	*Bakery/Eclectic*	22
Ledford Hse.	*Cal./Med.*	23
Little River Inn	*Cal./Seafood*	22
MacCallum	*Cal.*	24
Mendo Bistro	*Amer.*	23
Mendo Café	*Eclectic*	20
Mendo Hotel	*Cal.*	18
Moosse Café	*Cal.*	22
955 Ukiah	*Amer./French*	25
North Coast Brew	*Amer.*	18
Oco Time	*Japanese*	-
Patrona	*Cal.*	-
Piaci	*Pizza*	25
Ravens'	*Vegan*	26
Restaurant	*Amer./Eclectic*	25
Rest./Stevenswood	*Amer.*	21
Schat's/Bakery	*Bakery*	-
St. Orres	*Cal.*	23
Table 128	*Cal.*	-
Ukiah Brew	*Pub*	-

MILL VALLEY

Avatar's	*Indian*	22
Balboa Cafe	*Amer.*	19
☑ Buckeye	*Amer./BBQ*	24
Bungalow 44	*Amer.*	21
Dipsea Cafe	*Amer.*	18
NEW El Paseo	*Steak*	-
Frantoio	*Italian*	20
Harmony	*Chinese*	20
☑ In-N-Out	*Burgers*	21
Joe's Taco	*Mex.*	20
La Boulange	*Bakery*	21
La Ginestra	*Italian*	19
Pasta Pomodoro	*Italian*	16
Piatti	*Italian*	19
Piazza D'Angelo	*Italian*	20

Pizza Antica	Pizza	20
Robata Grill	Japanese	21
Toast	Amer.	19
Tsukiji Sushi	Japanese	22

NAPA

Alexis Baking	Bakery	22
Angèle	French	24
Azzurro Pizzeria	Pizza	23
BarBersQ	BBQ	21
Bistro Don Giovanni	Italian	24
Boon Fly	Cal.	21
Bounty Hunter	BBQ	21
Brix	Cal./Med.	23
Cafe Zoetrope/Mammarella's	Italian	19
C Casa	Mex.	24
Celadon	Amer./Eclectic	23
Cole's Chop	Steak	25
Cuvée	Amer.	22
Farm	Amer.	24
Fish Story	Seafood	18
Fumé Bistro	Amer.	19
Gott's Roadside	Diner	21
Z Hog Island	Seafood	25
Z In-N-Out	Burgers	21
NEW Kitchen Door	Eclectic	-
La Toque	French	26
Model Bakery	Bakery	22
Morimoto	Japanese	26
Napa General	Cal./Eclectic	18
Napa Wine Train	Cal.	18
Neela's	Indian	24
Norman Rose	Amer.	20
Oenotri	Italian	25
Oxbow Wine	Cal./Med.	18
Pearl	Cal.	24
Pica Pica Maize	Venez.	21
Rotisserie & Wine	Amer.	22
Ubuntu	Cal./Vegan	24
Uva Trattoria	Italian	21
Zinsvalley	Amer.	17
ZuZu	Spanish	25

NOVATO

Boca	Argent./Steak	22
La Boulange	Bakery	21
Anokha/Lotus	Indian	22
Toast	Amer.	19

OCCIDENTAL

Z Bistro/Copains	French	27

PETALUMA

Avatar's	Indian	22
Central Market	Cal./Med.	22
Cucina Paradiso	Italian	25
Della Fattoria	Bakery/Eclectic	26
Risibisi	Italian	20
Volpi's Rist.	Italian	19
Water St. Bistro	French	22

ROSS

Marché/Fleurs	French	25

RUTHERFORD

Z Auberge/Soleil	Cal./French	27
Rutherford Grill	Amer.	23

SAN ANSELMO

Cucina Rest.	Italian	22
Insalata's	Med.	24
Marinitas	Mex./Pan-Latin	20

SAN RAFAEL

Amici's	Pizza	20
Arizmendi	Bakery/Pizza	26
Barney's	Burgers	19
Café Gratitude	Vegan	17
Il Davide	Italian	24
Las Camelias	Mex.	20
Anokha/Lotus	Indian	22
Royal Thai	Thai	23
Sol Food	Puerto Rican	23
Vin Antico	Italian	23

SANTA ROSA/ ROHNERT PARK

Betty's Fish	British/Seafood	21
Cheese Steak Shop	Cheesestks.	20
Flavor	Cal./Eclectic	20
NEW Fresh/Lisa	Cal./French	24
Gary Chu's	Chinese	22
Hana	Japanese	25
John Ash	Cal.	24
La Gare	French	21
Monti's	Amer./Med.	20
Osake	Cal./Japanese	24
NEW Petite Syrah	Cal.	-
Rosso Pizzeria	Italian/Pizza	25
NEW Sazon	Peruvian	-
Stark's	Steak	-
Willi's Wine	Eclectic	25
Zazu	Amer./Italian	25

SAUSALITO

Avatar's	Indian	22
NEW Bar Bocce	Pizza	-
Fish	Seafood	24
Murray Circle	Cal.	24
NEW Plate Shop	Cal.	-
Poggio	Italian	23

Vote at ZAGAT.com

| | Scoma's | *Seafood* | 23 |
| | Sushi Ran | *Japanese* | 28 |

SEBASTOPOL/ GRATON

Hopmonk Tav.	*Eclectic*	18
K&L Bistro	*French*	24
Peter Lowell	*Italian*	23
Starlight	*Amer.*	22
Underwood Bar	*Med.*	23
Willow Wood	*Eclectic/Med.*	23

SONOMA

	Cafe La Haye	*Amer./Cal.*	27
Carneros Bistro	*Cal.*	24
Della Santina	*Italian*	22
El Dorado	*Cal./Med.*	22
Estate	*Cal./Italian*	21
Fremont Diner	*Diner*	21
Girl & the Fig	*French*	23
Harvest Moon	*Cal./Med.*	24
Hopmonk Tav.	*Eclectic*	18
Hot Box Grill	*Cal.*	23
LaSalette	*Portug.*	24
Meritage Martini	*Italian*	22
	Santé	*Cal./French*	26

ST. HELENA

Cindy's	*Cal.*	24
Cook St. Helena	*Italian*	26
Farmstead	*Cal.*	20
Gott's Roadside	*Diner*	21
Market	*Amer.*	23
Meadowood Grill	*Cal.*	22
	Meadowood Rest.	*Cal.*	28
Model Bakery	*Bakery*	22
Pizzeria Tra Vigne	*Pizza*	21
Press	*Amer./Steak*	24
	Terra	*Amer.*	27
Tra Vigne	*Italian*	24
Wine Spectator	*Cal.*	21

TIBURON

| Caprice | *Amer.* | 22 |
| Guaymas | *Mex.* | 17 |

VALLEY FORD

| Rocker Oyster | *Amer.* | 21 |

WEST MARIN/OLEMA

Drake's	*Cal.*	21
Nick's Cove	*Cal.*	19
Olema Inn	*Cal.*	18
Osteria Stellina	*Italian*	23
Pine Cone Diner	*Diner*	23
Station House	*Cal.*	18

YOUNTVILLE

	Ad Hoc/Addendum	*Amer.*	27
Bardessono	*Amer.*	21
	Bistro Jeanty	*French*	25
	Bottega	*Italian*	25
	Bouchon	*French*	25
Étoile	*Cal.*	25
	French Laundry	*Amer./French*	29
Hurley's	*Cal./Med.*	21
	Mustards	*Amer./Cal.*	25
	Redd	*Cal.*	27

South of San Francisco

BIG SUR

Big Sur	*Amer./Bakery*	22
Deetjen's Big Sur	*Cal.*	23
Nepenthe	*Amer.*	16
Rest./Ventana	*Cal.*	21
	Sierra Mar	*Cal./Eclectic*	27

BURLINGAME

Benihana	*Japanese*	17
Burger Joint	*Burgers*	18
Ecco	*Cal./Continental*	23
Il Fornaio	*Italian*	20
Isobune	*Japanese*	19
Juban	*Japanese*	18
Kabul Afghan	*Afghan*	22
La Corneta	*Mex.*	21
Max's	*Deli*	17
Roti Indian	*Indian*	21
Sakae Sushi	*Japanese*	26
Stacks	*Amer.*	18
Straits	*Singapor.*	20

CAMPBELL

| Buca di Beppo | *Italian* | 15 |
| Twist | *Amer./French* | 18 |

CARMEL/MONTEREY PENINSULA

Anton/Michel	*Continental*	23
	Aubergine	*Cal.*	28
Bistro Moulin	*French*	25
Cannery/Brew	*Amer.*	17
Cantinetta Luca	*Italian*	21
Casanova	*French/Italian*	23
	Club XIX	*Cal./French*	23
Duck Club	*Amer.*	20
Fandango	*Med.*	23
Fishwife	*Cal./Seafood*	20
Flying Fish	*Cal./Seafood*	24
Grasing's Coastal	*Cal.*	23
Hula's	*Hawaiian*	18

Il Fornaio	*Italian*	20
Montrio Bistro	*Cal.*	23
Mundaka	*Spanish*	24
☑ Pacific's Edge	*Amer./French*	24
☑ Passionfish	*Cal./Seafood*	27
Rio Grill	*Cal.*	21
Roy's	*Hawaiian*	24
Sardine Factory	*Amer./Seafood*	21
Tarpy's	*Amer.*	20

CARMEL VALLEY

Café Rustica	*Cal.*	24
☑ Marinus	*Cal./French*	27
Wicket's	*Cal.*	–
Will's Fargo	*Seafood/Steak*	21

CUPERTINO

Alexander's	*Japanese/Steak*	26
Amici's	*Pizza*	20
Benihana	*Japanese*	17
Gochi	*Japanese*	25

HALF MOON BAY/ COAST

Barbara's	*Seafood*	21
☑ Cafe Gibraltar	*Med.*	26
Cetrella	*Med.*	22
Chez Shea	*Eclectic*	23
Davenport	*Cal./Coffee*	16
Duarte's	*Amer.*	20
Flying Fish	*Cal./Seafood*	22
Half Moon Brew	*Pub/Seafood*	16
La Costanera	*Peruvian*	21
Mezza Luna	*Italian*	22
Navio	*Amer.*	25
Pasta Moon	*Italian*	24
Sam's Chowder	*Seafood*	20

LOS ALTOS

Chef Chu's	*Chinese*	20
Hunan	*Chinese*	22
Muracci's	*Japanese*	21
Sumika	*Japanese*	22

LOS GATOS

Andalé	*Mex.*	21
Dio Deka	*Greek*	26
Forbes Mill	*Steak*	22
☑ Manresa	*Amer.*	28
Nick's on Main	*Amer.*	26

MENLO PARK

Applewood Pizza	*Pizza*	21
Cool Café	*Cal.*	20
Flea St. Café	*Cal.*	26
Iberia	*Spanish*	22

Juban	*Japanese*	18
☑ Kaygetsu	*Japanese*	27
Left Bank	*French*	19
Madera	*Amer.*	22
Naomi Sushi	*Japanese*	20
Stacks	*Amer.*	18

MILLBRAE

HK Flower/Mayflower	*Chinese*	20
☑ In-N-Out	*Burgers*	21
Kitchen	*Chinese*	19

MILPITAS

HK Flower/Mayflower	*Chinese*	20

MOUNTAIN VIEW

☑ Amber India	*Indian*	24
Amici's	*Pizza*	20
Cascal	*Pan-Latin*	21
Chez TJ	*French*	24
☑ In-N-Out	*Burgers*	21
Krung Thai	*Thai*	19
Sakoon	*Indian*	23
Xanh	*Viet.*	21

PALO ALTO/ EAST PALO ALTO

☑ Baumé	*French*	27
Buca di Beppo	*Italian*	15
Café Brioche	*Cal./French*	21
Calafia	*Cal.*	17
Cheesecake	*Amer.*	17
☑ Evvia	*Greek*	27
Fuki Sushi	*Japanese*	23
Gordon Biersch	*Pub*	15
Hunan	*Chinese*	22
Il Fornaio	*Italian*	20
Jin Sho	*Japanese*	23
Joya	*Nuevo Latino*	21
Junnoon	*Indian*	22
Kanpai	*Japanese*	22
La Strada	*Italian*	19
Lavanda	*Med.*	20
MacArthur Pk.	*Amer.*	17
Mantra	*Cal./Indian*	21
Max's	*Deli*	17
Mayfield	*Bakery/Cal.*	20
Osteria	*Italian*	23
Pampas	*Brazilian*	22
Patxi's Pizza	*Pizza*	22
Pluto's	*Amer.*	21
Quattro	*Italian*	22
Scott's	*Seafood*	20
Shokolaat	*Cal.*	17
St. Michael's	*Cal.*	22

Vote at ZAGAT.cor

Straits	*Singapor.*	20
Tai Pan	*Chinese*	22
Tamarine	*Viet.*	26
Three Seasons	*Viet.*	19
Trader Vic's	*Polynesian*	17
Zibibbo	*Med.*	19

REDWOOD CITY

Chantilly	*French/Italian*	25
Crouching Tiger	*Chinese*	19
Donato	*Italian*	22
Ike's	*Sandwiches*	24
John Bentley	*Cal.*	26
Mandaloun	*Cal./Med.*	20
Martins West	*Scottish*	22
Max's	*Deli*	17
Old Port Lobster	*Seafood*	21
Pasta Pomodoro	*Italian*	16

REDWOOD SHORES

Amici's	*Pizza*	20
Ike's	*Sandwiches*	24
Mistral	*French/Italian*	20

SAN BRUNO

Don Pico	*Mex.*	17
Pasta Pomodoro	*Italian*	16

SAN CARLOS

Izzy's Steak	*Steak*	20
Kabul Afghan	*Afghan*	22
La Corneta	*Mex.*	21
NEW Locanda Positano	*Pizza*	-

SAN JOSE

Z Amber India	*Indian*	24
Amici's	*Pizza*	20
Arcadia	*Amer.*	20
Blowfish Sushi	*Japanese*	21
Buca di Beppo	*Italian*	15
Cheesecake	*Amer.*	17
Cheese Steak Shop	*Cheesestks.*	20
Gordon Biersch	*Pub*	15
Il Fornaio	*Italian*	20
Z In-N-Out	*Burgers*	21
Krung Thai	*Thai*	19
Z La Forêt	*Continental/French*	27
LB Steak	*Steak*	20
Left Bank	*French*	19
Z Le Papillon	*French*	27
McCormick/Schmick	*Seafood*	21
Morton's	*Steak*	23
Original Joe's	*Amer./Italian*	22
Pasta Pomodoro	*Italian*	16
Pizza Antica	*Pizza*	20

Pluto's	*Amer.*	21
Scott's	*Seafood*	20
71 St. Peter	*Cal./Med.*	20
Sino	*Chinese*	19
Straits	*Singapor.*	20
Taqueria Tlaquepaque	*Mex.*	20
Thea Med.	*Greek/Med.*	19
Yankee Pier	*New Eng./Seafood*	18

SAN MATEO

Acqua Pazza	*Italian*	21
NEW All Spice	*Indian*	24
Amici's	*Pizza*	20
Attic	*Asian*	18
NEW Café Tradition	*French/Moroccan*	-
Cha Cha	*Carib./Cuban*	20
Espetus	*Brazilian*	22
Happy Cafe	*Chinese*	21
Hotaru	*Japanese*	20
La Cumbre	*Mex.*	22
Melting Pot	*Fondue*	16
North Bch. Pizza	*Pizza*	19
NEW Osteria Coppa	*Italian/Pizza*	24
Pancho Villa	*Mex.*	22
Pasta Pomodoro	*Italian*	16
Rist. Capellini	*Italian*	20
231 Ellsworth	*Amer.*	23
Viognier	*Cal./French*	23
Wakuriya	*Japanese*	27
Yuzu Sushi	*Japanese*	22

SANTA CLARA

Cheesecake	*Amer.*	17
Dasaprakash	*Indian*	22
Parcel 104	*Cal.*	23
Piatti	*Italian*	19

SANTA CRUZ/ APTOS/CAPITOLA/ SOQUEL

Aquarius	*Amer.*	21
Cellar Door Café	*Cal.*	26
Gabriella Café	*Cal./Italian*	22
Gayle's Bakery	*Bakery*	23
Hula's	*Hawaiian*	18
La Posta	*Italian*	26
Ma Maison	*French*	24
O'mei	*Chinese*	20
Oswald	*Amer.*	25
Rist. Avanti	*Cal./Italian*	24
Shadowbrook	*Cal.*	18
Soif Wine Bar	*Cal.*	25

LOCATIONS

SARATOGA

Basin | *Amer.* — 20
Hachi Ju Hachi | *Japanese* — 23
Ⓩ Plumed Horse | *Cal.* — 26
Sent Sovi | *Cal.* — 23

SOUTH SF/ DALY CITY

Andalé | *Mex.* — 21
Basque Cultural | *French* — 19
Burger Joint | *Burgers* — 18
BurgerMeister | *Burgers* — 20
Ebisu | *Japanese* — 24
Emporio Rulli | *Dessert/Italian* — 24
Ⓩ In-N-Out | *Burgers* — 21
Koi | *Chinese* — 24
Yankee Pier | *New Eng./Seafood* — 18

STANFORD

Cool Café | *Cal.* — 20
Ike's | *Sandwiches* — 24

SUNNYVALE

Cheese Steak Shop | *Cheesestks.* — 20
Dishdash | *Mideast.* — 22
Il Postale | *Italian* — 21
Lion/Compass | *Amer.* — 21
Shalimar | *Indian/Pakistani* — 22
Udupi Palace | *Indian/Veg.* — 21

WOODSIDE

Bella Vista | *Continental* — 22
NEW Station 1 | *Cal.* — 25
Village Pub | *Amer.* — 26

COW HOLLOW · MARINA

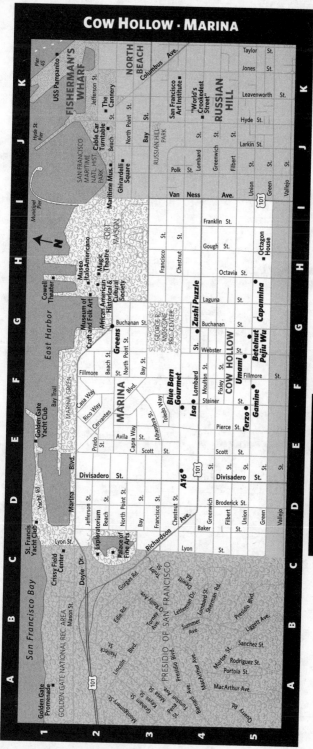

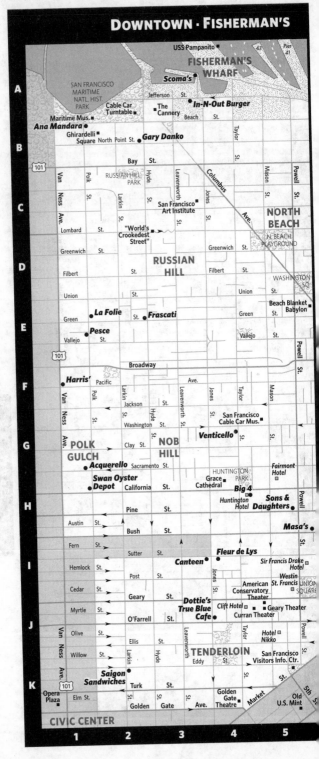

DOWNTOWN · FISHERMAN'S

USS Pampanito ■

43   Pier 41

FISHERMAN'S WHARF

Scoma's ■

A

Jefferson   St.

SAN FRANCISCO MARITIME NATL. HIST. PARK

Cable Car Turntable ■   ■ The Cannery   ■ In-N-Out Burger

Maritime Mus. ■   Beach   St.

Ana Mandara ●

Ghirardelli ■   Taylor   St.

B   Square   North Point St.   ● **Gary Danko**

Bay   St.

101

Van   Polk   RUSSIAN HILL PARK   Leavenworth   Columbus   Mason   Powell

C   Ness   St.   Larkin   Hyde   Jones   St.   St.

San Francisco Art Institute

NORTH BEACH

Ave.   Lombard   St.   N. BEACH PLAYGROUND

"World's Crookedest Street"   Greenwich   St.

Greenwich   St.   **RUSSIAN HILL**

D   Filbert   St.   Filbert   St.   WASHINGTON SQ

Union   St.   Union   St.

Beach Blanket Babylon ■

La Folie ●   St.   ● **Frascati**

E   Green   Green   St.   Powell

Pesce ●   Vallejo   St.   Vallejo   St.

101   Broadway

Broadway   Ave.

F   **Harris'** ●   Pacific   Jones   Taylor   Mason

Van   Polk   Larkin   Leavenworth

Ness   St.   Jackson   St.

Ave.   Washington   St.   San Francisco Cable Car Mus. ■

G   Clay St.   **NOB HILL**   ● **Venticello**   St.   St.

POLK GULCH   Fairmont Hotel ■

● **Acquerello**   Sacramento St.   HUNTINGTON PARK   ■

Swan Oyster Depot ●   Grace Cathedral ■   **Big 4** ■

H   California   St.   Huntington Hotel ■   **Sons & Daughters** ●

Pine   St.   Powell

Austin   St.   →   **Masa's** ●

Bush   St.   ↓   St.

Fern   St.   →

Sutter   St.   **Fleur de Lys** ●

I   Hemlock   St.   →   **Canteen** ●   Jones   Sir Francis Drake Hotel

Post   St.   Westin St. Francis ■

Cedar   St.   Geary   St.   American Conservatory Theater   UNION SQUARE

Myrtle   St.   **Dottie's True Blue Cafe** ●   Clift Hotel ■ ■ Geary Theater

O'Farrell   St.   Curran Theater   Taylor

J   Van   Olive   St.   Hotel Nikko ■

Ness   Ellis   St.   Leavenworth   Powell

Willow   St.   Larkin   Hyde   **TENDERLOIN**   San Francisco Visitors Info. Ctr. ■

Ave.   Eddy   St.   St.

K   **Saigon Sandwiches** ●   Turk   St.   St.

101   Opera Plaza   Elm   St.   Golden Gate Theatre ■   Market   Old U.S. Mint ■   5th St.

Golden   Gate   Ave.

CIVIC CENTER

1   2   3   4   5

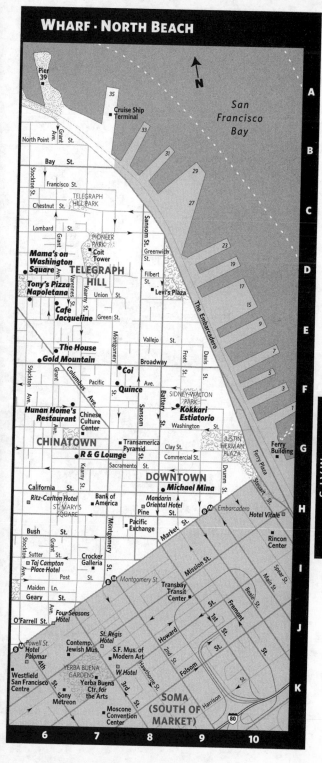

A

B

C

D

E

F

G

H

I

J

K

San
Francisco
Bay

Pier 39

35

Cruise Ship
Terminal

33

31

29

27

North Point Ave.

Grant St.

Bay St.

Stockton St.

Francisco St.

TELEGRAPH
HILL PARK

Chestnut St.

Lombard St.

Grant Ave.

PIONEER
PARK

Coit
Tower

23

19

17

15

9

7

**Mama's on
Washington
Square**

TELEGRAPH
HILL

Sansom St.

Greenwich St.

Varennes St.

**Tony's Pizza
Napoletana**

Kearny St.

Filbert
St.

Levi's Plaza

**Cafe
Jacqueline**

Union St.

Green St.

The Embarcadero

The House

Montgomery St.

Vallejo St.

Front St.

Davis St.

5

3

1

Gold Mountain

Broadway

Stockton St.

Grant Ave.

Columbus Ave.

Pacific Ave.

Coi

Quince

Sansom St.

Battery St.

SIDNEY WALTON
PARK

**Hunan Home's
Restaurant**

Chinese
Culture
Center

**Kokkari
Estiatorio**

Washington St.

CHINATOWN

Transamerica
Pyramid

Clay St.

JUSTIN
HERMAN
PLAZA

Ferry
Building

R & G Lounge

Kearny St.

Sacramento St.

Commercial St.

DOWNTOWN

Drumm St.

Ferry Plaza

California St.

Montgomery St.

Michael Mina

Steuart St.

Ritz-Carlton Hotel

ST. MARY'S
SQUARE

Bank of
America

**Mandarin
Oriental Hotel**

Pine St.

Embarcadero

Hotel Vitale

Bush St.

Stockton St.

Grant Ave.

Pacific
Exchange

Market St.

Rincon
Center

Sutter St.

Crocker
Galleria

Montgomery St.

Spear St.

Taj Campton
Place Hotel

Post St.

Montgomery St.

Mission St.

Main St.

Maiden Ln.

Transbay
Transit
Center

Beale St.

Geary St.

Four Seasons
Hotel

Howard St.

Fremont St.

1st St.

O'Farrell St.

Ave.

St. Regis
Hotel

2nd St.

Folsom St.

Powell St.

Hotel
Polomar

Contemp.
Jewish Mus.

S.F. Mus. of
Modern Art

Hawthorne St.

4th St.

**Westfield
San Francisco
Centre**

YERBA BUENA
GARDENS

W Hotel

3rd St.

Harrison St.

80

Sony
Metreon

Yerba Buena
Ctr. for
the Arts

**SoMa
(SOUTH OF
MARKET)**

Moscone
Convention
Center

6   7   8   9   10

MAPS

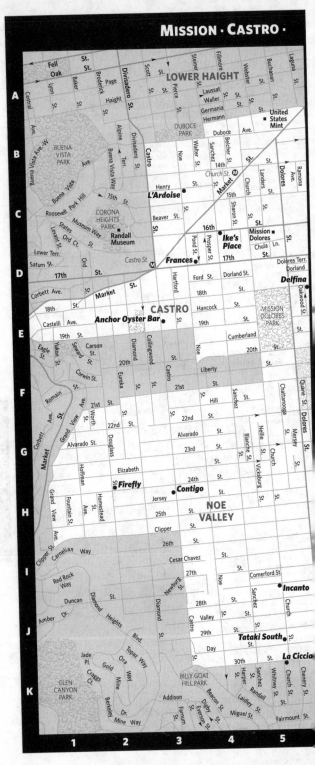

LOWER HAIGHT

Fell St.
Oak St.
Page St.
Haight St.
Lyon St.
Baker St.
Broderick St.
Divisadero St.
Scott St.
Pierce St.
Steiner St.
Fillmore St.
Webster St.
Buchanan St.
Laguna St.
Laussat
Waller St.
Germania
Hermann

Central Ave.
Buena Vista Ave. W
Alpine Terr.
Castro St.
Noe St.
Walter St.
Sanchez St.
Duboce Ave.
Belcher St.
United States Mint

DUBOCE PARK

BUENA VISTA PARK

Buena Vista Ave.
Buena Vista Terr.
Divisadero St.
14th St.
Church St.
Landers St.
Dolores St.
Ramona Ave.

Buena Vista
15th St.
L'Ardoise
Henry St.
Market St.
15th
Church St.
Sharon St.
Dolores St.

Roosevelt
Park Hill
Museum Way
CORONA HEIGHTS PARK
Beaver St.
16th
Ike's Place
Mission Dolores

States St.
Levant St.
Ord Ct.
Randall Museum
Castro St.
Pond St.
Prosper St.
17th
Chula Ln.
St.

Lower Terr.
Saturn St.
Ord St.
Castro St.
Frances
Dolores Terr.
Dorland
Delfina

17th St.
Hartford St.
Ford St.
Dorland St.
Oakwood St.

Corbett Ave.
Market
18th St.

18th St.
CASTRO
Hancock St.
MISSION DOLORES PARK

Castelli Ave.
Anchor Oyster Bar
19th St.

19th St.
Carson St.
Diamond St.
Collingwood St.
Noe St.
Cumberland St.

Eagle St.
Yukon St.
Seward St.
20th St.
Castro St.
20th St.

Corwin St.
Liberty St.

Romain
Eureka St.
21st St.
Hill St.
Sanchez St.
Chattanooga St.
Quane St.
Dolores St.

Corbett Ave.
21st St.
Worth St.
22nd St.
Alvarado St.
Nellie St.
Blanche St.
Vicksburg St.
Church St.
Mersey St.

Grand View Ave.
Grand View
Alvarado St.
Douglass St.
23rd St.

Market St.
Hoffman Ave.
Elizabeth
24th St.
NOE VALLEY

Firefly
Contigo
Jersey St.
25th St.

Homestead St.
Fountain St.
Clipper St.
26th St.

Grand View Ave.
Carnelian Way
Cesar Chavez St.

Clipper St.
27th St.
Noe St.
Comerford St.
Incanto

Red Rock Way
Newburg St.
Sanchez St.
Church St.

Duncan St.
28th St.

Amber Dr.
Diamond Heights
Castro St.
Valley St.
29th St.
Tataki South

Jade Pl.
Topaz Way
Ora Way
Day St.
30th St.
La Ciccia

Gold Mine
Craggs Ct.
Berkeley
BILLY GOAT HILL PARK
Harper St.
Randall St.
Sanchez St.
Whitney St.
Church St.
Chenery St.

GLEN CANYON PARK
Addison St.
Farnum St.
Beacon St.
Digby St.
Everson St.
Laidley St.
Miguel St.
Fairmount St.

Mine Way

1   2   3   4   5

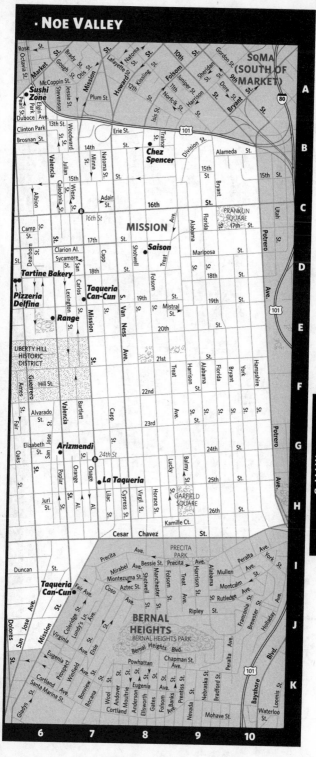

· NOE VALLEY

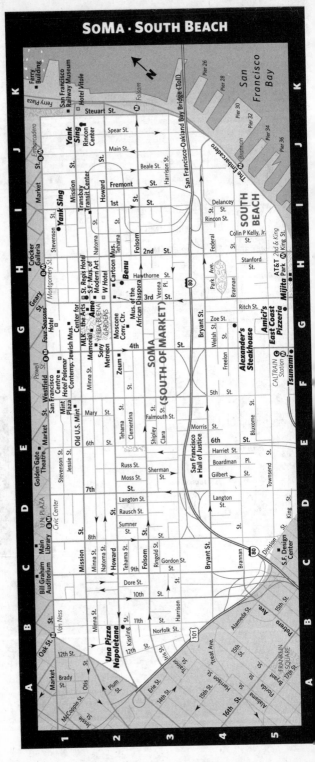

SoMa · South Beach

Special Features

Listings cover the best in each category and include names, locations and Food ratings. Multi-location restaurants' features may vary by branch.

BREAKFAST

(See also Hotel Dining)

Alexis Baking	Napa/N	22
Bette's Oceanview	Berkeley/E	23
Big Sur	Big Sur/S	22
Blackberry Bistro	Oakland/E	21
Boulette Larder	Embarcadero	25
Butler & The Chef Bistro	SoMa	22
Café Fanny	Berkeley/E	23
Chloe's Cafe	Noe Valley	24
Dipsea Cafe	Mill Valley/N	18
Dottie's	Tenderloin	26
Downtown Bakery	Healdsburg/N	25
Ella's	Presidio Hts	21
Emporio Rulli	Downtown	24
FatApple's	multi.	18
Gayle's Bakery	Capitola/S	23
Il Fornaio	multi.	20
Jimmy Beans	Berkeley/E	20
Jimtown Store	Healdsburg/N	21
Kate's Kitchen	Lower Haight	21
Koi	Daly City/S	24
La Boulange	multi.	21
La Note	Berkeley/E	22
Mama's on Wash.	N Beach	25
Mama's Royal	Oakland/E	22
Mel's Drive-In	multi.	13
Model Bakery	St. Helena/N	22
Napa General	Napa/N	18
Oliveto	Oakland/E	24
Pork Store	multi.	19
Red's Java	Embarcadero	15
Rick & Ann	Berkeley/E	21
Rose's Cafe	Cow Hollow	21
Savor	Noe Valley	18
Sears	Downtown	19
☑ Tartine	Mission	27
Town's End	Embarcadero	21
Venus	Berkeley/E	23
Water St. Bistro	Petaluma/N	22
Willow Wood	Graton/N	23
Zazie	Cole Valley	23

BRUNCH

☑ Absinthe	Hayes Valley	22
☑ Ahwahnee	Yosemite/E	18
Alexis Baking	Napa/N	22
Anzu	Downtown	22
Baker St. Bistro	Marina	19
Balboa Cafe	Cow Hollow	19
Beach Chalet	Outer Sunset	15
Bistro Liaison	Berkeley/E	22
Blackhawk Grille	Danville/E	20
Brenda's	Civic Ctr	24
☑ Buckeye	Mill Valley/N	24
Campton Place	Downtown	25
☑ Canteen	Tenderloin	27
Catch	Castro	18
Spencer/Go	Potrero Hill	23
Chloe's Cafe	Noe Valley	24
Chow	multi.	20
Delancey St.	Embarcadero	18
Dottie's	Tenderloin	26
Duck Club	Lafayette/E	20
Elite Cafe	Pacific Hts	19
Ella's	Presidio Hts	21
☑ Erna's	Oakhurst/E	27
Estate	Sonoma/N	21
Fandango	Pacific Grove/S	23
Five	Berkeley/E	20
☑ Foreign Cinema	Mission	24
Gabriella Café	Santa Cruz/S	22
☑ Garden Ct.	Downtown	19
Gayle's Bakery	Capitola/S	23
Girl & the Fig	Sonoma/N	23
Grand Cafe	Downtown	19
☑ Greens	Marina	24
Insalata's	San Anselmo/N	24
Kate's Kitchen	Lower Haight	21
☑ La Forêt	San Jose/S	27
La Note	Berkeley/E	22
Lark Creek	Walnut Creek/E	22
Liberty Cafe	Bernal Hts	23
Luna Park	Mission	19
Madera	Menlo Pk/S	22
Marinitas	San Anselmo/N	20
Mayfield	Palo Alto/S	20
Mission Bch. Café	Mission	22
MoMo's	S Beach	18
Navio	Half Moon Bay/S	25
Nob Hill Café	Nob Hill	20
Park Chalet	Outer Sunset	15
Piazza D'Angelo	Mill Valley/N	20
Picante Cocina	Berkeley/E	23
Q Rest.	Inner Rich	20
Rest. LuLu	SoMa	19
Rick & Ann	Berkeley/E	21
Rio Grill	Carmel/S	21

Rose's Cafe | **Cow Hollow**	21
Savor | **Noe Valley**	18
Scott's | **multi.**	20
Z Seasons | **Downtown**	24
Slow Club | **Mission**	22
Tarpy's | **Monterey/S**	20
Tav./Lark Creek | **Larkspur/N**	20
1300/Fillmore | **W Addition**	21
Tipsy Pig | **Marina**	18
Town's End | **Embarcadero**	21
Trader Vic's | **Emeryville/E**	17
Tra Vigne | **St. Helena/N**	24
2223 | **Castro**	22
Universal Cafe | **Mission**	24
Venus | **Berkeley/E**	23
Wente Vineyards | **Livermore/E**	24
Willow Wood | **Graton/N**	23
Z Yank Sing | **SoMa**	26
Zazie | **Cole Valley**	23
Z Zuni Café | **Hayes Valley**	25

BUFFET

(Check availability)

Z Ahwahnee | **Yosemite/E**	18
Z Amber India | **multi.**	24
Anzu | **Downtown**	22
Brix | **Napa/N**	23
Café Fanny | **Berkeley/E**	23
Cliff House | **Outer Rich**	18
Duck Club | **Lafayette/E**	20
Farmerbrown | **Tenderloin**	20
Z Garden Ct. | **Downtown**	19
Gaylord India | **Downtown**	18
Lake Chalet | **Oakland/E**	14
Anokha/Lotus | **multi.**	22
Mantra | **Palo Alto/S**	21
Naan/Curry | **Downtown**	17
Navio | **Half Moon Bay/S**	25
Pakwan | **Hayward/E**	22
Park Chalet | **Outer Sunset**	15
Sakoon | **Mtn View/S**	23
Scott's | **Walnut Creek/E**	20
Shabu-Sen | **Japantown**	21
Z Sutro's | **Outer Rich**	22
Tonga Rm. | **Nob Hill**	13
Udupi Palace | **Sunnyvale/S**	21
Xanh | **Mtn View/S**	21

BUSINESS DINING

Alexander's | **multi.**	26
Alfred's Steak | **Downtown**	23
Z Amber India | **multi.**	24
Ame | **SoMa**	26
Americano | **Embarcadero**	18
Anchor & Hope | **SoMa**	21

Anzu | **Downtown**	22
Z Barbacco | **Downtown**	24
Basin | **Saratoga/S**	20
Z Big 4 | **Nob Hill**	23
Boca | **Novato/N**	22
Z Bottega | **Yountville/N**	25
Z Boulevard | **Embarcadero**	27
NEW Bourbon | **Downtown**	24
Bushi-tei | **Japantown**	22
Campton Place | **Downtown**	25
Cha Am Thai | **SoMa**	19
Chantilly | **Redwood City/S**	25
Chaya | **Embarcadero**	20
Chef Chu's | **Los Altos/S**	20
Chez Papa Resto | **SoMa**	24
Cole's Chop | **Napa/N**	25
Cool Café | **Stanford/S**	20
Cosmopolitan | **SoMa**	18
Dio Deka | **Los Gatos/S**	26
Donato | **Redwood City/S**	22
Z Evvia | **Palo Alto/S**	27
Z Farallon | **Downtown**	24
Five | **Berkeley/E**	20
5A5 Steak | **Downtown**	23
Flea St. Café | **Menlo Pk/S**	26
Fuki Sushi | **Palo Alto/S**	23
Gaylord India | **Downtown**	18
Georges | **Downtown**	19
Gitane | **Downtown**	23
Grand Cafe | **Downtown**	19
Harris' | **Polk Gulch**	26
Heaven's Dog | **SoMa**	20
Z House/Prime | **Polk Gulch**	25
Iberia | **Menlo Pk/S**	22
Il Fornaio | **multi.**	20
Izzy's Steak | **multi.**	20
Jin Sho | **Palo Alto/S**	23
Joya | **Palo Alto/S**	21
Junnoon | **Palo Alto/S**	22
Kanpai | **Palo Alto/S**	22
Z Kaygetsu | **Menlo Pk/S**	27
Z Kokkari | **Downtown**	27
Kuleto's | **Downtown**	21
Kyo-Ya | **Downtown**	23
Z La Forêt | **San Jose/S**	27
Lark Creek Steak | **Downtown**	23
Lavanda | **Palo Alto/S**	20
LB Steak | **San Jose/S**	20
Le Central Bistro | **Downtown**	21
Z Le Papillon | **San Jose/S**	27
Lion/Compass | **Sunnyvale/S**	21
Luce | **SoMa**	21
MacArthur Pk. | **Palo Alto/S**	17
Madera | **Menlo Pk/S**	22

Manzanita	**Truckee/E**	23	🛛 Tadich Grill	**Downtown**	23
🛛 Marinus	**Carmel Valley/S**	27	Tommy Toy	**Downtown**	23
MarketBar	**Embarcadero**	16	Tony's Coal-Fired Pizza	**N Beach**	24
Martins West	**Redwood City/S**	22	Townhouse B&G	**Emeryville/E**	21
🛛 Masa's	**Downtown**	28	🛛 NEW 25 Lusk	**SoMa**	20
Meadowood Grill	**St. Helena/N**	22	231 Ellsworth	**San Mateo/S**	23
Meritage/Claremont	**Berkeley/E**	25	Urban Tavern	**Downtown**	16
Mexico DF	**Embarcadero**	20	Viognier	**San Mateo/S**	23
🛛 NEW Michael Mina	**Downtown**	26	Waterfront	**Embarcadero**	20
Mistral	**Redwood Shores/S**	20	🛛 Yank Sing	**SoMa**	26
Mixt Greens	**Downtown**	20	Zaré/Fly Trap	**SoMa**	22
MoMo's	**S Beach**	18	Zibibbo	**Palo Alto/S**	19
Morton's	**multi.**	23	🛛 Zuni Café	**Hayes Valley**	25
Moss Room	**Inner Rich**	22	Zuppa	**SoMa**	19
Muracci's	**Downtown**	21		

CATERING

Murray Circle	**Sausalito/N**	24	🛛 Acquerello	**Polk Gulch**	28
O Izakaya	**Japantown**	18	Adagia	**Berkeley/E**	20
One Market	**Embarcadero**	24	Alexis Baking	**Napa/N**	22
Osha Thai	**multi.**	21	All Seasons	**Calistoga/N**	23
Osteria	**Palo Alto/S**	23	Americano	**Embarcadero**	18
Ozumo	**multi.**	23	Asqew Grill	**multi.**	17
Palio d'Asti	**Downtown**	20	Barndiva	**Healdsburg/N**	23
Pampas	**Palo Alto/S**	22	Betelnut Pejiu	**Cow Hollow**	23
Pazzia	**SoMa**	23	Bistro Liaison	**Berkeley/E**	22
Peasant & the Pear	**Danville/E**	22	🛛 Bix	**Downtown**	24
🛛 Perbacco	**Downtown**	25	Blowfish Sushi	**multi.**	21
Picco	**Larkspur/N**	25	Bocadillos	**N Beach**	23
Piperade	**Downtown**	25	🛛 Buckeye	**Mill Valley/N**	24
🛛 Plumed Horse	**Saratoga/S**	26	César	**Berkeley/E**	22
Poggio	**Sausalito/N**	23	Cha Cha	**multi.**	20
Postrio	**Downtown**	23	Charanga	**Mission**	21
Presidio Social	**Presidio**	19	Chef Chu's	**Los Altos/S**	20
Press	**St. Helena/N**	24	Chenery Park	**Glen Pk**	21
Prospect	**SoMa**	24	Chez Papa Bistrot	**Potrero Hill**	23
Quattro	**E Palo Alto/S**	22	Chez Spencer	**Mission**	25
Rest. LuLu	**SoMa**	19	Cucina Paradiso	**Petaluma/N**	25
Rist. Umbria	**SoMa**	18	Destino	**Castro**	22
Ritz-Carlton	**Nob Hill**	-	Ebisu	**Inner Sunset**	24
RN74	**SoMa**	23	Eos	**Cole Valley**	23
Roy's	**SoMa**	23	Fig Cafe/Wine	**Glen Ellen/N**	25
Ruth's Chris	**Polk Gulch**	24	Fresca	**W Portal**	22
Salt House	**SoMa**	21	Gayle's Bakery	**Capitola/S**	23
Sam's Grill	**Downtown**	22	Grasing's Coastal	**Carmel/S**	23
Sanraku	**multi.**	22	🛛 Greens	**Marina**	24
🛛 Seasons	**Downtown**	24	Hana	**Rohnert Pk/N**	25
Sens	**Downtown**	17	Iberia	**Menlo Pk/S**	22
71 St. Peter	**San Jose/S**	20	Il Davide	**San Rafael/N**	24
NEW Shimo	**Healdsburg/N**	-	Il Fornaio	**San Jose/S**	20
Silks	**Downtown**	23	Insalata's	**San Anselmo/N**	24
Sino	**San Jose/S**	19	Jimtown Store	**Healdsburg/N**	21
Solbar	**Calistoga/N**	26	🛛 Kokkari	**Downtown**	27
South Park	**SoMa**	22	La Méditerranée	**multi.**	20
St. Michael's	**Palo Alto/S**	22	La Strada	**Palo Alto/S**	19

Lavanda | Palo Alto/S	20
Left Bank | multi.	19
☑ Marinus | Carmel Valley/S	27
Max's | Downtown	17
Memphis Minnie | Lower Haight	19
Mochica | SoMa	25
Moki's Sushi | Bernal Hts	26
Monti's | Santa Rosa/N	20
Napa General | Napa/N	18
Nick's Crispy | Russian Hill	22
Ozumo | Embarcadero	23
Piatti | multi.	19
Piazza D'Angelo | Mill Valley/N	20
Picante Cocina | Berkeley/E	23
Pizza Antica | Lafayette/E	20
Pizza Rustica | Oakland/E	20
Pomelo | Inner Sunset	21
Rest. LuLu | SoMa	19
Rick & Ann | Berkeley/E	21
Roy's | SoMa	23
Saul's Rest./Deli | Berkeley/E	19
Shalimar | multi.	22
St. Michael's | Palo Alto/S	22
Straits | multi.	20
Town's End | Embarcadero	21
☑ Tratt. La Sicil. | Berkeley/E	25
Tra Vigne | St. Helena/N	24
Truly Med. | Mission	22
Village Pub | Woodside/S	26
Wente Vineyards | Livermore/E	24
Willi's Seafood | Healdsburg/N	24
Willi's Wine | Santa Rosa/N	25
☑ Yank Sing | SoMa	26
Yumma's | Inner Sunset	21
Zatar | Berkeley/E	23
Zazu | Santa Rosa/N	25
Zibibbo | Palo Alto/S	19
Zin | Healdsburg/N	23
Zuppa | SoMa	19

CELEBRITY CHEFS

Gastón Acurio	
La Mar | Embarcadero	25
Jan Birnbaum	
Epic Roasthse. | Embarcadero	21
Wendy Brucker	
☑ Rivoli | Berkeley/E	26
Trattoria Corso | Berkeley/E	24
Michael Chiarello	
☑ Bottega | Yountville/N	25
Lawrence Chu	
Chef Chu's | Los Altos/S	20

Tom Colicchio	
'Wichcraft | Downtown	18
Jesse Cool	
Cool Café | Stanford/S	20
Flea St. Café | Menlo Pk/S	26
Chris Cosentino	
Boccalone | Embarcadero	26
Incanto | Noe Valley	25
Dominique Crenn	
NEW Atelier Crenn | Marina	26
Gary Danko	
☑ Gary Danko | Fish. Wharf	29
Traci Des Jardins	
☑ Jardinière | Civic Ctr	26
Manzanita | Truckee/E	23
Mijita | multi.	19
Public House | S Beach	16
Elizabeth Falkner	
Citizen Cake | Upper Fillmore	21
Orson | SoMa	18
Ryan Farr	
4505 Meats | Embarcadero	27
Tyler Florence	
NEW El Paseo | Mill Valley/N	-
Rotisserie & Wine | Napa/N	22
Wayfare Tav. | Downtown	22
Ken Frank	
La Toque | Napa/N	26
Mark Franz	
☑ Farallon | Downtown	24
Nick's Cove | Marshall/N	19
Waterbar | Embarcadero	21
Ruggero Gadaldi	
Beretta | Mission	22
Delarosa | Marina	22
Pesce | Russian Hill	25
Tony Gemignani	
Tony's Coal-Fired Pizza | N Beach	24
Tony's Pizza | N Beach	25
Charlie Hallowell	
Boot/Shoe | Oakland/E	24
☑ Pizzaiolo | Oakland/E	26
Bruce Hill	
☑ Bix | Downtown	24
Picco | Larkspur/N	25
☑ Pizzeria Picco | Larkspur/N	27
Zero Zero | SoMa	24
Gerald Hirigoyen	
Bocadillos | N Beach	23
Piperade | Downtown	25
Scott Howard	
Brick/Bottle | Corte Madera/N	1

Todd Humphries		
NEW Kitchen Door	Napa/N	–
Philippe Jeanty		
Z Bistro Jeanty	Yountville/N	25
Laurence Jossel		
Z Nopa	W Addition	25
Nopalito	W Addition	22
Shotaro "Sho" Kamio		
Yoshi's	Oakland/E	20
Yoshi's SF	W Addition	21
Laurent Katgely		
Chez Spencer	Mission	25
Spencer/Go	SoMa	26
Douglas Keane		
Z Cyrus	Healdsburg/N	28
Healdsburg B&G	Healdsburg/N	18
NEW Shimo	Healdsburg/N	–
Hubert Keller		
Burger Bar	Downtown	19
Z Fleur de Lys	Downtown	27
Loretta Keller		
Coco500	SoMa	24
Moss Room	Inner Rich	22
Thomas Keller		
Z Ad Hoc/Addendum	Yountville/N	27
Z Bouchon	Yountville/N	25
Z French Laundry	Yountville/N	29
Christopher Kump		
Fort Bragg	Ft Bragg/N	22
Mourad Lahlou		
Z Aziza	Outer Rich	26
Dennis Leary		
Z Canteen	Tenderloin	27
Golden West	Downtown	24
Sentinel	SoMa	24
Corey Lee		
Benu	SoMa	26
Anthony Mangieri		
NEW Una Pizza	SoMa	26
Joseph Manzare		
Globe	Downtown	18
NEW Hecho	Downtown	–
Zuppa	SoMa	19
Michael Mina		
Arcadia	San Jose/S	20
NEW Bourbon	Downtown	24
Z NEW Michael Mina	Downtown	26
RN74	SoMa	23
Masaharu Morimoto		
Morimoto	Napa/N	26

Nancy Oakes		
Z Boulevard	Embarcadero	27
Prospect	SoMa	24
Daniel Olivella		
Barlata	Oakland/E	21
B44	Downtown	21
Charlie Palmer		
Dry Creek	Healdsburg/N	24
Roland Passot		
Z La Folie	Russian Hill	28
LB Steak	San Jose/S	20
Daniel Patterson		
Coi	N Beach	26
Plum	Oakland/E	24
Cindy Pawlcyn		
Cindy's	St. Helena/N	24
Z Mustards	Yountville/N	25
Charles Phan		
Academy Cafe	Inner Rich	19
Heaven's Dog	SoMa	20
Out the Door	multi.	22
Z Slanted Door	Embarcadero	25
Wolfgang Puck		
Postrio	Downtown	23
Richard Reddington		
Z Redd	Yountville/N	27
Judy Rodgers		
Z Zuni Café	Hayes Valley	25
Mitchell and Steven Rosenthal		
Anchor & Hope	SoMa	21
Salt House	SoMa	21
Town Hall	SoMa	22
Gregory Short		
Z Masa's	Downtown	28
Ron Siegel		
Ritz-Carlton	Nob Hill	–
Hiro Sone		
Ame	SoMa	26
Z Terra	St. Helena/N	27
Cal Stamenov		
Z Marinus	Carmel Valley/S	27
Wicket's	Carmel Valley/S	–
Will's Fargo	Carmel Valley/S	21
Craig Stoll		
Z Delfina	Mission	26
NEW Locanda	Mission	–
Pizzeria Delfina	multi.	25
Luke Sung		
Prime Rib Shabu	Inner Rich	20
James Syhabout		
Z Commis	Oakland/E	27
NEW Hawker Fare	Oakland/E	–

Alice Waters
  Café Fanny | **Berkeley/E** — 23
  🄩 Chez Panisse | **Berkeley/E** — 28
  🄩 Chez Panisse Café | **Berkeley/E** — 27
Roy Yamaguchi
  Roy's | **SoMa** — 23
  Roy's | **Pebble Bch/S** — 24
Chris Yeo
  Sino | **San Jose/S** — 19
  Straits | **multi.** — 20

CHILD-FRIENDLY

(Alternatives to the usual fast-food places; * children's menu available)

🄩 Ahwahnee*	**Yosemite/E**	18
Alexis Baking	**Napa/N**	22
Alice's	**Noe Valley**	19
Alioto's*	**Fish. Wharf**	18
Amici's*	**multi.**	20
Aperto*	**Potrero Hill**	23
Arcadia*	**San Jose/S**	20
Asqew Grill*	**multi.**	17
Azzurro Pizzeria	**Napa/N**	23
Barbara's*	**Princeton Sea/S**	21
Barney's*	**multi.**	19
Basque Cultural*	**S San Francisco/S**	19
Beach Chalet*	**Outer Sunset**	15
Bellanico	**Oakland/E**	23
Bette's Oceanview	**Berkeley/E**	23
Bistro Boudin*	**Fish. Wharf**	20
Brandy Ho's	**multi.**	19
Buca di Beppo*	**multi.**	15
🄩 Buckeye*	**Mill Valley/N**	24
Bungalow 44*	**Mill Valley/N**	21
Burger Joint	**Mission**	18
🄩 Burma Superstar	**Inner Rich**	24
Cactus Taqueria*	**multi.**	20
Caffe Delle Stelle	**Hayes Valley**	17
Caffè Macaroni*	**N Beach**	19
Caffè Museo	**SoMa**	18
Caspers Hot Dogs	**multi.**	20
Cetrella*	**Half Moon Bay/S**	22
Cheesecake*	**multi.**	17
Chenery Park	**Glen Pk**	21
Chow*	**multi.**	20
Cindy's*	**St. Helena/N**	24
Citrus Club	**Haight-Ashbury**	22
Cook St. Helena	**St. Helena/N**	26
Cool Café	**Stanford/S**	20
Delancey St.	**Embarcadero**	18
Dipsea Cafe*	**Mill Valley/N**	18
Dottie's	**Tenderloin**	26
Duarte's*	**Pescadero/S**	20

Eliza's	**Pacific Hts**	21
Ella's	**Presidio Hts**	21
Emmy's Spaghetti*	**Bernal Hts**	20
Eric's	**Noe Valley**	20
FatApple's*	**multi.**	18
Fentons*	**Oakland/E**	20
Fish*	**Sausalito/N**	24
Flavor*	**Santa Rosa/N**	20
Fog City Diner*	**Embarcadero**	18
Forbes Mill*	**Danville/E**	22
🄩 Foreign Cinema*	**Mission**	24
Front Porch*	**Bernal Hts**	20
Gar Woods*	**Carnelian Bay/E**	17
Giordano	**N Beach**	23
Giorgio's	**Inner Rich**	20
Goat Hill Pizza	**Potrero Hill**	18
Gott's Roadside	**multi.**	21
Great China	**Berkeley/E**	24
Great Eastern	**Chinatown**	21
Guaymas*	**Tiburon/N**	17
Healdsburg B&G*	**Healdsburg/N**	18
Henry's Hunan	**multi.**	21
Hurley's	**Yountville/N**	21
Il Fornaio*	**multi.**	20
Insalata's*	**San Anselmo/N**	24
Jay's*	**multi.**	17
Jimmy Beans*	**Berkeley/E**	20
Joe's Cable Car	**Excelsior**	19
Joe's Taco*	**Mill Valley/N**	20
Juan's	**Berkeley/E**	18
Juban	**multi.**	18
Koi	**Daly City/S**	24
Koryo BBQ	**Oakland/E**	21
Kuleto's	**Downtown**	21
La Boulange	**multi.**	21
La Cumbre	**Mission**	22
La Méditerranée*	**multi.**	20
Lark Creek*	**Walnut Creek/E**	22
Lark Creek Steak*	**Downtown**	23
La Taqueria	**Mission**	25
Left Bank*	**multi.**	19
Lo Coco	**Berkeley/E**	2
Lovejoy's Tea*	**Noe Valley**	2
Luella*	**Russian Hill**	2
Mama's on Wash.	**N Beach**	2
Market	**St. Helena/N**	2
Max's*	**multi.**	1
Mel's Drive-In*	**multi.**	1
Model Bakery*	**St. Helena/N**	2
Napa General*	**Napa/N**	1
Nepenthe*	**Big Sur/S**	1
North Bch. Pizza	**multi.**	1
O'mei	**Santa Cruz/S**	2

Original Joe's* | San Jose/S	22	Dosa | multi.	22
Pacific Catch* | multi.	19	15 Romolo | N Beach	20
Pancho Villa | multi.	22	Flora | Oakland/E	21
Parcel 104* | Santa Clara/S	23	Heaven's Dog | SoMa	20
Park Chalet* | Outer Sunset	15	Hog & Rocks | Mission	21
Pasta Pomodoro* | multi.	16	Z Jardinière | Civic Ctr	26
Piatti* | multi.	19	Le Colonial | Downtown	22
Picante Cocina* | Berkeley/E	23	Nihon | Mission	19
Pizza Antica* | multi.	20	Nombe | Mission	21
Pizza Rustica* | Oakland/E	20	Orson | SoMa	18
Pizzeria Tra Vigne* | St. Helena/N	21	NEW Plate Shop | Sausalito/N	-
Q Rest. | Inner Rich	20	Prospect | SoMa	24
Quattro* | E Palo Alto/S	22	Z Range | Mission	27
R&G Lounge | Chinatown	24	Revival Bar | Berkeley/E	20
Rest. Peony | Oakland/E	21	Sidebar | Oakland/E	22
Rick & Ann* | Berkeley/E	21	Spoonbar | Healdsburg/N	18
Robata Grill | Mill Valley/N	21	Starbelly | Castro	21
Rosso Pizzeria* | Santa Rosa/N	25	Thermidor | SoMa	20
Roy's* | Pebble Bch/S	24	Tres | S Beach	17
Sam's Chowder* | Half Moon Bay/S	20	Wayfare Tav. | Downtown	22
		Z Wood Tavern | Oakland/E	26
Saul's Rest./Deli* | Berkeley/E	19	Zero Zero | SoMa	24
Savor* | Noe Valley	18		

DANCING

Z Scoma's* | multi.	23	AsiaSF | SoMa	17
Sears | Downtown	19	NEW Asiento | Mission	-
Shen Hua | Berkeley/E	22	NEW Ki | SoMa	-
Taqueria Can Cun | multi.	25	Le Colonial | Downtown	22
Tarpy's* | Monterey/S	20	Luka's Taproom | Oakland/E	20
Tommaso's | N Beach	25	Tonga Rm. | Nob Hill	13
Ton Kiang | Outer Rich	23	Uva Trattoria | Napa/N	21
Tony's Pizza* | N Beach	25		

DELIVERY

Venezia* | Berkeley/E	18	Alexis Baking | Napa/N	22
Willow Wood | Graton/N	23	Amici's | multi.	20
Yankee Pier* | multi.	18	Angkor Borei | Bernal Hts	22
Z Yank Sing | SoMa	26	Basil | SoMa	23
Zachary's Pizza | Oakland/E	24	Brandy Ho's | Chinatown	19
		Gary Chu's | Santa Rosa/N	22

COCKTAIL SPECIALISTS

		Goat Hill Pizza | SoMa	18
Z Absinthe | Hayes Valley	22	Henry's Hunan | SoMa	21
Z À Côté | Oakland/E	24	Max's | multi.	17
Adesso | Oakland/E	24	Mission Chinese | Mission	21
Alembic | Haight-Ashbury	23	North Bch. Pizza | multi.	19
Z Aziza | Outer Rich	26	Pizza Rustica | Oakland/E	20
Bar Agricole | SoMa	21	Z Swan Oyster | Polk Gulch	27
Beretta | Mission	22	Ton Kiang | Outer Rich	23
Betelnut Pejiu | Cow Hollow	23	Zante | Bernal Hts	20
Z Bix | Downtown	24		

DINING ALONE

Boot/Shoe | Oakland/E	24	(Other than hotels and places with counter service)	
Brick/Bottle | Corte Madera/N	19		
Café des Amis | Cow Hollow	19	Z Absinthe | Hayes Valley	22
Coco500 | SoMa	24	Anchor & Hope | SoMa	21
Comstock | N Beach	16	Ariake | Outer Rich	23
Delarosa | Marina	22		

Restaurant	Location	Rating
Z Barbacco	Downtown	24
Bar Crudo	W Addition	25
Barlata	Oakland/E	21
Bar Tartine	Mission	24
Beretta	Mission	22
Bette's Oceanview	Berkeley/E	23
Bistro Central Parc	W Addition	24
Z Bistro Jeanty	Yountville/N	25
Bistro Ralph	Healdsburg/N	24
Blowfish Sushi	multi.	21
Blue Barn	Marina	24
Bocadillos	N Beach	23
Z Bouchon	Yountville/N	25
Z Boulevard	Embarcadero	27
Bovolo	Healdsburg/N	22
Z Buckeye	Mill Valley/N	24
Bungalow 44	Mill Valley/N	21
NEW Bun Mee	Upper Fillmore	-
BurgerMeister	Berkeley/E	20
Café Claude	Downtown	22
Café de la Presse	Downtown	18
Café Gratitude	multi.	17
Café Rouge	Berkeley/E	22
Z Canteen	Tenderloin	27
Cascal	Mtn View/S	21
Cellar Door Café	Santa Cruz/S	26
César	Berkeley/E	22
Cetrella	Half Moon Bay/S	22
Cheese Steak Shop	Concord/E	20
Spencer/Go	Potrero Hill	23
Chez Papa Bistrot	Potrero Hill	23
Chile Pies	W Addition	22
Chop Bar	Oakland/E	22
Citizen Cake	Upper Fillmore	21
Coco500	SoMa	24
Contigo	Noe Valley	24
Cook St. Helena	St. Helena/N	26
Cuvée	Napa/N	22
Delarosa	Marina	22
DeLessio	multi.	20
Della Fattoria	Petaluma/N	26
Dinosaurs	Castro	-
Domo Sushi	Hayes Valley	24
Dosa	Mission	22
Duarte's	Pescadero/S	20
Ebisu	multi.	24
Emporio Rulli	Larkspur/N	24
Encuentro	Oakland/E	23
Eos	Cole Valley	23
Eve	Berkeley/E	25
Z Evvia	Palo Alto/S	27
Farmerbrown	Tenderloin	20
Farmstead	St. Helena/N	20
Firefly	Noe Valley	25
Flora	Oakland/E	21
Fog City Diner	Embarcadero	18
Fort Bragg	Ft Bragg/N	22
4505 Meats	Embarcadero	27
Fremont Diner	Sonoma/N	21
NEW Fresh/Lisa	Santa Rosa/N	24
Fringale	SoMa	24
Frjtz Fries	multi.	17
Gamine	Cow Hollow	24
Georges	Downtown	19
Godzila Sushi	Pacific Hts	20
Gott's Roadside	Napa/N	21
Gracias	Mission	21
Grandeho Kamekyo	Fish. Wharf	25
Grand Pu Bah	Potrero Hill	19
Green Chile	W Addition	23
Grégoire	Oakland/E	21
Hachi Ju Hachi	Saratoga/S	23
Hamano Sushi	Noe Valley	20
Hana	Rohnert Pk/N	25
Heart	Mission	19
Hibiscus	Oakland/E	20
Z Hog Island	Embarcadero	25
Home of Chicken	Oakland/E	16
Hopmonk Tav.	Sebastopol/N	18
Hula's	Monterey/S	18
Hurley's	Yountville/N	21
Izakaya Sozai	Inner Sunset	22
Kabuto	Outer Rich	25
Kanpai	Palo Alto/S	22
Z Kaygetsu	Menlo Pk/S	27
King of Thai	multi.	19
Kirala	Berkeley/E	25
Z Kiss Seafood	Japantown	28
Kitchenette SF	Dogpatch	24
Z Koo	Inner Sunset	27
Krung Thai	San Jose/S	19
La Boulange	multi.	21
La Costanera	Montara/S	21
Lafitte	Embarcadero	20
La Note	Berkeley/E	22
La Trappe	N Beach	16
Left Bank	Menlo Pk/S	19
Little Chihuahua	W Addition	21
Local Mission	Mission	23
Mario's Bohemian	N Beach	17
MarketBar	Embarcadero	1
Marlowe	SoMa	2
Marzano	Oakland/E	2
Maverick	Mission	2
Mayfield	Palo Alto/S	2
Meritage Martini	Sonoma/N	2
Mission Bch. Café	Mission	2
Model Bakery	Napa/N	2

Monk's Kettle | **Mission**	20
☑ Mustards | **Yountville/N**	25
Naan/Curry | **Downtown**	17
Naked Lunch | **N Beach**	19
Namu | **Embarcadero**	22
Naomi Sushi | **Menlo Pk/S**	20
Nombe | **Mission**	21
Nopalito | **W Addition**	22
Oliveto | **Oakland/E**	24
Orson | **SoMa**	18
Ottimista | **Cow Hollow**	19
Outerlands | **Outer Sunset**	23
Out the Door | **multi.**	22
Oxbow Wine | **Napa/N**	18
Oyaji | **Outer Rich**	24
Pacific Catch | **multi.**	19
Papito | **Potrero Hill**	25
Parada 22 | **Haight-Ashbury**	21
Pasta Pomodoro | **multi.**	16
Patrona | **Ukiah/N**	-
Peter Lowell | **Sebastopol/N**	23
Pi Bar | **Mission**	18
Pica Pica Maize | **Napa/N**	21
Piccino | **Dogpatch**	23
Pine Cone Diner | **Pt Reyes/N**	23
Piperade | **Downtown**	25
Pizzeria Delfina | **Pacific Hts**	25
Plant Cafe Organic | **multi.**	21
Radius | **SoMa**	23
☑ Redd | **Yountville/N**	27
Robata Grill | **Mill Valley/N**	21
Samovar Tea | **multi.**	18
Schat's/Bakery | **Ukiah/N**	-
Sebo | **Hayes Valley**	26
Serpentine | **Dogpatch**	22
Shabu-Sen | **Japantown**	21
NEW Shimo | **Healdsburg/N**	-
Sino | **San Jose/S**	19
Spork | **Mission**	20
SPQR | **Pacific Hts**	24
Stable Café | **Mission**	20
Starbelly | **Castro**	21
NEW Summit | **Mission**	-
Super Duper | **Castro**	21
Suppenküche | **Hayes Valley**	22
☑ Sushi Ran | **Sausalito/N**	28
☑ Sushi Zone | **Castro**	27
☑ Swan Oyster | **Polk Gulch**	27
Table Café | **Larkspur/N**	22
Tacolicious | **Marina**	22
Tataki | **Pacific Hts**	24
Terzo | **Cow Hollow**	24
Town Hall | **SoMa**	22
Trattoria Corso | **Berkeley/E**	24
Tra Vigne | **St. Helena/N**	24
Trueburger | **Oakland/E**	20
Tsunami | **W Addition**	21
Uva Enoteca | **Lower Haight**	22
Vanessa's Bistro | **Berkeley/E**	23
Viognier | **San Mateo/S**	23
Wild Goose | **Tahoe Vista/E**	23
Willi's Seafood | **Healdsburg/N**	24
Will's Fargo | **Carmel Valley/S**	21
Woodhse. | **Castro**	21
Xanh | **Mtn View/S**	21
Yoshi's | **Oakland/E**	20
Yoshi's SF | **W Addition**	21
Zazie | **Cole Valley**	23
Zibibbo | **Palo Alto/S**	19
☑ Zuni Café | **Hayes Valley**	25
Zushi Puzzle | **Marina**	26

ENTERTAINMENT

(Call for days and times of
performances)

☑ Ahwahnee | piano | **Yosemite/E**	18
Albion River Inn | piano | **Albion/N**	23
Ana Mandara | jazz | **Fish. Wharf**	21
AsiaSF | gender illusionists | **SoMa**	17
Beach Chalet | live music | **Outer Sunset**	15
☑ Big 4 | piano | **Nob Hill**	23
☑ Bix | live music | **Downtown**	24
Blowfish Sushi | DJ | **San Jose/S**	21
Butterfly | jazz | **Embarcadero**	21
Cascal | Spanish music | **Mtn View/S**	21
Cetrella | jazz | **Half Moon Bay/S**	22
☑ Cheese Board | jazz/pop | **Berkeley/E**	27
Everett/Jones | jazz | **Oakland/E**	20
☑ Foreign Cinema | films | **Mission**	24
☑ Garden Ct. | live music | **Downtown**	19
Giordano | live music | **N Beach**	23
Harris' | live music | **Polk Gulch**	26
Katia's Tea | accordion | **Inner Rich**	20
La Note | accordion | **Berkeley/E**	22
Ledford Hse. | jazz | **Albion/N**	23
☑ Marinus | jazz piano | **Carmel Valley/S**	27
Max's | varies | **multi.**	17
Navio | jazz | **Half Moon Bay/S**	25
Olema Inn | jazz | **Olema/N**	18
☑ Plumed Horse | piano | **Saratoga/S**	26
Rose Pistola | jazz | **N Beach**	21

SPECIAL FEATURES

Z Santé	piano	Sonoma/N	26
Sardine Factory	piano	Monterey/S	21
Scott's	varies	multi.	20
Straits	varies	multi.	20
Sushi Groove	DJ	SoMa	21
Tonga Rm.	live music	Nob Hill	13
Townhouse B&G	live music	Emeryville/E	21
Uva Trattoria	jazz	Napa/N	21
Vic Stewart	piano	Walnut Creek/E	22
Yoshi's	jazz	Oakland/E	20
Yoshi's SF	jazz	W Addition	21
Z Zuni Café	piano	Hayes Valley	25

FIREPLACES

Adagia	Berkeley/E	20
Z Ahwahnee	Yosemite/E	18
Albion River Inn	Albion/N	23
Alexander's	Cupertino/S	26
NEW All Spice	San Mateo/S	24
Ame	SoMa	26
Anton/Michel	Carmel/S	23
Applewood Inn	Guerneville/N	25
Z Auberge/Soleil	Rutherford/N	27
Bardessono	Yountville/N	21
Barney's	Berkeley/E	19
Bella Vista	Woodside/S	22
Betelnut Pejiu	Cow Hollow	23
Z Big 4	Nob Hill	23
Bistro Don Giovanni	Napa/N	24
Z Bistro Jeanty	Yountville/N	25
Boca	Novato/N	22
NEW Branches	Ukiah/N	-
Brannan's Grill	Calistoga/N	18
Brix	Napa/N	23
NEW Brixton	Cow Hollow	15
Z Buckeye	Mill Valley/N	24
Cafe Citti	Kenwood/N	22
Café des Amis	Cow Hollow	19
Café Gratitude	Berkeley/E	17
Caffè Macaroni	N Beach	19
Camino	Oakland/E	22
Caprice	Tiburon/N	22
Casanova	Carmel/S	23
Casa Orinda	Orinda/E	18
Cetrella	Half Moon Bay/S	22
Chantilly	Redwood City/S	25
Chapter & Moon	Ft Bragg/N	21
Chez Spencer	Mission	25
Chez TJ	Mtn View/S	24
Chow	multi.	20
Comstock	N Beach	16
Cottonwood	Truckee/E	26

Cuvée	Napa/N	22
Davenport	Davenport/S	16
Deetjen's Big Sur	Big Sur/S	23
Della Santina	Sonoma/N	22
Dio Deka	Los Gatos/S	26
Dipsea Cafe	Mill Valley/N	18
Duck Club	Bodega Bay/N	20
El Dorado	Sonoma/N	22
NEW El Paseo	Mill Valley/N	-
Epic Roasthse.	Embarcadero	21
Z Erna's	Oakhurst/E	27
Étoile	Yountville/N	25
Z Evvia	Palo Alto/S	27
Fandango	Pacific Grove/S	23
Farm	Napa/N	24
Z Farmhse. Inn	Forestville/N	27
Farmstead	St. Helena/N	20
5A5 Steak	Downtown	23
Flavor	Santa Rosa/N	20
Z Fleur de Lys	Downtown	27
Flying Fish	Carmel/S	24
Forbes Island	Fish. Wharf	15
Forbes Mill	Los Gatos/S	22
Z Foreign Cinema	Mission	24
Z French Laundry	Yountville/N	29
Gar Woods	Carnelian Bay/E	17
NEW Guamenkitzel	Berkeley/E	-
Gayle's Bakery	Capitola/S	23
Guaymas	Tiburon/N	17
Half Moon Brew	Half Moon Bay/S	16
Harris'	Polk Gulch	26
Z House/Prime	Polk Gulch	25
Iberia	Menlo Pk/S	22
Il Fornaio	multi.	20
Izzy's Steak	Marina	20
Jake's/Lake	Tahoe City/E	18
John Ash	Santa Rosa/N	24
Kenwood	Kenwood/N	23
Another Monkey/Koh	Mission	20
Z Kokkari	Downtown	27
Kuleto's	Downtown	21
Lake Chalet	Oakland/E	14
La Terrasse	Presidio	17
La Toque	Napa/N	26
LB Steak	San Jose/S	20
Ledford Hse.	Albion/N	2
Left Bank	Larkspur/N	1
Le Soleil	Inner Rich	2
Lupa Trattoria	Noe Valley	2
MacArthur Pk.	Palo Alto/S	1
MacCallum	Mendocino/N	2
Madera	Menlo Pk/S	2
Z Madrona	Healdsburg/N	2

Vote at ZAGAT.co

Ma Maison | **Aptos/S**	24
Mandaloun | **Redwood City/S**	20
🔲 Manresa | **Los Gatos/S**	28
🔲 Marinus | **Carmel Valley/S**	27
🔲 Meadowood Rest. | **St. Helena/N**	28
Mendo Hotel | **Mendocino/N**	18
Metro | **Lafayette/E**	21
Mezza Luna | **Princeton Sea/S**	22
Monti's | **Santa Rosa/N**	20
Moosse Café | **Mendocino/N**	22
Murray Circle | **Sausalito/N**	24
Napa General | **Napa/N**	18
Navio | **Half Moon Bay/S**	25
Nepenthe | **Big Sur/S**	16
Nick's Cove | **Marshall/N**	19
Osha Thai | **multi.**	21
🔲 Pacific's Edge | **Carmel/S**	24
Parcel 104 | **Santa Clara/S**	23
Park Chalet | **Outer Sunset**	15
Piatti | **multi.**	19
Piazza D'Angelo | **Mill Valley/N**	20
Plouf | **Downtown**	21
🔲 Plumed Horse | **Saratoga/S**	26
PlumpJack | **Olympic Valley/E**	23
Postino | **Lafayette/E**	22
Press | **St. Helena/N**	24
Prima | **Walnut Creek/E**	24
Quattro | **E Palo Alto/S**	22
Ravenous | **Healdsburg/N**	23
Ravens' | **Mendocino/N**	26
Rest./Stevenswood | **Little River/N**	21
Rest. LuLu | **SoMa**	19
Rio Grill | **Carmel/S**	21
Samovar Tea | **Hayes Valley**	18
Sam's Chowder | **Half Moon Bay/S**	20
🔲 Santé | **Sonoma/N**	26
Sardine Factory | **Monterey/S**	21
Savor | **Noe Valley**	18
Scott's | **Palo Alto/S**	20
Shadowbrook | **Capitola/S**	18
🔲 Sierra Mar | **Big Sur/S**	27
Soule Domain | **Kings Bch/E**	24
🔲 Spruce | **Presidio Hts**	25
Stark's | **Santa Rosa/N**	-
St. Orres | **Gualala/N**	23
Sunnyside | **Tahoe City/E**	18
Table 128 | **Boonville/N**	-
Tarpy's | **Monterey/S**	20
Terzo | **Cow Hollow**	24
Toast | **Novato/N**	19
Townhouse B&G | **Emeryville/E**	21
Troya | **Inner Rich**	21

Tsukiji Sushi | **Mill Valley/N**	22
Venticello | **Nob Hill**	23
Vic Stewart | **Walnut Creek/E**	22
Village Pub | **Woodside/S**	26
Viognier | **San Mateo/S**	23
Wayfare Tav. | **Downtown**	22
Wild Goose | **Tahoe Vista/E**	23
Will's Fargo | **Carmel Valley/S**	21
Wine Spectator | **St. Helena/N**	21
Zibibbo | **Palo Alto/S**	19
Zinsvalley | **Napa/N**	17

FOOD TRUCKS

Chairman Bao Bun | **Loc varies**	25
Curry Up Now | **Loc varies**	25
El Tonayense | **multi.**	24
Fivetenburger | **Loc varies**	25
Liba Falafel | **multi.**	25
NEW Mama's Empanadas | **Loc varies**	26
RoliRoti | **Embarcadero**	25
Spencer/Go | **SoMa**	26

GREEN/LOCAL/ORGANIC

(Specializing in organic, local ingredients)

Academy Cafe | **Inner Rich**	19
Adagia | **Berkeley/E**	20
🔲 Ad Hoc/Addendum | **Yountville/N**	27
Ajanta | **Berkeley/E**	25
Aquarius | **Santa Cruz/S**	21
Artisan Bistro | **Lafayette/E**	24
NEW Atelier Crenn | **Marina**	26
🔲 Aubergine | **Carmel/S**	28
Bar Agricole | **SoMa**	21
Bardessono | **Yountville/N**	21
Bar Jules | **Hayes Valley**	23
Barndiva | **Healdsburg/N**	23
Beautifull | **multi.**	17
Bellanico | **Oakland/E**	23
🔲 Bistro/Copains | **Occidental/N**	27
Bistro Don Giovanni | **Napa/N**	24
Blue Barn | **Marina**	24
Blue Plate | **Mission**	24
🔲 Bottega | **Yountville/N**	25
Boulette Larder | **Embarcadero**	25
🔲 Boulevard | **Embarcadero**	27
Bovolo | **Healdsburg/N**	21
Breads/India | **multi.**	19
Brix | **Napa/N**	23
Butler & The Chef Bistro | **SoMa**	22
Cafe Beaujolais | **Mendocino/N**	25
Café Fanny | **Berkeley/E**	23

☑ Cafe Gibraltar	El Granada/S	26
Café Gratitude	multi.	17
☑ Cafe La Haye	Sonoma/N	27
Camino	Oakland/E	22
☑ Canteen	Tenderloin	27
Cellar Door Café	Santa Cruz/S	26
☑ Chez Panisse	Berkeley/E	28
☑ Chez Panisse Café	Berkeley/E	27
Chez Shea	Half Moon Bay/S	23
Chow	Inner Sunset	20
Coi	N Beach	26
☑ Commis	Oakland/E	27
Commonwealth	Mission	24
Contigo	Noe Valley	24
Cool Café	Stanford/S	20
Cotogna	Downtown	26
☑ Cyrus	Healdsburg/N	28
Deetjen's Big Sur	Big Sur/S	23
☑ Delfina	Mission	26
Della Fattoria	Petaluma/N	26
Della Santina	Sonoma/N	22
Donato	Redwood City/S	22
Doña Tomás	Oakland/E	22
Dopo	Oakland/E	25
Dosa	multi.	22
Dragonfly	Truckee/E	22
Drake's	Inverness/N	21
Dry Creek	Healdsburg/N	24
☑ Dynamo Donut	Mission	24
Encuentro	Oakland/E	23
Eos	Cole Valley	23
Epic Roasthse.	Embarcadero	21
☑ Erna's	Oakhurst/E	27
Étoile	Yountville/N	25
Eureka	Castro	20
☑ Farallon	Downtown	24
Farm	Napa/N	24
Farmerbrown	multi.	20
☑ Farmhse. Inn	Forestville/N	27
Farmstead	St. Helena/N	20
Fifth Floor	SoMa	23
Firefly	Noe Valley	25
Fish	Sausalito/N	24
Fish & Farm	Downtown	20
Flea St. Café	Menlo Pk/S	26
☑ Fleur de Lys	Downtown	27
☑ Flour + Water	Mission	24
☑ Foreign Cinema	Mission	24
4505 Meats	Embarcadero	27
☑ French Laundry	Yountville/N	29
Gabriella Café	Santa Cruz/S	22
Garibaldis	Presidio Hts	22
☑ Gary Danko	Fish. Wharf	29
Gialina	Glen Pk	25

Gioia Pizzeria	Berkeley/E	25
Globe	Downtown	18
Grasing's Coastal	Carmel/S	23
Green Chile	W Addition	23
☑ Greens	Marina	24
Harmony	Mill Valley/N	20
Harvest Moon	Sonoma/N	24
Hayes St. Grill	Hayes Valley	23
Heaven's Dog	SoMa	20
Herbivore	multi.	17
Il Cane Rosso	Embarcadero	23
Imperial Tea Ct.	Embarcadero	19
Incanto	Noe Valley	25
Insalata's	San Anselmo/N	24
☑ Jardinière	Civic Ctr	26
Jimtown Store	Healdsburg/N	21
John Ash	Santa Rosa/N	24
Junnoon	Palo Alto/S	22
Kiji Sushi Bar	Mission	25
La Ciccia	Noe Valley	26
☑ La Folie	Russian Hill	28
Lalime's	Berkeley/E	25
Lark Creek	Walnut Creek/E	22
Las Camelias	San Rafael/N	20
La Toque	Napa/N	26
Ledford Hse.	Albion/N	23
Local Kitchen	SoMa	18
Local Mission	Mission	23
NEW Locavore	Bernal Hts	20
Anokha/Lotus	San Rafael/N	22
Luella	Russian Hill	21
MacCallum	Mendocino/N	24
Madera	Menlo Pk/S	22
☑ Madrona	Healdsburg/N	27
Magnolia	Haight-Ashbury	20
☑ Manresa	Los Gatos/S	28
Marché/Fleurs	Ross/N	25
Marinitas	San Anselmo/N	20
☑ Marinus	Carmel Valley/S	27
MarketBar	Embarcadero	16
Martins West	Redwood City/S	22
Marzano	Oakland/E	23
☑ Masa's	Downtown	28
Maverick	Mission	24
Meadowood Grill	St. Helena/N	22
☑ Meadowood Rest.	St. Helena/N	28
Mendo Bistro	Ft Bragg/N	23
Mijita	multi.	19
Millennium	Downtown	25
Mixt Greens	Downtown	20
Montrio Bistro	Monterey/S	23
Moss Room	Inner Rich	22
Navio	Half Moon Bay/S	25

Nick's Cove | **Marshall/N** 19
Nick's Crispy | **Russian Hill** 22
Z Nopa | **W Addition** 25
Nopalito | **W Addition** 22
North Bch. Rest. | **N Beach** 22
O Chamé | **Berkeley/E** 24
Olema Inn | **Olema/N** 18
Oliveto | **Oakland/E** 24
Oliveto Rest. | **Oakland/E** 25
One Market | **Embarcadero** 24
Oola | **SoMa** 19
Osteria Stellina | **Pt Reyes/N** 23
Pacific Catch | **Marina** 19
Z Pacific's Edge | **Carmel/S** 24
Parcel 104 | **Santa Clara/S** 23
Z Passionfish | **Pacific Grove/S** 27
Pauline's | **Mission** 23
Pearl | **Napa/N** 24
Peter Lowell | **Sebastopol/N** 23
Piccino | **Dogpatch** 23
Picco | **Larkspur/N** 25
Pine Cone Diner | **Pt Reyes/N** 23
Pizza Antica | **Lafayette/E** 20
Z Pizzaiolo | **Oakland/E** 26
Z Pizzeria Picco | **Larkspur/N** 27
Pizzeria Tra Vigne | **St. Helena/N** 21
Pizzetta 211 | **Outer Rich** 25
Plant Cafe Organic | **multi.** 21
NEW Plate Shop | **Sausalito/N** -
Press | **St. Helena/N** 24
Z Quince | **Downtown** 26
Radius | **SoMa** 23
Z Range | **Mission** 27
Ravenous | **Healdsburg/N** 23
Ravens' | **Mendocino/N** 26
Regalito Rosticeria | **Mission** 23
Rest./Stevenswood | **Little River/N** 21
Revival Bar | **Berkeley/E** 20
Richmond Rest. | **Inner Rich** 24
Rist. Avanti | **Santa Cruz/S** 24
Ritz-Carlton | **Nob Hill** -
Z Rivoli | **Berkeley/E** 26
Rocker Oyster | **Valley Ford/N** 21
Saison | **Mission** 26
Sebo | **Hayes Valley** 26
Serpentine | **Dogpatch** 22
Z Sierra Mar | **Big Sur/S** 27
Z Slanted Door | **Embarcadero** 25
Slow Club | **Mission** 22
Sol Food | **San Rafael/N** 23
Spoonbar | **Healdsburg/N** 18
SPQR | **Pacific Hts** 24
Z Spruce | **Presidio Hts** 25

NEW Station 1 | **Woodside/S** 25
St. Orres | **Gualala/N** 23
Z Sutro's | **Outer Rich** 22
Table Café | **Larkspur/N** 22
Tacubaya | **Berkeley/E** 23
Tamarine | **Palo Alto/S** 26
Z Tartine | **Mission** 27
Tav./Lark Creek | **Larkspur/N** 20
Terzo | **Cow Hollow** 24
Tipsy Pig | **Marina** 18
Tra Vigne | **St. Helena/N** 24
T Rex BBQ | **Berkeley/E** 18
2223 | **Castro** 22
Ubuntu | **Napa/N** 24
Underdog | **Inner Sunset** 22
Underwood Bar | **Graton/N** 23
Village Pub | **Woodside/S** 26
Viognier | **San Mateo/S** 23
Warming Hut | **Presidio** 14
Water St. Bistro | **Petaluma/N** 22
Weird Fish | **Mission** -
Wente Vineyards | **Livermore/E** 24
Willi's Seafood | **Healdsburg/N** 24
Willi's Wine | **Santa Rosa/N** 25
Wolfdale's | **Tahoe City/E** 24
Woodward's Gdn. | **Mission** 24
Yankee Pier | **San Jose/S** 18
Zaré/Fly Trap | **SoMa** 22
Zatar | **Berkeley/E** 23
Zazu | **Santa Rosa/N** 25
Zin | **Healdsburg/N** 23
Z Zuni Café | **Hayes Valley** 25

HISTORIC PLACES

(Year opened; * building)
1800 | Market* | **St. Helena/N** 23
1800 | Stable Café* | **Mission** 20
1848 | Cindy's* | **St. Helena/N** 24
1848 | La Forêt* | **San Jose/S** 27
1849 | Tadich Grill | **Downtown** 23
1856 | Garden Ct.* | **Downtown** 19
1857 | Little River Inn* | **Little River/N** 22
1860 | Della Fattoria* | **Petaluma/N** 26
1860 | Pizza Antica* | **Lafayette/E** 20
1863 | Cliff House | **Outer Rich** 18
1863 | Sutro's* | **Outer Rich** 22
1864 | Rocker Oyster* | **Valley Ford/N** 21
1864 | Table 128* | **Boonville/N** -
1867 | Sam's Grill | **Downtown** 22
1870 | Bottega* | **Yountville/N** 25
1870 | Murray Circle* | **Sausalito/N** 24

1873 | Farmhse. Inn* | Forestville/N — 27

1875 | La Note* | Berkeley/E — 22

1876 | Olema Inn* | Olema/N — 18

1878 | Mendo Hotel* | Mendocino/N — 18

1880 | Estate* | Sonoma/N — 21

1880 | Pianeta* | Truckee/E — 24

1881 | Il Fornaio* | Carmel/S — 20

1881 | Madrona* | Healdsburg/N — 27

1882 | MacCallum* | Mendocino/N — 24

1883 | Celadon* | Napa/N — 23

1884 | Napa General* | Napa/N — 18

1884 | Terra* | St. Helena/N — 27

1886 | Cole's Chop* | Napa/N — 25

1886 | Fior d'Italia | N Beach — 18

1886 | Mendo Bistro* | Ft Bragg/N — 23

1886 | Willi's Wine* | Santa Rosa/N — 25

1888 | Bounty Hunter* | Napa/N — 21

1888 | Tav./Lark Creek* | Larkspur/N — 20

1889 | Boulevard* | Embarcadero — 27

1889 | Pacific Café* | Outer Rich — 23

1889 | Wine Spectator* | St. Helena/N — 21

1890 | Chez TJ* | Mtn View/S — 24

1890 | Eureka* | Castro — 20

1890 | Scoma's* | Sausalito/N — 23

1890 | Yankee Pier* | Larkspur/N — 18

1891 | Ubuntu* | Napa/N — 24

1893 | Cafe Beaujolais* | Mendocino/N — 25

1893 | Jimtown Store* | Healdsburg/N — 21

1894 | Duarte's* | Pescadero/S — 20

1894 | Fentons | Oakland/E — 20

1895 | La Posta* | Santa Cruz/S — 26

1895 | Restaurant* | Ft Bragg/N — 25

1898 | Slanted Door* | Embarcadero — 25

1900 | Axum Cafe* | Lower Haight — 23

1900 | Bar Agricole* | SoMa — 21

1900 | Bar Tartine* | Mission — 24

1900 | Central Market* | Petaluma/N — 22

1900 | Cha Cha* | Mission — 20

1900 | Diavola* | Geyserville/N — 25

1900 | Emporio Rulli* | Downtown — 24

1900 | Frances* | Castro — 27

1900 | French Laundry* | Yountville/N — 29

1900 | Girl & the Fig* | Sonoma/N — 23

1900 | La Ginestra* | Mill Valley/N — 19

1900 | Pauline's* | Mission — 23

1904 | Moosse Café* | Mendocino/N — 22

1904 | Paul K* | Hayes Valley — 22

1905 | Hopmonk Tav.* | Sebastopol/N — 18

1906 | Chez Shea* | Half Moon Bay/S — 23

1906 | Coco500* | SoMa — 24

1906 | Davenport* | Davenport/S — 16

1906 | Imperial Tea Ct.* | Embarcadero — 19

1906 | Pork Store* | Haight-Ashbury — 19

1906 | Tonga Rm.* | Nob Hill — 13

1906 | Wayfare Tav.* | Downtown — 22

1907 | Comstock* | N Beach — 16

1907 | Tony's Coal-Fired Pizza* | N Beach — 24

1907 | Tony's Pizza* | N Beach — 25

1907 | Town Hall* | SoMa — 22

1908 | Mezza Luna* | Princeton Sea/S — 22

1908 | Zaré/Fly Trap* | SoMa — 22

1909 | Campton Place* | Downtown — 25

1909 | Fort Bragg* | Ft Bragg/N — 22

1909 | Ironside* | S Beach — 17

1910 | Catch* | Castro — 18

1910 | Charanga* | Mission — 21

1910 | Élevé* | Walnut Creek/E — 21

1910 | Harris'* | Polk Gulch — 26

1910 | Rest. LuLu* | SoMa — 19

1910 | Sasa* | Walnut Creek/E — 23

1912 | Tipsy Pig* | Marina — 18

1912 | Swan Oyster | Polk Gulch — 27

1913 | Balboa Cafe | Cow Hollow — 19

1913 | Zuni Café* | Hayes Valley — 25

1914 | Healdsburg B&G* | Healdsburg/N — 18

1914 | Red's Java* | Embarcadero — 15

1914 | Wexler's* | Downtown — 22

1915 | Café des Amis* | Cow Hollow — 19

1915 | Napa Wine Train* | Napa/N — 18

1916 | Amer. Grilled Cheese* | SoMa — 22

1916 | Cafe Divine* | N Beach — 18

1917 | Pacific's Edge* | Carmel/S — 24

1917 | Tarpy's* | Monterey/S — 20

1918 | MacArthur Pk.* | Palo Alto/S — 17

1918 | St. Francis | Mission — 17

1919 | Albion River Inn* | Albion/N — 23

1919 | Ana Mandara* | **Fish. Wharf** [21]
1919 | Sauce* | **Hayes Valley** [17]
1920 | Acquerello* | **Polk Gulch** [28]
1920 | Albona Rist.* | **N Beach** [25]
1920 | Boogaloos* | **Mission** [17]
1920 | Commonwealth* | [24]
  Mission
1920 | Florio* | **Pacific Hts** [19]
1925 | Adagia* | **Berkeley/E** [20]
1925 | Alioto's | **Fish. Wharf** [18]
1925 | Farallon* | **Downtown** [24]
1925 | John Bentley* | [26]
  Redwood City/S
1925 | Rist. Capellini* | [20]
  San Mateo/S
1927 | Ahwahnee* | **Yosemite/E** [18]
1927 | Bella Vista* | **Woodside/S** [22]
1927 | Chop Bar* | **Oakland/E** [22]
1927 | Townhouse B&G* | [21]
  Emeryville/E
1928 | Alfred's Steak | **Downtown** [23]
1928 | Cottonwood* | **Truckee/E** [26]
1928 | Elite Cafe* | **Pacific Hts** [19]
1928 | Ma Maison* | **Aptos/S** [24]
1929 | Aubergine* | **Carmel/S** [28]
1930 | Big 4* | **Nob Hill** [23]
1930 | Caprice* | **Tiburon/N** [22]
1930 | Disco Volante* | [-]
  Oakland/E
1930 | Foreign Cinema* | [24]
  Mission
1930 | Guamenkitzel* | **Berkeley/E** [-]
1930 | Lalime's* | **Berkeley/E** [25]
1930 | Lo Coco* | **Oakland/E** [22]
1930 | Ravenous* | **Healdsburg/N** [23]
1930 | Soule Domain* | [24]
  Kings Bch/E
1930 | Willow Wood* | **Graton/N** [23]
1932 | Camino* | **Oakland/E** [22]
1932 | Casa Orinda* | **Orinda/E** [18]
1933 | Luka's Taproom* | [20]
  Oakland/E
1934 | Caspers Hot Dogs | [20]
  Oakland/E
1934 | Stark's* | **Santa Rosa/N** [-]
1935 | Tommaso's | **N Beach** [25]
1936 | Cafe La Haye* | **Sonoma/N** [27]
1936 | Gabriella Café* | [22]
  Santa Cruz/S
1937 | Buckeye | **Mill Valley/N** [24]
1937 | Deetjen's Big Sur* | [23]
  Big Sur/S
1937 | Postino* | **Lafayette/E** [22]
1937 | 231 Ellsworth* | [23]
  San Mateo/S
1938 | Sears | **Downtown** [19]

1947 | Shadowbrook | **Capitola/S** [18]
1948 | Evan's* | **S Lake Tahoe/E** [27]
1949 | Gott's Roadside | [21]
  St. Helena/N
1949 | House/Prime | **Polk Gulch** [25]
1949 | Nepenthe | **Big Sur/S** [16]
1950 | Alexis Baking* | **Napa/N** [22]
1950 | Café Zitouna* | [-]
  Polk Gulch
1952 | Plumed Horse | **Saratoga/S** [26]
1952 | Rivoli* | **Berkeley/E** [26]
1953 | Mel's Drive-In* | **Inner Rich** [13]
1955 | Breads/India* | **Berkeley/E** [19]
1956 | Original Joe's | **San Jose/S** [22]
1958 | Yank Sing | **SoMa** [26]
1959 | Red Hut | **S Lake Tahoe/E** [22]
1959 | St. Michael's | **Palo Alto/S** [22]
1959 | Will's Fargo | [21]
  Carmel Valley/S
1960 | Benihana | **Japantown** [17]
1960 | HRD Coffee | **SoMa** [20]

HOTEL DINING

Ahwahnee Hotel
  Z Ahwahnee | **Yosemite/E** [18]
Auberge du Soleil
  Z Auberge/Soleil | [27]
  Rutherford/N
Bardessono Hotel & Spa
  Bardessono | **Yountville/N** [21]
Basque Hotel
  15 Romolo | **N Beach** [20]
Bernardus Lodge
  Z Marinus | **Carmel Valley/S** [27]
  Wicket's | **Carmel Valley/S** [-]
Blue Heron Inn
  Moosse Café | **Mendocino/N** [22]
Blue Rock Inn
  Left Bank | **Larkspur/N** [19]
Boonville Hotel
  Table 128 | **Boonville/N** [-]
California, Hotel
  Millennium | **Downtown** [25]
Carlton Hotel
  Saha | **Tenderloin** [26]
Carneros Inn
  Boon Fly | **Napa/N** [21]
  Farm | **Napa/N** [24]
Casa Madrona
  Poggio | **Sausalito/N** [23]
Cavallo Pt. Resort in Fort Baker
  Murray Circle | **Sausalito/N** [24]
Château du Sureau
  Z Erna's | **Oakhurst/E** [27]

SPECIAL FEATURES

Claremont Hotel
Meritage/Claremont | **Berkeley/E** _25_

Dina's Garden Hotel
Trader Vic's | **Palo Alto/S** _17_

El Dorado Hotel
El Dorado | **Sonoma/N** _22_

Fairmont San Francisco
Tonga Rm. | **Nob Hill** _13_

Fairmont San Jose
McCormick/Schmick | **San Jose/S** _21_

Fairmont Sonoma
Mission Inn & Spa
🅱 Santé | **Sonoma/N** _26_

Farmhouse Inn
🅱 Farmhse. Inn | **Forestville/N** _27_

Four Seasons Hotel
Quattro | **E Palo Alto/S** _22_
🅱 Seasons | **Downtown** _24_

Frank, Hotel
Max's | **Downtown** _17_

Garden Ct. Hotel
Il Fornaio | **Palo Alto/S** _20_

H2hotel
Spoonbar | **Healdsburg/N** _18_

Healdsburg, Hotel
Dry Creek | **Healdsburg/N** _24_

Hilton San Francisco Union Sq.
Urban Tavern | **Downtown** _16_

Huntington Hotel
🅱 Big 4 | **Nob Hill** _23_

Hyatt Highlands Inn
🅱 Pacific's Edge | **Carmel/S** _24_

Inn at Southbridge
Pizzeria Tra Vigne | **St. Helena/N** _21_

Inn at Spanish Bay
Roy's | **Pebble Bch/S** _24_

InterContinental Hotel
Luce | **SoMa** _21_

Kabuki, Hotel
O Izakaya | **Japantown** _18_

Lafayette Park Hotel & Spa
Duck Club | **Lafayette/E** _20_

L'Auberge Carmel
🅱 Aubergine | **Carmel/S** _28_

Les Mars Hotel
🅱 Cyrus | **Healdsburg/N** _28_

Little River Inn
Little River Inn | **Little River/N** _22_

Lodge at Pebble Beach
🅱 Club XIX | **Pebble Bch/S** _23_

Lodge at Sonoma
Carneros Bistro | **Sonoma/N** _24_

Los Gatos, Hotel
Dio Deka | **Los Gatos/S** _26_

MacCallum House Inn
MacCallum | **Mendocino/N** _24_

Madrona Manor
🅱 Madrona | **Healdsburg/N** _27_

Mandarin Oriental Hotel
Silks | **Downtown** _23_

Meadowood Napa Valley
Meadowood Grill | **St. Helena/N** _22_
🅱 Meadowood Rest. | **St. Helena/N** _28_

Mendocino Hotel
Mendo Hotel | **Mendocino/N** _18_

Monaco, Hotel
Grand Cafe | **Downtown** _19_

Monterey Plaza Hotel & Spa
Duck Club | **Monterey/S** _20_

Mount View Hotel
Jole | **Calistoga/N** _27_

Nick's Cove & Cottages
Nick's Cove | **Marshall/N** _19_

Nikko, Hotel
Anzu | **Downtown** _22_

Olema Inn
Olema Inn | **Olema/N** _18_

Palace Hotel
🅱 Garden Ct. | **Downtown** _19_
Kyo-Ya | **Downtown** _23_

Palomar, Hotel
Fifth Floor | **SoMa** _23_

Phoenix Hotel
NEW Chambers | **Tenderloin** _-_

Pine Inn
Il Fornaio | **Carmel/S** _20_

PlumpJack Squaw Valley Inn
PlumpJack | **Olympic Valley/E** _23_

Post Ranch Inn
🅱 Sierra Mar | **Big Sur/S** _27_

Prescott Hotel
Postrio | **Downtown** _23_

Ritz-Carlton Half Moon Bay
Navio | **Half Moon Bay/S** _25_

Ritz-Carlton Lake Tahoe
Manzanita | **Truckee/E** _23_

Ritz-Carlton San Francisco
Ritz-Carlton | **Nob Hill** _-_

Rosewood Sand Hill
Madera | **Menlo Pk/S** _22_

Sainte Claire Hotel	
Il Fornaio | **San Jose/S**	20
San Jose Marriott	
Arcadia | **San Jose/S**	20
San Remo Hotel	
Fior d'Italia | **N Beach**	18
Santa Clara Marriott	
Parcel 104 | **Santa Clara/S**	23
Santa Cruz Dream Inn	
Aquarius | **Santa Cruz/S**	21
Serrano Hotel	
NEW Jasper's Corner | **Downtown**	–
Shattuck Plaza	
Five | **Berkeley/E**	20
Sir Francis Drake Hotel	
Scala's Bistro | **Downtown**	21
Solage Resort	
Solbar | **Calistoga/N**	26
Sonoma Hotel	
Girl & the Fig | **Sonoma/N**	23
Stanford Inn & Spa	
Ravens' | **Mendocino/N**	26
Stevenswood Lodge	
Rest./Stevenswood | **Little River/N**	21
St. Orres Hotel	
St. Orres | **Gualala/N**	23
St. Regis	
Ame | **SoMa**	26
Vitrine | **SoMa**	24
Taj Campton Pl. Hotel	
Campton Place | **Downtown**	25
Truckee Hotel	
Moody's Bistro | **Truckee/E**	25
Valley Ford Hotel	
Rocker Oyster | **Valley Ford/N**	21
Ventana Inn & Spa	
Rest./Ventana | **Big Sur/S**	21
Villa Florence Hotel	
Kuleto's | **Downtown**	21
Vintage Ct., Hotel	
Z Masa's | **Downtown**	28
Vitale, Hotel	
Americano | **Embarcadero**	18
Warwick Regis	
La Scene | **Downtown**	19
Waterfront Plaza Hotel	
Miss Pearl's | **Oakland/E**	18
Westin St. Francis	
NEW Bourbon | **Downtown**	24
Westin Verasa	
La Toque | **Napa/N**	26

LATE DINING

(Weekday closing hour)

Z Absinthe | 12 AM | **Hayes Valley**	22
Acme Burger | varies | **W Addition**	20
Adesso | varies | **Oakland/E**	24
Alembic | 12 AM | **Haight-Ashbury**	23
NEW Asiento | varies | **Mission**	–
Beretta | 12 AM | **Mission**	22
NEW Boxing Rm. | varies | **Hayes Valley**	–
Brazen Head | 1 AM | **Cow Hollow**	21
Broken Record | 12 AM | **Excelsior**	24
Brother's Korean | varies | **Inner Rich**	24
Caspers Hot Dogs | 11:30 PM | **multi.**	20
César | 11:30 PM | **Berkeley/E**	22
Comstock | 1 AM | **N Beach**	16
Cuvée | varies | **Napa/N**	22
Delarosa | 1 AM | **Marina**	22
El Zocalo | 3:45 AM | **Bernal Hts**	19
Emporio Rulli | 12 AM | **S San Francisco/S**	24
15 Romolo | 1:30 AM | **N Beach**	20
Fonda Solana | 12:30 AM | **Albany/E**	23
Globe | 1 AM | **Downtown**	18
Gordon Biersch | 12 AM | **Embarcadero**	15
Great Eastern | 12 AM | **Chinatown**	21
NEW Grub | 12:30 AM | **Mission**	16
Heaven's Dog | 1 AM | **SoMa**	20
Hog & Rocks | 12 AM | **Mission**	21
Home of Chicken | varies | **multi.**	16
Incontro | 12 AM | **San Ramon/E**	24
Z In-N-Out | varies | **multi.**	21
NEW Jones | varies | **Tenderloin**	–
Katana-Ya | 11:30 PM | **Downtown**	22
King of Thai | varies | **multi.**	19
Kitchen | 1 AM | **Millbrae/S**	19
Lanesplitter | 12 AM | **multi.**	17
Lers Ros Thai | 12 AM | **Tenderloin**	23
NEW Locanda | 12 AM | **Mission**	–
Luka's Taproom | varies | **Oakland/E**	20
Magnolia | 12 AM | **Haight-Ashbury**	20
Mel's Drive-In | varies | **multi.**	13
Monk's Kettle | 1 AM | **Mission**	20
Naan/Curry | varies | **multi.**	17
Z Nopa | 1 AM | **W Addition**	25
Oola | 1 AM | **SoMa**	19
Original Joe's | varies | **San Jose/S**	22

Osha Thai | varies | multi.	21
Pancho Villa | varies | Mission	22
NEW Pause | 12 AM | Hayes Valley	-
Pi Bar | 12 AM | Mission	18
Rudy's | 1 AM | multi.	20
Ryoko's | 2 AM | Downtown	24
Sam Wo's | 3 AM | Chinatown	18
Sauce | 12 AM | Hayes Valley	17
Shalimar | 11:30 PM | Tenderloin	22
NEW Summit | 2 AM | Mission	-
Taqueria Can Cun | varies | Mission	25
Thai House | varies | Tenderloin	21
Tsunami | 12 AM | multi.	21
Zeitgeist | 2 AM | Mission	14
Zinsvalley | 12 AM | Napa/N	17

MEET FOR A DRINK

Z Absinthe | Hayes Valley	22
Adesso | Oakland/E	24
Alembic | Haight-Ashbury	23
Alexander's | SoMa	26
Amber Bistro | Danville/E	21
Z Amber India | SoMa	24
Americano | Embarcadero	18
Ana Mandara | Fish. Wharf	21
Anchor & Hope | SoMa	21
Andalu | Mission	21
Arizmendi | Mission	26
AsiaSF | SoMa	17
Baci Cafe | Healdsburg/N	22
Balboa Cafe | Cow Hollow	19
Bar Agricole | SoMa	21
Z Barbacco | Downtown	24
Bar Bambino | Mission	24
Bardessono | Yountville/N	21
Barlata | Oakland/E	21
Barndiva | Healdsburg/N	23
Beach Chalet | Outer Sunset	15
Bellanico | Oakland/E	23
Beretta | Mission	22
Betelnut Pejiu | Cow Hollow	23
Z Big 4 | Nob Hill	23
Z Bistro/Copains | Occidental/N	27
Bistro Don Giovanni | Napa/N	24
Z Bix | Downtown	24
NEW Bluestem Brass. | SoMa	-
Z Bottega | Yountville/N	25
Z Bouchon | Yountville/N	25
Z Boulevard | Embarcadero	27
Brazen Head | Cow Hollow	21
Brick/Bottle | Corte Madera/N	19
Bridgetender | Tahoe City/E	18

NEW Brixton | Cow Hollow	15
Broken Record | Excelsior	24
Z Buckeye | Mill Valley/N	24
Bungalow 44 | Mill Valley/N	21
Butterfly | Embarcadero	21
Café des Amis | Cow Hollow	19
Café Flore | Castro	17
Café Rouge | Berkeley/E	22
Cannery/Brew | Monterey/S	17
Cascal | Mtn View/S	21
Cellar Door Café | Santa Cruz/S	26
César | Berkeley/E	22
NEW Chambers | Tenderloin	-
Cheese Steak Shop | Concord/E	20
Chop Bar | Oakland/E	24
NEW Chotto | Marina	21
Colibrí | Downtown	16
Comstock | N Beach	18
Cosmopolitan | SoMa	16
Davenport | Davenport/S	22
Delarosa | Marina	26
Dio Deka | Los Gatos/S	-
NEW Disco Volante | Oakland/E	22
Donato | Redwood City/S	22
Doña Tomás | Oakland/E	20
E&O Trading | Downtown	19
Elite Cafe | Pacific Hts	23
Encuentro | Oakland/E	22
Della Santina | Sonoma/N	-
NEW Enoteca Molinari | Oakland/E	
Eos | Cole Valley	23
Epic Roasthse. | Embarcadero	21
Eureka | Castro	20
Z Farallon | Downtown	24
Farm | Napa/N	24
15 Romolo | N Beach	20
54 Mint | SoMa	21
Fig Cafe/Wine | Glen Ellen/N	25
Five | Berkeley/E	20
5A5 Steak | Downtown	23
Flora | Oakland/E	21
Florio | Pacific Hts	19
Fonda Solana | Albany/E	23
Z Foreign Cinema | Mission	24
Garibaldis | Presidio Hts	22
Gar Woods | Carnelian Bay/E	17
Gitane | Downtown	23
Gordon Biersch | multi.	15
Guaymas | Tiburon/N	17
Half Moon Brew | Half Moon Bay/S	16
Hapa Ramen | Loc varies	20
Heart | Mission	19

Heaven's Dog | SoMa	20
NEW Hecho | Downtown	-
Heirloom | Mission	23
Hog & Rocks | Mission	21
Hopmonk Tav. | Sebastopol/N	18
HRD Coffee | SoMa	20
Hula's | Santa Cruz/S	18
Iberia | Menlo Pk/S	22
Izakaya Sozai | Inner Sunset	22
Jake's/Lake | Tahoe City/E	18
Z Jardinière | Civic Ctr	26
NEW Jasper's Corner | Downtown	-
NEW Jones | Tenderloin	-
Joya | Palo Alto/S	21
Junnoon | Palo Alto/S	22
Z Kokkari | Downtown	27
La Costanera | Montara/S	21
La Mar | Embarcadero	25
Lanesplitter | Oakland/E	17
La Trappe | N Beach	16
Lavanda | Palo Alto/S	20
Le Colonial | Downtown	22
Left Bank | multi.	19
Luce | SoMa	21
Luka's Taproom | Oakland/E	19
Luna Park | Mission	17
NEW Ma*Velous | Civic Ctr	-
Magnolia | Haight-Ashbury	20
Mamacita | Marina	22
Mantra | Palo Alto/S	21
Manzanita | Truckee/E	23
Marinitas | San Anselmo/N	20
MarketBar | Embarcadero	16
Martins West | Redwood City/S	22
Mendo Hotel | Mendocino/N	18
Meritage/Claremont | Berkeley/E	25
Meritage Martini | Sonoma/N	22
Z NEW Michael Mina | Downtown	26
Mijita | S Beach	19
Miss Pearl's | Oakland/E	18
MoMo's | S Beach	18
Monk's Kettle | Mission	20
Moody's Bistro | Truckee/E	25
Mundaka | Carmel/S	24
Murray Circle | Sausalito/N	24
Z Mustards | Yountville/N	25
Nettie's Crab | Cow Hollow	18
Nihon | Mission	19
Nombe | Mission	21
Z Nopa | W Addition	25
Norman Rose | Napa/N	20
North Coast Brew | Ft Bragg/N	18
O Izakaya | Japantown	18
Oliveto | Oakland/E	24
One Market | Embarcadero	24
Orson | SoMa	18
Oswald | Santa Cruz/S	25
Ottimista | Cow Hollow	19
Oxbow Wine | Napa/N	18
Oyaji | Outer Rich	24
Ozumo | multi.	23
Pacific Crest | Truckee/E	-
Palio d'Asti | Downtown	20
Park Chalet | Outer Sunset	15
Patrona | Ukiah/N	-
NEW Pause | Hayes Valley	-
Z Perbacco | Downtown	25
Pi Bar | Mission	18
Picán | Oakland/E	22
Picco | Larkspur/N	25
Z Plumed Horse | Saratoga/S	26
Presidio Social | Presidio	19
Prima | Walnut Creek/E	24
Prospect | SoMa	24
Public House | S Beach	16
Radius | SoMa	23
Z Range | Mission	27
Z Redd | Yountville/N	27
Rest./Ventana | Big Sur/S	21
Rest. LuLu | SoMa	19
Revival Bar | Berkeley/E	20
Rist. Avanti | Santa Cruz/S	24
RN74 | SoMa	23
Rose Pistola | N Beach	21
Rose's Cafe | Cow Hollow	21
Rosso Pizzeria | Santa Rosa/N	25
Rustic | Geyserville/N	19
Sardine Factory | Monterey/S	21
Sea Salt | Berkeley/E	21
Sens | Downtown	17
Serpentine | Dogpatch	22
Sidebar | Oakland/E	22
Sino | San Jose/S	19
Slow Club | Mission	22
Social Kit. | Inner Sunset	15
Soif Wine Bar | Santa Cruz/S	25
Solbar | Calistoga/N	26
Spoonbar | Healdsburg/N	18
Starbelly | Castro	21
Starlight | Sebastopol/N	22
Sunnyside | Tahoe City/E	18
Sushi Groove | Russian Hill	21
Tamarine | Palo Alto/S	26
Tav./Lark Creek | Larkspur/N	20
Terzo | Cow Hollow	24
Thermidor | SoMa	20
1300/Fillmore | W Addition	21

Tipsy Pig | **Marina**	18
Tokyo Go Go | **Mission**	20
Tommy's Mex. | **Outer Rich**	15
Tonga Rm. | **Nob Hill**	13
Town Hall | **SoMa**	22
Townhouse B&G | **Emeryville/E**	21
Trader Vic's | **Emeryville/E**	17
Tra Vigne | **St. Helena/N**	24
Tres | **S Beach**	17
Z NEW 25 Lusk | **SoMa**	20
2223 | **Castro**	22
Ukiah Brew | **Ukiah/N**	–
Umami | **Cow Hollow**	24
Underwood Bar | **Graton/N**	23
Uva Enoteca | **Lower Haight**	22
Va de Vi | **Walnut Creek/E**	24
Vin Antico | **San Rafael/N**	23
Waterbar | **Embarcadero**	21
Wayfare Tav. | **Downtown**	22
Wexler's | **Downtown**	22
Wicket's | **Carmel Valley/S**	–
Wild Goose | **Tahoe Vista/E**	23
Willi's Seafood | **Healdsburg/N**	24
Will's Fargo | **Carmel Valley/S**	21
Wine Spectator | **St. Helena/N**	21
Z Wood Tavern | **Oakland/E**	26
Xanh | **Mtn View/S**	21
Yoshi's SF | **W Addition**	21
Zaré/Fly Trap | **SoMa**	22
Zibibbo | **Palo Alto/S**	19
Zin | **Healdsburg/N**	23
Z Zuni Café | **Hayes Valley**	25
ZuZu | **Napa/N**	25

NEWCOMERS

Addie's | **Berkeley/E**	21
All Spice | **San Mateo/S**	24
Asiento | **Mission**	–
Atelier Crenn | **Marina**	26
Bar Bocce | **Sausalito/N**	–
Beast/Hare | **Mission**	20
Bistro SF Grill | **Pacific Hts**	–
Bluestem Brass. | **SoMa**	–
Bottle Cap | **N Beach**	–
Bourbon | **Downtown**	24
Boxing Rm. | **Hayes Valley**	–
Branches | **Ukiah/N**	–
Brixton | **Cow Hollow**	15
Bun Mee | **Upper Fillmore**	–
Café Tradition | **San Mateo/S**	–
Campanula | **N Beach**	–
Chambers | **Tenderloin**	–
Chotto | **Marina**	24
Cosecha Café | **Oakland/E**	–

Criolla Kitchen | **Castro**	–
Cupola Pizzeria | **Downtown**	–
Disco Volante | **Oakland/E**	–
El Paseo | **Mill Valley/N**	–
Enoteca Molinari | **Oakland/E**	–
Frank/Ernie's | **Healdsburg/N**	–
Fresh/Lisa | **Santa Rosa/N**	24
Guamenkitzel | **Berkeley/E**	–
Greenburgers | **Lower Haight**	–
Grub | **Mission**	16
Hawker Fare | **Oakland/E**	–
Hecho | **Downtown**	–
Hodo Soy | **Embarcadero**	–
Homeroom | **Oakland/E**	–
Hudson | **Oakland/E**	20
Ichi Sushi | **Bernal Hts**	23
Jane | **Upper Fillmore**	–
Jones | **Tenderloin**	–
Ki | **SoMa**	–
Kitchen Door | **Napa/N**	–
Leopold's | **Russian Hill**	23
Locanda | **Mission**	–
Locanda Positano | **San Carlos/S**	–
Locavore | **Bernal Hts**	20
Ma*Velous | **Civic Ctr**	17
Mama's Empanadas | **Loc varies**	26
Mamma Pig's | **Windsor/N**	–
Z Michael Mina | **Downtown**	26
Mission Cheese | **Mission**	–
Nojo | **Hayes Valley**	–
Osteria Coppa | **San Mateo/S**	24
Pasión | **Inner Sunset**	22
Pause | **Hayes Valley**	–
Petite Syrah | **Santa Rosa/N**	–
Plate Shop | **Sausalito/N**	–
Plow | **Potrero Hill**	25
Prickly Pear | **Danville/E**	–
Radish | **Mission**	–
Ragazza | **W Addition**	24
Sazon | **Santa Rosa/N**	–
Seven Hills | **Nob Hill**	24
Shimo | **Healdsburg/N**	–
Source | **Potrero Hill**	–
Southie | **Oakland/E**	–
Station 1 | **Woodside/S**	25
Straw | **Hayes Valley**	–
Summit | **Mission**	–
Sushirrito | **SoMa**	–
Table 24 | **Orinda/E**	18
Tacko | **Cow Hollow**	–
Z 25 Lusk | **SoMa**	20
Txoko | **N Beach**	–
Una Pizza | **SoMa**	26

Vote at ZAGAT.com

Wise Sons	Loc varies	23
Xolo Taqueria	Oakland/E	-
Zut!	Berkeley/E	20

OFFBEAT

Ace Wasabi's	Marina	19
Albona Rist.	N Beach	25
AsiaSF	SoMa	17
Avatar's	Sausalito/N	22
Basque Cultural	S San Francisco/S	19
Benihana	Japantown	17
Blowfish Sushi	Mission	21
Boogaloos	Mission	17
Broken Record	Excelsior	24
Buca di Beppo	multi.	15
Café Gratitude	multi.	17
Candybar	W Addition	20
Cellar Door Café	Santa Cruz/S	26
Cha Cha	multi.	20
Cha-Ya Veg.	multi.	23
Don Pico	San Bruno/S	17
Duarte's	Pescadero/S	20
Fish	Sausalito/N	24
Forbes Island	Fish. Wharf	15
Home of Chicken	Oakland/E	16
Jimtown Store	Healdsburg/N	21
Joe's Cable Car	Excelsior	19
Kitchenette SF	Dogpatch	24
Loló	Mission	24
Lovejoy's Tea	Noe Valley	20
Nick's Crispy	Russian Hill	22
Oyaji	Outer Rich	24
Ravens'	Mendocino/N	26
Red's Java	Embarcadero	15
St. Orres	Gualala/N	23
Thai Buddhist	Berkeley/E	21
Tonga Rm.	Nob Hill	13
Trader Vic's	Emeryville/E	17

OUTDOOR DINING

(G=garden; P=patio; S=sidewalk;
T=terrace; W=waterside)

☑ Absinthe	S	Hayes Valley	22
☑ À Côté	P	Oakland/E	24
Adagia	P	Berkeley/E	20
Alexis Baking	S	Napa/N	22
Angèle	P, W	Napa/N	24
Anton/Michel	G, P	Carmel/S	23
Aperto	S	Potrero Hill	23
Applewood Inn	G, T	Guerneville/N	25
☑ Auberge/Soleil	T	Rutherford/N	27
Baker St. Bistro	S	Marina	19

Bar Agricole	P	SoMa	21
Barbara's	P, S, W	Princeton Sea/S	21
Barndiva	G, P	Healdsburg/N	23
Barney's	P	multi.	19
Basin	P	Saratoga/S	20
Beach Chalet	W	Outer Sunset	15
Betelnut Pejiu	S	Cow Hollow	23
B44	S	Downtown	21
Bistro Boudin	P, W	Fish. Wharf	20
Bistro Don Giovanni	P, T	Napa/N	24
☑ Bistro Jeanty	P	Yountville/N	25
Bistro Liaison	P	Berkeley/E	22
Blackhawk Grille	P, T, W	Danville/E	20
Blue Bottle	S	SoMa	23
Blue Plate	G, P	Mission	24
Boca	P	Novato/N	22
Bo's BBQ	T	Lafayette/E	22
☑ Bouchon	P	Yountville/N	25
Bridges	P	Danville/E	23
Bucci's	P	Emeryville/E	21
☑ Buckeye	P	Mill Valley/N	24
Bungalow 44	P	Mill Valley/N	21
Cafe Bastille	S, T	Downtown	20
Cafe Citti	P	Kenwood/N	22
Café Claude	P, S	Downtown	22
Café Fanny	P	Berkeley/E	23
Café Rouge	P	Berkeley/E	22
Café Tiramisu	P, S	Downtown	22
Caffè Museo	S	SoMa	18
Casanova	P	Carmel/S	23
Cascal	P	Mtn View/S	21
Catch	P	Castro	18
Celadon	G, T	Napa/N	23
César	P	Oakland/E	22
Charanga	P	Mission	21
Chaya	P	Embarcadero	20
Cheesecake	P, T	Downtown	17
Spencer/Go	S	Potrero Hill	23
Chez Papa Bistrot	S	Potrero Hill	23
Chez Spencer	G, P	Mission	25
Chez TJ	P	Mtn View/S	24
Chloe's Cafe	S	Noe Valley	24
Chow	P, S	multi.	20
Cindy's	P	St. Helena/N	24
☑ Club XIX	P, W	Pebble Bch/S	24
Cole's Chop	P	Napa/N	25
Cool Café	P	Stanford/S	20
Delancey St.	P, S	Embarcadero	18
Della Santina	P	Sonoma/N	22
Doña Tomás	P	Oakland/E	22
Dopo	S	Oakland/E	25

SPECIAL FEATURES

Dry Creek | P | **Healdsburg/N** 24	Mezze | S | **Oakland/E** 23
El Dorado | P, W | **Sonoma/N** 22	Mistral | P, W | **Redwood Shores/S** 20
Emporio Rulli | G, P, S, T | multi. 24	MoMo's | T | **S Beach** 18
Epic Roasthse. | P | **Embarcadero** 21	Monti's | P | **Santa Rosa/N** 20
Étoile | P, T | **Yountville/N** 25	Moosse Café | T, W | 22
Everett/Jones | S | multi. 20	**Mendocino/N**
Fentons | P | **Oakland/E** 20	Murray Circle | P | **Sausalito/N** 24
Fish | T, W | **Sausalito/N** 24	Napa General | T, W | **Napa/N** 18
Flavor | P | **Santa Rosa/N** 20	Nepenthe | P, W | **Big Sur/S** 16
Fog City Diner | P, S | 18	O Chamé | P | **Berkeley/E** 24
Embarcadero	Olema Inn | P | **Olema/N** 18
Fonda Solana | S | **Albany/E** 23	Oliveto | S | **Oakland/E** 24
❷ Foreign Cinema | P | **Mission** 24	Parcel 104 | P | **Santa Clara/S** 23
Frantoio | P | **Mill Valley/N** 20	Park Chalet | G, P, W | 15
Fumé Bistro | P | **Napa/N** 19	**Outer Sunset**
Gabriella Café | G, P | 22	Pasta Moon | P | **Half Moon Bay/S** 24
Santa Cruz/S	Pazzia | P | **SoMa** 23
Girl & the Fig | G, P | **Sonoma/N** 23	Piatti | P, W | multi. 19
Gott's Roadside | G, P | multi. 21	Piazza D'Angelo | P | **Mill Valley/N** 20
Grasing's Coastal | P | **Carmel/S** 23	Picante Cocina | P | **Berkeley/E** 23
Grégoire | S | **Berkeley/E** 21	Piperade | P | **Downtown** 25
Guaymas | P, T, W | **Tiburon/N** 17	Pizza Antica | P | multi. 20
❷ Hog Island | P, W | 25	Pizzeria Tra Vigne | P | 21
Embarcadero	**St. Helena/N**
Hurley's | P | **Yountville/N** 21	Pizzetta 211 | S | **Outer Rich** 25
Iberia | P | **Menlo Pk/S** 22	Plouf | T | **Downtown** 21
Il Davide | P | **San Rafael/N** 24	PlumpJack | P | **Olympic Valley/E** 23
Il Fornaio | P | multi. 20	Poggio | S | **Sausalito/N** 23
Isa | P | **Marina** 26	Postino | P | **Lafayette/E** 22
Jimmy Beans | S | **Berkeley/E** 20	Press | P | **St. Helena/N** 24
Jimtown Store | P | **Healdsburg/N** 21	Prima | P | **Walnut Creek/E** 24
John Ash | P | **Santa Rosa/N** 24	Ravenous | P | **Healdsburg/N** 23
Kenwood | G | **Kenwood/N** 23	Red's Java | P, W | **Embarcadero** 15
La Boulange | S | multi. 21	Rick & Ann | P | **Berkeley/E** 21
Lake Chalet | T, W | **Oakland/E** 14	Rose Pistola | S | **N Beach** 21
La Mar | P, W | **Embarcadero** 25	Rose's Cafe | S | **Cow Hollow** 21
La Note | P | **Berkeley/E** 22	Roy's | P, W | **Pebble Bch/S** 24
Lark Creek | P | **Walnut Creek/E** 22	Rustic | P | **Geyserville/N** 19
LaSalette | P | **Sonoma/N** 24	Rutherford Grill | P | **Rutherford/N** 23
La Strada | T | **Palo Alto/S** 19	Sam's Chowder | P, W | 20
Le Charm Bistro | P | **SoMa** 23	**Half Moon Bay/S**
Le Colonial | P | **Downtown** 22	Savor | P | **Noe Valley** 18
Left Bank | P, S | multi. 19	❷ Scoma's | P, W | **Sausalito/N** 23
Lion/Compass | P | **Sunnyvale/S** 21	Sea Salt | P | **Berkeley/E** 21
MacCallum | T | **Mendocino/N** 24	71 St. Peter | P | **San Jose/S** 20
Madera | T | **Menlo Pk/S** 22	❷ Sierra Mar | T, W | **Big Sur/S** 27
❷ Madrona | T | **Healdsburg/N** 27	Skool | P | **Potrero Hill** 22
Marché/Fleurs | P | **Ross/N** 25	Slow Club | S | **Mission** 22
MarketBar | P | **Embarcadero** 16	Sociale | G, P | **Presidio Hts** 23
Meadowood Grill | T | 22	South Park | S | **SoMa** 22
St. Helena/N	Straits | P | multi. 20
❷ Meadowood Rest. | T | 28	❷ Sushi Ran | P | **Sausalito/N** 28
St. Helena/N	Tarpy's | P | **Monterey/S** 20
Meritage Martini | G, P | 22	❷ Tartine | S | **Mission** 27
Sonoma/N	

     Vote at ZAGAT.com

Townhouse B&G | P | Emeryville/E	21	Café de la Presse | Downtown	18
Town's End | P | Embarcadero	21	Café Flore | Castro	17
Trader Vic's | T | Palo Alto/S	17	Candybar | W Addition	20
Tra Vigne | G, T | St. Helena/N	24	Cannery/Brew | Monterey/S	17
Underwood Bar | P | Graton/N	23	Cascal | Mtn View/S	21
Universal Cafe | P | Mission	24	Catch | Castro	18
Va de Vi | S, T | Walnut Creek/E	24	Central Market | Petaluma/N	22
Waterbar | P, W | Embarcadero	21	César | Berkeley/E	22
Waterfront | P, W | Embarcadero	20	Cha Cha | multi.	20
Water St. Bistro | P, W | Petaluma/N	22	Chaya | Embarcadero	20
Wente Vineyards | P | Livermore/E	24	☑ Chez Panisse Café | Berkeley/E	27
		Chez Papa Resto | SoMa	24
Willi's Seafood | P | Healdsburg/N	24	Comstock | N Beach	16
Willi's Wine | P, T | Santa Rosa/N	25	Cottonwood | Truckee/E	26
Wine Spectator | T | St. Helena/N	21	Delarosa | Marina	22
Yankee Pier | P, T | multi.	18	Dio Deka | Los Gatos/S	26
Yumma's | G | Inner Sunset	21	Donato | Redwood City/S	22
Zazie | G | Cole Valley	23	Dosa | multi.	22
Zibibbo | G, P | Palo Alto/S	19	Downtown Bakery | Healdsburg/N	25
Zinsvalley | P | Napa/N	17	Dragonfly | Truckee/E	22
☑ Zuni Café | S | Hayes Valley	25	NEW El Paseo | Mill Valley/N	–
		Epic Roasthse. | Embarcadero	21

PEOPLE-WATCHING

☑ Absinthe | Hayes Valley	22	☑ Evvia | Palo Alto/S	27
Ace Wasabi's | Marina	19	Farina | Mission	23
☑ À Côté | Oakland/E	24	Farmstead | St. Helena/N	20
Ana Mandara | Fish. Wharf	21	54 Mint | SoMa	21
Anchor & Hope | SoMa	21	Fish & Farm | Downtown	20
AsiaSF | SoMa	17	Five | Berkeley/E	20
Balboa Cafe | multi.	19	5A5 Steak | Downtown	23
☑ Barbacco | Downtown	24	Flea St. Café | Menlo Pk/S	26
Barlata | Oakland/E	21	Flora | Oakland/E	21
Barndiva | Healdsburg/N	23	☑ Flour + Water | Mission	24
Bar Tartine | Mission	24	☑ Foreign Cinema | Mission	24
Beretta | Mission	22	Frjtz Fries | multi.	17
Betelnut Pejiu | Cow Hollow	23	Front Porch | Bernal Hts	20
Bistro Don Giovanni | Napa/N	24	Gar Woods | Carnelian Bay/E	17
☑ Bistro Jeanty | Yountville/N	25	Gitane | Downtown	23
☑ Bix | Downtown	24	Gott's Roadside | Napa/N	21
Blowfish Sushi | Mission	21	Grand Pu Bah | Potrero Hill	19
Blue Bottle | multi.	23	Heaven's Dog | SoMa	20
Bocanova | Oakland/E	21	☑ Hog Island | Napa/N	25
Boogaloos | Mission	17	Hopmonk Tav. | Sebastopol/N	18
☑ Bottega | Yountville/N	25	Ironside | S Beach	17
☑ Bouchon | Yountville/N	25	Jake's/Lake | Tahoe City/E	18
☑ Boulevard | Embarcadero	27	☑ Jardinière | Civic Ctr	26
Bridgetender | Tahoe City/E	18	Joya | Palo Alto/S	21
Brix | Napa/N	23	Junnoon | Palo Alto/S	22
NEW Brixton | Cow Hollow	15	La Boulange | Noe Valley	21
Bungalow 44 | Mill Valley/N	21	La Mar | Embarcadero	25
Burger Bar | Downtown	19	LB Steak | San Jose/S	20
Cafe Bastille | Downtown	20	Left Bank | Larkspur/N	19
Café Claude | Downtown	22	Lion/Compass | Sunnyvale/S	21
		Madera | Menlo Pk/S	22

Magnolia | **Haight-Ashbury**	20
Mamacita | **Marina**	22
Manzanita | **Truckee/E**	23
Marinitas | **San Anselmo/N**	20
Mario's Bohemian | **N Beach**	17
MarketBar | **Embarcadero**	16
Martins West | **Redwood City/S**	22
Miss Pearl's | **Oakland/E**	18
Moody's Bistro | **Truckee/E**	25
Morimoto | **Napa/N**	26
☑ Mustards | **Yountville/N**	25
Nettie's Crab | **Cow Hollow**	18
Nihon | **Mission**	19
☑ Nopa | **W Addition**	25
Oliveto | **Oakland/E**	24
Orson | **SoMa**	18
Ottimista | **Cow Hollow**	19
Ozumo | **Oakland/E**	23
Pampas | **Palo Alto/S**	22
Picán | **Oakland/E**	22
Picco | **Larkspur/N**	25
☑ Plumed Horse | **Saratoga/S**	26
Poesia | **Castro**	21
Poggio | **Sausalito/N**	23
Postino | **Lafayette/E**	22
Postrio | **Downtown**	23
Prospect | **SoMa**	24
Public House | **S Beach**	16
Quattro | **E Palo Alto/S**	22
☑ Redd | **Yountville/N**	27
Rest. LuLu | **SoMa**	19
RN74 | **SoMa**	23
Rose Pistola | **N Beach**	21
Rose's Cafe | **Cow Hollow**	21
Scala's Bistro | **Downtown**	21
Serpentine | **Dogpatch**	22
Sidebar | **Oakland/E**	22
Sino | **San Jose/S**	19
Solbar | **Calistoga/N**	26
Starbelly | **Castro**	21
Sunnyside | **Tahoe City/E**	18
Sushi Groove | **multi.**	21
Tamarine | **Palo Alto/S**	26
Tipsy Pig | **Marina**	18
Tokyo Go Go | **Mission**	20
Town Hall | **SoMa**	22
Tra Vigne | **St. Helena/N**	24
Tres | **S Beach**	17
Tsunami | **W Addition**	21
☑ **NEW** 25 Lusk | **SoMa**	20
2223 | **Castro**	22
Umami | **Cow Hollow**	24
Urban Tavern | **Downtown**	16
Va de Vi | **Walnut Creek/E**	24

Village Pub | **Woodside/S**	26
Viognier | **San Mateo/S**	23
Waterbar | **Embarcadero**	21
☑ Wood Tavern | **Oakland/E**	26
Xanh | **Mtn View/S**	21
Yoshi's SF | **W Addition**	21
Zibibbo | **Palo Alto/S**	19
☑ Zuni Café | **Hayes Valley**	25

POWER SCENES

Alexander's | **multi.**	26
Ana Mandara | **Fish. Wharf**	21
Arcadia | **San Jose/S**	20
☑ Auberge/Soleil | **Rutherford/N**	27
Balboa Cafe | **Mill Valley/N**	19
☑ Barbacco | **Downtown**	24
☑ Big 4 | **Nob Hill**	23
Blackhawk Grille | **Danville/E**	20
☑ Bouchon | **Yountville/N**	25
☑ Boulevard | **Embarcadero**	27
Chaya | **Embarcadero**	20
Chef Chu's | **Los Altos/S**	20
Dio Deka | **Los Gatos/S**	26
Epic Roasthse. | **Embarcadero**	21
☑ Evvia | **Palo Alto/S**	27
Fifth Floor | **SoMa**	23
☑ Fleur de Lys | **Downtown**	27
Forbes Mill | **multi.**	22
☑ Gary Danko | **Fish. Wharf**	29
Il Fornaio | **Palo Alto/S**	20
☑ Jardinière | **Civic Ctr**	26
☑ Kokkari | **Downtown**	27
Le Central Bistro | **Downtown**	21
Le Colonial | **Downtown**	22
Lion/Compass | **Sunnyvale/S**	21
Manzanita | **Truckee/E**	23
Martins West | **Redwood City/S**	22
☑ Masa's | **Downtown**	28
☑ **NEW** Michael Mina | **Downtown**	26
Mistral | **Redwood Shores/S**	20
Morton's | **multi.**	23
One Market | **Embarcadero**	24
Ottimista | **Cow Hollow**	19
Ozumo | **Embarcadero**	23
Parcel 104 | **Santa Clara/S**	23
☑ Perbacco | **Downtown**	25
☑ Plumed Horse | **Saratoga/S**	26
Postrio | **Downtown**	23
Press | **St. Helena/N**	24
Prospect | **SoMa**	24
Quattro | **E Palo Alto/S**	22
☑ Redd | **Yountville/N**	27

Ritz-Carlton | **Nob Hill**	–
RN74 | **SoMa**	23
Sam's Grill | **Downtown**	22
☑ Seasons | **Downtown**	24
Sens | **Downtown**	17
Silks | **Downtown**	23
☑ Spruce | **Presidio Hts**	25
☑ Tadich Grill | **Downtown**	23
Tommy Toy | **Downtown**	23
Tony's Coal-Fired Pizza | **N Beach**	24
Town Hall | **SoMa**	22
Urban Tavern | **Downtown**	16
Village Pub | **Woodside/S**	26
Viognier | **San Mateo/S**	23
Waterbar | **Embarcadero**	21
Wayfare Tav. | **Downtown**	22
☑ Zuni Café | **Hayes Valley**	25

PRE-THEATER

☑ Absinthe | **Hayes Valley**	22
Arlequin | **Hayes Valley**	19
Bistro Liaison | **Berkeley/E**	22
Colibrí | **Downtown**	21
Fish & Farm | **Downtown**	20
Grand Cafe | **Downtown**	19
Hayes St. Grill | **Hayes Valley**	23
☑ Jardinière | **Civic Ctr**	26
La Scene | **Downtown**	19
Paul K | **Hayes Valley**	22
Sauce | **Hayes Valley**	17
Scala's Bistro | **Downtown**	21
Venus | **Berkeley/E**	23

PRIVATE ROOMS

(Restaurants charge less at off times; call for capacity)

☑ Absinthe | **Hayes Valley**	22
☑ À Côté | **Oakland/E**	24
☑ Acquerello | **Polk Gulch**	28
Adagia | **Berkeley/E**	20
Alegrias | **Marina**	21
Alexander's | **Cupertino/S**	26
Alfred's Steak | **Downtown**	23
Ana Mandara | **Fish. Wharf**	21
Andalu | **Mission**	21
Angèle | **Napa/N**	24
Anton/Michel | **Carmel/S**	23
Arcadia | **San Jose/S**	20
☑ Auberge/Soleil | **Rutherford/N**	27
☑ Aubergine | **Carmel/S**	28
☑ Aziza | **Outer Rich**	26
Barndiva | **Healdsburg/N**	23
Basin | **Saratoga/S**	20
☑ BayWolf | **Oakland/E**	26

Bella Vista | **Woodside/S**	22
Betelnut Pejiu | **Cow Hollow**	23
☑ Big 4 | **Nob Hill**	23
Bistro Liaison | **Berkeley/E**	22
Blackhawk Grille | **Danville/E**	20
Blue Plate | **Mission**	24
Boca | **Novato/N**	22
Boulette Larder | **Embarcadero**	25
☑ Boulevard | **Embarcadero**	27
Buca di Beppo | **multi.**	15
☑ Buckeye | **Mill Valley/N**	24
Café Rouge | **Berkeley/E**	22
Caprice | **Tiburon/N**	22
Carneros Bistro | **Sonoma/N**	24
Casanova | **Carmel/S**	23
Cetrella | **Half Moon Bay/S**	22
Cha Cha | **Mission**	20
Chantilly | **Redwood City/S**	25
Chez TJ | **Mtn View/S**	24
Cindy's | **St. Helena/N**	24
☑ Club XIX | **Pebble Bch/S**	23
Cosmopolitan | **SoMa**	18
☑ Cyrus | **Healdsburg/N**	28
Dry Creek | **Healdsburg/N**	24
Eos | **Cole Valley**	23
☑ Erna's | **Oakhurst/E**	27
Fandango | **Pacific Grove/S**	23
☑ Farallon | **Downtown**	24
Fifth Floor | **SoMa**	23
Flea St. Café | **Menlo Pk/S**	26
☑ Fleur de Lys | **Downtown**	27
Florio | **Pacific Hts**	19
☑ Foreign Cinema | **Mission**	24
Frantoio | **Mill Valley/N**	20
Gary Chu's | **Santa Rosa/N**	22
☑ Gary Danko | **Fish. Wharf**	29
Grand Cafe | **Downtown**	19
Grasing's Coastal | **Carmel/S**	23
Harris' | **Polk Gulch**	26
Hurley's | **Yountville/N**	21
Iberia | **Menlo Pk/S**	22
Il Fornaio | **multi.**	20
Incanto | **Noe Valley**	25
Indigo | **Civic Ctr**	20
Insalata's | **San Anselmo/N**	24
☑ Jardinière | **Civic Ctr**	26
John Bentley | **Redwood City/S**	26
Kenwood | **Kenwood/N**	23
Khan Toke | **Outer Rich**	21
☑ Kokkari | **Downtown**	27
☑ La Folie | **Russian Hill**	28
☑ La Forêt | **San Jose/S**	27
La Strada | **Palo Alto/S**	19
Lavanda | **Palo Alto/S**	20

Le Colonial	**Downtown**	22
Left Bank	**multi.**	19
☑ Le Papillon	**San Jose/S**	27
Lion/Compass	**Sunnyvale/S**	21
Little River Inn	**Little River/N**	22
MacCallum	**Mendocino/N**	24
☑ Madrona	**Healdsburg/N**	27
☑ Manresa	**Los Gatos/S**	28
☑ Marinus	**Carmel Valley/S**	27
☑ Masa's	**Downtown**	28
Maya	**SoMa**	20
Millennium	**Downtown**	25
Montrio Bistro	**Monterey/S**	23
Morton's	**Downtown**	23
Moss Room	**Inner Rich**	22
Navio	**Half Moon Bay/S**	25
North Bch. Rest.	**N Beach**	22
Olema Inn	**Olema/N**	18
One Market	**Embarcadero**	24
Orson	**SoMa**	18
Ozumo	**Embarcadero**	23
☑ Pacific's Edge	**Carmel/S**	24
Palio d'Asti	**Downtown**	20
Parcel 104	**Santa Clara/S**	23
☑ Passionfish	**Pacific Grove/S**	27
Pauline's	**Mission**	23
☑ Perbacco	**Downtown**	25
Pesce	**Russian Hill**	25
Piatti	**Mill Valley/N**	19
Piazza D'Angelo	**Mill Valley/N**	20
☑ Plumed Horse	**Saratoga/S**	26
PlumpJack	**Olympic Valley/E**	23
Poggio	**Sausalito/N**	23
Postino	**Lafayette/E**	22
Postrio	**Downtown**	23
Press	**St. Helena/N**	24
Prima	**Walnut Creek/E**	24
Prospect	**SoMa**	24
R&G Lounge	**Chinatown**	24
Rest. LuLu	**SoMa**	19
Rio Grill	**Carmel/S**	21
Ritz-Carlton	**Nob Hill**	-
Rose Pistola	**N Beach**	21
Roy's	**SoMa**	23
Ruth's Chris	**Polk Gulch**	24
Sardine Factory	**Monterey/S**	21
Sauce	**Hayes Valley**	17
Scala's Bistro	**Downtown**	21
Scott's	**multi.**	20
☑ Seasons	**Downtown**	24
71 St. Peter	**San Jose/S**	20
Shadowbrook	**Capitola/S**	18
Silks	**Downtown**	23
☑ Slanted Door	**Embarcadero**	25

Soi4	**Oakland/E**	24
Sons/Daughters	**Nob Hill**	25
☑ Spruce	**Presidio Hts**	25
St. Orres	**Gualala/N**	23
Straits	**San Jose/S**	20
Table 128	**Boonville/N**	-
Tamarine	**Palo Alto/S**	26
Tarpy's	**Monterey/S**	20
☑ Terra	**St. Helena/N**	27
Tommy Toy	**Downtown**	23
Town Hall	**SoMa**	22
Trader Vic's	**multi.**	17
Tra Vigne	**St. Helena/N**	24
231 Ellsworth	**San Mateo/S**	23
2223	**Castro**	22
Vic Stewart	**Walnut Creek/E**	22
Village Pub	**Woodside/S**	26
Viognier	**San Mateo/S**	23
Waterbar	**Embarcadero**	21
Wente Vineyards	**Livermore/E**	24
☑ Yank Sing	**SoMa**	26
Zarzuela	**Russian Hill**	24
Zibibbo	**Palo Alto/S**	19
Zuppa	**SoMa**	19

PRIX FIXE MENUS

(Call for prices and times)

☑ Acquerello	**Polk Gulch**	28
☑ Ad Hoc/Addendum	**Yountville/N**	27
Ajanta	**Berkeley/E**	25
Alamo Sq.	**W Addition**	18
Amber Bistro	**Danville/E**	21
Ana Mandara	**Fish. Wharf**	21
AsiaSF	**SoMa**	17
☑ Auberge/Soleil	**Rutherford/N**	27
☑ Aubergine	**Carmel/S**	28
Axum Cafe	**Lower Haight**	23
☑ Aziza	**Outer Rich**	26
Baker St. Bistro	**Marina**	19
Basque Cultural	**S San Francisco/S**	19
☑ Baumé	**Palo Alto/S**	27
Bistro Central Parc	**W Addition**	24
☑ Bistro/Copains	**Occidental/N**	27
Bistro Liaison	**Berkeley/E**	22
☑ Bix	**Downtown**	24
Cafe Bastille	**Downtown**	20
☑ Cafe Gibraltar	**El Granada/S**	26
Caffe Delle Stelle	**Hayes Valley**	17
☑ Canteen	**Tenderloin**	27
Capannina	**Cow Hollow**	25
Caprice	**Tiburon/N**	22
Cellar Door Café	**Santa Cruz/S**	26

Chantilly	**Redwood City/S**	25
Z Chapeau!	**Inner Rich**	26
Charcuterie	**Healdsburg/N**	21
Z Chez Panisse	**Berkeley/E**	28
Z Chez Panisse Café	**Berkeley/E**	27
Chez Papa Bistrot	**Potrero Hill**	23
Chez Papa Resto	**SoMa**	24
Chez Spencer	**Mission**	25
Chez TJ	**Mtn View/S**	24
Cliff House	**Outer Rich**	18
Coi	**N Beach**	26
Z Commis	**Oakland/E**	27
Cuvée	**Napa/N**	22
Z Cyrus	**Healdsburg/N**	28
Dry Creek	**Healdsburg/N**	24
Duck Club	**Lafayette/E**	20
Ecco	**Burlingame/S**	23
Erna's	**Oakhurst/E**	27
Z Esin	**Danville/E**	25
Espetus	**Hayes Valley**	22
Étoile	**Yountville/N**	25
Eve	**Berkeley/E**	25
Z Farallon	**Downtown**	24
Firefly	**Noe Valley**	25
Z Fleur de Lys	**Downtown**	27
Z French Laundry	**Yountville/N**	29
Garibaldis	**Presidio Hts**	22
Z Gary Danko	**Fish. Wharf**	29
Girl & the Fig	**Sonoma/N**	23
Grand Cafe	**Downtown**	19
Grand Pu Bah	**Potrero Hill**	19
Grasing's Coastal	**Carmel/S**	23
Great China	**Berkeley/E**	24
Z Greens	**Marina**	24
Hana	**Rohnert Pk/N**	25
Hurley's	**Yountville/N**	21
Hyde St. Bistro	**Russian Hill**	21
Indigo	**Civic Ctr**	20
Isa	**Marina**	26
Isobune	**Burlingame/S**	19
Z Jardinière	**Civic Ctr**	26
Jimmy Beans	**Berkeley/E**	20
Jin Sho	**Palo Alto/S**	23
Junnoon	**Palo Alto/S**	22
Kyo-Ya	**Downtown**	23
Z La Forêt	**San Jose/S**	27
Lark Creek Steak	**Downtown**	23
La Scene	**Downtown**	19
La Terrasse	**Presidio**	17
La Toque	**Napa/N**	26
Lavanda	**Palo Alto/S**	20
Le Charm Bistro	**SoMa**	23
Ledford Hse.	**Albion/N**	23
Z Le Papillon	**San Jose/S**	27
Le P'tit Laurent	**Glen Pk**	23
MacCallum	**Mendocino/N**	24
Z Madrona	**Healdsburg/N**	27
Z Manresa	**Los Gatos/S**	28
Mantra	**Palo Alto/S**	21
MarketBar	**Embarcadero**	16
Z Masa's	**Downtown**	28
Z Meadowood Rest.	**St. Helena/N**	28
Metro	**Lafayette/E**	21
Mezze	**Oakland/E**	23
Millennium	**Downtown**	25
MoMo's	**S Beach**	18
Navio	**Half Moon Bay/S**	25
One Market	**Embarcadero**	24
Z Pacific's Edge	**Carmel/S**	24
Palio d'Asti	**Downtown**	20
Parcel 104	**Santa Clara/S**	23
Piperade	**Downtown**	25
Plouf	**Downtown**	21
Z Plumed Horse	**Saratoga/S**	26
Postrio	**Downtown**	23
Rick & Ann	**Berkeley/E**	21
Risibisi	**Petaluma/N**	20
Ritz-Carlton	**Nob Hill**	-
Roy's	**SoMa**	23
Saison	**Mission**	26
Sanraku	**Downtown**	22
Z Santé	**Sonoma/N**	26
Scala's Bistro	**Downtown**	21
Z Scoma's	**Fish. Wharf**	23
Z Seasons	**Downtown**	24
Sens	**Downtown**	17
Sent Sovi	**Saratoga/S**	23
Z Sierra Mar	**Big Sur/S**	27
Silks	**Downtown**	23
Z Slanted Door	**Embarcadero**	25
South Park	**SoMa**	22
St. Orres	**Gualala/N**	23
Table 128	**Boonville/N**	-
Tarpy's	**Monterey/S**	20
Tommy Toy	**Downtown**	23
Ton Kiang	**Outer Rich**	23
Town's End	**Embarcadero**	21
231 Ellsworth	**San Mateo/S**	23
Unicorn	**Downtown**	22
Vik's Chaat	**Berkeley/E**	23
Waterbar	**Embarcadero**	21
Waterfront	**Embarcadero**	20
Zazie	**Cole Valley**	23
Zibibbo	**Palo Alto/S**	19

SPECIAL FEATURES

QUIET CONVERSATION

- ☑ Acquerello | **Polk Gulch** 28
- Alexander's | **multi.** 26
- Applewood Inn | **Guerneville/N** 25
- Arcadia | **San Jose/S** 20
- 🆕 Atelier Crenn | **Marina** 26
- ☑ Auberge/Soleil | **Rutherford/N** 27
- ☑ Aubergine | **Carmel/S** 28
- ☑ Baumé | **Palo Alto/S** 27
- ☑ BayWolf | **Oakland/E** 26
- Bella Vista | **Woodside/S** 22
- Bushi-tei | **Japantown** 22
- Cafe Jacqueline | **N Beach** 26
- Campton Place | **Downtown** 25
- Casanova | **Carmel/S** 23
- Chantilly | **Redwood City/S** 25
- ☑ Chez Panisse | **Berkeley/E** 28
- Chez TJ | **Mtn View/S** 24
- ☑ Cyrus | **Healdsburg/N** 28
- Duck Club | **multi.** 20
- Ecco | **Burlingame/S** 23
- Estate | **Sonoma/N** 21
- ☑ Farmhse. Inn | **Forestville/N** 27
- Fifth Floor | **SoMa** 23
- Five | **Berkeley/E** 20
- Flea St. Café | **Menlo Pk/S** 26
- ☑ Fleur de Lys | **Downtown** 27
- Forbes Mill | **multi.** 22
- ☑ Gary Danko | **Fish. Wharf** 29
- Kyo-Ya | **Downtown** 23
- Lalime's | **Berkeley/E** 25
- L'Ardoise | **Castro** 24
- La Toque | **Napa/N** 26
- ☑ Le Papillon | **San Jose/S** 27
- Lovejoy's Tea | **Noe Valley** 20
- Luce | **SoMa** 21
- ☑ Madrona | **Healdsburg/N** 27
- ☑ Manresa | **Los Gatos/S** 28
- Manzanita | **Truckee/E** 23
- Marché/Fleurs | **Ross/N** 25
- ☑ Masa's | **Downtown** 28
- ☑ Meadowood Rest. | **St. Helena/N** 28
- Mescolanza | **Outer Rich** 23
- Morton's | **San Jose/S** 23
- Moss Room | **Inner Rich** 22
- Murray Circle | **Sausalito/N** 24
- O Chamé | **Berkeley/E** 24
- ☑ Pacific's Edge | **Carmel/S** 24
- ☑ Plumed Horse | **Saratoga/S** 26
- Postino | **Lafayette/E** 22
- Quattro | **E Palo Alto/S** 22
- ☑ Quince | **Downtown** 26
- Rest./Ventana | **Big Sur/S** 21
- Richmond Rest. | **Inner Rich** 24
- Scott's | **Palo Alto/S** 20
- ☑ Seasons | **Downtown** 24
- Silks | **Downtown** 23
- Solbar | **Calistoga/N** 26
- Soule Domain | **Kings Bch/E** 24
- St. Orres | **Gualala/N** 23
- Urban Tavern | **Downtown** 16
- Zaré/Fly Trap | **SoMa** 22

RAW BARS

- ☑ Absinthe | **Hayes Valley** 22
- Ame | **SoMa** 26
- Anchor Oyster | **Castro** 25
- Bar Crudo | **W Addition** 25
- ☑ Bouchon | **Yountville/N** 25
- 🆕 Boxing Rm. | **Hayes Valley** –
- Café des Amis | **Cow Hollow** 19
- Café Rouge | **Berkeley/E** 22
- Central Market | **Petaluma/N** 22
- 🆕 Chotto | **Marina** 24
- Cliff House | **Outer Rich** 18
- Dragonfly | **Truckee/E** 22
- El Dorado | **Sonoma/N** 22
- ☑ Farallon | **Downtown** 24
- Fish Story | **Napa/N** 18
- Fog City Diner | **Embarcadero** 18
- ☑ Foreign Cinema | **Mission** 24
- Fresca | **Noe Valley** 22
- Georges | **Downtown** 19
- Grand Cafe | **Downtown** 19
- Grand Pu Bah | **Potrero Hill** 19
- Hog & Rocks | **Mission** 21
- ☑ Hog Island | **multi.** 25
- 🆕 Ichi Sushi | **Bernal Hts** 23
- 🆕 Ki | **SoMa** –
- Lake Chalet | **Oakland/E** 14
- Luka's Taproom | **Oakland/E** 20
- Meritage Martini | **Sonoma/N** 22
- Metro | **Lafayette/E** 21
- Monti's | **Santa Rosa/N** 20
- Nick's Cove | **Marshall/N** 19
- Pesce | **Russian Hill** 25
- Rocker Oyster | **Valley Ford/N** 21
- Sam's Chowder | **Half Moon Bay/S** 20
- ☑ Slanted Door | **Embarcadero** 25
- Station House | **Pt Reyes/N** 18
- ☑ Sushi Ran | **Sausalito/N** 28
- ☑ Sutro's | **Outer Rich** 22
- ☑ Swan Oyster | **Polk Gulch** 27
- Tataki | **Noe Valley** 24

Waterbar	**Embarcadero**	21
Wayfare Tav.	**Downtown**	22
Willi's Seafood	**Healdsburg/N**	24
Wine Spectator	**St. Helena/N**	21
Woodhse.	**Castro**	21
Yankee Pier	**multi.**	18
Zibibbo	**Palo Alto/S**	19
☑ Zuni Café	**Hayes Valley**	25

ROMANTIC PLACES

☑ Acquerello	**Polk Gulch**	28
☑ Ahwahnee	**Yosemite/E**	18
Albion River Inn	**Albion/N**	23
Alexander's	**Cupertino/S**	26
☑ Amber India	**SoMa**	24
Ana Mandara	**Fish. Wharf**	21
Anton/Michel	**Carmel/S**	23
Applewood Inn	**Guerneville/N**	25
☑ Auberge/Soleil	**Rutherford/N**	27
☑ Aubergine	**Carmel/S**	28
☑ Aziza	**Outer Rich**	26
Barndiva	**Healdsburg/N**	23
☑ Baumé	**Palo Alto/S**	27
Bella Vista	**Woodside/S**	22
☑ Big 4	**Nob Hill**	23
Bistro Central Parc	**W Addition**	24
☑ Bistro/Copains	**Occidental/N**	27
☑ Bix	**Downtown**	24
☑ Bottega	**Yountville/N**	25
☑ Boulevard	**Embarcadero**	27
Brix	**Napa/N**	23
Bushi-tei	**Japantown**	22
Cafe Beaujolais	**Mendocino/N**	25
Cafe Jacqueline	**N Beach**	26
Candybar	**W Addition**	20
Caprice	**Tiburon/N**	22
Casanova	**Carmel/S**	23
Chantilly	**Redwood City/S**	25
☑ Chapeau!	**Inner Rich**	26
☑ Chez Panisse	**Berkeley/E**	28
Chez Papa Resto	**SoMa**	24
Chez Spencer	**Mission**	25
Chez TJ	**Mtn View/S**	24
Christy Hill	**Tahoe City/E**	22
Coi	**N Beach**	26
Cool Café	**Stanford/S**	20
☑ Cyrus	**Healdsburg/N**	28
Deetjen's Big Sur	**Big Sur/S**	23
Donato	**Redwood City/S**	22
Duck Club	**multi.**	20
Ecco	**Burlingame/S**	23
☑ Erna's	**Oakhurst/E**	27
Estate	**Sonoma/N**	21
Étoile	**Yountville/N**	25

☑ Farmhse. Inn	**Forestville/N**	27
Fifth Floor	**SoMa**	23
Flea St. Café	**Menlo Pk/S**	26
☑ Fleur de Lys	**Downtown**	27
Forbes Island	**Fish. Wharf**	15
☑ French Laundry	**Yountville/N**	29
Gabriella Café	**Santa Cruz/S**	22
☑ Garden Ct.	**Downtown**	19
☑ Gary Danko	**Fish. Wharf**	29
Gitane	**Downtown**	23
Harvest Moon	**Sonoma/N**	24
Incanto	**Noe Valley**	25
Indigo	**Civic Ctr**	20
☑ Jardinière	**Civic Ctr**	26
John Ash	**Santa Rosa/N**	24
Katia's Tea	**Inner Rich**	20
Khan Toke	**Outer Rich**	21
La Corneta	**Burlingame/S**	21
La Costanera	**Montara/S**	21
☑ La Folie	**Russian Hill**	28
☑ La Forêt	**San Jose/S**	27
Lalime's	**Berkeley/E**	25
La Mar	**Embarcadero**	25
La Note	**Berkeley/E**	22
L'Ardoise	**Castro**	24
La Toque	**Napa/N**	26
☑ Le Papillon	**San Jose/S**	27
Little River Inn	**Little River/N**	22
Luce	**SoMa**	21
MacCallum	**Mendocino/N**	24
Madera	**Menlo Pk/S**	22
☑ Madrona	**Healdsburg/N**	27
Ma Maison	**Aptos/S**	24
Mantra	**Palo Alto/S**	21
Manzanita	**Truckee/E**	23
Marché/Fleurs	**Ross/N**	25
☑ Marinus	**Carmel Valley/S**	27
☑ Masa's	**Downtown**	28
Matterhorn Swiss	**Russian Hill**	22
☑ Meadowood Rest.	**St. Helena/N**	28
Moosse Café	**Mendocino/N**	22
Moss Room	**Inner Rich**	22
Murray Circle	**Sausalito/N**	24
Napa Wine Train	**Napa/N**	18
Nick's Cove	**Marshall/N**	19
O Chamé	**Berkeley/E**	24
Olema Inn	**Olema/N**	18
Ozumo	**Oakland/E**	23
☑ Pacific's Edge	**Carmel/S**	24
Pampas	**Palo Alto/S**	22
Peasant & the Pear	**Danville/E**	22
Pianeta	**Truckee/E**	24
Picco	**Larkspur/N**	25

Quince	Downtown	26
Rest./Stevenswood	Little River/N	21
Rest./Ventana	Big Sur/S	21
Risibisi	Petaluma/N	20
Ritz-Carlton	Nob Hill	-
Roy's	Pebble Bch/S	24
Sea Salt	Berkeley/E	21
Sent Sovi	Saratoga/S	23
71 St. Peter	San Jose/S	20
Shadowbrook	Capitola/S	18
Shokolaat	Palo Alto/S	17
Sierra Mar	Big Sur/S	27
Silks	Downtown	23
Slow Club	Mission	22
Solbar	Calistoga/N	26
Soule Domain	Kings Bch/E	24
Starlight	Sebastopol/N	22
St. Michael's	Palo Alto/S	22
St. Orres	Gualala/N	23
Sunnyside	Tahoe City/E	18
Tav./Lark Creek	Larkspur/N	20
Terra	St. Helena/N	27
Terzo	Cow Hollow	24
1300/Fillmore	W Addition	21
NEW 25 Lusk	SoMa	20
Venticello	Nob Hill	23
Viognier	San Mateo/S	23
Wente Vineyards	Livermore/E	24
Wild Goose	Tahoe Vista/E	23
Wolfdale's	Tahoe City/E	24
Woodward's Gdn.	Mission	24
Zarzuela	Russian Hill	24

SENIOR APPEAL

Acquerello	Polk Gulch	28
Alexander's	SoMa	26
Alfred's Steak	Downtown	23
Alioto's	Fish. Wharf	18
Anton/Michel	Carmel/S	23
Baker/Banker	Upper Fillmore	25
Baumé	Palo Alto/S	27
Bella Vista	Woodside/S	22
Big 4	Nob Hill	23
NEW Bourbon	Downtown	24
Caprice	Tiburon/N	22
Chantilly	Redwood City/S	25
Christy Hill	Tahoe City/E	22
Cole's Chop	Napa/N	25
Cook St. Helena	St. Helena/N	26
Cyrus	Healdsburg/N	28
Duck Club	multi.	20
Epic Roasthse.	Embarcadero	21
Estate	Sonoma/N	21

Fior d'Italia	N Beach	18
Fleur de Lys	Downtown	27
Forbes Mill	multi.	22
Garden Ct.	Downtown	19
Harris'	Polk Gulch	26
Hayes St. Grill	Hayes Valley	23
House/Prime	Polk Gulch	25
Izzy's Steak	Marina	20
La Ginestra	Mill Valley/N	19
Lalime's	Berkeley/E	25
LB Steak	San Jose/S	20
Le Central Bistro	Downtown	21
Manzanita	Truckee/E	23
Masa's	Downtown	28
Meadowood Rest.	St. Helena/N	28
Morton's	multi.	23
North Bch. Rest.	N Beach	22
Plumed Horse	Saratoga/S	26
Rest./Ventana	Big Sur/S	21
Rotunda	Downtown	22
Sardine Factory	Monterey/S	21
Scoma's	Fish. Wharf	23
Sens	Downtown	17
Solbar	Calistoga/N	26
Soule Domain	Kings Bch/E	24
Tadich Grill	Downtown	23
Urban Tavern	Downtown	16
Vic Stewart	Walnut Creek/E	22
Waterbar	Embarcadero	21
Wayfare Tav.	Downtown	22
Zaré/Fly Trap	SoMa	22

SINGLES SCENES

Ace Wasabi's	Marina	19
Anchor & Hope	SoMa	21
Andalu	Mission	21
Balboa Cafe	multi.	19
Barbacco	Downtown	24
Barlata	Oakland/E	21
Barndiva	Healdsburg/N	23
Beach Chalet	Outer Sunset	15
Beretta	Mission	22
Betelnut Pejiu	Cow Hollow	21
Bix	Downtown	24
Blowfish Sushi	Mission	20
Blue Plate	Mission	24
NEW Brixton	Cow Hollow	17
Broken Record	Excelsior	25
Butterfly	Embarcadero	21
Cafe Bastille	Downtown	18
Café Claude	Downtown	21
Café Flore	Castro	18
Cannery/Brew	Monterey/S	17

Cascal | **Mtn View/S**	21
Catch | **Castro**	18
Cha Cha | **multi.**	20
NEW Chambers | **Tenderloin**	–
Cheese Steak Shop | **Concord/E**	20
Comstock | **N Beach**	16
Cosmopolitan | **SoMa**	18
Cottonwood | **Truckee/E**	26
Davenport | **Davenport/S**	16
NEW Disco Volante | **Oakland/E**	–
Dosa | **Upper Fillmore**	22
Dragonfly | **Truckee/E**	22
E&O Trading | **Downtown**	20
Elite Cafe | **Pacific Hts**	19
Emmy's Spaghetti | **Bernal Hts**	20
15 Romolo | **N Beach**	20
5A5 Steak | **Downtown**	23
Flora | **Oakland/E**	21
Z Foreign Cinema | **Mission**	24
Frjtz Fries | **multi.**	17
Gar Woods | **Carnelian Bay/E**	17
Georges | **Downtown**	19
Gitane | **Downtown**	23
Gordon Biersch | **multi.**	15
Grand Pu Bah | **Potrero Hill**	19
Guaymas | **Tiburon/N**	17
Half Moon Brew | **Half Moon Bay/S**	16
Heart | **Mission**	19
Heaven's Dog | **SoMa**	20
Hog & Rocks | **Mission**	21
Hopmonk Tav. | **Sebastopol/N**	18
Hula's | **multi.**	18
Ironside | **S Beach**	17
Jake's/Lake | **Tahoe City/E**	18
Joya | **Palo Alto/S**	21
Junnoon | **Palo Alto/S**	22
La Trappe | **N Beach**	16
Local Kitchen | **SoMa**	18
Luce | **SoMa**	21
Luna Park | **Mission**	19
Magnolia | **Haight-Ashbury**	20
Marlowe | **SoMa**	23
Martins West | **Redwood City/S**	22
Miss Pearl's | **Oakland/E**	18
MoMo's | **S Beach**	18
Monk's Kettle | **Mission**	20
Moody's Bistro | **Truckee/E**	25
Nettie's Crab | **Cow Hollow**	18
Nihon | **Mission**	19
Orson | **SoMa**	18
Ottimista | **Cow Hollow**	19
Ozumo | **multi.**	23
Poesia | **Castro**	21

Quattro | **E Palo Alto/S**	22
Rose Pistola | **N Beach**	21
Serpentine | **Dogpatch**	22
Sino | **San Jose/S**	19
Slow Club | **Mission**	22
Starbelly | **Castro**	21
Sunnyside | **Tahoe City/E**	18
Sushi Groove | **multi.**	21
Tipsy Pig | **Marina**	18
Tokyo Go Go | **Mission**	20
Tommy's Mex. | **Outer Rich**	15
Tres | **S Beach**	17
Tsunami | **W Addition**	21
Z NEW 25 Lusk | **SoMa**	20
2223 | **Castro**	22
Umami | **Cow Hollow**	24
Universal Cafe | **Mission**	24
Xanh | **Mtn View/S**	21
Zibibbo | **Palo Alto/S**	19
Z Zuni Café | **Hayes Valley**	25

SLEEPERS

(Good food, but little known)

Broken Record | **Excelsior**	24
Café Fiore | **S Lake Tahoe/E**	24
Carneros Bistro | **Sonoma/N**	24
Cellar Door Café | **Santa Cruz/S**	26
Cottonwood | **Truckee/E**	26
Domo Sushi | **Hayes Valley**	24
Eiji | **Castro**	26
El Porteno | **Loc varies**	24
Emilia's | **Berkeley/E**	27
Evan's | **S Lake Tahoe/E**	27
Fivetenburger | **Loc varies**	25
Golden West | **Downtown**	24
Grandeho Kamekyo | **Fish. Wharf**	25
Hakka Restaurant | **Outer Rich**	24
Incontro | **San Ramon/E**	24
Jai Yun | **Chinatown**	26
Jole | **Calistoga/N**	27
Kappou Gomi | **Outer Rich**	28
Kiji Sushi Bar | **Mission**	25
Kitchenette SF | **Dogpatch**	24
La Posta | **Santa Cruz/S**	26
Ma Maison | **Aptos/S**	24
Marica | **Oakland/E**	27
Moki's Sushi | **Bernal Hts**	26
Moody's Bistro | **Truckee/E**	25
Mr. Pollo | **Mission**	24
Mundaka | **Carmel/S**	24
Osake | **Santa Rosa/N**	24
Oswald | **Santa Cruz/S**	25
Oyaji | **Outer Rich**	24
Pappo | **Alameda/E**	24

SPECIAL FEATURES

Pearl | **Napa/N**	24
Piaci | **Ft Bragg/N**	25
Pianeta | **Truckee/E**	24
Ravens' | **Mendocino/N**	26
Restaurant | **Ft Bragg/N**	25
Rist. Avanti | **Santa Cruz/S**	24
Ryoko's | **Downtown**	24
Saha | **Tenderloin**	26
Sakae Sushi | **Burlingame/S**	26
Soif Wine Bar | **Santa Cruz/S**	25
Soule Domain | **Kings Bch/E**	24
Suriya Thai | **SoMa**	25
Terrapin Creek | **Bodega Bay/N**	25
Vitrine | **SoMa**	24
Wakuriya | **San Mateo/S**	27
Z & Y | **Chinatown**	24

TASTING MENUS

Z Acquerello | **Polk Gulch**	28
Alexander's | **multi.**	26
Ame | **SoMa**	26
Applewood Inn | **Guerneville/N**	25
Z Auberge/Soleil | **Rutherford/N**	27
Z Aubergine | **Carmel/S**	28
Z Aziza | **Outer Rich**	26
Baker/Banker | **Upper Fillmore**	25
Bardessono | **Yountville/N**	21
Benu | **SoMa**	26
Bushi-tei | **Japantown**	22
Z Cafe Gibraltar | **El Granada/S**	26
Z Chevalier | **Lafayette/E**	25
Chez Spencer | **Mission**	25
Chez TJ | **Mtn View/S**	24
Z Club XIX | **Pebble Bch/S**	23
Coi | **N Beach**	26
Commonwealth | **Mission**	24
Contigo | **Noe Valley**	24
Z Cyrus | **Healdsburg/N**	28
Donato | **Redwood City/S**	22
Dosa | **multi.**	22
Dragonfly | **Truckee/E**	22
Dry Creek | **Healdsburg/N**	24
Ecco | **Burlingame/S**	23
El Dorado | **Sonoma/N**	22
Estate | **Sonoma/N**	21
Étoile | **Yountville/N**	25
Z Farallon | **Downtown**	24
Fifth Floor | **SoMa**	23
Frantoio | **Mill Valley/N**	20
Z French Laundry | **Yountville/N**	29
Z Gary Danko | **Fish. Wharf**	29
Hana | **Rohnert Pk/N**	25
NEW Ichi Sushi | **Bernal Hts**	23
Z Jardinière | **Civic Ctr**	26

Juban | **multi.**	18
Kanpai | **Palo Alto/S**	22
Z Kaygetsu | **Menlo Pk/S**	27
Kiji Sushi Bar | **Mission**	25
Z Kiss Seafood | **Japantown**	28
Koi | **Daly City/S**	24
Z La Folie | **Russian Hill**	28
Z La Forêt | **San Jose/S**	27
La Toque | **Napa/N**	26
Z Le Papillon | **San Jose/S**	27
MacCallum | **Mendocino/N**	24
Z Madrona | **Healdsburg/N**	27
Z Manresa | **Los Gatos/S**	28
Z Marinus | **Carmel Valley/S**	27
Z Masa's | **Downtown**	28
Z Meadowood Rest. | **St. Helena/N**	28
Meritage/Claremont | **Berkeley/E**	25
Meritage Martini | **Sonoma/N**	22
Z NEW Michael Mina | **Downtown**	26
Millennium | **Downtown**	25
Mr. Pollo | **Mission**	24
Murray Circle | **Sausalito/N**	24
Navio | **Half Moon Bay/S**	25
One Market | **Embarcadero**	24
Ozumo | **Embarcadero**	23
Z Pacific's Edge | **Carmel/S**	24
Z Plumed Horse | **Saratoga/S**	26
PlumpJack | **Olympic Valley/E**	23
Postrio | **Downtown**	23
Prima | **Walnut Creek/E**	24
Quattro | **E Palo Alto/S**	22
Z Redd | **Yountville/N**	27
Richmond Rest. | **Inner Rich**	24
Ritz-Carlton | **Nob Hill**	-
Saison | **Mission**	26
Sakae Sushi | **Burlingame/S**	26
Sakoon | **Mtn View/S**	23
Sanraku | **Downtown**	22
Z Santé | **Sonoma/N**	26
Z Seasons | **Downtown**	24
Sent Sovi | **Saratoga/S**	23
Silks | **Downtown**	23
Soif Wine Bar | **Santa Cruz/S**	25
Tommy Toy | **Downtown**	23
231 Ellsworth | **San Mateo/S**	23
Vanessa's Bistro | **Berkeley/E**	23
Viognier | **San Mateo/S**	23

TEEN APPEAL

NEW Addie's | **Berkeley/E**	21
Amici's | **multi.**	20
Asqew Grill | **Laurel Hts**	17
Barney's | **multi.**	19

Beach Chalet | **Outer Sunset**	15
Buca di Beppo | **multi.**	15
Burger Bar | **Downtown**	19
Burger Joint | **Mission**	18
BurgerMeister | **multi.**	20
Cactus Taqueria | **multi.**	20
Cheesecake | **multi.**	17
Ebisu | **S San Francisco/S**	24
El Tonayense | **multi.**	24
FatApple's | **multi.**	18
Fentons | **Oakland/E**	20
Fog City Diner | **Embarcadero**	18
Fremont Diner | **Sonoma/N**	21
Gar Woods | **Carnelian Bay/E**	17
NEW Guamenkitzel | **Berkeley/E**	-
Goat Hill Pizza | **Potrero Hill**	18
Gott's Roadside | **St. Helena/N**	21
NEW Hecho | **Downtown**	-
Hula's | **multi.**	18
Jake's/Lake | **Tahoe City/E**	18
Jake's Steaks | **Marina**	19
Joe's Cable Car | **Excelsior**	19
La Corneta | **multi.**	21
Lanesplitter | **Oakland/E**	17
Little Chihuahua | **W Addition**	21
MacArthur Pk. | **Palo Alto/S**	17
Max's | **multi.**	17
Mel's Drive-In | **multi.**	13
Mijita | **S Beach**	19
Miller's Deli | **Polk Gulch**	20
Park Chalet | **Outer Sunset**	15
Pasta Pomodoro | **multi.**	16
Patxi's Pizza | **Cow Hollow**	22
Pauline's | **Mission**	23
Piaci | **Ft Bragg/N**	25
Pi Bar | **Mission**	18
Picante Cocina | **Berkeley/E**	23
Pizza Antica | **Lafayette/E**	20
Pizza Nostra | **Potrero Hill**	19
Z Pizzeria Picco | **Larkspur/N**	27
Plant Cafe Organic | **Marina**	21
Rosso Pizzeria | **Santa Rosa/N**	25
Rudy's | **Emeryville/E**	20
Rutherford Grill | **Rutherford/N**	23
Sardine Factory | **Monterey/S**	21
Shen Hua | **Berkeley/E**	22
Stinking Rose | **N Beach**	18
NEW Straw | **Hayes Valley**	-
Sunnyside | **Tahoe City/E**	18
Super Duper | **Castro**	21
TacoBar | **Pacific Hts**	17
Tacolicious | **multi.**	22
Tonga Rm. | **Nob Hill**	13
Trueburger | **Oakland/E**	20

THEME RESTAURANTS

Benihana | **multi.**	17
Buca di Beppo | **multi.**	15
Hula's | **multi.**	18
Max's | **multi.**	17
Miss Pearl's | **Oakland/E**	18
Napa Wine Train | **Napa/N**	18
Stinking Rose | **N Beach**	18

TRENDY

Ace Wasabi's | **Marina**	19
Z À Côté | **Oakland/E**	24
Adesso | **Oakland/E**	24
Anchor & Hope | **SoMa**	21
Z A16 | **Marina**	24
Balboa Cafe | **Cow Hollow**	19
Bar Agricole | **SoMa**	21
Barndiva | **Healdsburg/N**	23
Bar Tartine | **Mission**	24
Beretta | **Mission**	22
Betelnut Pejiu | **Cow Hollow**	23
Bistro Don Giovanni | **Napa/N**	24
Z Bix | **Downtown**	24
Blowfish Sushi | **Mission**	21
Bocadillos | **N Beach**	23
Boot/Shoe | **Oakland/E**	24
Z Bottega | **Yountville/N**	25
Z Bouchon | **Yountville/N**	25
Bungalow 44 | **Mill Valley/N**	21
Café des Amis | **Cow Hollow**	19
Café Flore | **Castro**	17
Café Rouge | **Berkeley/E**	22
Cascal | **Mtn View/S**	21
César | **Berkeley/E**	22
Cha Cha | **multi.**	20
Charanga | **Mission**	21
Chaya | **Embarcadero**	20
Coco500 | **SoMa**	24
Z Commis | **Oakland/E**	27
Commonwealth | **Mission**	24
Delarosa | **Marina**	22
Z Delfina | **Mission**	26
NEW Disco Volante | **Oakland/E**	-
Doña Tomás | **Oakland/E**	22
Dosa | **multi.**	22
Emmy's Spaghetti | **Bernal Hts**	20
Farina | **Mission**	23
15 Romolo | **N Beach**	20
5A5 Steak | **Downtown**	23
Flora | **Oakland/E**	21
Z Flour + Water | **Mission**	24
Fonda Solana | **Albany/E**	23
Z Foreign Cinema | **Mission**	24

SPECIAL FEATURES

Front Porch | **Bernal Hts** 20
Gitane | **Downtown** 23
Grand Pu Bah | **Potrero Hill** 19
Heart | **Mission** 19
Heaven's Dog | **SoMa** 20
Hog & Rocks | **Mission** 21
Hopmonk Tav. | **Sebastopol/N** 18
Z Jardinière | **Civic Ctr** 26
NEW Jones | **Tenderloin** –
Joya | **Palo Alto/S** 21
Junnoon | **Palo Alto/S** 22
NEW Ki | **SoMa** –
Limón | **Mission** 22
Mamacita | **Marina** 22
Mantra | **Palo Alto/S** 21
Maverick | **Mission** 24
Miss Pearl's | **Oakland/E** 18
Morph | **Outer Rich** –
Z Mustards | **Yountville/N** 25
Naked Fish | **S Lake Tahoe/E** 23
Nihon | **Mission** 19
Z Nopa | **W Addition** 25
Orson | **SoMa** 18
Osha Thai | **multi.** 21
Ottimista | **Cow Hollow** 19
Ozumo | **multi.** 23
Piazza D'Angelo | **Mill Valley/N** 20
Picán | **Oakland/E** 22
Picco | **Larkspur/N** 25
Pizzeria Delfina | **Mission** 25
Z Pizzeria Picco | **Larkspur/N** 27
Postrio | **Downtown** 23
Revival Bar | **Berkeley/E** 20
Salt House | **SoMa** 21
Sebo | **Hayes Valley** 26
Serpentine | **Dogpatch** 22
Sidebar | **Oakland/E** 22
Sino | **San Jose/S** 19
Z Slanted Door | **Embarcadero** 25
Slow Club | **Mission** 22
Social Kit. | **Inner Sunset** 15
Spork | **Mission** 20
SPQR | **Pacific Hts** 24
Starbelly | **Castro** 21
Sushi Groove | **multi.** 21
Tamarine | **Palo Alto/S** 26
Terzo | **Cow Hollow** 24
1300/Fillmore | **W Addition** 21
Tipsy Pig | **Marina** 18
Town Hall | **SoMa** 22
Trattoria Corso | **Berkeley/E** 24
Tres | **S Beach** 17
Tsunami | **W Addition** 21
Z NEW 25 Lusk | **SoMa** 20

Umami | **Cow Hollow** 24
Underwood Bar | **Graton/N** 23
Waterbar | **Embarcadero** 21
Z Wood Tavern | **Oakland/E** 26
Xanh | **Mtn View/S** 21
Yoshi's SF | **W Addition** 21
Zibibbo | **Palo Alto/S** 19
Z Zuni Café | **Hayes Valley** 25
ZuZu | **Napa/N** 25

VALET PARKING

Z Absinthe | **Hayes Valley** 22
Z Ahwahnee | **Yosemite/E** 18
Albona Rist. | **N Beach** 25
Amber Bistro | **Danville/E** 21
Ame | **SoMa** 26
Americano | **Embarcadero** 18
Ana Mandara | **Fish. Wharf** 21
Andalu | **Mission** 21
Anzu | **Downtown** 22
Aquarius | **Santa Cruz/S** 21
Arcadia | **San Jose/S** 20
Z Auberge/Soleil | **Rutherford/N** 27
Z Aubergine | **Carmel/S** 28
Z Aziza | **Outer Rich** 26
Baker/Banker | **Upper Fillmore** 25
Balboa Cafe | **Cow Hollow** 19
Z Barbacco | **Downtown** 24
Bardessono | **Yountville/N** 21
Benihana | **Burlingame/S** 17
Z Big 4 | **Nob Hill** 23
Z Bix | **Downtown** 24
Blowfish Sushi | **San Jose/S** 21
Boccalone | **Embarcadero** 26
Z Boulevard | **Embarcadero** 27
NEW Bourbon | **Downtown** 24
NEW Branches | **Ukiah/N** –
Bridges | **Danville/E** 23
Z Buckeye | **Mill Valley/N** 24
Café des Amis | **Cow Hollow** 19
Campton Place | **Downtown** 25
Cantinetta Luca | **Carmel/S** 21
Casa Orinda | **Orinda/E** 18
Cha Am Thai | **SoMa** 19
Chantilly | **Redwood City/S** 25
Chaya | **Embarcadero** 20
Cheesecake | **Santa Clara/S** 17
Cliff House | **Outer Rich** 18
Z Club XIX | **Pebble Bch/S** 23
Coi | **N Beach** 26
Cole's Chop | **Napa/N** 25
Cotogna | **Downtown** 26
Crustacean | **Polk Gulch** 24
NEW Cupola Pizzeria | **Downtown** –

Delancey St. | **Embarcadero**	18
Delica | **Embarcadero**	21
Dio Deka | **Los Gatos/S**	26
Donato | **Redwood City/S**	22
Duck Club | **Lafayette/E**	20
Elite Cafe | **Pacific Hts**	19
Epic Roasthse. | **Embarcadero**	21
🛿 Evvia | **Palo Alto/S**	27
🛿 Farallon | **Downtown**	24
Farina | **Mission**	23
Fifth Floor | **SoMa**	23
Fior d'Italia | **N Beach**	18
Fish & Farm | **Downtown**	20
Five | **Berkeley/E**	20
5A5 Steak | **Downtown**	23
🛿 Fleur de Lys | **Downtown**	27
Florio | **Pacific Hts**	19
🛿 Foreign Cinema | **Mission**	24
Garibaldis | **Presidio Hts**	22
🛿 Gary Danko | **Fish. Wharf**	29
Grand Cafe | **Downtown**	19
Harris' | **Polk Gulch**	26
Hayes St. Grill | **Hayes Valley**	23
🛿 House/Prime | **Polk Gulch**	25
Hunan | **Chinatown**	22
Il Fornaio | **multi.**	20
Insalata's | **San Anselmo/N**	24
🛿 Jardinière | **Civic Ctr**	26
NEW Jasper's Corner | **Downtown**	-
🛿 Kokkari | **Downtown**	27
Kuleto's | **Downtown**	21
Kyo-Ya | **Downtown**	23
🛿 La Folie | **Russian Hill**	28
La Scene | **Downtown**	19
La Toque | **Napa/N**	26
LB Steak | **San Jose/S**	20
LCX/Le Cheval | **Oakland/E**	20
Lion/Compass | **Sunnyvale/S**	21
Luce | **SoMa**	21
MacArthur Pk. | **Palo Alto/S**	17
Manzanita | **Truckee/E**	23
Marinitas | **San Anselmo/N**	20
🛿 Marinus | **Carmel Valley/S**	27
🛿 Masa's | **Downtown**	28
Matterhorn Swiss | **Russian Hill**	22
Maykadeh | **N Beach**	23
Meritage/Claremont | **Berkeley/E**	25
Mexico DF | **Embarcadero**	20
🛿**NEW** Michael Mina | **Downtown**	26
Millennium | **Downtown**	25
Miss Pearl's | **Oakland/E**	18
MoMo's | **S Beach**	18
Morton's | **multi.**	23
Navio | **Half Moon Bay/S**	25
North Bch. Rest. | **N Beach**	22
O Izakaya | **Japantown**	18
One Market | **Embarcadero**	24
NEW Osteria Coppa | **San Mateo/S**	24
Ozumo | **Embarcadero**	23
🛿 Pacific's Edge | **Carmel/S**	24
Parcel 104 | **Santa Clara/S**	23
🛿 Perbacco | **Downtown**	25
Picco | **Larkspur/N**	25
🛿 Pizzeria Picco | **Larkspur/N**	27
🛿 Plumed Horse | **Saratoga/S**	26
Poggio | **Sausalito/N**	23
Postino | **Lafayette/E**	22
Postrio | **Downtown**	23
Prima | **Walnut Creek/E**	24
Prospect | **SoMa**	24
Quattro | **E Palo Alto/S**	22
🛿 Quince | **Downtown**	26
Rest. LuLu | **SoMa**	19
Rist. Capellini | **San Mateo/S**	20
Ritz-Carlton | **Nob Hill**	-
Rose Pistola | **N Beach**	21
Roy's | **Pebble Bch/S**	24
Ruth's Chris | **multi.**	24
🛿 Santé | **Sonoma/N**	26
🛿 Scoma's | **Fish. Wharf**	23
Scott's | **Walnut Creek/E**	20
🛿 Seasons | **Downtown**	24
🛿 Sierra Mar | **Big Sur/S**	27
Silks | **Downtown**	23
🛿 Slanted Door | **Embarcadero**	25
Solbar | **Calistoga/N**	26
🛿 Spruce | **Presidio Hts**	25
Straits | **Downtown**	20
Sunnyside | **Tahoe City/E**	18
Suppenküche | **Hayes Valley**	22
🛿 Sutro's | **Outer Rich**	22
NEW Table 24 | **Orinda/E**	18
Tav./Lark Creek | **Larkspur/N**	20
Terzo | **Cow Hollow**	24
Thanh Long | **Outer Sunset**	24
Tokyo Go Go | **Mission**	20
Tommy Toy | **Downtown**	23
Townhouse B&G | **Emeryville/E**	21
Trader Vic's | **Emeryville/E**	17
🛿**NEW** 25 Lusk | **SoMa**	20
231 Ellsworth | **San Mateo/S**	23
Ubuntu | **Napa/N**	24
Urban Tavern | **Downtown**	16
Venticello | **Nob Hill**	23
Vitrine | **SoMa**	24

Waterbar | **Embarcadero**	21
Waterfront | **Embarcadero**	20
Wayfare Tav. | **Downtown**	22
Wente Vineyards | **Livermore/E**	24
Wicket's | **Carmel Valley/S**	–
Wine Spectator | **St. Helena/N**	21
Yankee Pier | **multi.**	18
Zibibbo | **Palo Alto/S**	19
☑ Zuni Café | **Hayes Valley**	25

VIEWS

☑ Ahwahnee | **Yosemite/E**	18
Albion River Inn | **Albion/N**	23
Alioto's | **Fish. Wharf**	18
Americano | **Embarcadero**	18
Angèle | **Napa/N**	24
Applewood Inn | **Guerneville/N**	25
Aquarius | **Santa Cruz/S**	21
☑ Auberge/Soleil | **Rutherford/N**	27
Barbara's | **Princeton Sea/S**	21
NEW Bar Bocce | **Sausalito/N**	–
Barndiva | **Healdsburg/N**	23
Beach Chalet | **Outer Sunset**	15
Bella Vista | **Woodside/S**	22
Big Sur | **Big Sur/S**	22
Bistro Boudin | **Fish. Wharf**	20
Bistro Don Giovanni | **Napa/N**	24
Blackhawk Grille | **Danville/E**	20
Boulette Larder | **Embarcadero**	25
Brick/Bottle | **Corte Madera/N**	19
Bridgetender | **Tahoe City/E**	18
Brix | **Napa/N**	23
Butterfly | **Embarcadero**	21
Cafe Beaujolais | **Mendocino/N**	25
Cafe Citti | **Kenwood/N**	22
Café de la Presse | **Downtown**	18
Café des Amis | **Cow Hollow**	19
Cafe Divine | **N Beach**	18
☑ Cafe Gibraltar | **El Granada/S**	26
☑ Cafe La Haye | **Sonoma/N**	27
Café Rustica | **Carmel Valley/S**	24
Café Zitouna | **Polk Gulch**	–
Caprice | **Tiburon/N**	22
Catch | **Castro**	18
C Casa | **Napa/N**	24
Cellar Door Café | **Santa Cruz/S**	26
Chapter & Moon | **Ft Bragg/N**	21
Charanga | **Mission**	21
Chaya | **Embarcadero**	20
Cheesecake | **Downtown**	17
☑ Chevalier | **Lafayette/E**	25
Chez TJ | **Mtn View/S**	24
Christy Hill | **Tahoe City/E**	22
Cliff House | **Outer Rich**	18

☑ Club XIX | **Pebble Bch/S**	23
Cool Café | **Stanford/S**	20
Cottonwood | **Truckee/E**	26
Cucina Paradiso | **Petaluma/N**	25
Cuvée | **Napa/N**	22
Davenport | **Davenport/S**	16
Delancey St. | **Embarcadero**	18
Delica | **Embarcadero**	21
NEW Disco Volante | **Oakland/E**	–
Downtown Bakery | **Healdsburg/N**	25
Dragonfly | **Truckee/E**	22
Drake's | **Inverness/N**	21
Dry Creek | **Healdsburg/N**	24
Duck Club | **multi.**	20
Élevé | **Walnut Creek/E**	21
Eos | **Cole Valley**	23
Epic Roasthse. | **Embarcadero**	21
☑ Erna's | **Oakhurst/E**	27
Étoile | **Yountville/N**	25
Farm | **Napa/N**	24
☑ Farmhse. Inn | **Forestville/N**	27
Fish | **Sausalito/N**	24
Fishwife | **Pacific Grove/S**	20
Flavor | **Santa Rosa/N**	20
Forbes Island | **Fish. Wharf**	15
Frascati | **Russian Hill**	26
Gar Woods | **Carnelian Bay/E**	17
Gordon Biersch | **Embarcadero**	15
☑ Greens | **Marina**	24
Guaymas | **Tiburon/N**	17
Half Moon Brew | **Half Moon Bay/S**	16
☑ Hog Island | **Embarcadero**	25
HRD Coffee | **SoMa**	20
Ike's | **Stanford/S**	24
Il Cane Rosso | **Embarcadero**	23
Il Fornaio | **Carmel/S**	20
Imperial Tea Ct. | **Berkeley/E**	19
Jake's/Lake | **Tahoe City/E**	18
John Ash | **Santa Rosa/N**	24
NEW Jones | **Tenderloin**	–
Kenwood | **Kenwood/N**	23
La Costanera | **Montara/S**	21
Lafitte | **Embarcadero**	20
☑ La Forêt | **San Jose/S**	27
La Mar | **Embarcadero**	25
La Terrasse | **Presidio**	17
Ledford Hse. | **Albion/N**	23
Lion/Compass | **Sunnyvale/S**	21
Little River Inn | **Little River/N**	22
Madera | **Menlo Pk/S**	22
Mama's on Wash. | **N Beach**	25
Manzanita | **Truckee/E**	23

Marinus | **Carmel Valley/S** 27

McCormick/Kuleto | **Fish. Wharf** 20

Meadowood Grill | **St. Helena/N** 22

☒ Meadowood Rest. | 28
St. Helena/N

Melting Pot | **San Mateo/S** 16

Mendo Café | **Mendocino/N** 20

Mendo Hotel | **Mendocino/N** 18

Meritage/Claremont | **Berkeley/E** 25

Mezza Luna | **Princeton Sea/S** 22

Mijita | **Embarcadero** 19

Mistral | **Redwood Shores/S** 20

MoMo's | **S Beach** 18

Moosse Café | **Mendocino/N** 22

Murray Circle | **Sausalito/N** 24

Napa General | **Napa/N** 18

Napa Wine Train | **Napa/N** 18

Navio | **Half Moon Bay/S** 25

Nepenthe | **Big Sur/S** 16

Nick's Cove | **Marshall/N** 19

One Market | **Embarcadero** 24

Ozumo | **Embarcadero** 23

☒ Pacific's Edge | **Carmel/S** 24

Park Chalet | **Outer Sunset** 15

Piatti | **Mill Valley/N** 19

Picco | **Larkspur/N** 25

Press | **St. Helena/N** 24

Ravens' | **Mendocino/N** 26

Red's Java | **Embarcadero** 15

Rest./Stevenswood | 21
Little River/N

Rest./Ventana | **Big Sur/S** 21

☒ Rivoli | **Berkeley/E** 26

☒ Rotunda | **Downtown** 22

Roy's | **Pebble Bch/S** 24

Rustic | **Geyserville/N** 19

Sam's Chowder | 20
Half Moon Bay/S

☒ Scoma's | **multi.** 23

Scott's | **multi.** 20

Shadowbrook | **Capitola/S** 18

☒ Sierra Mar | **Big Sur/S** 27

☒ Slanted Door | **Embarcadero** 25

St. Orres | **Gualala/N** 23

Sunnyside | **Tahoe City/E** 18

☒ Sutro's | **Outer Rich** 22

Tony's Pizza | **N Beach** 25

Trader Vic's | **multi.** 17

Venticello | **Nob Hill** 23

Warming Hut | **Presidio** 14

Waterbar | **Embarcadero** 21

Waterfront | **Embarcadero** 20

Water St. Bistro | **Petaluma/N** 22

Wente Vineyards | **Livermore/E** 24

Wicket's | **Carmel Valley/S** -

Wild Goose | **Tahoe Vista/E** 23

Willi's Seafood | **Healdsburg/N** 24

Wine Spectator | **St. Helena/N** 21

Wolfdale's | **Tahoe City/E** 24

Zazu | **Santa Rosa/N** 25

VISITORS ON EXPENSE ACCOUNT

☒ Acquerello | **Polk Gulch** 28

Alexander's | **multi.** 26

NEW Atelier Crenn | **Marina** 26

☒ Auberge/Soleil | **Rutherford/N** 27

☒ Aubergine | **Carmel/S** 28

☒ Barbacco | **Downtown** 24

Bardessono | **Yountville/N** 21

☒ Baumé | **Palo Alto/S** 27

Benu | **SoMa** 26

☒ Bottega | **Yountville/N** 25

☒ Boulevard | **Embarcadero** 27

NEW Bourbon | **Downtown** 24

Burger Bar | **Downtown** 19

Campton Place | **Downtown** 25

☒ Chez Panisse | **Berkeley/E** 28

Chez TJ | **Mtn View/S** 24

☒ Club XIX | **Pebble Bch/S** 23

☒ Cyrus | **Healdsburg/N** 28

Deetjen's Big Sur | **Big Sur/S** 23

Dry Creek | **Healdsburg/N** 24

NEW El Paseo | **Mill Valley/N** -

Epic Roasthse. | **Embarcadero** 21

☒ Erna's | **Oakhurst/E** 27

☒ Evvia | **Palo Alto/S** 27

Fifth Floor | **SoMa** 23

Flea St. Café | **Menlo Pk/S** 26

☒ Fleur de Lys | **Downtown** 27

Forbes Mill | **Los Gatos/S** 22

☒ French Laundry | **Yountville/N** 29

☒ Gary Danko | **Fish. Wharf** 29

☒ Greens | **Marina** 24

Harris' | **Polk Gulch** 26

☒ Jardinière | **Civic Ctr** 26

John Ash | **Santa Rosa/N** 24

NEW Jones | **Tenderloin** -

☒ Kaygetsu | **Menlo Pk/S** 27

☒ Kokkari | **Downtown** 27

Kyo-Ya | **Downtown** 23

☒ La Folie | **Russian Hill** 28

☒ La Forêt | **San Jose/S** 27

La Toque | **Napa/N** 26

☒ Manresa | **Los Gatos/S** 28

Manzanita | **Truckee/E** 23

☒ Marinus | **Carmel Valley/S** 27

☒ Masa's | **Downtown** 28

SPECIAL FEATURES

McCormick/Kuleto | Fish. Wharf	20
☑ Meadowood Rest. | St. Helena/N	28
☑ NEW Michael Mina | Downtown	26
Morimoto | Napa/N	26
Morton's | Downtown	23
Napa Wine Train | Napa/N	18
Oliveto Rest. | Oakland/E	25
☑ Pacific's Edge | Carmel/S	24
☑ Plumed Horse | Saratoga/S	26
Press | St. Helena/N	24
Prospect | SoMa	24
Rest./Ventana | Big Sur/S	21
Ritz-Carlton | Nob Hill	-
Roy's | SoMa	23
Roy's | Pebble Bch/S	24
☑ Santé | Sonoma/N	26
☑ Seasons | Downtown	24
Sent Sovi | Saratoga/S	23
71 St. Peter | San Jose/S	20
☑ Sierra Mar | Big Sur/S	27
Silks | Downtown	23
Sino | San Jose/S	19
Tommy Toy | Downtown	23
Village Pub | Woodside/S	26
Wakuriya | San Mateo/S	27
Waterbar | Embarcadero	21
Wayfare Tav. | Downtown	22

WINE BARS

All Seasons | Calistoga/N	23
☑ A16 | Marina	24
☑ Barbacco | Downtown	24
Bar Bambino | Mission	24
Bar Tartine | Mission	24
Bocadillos | N Beach	23
Bounty Hunter | Napa/N	21
NEW Café Tradition | San Mateo/S	-
Cafe Zoetrope/Mammarella's | N Beach	19
Candybar | W Addition	20
Cantinetta Luca | Carmel/S	21
Carneros Bistro | Sonoma/N	24
Cucina Rest. | San Anselmo/N	22
Emporio Rulli | Larkspur/N	24
Encuentro | Oakland/E	23
NEW Enoteca Molinari | Oakland/E	-
Eos | Cole Valley	23
Étoile | Yountville/N	25
Fig Cafe/Wine | Glen Ellen/N	25
Frascati | Russian Hill	26
Incanto | Noe Valley	25

Kuleto's | Downtown	21
La Toque | Napa/N	26
Liberty Cafe | Bernal Hts	23
Maverick | Mission	24
Napa General | Napa/N	18
Napa Wine Train | Napa/N	18
Ottimista | Cow Hollow	19
Pauline's | Mission	23
NEW Pause | Hayes Valley	-
Picco | Larkspur/N	25
Prima | Walnut Creek/E	24
Q Rest. | Inner Rich	20
Rest. LuLu | SoMa	19
Rist. Avanti | Santa Cruz/S	24
RN74 | SoMa	23
Rosso Pizzeria | Santa Rosa/N	25
Soif Wine Bar | Santa Cruz/S	25
Starlight | Sebastopol/N	22
Stomp | Danville/E	16
☑ Sushi Ran | Sausalito/N	28
Urban Tavern | Downtown	16
Uva Enoteca | Lower Haight	22
Va de Vi | Walnut Creek/E	24
Vin Antico | San Rafael/N	23
Viognier | San Mateo/S	23
Wente Vineyards | Livermore/E	24
Willi's Wine | Santa Rosa/N	25
Zibibbo | Palo Alto/S	19
Zin | Healdsburg/N	23
ZuZu | Napa/N	25

WINNING WINE LISTS

☑ Absinthe | Hayes Valley	22
☑ À Côté | Oakland/E	24
☑ Acquerello | Polk Gulch	28
Adesso | Oakland/E	24
Albion River Inn | Albion/N	23
Alembic | Haight-Ashbury	23
Alexander's | Cupertino/S	26
Alioto's | Fish. Wharf	18
All Seasons | Calistoga/N	23
Ame | SoMa	26
Angèle | Napa/N	24
Anton/Michel | Carmel/S	23
☑ A16 | Marina	24
☑ Auberge/Soleil | Rutherford/N	27
☑ Aubergine | Carmel/S	28
Baker/Banker | Upper Fillmore	25
Balboa Cafe | Mill Valley/N	19
☑ Barbacco | Downtown	24
Bar Bambino | Mission	24
Bardessono | Yountville/N	21
Barlata | Oakland/E	21

Bar Tartine | **Mission**	24
Z BayWolf | **Oakland/E**	26
Bella Vista | **Woodside/S**	22
Beretta | **Mission**	22
Bistro Aix | **Marina**	22
Bistro Don Giovanni | **Napa/N**	24
Bistro Ralph | **Healdsburg/N**	24
Blackhawk Grille | **Danville/E**	20
Bocadillos | **N Beach**	23
Z Bottega | **Yountville/N**	25
Z Bouchon | **Yountville/N**	25
Z Boulevard | **Embarcadero**	27
NEW Bourbon | **Downtown**	24
Bridges | **Danville/E**	23
Brix | **Napa/N**	23
Butterfly | **Embarcadero**	21
Z Cafe La Haye | **Sonoma/N**	27
Camino | **Oakland/E**	22
Campton Place | **Downtown**	25
Cantinetta Luca | **Carmel/S**	21
Carneros Bistro | **Sonoma/N**	24
Casanova | **Carmel/S**	23
Celadon | **Napa/N**	23
Central Market | **Petaluma/N**	22
César | **Berkeley/E**	22
Cetrella | **Half Moon Bay/S**	22
Z Chapeau! | **Inner Rich**	26
Z Chez Panisse | **Berkeley/E**	28
Z Chez Panisse Café | **Berkeley/E**	27
Chez Papa Resto | **SoMa**	24
Chez TJ | **Mtn View/S**	24
Z Club XIX | **Pebble Bch/S**	23
Cole's Chop | **Napa/N**	25
Contigo | **Noe Valley**	24
Cuvée | **Napa/N**	22
Z Cyrus | **Healdsburg/N**	28
Dio Deka | **Los Gatos/S**	26
Donato | **Redwood City/S**	22
Dry Creek | **Healdsburg/N**	24
NEW El Paseo | **Mill Valley/N**	-
Eos | **Cole Valley**	23
Epic Roasthse. | **Embarcadero**	21
Z Erna's | **Oakhurst/E**	27
Estate | **Sonoma/N**	21
Étoile | **Yountville/N**	25
Fandango | **Pacific Grove/S**	23
Z Farallon | **Downtown**	24
Farm | **Napa/N**	24
Z Farmhse. Inn | **Forestville/N**	27
Farmstead | **St. Helena/N**	20
Fifth Floor | **SoMa**	23
54 Mint | **SoMa**	21
Fig Cafe/Wine | **Glen Ellen/N**	25
Five | **Berkeley/E**	20

Flea St. Café | **Menlo Pk/S**	26
Z Fleur de Lys | **Downtown**	27
Forbes Mill | **multi.**	22
Z French Laundry | **Yountville/N**	29
Gabriella Café | **Santa Cruz/S**	22
Z Gary Danko | **Fish. Wharf**	29
Georges | **Downtown**	19
Girl & the Fig | **Sonoma/N**	23
Gott's Roadside | **Napa/N**	21
Grasing's Coastal | **Carmel/S**	23
Z Greens | **Marina**	24
Heirloom | **Mission**	23
Incanto | **Noe Valley**	25
Indigo | **Civic Ctr**	20
Z Jardinière | **Civic Ctr**	26
John Ash | **Santa Rosa/N**	24
Jole | **Calistoga/N**	27
Kenwood | **Kenwood/N**	23
Z Kokkari | **Downtown**	27
Kuleto's | **Downtown**	21
Z La Folie | **Russian Hill**	28
Z La Forêt | **San Jose/S**	27
La Mar | **Embarcadero**	25
Lark Creek Steak | **Downtown**	23
LaSalette | **Sonoma/N**	24
La Toque | **Napa/N**	26
Lavanda | **Palo Alto/S**	20
LB Steak | **San Jose/S**	20
Ledford Hse. | **Albion/N**	23
Z Le Papillon | **San Jose/S**	27
Liberty Cafe | **Bernal Hts**	23
Local Kitchen | **SoMa**	18
Luce | **SoMa**	21
Luella | **Russian Hill**	21
Z Madrona | **Healdsburg/N**	27
Z Manresa | **Los Gatos/S**	28
Manzanita | **Truckee/E**	23
Marinitas | **San Anselmo/N**	20
Z Marinus | **Carmel Valley/S**	27
Martins West | **Redwood City/S**	22
Z Masa's | **Downtown**	28
Meadowood Grill | **St. Helena/N**	22
Z Meadowood Rest. | **St. Helena/N**	28
Mendo Bistro | **Ft Bragg/N**	23
Z NEW Michael Mina | **Downtown**	26
Millennium | **Downtown**	25
Monk's Kettle | **Mission**	20
Monti's | **Santa Rosa/N**	20
Montrio Bistro | **Monterey/S**	23
Moss Room | **Inner Rich**	22
Z Mustards | **Yountville/N**	25
Naomi Sushi | **Menlo Pk/S**	20

Napa Wine Train | **Napa/N**	18
Navio | **Half Moon Bay/S**	25
Nick's Cove | **Marshall/N**	19
955 Ukiah | **Mendocino/N**	25
North Bch. Rest. | **N Beach**	22
Oliveto | **Oakland/E**	24
Oliveto Rest. | **Oakland/E**	25
One Market | **Embarcadero**	24
Ottimista | **Cow Hollow**	19
Oxbow Wine | **Napa/N**	18
☑ Pacific's Edge | **Carmel/S**	24
Palio d'Asti | **Downtown**	20
Pampas | **Palo Alto/S**	22
☑ Passionfish | **Pacific Grove/S**	27
Picán | **Oakland/E**	22
Picco | **Larkspur/N**	25
Piperade | **Downtown**	25
☑ Plumed Horse | **Saratoga/S**	26
PlumpJack | **Olympic Valley/E**	23
Poggio | **Sausalito/N**	23
Postrio | **Downtown**	23
Prima | **Walnut Creek/E**	24
☑ Quince | **Downtown**	26
☑ Redd | **Yountville/N**	27
Rest./Ventana | **Big Sur/S**	21
Rest. LuLu | **SoMa**	19
Rio Grill | **Carmel/S**	21
Ristobar | **Marina**	21
Ritz-Carlton | **Nob Hill**	-
☑ Rivoli | **Berkeley/E**	26
RN74 | **SoMa**	23
Rose Pistola | **N Beach**	21
Roy's | **SoMa**	23
Roy's | **Pebble Bch/S**	24
Rustic | **Geyserville/N**	19
☑ Santé | **Sonoma/N**	26
Sardine Factory | **Monterey/S**	21
Scala's Bistro | **Downtown**	21
☑ Seasons | **Downtown**	24
Sent Sovi | **Saratoga/S**	23
☑ Sierra Mar | **Big Sur/S**	27
Silks | **Downtown**	23
☑ Slanted Door | **Embarcadero**	25
Soif Wine Bar | **Santa Cruz/S**	25
Solbar | **Calistoga/N**	26
SPQR | **Pacific Hts**	24
St. Michael's | **Palo Alto/S**	22
St. Orres | **Gualala/N**	23
Sushi Groove | **multi.**	21
☑ Sushi Ran | **Sausalito/N**	28
Tav./Lark Creek | **Larkspur/N**	20
☑ Terra | **St. Helena/N**	27
Terzo | **Cow Hollow**	24

Tipsy Pig | **Marina**	18
Town Hall | **SoMa**	22
Tra Vigne | **St. Helena/N**	24
231 Ellsworth | **San Mateo/S**	23
Urban Tavern | **Downtown**	16
Uva Enoteca | **Lower Haight**	22
Va de Vi | **Walnut Creek/E**	24
Vic Stewart | **Walnut Creek/E**	22
Village Pub | **Woodside/S**	26
Vin Antico | **San Rafael/N**	23
Viognier | **San Mateo/S**	23
Waterbar | **Embarcadero**	21
Wente Vineyards | **Livermore/E**	24
Willi's Seafood | **Healdsburg/N**	24
Wine Spectator | **St. Helena/N**	21
Zaré/Fly Trap | **SoMa**	22
Zibibbo | **Palo Alto/S**	19
Zin | **Healdsburg/N**	23
Zinsvalley | **Napa/N**	17
☑ Zuni Café | **Hayes Valley**	25

WORTH A TRIP

Albion	
Albion River Inn	23
Ledford Hse.	23
Berkeley	
César	22
☑ Chez Panisse	28
☑ Chez Panisse Café	27
Lalime's	25
☑ Rivoli	26
Zachary's Pizza	24
Big Sur	
Deetjen's Big Sur	23
Rest./Ventana	21
☑ Sierra Mar	27
Carmel	
☑ Aubergine	28
Cantinetta Luca	21
☑ Pacific's Edge	24
Carmel Valley	
☑ Marinus	27
El Granada	
☑ Cafe Gibraltar	26
Forestville	
☑ Farmhse. Inn	27
Gualala	
St. Orres	23
Half Moon Bay	
Navio	25
Healdsburg	
☑ Cyrus	28
Dry Creek	24
☑ Madrona	27

SPECIAL FEATURES

ALPHABETICAL
PAGE INDEX

All places are in San Francisco unless otherwise noted (East of San Francisco=E; North of San Francisco=N; South of San Francisco=S).

Latest openings, menus, photos and more – free at ZAGAT.com   351

Wine Vintage Chart

This chart is based on our 0 to 30 scale. The ratings (by U. of South Carolina law professor **Howard Stravitz**) reflect vintage quality and the wine's readiness to drink. A dash means the wine is past its peak or too young to rate. Loire ratings are for dry whites.

Whites	95	96	97	98	99	00	01	02	03	04	05	06	07	08	0
France:															
Alsace	24	23	23	25	23	25	26	23	21	24	25	24	26	25	2
Burgundy	27	26	22	21	24	24	24	27	23	26	27	25	26	25	2
Loire Valley	-	-	-	-	-	-	-	26	21	23	27	23	24	24	2
Champagne	26	27	24	23	25	24	21	26	21	-	-	-	-	-	-
Sauternes	21	23	25	23	24	24	29	24	26	21	26	24	27	25	2
California:															
Chardonnay	-	-	-	-	22	21	25	26	22	26	29	24	27	25	-
Sauvignon Blanc	-	-	-	-	-	-	-	-	26	25	27	25	24	2	
Austria:															
Grüner V./Riesl.	22	-	25	22	25	21	22	25	26	25	24	26	25	23	2
Germany:	21	26	21	22	24	20	29	25	26	27	28	25	27	25	2

Reds	95	96	97	98	99	00	01	02	03	04	05	06	07	08	0
France:															
Bordeaux	26	25	23	25	24	29	26	24	26	25	28	24	23	25	2
Burgundy	26	27	25	24	27	22	24	27	25	23	28	25	25	24	26
Rhône	26	22	23	27	26	27	26	-	26	25	27	25	26	23	26
Beaujolais	-	-	-	-	-	-	-	-	-	27	24	25	23	2	
California:															
Cab./Merlot	27	25	28	23	25	-	27	26	25	24	26	23	26	23	25
Pinot Noir	-	-	-	-	-	-	25	26	25	26	24	23	27	25	24
Zinfandel	-	-	-	-	-	25	23	27	22	24	21	21	25	2	
Oregon:															
Pinot Noir	-	-	-	-	-	-	26	24	26	25	24	23	27	25	
Italy:															
Tuscany	25	24	29	24	27	24	27	-	25	27	26	26	25	24	-
Piedmont	21	27	26	25	26	28	27	-	24	27	26	25	26	26	-
Spain:															
Rioja	26	24	25	-	25	24	28	-	23	27	26	24	24	-	26
Ribera del Duero/ Priorat	26	27	25	24	25	24	27	-	24	27	26	24	26	-	-
Australia:															
Shiraz/Cab.	24	26	25	28	24	24	27	27	25	26	27	25	23	-	-
Chile:	-	-	-	-	25	23	26	24	25	24	27	25	24	26	-
Argentina:															
Malbec	-	-	-	-	-	-	-	-	25	26	27	25	24	-